HANDBOOK OF FAMILY THEORIES

"[This book] ... should inspire scholars to advance their theoretical contributions and thus foster better theorizing in the...field. Graduate students should find the book particularly helpful....[The] chapters I reviewed are written in a clear and engaging manner. ...I would ...recommend [it] to ... students and other family professionals."– Charles B. Hennon, Miami University, USA

"[This] ... book ... is needed ... to illustrate ... links between theory and research ... to move the field forward ... and ...to overcome some of the limitations of textbooks/handbooks currently in use....The editors...are eminent researchers in the field and have ...assembled a list of ...authors that are at the top of their...area of specialization. I would very much welcome this handbook and use it in my graduate family theories course." – Sylvia Niehuis, Texas Tech University, USA

HANDBOOK OF FAMILY THEORIES

A Content-Based Approach

EDITED BY

MARK A. FINE
The University of North Carolina at Greensboro

FRANK D. FINCHAM
Florida State University

Routledge
Taylor & Francis Group

NEW YORK AND LONDON

First published 2013
by Routledge
711 Third Avenue,
New York, NY 10017

Simultaneously published in the UK
by Routledge
27 Church Road,
Hove, East Sussex BN3 2FA

Routledge is an imprint of the Taylor & Francis Group, an Informa business

© 2013 Taylor & Francis

Library of Congress Cataloging in Publication Data
Handbook of family theories : a content-based approach / edited by Mark A. Fine,
Frank D. Fincham.
    p. cm.
Includes bibliographical references and index.
1. Families. 2. Marriage. I. Fine, Mark A. II. Fincham, Frank D.
HQ728.H275
2013306.85–dc23   2012025155

ISBN: 978-0-415-87945-3 (hbk)
ISBN: 978-0-415-65722-8 (pbk)
ISBN: 978-0-203-07518-0 (ebk)

Typeset in Times New Roman
by Cenveo Publisher Services

SFI Certified Sourcing
www.sfiprogram.org
SFI-00453

Printed and bound in the United States of America
by Edwards Brothers, Inc.

Contents

SECTION I   Parenting and Parent–Child Relations

SECTION II   Dating, Cohabiting, and Marital Relationships

SECTION VI   *Families and Extrafamilial Institutions*

Preface

Between the two of us, we have engaged in decades of teaching about family theories, constructing and evaluating family theories, and doing theory-based research. This book arose out of the need for a family theory text that offered a content-based alternative to the typical theory-by-theory organizational approach. Family theories courses typically present theories separately and sequentially, with some attention devoted to how the theory might be used in research. Our experience shows that it makes more sense to teach theories *in situ*—as they are used in actual research in family-related content areas. This approach helps students make clearer and stronger connections between theories and the empirical literature. Because most researchers use multiple theories in their work, and even in a particular study, this approach also allowed us to introduce more theories than the 10–15 that are typically covered in courses using the "theory of the week approach."

To convey a sense of how theory underlies specific family-related domains, we organized the book around the most important domains in the field: parenting and parent–child relationships, romantic relationships, conflict and aggression, structural variation and transitions, demographic variations, and families and extrafamilial institutions. Thus, in this volume, our aim was to have scholars in particular content areas (within the domains listed above), such as parenting young children, the transition to parenthood, intergenerational relationships, and divorce, describe how theory has been used to generate new knowledge in their field, and to suggest future directions for how theory may be used to extend our knowledge base. The goal is to help readers: (1) acquire a good working understanding of a number of theories relevant to family science; (2) understand how leading scholars in the field make use of these theories in their empirical efforts; and (3) acquire a cutting edge understanding of the key findings and issues in important family-related content areas.

A great deal of effort went into making this book as accessible as possible. To accomplish that goal, readers will find a consistent organizational structure in the chapters. Each chapter features: an introduction to the content area; a brief review of key topics/issues/findings in the content area; descriptions of the theories that have been used to study these topics; limitations of how theory has been used in this content area; suggestions for better use of theory in this content area and/or new theoretical advances, and a conclusion about future theoretical developments in the content area.

The book is primarily intended for use in family theories courses that are taught at the advanced undergraduate and/or graduate level in a variety of disciplines, including, but not limited to, family studies, human development, psychology, sociology, education, communication studies, social work and nursing. In addition, scholars who are interested in how family theories are and have been applied to the study of families will appreciate the book's comprehensiveness and currency.

Mark Fine shared this vision with Debra Riegert, a Senior Editor at Taylor & Francis, who was very supportive of the idea and patiently waited over a year for a proposal to be developed. Frank Fincham graciously agreed to be co-editor and we subsequently shared in all editing activities, including giving each of our 23 sets of authors extensive feedback on two and sometimes three drafts of their chapters. For their part, our authors were very responsive to our comments and suggestions and typically provided relatively quick turnarounds on their chapters. The most frequent suggestion that we made to authors was to follow as closely as they could the organizational structure that we described earlier. We very much appreciate that most authors found this organizational structure to their liking and, thus, virtually all chapters follow this general structure.

This volume contains an introductory chapter by the editors, which is followed by 23 other chapters on different family-related content areas written by noted scholars in each of these topical areas. We used the 2000 and 2010 Decade-in-Review issues of the *Journal of Marriage and Family* as a resource to help identify the most critical issues and topics. We hope that readers of this volume come away not only with extensive information about how theory has been used in the 23 content areas represented in this book, but also with new ideas and strategies for how to incorporate theory more effectively into their own research.

Mark A. Fine
Frank D. Fincham
2012

Acknowledgments

We thank Debra Riegert for her ongoing support of this project; our authors for working so hard to write chapters that place theory in the foreground and research findings in the background—a format that is not usually followed in scholarly writings and that, therefore, represents, in teaching terms, a "new prep"; our Production Editor, Kristin Susser, and our Project Manager, Apurupa Mallik. The editors are also grateful to Deans Stephen Jorgensen and Celia Hooper at the University of Missouri and The University of North Carolina at Greensboro, respectively, who each provided resources that supported the project from start to finish. Finally, Dave Demo provided extremely helpful guidance on topics to cover, partly based on his experience as the Editor of the *Journal of Marriage and Family*'s 2010 Decade-in-Review.

We would also like to thank those who reviewed the project along the way: Thomas Bradbury (UCLA), David Eggebeen (Pennsylvania State University), Sylvia Niehuis (Texas Tech University), Selva Lewin-Bizan (Tufts University), Joe F. Pittman (Auburn University), Charles Hennon (Miami University), and Laura KM Donorfio (University of Connecticut).

Mark Fine thanks his children: Aubrey, Julia, Kenyon, and Keaton—and wife, Loreen Olson, for giving him the support and time needed to work on this book. He also thanks his mother, Marilynn Fine, and father, Burril Fine, who died as this project was coming to a close, and to whom he dedicates this book.

Frank Fincham is grateful to his wife Susan who has shouldered more than her fair share of family responsibilities to allow him to work on this project. He dedicates this book to his mother, Colleen Ann Valerie Fincham, who passed away shortly after work on the book commenced.

Editors

Mark A. Fine received a PhD from the Ohio State University in Clinical Psychology and is currently Professor and Chair of the Department of Human Development and Family Studies at The University of North Carolina at Greensboro. He was editor of *Family Relations* from 1993 to 1996 and the *Journal of Social and Personal Relationships* from 1999 to 2004. He has published almost 200 peer-reviewed journal articles and book chapters, as well as nine books. In 2000, he was selected as a fellow of the National Council on Family Relations. He is on the editorial boards of nine peer-review journals in family studies, relationship science, and human development.

Frank D. Fincham obtained a doctoral degree in Social Psychology as a Rhodes Scholar at Oxford University and then completed postdoctoral training in clinical psychology at Stony Brook University. He is currently Eminent Scholar and Director of the Family Institute at Florida State University. The author of more than 200 publications, his research has been widely recognized by numerous awards, including the Berscheid–Hatfield Award for "sustained, substantial, and distinguished contributions to the field of personal relationships" from the International Network on Personal Relationships, and the President's Award for "distinguished contributions to psychological knowledge" from the British Psychological Society. A Fellow of five different professional societies, Frank has been listed among the top 25 psychologists in the world in terms of impact (defined as number of citations per paper).

Contributors

David C. Atkins
University of Washington

James S. Bates
South Dakota State University

Brian R. Baucom
University of Southern California

Lisa Baumwell
New York University

Kira S. Birditt
University of Michigan

Gary L. Bowen
University of North Carolina at Chapel Hill

Cheryl Buehler
University of North Carolina at
Greensboro

Susan S. Chuang
University of Guelph

Catherine L. Cohan
The Pennsylvania State University

Katherine J. Conger
University of California at Davis

Rand D. Conger
University of California at Davis

Teresa M. Cooney
University of Missouri

Tamara Del Vecchio
St. John's University

David H. Demo
University of North Carolina at Greensboro

Lisa M. Diamond
University of Utah

M. Brent Donnellan
Michigan State University

Pearl A. Dykstra
Erasmus University

Ann C. Eckardt-Erlanger
New York University

Barbara H. Fiese
University of Illinois

Frank D. Fincham
Florida State University

Mark A. Fine
The University of North Carolina at
Greensboro

Karen L. Fingerman
University of Texas

Bethany Fisackerly
Baptist Hospital of South Florida

Heather M. Foran
Technische Universität Braunschweig

Peggy C. Giordano
Bowling Green State University

John Grych
Marquette University

Amber Hammons
University of Illinois

Richard E. Heyman
New York University

Michael E. Lamb
Cambridge University

Ashley Smith Leavell
New York University

Monica A. Longmore
Bowling Green State University

Mark Lynn
Marquette University

Shelly M. MacDermid
Purdue University

Jay A. Mancini
University of Georgia

Wendy D. Manning
Bowling Green State University

Claudia Manzi
Catholic University of Milan

Gayla Margolin
University of Southern California

James A. Martin
Brynmawr University

Monica J. Martin
University of California at Davis

Robert P. Moreno
Syracuse University

Claire Oxtoby
Marquette University

Maureen Perry-Jenkins
University of Massachusetts-Amherst

Kendrick A. Rith
University of Utah

Camillo Regalia
Catholic University of Milan

Mihaela Robila
Queens College

Aubrey J. Rodriguez
University of Southern California

Darby E. Saxbe
University of Southern California

Eugenia Scabini
Catholic University of Milan

Jacqueline D. Shannon
Brooklyn College of the City University
of New York

Amy M. Smith Slep
New York University

Catherine S. Tamis-LeMonda
New York University

Alan C. Taylor
East Carolina University

Jesse L. Wilkinson
Stony Brook University

Julia T. Wood
University of North Carolina at Chapel Hill

1 Introduction

The Role of Theory in Family Science

Mark A. Fine and Frank D. Fincham

There is nothing so practical as a good theory.

Lewin, 1951, p. 169

This book focuses on theoretical perspectives that inform research in key topical areas of family science.[1] Along with most scholars, we share a strong belief in the value of theory in the empirical process. Conducting research without theory is analogous to building a new house without a set of blueprints. In fact, we argue that one cannot conduct research without at least an implicit theoretical orientation, just as one cannot build a house without having some type of blueprint, no matter how poorly defined. Builders (and researchers) may think that they can engage in their craft without having an underlying blueprint (or theoretical perspective), but every step in the construction (or empirical) process requires some foundational sense of future direction. The lack of a theoretical perspective is not an option; the choice is the extent to which one uses theory explicitly and deliberately versus implicitly and outside of conscious awareness.

WHAT ARE THEORIES?

We follow in the tradition of many others (e.g., White & Klein, 2008; Boss, Doherty, LaRossa, Schumm, & Steinmetz, 1993) who have described theories as socially constructed explanations of why certain phenomena occur as they do. Definitions of theories often refer to constructs, logical relations among these constructs or statements the theory purports to be truths, and testable hypotheses logically derived from the theory that empirically will either be consistent or inconsistent with the theory. Ideally, theories also specify the relations between and among unobservable constructs and variables that can be observed. In short, good theories specify relations between observables (e.g., a punch, slap, kick) and underlying constructs (e.g., aggression, hostility), as well as relations among the constructs, are internally consistent, useful, explanatory, evidence-based, falsifiable, broadly applicable, and consistent with other accepted theories. All of these features are important aspects of theories in family science, and they serve to explain why or how some (family) phenomenon occurs the way that it does.

---

[1] We will use the term *family science* in this book to refer to all research on families. This term includes such subdisciplines as psychology, sociology, family studies, communication, and nursing

For example, consider Rusbult's (1983) investment model, which is an extension of social exchange theory. Her model attempts to explain relationship stability (i.e., whether a relationship continues or discontinues). In her model, rewards, costs, and comparison level predict relationship satisfaction. In turn, relationship satisfaction (positively), investments (positively), and the quality of available alternatives (negatively) predict each individual's level of commitment to the relationship. Finally, level of commitment predicts relationship stability. The model contains a series of key constructs, delineates how the constructs are related to each other, and leads to a wealth of empirically testable hypotheses that have been studied in previous research. However, it is important not to lose sight of the key function of the investment model: to predict which relationships will continue and which will break up. To the extent that it does so (and research suggests that it does so quite well), the model can be said to explain the future course of relationships. Of course, the model needs to (and empirically does in research) predict relationship stability better than pure chance alone (if 70% of relationships remain intact, one could predict which relationships will continue with a 70% success rate merely by predicting that every relationship will continue).

Several points are important to note regarding how *theory* is used in this volume. First, we imposed no restrictions on how our authors could define *theory*. Authors were free to use the term, and similar ones, as they wished with no attempt on our part to ensure that a consensually agreed upon definition was used in every chapter. We felt that it was more desirable for readers to be exposed to how scholars in family science themselves use terms like *theory* than for us to impose a definition on experienced and successful scholars. Nevertheless, we believe that all authors defined and used theory in a manner consistent with what was depicted earlier—as an explanation of why and how certain phenomena occur as they do.

Second, and related to the definitional freedom given to our authors, we also imposed no constraints on the terms that authors could use as synonyms for *theory*. While some theorists have attempted to delineate distinctions among such terms as conceptual framework, theory, model, perspective, causal models, and so forth, there is no consensus among theorists on the nature of many of these distinctions and, thus, we allowed authors to use these terms in any way that they wished to do so. If there is a somewhat consistent distinction that is used in this book, it is the distinction between a *theory/model* and a *perspective*. A theory or model is designed to explain a particular phenomenon and to make predictions about what might happen in the future. By contrast, a perspective is broader and involves a world view or lens through which one views families and relationships. For example, social exchange is a theory in the sense that it allows one to explain certain behaviors and to predict how one will act in the future. However, many consider the life course approach to be a perspective in the sense that it is not designed to explain why certain phenomena unfold as they do and it makes no specific predictions about family-related events, but provides a lens through which one can gain perspective on family events.

Finally, although we use the term *theory*, we are actually referring to *deductively-derived theory*. Family scientists use both deductively-derived and inductively-derived theories in their work, but the vast majority of the research reviewed in this volume is based on deductively-derived theories that are typically used to ground quantitative studies. Inductively-derived theories are frequently generated from qualitative studies and have made extremely important contributions to family science. However, as do all other books on family theories that we are aware of, we focus primarily on theories derived from the deductive process.

WHY ARE THEORIES IMPORTANT TO THE RESEARCH ENDEAVOR?

Theories provide guidance to investigators throughout the empirical endeavor, from selecting a research topic, to carefully reviewing the relevant literature(s), to formulating hypotheses and/or questions, to designing the study and choosing measures, to choosing one's sample, to analyzing and interpreting results, and to drawing implications for future research and for practice. It is clearly as important for scholars to have expertise in the use of theory as it is to have sophisticated method-ological and statistical skills. Indeed, without theory, even the most sophisticated methods can be counter-productive as "conceptual clarification [theory] is a pre-requisite for efficient experimenta-tion [data collection]" (Heider, 1958, p. 4). In short, "good theory construction, with its attendant methods, has the resources to provide the types of conceptual analyses (better theoretical analyses) that really matter to science" (Bennett & Hacker, 2003, p. 565).

In what ways do theories influence steps in the research process? The first point to note is that no decisions regarding methodology are objective and mechanical in the sense that they are indepen-dent of the researcher's underlying values, world view, conceptual lens and (implicit or explicit) theory. Even something as apparently simple as choosing a measure of a particular construct is based on theoretical assumptions. For example, depression is a construct relevant to many family scholars, such as in work related to how parental depression affects parenting and how depression affects couple dynamics. However, some measures of depression are more focused on cognitive symptoms (e.g., the Beck Depression Inventory), whereas others emphasize somatic symptoms (e.g., Zung Depression Scale). Some people may score higher on one type of depression scale than another, depending on the nature of their symptoms. The choice of whether one prefers to measure primarily (but not exclusively) cognitive symptoms or primarily (but not exclusively) somatic symptoms should be based on the particular theoretical underpinnings of one's study. If one's theoretical perspective is based on the notion that depressed parents become less *physically* available to their children, then one may prefer a more somatic-based measure. However, if one considers the *modeling of depressive thinking* as the key mechanism by which parental depression affects children, one may decide to use a measure such as the Beck Depression Inventory. We argue that all of the various decisions made in the research endeavor, however seemingly minor they may appear to be, are affected by theoretical thinking. Even such choices as which sample to gather data from and how to recruit participants, should be based on underlying theory.

We recognize that empirical studies as they typically unfold are not always based on careful theoretical thinking at each and every step. However, even if a particular choice is not made with a carefully thought out theoretical rationale, one should at least make sure that one's choice is not *inconsistent* with one's theoretical approach. For example, some data analysis decisions seem quite clear cut and may not require much thought (e.g., comparing the means of two groups with a *t-test*), but at the very least such decisions should not be inconsistent with one's theoretical perspective. However, many data analytic decisions do need to be based on theoretical consider-ations, such as deciding to use growth curve modeling because one has hypothesized that parental depression affects *later* parental availability. As an obvious example of a decision that would be inconsistent with underlying theory—if one's theory is that parental depression, through the mechanism of depressed parents being unavailable to school-age children who are still quite dependent on their parents, negatively affects children's well-being, one should not gather a sample of high school juniors and seniors. Thus, researchers need to review all of their method-ological choices not only with an eye toward what seems most feasible and logical, but also with an eye towards ensuring that decisions are, at minimum, not inconsistent with one's theoretical perspective.

APPROACHES TO TEACHING ABOUT THEORIES

The traditional approach to teaching about theories has been labeled by Klein (personal communica-tion) as the "theory of the week" approach. With this approach, theories are learned one after the other, often from textbooks that devote single chapters to each of the theories covered. Whereas the "theory of the week" approach can provide a useful description of the various theories and how they have been used, it does not provide a clear sense of how theory is an integral part of the study of specific family-related topics. In other words, the traditional approach to presenting and teaching about theories, in general, and family theories, in particular, often leaves readers with a good sense of the tenets, strengths, and weaknesses of the various theories, but, importantly, not a good sense of the direct linkages between theory and research.

In this volume, we use a second and far less commonly used strategy—a content-based approach. We organize the book around content areas and show how theories have been used to further our knowledge in a variety of family-related areas. The rationale behind this approach is that readers will gain more insight into how theory is used in family science by organizing the presentation according to topics within family science, as opposed to devoting one theory to each chapter. Different content areas in family studies have different traditions with respect to how theories have grounded empirical research. Thus, to convey a rich and nuanced sense of how theory underlies specific family-related domains, we organize the book around the most important domains in the field. We carefully selected what we consider to be the topics that have received the most research attention in the last 10–15 years in family science, with guidance from tables of contents from the 2000 and 2010 decade-in-review issues of *Journal of Marriage and Family*, from colleagues, and from our ongoing exposure to the family science literature(s).

Only via this content-based approach can readers obtain a thorough and clear understanding of how empirical research in particular family-related areas, depends on the use of family theories. For example, most family-related content areas make use of multiple theories and this multifaceted use of theory will be conveyed in each chapter of this book, unlike the picture one obtains in more traditional books that present one and only one theory per chapter. A related benefit of the content-based approach is that readers are exposed to a much greater number of theories than are commonly included in books that cover one theory per chapter. As described below, readers of this book will learn about numerous theories, whereas more traditional books tend to cover at most 15 theories because there are typically 15 weeks in a typical university semester.

Thus, readers of this volume should realize three interrelated goals: (1) acquire a good working understanding of a number of theories relevant to family science; (2) see how leading scholars in the field make use of these theories in their empirical efforts; and (3) acquire a cutting edge understanding of the key findings and issues in important family-related content areas.

We know of only one other book that has attempted to use the content-based approach to covering family theories (Bengtson, Acock, Allen, Dilworth-Anderson, & Klein, 2005). Bengtson et al.'s *Sourcebook* was ground-breaking in its use of the content-based approach, its inclusion of authors representing numerous different theoretical and methodological orientations, and its attention to the implications that theories have for methodological decisions. However, compared with the *Sourcebook*, the present volume is more current (the *Sourcebook* was published in 2005), has a more consistent organizational structure across chapters, is considerably shorter and more amenable to coverage in a semester-long graduate seminar, is more focused on how theory has extended our knowledge base in particular content areas in family science (as opposed to addressing some methodological issues in detail), and has more reader-accessible material. Its accessibility stems from its greater organizational consistency across chapters and its strict and consistent devotion to theory throughout each chapter.

DESIGN OF THE BOOK

To meet these goals, we asked authors with high levels of expertise and strong reputations in particular areas to write a theory-based chapter on their content area. These authors were asked to address in their chapter, a common set of questions and issues pertaining to the use of theory in the relevant area. The core set of issues included the following:

1. Introduction to the content area
2. Brief review of key topics/issues/findings in this content area

3. Theories that have been used to study these topics in this content area, including a brief description of each theory, focusing primarily on those aspects of the theory that have been used to study this aspect of the content area
4. Limitations of how theory has been used in this content area
5. Suggestions for better use of theory in this content area and/or new theoretical advances
6. Conclusions about future theoretical developments in this content area.

Readers will find that most authors very carefully followed the proposed outline, whereas a few felt that their particular content areas required some deviation from the core outline. Even in these cases, however, authors did their best to address the key points in the outline and to adhere to the spirit of the organizational structure.

FAMILY SCIENCE CONTENT AREAS COVERED

This book includes six broad content areas: *Parenting and Parent–Child Relations* (five chapters); *Romantic Relationships* (three chapters); *Conflict and Aggression in Families* (four chapters); *Structural Variations and Transitions in Families* (three chapters); *Demographic Variations in Families* (four chapters), and *Families and Extrafamilial Institutions* (four chapters).

The *Parenting and Parent–Child Relations* chapters address parenting and parent–child relationships across the lifespan. Tamis-LeMonda, Smith Leavell, and Tamis LeMonda address theoretical underpinnings of research on parenting *infants and young children*; Longmore, Manning, and Giordano review theory and research in the area of parenting *adolescents*; and Birditt and Fingerman cover parent–child and intergenerational relationships in *adulthood*. Two particularly salient issues in parenting have been extensively studied by researchers and are included in this section: relationships between grandparents and grandchildren (Bates and Taylor, Chapter 4), who increasingly find themselves living together; and fathering (Chapter 6 authored by Lamb). These excellent chapters show that numerous theoretical perspectives have been used to help us understand how parents and children relate to and mutually influence each other.

The section on *Dating, Cohabiting, and Marital Relationships* addresses theoretical perspectives on a variety of types of romantic relationships. In Chapter 7, Cohan reviews theory and research on cohabitation in heterosexual relationships, while Rith and Diamond cover cohabitation in gay and lesbian relationships, in Chapter 8. The final chapter (Chapter 9) in this section, authored by Baucom and Atkins, focuses on marriage in general and polarization in marriage in particular. Most of the material in Baucom and Atkins' chapter is based on research conducted on heterosexual married couples. With the increasing prevalence of gay and lesbian marriages, hopefully this research in the future will expand to consider marriage in both heterosexual and homosexual couples.

The *Conflict and Aggression in Families* section includes chapters on a wide variety of types of conflict and aggression in romantic relationships and families. Saxbe, Rodriguez, and Margolin (Chapter 10) explore conflict in families; Heyman, Foran, and Wilkinson examine intimate partner violence in Chapter 11, and Del Vecchio, Eckardt-Erlanger, and Smith-Slep reviews the area of child abuse in Chapter 12. Chapter 13, authored by Grych, Oxtoby, and Lynn, focuses on perhaps the most widely studied area on the consequences of conflict and aggression—the effects of marital conflict on children.

The section on *Structural Variations and Transitions in Families* addresses common changes that families make over their life course. Chapter 14, written by Shannon, Baumwell, and Tamis-LeMonda, reviews the literature on the transition to parenthood with a particular emphasis on how contextual factors influence this important period of change. Demo and Buehler, in Chapter 15, cover divorce and relationship dissolution; and Taylor, Robila, and Fisackerly address how theories have been used to help us understand remarriages and stepfamilies in Chapter 16.

The next section, *Demographic Variations in Families*, examines how theory has been used to help us understand a variety of demographic (broadly defined) variations in families. Wood, in Chapter 17, discusses theoretical underpinnings of research on gender, whereas Chuang and Moreno review theory and research on immigrant families. Donnellan, Martin, K. Conger, and R. Conger cover the topic of economic distress and poverty in families, in Chapter 19, certainly a salient topic in the present economic climate. The final chapter in this section (Chapter 20), authored by Cooney and Dykstra, addresses a growing segment of the population (the elderly) that is often underrepresented in family science.

The final section of this volume, *Families and Extrafamilial Institutions*, deals with the interface between families and institutions. Perry-Jenkins and MacDermid, in Chapter 21, review the important area of work and families; Fiese and Hammons examine families and healthcare in Chapter 22; and families and the military is covered by Bowen, Martin, and Mancini in Chapter 23. The volume concludes with Chapter 24, written by Regalia, Manzi, and Scabini, and focuses on individuation and differentiation in families from a cross-cultural and global perspective. We encouraged all of our authors to consider international research to the extent that it was available, and they did, but the focus is even more strongly cross-cultural in Regalia et al.'s chapter.

THEORY USAGE IN FAMILY SCIENCE

As the reader will readily observe as he or she progresses through this volume, an impressively large number of theories "have been used or might be used, to study families". Among many others, the following theories and/or perspectives are described and applied in this volume: social learning, family systems, social exchange, attachment, life course, lifespan, behavioral, social cognitive, cognitive behavioral, ecological, symbolic interactionism, identity, feminist, stress and resiliency, conflict structure, social capital, evolutionary, conflict, relationship enhancement, attribution theory, parenting, minority stress, gender-role, interpersonal process model of intimacy, investment, commitment, coercion, polarization, vulnerability-stress-adaptation, cascade model of marital dissolution, and demand withdraw. Some of these theories are grand in scale (i.e., they attempt to explain a wide array of phenomena, such as family systems theory), whereas others are somewhat more narrow in scope (e.g., middle-range theories, such as the interpersonal process model of intimacy). As an aid for the reader, we place the name of each theory in *italics* the first time it is mentioned in each chapter.

To what extent is the use of so many different theories and perspectives helpful in family studies? We believe that the use of so many theories is both helpful and detrimental. It is helpful because diversity in theories (and methods) often leads to more creative, innovative, and rich solutions to research questions. Especially in the social sciences, it is quite likely the case that there are multiple causal explanations of why phenomena occur as they do. Thus, no single theoretical perspective is likely to be able to address the range of possible causes of family-related phenomena. If the multiple theories are not only consistent with each other, but are also complementary and even synergistic, our knowledge base is likely to benefit all that much more.

By contrast, having so many theories is detrimental because the lack of a singular, unifying perspective makes it more difficult to integrate findings across studies. Despite the benefits of multiple theoretical perspectives being brought to bear on research questions, there is some benefit to having some uniformity in theoretical perspectives. For example, it is easier to aggregate across studies when researchers employ similar definitions of key constructs and, thus, use the same or similar measures. The use of so many theories is analogous to the proliferation of different computer hardware and software products. The computing world is probably a better place with both PCs and Macs and with different software programs attempting to perform similar tasks; however, for some purposes, it is more efficient if there is compatibility and convention across different types of computer and software programs. As an example of a construct that has been defined in multiple ways, *relationship stability* has been defined both in terms of whether or not the relationship continues over time and, by different scholars, as the extent to which each partner has thoughts of ending the relationship. To their credit, many of the authors in this volume have developed integrative theoretical models of their own to bring greater clarity and integration to their topic.

INTENDED AUDIENCES

This book is intended for scholars, graduate students, and advanced undergraduates who are interested in how family theories are and have been applied to the study of families. Its primary audience includes those who want to extend their knowledge of, or have a good resource on family theories, but there is also a very relevant secondary audience—individuals who are interested in particular family-related content areas and who want current reviews of how different theoretical perspectives have been used by prominent researchers. Such readers are spread across multiple disciplines, including, but not limited to, psychology, sociology, communication studies, social work, nursing, and family studies.

REFERENCES

Bennett, M. R., & Hacker, P. M. S. (2003). *Philosophical foundations of neuroscience*. Oxford, England: Blackwell.

Bengtson, V. L., Acock, A. C., Allen, K. R., Dilworth-Anderson, P., & Klein, D. M. (Eds.) (2005). *Sourcebook of family theory and research*. Thousand Oaks, CA: Sage.

Boss, P.G., Doherty, W.J., LaRossa, R., Schumm, W. R., & Steinmetz, S. K. (1993). *Sourcebook of family Theory and Methods: A Contextual Approach*. New York: Plenum Press.

Heider, F. (1958). *The Psychology of Interpersonal Relations*. New York: Wiley.

Lewin, K. (1951). *Field theory in social science; selected theoretical papers*. In D. Cartwright (Ed.), New York: Harper & Row.

Rusbult, C. E. (1983). A longitudinal test of the investment model: The development (and deterioration) of satisfaction and commitment in heterosexual involvements. *Journal of Personality and Social Psychology, 45*, 101–117.

White, J. W., & Klein, D. M. (2008). *Family theories* (3rd ed.). Thousand Oaks, CA: Sage.

Section I

Parenting and Parent–Child Relations

2 Parenting in Infancy and Early Childhood

A Focus on Gender Socialization

Ashley Smith Leavell and Catherine S. Tamis-LeMonda[1]

Vygotsky's *sociocultural theories* of development ignited interest in the role of parents in young children's learning and development (e.g., Rogoff, 2003). Vygotsky's writings diverged from those of Piaget (1932, 1952) by shifting focus from intra-psychological processes of learning and development to interpersonal processes. This sociocultural revolution was also echoed in the writings of Bruner (1991, 1992), Wertsch (1991), and Luria (1976), who commonly highlighted the importance of social and cultural contexts in the co-construction of knowledge. However, much developmental research from this sociocultural tradition has focused on *dyadic* interactions—most notably young children's interactions with their mothers (and in rare instances, fathers). Children's early development is the product of multiple converging forces within the larger family system, and even though *direct* interactions between parents and children are a powerful force in early development, indirect influences should also be considered.

In particular, *family systems theory* (e.g., Bowen, 1978) underscores the need to consider reciprocal influences among all members of the family unit, including relationships among parents and children, mother and father, siblings, extended kin, and so on. Each person within the system enacts roles that reflect expectations and norms regarding appropriate ways to relate to and interact with other members of the family. As such, the family system channels and defines patterns of interpersonal relationships that in turn shape the course of children's early development.

Similarly, *economic theories* (e.g., Becker, 1991) consider broader systems of influence on developmental processes through examination of family members' connections to the labor market, for example by asking how work status and work roles influence parents and children's lives. More recently, economic theories have been extended to the study of labor distribution within the home as well, such as how mothers and fathers negotiate childcare and housework. Together, the worlds of work within and outside the home present significant contextual influences on young children's development.

In this chapter, we therefore refer to three theories that offer useful frameworks for understanding social forces in young children's development: sociocultural, family systems, and economic theory. These theories present unique but complementary lenses onto the ways that parents socialize their children, through direct interactions (sociocultural), through the influence of multiple, dynamic relationships (family systems), and through their connections to economic processes that affect the contexts in which children develop (economic theory).

---

[1] The authors acknowledge support from the National Science Foundation, BCS grant #021859 and NSF IRADS grant #0721383.

KEY ISSUES IN EARLY GENDER DEVELOPMENT

To concretely illustrate the relevance of these theories to an understanding of early development, we focus specifically on the topic of *gender socialization* in infancy and early childhood. As a model system, gender socialization provides fertile ground for exploring the multiple pathways through which parents influence their children's behavioral and psychological expressions of self. Accordingly, we begin by providing a brief overview of early gender development.

It has long been recognized that boys and girls behave in different ways, have different likes and dislikes, and display strong preferences for toy types and play partners. A central question, therefore, concerns the early origins of these views and behaviors. Why do boys and girls adopt gendered patterns of behaviors, likes and dislikes, and evaluative stances? Compelling evidence exists for the influence of both biology and socialization. For example, girls exposed to high levels of prenatal androgen (congenital adrenal hyperplasia, CAH) have genitalia that are masculinized but also have working ovaries and a uterus. Although raised as females, girls with CAH display more masculine preferences, play, occupational interests, emotions and behaviors compared to non-CAH girls (Berenbaum, 1999; Ruble, Martin, & Berenbaum, 2006; Servin, Nordenstrom, Larsson, & Bohlin, 2003). Studies of Rhesus monkeys yielded similar findings: female monkeys exposed to prenatal androgens for more than 35 days display high levels of foot-clasp mounting and rough and tumble play as juveniles, behaviors typically seen in male juvenile monkeys (Wallen, 1996).

However, biological evidence does not preclude the importance of socialization. For instance, biology may predispose an individual to obesity but with simple modifications of diet, the biological predisposition will not be expressed. Gender development operates in much the same way. Gender roles are often so ingrained that it is easy to appeal to "innate" processes and forget that these roles are the learned outcomes of socialization. Indeed, countless studies indicate that boys and girls are treated differently from infancy: parents decorate their infants' rooms differently; dress girls and boys in different clothes; and describe their infants in gender-stereotyped terms within hours of the infant's birth (Karraker, Vogel, & Lake, 1995; Pomerleau, Bolduc, Malcuit, & Cossette, 1990; Rheingold & Cook, 1975; Rubin, Provenzano, & Lauria, 1974; Sweeney & Bradbard, 1988).

The differential treatment of boys and girls comes to be reflected in their behaviors and emerging knowledge about gender. There is evidence of gender awareness by 3–4 months (Quinn, Yahr, Kuhn, Slater, & Pascalis, 2002), and by 2 years of age, children label themselves as a boy or a girl and can also generally categorize others by gender as well (Ruble et al., 2006; Zosuls et al., 2009). By 3 years of age, children have basic knowledge of gender stereotypes (Signorella, Bigler, & Liben, 1993), including knowledge about toys, physical appearance and activities (Leinbach, Hort, & Fagot, 1997; Weinraub et al., 1984). By 4 years of age, children have rigid beliefs about gender and gender-appropriate behavior, as expressed in their likes and dislikes, types of play, and choices of clothes and play partners (Ruble et al., 2006).

Traditionally, *social learning theory* (Bussey & Bandura, 1999; Mischel, 1966) and *cognitive developmental theory* (Kohlberg, 1966) have been used to explain social influences on children's gender development. Social learning theory emphasizes observational learning and the role of environmental rewards and punishments in shaping children's behaviors. Children imitate others' behaviors and learn which behaviors are appropriate for their gender through the rewards and punishments that they receive. For example, a boy may put on his mother's dress while playing at the age of 2 or 3, which results in his mother directing him to remove it before his father returns. Over time, the boy will learn that it is wrong for boys to wear dresses. Thus, according to this theory, behavior precedes cognition.

In contrast, cognitive developmental theories (Kohlberg, 1966) emphasize the mediating role of cognitions in the process of gender development. Children come to understand gender as part of their cognitive development, and once they recognize that they are a boy or a girl, and that this will not change, they actively seek information about appropriate behaviors for their sex by observing those around them (Ruble & Martin, 1998). Thus, in contrast to social learning theory, cognition precedes behavior.

Despite their differences, both theories emphasize the primary role of parents as key socializing agents in their children's development. Parents provide models to children in terms of what males versus females like and do and they also reward and punish children for particular behaviors. In the balance of the chapter, we will show that beyond modeling and rewarding/punishing gendered behaviors, parents interact with their boys and girls in ways that subtly, yet powerfully scaffold children towards gendered behaviors (i.e., a Vygotskian approach to *direct* effects) as well as *indirectly* influence children through the broader family context and their relationships to economic systems.

OVERVIEW OF THEORIES

We will first illustrate the ways in which Vygotsky's theory, particularly his emphases on language and play interactions, can be brought to bear on the topic of parents' role in early development. We then turn to family systems theory to explore how reciprocal relationships among multiple family members influence children's development. Finally, economic theories pertaining to divisions of labor within and outside the home are considered.

VYGOTSKY'S THEORY AND PARENT–CHILD INTERACTIONS

Vygotsky (1978, 1986) emphasized the ways in which direct interactions between (typically) adult caregivers and their young promote children's learning and development. According to Vygotsky, what happens "between minds" during parent–child interactions comes to be internalized by the child until it is "within" the child's mind. Moreover, play and language are central to these complementary processes of learning and development. Through play and language interactions, parents directly interact with and support children's developing cognitive abilities, while also teaching children how to be active members of their cultural communities.

How might Vygotskian principles be applied to the study of gender socialization? Although Vygotsky's theory is seldom referred to in the study of gender socialization, we show how parents use the tools of play and language in different ways with their girls and boys, and how these everyday interactions come to shape children's understanding of cultural norms related to gender roles and behavior.

Play

As children play, they internalize and learn the "scripts" of their culture. For example, as children "play house", roles are assigned, such as who will play the mother and who will be the father, and actions are appointed to these different roles (e.g., who does the dishes and who mows the lawn). These actions are clearly rooted in cultural norms around gender roles. Thus, as children work through these scripts, they further solidify and internalize their understanding of the roles of people around them.

Parents are integral to children's play enactments. They implicitly teach and model such scripts, and also directly engage in play with children in ways that further convey messages about gender. For example, parents "scaffold" different types of play with girls versus boys, by encouraging girls to hug their dollies and boys to push their trucks (Lindsey & Mize, 2001; Lytton & Romney, 1991). Observational studies of children on playgrounds indicate that mothers react differently to their sons and daughters in risky situations. Mothers of sons are more likely to *physically* redirect their children around hazards in the environment, whereas mothers of girls offer more *verbal* redirection (Morrongiello & Dawber, 1998). When children engage in risky behavior (e.g., reaching for, mounting and sliding down a firehouse pole), mothers provide sons with a more physical challenge (e.g., requesting the child to reach for the pole unassisted) relative to daughters, who in contrast, receive more physical assistance and verbal cautions (Morrongiello & Dawber, 1999). Additionally, mothers assist girls more than boys during tasks that contain physical risk (e.g., climbing across a 5-foot high catwalk), whereas boys are allowed more independence than girls (Hagan & Kuebli, 2007). In turn, parents' differential treatment of boys and girls results in different behaviors in children. For example, in the context of potentially hazardous objects, boys more often touch or retrieve the object, whereas girls look at the object, verbalize, and point to elicit mothers' attention (Morrongiello & Dawber, 1998).

Language Interactions

Parents also differ in their use of language with boys versus girls. For example, mothers of daughters are more talkative, emotionally supportive and responsive in their language compared with mothers of sons (Fagot, 1995; Leaper, Anderson, & Sanders, 1998). A meta-analysis exploring gender differences in parents' talk indicates that mothers use more socioemotional language with their children, whereas fathers use more instrumental language such as directives and informing statements (Leaper et al., 1998). As a result, children witness men and women communicating in very different ways.

Shared narratives provide particularly rich examples of gender differences in parent–child language interactions. When sharing narratives about sad events with their 3-year-olds, parents of girls use more emotion words compared with parents of boys (Fivush, Broatman, Buckner, & Goodman, 2000). When talking about past experiences with young children, parents use more elaboration and evaluations with girls compared to boys (Reese, Haden, & Fivush, 1996). In our research, we find that when Latino fathers of boys talk about past memories with their sons, they are more likely to talk about experiences characterized by high levels of activity (e.g., going to an amusement park) compared with Latino fathers of girls. In contrast, Latino fathers of girls focus on quiet or social activities, such as reading or birthday parties (Cristofaro & Tamis-LeMonda, 2008).

Such differences in shared narratives convey meaningful messages to children. For example, when parents' use evaluations, they are providing feedback, acknowledgment, and praise about the child's involvement in the conversation. As girls receive more evaluations in narratives about past experiences, they also receive more positive reinforcement for engaging in conversations about feelings. Girls and boys are also being implicitly instructed about what is appropriate to talk about, and how. Such subtle forms of socialization have received less attention in the literature than explicit forms of gender socialization, such as rough-housing with boys or buying girls dolls in frilly dresses.

FAMILY SYSTEMS THEORY

Whereas a Vygotskian framework highlights direct forms of socialization in parent–child interactions, family systems theory (e.g., Bowen, 1978; Sameroff, 1983) emphasizes how multiple relationships within a family influence children's development. This perspective has only recently been applied to the study of parenting practices broadly, and gender socialization specifically.

Family systems' theorists assert that the members of a family are pieces of a larger whole, who mutually influence one another: "the functioning of any one subsystem in the family is influenced by interactions within other subsystems" (Furman & Lanthier, 2002, p. 152). To date, the application of family systems theory has often focused on the treatment of psychopathology and the psychological outcomes of family members (e.g., Broderick, 1993). Here, we examine four ways in which the family system affects children's "normal" developmental outcomes, specifically gender development: through parenting roles (in differing family structures), the mother–father relationship, triadic relationships among parents and children, and sibling relationships.

Parent Roles and Family Structure

Different models of family roles are likely to result in different trajectories of gender development in children. For example, a child with a father who is the primary caregiver will have a very different experience from one whose mother is the primary caregiver. These roles will affect children's experience with both parents, as well as the relationship between parents. And indeed, children from more egalitarian families, where fathers share caregiving responsibilities, have less knowledge of gender stereotypes at age 4 than their peers raised in more traditional homes (Fagot & Leinbach, 1995).

Family structure often dictates roles within the family system. For example, single mothers might have significant responsibilities within the household as well as in the workforce. The child will therefore witness a female engaging in multiple roles—those associated with her gender and those that are not—which may affect the child's developing understanding of gender roles. Boys and girls who are raised in single parent, mother-run households are less sex-stereotyped than children from two-parent households (McHale, Crouter, & Whiteman, 2003; Roberts, Green, Williams, & Goodman, 1987; Russel & Ellis, 1991).

There is also evidence of small differences in gender development among children raised by gay or lesbian parents. One study found that girls with lesbian mothers have fewer feminine preferences in activity and dress choices (Green, Mandel, Hotvedt, Gray, & Smith, 1986). However, differences in the gender development of children from non-traditional (i.e., single-parent, lesbian and gay-parent families) versus intact families are small in magnitude, suggesting that family structure in and of itself is not a major influence on gender development (McHale et al., 2003). Thus, other aspects of the family system need to be considered, most notably relationships among family members.

Mother–Father Relationship

The mother–father relationship is perhaps the most influential on a child's development, second only to the child's direct relationship with each parent. For example, marital conflict predicts lower parental sensitivity (Erel & Burman, 1995; Wong, Mangelsdorf, Brown, Neff, & Schoppe-Sullivan, 2009), child behavior problems (Fincham & Hall, 2005; Buehler, Anthony, Krishnakumar, & Stone, 1997), disorganized attachment in infancy (Owen & Cox, 1997), and lower parent–child relationship quality (Shek, 1998; Cowan & Cowan, 2000). The relationship between marital quality and parenting practices is commonly referred to as the "spillover effect".

Notably, associations between marital quality and parenting may differ by child sex. For example, marital conflict is related to hostile-competitive co-parenting for parents of boys but not for parents of girls (McHale, 1995). For parents of girls, high levels of marital conflict lead to larger discrepancies in the levels of parental engagement when in a triadic situation, but this is not seen among parents of boys (McHale, 1995). These findings are in-line with other research that suggests that boys are more likely to be exposed to interparental conflict than girls (Block, Block, & Morrison, 1981), whereas fathers of girls are more likely to withdraw from their daughters when the marriage is in distress as compared with fathers of boys (Amato, 1986).

Mother–Father–Child Relationship

Research on the links between marital quality and parenting also highlights the importance of "triadic" relationships (i.e., father–mother–child). For example, both mothers and fathers talk less to their children and have less physical contact with them when they are all together versus when a parent is alone with the child (Belsky, 1979). In addition, while parental warmth remains the same across dyadic and triadic situations, parental engagement with children decreases in triadic situations (Johnson, 2001). Moreover, the triadic relationship appears to affect mothers and fathers differently. When in a triadic situation with both parents, mothers are more comfortable and behave in a more traditional mothering manner, while fathers are more likely to withdraw from the parenting role (Gjerde, 1986; Johnson, 2001).

Triadic relationships are critical to the exploration of gender socialization because they provide children opportunities to witness power differentials. At an extreme, a child who witnesses a father being abusive towards a mother is the recipient of potent messages about male aggression, control, and dominance. Additionally, in triadic relationships, power differences might adversely affect parents' sensitivity to children. For example, mothers are more emotionally supportive of their children in triadic interactions in marriages with a more traditional power balance compared with mothers who are in marriage relationships characterized by power-struggle (Lindahl & Malik, 1999).

Siblings

The birth of an additional child markedly changes subsystems and relationships within the family. Early research on sibling effects on parenting primarily focused on the effects of birth order, influenced largely by the work of Adler (1931). In early development, first-born children receive more care and attention than latter-born children, whereas parents of latter-born children express less positive affection and engage with their children less frequently (e.g., Belsky, Gilstrap, & Rovine, 1984; Ernst & Angst, 1983). Over time, parents express greater expectations of achievement for their first-born (e.g., Ernst & Angst, 1983), which often results in lower tolerance, greater control and intrusiveness, and more inconsistency in parenting compared with parents of latter-born children, particularly when the first born is a girl (Ernst & Angst, 1983). Moreover, because there are no differences in the behaviors of first- versus latter-born infants, these differences can be attributed to parents (Furman & Lanthier, 2002). Longitudinal studies, which compare parenting relationships with first- and latter-born siblings within the same family, support these findings (e.g., Dunn & Kendrick, 1980).

However, with rare exceptions (e.g., McHale, Updegraff, Helms-Erickson, & Crouter, 2001; Tucker, McHale, & Crouter, 2003), the influence of siblings on children's gender development has been relatively neglected. Yet siblings provide models of gendered behavior for children and serve as important points of comparison. In particular, the manner in which parents interact with male or female siblings may influence children's developing understanding of gender. This is where the family systems perspective is particularly helpful, because it focuses on looking at each part of the system: each parent, and each sibling, as both a separate input into the system as well as part of the larger whole (see Bornstein & Sawyer, 2006). A series of studies examining within-family comparisons of siblings found that parents of siblings of the same sex interact with their children differently from parents of different sex siblings. In families with boys and girls, parents tend to spend more time with children who are their gender; fathers spend more time with sons and mothers spend more time with daughters (Crouter, Helms-Erickson, Updegraff, & McHale, 1999). Because of the shared time in conversation and activities, parents of mixed gender siblings know more about children who are their same sex versus those who are the opposite sex (Crouter et al., 1999). The sex of siblings also has been found to relate to children's personalities, allocation of family chores, and children's overall feelings of fairness in treatment by their parents. In households in which parents hold traditional beliefs about gender and gender roles, there is evidence of greater sex typing in children's personalities when children are of the same gender (McHale, Crouter, & Tucker, 1999). For example, in such families, with two boys, the boys act in more masculine ways than boys in a family with a boy and a girl, but if the parents hold to less traditional beliefs, this difference disappears. In addition, children who live in families with siblings of the opposite sex are more likely to rate their parents as fair in treatment and allocation of family chores, compared with children in families with same-sex siblings (McHale, Updegraff, Jackson-Newsom, Tucker, & Crouter, 2000). All of these findings are more robust in families in which parents have traditional attitudes about gender.

Beyond parents' treatment of siblings, siblings themselves influence one another. First-born children are more likely to model their parents' behavior, but second-borns are more likely to model the behaviors of their older siblings (McHale et al., 2001). In addition, play between siblings is influenced by the older sibling's sex. When the older child is a boy, the play of the younger sibling takes on a more masculine style, whereas the younger sibling's play style is more feminine when the older sibling is a girl (Stoneman, Brody, & MacKinnon, 1986; Rust et al., 2000).

In addition, children who have siblings of the opposite sex hold less gender-stereotyped attitudes than children without opposite-sex siblings (Stoneman et al., 1986). Viewed through a family systems approach, this outcome could be viewed as a result of feedback from the family (see Klein & White, 1996). For example, if a 3-year-old boy has a 5-year-old sister, there is a good chance that his sister will be a primary play partner, and as an older play partner, she may dictate how they will play and with what toys. Thus, he may have a great deal of experience playing with dolls or playing in a more stereotypical female way than a 3-year-old boy with a 5-year-old brother. The boy might receive positive reinforcement from his sister for playing in the way she dictates, from his parents for being a cooperative play partner, and he may feel personally rewarded because he is not bored. The input and output of the system help to encourage engagement in types of play that would potentially be very different if the older sibling were a boy.

ECONOMIC THEORY

The family system does not operate in isolation, but rather is influenced by a variety of factors, including division of labor within and outside the family system. Household economics and division of labor play out in the daily lives of family members in a variety of ways, including who leaves for work and for how long and who manages children's schedules. Children are keen observers of these everyday dynamics, and family economic resources and labor will largely shape their own behaviors and attitudes regarding gender.

Surprisingly, scholars in the field of economics did not really begin to explore the family as a unit until the 1970s, as described in Becker's *Treatise on the Family* (1991). His work further pioneered economic models of parenting behavior, particularly how parents garner, organize, and allocate resources (Duncan & Magnuson, 2002). Based on a production model much like the production of a factory, Becker and others argue that the production in a household will be more efficient and rewarding if the members of the household (traditionally the husband and wife) divide the labor, with each having a specialty. Most often this is broken down into one member specializing in outside paid work while the other specializes in work inside the home, including childrearing (Becker, 1991). Thus, the two partners will "produce" more than they would if they lived separately. Although this division is not necessarily divided along gender lines, some economists argue that because of gender discrimination in the labor market, the earning potential of women may be less, thus making the male the more productive member in terms of paid work outside the home (see Bianchi, Milkie, Sayer, & Robinson, 2000).

Household Labor

How might division of labor within the home affect gender development? Parents who enact traditional division of labor will model gender differently than parents who take on more non-traditional roles, and thus this division can influence children's growing understanding of gender even in early childhood (e.g., Serbin, Powlishta, & Gulko, 1993). In our own work, we have found that the division of household labor within a family predicts how 4-year-old girls think others view their own gender. As disparities in the division of housework between mothers and fathers increase, girls are increasingly likely to believe that others think boys are better than girls. This is so powerful that an additional unit of housework (e.g., report of doing "some of it" versus "most of it") for mothers compared with fathers results in girls who are twice as likely to believe this, when compared with girls from households with equal division of labor (Halim, Ruble, Tamis-LeMonda, in press).

Much research on division of household labor can be classified under three major emphases: (1) time constraints; (2) relative resources; and (3) gender perspectives (Pinto & Coltrane, 2009). The time constraint theme stresses rational division of household labor based on family composition and outside work schedules (Almeida, Maggs, & Galambos, 1993; Pinto & Coltrane, 2009). The more people in the household, the more work there is in the household, but the more an individual works outside the home, the less time there is for engaging in household labor. The theme of relative resources (more recently termed "economic dependence", Gupta, 2006) asserts that individuals will use resources such as education, salary, or occupational prestige to be less involved in housework (Becker, 1991; Blood & Wolfe, 1960). Thus, the spouse with more of these resources will do less housework. Indeed, spouses who are more equal across these resources have more equal division of household labor (Blair & Lichter, 1991; Kamo & Cohen, 1998).

The gendered perspective on household labor asserts that neither the time constraint nor relative resource theory adequately capture the role of gender and cultural norms in the division of household labor. Because of the historical and cultural nature of gender and household labor, household labor is not gender neutral. For example, when it comes to childcare and the additional work that is inherent with the arrival of a new infant, time constraints are different for men and women. During infancy, and especially for breastfeeding mothers, infants will require more time with their mothers versus fathers, and mothers will respond to this need. Men on the other hand, do not necessarily change their work schedules to accommodate childcare in the same way.

In turn, the division of household labor is a powerful force of gender socialization within the home. Parents' engagement in certain types of housework and activities with their children has been linked to children's knowledge of gender, career aspirations, and penchant for playing with same-sex peers (Serbin et al., 1993). Moreover, these influences are already seen early in development. For example, children from families who display a traditional division of labor within and outside the household have more gender stereotype knowledge by 2–3 years old (Weinraub et al., 1984), whereas children with parents who are less traditional in these divisions have generally less stereo-typed gender schemas (Turner & Gervai, 1995).

Work Outside the Home

Research on work outside the home and parenting has largely been focused on mothers, due to the historical precedent of mothers being primary caregivers as well as the biological necessity that makes maternal investment much higher in the early years of a child's life, from conception through weaning (Keller & Chasiotis, 2007). However, the movement of mothers into the workplace led to a surge of studies on the effects of maternal work on child development, with many early studies indicating detrimental effects (e.g., Barglow, Vaughn, & Molitor, 1987; Belsky, 1988; Hoffman, 1980; Howes & Stewart, 1987). It has also been suggested that the timing of a mother's re-entry into the labor market matters. For example, the amount of time a mother works in the first year of a child's life is negatively related to cognitive development as measured by the Peabody Picture Vocabulary Test (PPVT), whereas time spent at work during a child's second and third year of life has no detrimental effect (Baydar & Brooks-Gunn, 1991; Blau & Grossberg, 1992; Brooks-Gunn, Han, & Waldfogel, 2002). Moreover, some studies suggest that mothers' work status outside of the home has little to no long-term influence on children's development when compared with children raised by stay-at-home mothers (Greenstein, 1995; Harvey, 1999; Nomaguchi, 2006; Parcel & Menaghan, 1994). Mothers who work outside the home often sacrifice other areas of their lives, such as volunteer work and sleep, to ensure that they are spending time with their children (McHale, Bartko, Crouter, & Perry-Jenkins, 1990). Additionally, in dual earner families, fathers take on more responsibilities of childcare and housework than in single earner families (Crouter, Head, Bumpus, & McHale, 2001).

Interestingly, the influence of maternal work status on children's development depends on children's gender. A consistent finding is that boys suffer more from a loss of maternal attention, which is often associated with a mother's return to work, than girls (Benn, 1986; Chase-Lansdale & Owen, 1987; Bornstein, Hahn, Gist, Haynes, 2006). A review of 50 years of research indicates that the greater disadvantage for boys has remained steady (Hoffman, 1984). Moreover, boys are more sensitive to the quality of childcare received than girls. Boys who receive childcare from a grandmother or relative are likely to have higher PPVT scores than if they were placed in center-based care (Baydar & Brooks-Gunn, 1991). Perhaps boys are more influenced by a lack of stability and less attached caregivers than girls (Baydar & Brooks-Gunn, 1991).

In contrast, maternal work status may have a positive effect on girls' cognitive development. Girls whose mothers return to work during their second year of life have higher PPVT scores than girls of mothers who never worked outside of the home (Desai, Chase-Lansdale, & Michael, 1989; Goldberg, Prause, Lucas-Thompson, & Himsel, 2008). Additionally, girls who are placed in non-maternal care have higher test scores than girls in maternal care (Mott, 1991). Babysitter care is beneficial for girls' behavioral and socioemotional outcomes, whereas maternal care supports these outcomes in boys (Mott, 1991).

What might explain differences in the effects of maternal work outside the home for boys versus girls? There is some suggestion that mothers' interactions with their children are influenced by mother-work status. When mothers are employed, they engage in more positive interactions with their daughters than unemployed mothers, who engage in more positive interactions with their sons (Zaslow, Pedersen, Suwalsky, & Rabinovich, 1989; see also Braungart-Rieker, Courtney, & Garwood, 1999). Mothers' views of their boys versus girls also differ with maternal-work status. For example, when asked to describe their children, both part-time and stay at home mothers talk about their sons' activity level in positive terms and "describe their sons as compliant and affectionate" (Alvarez, 1985, p. 356). On the other hand, mothers who are employed full-time describe their sons' activity level in negative terms, and "describe their sons as being demanding and noncompliant" (Alvarez, 1985, p. 356). Girls on the other hand are most often described in terms of their looks, and caring abilities. However, highly educated and employed mothers also favorably describe their daughters in terms of independence and intelligence. These findings indicate the complex ways in which maternal employment status and child sex interact in their effects on parenting and children's development.

LIMITATIONS OF THEORY FOR UNDERSTANDING EARLY GENDER ROLE SOCIALIZATION

In this chapter, we applied three complementary theories to an understanding of parents' gender socialization in children's early development. Nonetheless, each demonstrates limitations that point to future directions for research. In particular, under each broad theoretical umbrella there is need to consider the subtle and implicit behaviors of parents that convey potent messages to children about gender. Below, we provide some examples of these behaviors and how their study can yield valuable insight into early gender socialization within the family system and advance the current focus of all three theories.

EXPANDING VYGOTSKY'S THEORY

As noted above, language and play are core mediums for children's development. However, in the area of language interactions, research to date has been limited to studies on narratives and emotion talk during children's preschool years. This is perhaps influenced by Vygotsky's emphasis on cognitive developmental change over time, without taking into consideration the influence of social developmental change. There is strong reason to believe that parents talk with boys and girls in different ways already from infancy. For example, mothers of 6-month old girls ask more interpretive questions of their infants (e.g., "You're playing with the octopus. You like that, right?") than mothers of boys—well before children can actually respond to such questions (Clearfield & Nelson, 2006). These early ways of talking might pave the way for different ways of viewing the world and interacting with others. Vygotsky's theories could benefit from an inclusion of looking at how talk and narratives between parent's and children change over an extended period of time as children develop. In particular, children's growing awareness and understanding of gender will almost certainly influence their interactions with their parents, and perhaps will influence parents as well in terms of their verbal interactions with their child. While Vygotskian theory is rarely applied to the study of gender socalization, the influence of our understanding of methods of gender socialization could in turn help to expand Vygotskian theory to emphasize the ways that parents' expectations, beliefs, social norms, etc., come to shape the process of "scaffolding" in early development.

Play interactions provide an illustration of how Vygotskian theory might be expanded to include a focus on gender. Most research on mother–child play focuses on *what* is played with (toys, dolls), rather than styles of play. This work shows that boys engage in more rough and tumble play than girls (Ruble et al., 2006), and parents of boys more often promote this style of play than parents of girls (Fagot, 1978). However, the study of parent–child play leaves much to be examined in terms of gendered differences in other aspects of play, including styles and types of play, particularly since gendered choices about *which* toys to play with may have broader implications for the types of play displayed. For example, dolls engender nurturance and care, whereas trucks elicit active types of play. Recent work indicates an association between preferences for toys that allow for propulsion (forward movement) and masculinity, as rated by teachers (Benenson, Liroff, Pascal, & Cioppa, 1997). There is limited work, however, on how parents encourage or discourage these particular play forms in their children. Therefore, building on Vygotsky's theoretical emphasis on the role of play on cognitive development, how does gender socialization fit into the picture? Applying Vygotskian theory to the study of gender socialization not only provides a new perspective of how boys and girls come to understand gender roles, but also potentially expands Vygotskian theory as well.

EXPANDING FAMILY SYSTEMS THEORY

As previously shown, family systems' theorists describe the ways in which multiple family members interact with one another and how this then affects children's development. Although we have extended family systems theory to gender socialization and early gender development, such an application is rare. As noted above, family systems theorists often focus on psychological dysfunction within families. However, their emphasis on the family as a system, which presents individuals with psychological and social input, output and feedback, could certainly be applied to look at more normative developmental outcomes, such as gender socialization. There is a dearth of studies on the ways that relationships among family members, as well as the participatory structures of households—in terms of the activities of which children are participants and those they are not—might come to shape gender development. For example, if a father takes his son grocery shopping, or asks his son to help out with the feeding and bathing of an infant sibling, his son has the opportunity to participate in activities typically defined as within the jurisdiction of women, while also witnessing a male role model in these non-traditional settings. These are all important sources of input in a family system's view. In contrast, in a family that ascribes more to gender attitudes and beliefs, daughters might assist with grocery shopping and childcare, solidifying messages about these gendered roles. As such, families create "affordances for action" (Gibson, 1979) that provide opportunities for particular kinds of behavior (Chemero, 2008).

In our own work, we have begun to explore gender differences in other areas of action affordances created within the family system, as for example, in opportunities for movement in infancy. When infants are as young as 5 months, first-time mothers of boys provide different affordances for movement than first-time mothers of girls. As one example, during everyday interactions with their infants, mothers place infant girls in restricted movement environments, such as being strapped to high chairs or swings, more often than mothers of boys, well before any differences in motor skills are seen (Smith Leavell, Tamis-LeMonda, Ruble, Scherer, & Scudellari, 2010). Such work highlights the need to consider the ways that family systems create different affordances for action for boys and girls early in the developmental process.

EXPANDING ECONOMIC THEORY

Studies out of an economic tradition highlight the ways that labor market participation and household labor differ by parent gender, as well as how household structure might affect parents' roles in these two worlds of work. However, researchers rarely examine how these divisions of labor and family structures directly affect children's early gendered experiences and development. Moreover, there is again need for focus on ways in which very nuanced forms of economic behavior might affect children's development. For example, even when both parents work outside the home, and share household and childcare duties, they likely engage in gendered behaviors in the absence of explicit awareness. As one example, when a family goes to dinner, the check is typically set down in front of the father, who will respond by pulling out his wallet, even if the money comes from shared economic contributions. These subtle behaviors contain implicit messages about power and gender that may be transmitted to children who witness such economic transactions on a daily basis. Economic theory would benefit from expansion to these micro-contexts of children's gender development, which in turn may shape future academic and career choices in boys and girls (indeed, it is noteworthy that men are largely the economists and business majors of the world!).

SUGGESTIONS FOR FUTURE THEORY USE

THEORY IN A CULTURAL CONTEXT

This chapter highlights the value of considering parenting and gender socialization in early childhood from multiple theoretical approaches. Much of the literature on gender development has traditionally targeted the historical debate of nature versus nurture, with studies of gender socialization focusing on children's observational learning (*social learning theory*) and understanding of gender (*cognitive developmental theory*). Here, we demonstrated the value of also considering sociocultural, family systems, and economic theories in the study of early gender socialization and development.

As shown, each theory has merit. Vygotsky and neo-Vygotskian theorists point to the importance of direct social exchanges between parents and children in shaping children's development. A family systems approach extends this work to consideration of multiple family members and relationships. Economic theory further expands focus to the ways that economic dynamics and structures within and outside of households shape everyday contexts of development.

However, the various theories each have limitations: there is a need for a more nuanced approach to the study of gender socialization and development, as well as call for attention to very early developmental processes. However, beyond the specific limitations and suggestions indicated in this chapter, there is a need to consider the role of *culture* across all theories, as culture permeates the everyday structures and relationships in children's lives. From a Vygotskian perspective, interactions between parents and their young reflect a common cultural goal of raising children to fit within and become active contributors to their cultural communities. Thus, gendered interactions between parents and children might serve a useful function in certain cultural contexts (e.g., hunter-gatherer communities where specialization is critical to survival), yet be disadvantageous in others (e.g., societies that espouse equality between the sexes in education and the labor market). Relatedly, the economic processes of households will vary across cultural communities, if for example, there are different needs and beliefs regarding women's and men's work within and outside the home. The reality is that all of the research reviewed in this chapter is based on studies of families in the US, largely from White middle-class backgrounds. There is therefore a need to consider similarities and differences in patterns of parenting and child development across families from different cultural backgrounds within the US, as well as across the globe.

In our own work, we examined ethnic variation in how fathers from low-income backgrounds within the US differ in their everyday activities with their young children (Smith Leavell, Tamis-LeMonda, Ruble, Zoslus, & Cabrrera, 2012). Ethnic similarities in gendered patterns of father–child activities were observed; regardless of ethnic background, fathers of girls engaged in more literacy activities with their children than fathers of boys, whereas fathers of boys engaged in more physical play than fathers of girls. Nonetheless, ethnic differences were also seen. For example, Black fathers of sons reported higher levels of engagement in three out of four types of daily activities than did Black fathers of daughters. This gender difference was not seen among White and Latino fathers. Black fathers of sons also engaged in higher levels of physical play and social activities with their children than did White fathers of sons. These differences might be attributed to fathers' concerns about the plight of Black boys in the US context, leading these involved fathers to spend more time with their sons than daughters.

CONCLUSION

Vygotsky's sociocultural, family systems, and economic theories have been peripheral to the study of early gender development, as most work in this area has been framed by social learning theory and cognitive-developmental theory. In part, this division reflects differential emphases on "developing children" versus the "context of children's development". Moreover, most work on gender development and socialization neglects foundational processes during infancy and early childhood. Scholarly advances rest on increasing integrative approaches, in which multiple theories are brought to bear in the study of young children's development in context. Early in children's lives, nuanced patterns of parent–child interactions, the roles and relationships of different family members, and divisions of labor within and outside the household communicate potent messages about the behaviors that are expected of girls and boys and the relative power of the two genders. Over developmental time, even small differences in parents' views and practices, and children's own behaviors and attitudes, will evolve into large effects that may alter the trajectories of children's development.

REFERENCES

Adler, A. (1931). *What life should mean to you*. Oxford, England: Little, Brown.

Almeida, D. M., Maggs, J. L., & Galambos, N. L. (1993). Wives' employment hours and spousal participation in family work. *Journal of Family Psychology, 7*, 233–244.

Alvarez, W. F. (1985). The meaning of maternal employment for mothers and their perceptions of their three-year-old children. *Child Development. Special Issue: Family Development, 56*, 350–360.

Amato, P. R. (1986). Marital conflict, the parent–child relationship and child self-esteem. *Family Relations: An Interdisciplinary Journal of Applied Family Studies, 35*, 403–410.

Barglow, P., Vaughn, B. E., & Molitor, N. (1987). Effects of maternal absence due to employment on the quality of infant–mother attachment in a low-risk sample. *Child Development, 58*, 945–954.

Baydar, N., & Brooks-Gunn, J. (1991). Effects of maternal employment and child-care arrangements on preschoolers' cognitive and behavioral outcomes: Evidence from the children of the national longitudinal survey of youth. *Developmental Psychology, 27*, 932–945.

Becker, G. S. (1991). *A treatise on the family*. Cambridge, MA: Harvard University Press.

Belsky, J. (1979). Mother–father–infant interaction: A naturalistic observational study. *Developmental Psychology, 15*, 601–607.

Belsky, J. (1988). The "effects" of infant day care reconsidered. *Early Childhood Research Quarterly. Special Issue: Infant Day Care, 3*, 235–272.

Belsky, J., Gilstrap, B., & Rovine, M. (1984). The Pennsylvania infant and family development project: I. stability and change in mother–infant and father–infant interaction in a family setting at one, three, and nine months. *Child Development, 55*, 692–705.

Benenson, J. F., Liroff, E. R., Pascal, S. J., & Cioppa, G. D. (1997). Propulsion: A behavioural expression of masculinity. *British Journal of Developmental Psychology, 15*, 37–50.

Benn, R. K. (1986). Factors promoting secure attachment relationships between employed mothers and their sons. *Child Development, 57*, 1224–1231.

Berenbaum, S. A. (1999). Effects of early androgens on sex-typed activities and interests in adolescents with congenital adrenal hyperplasia. *Hormones and Behavior, 35*, 102–110.

Bianchi, S. M., Milkie, M. A., Sayer, L. C., & Robinson, J. P. (2000). Is anyone doing the housework? Trends in the gender division of household labor. *Social Forces, 79*, 191–228.

Blair, S. L., & Lichter, D. T. (1991). Measuring the division of household labor: Gender segregation of housework among American couples. *Journal of Family Issues, 12*, 91–113.

Blau, F. D., & Grossberg, A. J. (1992). Maternal labor supply and children's cognitive development. *Review of Economics and Statistics, 74*, 474–481.

Block, J. H., Block, J., & Morrison, A. (1981). Parental agreement–disagreement on child-rearing orientations and gender-related personality correlates in children. *Child Development, 52*, 965–974.

Blood, R. O. Jr., & Wolfe, D. M. (1960). *Husbands and wives: The dynamics of family living*. Oxford, England: Free Press Glencoe.

Bornstein, M. H., Hahn, C., Gist, N. F., & Haynes, O. M. (2006). Long-term cumulative effects of childcare on children's mental development and socioemotional adjustment in a non-risk sample: The moderating effects of gender. *Early Child Development and Care, 176*, 129–156.

Bornstein, M. H. & Sawyer, J. (2006). Family systems. In K. McCarthy, & D. Phillips (Eds.), *Blackwell handbook of early childhood development* (pp. 381–398). Malden, MA: Blackwell.

Bowen, M. (1978). *Family therapy in clinical practice*. New York: Jason Aronson.

Braungart-Rieker, J., Courtney, S., & Garwood, M. M. (1999). Mother– and father–infant attachment: Families in context. *Journal of Family Psychology, 13*, 535–553.

Broderick, C. B. (1993). *Understanding family process: Basics of family systems theory*. Thousand Oaks, CA: Sage.

Brooks-Gunn, J., Han, W., & Waldfogel, J. (2002). Maternal employment and child cognitive outcomes in the first three years of life: The NICHD study of early child care. *Child Development, 73*, 1052–1072.

Bruner, J. S. (1991). *Nature and uses of immaturity*. Florence, KY: Taylor & Frances/Routledge.

Bruner, J. S. (1992). The narrative construction of reality. In H. Beilin, & P. B. Pufall (Eds.), *Piaget's theory: Prospects and possibilities* (pp. 229–248). Hillsdale, NJ: Lawrence Erlbaum.

Buehler, C., Anthony, C., Krishnakumar, A., & Stone, G. (1997). Interparental conflict and youth problem behaviors: A meta-analysis. *Journal of Child and Family Studies, 6*, 223–247.

Bussey, K., & Bandura, A. (1999). Social cognitive theory of gender development and differentiation. *Psychological Review, 106*, 676–713.

Chase-Lansdale, P. L., & Owen, M. T. (1987). Maternal employment in a family context: Effects on infant-mother and infant-father attachments. *Child Development, 58*, 1505–1512.

Chemero, A. (2008). Self-organization, writ large. *Ecological Psychology, 20*, 257–269.

Cristofaro, T. N., & Tamis-LeMonda, C. S. (2008). Mother-Child and Father-Child Personal Narratives in Latino Families. In A. McCabe, A. L. Bailey, & G. Melzi (Eds.), *Spanish-language narration and literacy* (pp. 54–91). New York: Cambridge University Press.

Clearfield, M. W., & Nelson, N. M. (2006). Sex differences in mothers' speech and play behavior with 6-, 9-, and 14-month-old infants. *Sex Roles, 54*, 127–137.

Cowan, C. P., & Cowan, P. A. (2000). *When partners become parents: The big life change for couples*. Mahwah, NJ: Lawrence Erlbaum.

Crouter, A. C., Head, M. R., Bumpus, M. F., & McHale, S. M. (2001). Household chores: Under what conditions do mothers lean on daughters? In A. J. Fuligni (Ed.), *Biennial meeting of the society for research on adolescence, April 2000, Chicago, IL, US; an earlier version of this article was presented at the aforementioned conference* (pp. 23–41). San Francisco, CA: Jossey-Bass.

Crouter, A. C., Helms-Erickson, H., Updegraff, K., & McHale, S. M. (1999). Conditions underlying parents' knowledge about children's daily lives in middle childhood: Between-and within-family comparisons. *Child Development, 70*, 246–259.

Desai, S., Chase-Lansdale, P. L., & Michael, R. T. (1989). Mother or market? effects of maternal employment on the intellectual ability of 4-year-old children. *Demography, 26*, 545–561.

Duncan, G. J., & Magnuson, K. A. (2002). Economics and parenting. *Parenting: Science and Practice, 2*, 437–450.

Dunn, J., & Kendrick, C. (1980). The arrival of a sibling: Changes in patterns of interaction between mother and first-born child. *Journal of Child Psychology and Psychiatry, 21*, 119–132.

Erel, O., & Burman, B. (1995). Interrelatedness of marital relations and parent–child relations: A meta-analytic review. *Psychological Bulletin, 118*, 108–132.

Ernst, C., & Angst, J. (1983). *Birth order: Its influence on personality*. New York: Springer-Verlag.

Fagot, B. I. (1978). The influence of sex of child on parental reactions to toddler children. *Child Development, 49*, 459–465.

Fagot, B. I. (1995). Parenting boys and girls. In M. H. Bornstein (Ed.), *Handbook of parenting, Vol. 1: Children and parenting* (pp. 163–183). Hillsdale, NJ: Lawrence Erlbaum.

Fagot, B. I., & Leinbach, M. D. (1995). Gender knowledge in egalitarian and traditional families. *Sex Roles, 32*, 513–526.

Fincham, F. D., & Hall, J. H. (2005). Parenting and the marital relationship. In T. Luster, & L. Okagaki (Eds.), *Parenting: An ecological perspective* (2nd ed.) (pp. 205–233). Mahwah, NJ: Lawrence Erlbaum.

Fivush, R., Brotman, M. A., Buckner, J. P., & Goodman, S. H. (2000). Gender differences in parent–child emotion narratives. *Sex Roles, 42*, 233–253.

Furman, W., & Lanthier, R. (2002). Parenting siblings. In M. H. Bornstein (Ed.), *Handbook of parenting: Vol. 1: Children and parenting* (2nd ed.) (pp. 165–188). Mahwah, NJ: Lawrence Erlbaum.

Gibson, J. J. (1979). *The ecological approach to visual perception*. Boston, MA: Houghton, Mifflin.

Gjerde, P. F. (1986). The interpersonal structure of family interaction settings: Parent–adolescent relations in dyads and triads. *Developmental Psychology, 22*, 297–304.

Goldberg, W. A., Prause, J., Lucas-Thompson, R., & Himsel, A. (2008). Maternal employment and children's achievement in context: A meta-analysis of four decades of research. *Psychological Bulletin, 134*, 77–108.

Green, R., Mandel, J., Hotvedt, M., Gray, J., & Smith, L. (1986). Lesbian mothers and their children: A comparison with solo parent heterosexual mothers and their children. *Archives of Sexual Behavior, 15*, 167–184.

Greenstein, T. N. (1995). Are the "most advantaged" children truly disadvantaged by early maternal employment? Effects on child cognitive outcomes. *Journal of Family Issues, 16*, 149–169.

Gupta, S. (2006). Her money, her time: Women's earnings and their housework hours. *Social Science Research, 35*, 975–999.

Hagan, L. K., & Kuebli, J. (2007). Mothers' and fathers' socialization of preschoolers' physical risk taking. *Journal of Applied Developmental Psychology, 28*, 2–14.

Halim, M. L., Ruble, D. N., Tamis-LeMonda, C. S. (2012). Four-year-olds' beliefs about how others regard males and females. *British Journal of Developmental Psychology*. doi: 10.1111/j.2044-835X.2012.02084.x

Harvey, E. (1999). Short-term and long-term effects of early parental employment on children of the national longitudinal survey of youth. *Developmental Psychology, 35*, 445–459.

Hoffman, L. W. (1980). The effects of maternal employment on the academic attitudes and performance of school-aged children. *School Psychology Review, 9*, 319–335.

Hoffman, L. W. (1984). Maternal employment and the young child. In M. Perlmutter (Ed.), *Minnesota symposium in child psychology* (pp. 101–127). Hillside, NJ: Lawrence Erlbaum.

Howes, C., & Stewart, P. (1987). Child's play with adults, toys, and peers: An examination of family and child-care influences. *Developmental Psychology, 23*, 423–430.

Johnson, V. K. (2001). Marital interaction, family organization, and differences in parenting behavior: Explaining variations across family interaction contexts. *Family Process, 40*, 333–342.

Kamo, Y., & Cohen, E. L. (1998). Division of household work between partners: A comparison of black and white couples. *Journal of Comparative Family Studies. Special Issue: Comparative Perspectives on Black Family Life, 29*, 131–145.

Karraker, K. H., Vogel, D. A., & Lake, M. A. (1995). Parents' gender-stereotyped perceptions of newborns: The eye of the beholder revisited. *Sex Roles, 33*, 687–701.

Keller, H., & Chasiotis, A. (2007). Maternal investment. In C. A. Salmon, & T. K. Shackelford (Eds.), *Family relationships: An evolutionary perspective.* (pp. 91–114). New York: Oxford University Press.

Klein, D. M., & White, J. M. (1996). *Family theories: An introduction*. Thousand Oaks, CA: Sage.

Kohlberg, L. A. (1966). A cognitive-developmental analysis of children's sex-role concepts and attitudes. In E. E. Maccoby (Ed.), *The development of sex differences*. Stanford, CA: Stanford University Press.

Leaper, C., Anderson, K. J., & Sanders, P. (1998). Moderators of gender effects on parents' talk to their children: A meta-analysis. *Developmental Psychology, 34*, 3–27.

Leinbach, M. D., Hort, B. E., & Fagot, B. I. (1997). Bears are for boys: Metaphorical associations in young children's gender stereotypes. *Cognitive Development, 12*, 107–130.

Lindahl, K. M., & Malik, N. M. (1999). Marital conflict, family processes, and boys' externalizing behavior in Hispanic American and European American families. *Journal of Clinical Child Psychology, 28,* 12–24.

Lindsey, E. W., & Mize, J. (2001). Contextual differences in parent-child play: Implications for children's gender role development. *Sex Roles, 44,* 155–176.

Luria, A. R. (1976). *Cognitive development: Its cultural and social foundations. (trans M. Lopez-Morillas & L. Solotaroff).* Oxford, England: Harvard University Press.

Lytton, H., & Romney, D. M. (1991). Parents' differential socialization of boys and girls: A meta-analysis. *Psychological Bulletin, 109,* 267–296.

McHale, J. P. (1995). Coparenting and triadic interactions during infancy: The roles of marital distress and child gender. *Developmental Psychology, 31,* 985–996.

McHale, S. M., Bartko, W. T., Crouter, A. C., & Perry-Jenkins, M. (1990). Children's housework and psychosocial functioning: The mediating effects of parents' sex-role behaviors and attitudes. *Child Development, 61,* 1413–1426.

McHale, S. M., Crouter, A. C., & Tucker, C. J. (1999). Family context and gender role socialization in middle childhood: Comparing girls to boys and sisters to brothers. *Child Development, 70,* 990–1004.

McHale, S. M., Crouter, A. C., & Whiteman, S. D. (2003). The family contexts of gender development in childhood and adolescence. *Social Development, 12,* 125–148.

McHale, S. M., Updegraff, K. A., Helms-Erikson, H., & Crouter, A. C. (2001). Sibling influences on gender development in middle childhood and early adolescence: A longitudinal study. *Developmental Psychology, 37,* 115–125.

McHale, S. M., Updegraff, K. A., Jackson-Newsom, J., Tucker, C. J., & Crouter, A. C. (2000). When does parents' differential treatment have negative implications for siblings? *Social Development, 9,* 149–172.

Mischel, W. (1966). A social learning view of sex differences in behavior. In E. E. Maccoby (Ed.), *The development of sex differences* (pp. 56–81). Stanford, CA: Stanford University Press.

Morrongiello, B. A., & Dawber, T. (1998). Toddlers' and mothers' behaviors in an injury-risk situation: Implications for sex differences in childhood injuries. *Journal of Applied Developmental Psychology, 19,* 625–639.

Morrongiello, B. A., & Dawber, T. (1999). Parental influences on toddlers' injury-risk behaviors: Are sons and daughters socialized differently? *Journal of Applied Developmental Psychology, 20,* 227–251.

Mott, F. L. (1991). Developmental effects of infant care: The mediating role of gender and health. *Journal of Social Issues, 47,* 139–158.

Nomaguchi, K. M. (2006). Maternal employment, nonparental care, mother-child interactions, and child outcomes during preschool years. *Journal of Marriage and Family, 68,* 1341–1369.

Owen, M. T., & Cox, M. J. (1997). Marital conflict and the development of infant–parent attachment relationships. *Journal of Family Psychology, 11,* 152–164.

Parcel, T. L., & Menaghan, E. G. (1994). Early parental work, family social capital, and early childhood outcomes. *American Journal of Sociology, 99,* 972–1009.

Piaget, J. (1932). *The moral judgment of the child.* Oxford, England: Harcourt, Brace.

Piaget, J. (1952). *The origins of intelligence in children.* Oxford, England: International Universities Press.

Pinto, K. M., & Coltrane, S. (2009). Divisions of labor in Mexican origin and Anglo families: Structure and culture. *Sex Roles, 60,* 482–495.

Pomerleau, A., Bolduc, D., Malcuit, G., & Cossette, L. (1990). Pink or blue: Environmental gender stereotypes in the first two years of life. *Sex Roles, 22,* 359–367.

Quinn, P. C., Yahr, J., Kuhn, A., Slater, A. M., & Pascalis, O. (2002). Representation of the gender of human faces by infants: A preference for female. *Perception, 31,* 1109–1121.

Reese, E., Haden, C. A., & Fivush, R. (1996). Mothers, fathers, daughters, sons: Gender differences in autobiographical reminiscing. *Research on Language and Social Interaction. Special Issue: Constituting Gender through Talk in Childhood: Conversations in Parent-Child, Peer, and Sibling Relationships, 29,* 27–56.

Rheingold, H. L., & Cook, K. V. (1975). The contents of boys' and girls' rooms as an index of parents' behavior. *Child Development, 46,* 459–463.

Roberts, C. W., Green, R., Williams, K., & Goodman, M. (1987). Boyhood gender identity development: A statistical contrast of two family groups. *Developmental Psychology, 23,* 544–557.

Rogoff, B. (2003). *The cultural nature of human development.* New York: Oxford University Press.

Rubin, J. S., Provenzano, F., & Lauria, Z. (1974). The eye of the beholder: Parents' views on sex of newborns. *American Journal of Orthopsychiatry, 44*, 512–519.

Ruble, D. N., & Martin, C. L. (1998). Gender development. In W. Damon, & N. Eisenberg (Eds.), *Handbook of child psychology* (5th ed., pp. 933–1016). New York: John Wiley.

Ruble, D. N., Martin, C. L., & Berenbaum, S. A. (2006). Gender development. In N. Eisenberg, W. Damon & R. M. Lerner (Eds.), *Handbook of child psychology: Vol. 3, Social, emotional, and personality development* (6th ed., pp. 858–932). Hoboken, NJ: John Wiley.

Russell, C. D., & Ellis, J. B. (1991). Sex-role development in single parent households. *Social Behavior and Personality, 19*, 5–9.

Rust, J., Golombok, S., Hines, M., Johnston, K., Golding, J., & ALSPAC Study Team. (2000). The role of brothers and sisters in the gender development of preschool children. *Journal of Experimental Child Psychology. Special Issue: Sex and Gender Development, 77*, 292–303.

Sameroff, A. J. (1983). Developmental systems: Context and evolution. In P. H. Mussen, & W. Kessen (Eds.), *Handbook of child psychology: History, theory, and methods, Vol. 1* (pp. 237–294). New York: John Wiley.

Serbin, L. A., Powlishta, K. K., & Gulko, J. (1993). The development of sex typing in middle childhood. *Monographs of the Society for Research in Child Development, 58*, 5–74.

Servin, A., Nordenström, A., Larsson, A., & Bohlin, G. (2003). Prenatal androgens and gender-typed behavior: A study of girls with mild and severe forms of congenital adrenal hyperplasia. *Developmental Psychology, 39*, 440–450.

Shek, D. T. L. (1998). Linkage between marital quality and parent–child relationship. *Journal of Family Issues, 19*, 687–704.

Signorella, M. L., Bigler, R. S., & Liben, L. S. (1993). Developmental differences in children's gender schemata about others: A meta-analytic review. *Developmental Review. Special Issue: Early Gender-Role Development, 13*, 147–183.

Smith Leavell, A., Tamis-LeMonda, C. S., Ruble, D. N., Zosuls, K, & Cabrrera, N. (2012). African American White and Latino fathers' activities with their sons and daughters in early childhood. *Sex Roles, 66*, 53–65. doi: 10.1007/s11199-011-0080-8

Smith Leavell, A., Tamis-LeMonda, C. S., Ruble, D., Scherer, L., & Scudellari, L. (2010, April). *Gender differences in movement opportunities for infants at 5 and 9 months.* Poster presented at the Gender Development Research Conference, San Francisco, CA.

Stoneman, Z., Brody, G. H., & MacKinnon, C. E. (1986). Same-sex and cross-sex siblings: Activity choices, roles, behavior, and gender stereotypes. *Sex Roles, 15*, 495–511.

Sweeney, J., & Bradbard, M. R. (1988). Mothers' and fathers' changing perceptions of their male and female infants over the course of pregnancy. *Journal of Genetic Psychology, 149*, 393–404.

Tucker, C. J., McHale, S. M., & Crouter, A. C. (2003). Dimensions of mothers' and fathers' differential treatment of siblings: Links with adolescents' sex-typed personal qualities. *Family Relations: An Interdisciplinary Journal of Applied Family Studies, 52*, 82–89.

Turner, P. J., & Gervai, J. (1995). A multidimensional study of gender typing in preschool children and their parents: Personality, attitudes, preferences, behavior, and cultural differences. *Developmental Psychology, 31*, 759–772.

Vygotsky, L. S. (1978). *Mind in society: The development of higher psychological processes.* Cambridge, MA: Harvard University Press.

Vygotsky, L. S. (1986). *Thought and language.* Cambridge, MA: MIT Press.

Wallen, K. (1996). Nature needs nurture: The interaction of hormonal and social influences on the development of behavioral sex differences in rhesus monkeys. *Hormones and Behavior, 30*, 364–378.

Weinraub, M., Clemens, L., Sockloff, A., Ethridge, T., Gracely, E., & Myers, B. (1984). The development of sex role stereotypes in the third year: Relationships to gender labeling, gender identity, sex-typed toy preference, and family characteristics. *Child Development, 55*, 1493–1503.

Wertsch, J. V. (1991). *Voices of the mind: A sociocultural approach to mediated action.* Cambridge, MA: Harvard University Press.

Wong, M. S., Mangelsdorf, S. C., Brown, G. L., Neff, C., & Schoppe-Sullivan, S. J. (2009). Parental beliefs, infant temperament, and marital quality: Associations with infant–mother and infant–father attachment. *Journal of Family Psychology, 23*, 828–838.

Zaslow, M. J., Pedersen, F. A., Suwalsky, J. T., & Rabinovich, B. A. (1989). Maternal employment and parent-infant interaction at one year. *Early Childhood Research Quarterly*, *4*, 459–478.

Zosuls, K. M., Ruble, D. N., Tamis-LeMonda, C. S., Shrout, P. E., Bornstein, M. H., & Greulich, F. K. (2009). The acquisition of gender labels in infancy: Implications for gender-typed play. *Developmental Psychology*, *45*, 688–701.

3 Parent–Child Relationships in Adolescence

Monica A. Longmore, Wendy D. Manning, and Peggy C. Giordano[1]

In this chapter, we review theory and research on parent–child relationships in adolescence, emphasizing the role that parents play to enhance adolescents' well-being and to decrease their likelihood of engaging in risk behaviors. Given the extensive literature on parent–teen relationships, we focus mostly on work during the past decade. Compared with childhood, adolescence involves distinct challenges. Parents' challenges include keeping the lines of communication open, providing support, and managing their children's behavior—all practices that ease the transition to adolescence. Adolescents must deal with issues surrounding identity exploration, peer pressure, bullying, dating, sexual activity, and substance abuse, to name a few core concerns (Zaff & Moore, 2002). How parents and adolescents handle these years is critical because this period is a 'launching' point with long-lasting consequences for the next stage of development—emerging adulthood (Arnett, 1996, 2010; Heard, Gorman, & Kapinus, 2008; Oesterle, Hawkins, Hill, & Bailey, 2010).

We begin by describing some distinguishing parent–adolescent dynamics. Next, we review theoretical orientations including social control, social learning, parental investment, and ecological/life course/family system approaches. In describing these orientations, we rely on current research, exemplifying important influences on adolescent outcomes including parental support and control, shared communication, and parents' socioeconomic status. Throughout the chapter, we describe theoretical advances and corresponding research findings, which provide for more nuanced understandings of ways in which parents are influential in adolescents' lives. These topics include parenting practices during adolescence (e.g., negotiated unsupervised time, independence-giving) and behavioral domains that are new to this life stage (e.g., dating and intimate relationships). We conclude by providing suggestions for areas worthy of continued theoretical attention, such as the influence of family structure and multiple family transitions on adolescents' well-being.

KEY ISSUES IN PARENT–ADOLESCENT RELATIONSHIPS

There is a history of theory and research on parenting and adolescent well-being going back to the earliest recognition, among social scientists, of adolescence as a unique life stage (Hall, 1904). Adolescence spans, approximately, the years 10–18 and is a time of change, possibility, and risk (Barber, 2000; Barber, Maughan, & Olsen, 2005; Hall, 1904; Steinberg & Morris, 2001; Zaff & Moore, 2002). During this period, challenges are associated with parents and adolescents adapting

---

[1] This research was supported by grants from The Eunice Kennedy Shriver National Institute of Child Health and Human Development (HD036223 and HD044206), the Department of Health and Human Services (5APRPA006009), and by the Center for Family and Demographic Research, Bowling Green State University, which has core funding from The Eunice Kennedy Shriver National Institute of Child Health and Human Development (R24HD050959-01).

to adolescents' biological maturation, social life transitions, role shifts, and changes in self-identities, including adolescents' increasing, often exaggerated, sense of invulnerability (e.g., Gecas & Seff, 1990; Giordano, Longmore, Manning, & Northcutt, 2009; Graber & Brooks-Gunn, 1996; Greene, Kromar, Waters, Rubin, & Hale, 2000; Steinberg, 2001; Zaff & Moore, 2002). Due to these changes and adaptations, adolescence is a time when self-protective and prosocial as well as self-destructive and anti-social behaviors can begin, taper off, or escalate (Elliott, 2009; Steinberg, 2001). Adolescents also encounter new experiences that occur outside of parental purview including romantic and intimate experiences (Bulcroft, Carmody, & Bulcroft, 1998; Giordano, Longmore, & Manning, 2001). Consequently, much of the current theory and research, including our own, focuses on adolescents' behaviors when they are not overtly watched by parents, and how parents elicit or fail to elicit compliance especially regarding sexual and fertility-related activities, school performance and achievement, substance use, and involvement in delinquent activities and other problem behaviors.

Regarding the likelihood of involvement in risk behaviors, the significance of attachment bonds and the need for parental control during adolescence is well established in the literature. Equally important, adolescents must learn to take greater responsibility for making decisions; and, parents must let youths learn from their actions. Decision-making requires that youths distance themselves from parents—a process referred to as individuation. According to *separation-individuation theory* (Blos, 1967, 1979; Daniels, 1990; Grotevant & Cooper, 1986), the parent–child relationship is redefined as adolescents separating from parents and gaining greater individuality. Adolescents' key developmental task is learning to make decisions and to begin creating a less hierarchical, more equal relationship with parents based on caring and respect (Grotevant & Cooper, 1986). Parents may resist renegotiating relationship boundaries especially when adolescents' decisions and behaviors do not meet expectations.

Independent decision-making is manifest more in some domains than others; issues of popularity, style, social activities, and externalizing or minor delinquent behaviors more likely are influenced by peers, and longer-term goals influenced more by parents (Gecas & Seff, 1990; Reitz, Deković, Meijer, & Engels 2006; Simons, Chao, Conger, & Elder, 2001; Simons-Morton, Chen, Abroms, & Haynie, 2004; South & Haynie, 2004). For example, adolescents typically begin dating around ages 12–14 (Carver, Joyner, & Udry, 2003; Longmore, Manning, & Giordano, 2001; Padgham & Blyth, 1991); however, decisions to start dating often occur without parental knowledge (Longmore et al., 2001). Conversely, students likely to be accepted at selective colleges make decisions about their educational trajectories and put into action the prerequisite steps and develop the necessary sense of agency (e.g., Chang, Heckhausen, Greenberger, & Chen, 2010) with assistance from parents (Kim & Schneider, 2005). A dilemma, however, for many parents is that some domains such as dating could potentially benefit from their, albeit unwanted, input.

Tensions, then, can exist between adolescents' needs to make decisions, including figuring out which domains might benefit from parental input, and parents' desires to use their skills, foresight, experience, and judgment to aid adolescents with decision-making. Not surprisingly, adolescence is viewed often as a period of "*sturm und drang*" (Hall, 1904), although some scholars (e.g., Chubb, Fertman, & Ross, 1997; Hines & Paulson, 2006; Gecas & Seff, 1990; Rathunde & Csikszentmihalyi, 1991) have noted that relational stress and strain is felt mostly by parents and less so by adolescents.

OVERVIEW OF THE THEORIES ON PARENT–ADOLESCENT RELATIONSHIPS

SOCIAL CONTROL FRAMEWORKS: PARENTAL SUPPORT AND CONTROL

Parenting practices emphasizing support and control play a powerful role in the management of adolescent behavior.[2] Scholarship emphasizing the importance of parental support and control for

---

[2] We use the term parental support, but other terms used in various theories include warmth (e.g., Shanahan, McHale, Crouter, & Osgood, 2007), indirect control, parental autonomy-support (e.g., Lekes, Gingras, Philippe, Koestner, & Fang, 2010), social capital (e.g., Coleman, 1988), and family capital (e.g., Parcel, Dufur, & Zito, 2010).

adolescent socialization fits within broader sociological and psychological theories such as *social control* in criminology (Giordano, 2010), and *attachment theory* in developmental psychology (Dornbusch, Erickson, Laird, & Wong, 2001; Steinberg, 2001). According to social control theories, parents inhibit adolescents' behavior by: (a) expressing care, which leads to adolescents' sense of attachment, and feeling that they matter to parents (Elliott, 2009); and (b) constraining involvement in particular activities. It is generally viewed that non-compliant, deviant or delinquent individuals likely do not have strong bonds with conventional society, and attachment to parents is a fundamental social bond.

In developmental psychology, similar typologies have been conceptualized and empirically examined. Based on the concepts of parental warmth and control, Baumrind (1967, 1971, 1991) described childrearing styles that affect adolescents' competence, well-being, and compliance including: authoritative, authoritarian, and permissive parenting. Authoritative parenting is marked by warmth and support (reflecting that youths matter to parents), explanation of rules, use of inductive reasoning, and non-punitive punishment. Authoritarian parenting focuses on rule violation and harsh punishment; and permissive parenting is distinguished by a lack of control, either due to indulgence or neglectfulness (e.g., Lamborn, Mounts, Steinberg, & Dornbusch, 1991). Although some studies have suggested that authoritarian parenting has fewer negative consequences for Black and Asian-American teens, especially with regard to academic achievement (e.g., Slaughter-Defoe, Nakagawa, Takanishi, & Johnson 1990) for non-White teens, authoritative parenting generally is viewed as having the best outcomes for adolescents. Using two waves of data from the National Survey of Families and Households (NSFH), Amato and Fowler (2002) examined parent reports of support, monitoring, and harsh parenting and found that these practices did not interact with race, ethnicity, family structure, education, income, or gender in predicting adolescent self-esteem, grades, and delinquency involvement.

Whereas earlier work tended to focus on mothers' childrearing styles (e.g., Baumrind, 1991), it is now well accepted that both mothers and fathers are likely involved in parenting (Hawkins, Amato, & King, 2006). As such, some theory and research has included both mothers and fathers to assess "family parenting styles." Simons and Conger (2007), for example, found that two authoritative parents resulted in the best outcomes for adolescents, although one authoritative parent could buffer adolescents from the negative effects of the other parent expressing a less optimal childrearing style.

Although parenting practices revolving around expressions of support and control are far from a comprehensive roster of ways in which parents influence adolescents, these are critical dimensions mentioned, or implied, in nearly all empirical studies examining parent influences on adolescent outcomes regardless of theoretical orientation. In a variety of studies, indicators of support are associated with, both lower risk of adolescents' involvement in problem behaviors and better psychological well-being (e.g., Amato & Fowler, 2002; Jessor & Jessor, 1977; Laub & Sampson, 1988, 2003; Meadows, 2007; Parcel, Dufur, & Zito, 2010; Steinberg & Silk, 2002). Using data from the Longitudinal Study of Adolescent Health (Add Health), Meadows (2007) recently showed that parental support protected adolescents against the likelihood of involvement in delinquent behaviors and experiencing depressive symptoms. Also based on data from the Add Health, indicators of parental involvement (i.e., shared dinnertimes, shared activities, sexual communication, and relationship quality) are associated with adolescents' delayed sexual activity (Pearson, Muller, & Frisco, 2006). Consistent with these prior studies, we found in a longitudinal study that parental caring is associated with lower likelihood of teens' sexual debut net of frequency of dating disagreements, sexual communication, demographic background, religiosity, presence of dating itself, parental monitoring, and adolescents' independent decision-making (Longmore, Eng, Giordano, & Manning, 2009).

Taken as a whole, this body of theory and research demonstrates that while striving for independence, teens still need parental support (Hair, Moore, Garrett, Ling, & Cleveland, 2008). Moreover, adolescents who feel cared for likely internalize parental values. As Baumrind (1967) noted, parental warmth and support provide the foundational bedrock for adolescents' compliance with expectations because emotional attachment facilitates parents' socialization attempts. Conversely, low emotional attachment likely increases the odds of adolescents' non-compliance with parental views and expectations.

Regarding conceptual advances, some scholars have distinguished parents' supportive behaviors and their expressions of support (e.g., Wright & Cullen, 2001). Yet others suggest that these are essentially synonymous in their effects on adolescent outcomes (e.g., Asendorpf & Wilpers, 2000; Elliott, 2009). Our view is that both instrumental and expressive indicators of support likely lead to adolescents feeling loved, which promotes emotional stability and encourages compliance. What is critical, however, is consistency (Benson, Buehler, & Gerard, 2008; Lamborn et al., 1991) between the expression of supportive feelings and actions, and that consistency occur across a range of inter-actions, especially as youths are pulling away from overt parental involvement in their lives.

In contrast to support, parental control refers to behavioral constraints. Parental control often is manifested as supervising and monitoring of adolescents' behavior in the context of clearly con-veyed rules. Parental control works by affecting whether interactions with negative peer influences likely occur and by limiting unsupervised time outside of the home or time spent home alone (e.g., Buhi & Goodson, 2007; Coley, Morris, & Hernandez, 2004; Sampson & Laub, 1994). Thus, con-trolling adolescents' behavior limits opportunities and provides dis-incentives (consequences for violating rules) for engaging in risky activities.

Compared with providing support, controlling behavior is more complicated because effects are not consistently positive, and adolescents often oppose control attempts leading to conflict, which may exacerbate the behavior that parents are trying to manage. For example, parents' attempts to control adolescents' involvement in risky activities can lead to *decreases* in control (e.g., Smetana & Daddis, 2002). Adolescents' early associations with delinquent peers can lead to increased conflict with parents. Rather than controlling adolescents' behavior, parents may withdraw to decrease conflict, which amplifies the effect of adolescents' initial involvement with delinquent peers. There is empirical support for these ideas; in an extensive review of *coercion theory*, Granic and Patterson (2006) reported findings from numerous studies concluding that poor parenting in early adolescence predicted problem behaviors such as delinquency and substance use, and that poor parenting mediated the impact of earlier involvement with delinquent peers on subsequent problem behaviors. Thus, while withdrawing from conflict may provide parents with relief from stress, abandoning attempts to control adolescents' behavior may lead to further problems. Similar points have been made in scholarship using *family stress models* (e.g., Brooks-Gunn, Duncan, Klebanov, & Sealand, 1993; Conger & Donnellan, 2007) to explain how family financial problems affect indicators of adolescent well-being, in part, by parents effectively withdrawing from super-vising and monitoring their children.

MONITORING, TEEN SELF-DISCLOSURE, AND NEGOTIATION

An important theoretical advance in the parent–adolescent literature is greater emphasis on system-atic conceptualization of control in terms of interrelated, and reciprocal, behaviors. In that vein, three foci, moving theory and research away from a strict focus on rules and rule violation include investigations of: (1) a range of monitoring strategies in the same study (e.g., providing attention, awareness, tracking, and structuring contexts); (2) parents eliciting from adolescents' self-disclo-sure of their free-time activities; and (3) parents managing of teens' behavior via negotiation (e.g., limit setting, independence-giving) (Bulcroft et al., 1998; Dishion & McMahon, 1998; Hayes, Hudson, & Matthews, 2007; Kerr & Stattin, 2000; Laird, Pettit, Bates, & Dodge, 2003; Stattin & Kerr, 2000). Consistent with control theory, attachment, separation-individuation processes, and the tenets of authoritative parenting, the relationship qualities of trust, closeness, and respect provide the foundation for the effectiveness of monitoring negotiation and teen self-disclosure (Dishion & McMahon, 1998; Hayes et al., 2007), but are also the outcomes of such processes. We review each in turn.

Monitoring

In much theoretical and empirical work, monitoring refers to parents' knowledge of adolescents' free-time activities, and conveying awareness of that knowledge to adolescents (e.g., Dishion & McMahon, 1998; Hayes et al., 2007). It involves the structuring of adolescents' social environments via peer, place, and activity monitoring.

Parents' lack of adequate monitoring, in both cross-sectional and longitudinal studies, is correlated with and predicts adolescents' poorer well-being and greater likelihood of engaging in a range of risky behaviors typically reflecting sensation seeking (e.g., Greene et al., 2000). Poor monitoring, for example, is associated with adolescents' involvement in delinquent activities, including use of alcohol and illicit substances (e.g., Barnes, Hoffman, Welte, Farrell, & Dintcheff, 2006; Barnes, Reifman, Farrell, & Dintcheff, 2000; Dodge, Coie, & Lynam, 2006; Li, Stanton, & Feigelman, 2000; Thomas, Reifman, Barnes, & Farrell, 2000; Steinberg, Fletcher & Darling, 1994;). Inadequate monitoring has negative consequences for the emotional and evaluative dimensions of adolescents' self-concepts including increased depressive symptoms and lower self-esteem (e.g., Gecas & Longmore, 2003; Gil-Rivas, Greenberger, Chen, & Lopez-Lena, 2003). Studies have found that poor monitoring is associated with adolescents' earlier sexual debut; Buhi and Goodson (2007) in an extensive review of early adolescent sexual behavior reported that time home alone is a stable predictor of sexual initiation. Among sexually experienced youths, poor monitoring is associated with greater sexual risk taking, less effective contraceptive use, inconsistent safe sex practices, and greater likelihood of involvement in coercive sex (e.g., DiClemente et al., 2001; Ikramullah, Manlove, Cui, & Moore, 2009; Landsford et al., 2010; Patrick, Snyder, Schrepferman, & Snyder 2005). Inadequate parental monitoring is also associated with poorer academic outcomes, and school behavior problems for adolescents (e.g., Crouter, MacDermid, McHale, & Perry-Jenkins, 1990; Parcel & Dufur, 2001; Parcel et al., 2010; Vandivere, Tout, Zaslow, Calkins, & Capizzano, 2003; Wright & Fitzpatrick, 2006). Thus, parents need to monitor peer involvement, and track where and what adolescents are doing because these activities effectively curtail the likelihood of adolescents' involvement in self-destructive and anti-social behaviors.

Eliciting Adolescents' Self-Disclosure

Kerr and Stattin (Kerr & Stattin, 2000; Stattin & Kerr, 2000) point out that parental knowledge of adolescents' free-time activities depends on adolescents' willingness to self-disclose to parents. Rather than focusing on parental activities (e.g., place, peer, and activity monitoring), their view of monitoring emphasizes understanding the factors that determine adolescents' willingness to disclose to parents. In general, close, supportive relationships promote adolescents' willingness to self-disclose, thus assisting in parents' control efforts.

Conceptualizing monitoring in terms of adolescents' self-disclosure provides a compelling explanation for findings demonstrating that monitoring influences internalizing of parental values and expectations, and results in adolescents' attitudes being consonant with those of parents (Hayes et al., 2007). For example, Sieverding, Adler, Witt, and Ellen (2005) examining over 300 youths who were not sexually active found that adolescents who reported that their parents' successfully monitored them (accurately knowing their whereabouts) expressed attitudes less favorable toward initiating sexual activity, and were less likely to intend to initiate sex. In contrast, teens who reported more unsupervised time expressed attitudes that favored sexual initiation and intentions to initiate sex. Thus, adolescents' willingness to self-disclose is likely important as a precursor to parents' effective monitoring of activities.

Negotiation

Although monitoring and encouraging adolescents to disclose information about free-time activities are both important, managing older adolescents' behavior through negotiation (e.g., parents might promise to stay out of the way, if adolescent has friends over rather than go out) is a common practice. Moreover, negotiation with adolescents is consistent with processes of individuation and trust-building.

Negotiating times in which adolescents are unsupervised, and negotiating the degree of independence permitted in specific domains, such as dating (e.g., Longmore et al., 2009), part-time employment (e.g., Staff & Mortimer, 2007), and time devoted to school work (deCastro & Catsambis, 2009) are critically important during this period. It is unclear, however, what kinds of parenting strategies work in various situations and studies have compared various parenting practices, including negotiated unsupervised time. For example, Borawski, Ievers-Landis, Lovegreen, and Trapl (2003) compared the effects of negotiated unsupervised time, monitoring, and perceived parental trust on adolescents' health risk behaviors and found that negotiated unsupervised time is associated positively with sexual activity and substance use, and positively associated with consistent condom use. For male adolescents, parental monitoring is associated with less alcohol use, and consistent condom use. Yet, monitoring is not associated with female adolescents' health risk behaviors. For adolescent girls, the perception that parents trusted them is negatively associated with sexual activity, cigarette smoking, and marijuana use. For adolescent boys, perceived trust is associated only with less alcohol use. In sum, this study showed that adolescents with a greater amount of negotiated unsupervised time engaged in activities that parents likely disapproved of, such as sexual activity, but also engaged in sex-related protective actions. The findings demonstrate that even non-coercive parenting practices do not result in unequivocally positive outcomes, but rather outcomes can be more of a 'mixed bag,' which is likely due to teens wanting to make independent choices.

The above findings also draw attention to gender differences. An important next step is to better understand why parenting practices may have different effects on sons and daughters. Future research should investigate whether the gender differences regarding monitoring and perceived trust hold for other domains apart from health risk behaviors (e.g., Booth, Farrell, & Varano, 2008), and why. The differential effects of parents (gender and behavior) on male and female adolescent outcomes, although an integral component of many studies on parental communication about sex (e.g., Guilamo-Ramos et al., 2009; Lefkowitz, Boone, Au, & Sigman, 2003), and some on aggressive behavior (e.g., MacKinnon-Lewis, Castellino, Brody, & Finchman, 2001), are limited in the area of parent–adolescent relations (for an exception, see Hawkins et al., 2006). This is surprising given the notion that a mother and father likely affect sons and daughters differently, and the availability of scholarship emphasizing the independent contributions mothers and fathers make to child development (e.g., Bussey & Bandura, 1999; Marsiglio, Amato, Day, & Lamb, 2000; McHale, Crouter, & Whiteman, 2003). Insights from literature on gender identity and the influence of gender on social interactions can be incorporated into theories of parent–adolescent relations and would be an important advancement.

Limiting Independent Choices

Another example of controlling behavior via negotiation concerns limiting adolescents' independent choices versus independence-giving—a perennial parental struggle. As noted, it is developmentally appropriate for adolescents to make independent decisions in various life domains. However, some domains are riskier than others. Dating is a domain in which greater independence may be problematic, and may be a source of parent–child conflict, because it is associated with availability of a sex partner (Blum, Beuhring, & Rinehart, 2000; Jaccard & Dittus, 2000; McNeely, Nonnemaker, & Blum, 2002). Research findings have found that dating is associated with greater frequency of disagreements with parents (Longmore et al., 2009), although sometimes the disagreements are due, not so much with dating, but other issues such as poor grades associated with dating (e.g., Joyner & Udry, 2000). Parents may attempt to control teens' dating by limiting independent choices, such as whom and how often to date. What is the likely effect of limiting choices at a time and in a domain that adolescents want greater control? Brehm and Brehm's (1981) *reactance theory* has posited that individuals react negatively to controlling tactics. Thus, we argue that limiting independent choices, but allowing for some choice, will likely result in greater compliance relative to curtailing adolescents' independent choices.

In prior work using longitudinal data from the Toledo Adolescent Relationships Study (TARS) based on adolescents who were not sexually active at the time of the first interview, we examined parents' attempts to monitor dating and to limit dating choices. The effect of limiting dating choices on delayed sexual initiation was stronger than that of monitoring (Longmore et al., 2009). However, it was not significant with the inclusion of age in multivariate models because older adolescents made more independent dating decisions, and were more likely to initiate sex. It is important to keep in mind that as adolescents get older it is increasingly likely that they will make independent decisions in various domains, including dating and sexual activity.

Other scholarship, however, questions whether the issue is one of independence-giving or autonomy-taking (e.g., Romich, Lundberg, & Tsang, 2009), with adolescents who exhibit impulsive tendencies more likely to make decisions without consulting parents; that is, they take autonomous action (with or without parental consent), and this effect is stronger among families with fewer economic resources. The influence of economic resources, and how economic resources affect parenting practices, is central to scholars using *social learning*, *investment*, and *ecological frame works*. In the next section, we review aspects of parenting from the perspective of social learning.

SOCIAL LEARNING: COMMUNICATION AND MODELING

A commonly researched question is how parents' attitudes and behavior influence those of adolescents. Primary mechanisms include social learning processes, such as observational learning and modeling. This approach sometimes is referred to as *social cognitive theory* (e.g., Bandura, 1986, 1989), or as a *family process approach* (e.g., Cavanagh, 2008), but for ease of presentation, we use the term social learning. Much prior theory and research on intergenerational family influences, e.g., regarding adolescents' intentions to cohabit and/or to marry have relied on social learning processes to interpret findings (e.g., Axinn & Thornton, 1996; Crissey, 2005; Ganong, Coleman, & Brown, 1981; Manning, Longmore, & Giordano, 2007; Paddock-Ellard & Thomas, 1981; Tasker & Richards, 1994). Studies have consistently shown that adolescents living in single parent and step-parent families, presumably via observational learning and modeling, reported more positive attitudes towards divorce and weaker support for marriage (e.g., Axinn & Thornton, 1996; Crissey, 2005; Martin, Martin, & Martin, 2001; Moore & Stief, 1991; Tasker & Richards, 1994). However, learning attitudes from parents may also be the result of parent–adolescent communication.

Communication dynamics are typically indexed by adolescents' or parents' reports of shared communication, ease of communication, topics that cause conflicts, and frequency of disagreements. Studies have also examined specific topics of discussion, and one important topic is sex. Theory and research on sexual communication includes parents' and adolescents' discussions of contraception, abstinence, and sexually transmitted infections. Lefkowitz, Boone, Au, and Sigman (2003) found that parents' and adolescents' communication about sex also included topics such as love, dating, romance, and opposite sex relationships. This finding suggests that when it comes to the topic of sex, parents' and adolescents' discussions are likely to be rather wide-ranging.

Given that much conversation about sex tends to be relatively broad, does communication result in compliance with parental views? Empirical results are mixed. For example, Davis and Friel's (2001) and Resnick et al.'s (1997) cross-sectional analyses of the first wave of the Add Health dataset found that maternal communication about sex is associated with earlier sexual initiation for both male and female adolescents. Conversely, Pearson, Muller, and Frisco (2006) using two waves of data from the same dataset reported that mother and daughter communication about sexual risk decreased the odds of daughters' sexual debut. Reviewing predictors of adolescents' intended sexual behavior, Buhi and Goodson (2007) reported a range of incongruent findings but, nevertheless, concluded that greater parental communication is related to greater odds of adolescents being sexually active. Lefkowitz, Romo, Corona, Kit-fong, and Sigman (2000), however, provided some clarity to these kinds of disparate results by emphasizing that the conclusion drawn may differ depending on who is reporting on the sexual communication. They found that parents primarily talked and youths listened. Consequently, parents believed conversations about sex have occurred, whereas youths often did not. Additionally, sexual communication deterred more effectively when it occurred prior to adolescents' sexual initiation (Meschke, Zweig, Barber, & Eccles, 2000). However, in cross-sectional studies it is difficult to assess causal ordering.

Similar to control strategies, attempts at communicating, sharing, and expressing attitudes and beliefs can result in parent–adolescent disagreements and conflict (Padilla-Walker, 2008). If parents and youths engage in hostile, confrontational, or disagreeable verbal interactions, teens are at risk of engaging in problematic behaviors. As noted earlier, one arena which seems to cause a lot of disagreement is dating. Quatman, Sampson, Robinson, and Watson (2001) and Dowdy and Kliewer (1998) found that adolescents who dated, compared with non-daters, reported more conflict with parents. In cross-sectional studies, dating rules affected the quality of relationship with parents (Madsen, 2008). Frequency of dating disagreements is associated with one of the central parental tasks, which is to control and guide youths' behavior, and they likely reflect disconnections between parental rules and adolescents' desires to comply. Not surprisingly, then, disagreements are a common form of communication as teens assert independence.

Modeling is another social learning process that likely affects adolescents' attitudes and behaviors. For example, parents' own early sexual history has likely influenced adolescents' sexual initiation (Giordano, 2010; Longmore et al., 2009; Rucibwa, Modeste, Montgomery, & Fox, 2003) suggesting, perhaps, parental acceptance of comparable behavior. That is, parents who had early sex may be less critical of teens engaging in earlier sexual activity. However, it can be difficult to disentangle the influence of parenting processes such as modeling from the influence of the advantages/ disadvantages associated with socioeconomic status.

Whether theory and research has focused on family processes, such as modeling, or socioeconomic status, has tended to reflect disciplinary backgrounds. Theories about processes of parenting are often conducted by social psychologists, criminologists, and human development specialists. The influence of parents' socioeconomic status and economic resources, which influence the likelihood of using various parenting practices, often is analyzed by demographers, sociologists, and economists. Research from both process and structural theoretical orientations, however, has generally supported the view that socially and economically disadvantaged adolescents are at increased risk for emotional and physical problems and poorer well-being based on a variety of indicators (e.g., Amato & Fowler, 2002; Leventhal & Brooks-Gunn, 2000; Parcel et al., 2010; Steinberg, 2001). In the next section, we review theory and scholarship that considers the influence of location in the social structure on parent–adolescent relationships.

ECONOMIC CHANGES AND PARENT–ADOLESCENT RELATIONSHIPS

Throughout much of this chapter, we have underscored the challenges experienced by *parents* during the adolescent period. However, over the past several decades in the US, growing income inequality (Bianchi, Cohen, Raley, & Nomaguchi, 2004); changes in the nature of the labor market (Lee & Mather, 2008), including the increasing prominence of the service sector; and changes in family structure, such as the increasing number of cohabiting relationships that include biological and step-children (Brown, 2010; Bulanda & Manning, 2008; Cavanagh, 2008), have resulted in developmental challenges for *adolescents*. One challenge is exploring personal, relational, educational and future work concerns and interests (i.e., issues of identity exploration associated with the adolescent period) within arenas of comfort. Relationships with parents are often an arena of comfort, which can provide a sense of certainty, security, and personal control (Barber, 2000; Call & Mortimer, 2001; Crockett & Silbereisen, 2000). However, changes in the structure of American society have resulted in parents being less available, but nevertheless critically important for assisting their children in successfully navigating adolescence.

The influence of economic and societal-level changes have been examined and incorporated in ongoing and new research on how parents' social position and economic resources and parenting practices affect adolescents (e.g., Amato & Fowler, 2002; Conger & Conger, 2002; Parcel et al., 2010; Schoon et al., 2002). *Parental investment, family stress, life course, ecological,* and *family systems frameworks* are useful for understanding structural influences on adolescent well-being. Each approach, while emphasizing the family's location in the social structure, provides a different lens: parental investment theory focusing on resources available to invest in children; family stress emphasizing the difficulties of parenting in the face of economic problems; life course stressing the intersection of parents' role transitions (e.g., change in union status) with that of their adolescents (e.g., change in schools, new neighborhoods); ecological focusing on the connections between social institutions such as family and school; and family systems highlighting the intersection of various subsets of family members (e.g., marital dyad, parent–adolescent dyad) on adolescents' outcomes. We examine these perspectives in turn.

PARENTAL INVESTMENT THEORY

Parental investment theory emphasizes that indicators of socioeconomic status, namely parental income, education, and occupational prestige, distinguish financial, human, and social capital. Parents' financial, human, and social capital investments influence adolescents' outcomes (e.g., Conger & Donnellan, 2007; Duncan & Magnuson, 2003; Furstenberg, 2000; Parcel & Dufur, 2001; Shanahan, 2000). Capital investments are often described in terms of: (a) an enriched home environment that provides educational resources (Guldi, Page, & Stevens, 2007); (b) enhanced education and achievement opportunities (Parcel et al., 2010); (c) an appropriate standard of living including safe neighborhoods (Sampson, Morenoff, & Earls, 1999); and (d) positive social contacts including peer groups (Knoester, Haynie, & Stephens, 2006; South & Haynie, 2004). Scholars such as Coleman (1988, 1990) and Parcel et al. (2010) have emphasized the importance of family capital, which appears to be similar to parental support and control, and is often associated with socioeconomic status. Family capital (i.e., close relationships) results in parents wanting to provide resources to children.

Parents advantaged by greater financial, human, and social capital have more to invest in children, while poorer parents are limited to investing in basic family needs, and have less access to resources and opportunities that potentially foster adolescents' well-being. There is much debate on exactly what, beyond basic parental financial investment, is consequential for adolescent well-being (e.g., Conger & Donnellan, 2007; Parcel et al., 2010), although it is generally agreed that low parental income is a risk factor for a variety of negative outcomes for children and adolescents.

Some scholarship, nevertheless, suggests that social class differences are, perhaps, over-emphasized. Santelli, Lowry, Brener, and Robin (2000), in their analysis of adolescents' sexual behaviors, concluded that differences by socioeconomic status do not fully account for pregnancy rate and sexually transmitted infection rate differences. Rather, it is essential to account for mediators, such as community factors (i.e., available health services and STD prevalence in the community) that enhance or derail adolescents' well-being. Blum, Beuhring, and Rinehart (2000) indicated that, in general, correlations between adolescent risk outcomes and parental economic resources are rather small. Resnick (2000) concluded that scholarship, and society in general, would be better off focusing on strengths and resiliency that reduce adolescents' risks for engaging in problem behaviors regardless of socioeconomic background.

Nonetheless, parents' financial, human, and social capital remains important because of the range of adolescents' outcomes that they influence. Test scores and cognitive development (Crosnoe, 2004; Parcel et al., 2010; Hill & Tyson, 2009); social competence (Steinberg, 2001); depressive symptoms, behavioral problems (Luster & Oh, 2001; Magnuson, 2007); poor physical health, lower physical activity (Babey, Hastert, & Brown, 2007); early sexual onset, teen childbearing

(Santelli, Lowry, Brener, & Robin, 2000); lower education attainment, school dropout, premature mortality (Laub & Vaillant, 2000); and bleaker future economic prospects (Thomas, 2003) are all influenced by parental investment of capital. Moreover, Starfield and colleagues (Starfield, 1989; Starfield, Riley, Witt, & Robertson, 2002) noted that severity is perhaps more important than the frequency of these outcomes. Thus in comparing social class and well-being outcomes, especially those associated with health, poor adolescents relative to non-poor adolescents often experience more severe outcomes and prognoses.

In addition to the outcomes listed above, parents' capital investment is positively related to child-rearing practices, which promote better outcomes for adolescents. Economically disadvantaged, compared with middle-class parents, are more likely to use an authoritarian parenting style as indicated by the use of physical punishment, emphasis on rule violation, and less reliance on explaining reasons behind rules (Conger & Donnellan, 2007; Patterson, 1982; Steinberg, 2001). Such parenting practices are associated with lower social competence for adolescents, and poorer outcomes.

Similar to financial capital, social (i.e., networks) and human capital (i.e., education) tend to be associated with positive outcomes for teens including indicators of achievement, and the lack of such capital is associated with negative outcomes including greater likelihood of involvement in delinquent and problem behaviors (Luster & Oh, 2001; Magnuson, 2007). Regarding parents' human capital and children's cognitive development, better educated parents, relative to their less educated counterparts, are likely to use more sophisticated vocabularies when talking with adolescents (Crosnoe, 2004; Hill & Tyson, 2009; Parcel et al., 2010). In addition to cognitive development and academic achievement, there is a social class gradient in health during adolescence (and beyond), with teens whose parents were better educated, employed, and have higher family income experiencing greater health satisfaction, and being in the best health overall (Cutler & Lleras-Muney, 2010). Similarly, regarding social capital, McNeal (1999) found that adolescent well-being was affected by parents' involvement in community and school activities such as PTA. Human and social capital are important for cognitive development, health behaviors, and ultimately health outcomes. Thus, all three types of capital have distinct effects, but the effects are in the same positive direction, and typically, the more capital invested in adolescents, the better the outcomes.

Findings on the influence of parental capital on adolescents' cognitive development and health outcomes are relatively straightforward, and not surprising. However, *parental investment models* have been used to understand some less straightforward outcomes such as adolescents' involvement in violent activities. Recent estimates from the Centers for Disease Control and Prevention (CDC, 2009) have indicated that about one-third of adolescents were involved in physical altercations during a 12-month period, and nearly 20% carried weapons including guns in a 30-day period. Adolescents from families with higher annual incomes are significantly less likely to engage in violent behavior than those from lower income families (Substance Abuse and Mental Health Services Administration, SAMHSA, 2010; Wright & Fitzpatrick, 2006). Self-report data indicated that 41% of adolescents in families with annual incomes less than $20,000, and 25% in families with annual incomes over $75,000 reported engaging in violent behaviors. Similarly, using Add Health data, Wright and Fitzpatrick (2006) found negative associations between a range of adolescent violence outcomes and the availability of social capital. Moreover, poor teens are more likely to be victims of violence and conflict (e.g., Mihalic & Elliott, 1997; Najman et al., 2010), including family violence (Mitchell & Finkelhor, 2001); to reside in neighborhoods with higher rates of violence (Jencks & Mayer, 1990; Leventhal & Brooks-Gunn, 2000); and to have greater odds of premature death (Laub & Vaillant, 2000; Starfield et al., 2002). Thus, a variety of sources of data demonstrate that parental capital influences violent activity involving adolescents.

The relationship between violence and family income is even stronger for adolescent girls. Historically, adolescent girls relative to boys have had significantly lower arrest rates. In recent years, that gap has decreased. In 2004, 30% of juvenile arrests were girls (SAMHSA, 2009). Youth self-report data indicated that violent behaviors were reported by 37% of adolescent girls whose family incomes were less than $20,000, and 21% of adolescent girls whose family incomes were more than $75,000. This may suggest, then, that the lack of financial capital is especially detrimental for adolescent girls with respect to engaging in violent behavior.

Family stress models draw attention to the myriad ways in which disadvantaged backgrounds affect family processes that influence adolescent development. Disadvantaged backgrounds adversely affect parents' emotional well-being, ability to cope, to engage in proactive behaviors and to sustain relationship quality, which in turn, negatively influence parenting strategies, including the ability to provide support and to monitor adolescents' behavior (Conger & Donnellan, 2007; Conger & Conger, 2002; Leventhal & Brooks-Gunn, 2000). That is, parents are distressed by their financial and personal problems, so they may demonstrate less affection, be less involved in adolescents' lives, and may be more likely to use harsh and inconsistent control attempts (Patterson, 1982; Steinberg, 2001). In effect, stressors exceed the resources available to parents.

Amato's (2000) conceptualization of resources and stressors emphasized that well-being depends on the quantity and quality of resources available including individual attributes such as knowledge and agency, instrumental and expressive support from significant others, and societal responsiveness in providing quality schools and government policies aimed at assisting economically marginalized families. Stressors refer to conditions that curtail parents' abilities to successfully manage day-to-day activities, and to plan for the future (Amato, 2000; Conger & Conger, 2002). When stressors exceed resources, parenting is likely compromised. As indicated above, evidence suggests that low income is associated with severe difficulties for adolescents including early sexual activity, drug and alcohol use, delinquency and lower academic achievement. Vandewater and Lansford (2005), for example, found that socioeconomic status influenced adolescents' involvement with violence through its effects on school stress, parental warmth, and family conflict. Adolescents from more affluent families experienced less stress at school, higher levels of parental warmth, and less exposure to familial conflict and violence.

Return on Investment

Two conceptual advances regarding *parental investment theory* are: (1) how parents might compensate for limited social and economic resources; and (2) discussion of instances in which capital does not provide the expected return on investment. Social capital with regard to adolescents' educational opportunities has been conceptualized as extra familial ties through which parents can effectively access resources and information to assist teens in making informed decisions about college. For example, parents' active involvement in school programs, which offered information on postsecondary education, was more beneficial to students whose parents had lower educational attainment (Kim & Schneider, 2005). In other words, it is important for parents to take action to assist teens with college goals. This is what Kim and Schneider (2005, p. 1184) referred to as "social capital in action." But again, as other theories and studies have emphasized, this outcome is premised on a positive parent–adolescent relationship, in which parents' actions for the benefit of their adolescents align with adolescents' goals, educational agency (Chang et al., 2010), and behavior, including earning the prerequisite good grades.

Although parents' investment of resources is associated with the successful development of adolescents, some theoretical twists include better understanding of contexts in which capital does not result in the expected returns. For example, parental investment and socioeconomic resources had less of a return for teens with disabilities relative to non-disabled teens (Wells, Sandefur, & Hogan, 2003). Additionally, although it is generally found that parental school involvement such as PTA had positive consequences for teens (e.g., McNeal, 1999), Santos (2005) found that social capital with respect to being connected and knowing many families at predominantly Black schools did not necessarily yield positive results for Black teens. Thus, although parents can build social capital, especially in the absence of financial and human capital, other characteristics also affect returns on capital investment in adolescents' development.

LIFE COURSE, ECOLOGICAL, AND FAMILY SYSTEM PERSPECTIVES

The *life course*, *ecological*, and *family systems perspectives* emphasize the ongoing bidirectional relationships between individuals and families and the broader contexts that influence them (e.g., peers, schools, neighborhoods, communities). As such, they are especially relevant for understanding how changes in the institution of marriage, employment patterns, and variability in life course trajectories affect individuals' behaviors. These approaches also highlight analysis of individuals within relational contexts that change over time, nested within larger social contexts, which also change over time.

There are disciplinary differences in these perspectives with sociologists more likely to emphasize life course (influence of social contexts and timing of social roles), psychologists emphasizing lifespan (changes in emotional, cognitive, and motivational aspects of personality from birth to death) (see Shanahan & Porfelli, 2002, for a discussion of similarities and differences between life course and lifespan approaches), and developmental scholars more likely to focus on ecological connections (nested contexts). Here, we describe *life course*, *ecological*, and *family systems approaches*, focusing more so on commonalities rather than differences. In particular, both ecological and life course frameworks incorporate two important concepts that distinguish them from many other orientations: context and time.

Contexts

The *ecological framework*, in particular, highlights that adolescents and their parents are connected through nested contexts. Behavior (both parents and adolescents) is a result of a combination of personal characteristics, as well as influences from proximal contexts (e.g., dyadic relationships such as parents' marriages or cohabiting unions), and more distal contexts (e.g., schools, communities, and neighborhoods). Dornbusch, Erickson, Laird, and Wong (2001) using the Add Health dataset, for example, demonstrated that attachment to two important contexts during adolescence, family and school, tended to reduce frequency and intensity of adolescents' delinquent involvement net of the influence of living in an economically disadvantaged neighborhood, gender, and race. Of particular relevance here is that the ecological focus draws attention to the multiple contexts that likely affect well-being and a sense of belonging. While many theories and studies have demonstrated the significance of parental attachment, the ecological perspective highlights that adolescent attachments to school, teachers, and other students, (as well as to family) are all important. Thus, this approach is more explicit than many others about measuring multiple contexts.

Cook, Herman, Phillips, and Settersten (2002) using an ecological approach examined ways in which schools, neighborhoods, family factors, and peer groups jointly influenced a combined index of successful development (e.g., academic performance, mental health, and social behavior) during early adolescence. They found that each context influenced successful development, but the cumulative effect of the four contexts on successful development was larger than the sum of the individual effects. The authors concluded that early adolescence is best understood pan-contextually rather than in terms of individual contexts for specific outcomes (e.g., school context for grades).

Timing

The life course perspective, while recognizing the significance of context, emphasizes the importance of the timing and ordering of events that shape developmental trajectories across the life course (Elder, 1998; Shanahan, 2000). Life course frameworks emphasize that individuals live in a continually changing social environment and that individuals shape and are shaped by the timing of life events and role transitions (e.g., on-time or off-time), while taking into account the cultural and historical settings influencing life events.

Cavanagh (2008), for example, using a life course perspective, examined the timing of family structure arrangements on adolescent well-being using data from the Add Health. She found that family structure at adolescence, relative to earlier in childhood, predicted later emotional distress.

Thus, as both the individual changes (i.e., transitions from childhood to adolescence), and other relationships change (i.e., parents' marital status changes from married to divorced), both sets of changes in due course influence behaviors such as parenting practices and ultimately adolescents' outcomes.

The life course perspective's emphasis on time is especially relevant for understanding intergenerational similarities in parenting practices and child outcomes. In an extensive review of intergenerational studies of parenting and risk transfer from parent to offspring, Serbin and Karp (2003) concluded that poor parenting skills were the result of modeling ineffective parents, but were also influenced by the individual's own past adolescent aggressive and dysfunctional behavior. Thus, the older generation (i.e., grandparents), their offspring (i.e., parents), and the next generation tended to have comparable and continuing social, behavioral, and mental health problems. Although the life course draws attention to intergenerational transmission of attitudes and behaviors, theoretical advances include focusing on ways in which individuals' agency influences their own development as well. Shanahan and Flaherty's (2001) study of time use among adolescents, for example, emphasized the importance of understanding the range of contexts in which youths spend their discretionary time.

Another conceptual framework, which is compatible with the life course and ecological approaches, is *family systems theory*. This approach emphasizes that the family is a system of interconnected parts. Problems in a subsystem (e.g., parent–parent) can potentially spillover and affect other subsystems (e.g., parent–child) (Erel & Burman, 1995). Amato and Cheadle (2008), for example, described several mechanisms by which marital conflict had negative effects on children including: (1) experiencing spillover effects in which parents take their frustration and aggression out on children; (2) witnessing stress-inducing conflict; (3) being drawn into conflicts; and (4) learning to be verbally and or physically aggressive through parental modeling. Additionally, it is likely that adolescents may escape parental fighting by staying out of the house. Parents caught up in marital conflict are not focused on parenting, which could lead to neglectful parenting (e.g., Buehler & Gerard, 2002). It is possible that teens take on more of a caregiving role with respect to younger siblings (instrumental parentification), and possibly even meeting the emotional needs of parents (emotional parentification).

In addition to adolescents' taking on the social role responsibilities of parents, there is much supporting theoretical and empirical work demonstrating other mechanisms by which family subsystems affect other subsystems (e.g., Grych, Fincham, Jouriles, & McDonald, 2000; Harold, Fincham, Osborne, & Conger, 1997), especially with regard to parental conflict, discord, and divorce. Fosco and Grych (2010) examined factors associated with adolescents being drawn into parental conflicts, and how triangulation leads to adolescent maladjustment conflict. Interparental conflict was also associated with parent–adolescent conflict in a cross-sectional study of over 600 adolescents (Bradford, Vaughn, & Barber, 2008). Thus, conflict between parents may not only influence the parents themselves but can spill over and result in parent–adolescent conflict.

Lastly, the effects of marital conflict, discord, and divorce on children can be long term and can also depend on sex of the parent and child. For example, marital conflict is associated with greater odds of not being emotionally close with both parents during early adulthood (Sobolewski & Amato, 2007). Booth and Amato (1994) found that when divorce occurred during adolescence, young adult women tended to have closer relationships with their mothers and more distant relationships with their fathers. In sum, the family systems approach has advanced our understanding of how conflict between parents likely influences well-being for adolescents.

LIMITATIONS AND NEW APPLICATIONS OF THEORY

This chapter is broadly concerned with how parents influence a range of adolescent outcomes. We initially framed the discussion in terms of parental control and support, and then described various theories involving social psychological processes and demographic patterns. In general, theory and research demonstrated that while striving for independence, teens still need parents to provide support and to set behavioral limits. In terms of better understanding how parents control adolescents' behavior, an important theoretical advance is greater emphasis on systematic conceptualization of control in terms of interrelated, and reciprocal, behaviors including focusing on a range of monitoring strategies, factors affecting adolescents' self-disclosure of their free-time activities to parents, and parents managing of teens' behavior by negotiating unsupervised time and setting limits on independent decision-making. We also noted that the primary mechanisms by which many adolescents learn attitudes and behavior from parents include communication. Communication dynamics are indexed by adolescents' or parents' reports of shared communication, ease of communication, topics that cause conflicts, and frequency of disagreements. Although some studies pit social control against social learning, it is important to look at social control and social learning processes in tandem because both likely underlie adolescents' compliance with parental desires. An integrated approach better captures the 'push and pull' of adolescence as parents attempt to guide youths' behavior and youths try to gain greater independence. Our conclusion, then, is that a variety of explanations likely accurately reflect how parenting influences adolescents. A limitation of our review, however, is not explicitly dealing with the voluminous literature on race and ethnicity. Nor did we distinguish between early, middle, and late adolescence. Future theory and research needs to include race, ethnicity, and age as important contexts for understanding parent–adolescent relationships.

Additionally, we have briefly examined how location in the social structure, as conceptualized by the *family investment*, *life course*, and *ecological frameworks*, affects adolescent outcomes. The following comments explore our views on future research needs and research areas that have seen, and are continuing to see, greater application of theories, especially life course and ecological frameworks, on parent–adolescent relationships.

Family Transitions

One area where we have seen greater application of theory is in recent research on the influence of family transitions, including multiple transitions, on adolescent well-being and involvement in risk activities. For example, the divorce process involves multiple transitions that affect the family environment, including changes in parenting arrangements (Demo & Fine, 2010). Understanding diversity in family structure is critical to strengthen our ability to make generalizations about parent–adolescent relations. Drawing on conceptual models such as parental investment, life course, and family systems theories, scholars are examining the implications of family structures that were largely ignored in research a few decades ago. Increases in nonmarital fertility, cohabitation, and divorce have resulted in children and adolescents being born and raised in diverse family and parental relationship statuses including married, divorced, widowed, cohabiting, stepfamily, dating, and single (Crosnoe & Cavanagh, 2010). Understanding the implications of this more comprehensive range of family structures is important because, even though the majority of children reside with two biological parents, studies using life course theory and longitudinal data indicate that more than half will reside in another family or parental relationship status, or multiple structures/statuses, before reaching young adulthood (Crosnoe & Cavanagh, 2010; Kennedy & Bumpass, 2008).

Family structure typically reflects advantages/disadvantages in financial, human, and social capital (Heard et al., 2008). Thus, understanding family structure and parental relationship status diversity is important because these factors influence financial investment, time availability, communication, and parenting strategies associated with parent–adolescent relationships and ultimately adolescents' outcomes. Additionally, recent research demonstrates that the type of family structure in which an adolescent is living is likely to affect his or her attachment to peers and to schools through residential moves and reduced parental support (emotional and financial) that are associated with single parent, step, and step-cohabiting families (Engels, Deković, & Meeus, 2002; Heard et al., 2008; South & Haynie, 2004).

For example, children are increasingly being born and raised in cohabiting step-parent families (Bulanda & Manning, 2008; Bumpass & Lu, 2000; Smock, 2000; Smock & Gupta, 2002)—although cohabitations are often short-term living arrangements (Brown, 2002; Manning & Lamb, 2003; Raley, Frisco, & Wildsmith, 2005). Using data from the National Survey of Family Growth (NSFG), Bulanda and Manning (2008) found that living in cohabiting parent families during childhood is associated with adolescent girls' earlier sexual initiation, a greater likelihood of experiencing a teen birth, and a lower likelihood of graduating from high school. They provide several compelling explanations for why parental cohabitation negatively influences adolescents' well-being including union instability, and parents are typically from poorer economic backgrounds. Of special interest, however, is their discussion of individuals who select to cohabit. They suggest that mothers whose children have behavioral problems likely have greater difficulty than other women in selecting a good marriage partner, so they choose to cohabit. Additionally, it is possible that cohabitation may also be selective of individuals who have weaker parenting skills (Bulanda & Manning, 2008; Manning & Lamb, 2003). As such, an important theoretical advancement would be to distinguish the influence of family structure diversity from family instability and multiple family transitions.

Regarding multiple family and parental relationship status changes, more than 1 in 5 adolescents in the US have experienced two or more changes (Cavanagh, 2008). In a review of the literature on families and adolescents, Crosnoe and Cavanagh (2010) summarized a variety of studies examining how adolescents experience and are influenced by multiple parental relationship statuses and transitions and concluded that adolescents who experienced multiple transitions also experienced compromised well-being including greater involvement in risk behaviors, and greater likelihood of sexual experience. Brown (2006), using two waves of data from Add Health to assess family transitions, found that not all types of transitions have comparable negative effects on adolescents' well-being, with the transition from a single parent family to a cohabiting family perhaps having the most negative consequences for adolescents. These kinds of changes can result in adolescents' greater involvement in risk behavior. By framing these demographic trends in terms of implications for adolescents, scholars have been able to show that parental union transitions often result in residential and school changes for children (e.g., Cavanagh, Crissey, & Raley, 2008; Fomby & Sennott 2009; South, Haynie, & Bose, 2005). These moves have significant implications regarding new friendship groups, attachment to new schools, and dating.

Some of our research has examined dating and dating disagreements, and we indicated in our review that dating is an arena in which parents and adolescents are likely to experience conflict. What effect might societal-level changes in family structure have on adolescent dating, and dating disagreements? Using the Add Health dataset, Cavanagh et al. (2008) demonstrated that changes in family structure increased the odds of adolescent involvement in dating relationships as well as involvement with a greater numbers of relationships among daters. Also using data from Add Health, South, Haynie, and Bose (2005) demonstrated that residential moves are associated with adolescents' sexual initiation, which they attributed to the greater likelihood of delinquency and poorer academic performance among the new peer network. In other words, the new friends are likely bad influences. Thus, transitions directly affect dating and sexual activity, two arenas that are conventional sources of parental conflict. However, an area that still needs research is the influence of communication dynamics and parental relationship status on adolescent outcomes such as dating and sexual activity.

CONCLUSION

Researchers from a range of disciplines are using theories on parent–adolescent relationships to better understand the period of adolescence as an important launching point. Conversely, scholars studying adolescent development and parenting are also using new findings on family structure to better understand how family context influences adolescent and parents' ability to support and control teens while attending to the implications of family structure instability in their own lives. We expect that future research will continue to explore the interconnections and reciprocal influences of parenting processes, socioeconomic status, and family structure changes on adolescent well-being.

REFERENCES

Amato. P. R. (2000). The consequences of divorce for adults and children. *Journal of Marriage and Family*, *62*, 1269–1287.

Amato, P. R., & Cheadle, J. E. (2008). Parental divorce, marital conflict and children's problems: A comparison of adopted and biological children. *Social Forces 86*: 1139–1161.

Amato, P. R., & Fowler, F. (2002). Parenting practices, child adjustment, and family diversity. *Journal of Marriage and Family*, *64*, 703–716.

Arnett, J. J. (1996). Sensation seeking, aggressiveness, and adolescent reckless behavior. *Personality and Individual Differences*, *20*, 693–702.

Arnett, J. J. (2010, October). *New horizons in research on emerging and young adulthood*. Paper presented at the Early Adulthood in a Family Context, Penn State's annual symposium on family issues, University Park, PA.

Asendorpf, J. B., & Wilpers, S. (2000). Attachment security and available support: Closely linked relationship qualities. *Journal of Social and Personal Relationships*, *17*, 115–138.

Axinn, W. G., & Thornton, A. (1996). The influence of parents' marital dissolutions on children's attitudes toward family formation. *Demography*, *33*, 66–81.

Babey, S. H., Hastert, T. A., & Brown, E. R. (2007). *Teens living in disadvantaged neighborhoods lack access to parks and get less physical activity*. Los Angeles, CA: UCLA Center for Health Policy Research.

Bandura, A. (1986). *Social foundations of thought and action: A social cognitive theory*. Englewood Cliffs, NJ: Prentice Hall.

Bandura, A. (1989). Social cognitive theory. In R. Vasta (Ed.), *Annals of Child Development, 6. Six theories of child development* (pp. 1–60). Greenwich, CT: JAI Press.

Barber, B. K., Maughan, S. L., & Olsen, J. A. (2005). Patterns of parenting across adolescence. *New Directions for Child and Adolescent Development*, *108*, 5–15.

Barber, N. (2000). *Why parents matter: Parental investment and child outcomes*. Westport, CT: Greenwood.

Barnes, G. M., Hoffman, J. H., Welte, J. W., Farrell, M. P., & Dintcheff, B. A. (2006). Effects of parental monitoring and peer deviance on substance use and delinquency. *Journal of Marriage and Family*, *68*, 1084–1104.

Barnes, G. M., Reifman, A. S., Farrell, M. P., & Dintcheff, B. A. (2000). The effects of parenting on the development of adolescent alcohol misuse: A six-wave latent growth model. *Journal of Marriage and Family*, *62*, 175–186.

Baumrind, D. (1967). Child care practices anteceding three patterns of preschool behavior. *Genetic Psychology Monographs*, *75*, 43–88.

Baumrind, D. (1971). Current patterns of parental authority. *Developmental Psychology Monograph*, *4*, 1–103.

Baumrind, D. (1991). Effective parenting during the early adolescent transition. In P. A. Cowen & E. M. Hetherington (Eds.), *Family transitions: Family research consortium: Advances in family research* (pp. 111–164). Hillsdale, NJ: Lawrence Erlbaum.

Benson, M. J., Buehler, C., & Gerard, J. M. (2008). Interparental hostility and early adolescent problem behavior: Spillover via maternal acceptance, harshness, inconsistency, and intrusiveness. *Journal of Early Adolescence*, *28*, 428–454.

Bianchi, S., Cohen, P., Raley, S., & Nomaguchi, K. (2004). Inequality in parental investment in childrearing: Time, expenditures, and health. In K. Neckerman (Ed.), *Social inequality* (pp. 189–219). New York: Russell Sage Foundation.

Blos, P. (1967). The second individuation process of adolescence. *Psychoanalytic Study of the Child*, *22*, 162–186.

Blos, P. (1979). *The adolescent passage*. New York: International Universities Press.

Blum, R. W., Beuhring, T., & Rinehart, P. M. (2000). *Protecting teens: Beyond race, income, and family structure*. Minneapolis, MN: University of Minnesota.

Booth, A., & Amato, P. R. (1994). Parental marital quality, divorce, and relations with offspring in young adulthood. *Journal of Marriage and the Family*, *56*, 21–34.

Booth, J. A., Farrell, A., & Varano, S. P. (2008). Social control, serious delinquency, and risky behavior: A gendered analysis. *Crime and Delinquency*, *54*, 423–456.

Borawski, E. A., Ievers-Landis, C. E., Lovegreen, L. D., & Trapl, E. S. (2003). Parental monitoring, negotiated unsupervised time, and parental trust: The role of perceived parenting practices in adolescent health risk behaviors. *Journal of Adolescent Health*, *33*, 60–70.

Bradford, K., Vaughn, L. B., & Barber, B. K. (2008). When there is conflict: Interparental conflict, parent-child conflict, and youth problem behaviors. *Journal of Family Issues 29*, 780–805.

Brehm, S. S., & Brehm, J. W. (1981). *Psychological reactance: A theory of freedom and control*. New York: Academic Press.

Brooks-Gunn, J., Duncan, G. J., Klebanov, P. K., & Sealand, N. (1993). Do neighborhoods affect child and adolescent development? *American Journal of Sociology*, *99*, 353–95.

Brown, S. L. (2002). Child well-being in cohabiting families. In A. Booth & A. C. Crouter (Eds.), *Just living together: Implications for children, families, and public policy* (pp. 173–188). Mahwah, NJ: Lawrence Erlbaum.

Brown, S. L. (2006). Family structure transitions and adolescent well-being. *Demography*, *43*, 447–461.

Brown, S. L. (2010). Marriage and child well-being: Research and policy perspectives. *Journal of Marriage and Family*, *72*, 1059–1077.

Buehler, C., & Gerard, J. M. (2002). Marital conflict, ineffective parenting, and children's and adolescents' maladjustment. *Journal of Marriage and Family*, *64*, 78–92.

Buhi, E. R., & Goodson, P. (2007). Predictors of adolescent sexual behavior and intention: A theory-guided systematic review. *Journal of Adolescent Health*, *40*, 4–21.

Bulanda, R. E., & Manning, W. D. (2008). Parental cohabitation experience and adolescent behavioral outcomes. *Population Research and Policy Review*, *27*, 593–618.

Bulcroft, R. A., Carmody, D. C., & Bulcroft, K. A. (1998). Family structure and patterns of independence-giving to adolescents: Variations by age, race, and gender of child. *Journal of Family Issues*, *19*, 404–435.

Bumpass, L., & Lu, H. H. (2000). Trends in cohabitation and implications for children's family contexts in the United States. *Population Studies*, *54*, 29–41.

Bussey, K., & Bandura, A. (1999). Social cognitive theory of gender development and differentiation. *Psychological Review*, *106*, 676–713.

Call, K. T., & Mortimer, J. T. (2001). *Arenas of comfort in adolescence: A study of adjustment in context*. Mahwah, NJ: Lawrence Erlbaum.

Carver, K., Joyner, K., & Udry, J. R. (2003). National estimates of adolescent romantic relationships. In P. Florsheim (Ed.), *Adolescent romantic relations and sexual behavior: Theory, research, and practical implications* (pp. 23–56). Mahwah, NJ: Lawrence Erlbaum.

Cavanagh, S. (2008). Family structure history and adolescent adjustment. *Journal of Family Issues*, *29*, 944–980.

Cavanagh, S., E., Crissey, S. R., & Raley, R. K. (2008). Family structure history and adolescent romance. *Journal of Marriage and Family*, *70*, 698–714.

Centers for Disease Control and Prevention. (2009). Youth risk behavior surveillance – United States, 2009. *MMWR, Surveillance Summaries*, 59, no. SS–5.

Chang, E. S., Heckhausen, J., Greenberger, E., & Chen, C. (2010). Shared agency with parents for educational goals: Ethnic differences and implications for college adjustment. *Journal of Youth and Adolescence*, *39*, 1293–1304.

Chubb, N., Fertman, C., & Ross, J. (1997). Adolescent self-esteem and locus of control: A longitudinal study of gender differences. *Adolescence*, *32*, 113–129.

Coleman, J. S. (1988). Social capital and the creation of human capital. *American Journal of Sociology*, *94*, S95–S120.

Coleman, J. S. (1990). *Foundations of social theory*. Cambridge, MA: Harvard University Press.

Coley, R. L., Morris, J. E., & Hernandez, D. (2004). Out-of-school care and problem behavior trajectories among low-income adolescents: Individual, family, and neighborhood characteristics as added risks. *Child Development*, *75*, 948–965.

Conger, R. D., & Conger, K. J. (2002). Resilience in midwestern families: Selected findings from the first decade of a prospective, longitudinal study. *Journal of Marriage and Family*, *64*, 361–373.

Conger, R. D., & Donnellan, M. B. (2007). An interactions perspective on the socioeconomic context of human development. *Annual Review of Psychology*, *58*, 175–199.

Cook, T. D., Herman, M. R., Phillips, M., & Settersten, R. A. Jr. (2002). Some ways in which neighborhoods, nuclear families, friendship groups, and schools jointly affect changes in early adolescent development. *Child Development, 73*, 1283–1309.

Crissey, S. R. (2005). Race/ethnic differences in the marital expectations of adolescents: The role of romantic relationships. *Journal of Marriage and Family, 67*, 697–709.

Crockett, L. J., & Silbereisen, R. K. (Eds.) (2000). *Negotiating adolescence in times of social change.* New York: Cambridge University Press.

Crosnoe, R. (2004). Social capital and the interplay of families and school. *Journal of Marriage and Family, 66*, 267–280.

Crosnoe, R., & Cavanagh, S. E. (2010). Families with children and adolescents: A review, critique, and future agenda. *Journal of Marriage and Family, 72*, 594–611.

Crouter, A. C., MacDermid, S. M., McHale, S. M., & Perry-Jenkins, M. (1990). Parental monitoring and perceptions of children's school performance and conduct in dual-earner and single-earner families. *Developmental Psychology, 26*, 649–657.

Cutler, D. M., & Lleras-Muney, A. (2010). Understanding differences in health behaviors by education. *Journal of Health Economics, 29*, 1–28.

Daniels, J. A. (1990). Adolescent separation-individuation and family transitions. *Adolescence, 25*, 105–116.

Davis, E. C., & Friel, L. V. (2001). Adolescent sexuality: Disentangling the effects of family structure and family context. *Journal of Marriage and the Family, 63*, 669–681.

deCastro, B. S., & Catsambis, S. (2009). Parents still matter: Parental links to the behaviors and further outlook of high school seniors. In N. E. Hill, & R. K. Chao (Eds.), *Families, schools and the adolescent: Connecting research, policy and practice* (pp. 91–109). New York: Teachers College Press.

Demo, D.H., & Fine, M. A. (2010). *Beyond the average divorce.* Thousand Oaks, CA: Sage.

DiClemente, R. J., Wingood, G. M., Crosby, R., Sionean, C., Cobb, B. K., Harrington, K., … Oh, M. K. (2001). Parental monitoring: Association with adolescents' risk behaviors. *Pediatrics, 107*, 1363–1368.

Dishion, T. J., & McMahon, R. J. (1998). Parental monitoring and the prevention of child and adolescent problem behavior: A conceptual and empirical formulation. *Clinical Child and Family Psychology Review, 1*, 61–75.

Dodge, K.A., Coie, J.D., & Lynam, D. (2006). Aggression and antisocial behavior in youth. In W. Damon (Series Ed.) & N. Eisenberg (Vol. Ed.), *Handbook of child psychology: Vol. 3. Social, emotional, and personality development* (6th ed., pp. 719–788). New York: Wiley.

Dornbusch, S., Erickson, K.G., Laird, J. & Wong, C.A. (2001) The relation of family and school attachment to adolescent deviance in diverse groups and communities. *Journal of Adolescent Research, 16*, 396–422.

Dowdy, B. B., & Kliewer, W. (1998). Dating, parent-adolescent conflict, and behavioral autonomy. *Journal of Youth and Adolescence, 27*, 473–492.

Duncan, G. J., & Magnuson, K. A. (2003). Off with Hollingshead: Socioeconomic resources, parenting, and child development. In M. H. Bornstein, & R. H. Bradley (Eds.), *Socioeconomic status, parenting, and child development* (pp. 83–106). Mahwah, NJ: Lawrence Erlbaum.

Elder, G. H., Jr. (1998). The life course and human development. In W. Damon (Series Ed.) & R. M. Lerner, (Vol. Ed.), *Handbook of child psychology: Vol. 1* (pp. 939–991). New York: Wiley.

Elliottt, G. C. (2009). *Family matters: The importance of mattering to family in adolescence.* Hoboken, NJ: Wiley-Blackwell.

Engels, R. C. M. E., Deković, M., & Meeus, W. (2002). Parenting practices, social skills and peer relationships in adolescence. *Social Behavior and Personality: An International Journal, 30*, 3–17.

Erel, O., & Burman, B. (1995). Interrelatedness of marital relations and parent-child relations: a meta-analytic review. *Psychological Bulletin, 118*, 108–32.

Fincham, F. D. (1998). Child development and marital relations. *Child Development, 69*, 543–574.

Fletcher, A.C., Steinberg, L., & Williams-Wheeler, M. (2004). Parental influences on adolescent problem behavior: Revisiting Stattin and Kerr. *Child Development, 75*, 781–796.

Fomby, P., & Sennott, C. A. (2009, April). *Family instability, residential mobility, and adolescents' behavior.* Paper presented at the biennial meeting of the Society for Research in Child Development, Denver, CO.

Fosco, G. M., & Grych, J. H. (2010). Adolescent triangulation into parental conflicts: Longitudinal implications for appraisals and adolescent-parent relations. *Journal of Marriage and Family, 72*, 254–266.

Furstenberg, F. F. (2000). The sociology of adolescence and youth in the 1990s: A critical commentary. *Journal of Marriage and Family, 62*, 896–910.

Ganong, L., Coleman, M., & Brown, G. (1981). Effect of family structure on marital attitudes of adolescents. *Adolescence, 16*, 281–288.

Gecas, V., & Longmore, M. A. (2003). Self-esteem. In J. J. Ponzetti Jr. (Ed.), *International encyclopedia of marriage and family relationships* (2nd ed., pp. 1419–1424). New York: Macmillan Reference.

Gecas, V., & Seff, M. A. (1990). Families and adolescents: A review of the 1980s. *Journal of Marriage and Family, 52*, 941–958.

Gil-Rivas, V., Greenberger, E., Chen, C., & Lopez-Lena, M. M. (2003). Understanding depressed mood in the context of a family-oriented culture. *Adolescence, 38*, 93–109.

Giordano, P. C. (2010). *Legacies of crime: A follow-up of the children of highly delinquent girls and boys.* New York: Cambridge University Press.

Giordano, P. C., Longmore, M. A., & Manning, W. D. (2001). A conceptual portrait of adolescent romantic relationships. In D. A. Kinney (Ed.), *Sociological studies of children and youth* (pp. 111–139). London, England: Elsevier Science.

Giordano, P. C., Longmore, M. A., Manning, W. D., & Northcutt, M. J. (2009). Adolescent identities and sexual behavior: An examination of Anderson's 'player' hypothesis. *Social Forces, 87*, 1813–1844.

Graber, J. A., & Brooks-Gunn, J. (1996). Transitions and turning points: Navigating the passage from childhood through adolescence. *Developmental Psychology, 32*, 768–776.

Granic, I., & Patterson, G. R. (2006). Toward a comprehensive model of antisocial development: A dynamic systems approach. *Psychological Review, 113*, 101–131.

Greene, K., Kromar, M., Walters, L. H., Rubin, D. L., & Hale, J. L. (2000). Targeting adolescent risk-taking behaviors: The contributions of egocentrism and sensation-seeking. *Journal of Adolescence, 23*, 439–461.

Grotevant, H. D., & Cooper, C. (1986). Individuation in family relationships: A perspective on individuals differences in the development of identity and role-taking. *Human Development, 29*, 82–100.

Grych, J. H., Fincham, F. D., Jouriles, E. N., & McDonald, R. (2000). Interparental conflict and child adjustment: Testing the mediational role of appraisals in the cognitive-contextual framework. *Child Development, 71*, 1648–1661.

Guilamo-Ramos, V., Bouris, A., Jaccard, J., Lesesne, C., Gonzalez, B., & Kalogerogiannis, K. (2009). Family mediators of acculturation and adolescent sexual behavior among Latino youth. *Journal of Primary Prevention, 30*, 395–419.

Guldi, M., Page, M. E., & Stevens, A. H. (2007). Family background and children's transitions to adulthood over time. In S. Danziger & C. E. Rouse (Eds.), *The price of independence: The economics of early adulthood* (pp. 261–277). New York: Russell Sage.

Hall, G. S. (1904). *Adolescence: Its' psychology and its' relations to physiology, anthropology, sociology, sex, crime, religion, and education.* New York: Appleton.

Hair, E. C., Moore, K. A., Garrett, S. B., Ling, T., & Cleveland, K. (2008). The continued importance of quality parent-adolescent relationships during late adolescence. *Journal of Research on Adolescence, 18*, 187–200.

Harold, G. T., Fincham, F. D., Osborne, L. N., & Conger, R. D. (1997). Mom and dad are at it again: Adolescent perceptions of marital conflict and adolescent psychological distress. *Developmental Psychology, 33*, 333–350.

Hawkins, D. N., Amato, P. R., & King, V. (2006). Parent-adolescent involvement: The relative influence of parent gender and residence. *Journal of Marriage and Family, 68*, 125–136.

Hayes, L., Husdon, A., & Matthews, J. (2007). Understanding parental monitoring through analysis of monitoring episodes in context. *International Journal of Behavioral and Consultation Therapy, 3*, 96–108.

Heard, H. E., Gorman, B. K., & Kapinus, C. A. (2008). Family structure and self-rated health in adolescence and young adulthood. *Population Research and Policy Review, 27*, 773–797.

Hill, N. E., & Tyson, D. F. (2009). Parental involvement in middle school: A meta-analytic assessment of the strategies that promote achievement. *Developmental Psychology, 45*, 740–763.

Hines, A. R., & Paulson, S. E. (2006). Parents' and teachers' perceptions of adolescent storm and stress: Relations with parenting and teaching styles. *Adolescence, 41*, 597–614.

Ikramullah, E., Manlove, J., Cui, C., & Moore, K. A. (2009). *Parents matter: The role of parents in teens' decisions about sex* (Publication 2009–45). Retrieved from http://www.childtrends.org/Files/Child_Trends-2009_11_11_RB_Parents&TeenSex.pdf

Jaccard, J., & Dittus, P. J. (2000). Adolescent perceptions of maternal approval of birth control and sexual risk behavior. *American Journal of Public Health*, *90*, 1426–1430.

Jencks, C., & Mayer, C. R. (1990). The social consequences of growing up in a poor neighborhood. In L. E. Lynn & M. G. McGeary (Eds.), *Inner-city poverty in the United States* (pp. 111–186). Washington, DC: National Academy Press.

Jessor, R., & Jessor, S. L. (1977). *Problem behavior and psychosocial development: A longitudinal study of youth*. New York: Academic Press.

Joyner, K., & Udry, J. R. (2000). You don't bring me anything but down: Adolescent romance and depression. *Journal of Health and Social Behavior*, *41*, 369–391.

Kennedy, S., & Bumpass, L. (2008). Cohabitation and children's living arrangements: New estimates from the United States. *Demographic Research*, *19*, 1663–1692.

Kerr, M., & Stattin, H. (2000). What parents know, how they know it, and several forms of adolescent adjustment: Further support for a reinterpretation of monitoring. *Developmental Psychology*, *36*, 366–380.

Kim, D.H., & Schneider, B. (2005). Social capital in action: Alignment of parental support in adolescents' transition to postsecondary education. *Social Forces*, *84*, 1181–1206.

Knoester, C., Haynie, D. L., & Stephens, C. M. (2006). Parenting practices and adolescents' friendship networks. *Journal of Marriage and Family*, *68*, 1247–1260.

Laird, R. D., Pettit, G. S., Bates, J. E., & Dodge, K. A. (2003). Parents' monitoring-relevant knowledge and adolescents' delinquent behavior: Evidence of correlated developmental changes and reciprocal influences. *Child Development*, *74*, 752–768.

Lamborn, S. D., Mounts, N. S., Steinberg, L., & Dornbusch, S. M. (1991). Patterns of competence and adjustment among adolescents from authoritative, authoritarian, indulgent, and neglectful families. *Child Development*, *62*, 1049–1065.

Landsford, J. E., Yu, T., Erath, S. A., Pettit, G. S., Bates, J. E., & Dodge, K. A. (2010). Developmental precursors of number of sexual partners from ages 16 to 22. *Journal of Research on Adolescence*, *20*, 651–677.

Laub, J. H., & Sampson, R. J. (1988). Unraveling families and delinquency: A reanalysis of the Gluecks' data. *Criminology*, *26*, 355–380.

Laub, J. H., & Sampson, R. J. (2003). *Shared beginnings, divergent lives: Delinquent boys to age 70*. Cambridge, MA: Harvard University Press.

Laub, J. H., & Vaillant, G. E. (2000). Delinquency and mortality: A 50-year follow-up study of 1,000 delinquent and nondelinquent boys. *American Journal of Psychiatry*, *157*, 96–102.

Lee, M. A., & Mather, M. (2008). U.S. labor force trends. *Population Bulletin*, *63*, 3–16.

Lefkowitz, E. S., Boone, T. L., Au, T. K., & Sigman, M. (2003). No sex or safe sex? Mothers' and adolescents' discussions about abstinence and safer sex. *Health Education Research*, *18*, 341–351.

Lefkowitz, E. S., Romo, L. F., Corona, R., Kit-fong Au, T., & Sigman, M. (2000). How Latino American and European American adolescents discuss conflicts, sexuality, and AIDS with their mothers. *Developmental Psychology*, *36*, 315–325.

Lekes, N., Gingras, I., Philippe, F. L., Koestner, R., & Fang, J. (2010). Parental autonomy-support, intrinsic life goals, and well-being among adolescents in China and North America. *Journal of Youth and Adolescence*, *39*, 858–869.

Leventhal, T., & Brooks-Gunn, J. (2000). The neighborhoods they live in: The effects of neighborhood residence on child and adolescent outcomes. *Psychological Bulletin*, *126*, 309–317.

Li, X., Stanton, B., & Feigelman, S. (2000). Impact of perceived parental monitoring on adolescent risk behavior over 4 years. *Journal of Adolescent Health*, *27*, 49–56.

Longmore, M. A., Eng, A. L., Giordano, P. C., & Manning, W. D. (2009). Parenting and adolescents' sexual initiation. *Journal of Marriage and Family*, *71*, 969–982.

Longmore, M. A., Manning, W. D., & Giordano, P. C. (2001). Preadolescent parenting strategies and teens' dating and sexual initiation: A longitudinal analysis. *Journal of Marriage and the Family*, *63*, 322–335.

Luster, T., & Oh, S. M. (2001). Correlates of male adolescents carrying handguns among their peers. *Journal of Marriage and Family*, *63*, 714–726.

MacKinnon-Lewis, C., Castellino, D. R., Brody, G. H., & Finchman, F. D. (2001). A longitudinal examination of the associations between fathers' and children's attributions and negative interactions. *Social Development*, *10*, 473–487.

Madsen, S. D. (2008). Parents' management of adolescents' romantic relationships through dating rules: Gender variations and correlates of relationship qualities. *Journal of Youth and Adolescence*, *37*, 1044–1058.

Magnuson, K. (2007). Maternal education and children's academic achievement during middle childhood. *Developmental Psychology*, *43*, 1497–1512.

Manning, W. D., Longmore, M. A., & Giordano, P. C. (2007). The changing institution of marriage: Adolescents expectations to cohabit and to marry. *Journal of Marriage and Family*, *69*, 559–575.

Manning, W. D., & Lamb, K. A. (2003). Adolescent well-being in cohabiting, married, and single parent families. *Journal of Marriage and Family*, *65*, 846–893.

Marsiglio, W., Amato, P., Day, R. D., & Lamb, M. E. (2000). Scholarship on fatherhood in the 1990s and beyond. *Journal of Marriage and Family*, *62*, 1173–1191.

Martin, P. D., Martin, D., & Martin, M. (2001). Adolescent premarital sexual activity, cohabitation, and attitudes toward marriage. *Adolescence*, *36*, 601–609.

McHale, S. M., Crouter, A. C., & Whiteman, S. D. (2003). The family contexts of gender development in childhood and adolescence. *Social Development*, *12*, 125–148.

McNeal, R. B. Jr. (1999). Parental involvement as social capital: Differential effectiveness on science achievement, truancy, and dropping out. *Social Forces*, *78*, 117–144.

McNeely, C. A., Nonnemaker, J. M., & Blum, R. W. (2002). Promoting school connectedness: Evidence from the National Longitudinal Study of Adolescent Health. *Journal of School Health*, *72*, 138–146.

Meadows, S. O. (2007). Evidence of parallel pathways: Gender similarity in the impact of social support on adolescent depression and delinquency. *Social Forces*, *85*, 1143–1167.

Meschke, L. L., Zweig, J. M., Barber, B. L., & Eccles, J. S. (2000). Demographic, biological, psychological, and social predictors of the timing of first intercourse. *Journal of Research on Adolescence*, *10*, 315–338.

Mihalic, S. W., & Elliott, D. (1997). A social learning theory model of marital violence. *Journal of Family Issues*, *12*, 21–47.

Mitchell, K. J., & Finkelhor, D. (2001). Risk of crime victimization among youth exposed to domestic violence. *Journal of Interpersonal Violence*, *16*, 945–966.

Moore, K. A., & Stief, T. M. (1991). Changes in marriage and fertility behavior: Behavior versus attitudes of young adults. *Youth and Society*, *22*, 362–386.

Najman, J. M., Clavarino, A., McGee, T. R., Bor, W., Williams, G. M., & Hayatbakhsh, M. R. (2010). Timing and chronicity of family poverty and development of unhealthy behaviors in children: A longitudinal study. *Journal of Adolescent Health*, *46*, 538–544.

Oesterle, S., Hawkins, J. D., Hill, K. G., & Bailey, J. A. (2010). Men's and women's pathways to adulthood and their adolescent precursors. *Journal of Marriage and Family*, *72*, 1436–1453.

Paddock-Ellard, K., & Thomas, S. (1981). Attitudes of young adolescents toward marriage, divorce, and children of divorce. *Journal of Early Adolescence*, *1*, 303–310.

Padgham, J. J., & Blyth, D. A. (1991). Dating during adolescence. In R. M. Lerner, A. C. Petersen, & J. Brooks-Gunn (Eds.), *Encyclopedia of adolescence* (pp. 196–198). New York: Garland.

Padilla-Walker, L. M. (2008). "My mom makes me so angry!": Adolescents' perceptions of mother-child interactions as correlates of adolescents' emotions. *Social Development*, *17*, 306–325.

Parcel, T. L., & Dufur, M. J. (2001). Capital at home and at school: Effects on student achievement. *Social Forces*, *79*, 881–911.

Parcel, T. L., Dufur, M. J., & Zito, R. C. (2010). Capital at home and at school: A review and synthesis. *Journal of Marriage and Family*, *72*, 828–846.

Patrick, M. R., Snyder, J., Schrepferman, L. M., & Snyder, J. M. (2005). The joint effects of early parental warmth and communication and child conduct problems on later monitoring and child conduct problems. *Child Development*, *76*, 999–1014.

Patterson, G. R. (1982). *Coercive family processes*. Eugene, OR: Castalia.

Pearson, J., Muller, C., & Frisco, M. L. (2006). Parental involvement, family structure, and adolescent sexual decision making. *Sociological Perspectives*, *49*, 67–90.

Quatman, T., Sampson, K., Robinson, C., & Watson, C. M. (2001). Academic, motivational and emotional correlated of adolescent dating. *Genetic, Social, and General Psychology Monographs*, *127*, 211–234.

Raley, R. K., Frisco, M., & Wildsmith, E. (2005). Maternal cohabitation and educational success. *Sociology of Education*, *78*, 144–164.

Rathunde, K., & Csikszentmihalyi, M. (1991). Adolescent happiness and family interaction. In K. Pillemer & K. McCarthey (Eds.), *Parent-child relations throughout life* (pp. 143–162). Hillsdale, NJ: Erlbaum.

Reitz, E., Deković, M., Meijer, A. M., & Engels, R. C. M. E. (2006). Longitudinal relations among parenting, best friends, and early adolescent problem behavior: Testing bidirectional effects. *Journal of Early Adolescence, 26*, 272–295.

Resnick, M. D. (2000). Protective factors, resiliency, and healthy youth development. *Adolescent Medicine: State of the Art Reviews, 11*, 157–164.

Resnick, M. D., Bearman, P. S., Blum, R. W., Bauman, K. E., Harris, K. M., Jones, J., ... Udry, J. R. (1997). Protecting adolescents from harm. Findings from the National Longitudinal Study of Adolescent Health. *Journal of the American Medical Association, 278*, 823–832.

Romich, J., Lundberg, S., & Tsang, K. P. (2009). Independence giving or autonomy taking? Childhood predictors of decision-making patterns between youth adolescents and parents, *Journal of Research on Adolescence, 19*, 587–600.

Rucibwa, N. K., Modeste, N., Montgomery, S., & Fox, C. A. (2003). Exploring family factors and sexual behaviors in a group of African American and Hispanic adolescent males. *American Journal of Health Behaviors, 27*, 63–74.

Sampson, R. J., & Laub, J. H. (1994). Urban poverty and the family context of delinquency: A new look at structure and process in a classic study. *Child Development, 65*, 523–540.

Sampson, R. J., Morenoff, J., & Earls, F. (1999). Beyond social capital: Spatial dynamics of collective efficacy for children. *American Sociological Review, 64*, 633–660.

Santelli, J. S., Lowry, R., Brener, N. D., & Robin, L. (2000). The association of sexual behaviors with socioeconomic status, family structure, and race/ethnicity among U.S. adolescents. *American Journal of Public Health, 90*, 1582–1588.

Santos, M. (2005, August). *Reopening the debate on social capital: Parental intergenerational closure, school racial composition, and math achievement: A multilevel approach.* Paper presented at the annual conference of the American Sociological Association, Madison, WI.

Schoon, I., Bynner, J., Joshi, H., Parsons, S., Wiggins, R.D., & Sacker, A. (2002). The influence of context, timing, and duration of risk experiences for the passage from childhood to mid-adulthood. *Child Development, 73*, 1486–1504.

Serbin, L., & Karp, J. (2003). Intergenerational studies of parenting and the transfer of risk from parent to child. *Current Directions in Psychological Science, 12*, 138–142.

Shanahan, L., McHale, S. M., Crouter, A. C., & Osgood, D. W. (2007). Warmth with mothers and fathers from middle childhood to late adolescence: Within- and between-families comparisons. *Developmental Psychology, 43*, 551–563.

Shanahan, M. J. (2000). Pathways to adulthood in changing societies: Variability and mechanisms in life course perspective. *Annual Review of Sociology, 26*, 667–692.

Shanahan, M. J., & Flaherty, B. P. (2001). Dynamic patterns of time use in adolescence. *Child Development, 72*, 385–401.

Shanahan, M. J., & Porfelli, E. (2002). Integrating the life course and life-span: Formulating research questions with dual points of entry. *Journal of Vocational Behavior, 61*, 298–406.

Sieverding, J. A., Adler, N., Witt, S., & Ellen, J. (2005). The influence of monitoring on adolescent sexual initiation. *Archives of Pediatric and Adolescent Medicine, 159*, 724–729.

Simons, L. G., & Conger, R. D. (2007). Linking mother-father differences in parenting to a typology of family parenting styles and adolescent outcomes. *Journal of Family Issues, 28*, 212–241.

Simons, R. L., Chao, W., Conger, R. D., & Elder, G. H., Jr. (2001). Quality of parenting as a mediator of the effect of childhood defiance on adolescent friendship choices and delinquency: A growth curve analysis. *Journal of Marriage and the Family, 63*, 63–79.

Simons-Morton, B. G., Chen, R., Abroms, L., & Haynie, D. L. (2004). Latent growth curve analysis of peer and parent influences on smoking progression among early adolescents. *Healthy Psychology, 23*, 612–621.

Slaughter-Defoe, D. T., Nakagawa, K., Takanishi, R., & Johnson, D. J. (1990). Toward cultural/ecological perspectives on schooling and achievement in African- and Asian-American children. *Child Development, 61*, 363–370.

Smetana, J., & Daddis, C. (2002). Domain-specific antecedents of parental psychological control and monitoring: The role of parenting beliefs and practices. *Child Development, 73*, 563–580.

Smock, P. J. (2000). Cohabitation in the United States: An appraisal of research themes, findings, and implications. *Annual Review of Sociology, 26*, 1–20.

Smock, P. J., & Gupta, S. (2002). Cohabitation in contemporary North America. In A. Booth & A. C. Crouter (Eds.), *Just living together: Implications for children, families, and public policy* (pp. 53–84). Mahwah, NJ: Lawrence Erlbaum.

Sobolewski, J., & Amato, P. R. (2007). Parents' discord and divorce, parent-child relationships, and subjective well-being in early adulthood: Is feeling close to two parents always better than feeling close to one? *Social Forces, 85*, 1105–1124.

South, S. J., & Haynie, D. L. (2004). Friendship networks of mobile adolescents. *Social Forces, 83*, 315–350.

South, S. J., Haynie, D. L., & Bose, S. (2005). Residential mobility and the onset of adolescent sexual activity. *Journal of Marriage and Family, 67*, 499–514.

Staff, J., & Mortimer, J. T. (2007). Educational and work strategies from adolescence to early adulthood: Consequences for educational attainment. *Social Forces, 85*, 1169–1194.

Starfield, B. (1989). Child health and public policy. In L. Kopelman & J. Moskop (Eds.), *Children and health care: Moral and social issues* (pp. 7–21). Dordrecht, the Netherlands: Kluwer.

Starfield, B., Riley, A. W., Witt, W. P., & Robertson, J. (2002). Social class gradients in health during adolescence. *Journal of Epidemiology and Community Health, 56*, 354–361.

Stattin, H., & Kerr, M. (2000). Parental monitoring: A reinterpretation. *Child Development, 71*, 1072–1085.

Steinberg, L. (2001). We know some things: Parent-adolescent relationships in retrospect and prospect. *Journal of Research on Adolescence, 11*, 1–19.

Steinberg, L., Fletcher, A., & Darling, N. (1994). Parental monitoring and peer influences on adolescent substance use. *Pediatrics, 93*, 1060–1064.

Steinberg, L., & Morris, A. S. (2001). Adolescent development. *Journal of Cognitive Education and Psychology, 22*, 55–87.

Steinberg, L., & Silk, J. S. (2002). Parenting adolescents. In M. Bornstein (Ed.), *Handbook of parenting, vol. 1, Children and parenting* (2nd ed., pp. 135–164). Mahwah, NJ: Laurence Erlbaum.

SAMHSA Substance Abuse and Mental Health Services Administration, Office of Applied Studies. (December 17, 2009). *The NSDUH Report: Violent Behaviors among Adolescent Females*. Rockville, MD: Department of Health and Human Services.

Substance Abuse and Mental Health Services Administration, Office of Applied Studies. (August 19, 2010). *The NSDUH Report: Violent Behaviors and Family Income among Adolescents*. Rockville, MD: Department of Health and Human Services.

Tasker, F. L., & Richards, M. P. M. (1994). Adolescents' attitudes toward marriage and marital prospects after parental divorce: A review. *Journal of Adolescent Research, 9*, 340–362.

Thomas, G., Reifman, A., Barnes, G. M., & Farrell, M. P. (2000). Delayed onset of drunkenness as a protective factor for adolescent alcohol misuse and sexual risk taking: A longitudinal study. *Deviant Behavior, 21*, 181–209.

Thomas, S. L. (2003). Longer-term economic effects of college selectivity and control. *Research in Higher Education, 44*, 263–299.

Vandewater, A. E., & Lansford, J. E. (2005). A family process model of problem behaviors in adolescents. *Journal of Marriage and the Family, 67*, 100–109.

Vandivere, S., Tout, K., Zaslow, M., Calkins, J., & Capizzano, J. (2003). *Unsupervised time: Family and child factors associated with self-care*. Washington, DC: The Urban Institute.

Wells, T., Sandefur, G. D., & Hogan, D. P. (2003). What happens after the high school years among young persons with disabilities? *Social Forces, 82*, 803–832.

Wright, J. P., & Cullen, F. T. (2001). Parental efficacy and delinquent behavior: Do control and support matter? *Criminology, 39*, 677–706.

Wright, D. R., & Fitzpatrick, K. M. (2006). Social capital and adolescent violent behavior: Correlates of fighting and weapon use among secondary school students. *Social Forces, 84*, 1435–1453.

Zaff, J. F., & Moore, K. A. (2002). *Promoting well-being among America's teens: An executive summary of adolescent development research reviews completed for the John S. and James L. Knight Foundation.* Retrieved from http://www.childtrends.org/Files//Child_Trends-2002_10_01_ES_TeenWellbeing.pdf

4 Taking Stock of Theory in Grandparent Studies

James S. Bates and Alan C. Taylor

Modern research on grandparents traces its roots to Neugarten and Weinstein's (1964) classic study of 70 adult dyads who were interviewed about their grandparent role. This study described the degree of comfort experienced in the grandparent role, delineated the significance and meaning of grandparenthood, and outlined the first typology of grandparenting styles. More than two decades later, Cherlin and Furstenberg's (1986) now classic study identified similar grandparenting styles and also explored the symbolic meaning of the grandparent role. This study also explored the exchange of services and support, the functions of a grandparent, grandparents' selective investment behaviors, and broached the term intergenerational solidarity.

Notwithstanding their important empirical contributions, these watershed studies are emblematic of the lack of explicit or overt utilization of theory that occurred in grandparent research at the time. That is, instead of mentioning a theory by name, explaining which concepts were applied to the study, and interpreting results through the lens of theory, grandparent scholars tended to borrow a concept from this theory and a concept from that theory and plugged them in where they seemed to fit best. Thus, the terms role performance and meaning, exchange, function, investment, and solidarity are likely concepts borrowed from a number of well-established theories, namely, *symbolic interactionism, social exchange theory, structural-functionalism, bio-evolutionary theory,* and the emergent *family solidarity model.*

This view of the first generation of grandparent research (1964–1991) is consistent with Kivett's (1991b) observation: "Similar to other research on the family, investigations of the grandparent-grandchild connection have been largely atheoretical" (p. 269), and "few studies… have been theoretically based" (p. 270). Kivett further contends, "There have been few attempts … to integrate this knowledge [of the grandparent–grandchild link] either conceptually or empirically" (p. 286). Her recommended solution: "Increase the use of theoretical frameworks and develop mid-range theories" (p. 285). Not only was the literature atheoretical but it was also "noncumulative and fragmentary" (Kivett, p. 285). Indeed, when grandparents are not studied well, misrepresentations and uninformed claims about intergenerational family relationships result.

The purpose of this chapter is to take stock of theory utilization in a second generation of grandparent research (1991–2010). We recognize the possibility that in research on grandparents published during the 1990s and 2000s a number of different theories were likely used, that there likely were variations in how theories were used (i.e., frameworks, middle-range theories), and that there likely was (as there had been prior to 1991) limited theory building (i.e., "few attempts …", Kivett, 1991b, p. 286). Thus, we are guided in our review by three basic questions: (1) Which theories have scholars utilized to study grandparent phenomena? (2) How have theories been utilized? (3) What has been the extent of theory building?

We begin by reviewing key topic areas in the body of scholarship called grandparent studies and examine the theories used to study these topic areas. We then point out limitations of theory utilization in this body of work. Finally, we propose and discuss opportunities for theoretical advancement.

THEORIES UTILIZED IN GRANDPARENT STUDIES

There are three key topic areas that have remained of consistent interest to grandparent scholars over the past 50 years: (1) the demographic and personal characteristics of grandparents, parents, and grandchildren; (2) the behavioral and psychological aspects of grandparenthood; and (3) the outcomes (or results) of grandparenting for grandparents, parents, grandchildren, and family relationships. Figure 4.1 depicts a simplified process model of the empirical relations among these three topic areas.

In order to identify theories, we conducted a series of systematic searches of several electronic databases, including *PsychInfo, PsychArticles, Ageline, Social Services Abstracts*, and *Sociological Abstracts*. Because research on grandparents is a relatively small body of scholarship and because of the historically limited use of theory, our search covered 20 years (January 1991 through December 2010). Key search words/phrases were: *grandparent, grandchild, grandmother, grandfather, intergenerational relationships*, and derivations of each. We also reviewed the reference lists of numerous articles and review chapters and searched individual journals specific to the fields of family studies, psychology, sociology, gerontology, and social work. Several hundred articles were found; however, we pared this list down to those that were empirical (qualitative and quantitative), contained data collected from grandparents, and to those that focused on grandparenting, grandparenthood, or grandparent–grandchild relationships. Articles that reported data collected exclusively from grandchildren, parents, or surrogate, caregiving grandparents were removed. The final list contained 209 articles.

These articles were analyzed for overt and unambiguous utilization of theory, meaning that a theory was named and utilized in the study (Taylor & Bagdi, 2005, use the term *explicit*). Only 48.3% of the articles contained an overt utilization of theory, 11.5% implied the use of theory in the mention of concepts or ideas from a theory but did not give a theory name, and 40.2% had no mention of theory. We discovered great diversity in the theories used—over 55 different theories were mentioned overtly—and the manner by which a particular theory was used depended on whether the theory was exploited as a theoretical framework or "lens" (Abend, 2008) or whether relations among concepts were examined or tested as empirical generalizations, causal models, middle-range theories, or formal propositional theories (Doherty, Boss, LaRossa, Schumm, & Steinmetz, 1993).

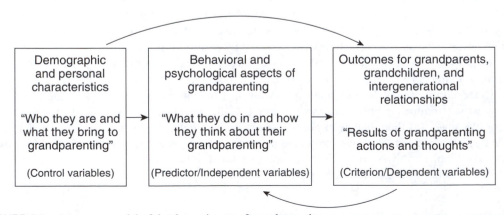

FIGURE 4.1   A process model of the determinants of grandparenting.

Such diversity likely reflects the international and multidisciplinary composition of grandparent scholars. Besides family studies, psychology, sociology, and gerontology, scholarship from 16 other disciplines was represented in these articles. Grandparent research was published by scholars from all inhabited continents, who, collectively, have studied more than 30 racial/ethnic groups, including all of the major racial groups in the US. Besides the dominant sociological and psychological issues, grandparent scholars have studied a diverse array of topics including feeding habits in intergenerational homes, grandparent–grandchild book reading, computer game leisure, grandchildhood, expatriated, international, and immigrant grandparenting, grandparent education, and so on.

DEMOGRAPHIC AND PERSONAL CHARACTERISTICS

Demographic information (e.g., age, sex, marital status, geographic distance from grandchild, race/ethnicity, lineage) is frequently utilized in grandparent research to categorize research participants and to draw comparisons on the basis of such categorizations. *Personal characteristics* refer to those aspects of self that people bring to family roles and relationships, such as personality traits and knowledge of the past.[1] Personal background and demographic data are often used as control variables (e.g., Chen, Short, & Entwisle, 2000), although they have also been used to predict the behavioral and psychological aspects of grandparenting (e.g., Baydar & Brooks-Gunn, 1998) and the outcomes of intergenerational relationships (e.g., Bengtson, Copen, Putney, & Silverstein, 2009) (see Figure 4.1). Following is a review of the theories used to study the demographic and personal characteristics of grandparents, parents, and grandchildren.

Grandparents

The most commonly used theory to study the demographic and personal characteristics of grandparents was *family systems theory*, also discussed as a *holistic perspective* (e.g., Ashton, 1996), which assumes an interconnectedness among family members and across generations (Whitchurch & Constantine, 1993). In every instance, family systems theory was used as a broad guiding perspective to justify the study of grandparents as a research population because, as members of the extended family, they are interconnected with grandchildren and parents of the nuclear family (Mirfin-Veitch, Bray, & Watson, 1996).

---

[1] The demographic features of grandparents that have been studied include: age; sex; marital status; race/ethnicity; education level; employment/retirement status; housing arrangements (e.g., assisted living facility, own home); neighborhood/community characteristics (e.g., rural, urban, nation); number of grandchildren; geographic distance from grandchildren; and age (timing) of first becoming a grandparent. The personal background characteristics of grandparents include: physical health; personality traits; religiosity; community involvement; and knowledge of own grandparents. In comparison to grandparents, the demographic characteristics of parents have been studied to a much lesser extent. However, scholars have investigated parental marital status, sex, age, neighborhood/community characteristics (e.g., rural, urban, country of origin), and consanguine (blood) and affinal (marriage) relation to grandparent. In the literature on grandparents raising grandchildren, there has been a strong emphasis on parental housing arrangements (i.e., three-generation households versus skip generation households) and on whether the parent is deceased, incarcerated, or has emigrated for employment. Scholars have also investigated the personal characteristics of parents and the parental nuclear family. Studies show that personality characteristics of parents, particularly depressive symptoms, delinquent behavioral tendencies, and parenting practices are transmitted across three generations (Bailey, Hill, Oesterle, & Hawkins, 2009; Barnes Nacoste & Wise, 1991; Kitamura, Shikai, Uji, Hiramura, Tanaka, & Shono, 2009). At the family-level, one important variable is the emotional closeness between the parent and the grandparent. Although the unit of analysis is the parent–grandparent relationship and not the parent specifically, emotional closeness is typically reported by the parent (e.g., King & Elder, 1995). Studied demographic characteristics of grandchildren include: sex; age (or life stage such as childhood, adolescence, or young adulthood); lineage (i.e., maternal, paternal); marital status; socioeconomic status; education level (i.e., used as a proxy for age or developmental ability); housing arrangements (i.e., a feature of the family); number of grandparents living; and geographic distance from grandparents. Personal characteristics of grandchildren include pubertal status, as well as aspects of personality (e.g., anger, tantrums, social competence, self-esteem, and depressive symptoms), which are often explored in multigenerational studies.

The *life course perspective* was also used to justify the study of grandparents as a population (Bengtson & Allen, 1993). In addition however, several studies adopted life course concepts and assumptions to frame their work. For instance, Kemp (2007), in using the concept of *linked lives*, or the interdependence of people's lives, in concert with the assumption that *life is embedded in time and place*, was able to highlight the interdependent nature of intergenerational family relationships and describe how such relationships simultaneously retain continuity and experience change across multiple generations in changing social and demographic contexts.

King's (2003) study of the effects of grandparent divorce on relationships with grandchildren was also guided by the concept of linked lives. She found that never-divorced grandparents reported significantly more contact and participation in shared activities and less conflict with grandchildren than ever-divorced grandparents. It was suggested that divorce in the grandparent generation weakened bonds between some grandparents and their adult children. As a result, grandchildren had less meaningful relationships with their ever-divorced grandparents. The strength of intergenerational ties in these families was thus a function of events that occurred in the grandparents' past and that divorce affects the development of meaningful relationships among those whose lives are linked genetically.

King and Elder (1997) utilized life course theory to examine whether grandparents' personal experiences and knowledge of their own grandparents was related to involvement in their grandchildren's lives. They found that grandparents who had known and learned about their own grandparents were more involved with their grandchildren. Data indicated that grandparents' lives were indeed linked with those of their grandchildren, even when the sources of influence extend beyond the grandparent.

Grandparent age and grandchild age were examined using the *intergenerational stake hypothesis*, which proposes that perceptions of intergenerational relationship quality are overstated by grandparents because they are motivated to minimize conflict and underestimated by grandchildren (typically young adults) who are motivated to overstate conflict (Giarrusso, Stallings, & Bengtson, 1995). In such cases, each has a different "stake" in the relationship. Harwood (2001) found support for this hypothesis in grandparents' ratings of emotional closeness that exceeded those of grandchildren's ratings. Hoff (2007) found support for asymmetrical exchanges in instrumental assistance and financial transfers such that grandparents gave more to younger generations than grandchildren gave to their grandparents. Giarrusso, Feng, Silverstein, and Bengtson (2001) further confirmed the hypothesis by finding that grandmothers showed greater affection to granddaughters than granddaughters did to their grandmothers.

The *socioemotional selectivity theory* (Cartensen, 1992) proposes that older adults express a greater interest in family relations because of their proximity to death than younger adults. Oppelaar and Dykstra (2004) utilized this theory to frame their investigation of contact differences as a function of grandparent age. It was anticipated that older grandparents would report greater amounts of contact than younger grandparents, although they found evidence to suggest the opposite. By contrast, Silverstein and Long (1998) found evidence to support the theory, where older grandparents had stronger levels of affection for grandchildren than younger grandparents. Future theoretical work should attempt to reconcile these discrepant findings.

The concept of *structural solidarity* from the *intergenerational solidarity model* (a framework of six broadly defined concepts; see Bengtson, 2001) refers to structural aspects of intergenerational family relationships that facilitate or inhibit solidarity. Structural solidarity is typically assessed as the geographic distance between grandparents and grandchildren (Silverstein & Long, 1998; Silverstein & Marenco, 2001), although it was used to justify the examination of the health status of grandparents, where more healthy grandparents had greater opportunities to provide functional assistance to grandchildren (Even-Zohar & Sharlin, 2009). While some studies found that geographic proximity facilitated closer emotional bonds and opportunities for grandchildren to assist grandparents (Silverstein & Long), Silverstein and Marenco found no evidence that structural solidarity affected emotional closeness.

Finally, the *cultural variant perspective* views racial divergences from norms of the dominant culture as adaptive behaviors rather than deviant (Allen, 1978). This perspective was utilized to justify making comparisons between Black and White grandparents on role conceptions and support networks (Kivett, 1993). Kivett found support for this perspective in which intergenerational exchanges were used by Black grandparents as a coping strategy to deal with the oppressive social environment.

Parents

Several theories helped frame studies in which the marital status of the parents was of direct relevance to the grandparent–grandchild relationship. Clingempeel, Colyar, Brand, and Hetherington (1992) tested the *latent function hypothesis*, a formal propositional theory that posits that grandparents assume a relatively passive, non-interferential role in the lives of adult children and grandchildren until there is a substantial disruption in family functioning (such as parental divorce) that prompts grandparents to increase involvement. Clingempeel et al. found that grandmothers and grandfathers increased involvement with grandchildren during such times of family crisis. Family systems theory (e.g., Jaskowski & Dellasega, 1993) and *critical role transitions theory* (e.g., Doyle, O'Dywer, & Timonen, 2010) were likewise applied to the study of parental divorce because in times of major transition all members of the family system negotiated new roles and responsibilities in order to return to normative functioning.

Social exchange theory is founded on the assumption that human thinking is rational and that individuals weigh the costs and rewards of their decisions and attempt to minimize costs and maximize rewards (Sabatelli & Shehan, 1993). When a divorced parent remarries, some grandparents experience a decrease in the number of visits with grandchildren (Gladstone, 1991). The remarriage *costs* or takes away grandparents' time and opportunities to maintain relationships with grandchildren who they had supported and grown close to during the parental divorce. This decrease in contact with grandchildren may also cost grandparents in their mental health as fewer visits may mean feelings of loss (Gladstone). Indeed, there may be few *rewards* for grandparents when parents remarry.

The notion of *gatekeeping* by parents was broached in a few studies of the personal characteristics of parents, although that term was not used specifically. *Parent-as-mediator theory* argues that parents broker relationships between grandparents and grandchildren (Doyle et al., 2010). Several studies found that the emotional closeness between parents (children and children-in-law) and grandparents affects the emotional closeness of grandparents and grandchildren, as well as grandparents' participation in recreational activities with the grandchild (Fingerman, 2004; Silverstein & Marenco, 2001).

Support was found for the *paternity uncertainty hypothesis*, a derivation of *evolutionary theory*, in the study of parent sex effects. This refers to the idea that grandparents on the mother's side invest more in grandchildren than paternal grandparents because of the certainty that maternal grandchildren carry their genes. Grandparent investment, assessed as frequent contact with grandchildren, was greater among those in the maternal line than in the paternal line (Pollet, Nettle, & Nelissen, 2006). Support for an alternative approach to studying parent sex effects is *kinkeeping theory* (Oppelaar & Dykstra, 2004). Like evolutionary theory, kinkeeping theory proposes that intergenerational ties are stronger among women than among men. Unlike evolutionary theory, kinkeeping is the learned behavior of nurturing and caregiving transmitted from grandmother to mother and from mother to daughter.

Grandchildren

Of the many demographic characteristics of grandchildren identified previously, socioeconomic status was the only characteristic studied with theory. Bengtson et al. (2009) framed processes of socialization across three generations of family members in terms of *status inheritance theory*. This theory states that parents provide status to their children in the form of wealth and education, and in doing so, they facilitate intergenerational similarity in values and beliefs. By extension, this study assumed that similarity in religious beliefs would more strongly follow those in the same family who had similar education levels. Unfortunately, the authors do not provide any information regarding the outcome of this hypothesis.

Only one personal characteristic, pubertal development, was examined with theory. According to the *emotional distancing hypothesis*, physical maturation of adolescents toward pubertal apex is associated with increased emotional distance and conflict with parents and grandparents (Clingempeel et al., 1992). By contrast, the *stress-buffering hypothesis*, a derivative of *attachment theory*, suggests that during stressful life changes such as maturational development, adolescents may develop emotionally closer relationships with parents and grandparents (Clingempeel et al., 1992). Empirical support was found for these opposing hypotheses. While grandsons developed closer relationships with grandparents, granddaughters distanced themselves from grandfathers but not grandmothers.

BEHAVIORAL AND PSYCHOLOGICAL ASPECTS OF GRANDPARENTHOOD

Behavioral

We use the term *grandparenting* to refer to the behavioral and interactive aspects of grandparenthood. Common interactive and behavioral topics of study include the frequency of grandparent–grandchild contact and participation in activities with grandchildren. Much less studied is the topic of intergenerational communication, which we discuss because of the potential for theoretical and empirical advancement. Following is a review of these topics and how theory has been used to study them.

Contact

Contact frequency is perhaps the most commonly studied aspect of grandparent–grandchild relationships. Indeed, in order for grandparents to perform their grandparental role and participate in relationship-building activities, they must first have contact with the grandchildren. Contact frequency is typically operationalized as the amount of face-to-face (e.g., visits) and non-face-to-face contact (e.g., letters, phone calls, e-mail) (Geurts, Poortman, van Tilburg, & Dykstra, 2009).

The *theory of the niche* (Dimmick, Kline, & Stafford, 2000) and the *theory of uses and gratifications* (Katz, Blumler, & Gurevitch, 1974) were proposed as formal propositional theories that were tested with a sample of grandparents to understand the frequency of contact with grandchildren as a function of new and traditional communication media (Quadrello, Hurme, Menzinger, Smith, Veisson, Vidal, & Westerback, 2005). The theory of the niche predicts that a new communication medium may or may not compete with the existing communication media but that competition depends on whether the new medium provides greater opportunities for gratification than the old. The theory of uses and gratifications proposes that new media should overlap and exceed the gratification of the old. In their application of these theories to contact frequency and contact type, Quadrello et al. did not find support for the theories but found that living geographically closer to their grandchild was associated with greater amounts of spoken communication and that living further apart was associated with more frequent contact through e-mail.

The concept of *associational solidarity* from the intergenerational solidarity model refers to the frequency of contact between grandparents and grandchildren (Bengtson, 2001) and was used in quantitative (Silverstein & Chen, 1999; Silverstein & Marenco, 2001; Williams & Guendouzi, 2005) and qualitative studies (Werner, Buchbinder, Lowenstein, & Livni, 2007). Presumably, the more grandparent–grandchild contact the stronger the relationship, although this relation may be moderated by feelings of ambivalence (Hebblethwaite & Norris, 2010). Of the theories reviewed, the intergenerational solidarity model is the only theory that contains the concept of contact frequency. Later in the chapter, however, we describe a new theoretical formulation that incorporates (as in incorporates) contact frequency.

Activities

Contact with grandchildren facilitates various documented interaction patterns and activities that grandparents participate in with grandchildren (Bates, 2009). Activities include playing together, teaching skills or mentoring, giving advice, exchanging assistance, providing emotional support or resources, showing affection, communicating and information sharing, and caregiving (Bates & Taylor, in press; Goodsell, Bates, & Behnke, 2011; Hagestad, 1985). Tinsley and Parke (1987) identified 13 different types of behaviors by grandparents during a 5-minute free play session with their infant grandchild, including object presentation, touching, kissing, demonstrating, laughing/smiling, positive verbalization, physical restriction, etc.

Social exchange theory was commonly utilized to guide investigations of grandparents providing assistance or emotional/social support to grandchildren. Studies investigated *reciprocity*, or the sharing of time and resources. For example, in a study of Chinese families, Cong and Silverstein (2008) found that when parents who had migrated from rural areas to work in urban centers financially compensated grandparents for providing full-time surrogate care of grandchildren, these grandparents experienced a statistically significant reduction in depressive symptoms. Time-for-money reciprocal transactions were also investigated in a study of Korean grandparents in which downward transfers of time, measured as caring for grandchildren, were compensated with either short-term financial support, long-term security, or not at all (Lee & Bauer, 2010). These authors use the *intergenerational transfer theory*, a derivative of exchange theory, to reconcile why some grandparents acted altruistically and simply did not expect payment for their time and effort in caregiving.

Social exchange theory was also used in concert with the concept of *functional solidarity* from the intergenerational solidarity model (Bengtson, 2001). Functional solidarity is typically operationalized in terms of the exchange or transfer of material resources and emotional or instrumental assistance (Hoff, 2007). In their investigation of grandchildhood, Even-Zohar and Sharlin (2009) found that grandchild identity was linked with expectations to "repay" grandparents for their lifelong help and support. Desires to repay grandparents for their investments demonstrate grandchildren's commitment and sense of obligation to their elders. Indeed, another intergenerational solidarity model concept comes into play here: *normative solidarity*. Normative solidarity refers to filial obligations and the importance of family values. Normative solidarity was also investigated in Even-Zohar and Sharlin's study and operates in concert with functional solidarity. While functional solidarity refers to exchanging assistance, normative solidarity is the motivation or filial obligation to do so.

Grandparents' participation in activities related to caregiving, recreation, mentoring, attending family celebrations and reunions, shopping together, and attending church together are operationalizations of the concept *associational solidarity* from the intergenerational solidarity model (Bengtson, 2001; Kivett, 1991a). Higher levels of associational solidarity were reported by more Black grandfathers than White grandfathers, even though the centrality of the role was based more strongly on affectionate types of behaviors (i.e., emotional closeness, getting along) than on associational activities and interactions (Kivett). Associational solidarity was implied in one study that utilized several concepts from the intergenerational solidarity model to develop a typology of grandparenting styles (Mueller & Elder, 2003). Grandparents who reported high levels of participation in activities were named *influential*. The influential style of grandparenting was more strongly correlated with emotionally close grandparent–grandchild relationships than any of the other four grandparenting styles.

Stress theory (Lazarus & Folkman, 1984) was utilized to describe reasons for grandparents' engagement in grandchildren's lives. Tenets of stress theory posit that in times of adjustment and adaptation to stressful situations, family members may modify their perceptions and behaviors to be able to adequately cope. Those with positive perceptions of a stressor event are more likely to help others adjust by providing support. In the case of families with a disabled grandchild, grandparents with positive perceptions of the disability may offer enhanced support to parents and the disabled grandchild (Katz & Kessel, 2002). Thus, in this instance, the performance of supportive behaviors is prompted by a stressor event.

Communication

One understudied topic in grandparent–grandchild research is communication and our searches yielded only three studies in which the authors utilized theory to examine it. These studies applied *communication accommodation theory* (CAT: Giles, Mulac, Bradac, & Johnson, 1987), which refers to (1) the behavioral changes that people make to attune their communication to their partner and (2) the extent to which people perceive their partner as appropriately attuning to them (Harwood, 2000). The premise of CAT is that communication partners adopt strategic behaviors, such as attuning their conversation topics and communication styles to be similar to or different from their partner's, in order to achieve various relational goals, such as interpersonal solidarity or group identification (Lin & Harwood, 2003). Overaccommodation occurs when grandchildren accommodate too much in their speech by using simplified vocabulary or increasing the volume of their speech. These behaviors inadvertently patronize grandparents (Lin & Harwood). Underaccommodating occurs when grandparents fail to consider that disclosing painful events or excessively complaining may be uncomfortable for grandchildren to listen to (Harwood). Because CAT has very specific premises, authors derived specific research questions and testable hypotheses (Ng & He, 2004). Studies found evidence that grandchildren overaccommodated and that grandparents underaccommodated in their communication but that perceptions of appropriate efforts to attune were associated with feelings of emotional closeness (Harwood).

Psychological

The psychological aspects of grandparenthood are those concepts and ideas related to internal processes of the mind, which are typically assessed as perceptions or cognitions. Commonly studied psychological aspects of grandparenthood include role identity, role-meaning making, and perceptions of self. Intimations of grandparent role meaning and identity were assessed nearly 50 years ago in the Neugarten and Weinstein (1964) study of grandparenthood. Since then, scholars have distinguished between the social and personal dimensions of the grandmother identity (Robertson, 1977), proposed meaning dimensions of grandparenthood (Kivnick, 1985), explored perceptions of grandfathers' role salience (Kivett, 1991a), and investigated grandparent identity meaning (Reitzes & Mutran, 2004b).

Other psychological concepts explored in grandparent research, although not to the same extent as meaning, identity, and perceptions of role, include ambivalence (Hebblethwaite & Norris, 2010) and learning and socialization (Seponski & Lewis, 2009). These concepts have largely been framed as cognitive processes that guide grandparent behaviors, which ultimately impact individual and relational outcomes.

Identity and meaning

The theoretical lens most prominent in investigations of identity and meaning was *symbolic interaction theory* and its close associates *identity theory* and *role theory* (see LaRossa & Reitzes, 1993, p. 142). Meaning arises through interaction with others and identities are based on the meanings humans ascribe to self within a given role (LaRossa & Reitzes). Grandparents thus develop meaning about their grandparental role through interaction with grandchildren (Vo-Thanh-Xuan & Liamputtong Rice, 2000) and may adopt grandparental subroles, including family historian, nurturer, and financial benefactor (Kornhaber, 1996). The grandparent role may intersect with other family roles such as in Reitzes and Mutran's (2004b) study that explored the overlapping meanings of the parent, grandparent, and intergenerational family roles. In testing symbolic interaction theory, Reitzes and Mutran (2004a) found that grandparent role identity meanings were significantly related to grandparent role satisfaction and grandfathers' frequency of contact with grandchildren.

Even-Zohar and Sharlin (2009) investigated the *role-taking* and *role-making* aspects of symbolic interactionism. Grandparents and grandchildren take and shape roles that are appropriate and functional for them in relation to other family members. Of particular interest in this study is the nuanced perspective on the grandchild identity and that the formation (role-making) of the grandchild role is based on intergenerational transfers and learning norms as well as behavior patterns demonstrated by parents.

Scholars working from a role theory perspective emphasized the multidimensionality of grandparenthood and the timing at which these roles are acquired and performed in the family. For instance, Kruk (1994) argued that grandparents may adopt a "great-parent" subrole to provide grandchildren and single parents with continuity, emotional support, and stability during and after a parental divorce. When stability returns to the family, grandparents may decrease their performance of this supportive role. In a similar vein, Kaufman and Elder (2003) found that those who enjoyed the role of grandparent indicated feeling younger, perceived old age to start later, and hoped to live longer. Additionally, those who made the transition to grandparenthood relatively early felt older than those who made the transition "on-time." These studies suggest that role acquisition and performance are a function of the temporal changes that occur in family relationships, and are an important focus of life course perspective (Elder, 1998).

Finally, Drew and Silverstein (2004), working from an identity theory perspective, operationalized grandparent role identity as a multidimensional construct. They argued that grandparents' role identities are comprised of self-evaluations of role salience, role satisfaction, and role performance. Role salience was operationalized as the importance of the role to the self and role satisfaction reflected overall satisfaction with being a grandparent. Reminiscent of *self-efficacy theory* (Bandura, 1982), role performance was framed as a judgment of how well participants felt they performed the grandparent role (see also King & Elder, 1998). Findings indicated strong correlations among the roles of great-grandparent with parent and grandparent, however, the performance, satisfaction, and salience of these roles did not individually predict psychological well-being (Drew & Silverstein).

Ambivalence

Ambivalence is a multifaceted concept that refers to the contradictions and tensions in relationships that cannot be reconciled (Lüscher & Pillemer, 1998). Although Lüscher and Pillemer refer to intergenerational ambivalence as a "'general orientation'... rather than as a formal theory" (p. 414), we include ambivalence in our discussion because of its potentially important theoretical contributions to the grandparent–grandchild literature that we will discuss later. Ambivalence was referred to as a concept in four of the five studies in which it was discussed. In one study, however, Hebblethwaite and Norris (2010) framed their study by what they termed the *intergenerational ambivalence model/framework*; with the words "model" and "framework" suggesting a more formalized characterization of ambivalence.

All of the studies that investigated ambivalence were qualitative, which allowed the authors to explore facets of the concept in great detail. Authors identified in their data the *social–structural* and *subjective–emotional* dimensions of ambivalence (Lüscher & Pillemer, 1998). The social–structural dimension refers to the contradictions and tensions in socially prescribed roles, such as grandparents who want to assist children and grandchildren but do not because social norms dictate it is not their place to "interfere" unless requested by parents (Kemp, 2004; Mason, May, & Clarke, 2007). The subjective–emotional dimension refers to contradictions and tensions in feelings and motivations within the individual about being a grandparent (Brannen, 2003; Scraton & Holland, 2006), as expressed in the adage "I'm happy to see them when they come and I'm happy to see them go." Hebblethwaite and Norris (2010) called this "the simultaneous positive and negative thoughts and emotions" (p. 492) of being a grandparent.

Learning processes

Theories about learning were represented in the literature. Two studies made explicit reference to *social learning theory* (Bandura, 1977). The concept of primary interest in these studies was *modeling*, which was theorized to be the mechanism by which teaching and thus learning occur. Bengtson et al. (2009) explored modeling in the transmission of religious preferences from grandparent to parent and from parent to grandchild and Teichman and Ziv (1998) explored modeling in the context of family patterns of cohesion and adaptability in children's adjustment to kindergarten. Both studies found evidence that what parents and grandchildren learned occurred via modeling.

Scholars referenced *theories of socialization* in studies that emphasized the congruence between grandmothers', mothers', and granddaughters' perceptions of grandparenthood (Werner et al., 2007) and the prevalence of mediation across three generations (Werner, Buchbinder, Lowenstein, Livni, 2005). In the former study, findings indicated that in relationships that were "connected," congruence of perceptions was greater than among those women who were "unconnected." Grandmothers in "unconnected" and "non-congruent" triads did not verbalize feelings of role satisfaction. Some mothers in this study functioned as gatekeepers between their children and their own mothers. This was typically due to incongruent perceptions of expectations about the potential meaningfulness of these relationships.

Werner et al. (2005) found that not only do mothers mediate between grandmothers and granddaughters but grandmothers mediate between mothers and granddaughters, and granddaughters mediate between their mothers and grandmothers. These findings suggest that perhaps gatekeeping is learned (through modeling), as it is performed by women at different stages of development in different roles and that it may transcend age hierarchies. Indeed, granddaughters' efforts to teach may be just as important to grandmother (and mother) learning as grandmother teaching is to granddaughter learning (Seponski & Lewis, 2009).

Finally, Vygotsky's *sociocultural theory* was applied to the grandparent–grandchild learning context but always in ways that placed the grandchild as the learner or apprentice (Gregory, Arju, Jessel, Kenner, & Ruby, 2007) and the grandparent as the expert (Ruby, Kenner, Jessel, Gregory, & Arju, 2007). Scholars referred to the concept of *scaffolding* in which grandparents structure learning activities carefully so as to nurture grandchild learning (Gregory et al., 2007). The *zone of proximal development* is a concept that refers to the ambiguous distance between the child's current developmental level and a higher level of potential development. Through interaction, grandparents scaffold young grandchildren from current problem-solving abilities to advanced developmental capabilities (Isman & Tzuriel, 2008).

Social cognitive

A collection of studies explored what we will refer to here, as *general social cognitive processes*. These studies neither specifically examined concepts from social cognitive theory (i.e., goals and expectations, attitudes, beliefs; Dix, 1992; Goodnow, 2002) nor overtly mention social cognitive theory. However, the theories we describe in this section were used to investigate human thinking in a social context (Okagaki & Bingham, 2005).

Consensual solidarity, from the intergenerational solidarity model, is defined as agreement in values, opinions, and orientations between generations (Bengtson, 2001), determined often through correlational analysis. The values, opinions, and orientations portion of the definition is a function of cognitive development in a social context of the intergenerational relationship. Giarrusso et al. (2001) examined consensual solidarity in attitudes and values between grandparents and their adult grandchildren and Kivett (1991a, 1993) explored consensual solidarity in grandparents' perceptions of similarity with grandchildren's views about life. Both studies found only modest support for consensual solidarity.

Two studies utilized *socioemotional selectivity theory* to investigate social cognitive processes. The socioemotional selectivity theory states that "reduced rates of interaction in late life are viewed as the result of lifelong selection processes by which people strategically and adaptively cultivate their social networks to maximize social and emotional gains and minimize social emotional risks" (Carstensen, 1992, p. 331). In one application of this theory, Hebblethwaite and Norris (2010) found that grandparents selected and presented positive events in relationships and expressed less ambivalence in relationships during participant interviews than grandchildren. Fung, Siu, Choy, and McBride-Chang (2005) operationalized the theory in a future time perspective. They assessed grandparents' perceptions of opportunities for the future, planning for the future, and the lack of time before death. Findings indicated that grandparents who perceived a greater lack of future time derived more meaning from their grandparent role. Thus, perceptions of the future likely influenced the social goals and expectations grandparents had for themselves and for their grandchildren.

Nehari, Grebler, and Toren (2007) explored grandparents' grief over grandchildren who had died of cancer. From their in-depth qualitative interviews, they developed the *grandparents' grief model*. Outlined within this theoretical model are the personal, familial, and cultural aspects of the grief process. Particularly salient in the context of grandchild death, is that grandparents often experience compounding grief; grief for themselves as grandparents in the loss of the grandchild and grief for the parents of the grandchild. In addition, upon the death of a grandchild, questions may arise about grandparents' roles and functions in the family. Thus, a third point of grief: the loss of the grandparent role. In such instances, the goals and expectations of grandparenthood are affected and must be reshaped by such loss. The grandparents' grief model brings conceptual clarity to the loss of this role and provides insight into the intersections among person, family, and cultural contexts.

Finally, stress and coping mechanisms among grandparents were investigated using *coping theory* (Folkman & Lazarus, 1988). Coping is defined as "an individual's efforts to manage the psychological demands of an environment" (Lumpkin, 2008, p. 360). Coping functions include regulating stressful emotions and regulating the environment that is causing the stress (Folkman & Lazarus). Grandparents involved in full-time or near-full-time care of grandchildren reported performing various coping strategies to manage the stresses of the caregiving context (Lumpkin).

OUTCOMES FOR GRANDPARENTS, GRANDCHILDREN, AND INTERGENERATIONAL RELATIONSHIPS

Scholars have explored the outcomes (or results) of grandparenthood at the individual level for grandparents and grandchildren, for grandparent–grandchild relationships, and for family relationships generally. Individual-level outcomes for grandparents include role satisfaction (Reitzes & Mutran, 2004a); grandparent mental health (e.g., depressive symptoms); grandparent well-being (e.g., quality-of-life, positive well-being, self-esteem) (Drew & Silverstein, 2004); and grandparent learning and social engagement (Armstrong, 2005; Seponski & Lewis, 2009). Grandchild outcomes include depressive symptoms (Ruiz & Silverstein, 2007) and grandparents' indirect influence on grandchildren's social–emotional development transmitted across three generations (Whitbeck, Hoyt, Simons, Conger, Elder, Lorenz, & Huck, 1992). Scholars have yet to adequately assess grandparents' direct and unique influence on grandchildren, except in studies of three-generation households where grandparents directly influence grandchildren's social–emotional development (Oyserman, Radin, & Benn, 1993).

Relationship-based and family outcomes include relationship satisfaction and relationship quality (emotional closeness), as reported by grandparents and grandchildren (Crosnoe & Elder, 2002; Taylor, Robila, & Lee, 2005). Additionally, some initial work has investigated family functioning and family communication in intergenerational households (Musil, Warner, Zauszniewski, Jeanblanc, & Kercher, 2006).

Grandparent Outcomes

Grandparent role satisfaction was the construct of interest in studies that utilized symbolic interactionism and identity theories. In one study, the frequency of contact between grandchildren and grandparents was found to be an important predictor of grandparent role satisfaction (Reitzes & Mutran, 2004a). In another study, although the grandparent role identity alone was not associated with psychological well-being, the concept of family identity (a combination of parent and great-grandparent role identities) was positively related to psychological well-being (Drew & Silverstein, 2004).

Armstrong (2005) drew upon *functional solidarity* from the intergenerational solidarity model, which refers to the assistance between the generations, to explore how grandchildren assist grandparents in becoming socially integrated and socially engaged in society. This study is interesting because it transcends the typical directional influence from grandparent to grandchild and brings to light the reciprocal learning outcomes that can occur in intergenerational relationships.

Bereavement theory suggests that the loss of a close, valued relationship may adversely affect mental health (Parkes, 1990). Testing the tenets of bereavement theory, Drew and Silverstein (2007) and Drew and Smith (2002) determined that the loss of contact with grandchildren negatively affected grandparents' depressive symptoms. The prevalence of depressive symptoms was also explored from the perspectives of *role stress theory* and *role enhancement theory* (Reid & Hardy, 1999). Role stress theory emphasizes that simultaneous roles (i.e., full-time caregiver, employee) create conflicts and stress that reduce well-being. By contrast, role enhancement theory suggests that multiple roles may have positive effects on well-being because of a multifaceted self. Interestingly, Szinovacz and Davey (2006) found no evidence in support of either of these theories in their comparisons of the depressive symptoms of retired and employed grandmothers.

Grandchild Outcomes

Topics of interest related to grandchild outcomes have centered on learning, specifically the transmission of religion (Bengtson et al., 2009), angry and aggressive behavior (Conger, Neppl, Kim, & Scaramella, 2003), and displays of anger in toddlers (Brook, Whiteman, & Brook, 1999). The predominant theory employed was social learning theory, and the concept of modeling was examined as the mechanism by which transmission occurred across three generations. These studies suggest that children learn through behaviors and attitudes modeled by their parents and grandparents.

Grandparent–Grandchild Relationship Outcomes

The intergenerational solidarity model was utilized to frame grandparent–grandchild relationship quality. The concept of *affectual solidarity* refers to feelings and evaluations expressed by family members about their relationships with other family members (Bengtson, 2001). In the studies we reviewed, affectual solidarity is typically operationalized with one or two items that assess emotional closeness and the degree of getting along. Affectual solidarity is utilized in these studies as a point-of-comparison variable by which Black and White grandfathers and grandmothers are evaluated (Kivett, 1991a, 1993) and by which grandparents and grandchildren assess their relationship (Harwood, 2001). Kivett (1991a) and Silverstein and Marenco (2001) found that emotional closeness is predicted by the frequency of contact with grandchildren.

Family Outcomes

Investigations into family-level outcomes centered on the use of family systems theory as a framework for studying how a disabled child affects family relationships (Mirfin-Veitch et al., 1996; Mirfin-Veitch, Bray, & Watson, 1997), and how intergenerational contact loss not only affects grandparents who grieve but the entire family (Drew & Smith, 2002). One exception was a study that assessed family functioning with the *resiliency model of stress, adjustment and adaptation* (Musil et al., 2006), which argues that family strains and stresses, if not mediated, may lead to problems in family functioning. The authors found that family functioning was related to complex interfacing between grandmothers' psychological, financial, and supportive resources and perceptions of family functioning.

LIMITATIONS OF THEORY USAGE

Scholars approach theory usage in three distinct ways, outlined here from least to most intensive: *theory application, theory assimilation*, and *theory expansion*.

The most prominent approach to theory utilization in grandparent studies is *theory application*. This involves using theory to justify the study of grandparents as a population such as when family systems theory was invoked to point out that grandparents should be studied because they are part of the family system (e.g., Mirfin-Veitch et al., 1996). Theory may also be applied to the formation of testable hypotheses and theory may also be applied in the explanation and interpretation of a finding such as when the researcher points out that a finding confirms or refutes an aspect of theory. Often, these studies lacked a clear interpretation of findings with the theory that was utilized to form the hypotheses. To be sure, the quality of theory application depends not so much on where (i.e., literature review, method, discussion) theory is used, but how thoroughly theory is applied to the study.

The second approach to theory utilization is *theory assimilation*. Theory assimilation includes all the aspects of theory application but assimilation operates at a level of integration—linking the theoretical perspective to the entire research process. For instance, scholars not only introduce and apply theory in their literature review but they also integrate and incorporate the theoretical concepts, principles, assumptions, and philosophical underpinning into their methods, analyses, results, discussion, and implications. The goal of theory assimilation is to embed and interweave theory throughout the investigative process. Therefore, theory is entrenched in the beginning, middle, and end of the research process. It is important to note that the primary purpose of theory assimilation is to magnify and to more clearly understand the specific phenomena being investigated. Those who assimilate theory do so believing that extensive theory integration would accomplish this purpose. We found that only a handful of scholars used the theory assimilation approach. One such example is Roberto, Allen, and Blieszner's (2001) qualitative study of grandfathers, in which the authors integrated social-constructivist and feminist approaches into the introductory, methodological, and interpretation of their findings.

The third approach to theory utilization is *theory expansion*. When purposely using theory expansion, scholars not only use theory to set up their research study (theory application) and integrate theory throughout the research process (theory assimilation), they take the additional step of building upon existing theory or attempt to develop theory from their empirical findings. The goal of theory expansion is not only to investigate the social phenomena and explain it through a theoretical lens, but to purposefully and substantively build theory. Scholars using this approach are aware that their research activities are intended for the growth, development, and extension of theoretical ideas. It is through these efforts that theory will advance in the area of grandparent studies. Although there was little use of this approach, Reese and Murray (1996) developed a *theory of transcendence* from qualitative data provided by 16 great-grandmothers. The authors first argued that Erikson's (1950) concluding life stage of ego integrity had salience to the notion of transcendence. Next, they developed interview questions about the meaning of life, life goals, the interpretation of interactions and relationships with descendants, influence, and death. Narrative responses to interview questions were interpreted inductively and pieced together in a type of theoretical process model proceeding from specific behaviors and attitudes, to domains of socialization and sharing, and ultimately to transcendence.

One reason for limited theory expansion may, in part, be due to the lack of theorizing specifically about grandparents. We know of only four theoretical frameworks (or conceptual models) indigenous to grandparent research. The first is Reese and Murray's (1996) *theory of transcendence*. The second is Strom and Strom's (1997) *theory of grandparent development*, which is a "formulation of assumptions, goals for guiding instruction, curriculum design, and a measurement tool to assess learning needs [of grandparents]" (p. 255). Nehari et al.'s (2007) *model of grandparents' grief* is the third theory, described in more detail in a previous section, was derived from qualitative interviews conducted with grandmothers and grandfathers who had a grandchild die of cancer. Finally, Bates (2009) proposed the *generative grandfathering conceptual framework*, which was derived from reviews of the grandfather and grandparent literatures. This framework describes domains in which grandfathers can participate in generative activities with and for grandchildren to help socialize, support, and nurture them (Bates & Goodsell, in press; Bates & Taylor, in press).

Family theory, as it is applied to grandparent–grandchild relationships, will only be enhanced when more scholars use the theory expansion approach. When theory is at the forefront of research, it can then be developed and built upon. Theories about grandparent–grandchild relationships will not emerge without increased effort to use more theory assimilation which will lay much of the groundwork for theory expansion.

NEW THEORETICAL OPPORTUNITIES

We now outline two new theoretical opportunities. The first is the *grandfather involvement conceptual framework* (Bates & Taylor, in press). It is comprised of three concepts, *contact frequency*, *participation in activities*, and *intergenerational commitment*. As discussed in a previous section, contact frequency refers to the amount of contact between the grandfather and the grandchild in a given time period. Participation in activities refers to the extent that grandfathers engage in in-person activities with and indirect support behaviors for the grandchild (Bates & Goodsell, in press; Bates & Taylor, in press). Intergenerational commitment is grounded in Johnson's (1973, 1999) concept of personal dedication and, as applied to grandfather–grandchild relationships, refers to grandfathers' level of commitment to the grandchild, the grandfather–grandchild relationship, and grandfathers' role identity. We have found that grandfathers who report more frequent contact and greater participation in activities also report higher levels of commitment than grandfathers with little contact and less participation in activities (Bates & Taylor, 2012). Elsewhere, we also note the empirical and hypothetical relations among these three concepts and the outcome variables, relationship satisfaction and relationship quality (Bates & Taylor, in press). Scholars can utilize concepts from this framework to guide their research and to test hypotheses. We also welcome extending the framework to grandmothers.

The second theoretical opportunity became apparent to us in the course of analyzing articles for this chapter. Among the understudied concepts and perspectives we thought could yield fruitful future research (e.g., communication, conflict, feminist perspective, gatekeeping), the concept of intergenerational ambivalence appealed to us because of the in-depth analysis it received in five of the studies we reviewed. Ambivalence is a psychological process and is thought to be caused by social-structural tensions and contradictions in social roles and by emotional tensions and contradictions in subjective experiences (Lüscher & Pillemer, 1998).

Speaking primarily of ambivalence in the grandparent role created at the structural level, scholars have acknowledged a contradiction in two normative expectations held by grandparents, parents, and grandchildren for intergenerational relationships. The first is called the *norm of noninterference*, a term coined by Cherlin and Furstenberg (1986) and a phenomenon noted by other scholars (Johnson, 1985), which refers to the expectation held by parents and grandparents that grandparental authority in their child's (and spouse's) nuclear family is contingent upon the request and/or sanctioning of the parents. Grandparents typically have little say in how the grandchild is raised, disciplined, and socialized unless parents authorize grandparents to participate in those ways. Thus, grandparents refrain from interfering unless asked.

The second has been referred to as the expectation of "being there" (Hagestad, 1985; Mason et al., 2007) or the expectation of teaching and mentoring (Kemp, 2004). This refers to the assumption held by parents, grandchildren, and grandparents that when requested, grandparents will spring into action to provide assistance, support, and resources to the parent's nuclear family (see also Clingempeel et al., 1992 and the latent function hypothesis). This expectation may be activated in grandchild caregiving situations (Scraton & Holland, 2006), in times of crisis such as parental divorce (Johnson, 1985), or whenever asked. We give this phenomenon the name of the *norm of avial obligation*. *Avo* is a Latin root for grandparent, just as *filio* is the Latin root for son/daughter. Similar to the notion of filial obligation, in *avial obligation*, grandparents are assumed and expected (obligated) to provide support to children and grandchildren.

These two contradictory social norms create situations where grandparents may experience ambivalence. For the sake of simplicity, under the norm of non-interference, grandparents who want to be involved in a grandchild's life cannot until the parents allow them to be. Under the norm of avial obligation, although grandparents desire autonomy from their children and grandchildren they cannot have it because of family stewardship expectations and obligations. Lest this be considered an over-generalization, three of the studies we analyzed (Hebblethwaite & Norris, 2010; Kemp, 2004; Mason et al., 2007) noted these precise "irreconcilable" contradictions (Lüscher & Pillemer, 1998).

Scholarship suggests that the quality of intergenerational relationships may be affected by high levels of ambivalence. In one study, grandchildren perceived more ambivalence in very emotionally close relationships with grandparents with whom they participated in more frequent leisure activities (Hebblethwaite & Norris, 2010). Grandparents in this study also reported that spending extensive amounts of time with grandchildren in leisure activities increased higher levels of ambivalence and conflict. Grandparents noted that time apart helped preserve positive feelings in the relationship (Hebblewaite & Norris). Hypothetically then, ambivalence may moderate the positive effects of being involved in activities with grandchildren and the quality of the relationship such that high ambivalence leads to decreased levels of emotional connectedness and low ambivalence gives way to less strain and greater emotional closeness. In sum, bringing these ideas and empirical observations together may give rise to a testable middle range theory we call the *intergenerational stewardship theory*.

CONCLUSION

We have taken stock of theory utilization in recent research on grandparents and found that over 55 theories were mentioned overtly and that utilization of theory varied by study. For instance, in a given study, scholars utilized a theory to provide an overarching framework to the research, and in another study, the same theory informed the development of hypotheses that were then tested. We also noted that theory building in grandparent studies is very limited.

We invite grandparent scholars to consider more carefully theory utilization in future research. Ideally, theory usage needs to move beyond superficial application to integration and assimilation into every aspect of the research process. What is more, scholars should not be satisfied with simply saying that findings support or oppose a given theory, but should attempt to theorize about their findings. To help in this endeavor, scholars may consider reflecting on the following questions: What makes my findings similar to or different from findings from other studies? What are the psychological, social, or behavioral mechanisms that influenced the outcomes of my study? What are frequently identified phenomena in the literature, why do these phenomena occur, and how are they linked? Are there unique ways to discuss and categorize an observed phenomenon? Answers to these questions will assist scholars in their creative endeavors of theorizing and to the development of conceptual frameworks and middle-range theories in a third generation of grandparent research.

REFERENCES

Abend, G. (2008). The meaning of 'theory'. *Sociological Theory, 26*, 173–199.

Allen, W. R. (1978). The search for applicable theories of Black family life. *Journal of Marriage and the Family, 40*, 117–129.

Armstrong, M. J. (2005). Grandchildren's influences on grandparents: A resource for integration of older people in New Zealand's aging society. *Journal of Intergenerational Relationships, 3*, 7–21.

Ashton, V. (1996). A study of mutual support between Black and White grandmothers and their adult grand-children. *Journal of Gerontological Social Work, 26*(1/2), 87–100.

Bailey, J. A., Hill, K. G., Oesterle, S., & Hawkins, J. D. (2009). Parenting practices and problem behavior across three generations: Monitoring, harsh discipline, and drug use in the intergenerational transmission of externalizing behavior. *Developmental Psychology, 45*, 1214–1226.

Bandura, A. (1977). *Social learning theory*. Englewood Cliffs, NJ: Prentice-Hall.

Bandura, A. (1982). The self and mechanisms of agency. In J. Suls (Ed.), *Psychological perspectives on the self* (pp. 3–39). Hillsdale, NJ: Lawrence Erlbaum.

Barnes Nacoste, D. R., & Wise, E. H. (1991). The relationship among negative life events, cognitions, and depression within three generations. *Gerontologist, 31*, 397–403.

Bates, J. S. (2009). Generative grandfathering: A conceptual framework for nurturing grandchildren. *Marriage and Family Review, 45*, 331–352.

Bates, J. S., & Goodsell, T. L. (in press). Male kin relationships: Grandfather, grandsons, and generativity. *Marriage and Family Review*.

Bates, J. S., & Taylor, A. C. (in press). Grandfather involvement: Contact frequency, participation in activities, and commitment. *International Journal of Aging and Human Development*.

Bates, J. S., & Taylor, A. C. (2012). Grandfather involvement and aging men's mental health. *American Journal of Men's Health, 6*, 229–239.

Baydar, N., & Brooks-Gunn, J. (1998). Profiles of grandmothers who help care for their grandchildren in the United States. *Family Relations, 47*, 385–393.

Bengtson, V. L. (2001). Beyond the nuclear family: The increasing importance of multigenerational bonds. *Journal of Marriage and Family, 63*, 1–16.

Bengtson, V. L., & Allen, K. R. (1993). The life course perspective applied to families over time. In P. G. Boss, W. J. Doherty, R. LaRossa, W. R. Schumm, & S. K. Steinmetz (Eds.), *Sourcebook of family theories and methods: A contextual approach* (pp. 469–499). New York: Plenum.

Bengtson, V. L., Copen, C. E., Putney, N. M., & Silverstein, M. (2009). A longitudinal study of the intergenerational transmission of religion. *International Sociology, 24*, 325–345.

Brannen, J. (2003). Towards a typology of intergenerational relations: Continuities and change in families. *Sociological Research Online*, 8. doi: 10.1111/j.1467–954X.2006.00605.x

Brook, J. S., Whiteman, M., & Brook, D. W. (1999). Transmission of risk factors across three generations. *Psychological Reports, 85*, 227–241.

Carstensen, L. L. (1992). Social and emotional patterns in adulthood: Support for socioemotional selectivity theory. *Psychology and Aging, 7*, 331–338.

Chen, F., Short, S. E., & Entwisle, B. (2000). The impact of grandparental proximity on maternal childcare in China. *Population Research and Policy Review, 19*, 571–590.

Cherlin, A. J., & Furstenberg, F. F., Jr. (1986). *The new American grandparent: A place in the family, a life apart*. New York: Basic Books.

Clingempeel, W. G., Colyar, J. J., Brand, E., & Hetherington, E. M. (1992). Children's relationships with maternal grandparents: A longitudinal study of family structure and pubertal status effects. *Child Development, 63*, 1404–1422.

Cong, Z., & Silverstein, M. (2008). Intergenerational time-for-money exchanges in rural China: Does reciprocity reduce depressive symptoms of older grandparents? *Research in Human Development, 5*, 6–25.

Conger, R. D., Neppl, T., Kim, K. J., & Scaramella, L. (2003). Angry and aggressive behavior across three generations: A prospective longitudinal study of parents and children. *Journal of Abnormal Child Psychology, 31*, 143–160.

Crosnoe, R., & Elder, G. H., Jr. (2002). Life course transitions, the generational stake, and grandparent-grandchild relationships. *Journal of Marriage and Family, 64*, 1089–1096.

Dimmick, J., Kline, S., Stafford, L. (2000). The gratification niches of personal e-mail and the telephone. *Communication Research, 27*, 227–248.

Dix, T. (1992). Parenting on behalf of the child: Empathic goals in the regulation of responsive parenting. In I. E. Sigel, A. V. McGillicuddy-DeLisi, & J. J. Goodnow (Eds.), *Parent belief systems: The psychological consequences for children* (2nd ed., pp. 319–346). Hillsdale, NJ: Erlbaum.

Doherty, W. J., Boss, P. G., LaRossa, R., Schumm, W. R., & Steinmetz, S. K. (1993). Family theories and methods: A contextual approach. In P. G. Boss, W. J. Doherty, R. LaRossa, W. R. Schumm, & S. K. Steinmetz (Eds.), *Sourcebook of family theories and methods: A contextual approach* (pp. 3–30). New York: Plenum.

Doyle, M., O'Dywer, C., & Timonen, V. (2010). "How can you just cut off a whole side of the family and say move on?" The reshaping of paternal grandparent-grandchild relationships following divorce or separation in the middle generation. *Family Relations, 59*, 587–598.

Drew, L. M., & Silverstein, M. (2004). Intergenerational role investments of great-grandparents: Consequences for psychological well-being. *Ageing and Society, 24*, 95–111.

Drew, L. M., & Silverstein, M. (2007). Grandparents' psychological well-being after loss of contact with their grandchildren. *Journal of Family Psychology, 21*, 372–379.

Drew, L. M., & Smith, P. K. (2002). Implications for grandparents when they lose contact with their grandchildren: Divorce, family feud, and geographical separation. *Journal of Mental Health and Aging, 8*, 95–119.

Elder, G. H., Jr. (1998). The life course and human development. In W. Damon (Series Ed.), & R. M. Lerner (Volume Ed.), *Handbook of child psychology: Vol. 1: Theoretical models of human development* (5th ed., pp. 939–991). Hoboken, NJ: Wiley.

Erikson, E. H. (1950). *Childhood and society*. New York, NY: Norton.

Even-Zohar, A., & Sharlin, S., (2009). Grandchildhood: Adult grandchildren's perception of their role towards their grandparents from an intergenerational perspective. *Journal of Comparative Family Studies, 40*, 167–185.

Fingerman, K. L. (2004). The role of offspring and in-laws in grandparents' ties to their grandchildren. *Journal of Family Issues, 25*, 1026–1049.

Folkman, S., & Lazarus, R. S. (1988). Coping as a mediator of emotion. *Journal of Personality and Social Psychology, 54*, 466–475.

Fung, H. H., Siu, C. M. Y., Choy, W. C. W., & McBride-Chang, C. (2005). Meaning of grandparenthood: Do concerns about time and mortality matter? *Ageing International, 30*(2), 122–146.

Geurts, T., Poortman, A-R., van Tilburg, T., & Dykstra, P. A. (2009). Contact between grandchildren and their grandparents in early adulthood. *Journal of Family Issues, 30*, 1698–1713.

Giarrusso, R., Feng, D., Silverstein, M., & Bengtson, V. L. (2001). Grandparent-adult grandchild affection and consensus: Cross-generational and cross ethnic comparisons. *Journal of Family Issues, 22*, 456–477.

Giarrusso, R., Stallings, M., & Bengtson, V. L. (1995). The "intergenerational stake" hypothesis revisited: Parent-child differences in perceptions of relationships 20 years later. In V. L. Bengtson, K. W. Schaie, & L. M. Burton (Eds.), *Adult intergenerational relationships: Effects of societal change* (pp. 227–296). New York: Springer.

Giles, H., Mulac, A., Bradac, J. J., & Johnson, P. (1987). Speech accommodation theory: The next decade and beyond. In M. McLaughlin (Ed.), *Communication Yearbook 10* (pp. 13–48). Newbury Park, CA: Sage.

Gladstone, J. W. (1991). An analysis of changes in grandparent-grandchild visitation following an adult child's remarriage. *Canadian Journal on Aging, 10*(2), 113–126.

Goodsell, T. L., Bates, J. S., & Behnke, A. O. (2011). Fatherhood stories: Grandparents, grandchildren, and gender. *Journal of Social and Personal Relationships, 28*, 134–154.

Goodnow, J. J. (2002). Parents' knowledge and expectations: Using what we know. In M. H. Bornstein (Ed.), *Handbook of parenting: Vol. 3. Being and becoming a parent* (pp. 439–460). Mahwah, NJ: Erlbaum.

Gregory, E., Arju, T., Jessel, J., Kenner, C., & Ruby, M. (2007). Snow White in different guises: Interlingual and intercultural exchanges between grandparents and young children at home in East London. *Journal of Early Childhood Literacy, 7*, 5–25.

Hagestad, G. O. (1985). Continuity and connectedness. In V. L. Bengtson & J. F. Robertson (Eds.), *Grandparenthood* (pp. 31–48). Beverly Hill, CA: Sage.

Harwood, J. (2000). Communicative predictors of solidarity in the grandparent-grandchild relationship. *Journal of Social and Personal Relationships, 17*, 743–766.

Harwood, J. (2001). Comparing grandchildren's and grandparent's stake in their relationship. *International Journal of Aging and Human Development, 53*, 195–210.

Hebblethwaite, S. & Norris, J. E. (2010). "You don't want to hurt his feelings …": Family leisure as a context for intergenerational ambivalence. *Journal of Leisure Research, 42*, 489–508.

Hoff, A. (2007). Patterns of intergenerational support in grandparent-grandchild and parent-child relationships in Germany. *Ageing & Society, 27*, 643–665.

Isman, E. B., & Tzuriel, D. (2008). The mediated learning experience in a three generational perspective. *British Journal of Developmental Psychology, 26*, 545–560.

Jaskowski, S. K., & Dellasega, C. (1993). Effects of divorce on the grandparent-grandchild relationship. *Issues in Comprehensive Pediatric Nursing, 16*, 125–133.

Johnson, C. L. (1985). Grandparenting options in divorcing families: An anthropological perspective. In V. L. Bengtson, & J. F. Robertson (Eds.), *Grandparenthood* (pp. 81–96). Beverly Hills, CA: Sage.

Johnson, M. P. (1973). Commitment: A conceptual structure and empirical application. *The Sociological Quarterly, 14*, 395–406.

Johnson, M. P. (1999). Personal, moral, and structural commitment to relationships: Experiences of choice and constraint. In J. M. Adams & W. H. Jones (Eds.), *Handbook of interpersonal commitment and relationship stability* (pp. 73–87). New York: Kluwer/Plenum.

Katz, E., Blumler, J., & Gurevitch, M. (1974). Uses and gratifications research. In J. Blumler, & E. Katz (Eds.), *The uses of mass communications*. Beverly Hills, CA: Sage.

Katz, S., & Kessel, L. (2002). Grandparents of children with developmental disabilities: Perceptions, beliefs, and involvement in their care. *Issues in Comprehensive Pediatric Nursing, 25*, 113–128.

Kaufman, G., & Elder, G. H., Jr. (2003). Grandparenting and age identity. *Journal of Aging Studies, 17*, 269–282.

Kemp, C. L. (2004). "Grand" expectations: The experiences of grandparents and adult grandchildren. *Canadian Journal of Sociology, 29*(4), 499–525.

Kemp, C. L. (2007). Grandparent-grandchild ties reflections on continuity and change across three generations. *Journal of Family Issues, 28*(7), 855–881.

King, V. (2003). The legacy of a grandparent's divorce: Consequences for ties between grandparents and grandchildren. *Journal of Marriage and Family, 65*, 170–183.

King, V., & Elder, G. H., Jr. (1995). American children view their grandparents: Linked lives across three rural generations. *Journal of Marriage and the Family, 57*, 165–178.

King, V., & Elder, G. H., Jr. (1997). The legacy of grandparenting: Childhood experiences with grandparents and current involvement with grandchildren. *Journal of Marriage and the Family, 59*, 848–859.

King, V., & Elder, G. H. Jr. (1998). Perceived self-efficacy and grandparenting. *Journals of Gerontology: Social Sciences, 53B*, S249–S257.

Kitamura, T., Shikai, N., Uji, M., Hiramura, H., Tanaka, N., & Shono, M. (2009). Intergenerational transmission of parenting style and personality: Direct influence or mediation? *Journal of Child and Family Studies, 18*, 541–556.

Kivett, V. R. (1991a). Centrality of the grandfather role among older rural Black and White men. *Journals of Gerontology: Social Sciences, 46*, S250–S258.

Kivett, V. R. (1991b). The grandparent-grandchild connection. *Marriage and Family Review, 16*, 267–290.

Kivett, V. R. (1993). Racial comparisons of the grandmother role: Implications for strengthening the family support system of older Black women. *Family Relations, 42*, 165–172.

Kivnick, H. Q. (1985). Grandparenthood and mental health: Meaning, behavior, and satisfaction. In V. L. Bengtson & J. F. Robertson (Eds.), *Grandparenthood* (pp. 151–158). Beverly Hills, CA: Sage.

Kornhaber, A. (1996). *Contemporary grandparenting*. Thousand Oaks, CA: Sage.

Kruk, E. (1994). Grandparent visitation disputes: Multigenerational approaches to family mediation. *Mediation Quarterly, 12*(1), 37–53.

LaRossa, R., & Reitzes, D. C. (1993). Symbolic interactionism and family studies. In P. G. Boss, W. J. Doherty, R. LaRossa, W. R. Schumm, & S. K. Steinmetz (Eds.). *Sourcebook of family theories and methods: A contextual approach* (pp. 135–166). New York: Plenum.

Lazarus, R. S., & Folkman, S. (1984). *Stress, appraisal and coping*. New York: Springer.

Lee, J & Bauer, J. W. (2010). Profiles of grandmothers providing child care to their grandchildren in South Korea. *Journal of Comparative Family Studies, 41*, 455–475.

Lin, M., & Harwood, J. (2003). Accommodation predictors of grandparent-grandchild relational solidarity in Taiwan. *Journal of Social and Personal Relationships, 20*, 537–563.

Lumpkin, J. R. (2008). Grandparents in a parental or near-parental role. *Journal of Family Issues, 29*(3), 357–372.

Lüscher, K., & Pillemer, K. (1998). Intergenerational ambivalence: A new approach to the study of parent-child relations in later life. *Journal of Marriage and the Family, 60*(2), 413–425.

Mason, J., May, V., & Clarke, L. (2007). Ambivalence and the paradoxes of grandparenting. *Sociological Review, 55*, 687–706.

Mirfin-Veitch, B., Bray, A., & Watson, M. (1996). "They really do care": Grandparents as informal support sources for families of children with disabilities. *New Zealand Journal of Disability Studies, 2*, 136–148.

Mirfin-Veitch, B., Bray, A., & Watson, M. (1997). "We're just that sort of family": Intergenerational relationships in families including children with disabilities. *Family Relations, 46*, 305–311.

Mueller, M. M., & Elder, G. H., Jr. (2003). Family contingencies across the generations: Grandparent-grandchild relationships in holistic perspective. *Journal of Marriage and Family, 65*, 404–417.

Musil, C. M., Warner, C. B., Zauszniewski, J. A., Jeanblanc, A. B., & Kercher, K. (2006). Grandmothers, caregiving, and family functioning. *Journal of Gerontology: Social Sciences, 61B*(2), S89–S98.

Nehari, M., Grebler, D., & Toren, A. (2007). A voice unheard: Grandparents' grief over children who died of cancer. *Mortality, 12*(1), 66–78.

Neugarten, B. L., & Weinstein, K. K. (1964). The changing American grandparent. *Journal of Marriage and the Family, 26*, 199–204.

Ng, S. H., & He, A. (2004). Code-switching in tri-generational family conversations among Chinese immigrants in New Zealand. *Journal of Language and Social Psychology, 23*, 28–48.

Okagaki, L., & Bingham, G. L. (2005). Parents' social cognitions and their parenting behaviors. In T. Luster, & L. Okagaki (Eds.), *Parenting: An ecological perspective* (2nd ed., pp. 3–33). Mahwah, NJ: Erlbaum.

Oppelaar, J., & Dykstra. P. (2004). Contacts between grandparents and grandchildren. *The Netherlands' Journal of Social Sciences, 40*(2), 91–113.

Oyserman, D., Radin, N., & Benn, R. (1993). Dynamics in a three-generational family: Teens, grandparents, and babies. *Developmental Psychology, 29*, 564–572.

Parkes, C. M. (1990). Risk factors in bereavement: Implications for the prevention and treatment of pathologic grief. *Psychiatric Annals, 20*, 308–313.

Pollet, T. V., Nettle, D., & Nelissen, M. (2006). Contact frequencies between grandparents and grandchildren in a modern society: Estimates of the impact of paternity uncertainty. *Journal of Culture and Evolutionary Psychology, 4*(3–4), 203–213.

Quadrello, T., Hurme, H., Menzinger, J., Smith, P. K., Veisson, M., Vidal, S., & Westerback, S. (2005). Grandparents use of new communication technologies in a European perspective. *European Journal of Ageing, 2*(3), 200–207.

Reese, C. G., & Murray, R. B. (1996). Transcendence: The meaning of great-grandmothering. *Archives of Psychiatric Nursing, 10*, 245–251.

Reid, J., & Hardy, M. (1999). Multiple roles and well-being among midlife women: Testing role strain and role enhancement theories. *Journal of Gerontology: Social Sciences, 54B*(6), S329–S338.

Reitzes, D. C., & Mutran, E. J. (2004a). Grandparenthood: Factors influencing frequency of grandparent-grandchildren contact and grandparent role satisfaction. *Journal of Gerontology: Social Sciences, 59B*, S9–S16.

Reitzes, D. C., & Mutran, E. J. (2004b). Grandparent identity, intergenerational family identity, and well-being. *Journals of Gerontology: Social Sciences, 59B*, S213–S219.

Roberto, K. A., Allen, K. R., & Blieszner, R. (2001). Grandfathers' perceptions and expectations of relationships with their adult grandchildren. *Journal of Family Issues, 22*, 407–426.

Robertson, J. F. (1977). Grandmotherhood: A study of role conceptions. *Journal of Marriage and the Family, 39*, 165–174.

Ruby, M., Kenner, C., Jessel, J., Gregory, E., & Arju, T. (2007). Gardening with grandparents: An early engagement with the science curriculum. *Early Years, 27*(2), 131–144.

Ruiz, S. A., & Silverstein, M. (2007). Relationships with grandparents and the emotional well-being of late adolescent and young adult grandchildren. *Journal of Social Issues, 63*, 793–808.

Sabatelli, R. M., & Shehan, C. L. (1993). Exchange and resource theories. In P. G. Boss, W. J. Doherty, R. LaRossa, W. R. Schumm, & S. K. Steinmetz (Eds.), *Sourcebook of family theories and methods: A contextual approach* (pp. 385–417). New York: Plenum.

Scraton, S., & Holland, S. (2006). Grandfatherhood and leisure. *Leisure Studies, 25*, 233–250.

Seponski, D. M., & Lewis, D. C. (2009). Caring for and learning from each other: A grounded theory study of grandmothers and adult granddaughters. *Journal of Intergenerational Relationships, 7*, 394–410.

Silverstein, M., & Chen, X. (1999). The impact of acculturation in Mexican American families on the quality of adult grandchild-grandparent relationships. *Journal of Marriage and the Family, 61*, 188–198.

Silverstein, M., & Long, J. D. (1998). Trajectories of grandparents' perceived solidarity with adult grandchildren: A growth curve analysis over 23 years. *Journal of Marriage and the Family, 60*, 912–923.

Silverstein, M., & Marenco, A. (2001). How Americans enact the grandparent role across the family life course. *Journal of Family Issues, 22*, 493–522.

Strom, R., & Strom, S. (1997). Building a theory of grandparent development. *International Journal of Aging & Human Development, 45*, 255–286.

Szinovacz, M. E., & Davey, A. (2006). Effects of retirement and grandchild care on depressive symptoms. *International Journal of Aging & Human Development, 62*, 1–20.

Taylor, A. C., & Bagdi, A. (2005). The lack of explicit theory in family research: A case analysis of the Journal of Marriage and the Family, 1990–1999. In V. L. Bengtson, A. C. Acock, K. R. Allen, P. Dilworth-Anderson, & D. M. Klein (Eds.), *Sourcebook of family theory and research* (pp. 22–25). Thousand Oaks, CA: Sage.

Taylor, A. C., Robila, M., & Lee, H. S. (2005). Distance, contact, and intergenerational relationships: Grandparents and adult grandchildren from an international perspective. *Journal of Adult Development, 12*, 33–41.

Teichman, Y., & Ziv, R. (1998). Grandparents' and parents' views about their family and children's adjustment to kindergarten. *Educational Gerontology, 24*, 115–128.

Tinsley, B. J., & Parke, R. D. (1987). Grandparents as interactive and social support agents for families with young infants. *International Journal of Aging & Human Development, 25*, 259–277.

Vo-Thanh-Xuan, J., & Rice, P. L. (2000). Vietnamese-Australian grandparenthood: The changing roles and psychological well-being. *Journal of Cross-Cultural Gerontology, 15*, 265–288.

Werner, P., Buchbinder, E., Lowenstein, A., & Livni, T. (2005). Mediation across generations: A tri-generational perspective. *Journal of Aging Studies, 19*, 489–502.

Werner, P., Buchbinder, E., Lowenstein, A., & Livni, T. (2007). Grandmothers', mothers' and granddaughters' perceptions of grandparenthood: A qualitative analysis of congruence across generations. *Journal of Intergenerational Relationships, 5*(3), 7–25.

Whitbeck, L. B., Hoyt, D. R., Simons, R. L., Conger, R. D., Elder, G. H., Jr., Lorenz, F. O., & Huck, S. (1992). Intergenerational continuity of parental rejection and depressed affect. *Journal of Personality and Social Psychology, 63*, 1036–1045.

Whitchurch, G. G., & Constantine, L. L. (1993). Systems theory. In P. G. Boss, W. J. Doherty, R. LaRossa, W. R. Schumm, & S. K. Steinmetz (Eds.), *Sourcebook of family theories and methods: A contextual approach* (pp. 325–352). New York: Plenum.

Williams, A., & Guendouzi, J. (2005). Constructing family relationships: Intimacy, harmony and social value in accounts of sheltered retirement community residents. *Journal of Aging Studies, 19*, 453–470.

5 Parent–Child and Intergenerational Relationships in Adulthood

Kira S. Birditt and Karen L. Fingerman

The parent–child relationship attracts considerable interest in both the mass media and scientific research. We know a great deal about parents and young children but considerably less about parents and grown children. It is particularly important to examine this relationship in adulthood and old age, not only because of its longevity, but also because it is often the only relationship in which two people from vastly different developmental stages and cohorts attempt to maintain a close and mutually supportive relationship across a lifetime.

Consider, for example, a mother–daughter relationship. It may last up to six decades, may span young adulthood to old age for mothers and almost the entire lifespan for daughters, and often involves multiple role transitions. For instance, the daughter may attend college, get married, move away, have children, get divorced, and retire while her mother simultaneously returns to work, divorces, remarries, retires, and develops chronic illness. All of these transitions may lead to changes in how close the mother and daughter live, how often they see each other or talk on the phone, the extent to which they feel emotionally close, experience conflict, as well as the types and amount of support they provide to one another.

Despite the longevity of this relationship and the multiple factors that may influence it over time, there has been much less research on the parent–child relationship in adulthood than in childhood or adolescence. Notwithstanding important theoretical developments in this area, there is little integration of the theoretical perspectives across disciplines. The purpose of this chapter is to provide an overview of theories and research regarding this emotionally complex relationship. We review key topics of inquiry, identify gaps in our current theoretical understandings of the parent–child tie, and provide some ideas for future theoretical developments and research.

KEY ISSUES IN THE STUDY OF ADULTS AND THEIR PARENTS

Research on the parent–child tie in adulthood tends to focus on structural changes in the tie as a result of demographic transitions, the emotional qualities of the tie, and/or the support exchange that occurs in this tie. We briefly discuss and provide definitions of the key topics in this research area below.

DEMOGRAPHIC TRANSITIONS AND STRUCTURAL FACTORS

Several demographic transitions have affected the parent–child tie in recent history including increased longevity, increased prevalence of chronic illness, declining fertility rates, and changes in marriage patterns. From 2008 to 2040, the proportion of individuals over aged 65 is projected to increase by 160% and the proportion of individuals over aged 85 to increase by 233% (Kinsella & He, 2009). Many older adults are in good health. Indeed, rates of disability in late life have decreased dramatically in the past two decades (Schoeni, Freedman, & Martin, 2008). This increased longevity and improved health has implications for the parent and adult child relationship. Parents often provide considerable help to grown children for several decades (Fingerman et al., 2010; Zarit & Eggebeen, 2002). Nonetheless, a significant number of older people (84% of people over age 65) have chronic health conditions (Anderson et al., 2002), which has led to an increase in the number of adult children who provide care to their parents (Family Caregiver Alliance, 2005; Wolff & Kasper, 2006). These trends lead to longer relationships between parents and children and families that often include multiple generations who provide care for one another (Bengtson, 2001).

The increased life expectancy is coupled with decreasing fertility rates (Center for Disease Control and Prevention, 2000; Hamilton, Martin, & Ventura, 2009). The fertility rate peaked during the US baby boom from 1946 to 1964, decreased until the 1970s, and has subsequently fluctuated slightly with the economy, increasing during times of prosperity and decreasing during recessions (Livingston & Cohn, 2010). As a result, the number of adult children available to provide assistance will most likely decline over time, reflecting the smaller family sizes of recent cohorts.

Marital and divorce patterns have shifted with a peak in the divorce rate in 1981 and a subsequent decline thereafter (Center for Disease Control and Prevention, 2009b; Clarke, 1995). This demographic change has lead to many different types of family arrangements including blended and stepfamilies that vary across generations of the family. Adult children today often have multiple sets of parents and grandparents. These shifts in marital patterns also have led to changes in the experience of caregiving in families and the expectations for caregiving are often more complicated in stepfamily arrangements (Ganong & Coleman, 2006).

Despite changing demographics, parents and children often live in close proximity (Lawton, Silverstein, & Bengtson, 1994). For example, in the national 2002 Health and Retirement study (the total sample size is over 20,000 individuals), 51% of the participants with adult children reported that one adult child lived within 10 miles. In addition, most parents and grown children are in frequent contact either by phone or in person (Fingerman, VanderDrift, Dotterer, Birditt, & Zarit, 2011; Kalmijn & De Vries, 2009). Of course, these ties are not always characterized by close proximity and frequent contact. Some parents and children report having minimal contact with one another, whereas others are in contact every day. Much of the variation in contact may be due to structural factors such as geographical proximity. However, the variations may also be due to differences in the importance and quality of the relationship.

RELATIONSHIP QUALITY AND SUPPORT EXCHANGE

Emotional qualities of these relationships also tend to remain intense. Parents and children experience positive and negative emotions regarding one another across the adult lifespan. Relationship quality is often defined in terms of positive, negative, or ambivalent (i.e., mixed) feelings. Positive quality includes the love, affection, and understanding parents and children feel for one another. In contrast, negative quality includes the extent to which parents and children get on one another's nerves, criticize one another, and make demands on one another. Ambivalence involves simultaneous feelings of positive and negative quality in the relationship or feeling mixed sentiments toward one another (Luescher & Pillemer, 1998).

Adult children and their parents also serve as primary sources of tangible and intangible support to one another across the lifespan (Fingerman, 2001; Fingerman et al., 2010; Silverstein, Gans, & Yang, 2006). Tangible support includes financial and instrumental help such as assistance with transportation and household chores. Intangible support includes providing affection, encouragement, and companionship such as listening to one another, discussing events, and socializing.

Parents also often rely on children to provide caregiving when they develop chronic illnesses. There is a large literature on caregiving, and offspring care for parents is becoming more frequent as parents are living longer. Caring for parents may include performing minor daily tasks and household chores as well as major duties such as bathing and feeding. US data indicate that older adults, especially those who are unmarried, tend to rely on their adult children for caregiving (Johnson & Wiener, 2006). Caregiving reduces the likelihood that older adults will enter a nursing home (Lo Sasso & Johnson, 2002), but is often considered a harmful and long-term chronic stress for caregivers (Epstein-Lubow, Davis, Miller, & Tremont, 2008; Pinquart, 2001; Zarit & Eggebeen, 2002).

THEORIES OF PARENT–CHILD TIES IN ADULTHOOD

The multitude of theories addressing this relationship tends to focus on a specific aspect of the tie (often called *middle range theories* because they address a circumscribed, as opposed to a global, family phenomenon), such as emotional qualities or provision of support. Because theories of relationship quality, aging and maturation, and support exchanges have been most frequently and most influentially used to study intergenerational relationships in adulthood, they are reviewed below.

THEORIES OF RELATIONSHIP QUALITY

Solidarity Theory

Homans (1950) first introduced the concept of solidarity to explain the influence of groups on its members. According to Homans, groups had greater cohesiveness with more frequent interactions, shared values, and affection. Bengtson used this theory to develop *intergenerational solidarity theory*, which proposes that there are six dimensions of the parent–child tie: associational (type and frequency of contact); consensual (degree of agreement in values); functional (support exchanges); normative (norms and beliefs about family behavior, including familial obligations); structural (geographical proximity), and finally, affective solidarity (emotional bonds), which is of particular relevance to relationship quality (Bengtson, 2001; Bengtson & Roberts, 1991). According to solidarity theory, parents and children vary in how positively they feel for one another (i.e., affective solidarity). Affective solidarity is defined as extent to which there is love, caring, and understanding in the relationship.

Many empirical studies have examined intergenerational solidarity theory. For example, a longitudinal study of three generations of family members revealed that all three generations reported high levels of solidarity and that the levels remained fairly stable over time (Bengtson, 2001). Bengtson and his colleagues identified five types of families based on the six dimensions: tight knit (high on all dimensions) and detached (low on all dimensions) at the two extremes and three types of families that are more varied (intimate but detached, obligatory, and sociable (Silverstein & Bengtson, 1997). Rossi and Rossi (1990) examined age of child effects on parents' feelings of affective solidarity and feelings of closeness using cross-sectional data. They found that parents experience the greatest feelings of closeness with infants, the least closeness with adolescents, and moderate to high closeness for young adult and middle-age children, especially among mothers and daughters.

The concept of the *intergenerational stake* emerged from solidarity theory to explain generational differences in affective solidarity. According to this hypothesis, parents are more invested in the parent–child relationship than are their offspring (Bengtson & Kuypers, 1971). Thus, parents report greater positive relationship quality than children across the lifespan (Giarrusso, Feng, & Bengtson, 2004; Shapiro, 2004).

Because parents are more invested, they tend to view their children as extensions of themselves, and their well-being is often tied to their offspring's success as adults. Indeed, parents tend to gain greater feelings of self-worth and more positive feelings from their more successful offspring (Birditt, Fingerman, & Zarit, 2010; Ryff, Lee, Essex, & Schmutte, 1994). For example, parents report higher relationship quality with children who are working, married, do not coreside with them, and who do not have problems considered voluntary (e.g., drug abuse; Belsky, Jaffee, Caspi, Moffitt, & Silva, 2003; Suitor & Pillemer, 2000).

Positive relationship quality is associated with greater individual well-being. Silverstein and Bengtson (1991) found that recently widowed parents who reported having more positive relationships with their children had lower mortality rates than those who reported less positive relationships. Parents also reported greater well-being when their children are more affectionate, supportive, and positive (Lang & Schutze, 2002; Ryan & Willits, 2007). Lowenstein (2007) found that solidarity predicted greater quality of life among parents across several countries, including England, Norway, Germany, Spain, and Israel.

Conflict Perspective

The *conflict perspective* recognizes that tensions and irritations are common and inevitable in the parent–child relationship across adulthood. According to the developmental schism hypothesis (Fingerman, 1996; 2001), which is an extension of the intergenerational stake concept, parents and children often experience tension due to having different developmental needs. This schism leads parents and children to report different topics of tension as well as use different strategies when handling those tensions. For example, parents tend to perceive fewer tensions than do offspring. But when parents do report problems, their irritations revolve around individual types of tensions (e.g., finances), whereas children tend to report tensions regarding the dynamics of the relationships or how parents and children interact (e.g., unsolicited advice; Birditt, Miller, Fingerman, & Lefkowitz, 2009; Fingerman, 1996).

When parents and children experience problems, they are most likely to report reacting with constructive strategies (e.g., calm discussion, listening) compared to avoidant (e.g., avoid talking about the topic, avoid talking to one another) and destructive (e.g., yelling, insulting) strategies (Birditt et al., 2009; Fingerman, 1995). Parents are more likely to report using constructive strategies than offspring. These generational differences in behaviors are consistent with the developmental stake perspective; parents are more emotionally invested in the relationship than are their children (Bengtson & Kuypers, 1971) and, thus, seek to resolve conflicts.

Gender differences also are evident in intergenerational conflicts. *Gender role theory* suggests that mothers are expected to provide more hands on care and to be more invested in the parental role than are fathers and thus there is more opportunity for stress and irritation (Simon, 1992). Mothers report more negative relationships (especially with daughters) than fathers (Fingerman, 2001; Umberson, 1992) and parents report lower levels of negative relationship quality over time (Birditt, Jackey, & Antonucci, 2009). Consistent with decreases in negative relationship qualities, older people report less negativity in the parent–child relationship than do younger adults (Akiyama, Antonucci, Takahashi, & Langfahl, 2003; Rossi & Rossi, 1990; Umberson, 1992).

Negative relationship quality is associated with poorer well-being. Umberson (1992) found that greater strain with mothers and fathers was associated with greater psychological distress among adult children.

Intergenerational Ambivalence Theory

Ambivalence theory emerged as a way of understanding simultaneous feelings of positive and negative affect in the relationship. According to ambivalence theory, roles or relationships that include contradictory norms for behavior cause feelings of psychological ambivalence (Connidis & McMullin, 2002). Psychological ambivalence is defined as having simultaneous positive and negative emotions or cognitions about the same object (Luescher & Pillemer, 1998). The intergenerational tie is particularly ambivalent because it is characterized by contradictory norms of closeness and independence. Parents and children are expected to provide one another with support and to have close ties but they are also expected to maintain some degree of separateness from one another's lives. For example, children are expected to become fully functioning and independent adults, but also to maintain intimacy with their parents. Studies show that approximately 40–50%

of parents and children report at least some mixed emotions regarding their relationships with one another (Fingerman, Hay, & Birditt, 2004; Pillemer & Suitor, 2002).

Parents and children report greater ambivalence when there are threats to the balance of independence and closeness. For instance, children tend to report more ambivalence when their parents have health problems, or when they are expected to provide caregiving for their parents (Willson, Shuey, & Elder, 2003). Parents, in contrast, report more ambivalence when their children have problems, when their children are not married, and when children are not invested in roles associated with adulthood (Birditt, Fingerman, & Zarit, 2010; Fingerman, Chen, Hay, Cichy, & Lefkowitz, 2006; Pillemer et al., 2007).

Research also indicates that ambivalence predicts poorer well-being among parents and children. Lowenstein (2007) found that greater intergenerational ambivalence predicted lower quality of life among parents in England, Norway, Germany, Spain, and Israel. Fingerman, Pitzer, Lefkowitz, Birditt, and Mroczek (2008) examined ambivalence and well-being among parents and offspring and found that ambivalence predicts lower psychological well-being among mothers, fathers, and offspring. Ward (2008) found that more ambivalent parents (i.e., low quality or infrequent contact with at least some children) reported greater depression. Uchino (2004) provided theoretical explanations for why ambivalent ties may evoke such deleterious outcomes. He postulated that ambivalent relationships may be harmful because they are unpredictable and people do not simply habituate to the negative aspects of their ambivalent relationships as they do with purely aversive ties. Similarly, individuals are invested in their ambivalent ties due to the positive aspects of the relationship, and therefore, may experience more frequent contact and emotional interactions than in purely negative ties.

THEORIES OF MATURATION AND AGING IN THE PARENT–CHILD TIE

Filial maturity, whereby the offspring ends the rebellion of adolescence and perceives parents from the perspective of a mature adult rather than a child, is hypothesized to begin in early adulthood and increase across adulthood (Blenkner, 1965; Nydegger, 1991). Blenkner (1965) described filial maturity as a major task in the relationship between adult offspring and parents. The filially mature adult offspring is able to understand the parent as a peer with a past history and limitations. Filial maturity goes beyond the adolescent concept of individuation. According to *individuation theory*, relationships between parents and children develop from hierarchical to more egalitarian over adolescence (Grotevant & Cooper, 1986; Youniss & Smollar, 1985). During adolescence, parents and offspring make efforts to increase autonomy while maintaining feelings of connectedness. This process involves the offspring's making his or her own decisions and deidealizing the parents, but at the same time feeling close and intimate. Autonomy is a precursor to filial maturity, which involves not only separation and intimacy, but also acceptance of the parent as a peer with imperfections.

Researchers have delineated two dimensions of filial maturity based on Blenkner's (1965) definition: accepting that the other party has weaknesses (i.e., distancing) and viewing the other as peer-like (i.e., comprehending; Birditt, Fingerman, Lefkowitz, & Kamp Dush, 2008; Nydegger, 1991). Distancing involves separation from parents and establishing an independent adult life and the perception of the parent objectively as a person with faults. Comprehending, which occurs subsequent to distancing, refers to the perception of the parent as an individual with a unique life history outside of the parent–child relationship. Fredricksen and Sharlach (1996) further clarified that filial maturity involves an empathetic parent–child relationship that includes an awareness of parents' needs and limitations.

Filial anxiety is another aspect of maturation that increases as children and parents grow older and it is defined as increased worry about parent's health, mortality, and potential caregiving needs (Cicirelli, 1988). Indeed, Hay, Fingerman, and Lefkowitz (2005) found that even young adults worry about their parents' health. By midlife, adults are surprisingly accurate in reporting their parents' health problems and functional status (Fingerman, Hay, Kamp Dush, Cichy, & Hosterman, 2005). Thus, as parents and children age together they experience developmental shifts in their perceptions. Parents tend to perceive their children with increasing positivity and children begin to perceive their parents as peers with faults and limitations.

Interestingly, some theories from the adult development literature have been slow to gain a foothold in family science. *Socioemotional selectivity theory* is a dominant theory in the study of adults' relationships (Carstensen, Fung, & Charles, 2003; Carstensen, Isaakowitz & Charles, 1999). The basic premise of this theory is that individuals alter their social behavior as a function of their future time perspective. When individuals perceive their future as open, they pursue a wide variety of social ties, including acquaintances and partners who provide information and opportunity. When individuals perceive time as limited, however, they tend to focus on their closest social partners (typically family) that offer emotional rewards (Lang, 2001). Many studies have examined this theory with regard to social networks broadly, and there is considerable empirical support documenting these shifts in preference for social partners (see Charles & Carstensen, 2010, for a review).

Although research using socioemotional selectivity theory to examine intergenerational ties is scant, this theory implicitly refers to parent–child ties by virtue of the fact that most adults nominate their parents and grown children among their most important social partners, following romantic ties (Antonucci & Akiyama, 1987; Fingerman, Hay, & Birditt, 2004). Applications of the theory to studies of the parent–child tie have been limited to consideration of the relative importance of the relationship. Because parents are near the end of life, and their grown children have more open time horizons, the value placed on the relationship may differ between parents and children. As stated previously, Fingerman (2001) referred to this phenomenon as a "developmental schism" and showed that tensions can arise when mothers place a greater value on ties to their grown children than the children do. Likewise, parental well-being is more sensitive to ambivalent relationships with grown children when parents place greater importance on ties to their grown children (Fingerman et al., 2008).

Research examining age differences and changes over time in relationship quality appears to support socioemotional selectivity theory. For example, several studies have shown that older people report more positive and less negative parent–child ties than younger people (Akiyama et al., 2003; Fingerman, Hay, & Birditt, 2004; Birditt et al., 2009; Rossi & Rossi, 1990). Additional research is needed to establish that time perspective accounts for such changes.

THEORIES OF SUPPORT EXCHANGE

In addition to possessing positive and negative emotional qualities, relationships between adults and their parents tend to be "resource rich" across adulthood. That is, both parties derive a great deal of tangible and non-tangible support from this tie. Nonetheless, the flow of support tends to be imbalanced, with greater support flowing downstream from parents to grown children than upwards from children to parents in Western nations (Fingerman et al., 2010; Grundy & Henretta, 2006). This pattern stems from historical patterns; in non-industrialized societies, parents were the principle source of economic position for their offspring, either through the inheritance of land or wealth or a profession (primarily for sons) or a dowry or marriage arrangement (for daughters). In the US and Europe today, this tradition persists in the flow of support from parents to grown children; most parents provide their grown children with considerable monetary and non-monetary support (Fingerman, Miller, Birditt, & Zarit, 2009; Kohli, 2005; Schoeni, 1997).

Interestingly, however, family theories regarding parent–child support disproportionately focus on support provided to aging parents. Theories regarding support of grown children have tended to focus on exceptional circumstances rather than everyday support. Because the literature is bifurcated and focuses on either support of grown children or on support of elderly parents, we cover these topics distinctly below.

Support of Grown Children

Theoretical perspectives regarding support of grown children have tended to focus on parental responses to grown children's needs. *Contingency theory* in sociology posits that parents and grown children provide assistance to one another in response to specific needs (Eggebeen & Davey, 1998). Social psychological research has noted that individuals respond to adults in distress under many circumstances, even to strangers (e.g., Dovidio, Piliavin, Schroeder, & Penner, 2006), and therefore, it is not surprising that parents would respond to their children's distress even after they are grown. Data support contingency theory for parental support of grown children; parents respond when offspring suffer health problems, financial difficulties, and other serious problems or crises (Fingerman et al., 2009; Suitor, Sechrist, & Pillemer, 2007a). Such support may reflect individuals' general willingness and feelings of obligation to support family members in need.

Related to contingency theory, theoretical perspectives on chronic stress have addressed parental support of grown children with exceptional circumstances of need, such as a developmental disability (Ha, Hong, Seltzer, & Greenberg, 2008), unemployment, or health problems (Milkie, Bierman, & Schieman, 2008). These models suggest that parents experience stress due not to only demands of supporting such grown children, but their feelings of empathy with the grown children. Studies also have found that children who suffer problems also may treat their parents more poorly, exacerbating the effects of the children's problems (Milkie et al., 2008). These models are informative for situations in which offspring exert exceptional demands on parents, but do not explain the everyday support pervasive in parent–child ties.

More specific to the relationship between adults and parents, however, parents also provide everyday support to grown children who occupy statuses that elicit support, such as being a student (Aquilino, 2006; Attias-Donfut & Wolff, 2000) or having young children of their own (Casper & Bianchi, 2002). The prolonged transition to adulthood in the US today has resulted in an increase in such circumstances of support over the past 20 years (Fingerman, Cheng, Tighe, Birditt, & Zarit, 2012).

Our own recent research found support for contingency theory with regard to distinct types of needs, namely, problems or crises and everyday issues (Fingerman et al., 2009). We studied the support that 633 middle-aged adults provided 1,374 grown children across a range of domains (financial, practical, emotional, advice). Consistent with the theory, support was higher for children who had suffered a problem in the past 2 years such as a divorce, being the victim of a crime, having a physical or psychiatric health problem, or other crises. Likewise, grown children who had everyday needs such as student status or were unmarried also received more support. Our findings extended prior theory, however, in that parents also provided greater support to grown children whom they deemed most successful. These children were often pursuing educational goals or involved in long term relationships that might become permanent ties (Fingerman et al., 2009). As we discuss later, to fully understand support between adults and parents, theory must go beyond an examination of needs to consider the personal meanings individuals derive from providing and receiving support in this family relationship.

Support of Aging Parents

Theory regarding support of aging parents is better developed than theory regarding support to grown children. Much of the theory addressing this topic pertains to caregiving for aging parents. Although the majority of support throughout life flows from parents to children, at the end of life, parents often incur health declines and their offspring increase assistance to them (Zarit & Eggebeen, 2002). At any given time in the US, approximately 20% of middle-aged adults provide care to their frail elderly parents (Grundy & Henretta, 2006; Fingerman et al., 2010). Explanations for such help are found in two theoretical perspectives already discussed in this chapter: contingency and solidarity theories, and in a third theoretical perspective not yet mentioned, *equity theory* (Silverstein, Conroy, Wang, Giarrusso, & Bengtson, 2002; Lowenstein, 2007).

Contingency theory applies to parent care to the extent that grown children step in and increase support to parents in response to parental needs. In a longitudinal study using national data, Eggebeen and Davey (1998) found that support increased in reaction to events in parents' lives (e.g., widowhood). Likewise, in an in-depth cross-sectional study of parents suffering differing degrees of health problems, offspring support and emotional reactions reflected objective features of the medical diagnosis such that offspring were more upset and involved with parents who were objectively more physically ill or frail (Fingerman, Hay, Kamp Dush, Cichy, & Hosterman, 2007).

With regard to solidarity theory, research has focused on affectional and normative solidarity (i.e., the emotional aspects of the relationship and beliefs about providing support). For example, Silverstein and colleagues (2006) used longitudinal data and found that declining parental health evoked assistance from offspring when the grown child held a stronger norm of obligation to support. Moreover, other studies have found that daughters tend to offer support to parents out of affection, whereas sons are more motivated by a sense of normative obligation (Dilworth-Anderson et al., 2005; Silverstein et al., 2006). Similarly, Pillemer and Suitor (2006) found that mothers' preferences for a grown child to provide support in the future depended on their feelings of closeness to the child and their shared values (normative solidarity) as well as the child's gender (i.e., daughters are preferred). Moreover, research conducted in the Netherlands found that parents and offspring benefited when offspring provided support in the context of high quality relationships, but did not benefit when support was provided in poorer quality ties (Merz, Consedine, Schulze, & Schuengel, 2009).

Social equity theory proposes that adults prefer to feel that their exchanges are equitable in any given relationship. That is, individuals like to feel as though what they give and receive in the relationship is equitable. This theory is supported by research, at least with regard to Western nations. For example, Lowenstein and colleagues (2007) analyzed data from the OASIS study of five nations (Norway, Germany, England, Spain, Israel) and found that older adults faired best when they were able to help their offspring as well as receive support from those offspring.

Equity theory also has been applied to offspring support of aging parents across the life course, with regard to reciprocity over time. The theory suggests that offspring may provide parents with support in late life as a means of paying back those parents for support the parents provided earlier in life. A longitudinal study from 1971 to 1985 found that grown children who provided support to aging parents were those who received support and affection from their parents earlier in adulthood (Silverstein et al., 2002). Likewise, Eggebeen and Davey (1998) found continuity in domains of assistance and exchanges over time. It is possible, however, that these findings do not reflect the "payback" proposed by this theoretical perspective, but rather, continuity in the qualities of offspring who receive support earlier in life and who provide support later. Our prior research revealed that in young adulthood, offspring who were deemed successful received greater support from their parents. But these young adults were also the children who provided the most support to their parents at that time (Fingerman et al., 2009). Likewise, in later life, parents often prefer to receive care from grown children whom they view as competent, with affection, and as having shared values (Pillemer & Suitor, 2006). Thus, the patterns observed may involve continuity in the types of offspring who help their parents in addition to a system of equity and reciprocity.

A NEW INTEGRATIVE MODEL: MULTIDIMENSIONAL INTERGENERATIONAL SUPPORT THEORY

We have proposed a model we refer to as the *multidimensional intergenerational support model* that suggests the middle-generation's decisions to support grown children or aging parents are multi-determined (Fingerman & Birditt, 2010; Fingerman et al., 2011). This model attempts to integrate theoretical perspectives from different fields to understand the factors that predict support and well-being in intergenerational relationships across generations of a family. According to this model, support is influenced by resources and demands, intrapsychic factors, and needs of family members. These factors all in turn influence well-being. The model also recognizes that there are bidirectional links between and among all of the constructs. We describe all aspects of the model below, along with a figure depicting the model (Figure 5.1).

First, support is constrained by available resources and demands. *Resource depletion theory* informs this theoretical perspective. Resource depletion theory was developed in response to the observation that children in larger families performed more poorly on indicators of academic achievement; the evidence suggested that the large number of children placed excessive demands on parental resources (Blake, 1981; Davey, Janke, & Savla, et al., 2005; Downey, 1995). We extended this theory to situations involving grown children and aging parents, as we proposed that demands from both generations and paid work may tax a middle-generation's ability to support members of either generation (Fingerman et al., 2010; Grundy & Henretta, 2006).

In the early twenty-first century, socioeconomically better-off families have fewer children and healthier elderly parents. It is less well-off families that have more children and thus, larger family size is also associated with fewer resources. Therefore, we propose that it is not only family size, but limited resources that contribute to lesser support of grown children in poorer families. Indeed, data suggest that middle-aged adults with adequate resources will find ways to expand their efforts when they confront demands from their aging parents and their grown children. They engage in what we call "resource expansion" (Fingerman et al., 2010). They may tap reserves of energy or use money to help pay for outside assistance. Families with insufficient resources may find the demands exceptionally demanding, experience high stress, or be unable to meet demands. Alternately, lower SES individuals may use extended family, community, or church ties to help bridge family needs.

Second, our model considers intrapsychic or cultural factors. That is, family members with comparable resources and demands make different decisions regarding support. Parents and grown children provide support in situations that they find personally rewarding, including ties that are emotionally closer (e.g., Fingerman et al., 2011; Suitor et al., 2007b), having offspring who may be successful in the future and who may reciprocate with support (e.g., Fingerman et al., 2009), and/or having culturally-shared values about personal meaning and fulfillment from providing such care (White, Townsend, & Stephens, 2000).

Likewise, cultural beliefs about support play a role in support patterns, with individuals from cultures with greater feelings of obligation to parents more likely to give help. Becker, Beyene,

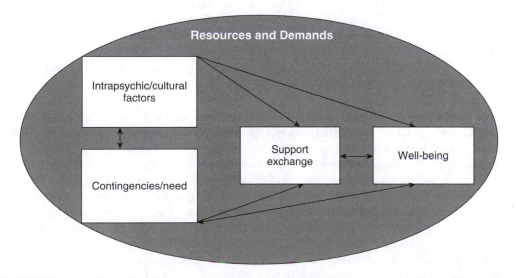

FIGURE 5.1 Multidimensional intergenerational support model.

Newsom, and Mayen (2003) conducted a qualitative longitudinal study of ethnic differences in beliefs about intergenerational support in the US. They found that Filipino, Latino, Cambodian, and African-American parents and children expressed differing preferences for coresidence, grand-parental provision of childcare, and the flow of financial support (from parent to child or from child to parent). For example, in the African-American community, family often included fictive kin who were not related by blood but who engaged in extensive support exchanges. In Cambodian families, older adults contributed to the family via provision of childcare, cooking, and cleaning while the middle generation worked. Filipino older adults still helped their children, but had a high expectation of support from those children later in life. Cultural preferences manifested different patterns of support and reactions to support.

Third, the multidimensional intergenerational support model incorporates *Contingency theory*, which suggests that parents and grown children provide assistance to one another in response to specific needs (Eggebeen & Davey, 1998). For example, parents or children may have health problems or financial difficulties that demand support.

These three dimensions—demands and resources, intrapsychic or cultural beliefs (e.g., sense of obligation, rewards from providing support), and contingencies or needs (e.g., health problems) may be interrelated. For example, Black and Hispanic families endorse intergenerational coresidence (Chatters, Taylor, Lincoln, & Schroepfer, 2002; Kamo, 2000). But an apparent cultural preference may arise from structural factors that limit access to independent housing, including larger family size, lower income, housing discrimination, and lack of access to mortgages.

Similarly, we observed that different factors helped explain racial differences in patterns of support to different family members (Fingerman et al., 2011). Structural factors such as demands and resources mediated racial differences in support of grown children. White parents reported giving more frequent support to grown children than Black parents did, but differences in opportunities for education and prolonged career exploration seemed to account for this racial difference. By contrast, Black middle-aged adults gave more support to elderly parents. Structural factors and greater parental need (i.e., worse health) did not explain this racial difference. Rather, cultural beliefs about providing support to parents and sense of personal rewards did.

THEORETICAL LIMITATIONS AND NEEDED THEORETICAL ADVANCES IN THE STUDY OF ADULTS AND PARENTS

Despite considerable advances in the past three decades, there are large gaps in the literature on the parent–child tie in adulthood with regard to theory and research. Family science might benefit from theories addressing relationships more broadly, and considering how such theory and research may apply to the specific features of parent–child relationships. Indeed, there are several aspects of the multidimensional intergenerational support model that need to be examined more carefully to understand the nature of the interrelationships among the constructs and the mechanisms that account for those links.

Although personal relationships research and theory has focused increasing attention on links to physical and emotional health (Berkman, Glass, Brisette, & Seeman 2000; Uchino, 2004), there is a lack of research and theory regarding the mechanisms that link constructs such as relationship quality between adults and their parents and health. For example, daily interactions that occur between parents and children, the emotions experienced, and the biological processes that occur are just some of the factors that may link relationships and individual well-being. Most diary studies of daily interactions that examine daily processes focus on spouses (Gleason, Iida, Bolger, & Shrout, 2003, 2008; Rafaeli, Cranford, Green, Shrout, & Bolger, 2008) and the few studies examining parent–child dyads have focused on caregiving (Savla, Almeida, Davey, & Zarit, 2008; Seltzer et al., 2009). Given the frequent contact many adults and parents share, these ties may also affect daily mood and symptoms, and longer term health and well-being. These aspects of daily life are absent from theory and research addressing adults and their parents. In addition, research rarely considers how constructs may be bidirectionally associated. For instance, greater conflict or negativity in the parent–child tie may lead to diminished parental well being. At the same time, poorer parental well-being may cause greater conflict in the parent–child tie.

It is also unclear how constructs are associated over the course of the relationship. We need longitudinal studies and daily process studies to understand how these relationships, mechanisms, and outcomes operate in a bidirectional manner over time. By examining these processes over time, we can test more complicated theoretical models that include how parent–child relationships and the links between relationship dynamics and well-being develop as parents and children age together.

In addition, we know little about how these constructs operate across all members of an immediate family and our theoretical models often do not consider these multiple perspectives. For example, we are just beginning to examine multiple generations and multiple offspring relationships in families (Fingerman et al., 2010; Suitor, Pillemer, & Sechrist, 2006). We know from our current research that there is a great deal of variability in how family members feel about one another and the support exchanged across family members. But we know little about how these variations between family members operate over time. For example, if one offspring tends to get more support than others or is viewed as more successful or problematic than others, does this differentiation remain consistent over time? If there are changes in the patterns of quality and support over time, what accounts for these changes?

CONCLUSION

Overall, the parent–child relationship in adulthood is often geographically proximal, involves frequent contact and support exchange, and tends to have negative as well as positive qualities. Theoretical developments in this area have delineated the dimensions of the parent–child tie and the predictors of variability in this tie, but there has been little integration of theoretical perspectives across disciplines. In addition, little is known about the mechanisms that account for links between and among constructs. We outline an integrated theory of parent–child relationships that attempts to combine theoretical perspectives. We hope that this new theory will lead to more research examining parent–child relationships over time. In order to move forward, we need a better understanding of the complex associations among relationship quality, support, and well-being and the dynamics of how these constructs change over time.

REFERENCES

Akiyama, H., Antonucci, T., Takahashi, K., & Langfahl, E. S. (2003). Negative interactions in close relationships across the life span. *Journals of Gerontology: Psychological Sciences, 58*, 70–79.

Anderson, G., Horvath, J., Herbert, R., Ridgway, K., Pavlovich, W., Harjai, G., …; GYMR Public Relations. (2002). *Chronic conditions: Making the case for ongoing care*. Johns Hopkins University. Retrieved from http://www.rwjf.org/files/research/chronicbook2002.pdf (accessed June 4, 2010).

Antonucci, T. C., & Akiyama, H. (1987). Social networks in adult life and a preliminary examination of the convoy model. *Journal of Gerontology, 42*, 519–527.

Aquilino, W. (2006). Family relationships and support systems in emerging adulthood. In J. J. Arnett & J. L. Tanner (Eds.), *Emerging adults in the America: Coming of age in the 21st Century* (pp. 193–217). Washington, DC: American Psychological Association.

Attias-Donfut, C., & Wolff, F. C. (2000). The redistributive effects of generational transfers. In S. Arbur & C. Attias-Donfut (Eds.), *The myth of generational conflict: The family and state in ageing societies* (pp. 22–46). New York: Routledge.

Becker, G., Beyene, Y., Newsom, E., & Mayen, N. (2003). Creating continuity through mutual assistance: Intergenerational reciprocity in four ethnic groups. *Journals of Gerontology: Social Sciences, 58*, S151–S159.

Belsky, J., Jaffee, S., Caspi, A., Moffitt, T., & Silva, P. (2003). Intergenerational relationships in young adult-hood and their life-course, mental-health, and personality correlates. *Journal of Family Psychology*, *17*, 460–471.

Bengtson, V. L. (2001). Beyond the nuclear family: The increasing importance of multigenerational bonds. *Journal of Marriage and Family*, *63*, 1–16. doi:10.1111/j1741–3737.2001.00001.x

Bengtson, V. L., & Kuypers, J. A. (1971). Generational differences and the developmental stake. *Aging and Human Development*, *2*, 249–260.

Bengtson, V. L., & Roberts, R. E. L. (1991). Intergenerational solidarity in aging families: An example of formal theory construction. *Journal of Marriage and the Family*, *53*, 856–870.

Berkman, L. F., Glass, T., Brisette, I., & Seeman, T. E. (2000). From social integration to health: Durkheim in the new millennium. *Social Science & Medicine*, *51*, 843–857.

Birditt, K. S., Fingerman, K. L., Lefkowitz, E. S., & Kamp Dush, C. M. (2008). Parents perceived as peers: Filial maturity in adulthood. *Journal of Adult Development*, *15*, 1–12.

Birditt, K. S., Fingerman, K. L., & Zarit, S. (2010). Adult children's problems and successes: Implications for intergenerational ambivalence. *Journals of Gerontology: Psychological Sciences*, *65B*, 145–153.

Birditt, K. S., Jackey, L. M. H., & Antonucci, T. C. (2009). Longitudinal patterns of negative relationship quality across adulthood. *Journals of Gerontology: Psychological Sciences*, *64B*, 55–64.

Birditt, K. S., Miller, L. M., Fingerman, K. L., & Lefkowitz, E. S. (2009). Tensions in the parent and adult child relationship: Links to solidarity and ambivalence. *Psychology and Aging*, *24*, 287–295.

Blake, J. (1981). Family size and the quality of children. *Demography 18*, 421–442.

Blenkner, M. (1965). Social work and family relationships in later life with some thoughts on filial maturity. In E. Shanas & G. Streib (Eds.), *Social structure and the family: Generational relations* (pp. 46–59). Englewood Cliffs: Prentice Hall.

Carstensen, L. L., Fung, H. H., & Charles, S. T. (2003). Socioemotional selectivity theory and the regulation of emotion in the second half of life. *Motivation and Emotion*, *27*, 103–123.

Carstensen, L. L., Isaacowitz, D. M., & Charles, S. T. (1999). Taking time seriously: A theory of socioemotional selectivity. *American Psychologist*, *54*, 165–181.

Casper, L. M., & Bianchi, S. M. (2002). *Continuity and change in the American family*. Thousand Oaks, CA: Sage.

Center for Disease Control and Prevention. (2000). Live births, birth rates, and fertility rates, by race: United States, 1909–2000 (Table 1–1). Retrieved from http://www.cdc.gov/nchs/data/statab/t001x01.pdf (accessed June 7, 2010).

Center for Disease Control and Prevention. (2009b). National marriage and divorce rate trends. Retrieved from http://www.cdc.gov/nchs/nvss/marriage_divorce_tables.html (accessed May 25, 2010).

Charles, S. T., & Carstensen, L. L. (2010). Social and emotional aging. *Annual Review of Psychology*, *61*, 383–409.

Chatters, L. M., Taylor, R. T., Lincoln, K. D., & Schroepfer, T. (2002). Patterns of informal support from family and church members among African Americans. *Journal of Black Studies*, *33*, 66–85.

Cicirelli, V. G. (1988). A measure of filial anxiety regarding anticipated care of elderly parents. *Gerontologist*, *28*, 478–482.

Clarke, S. C. (1995). Advance report of final divorce statistics, 1989 and 1990. *Monthly Vital Statistics Report*, *43*(8), National Center for Health Statistics. Retrieved from http://www.cdc.gov/nchs/data/mvsr/supp/mv43_09s.pdf (accessed May 25, 2010).

Connidis, I. A., & McMullin, J. A. (2002). Sociological ambivalence and family ties: A critical perspective. *Journal of Marriage and Family*, *64*, 558–567.

Davey, A., Janke, M., & Savla, J. (2005). Antecedents of intergenerational support: Families in contact and families as context. In M. Silversten (Ed.), *Intergenerational relations across time and place* (pp. 29–54). New York: Springer.

Dilworth-Anderson, P., Brummett, B. H., Goodwin, P., Williams, S. W., Williams, R. B., Siegler, I. C. (2005). Effect of race on cultural justifications for caregiving. *Journals of Gerontology, Series B, Psychological Sciences and Social Sciences*, *60*(S), 257–262.

Dovidio, J. F., Piliavin, J. A., Schroeder, D. A., & Penner, L. A. (2006). *The social psychology of prosocial behavior*. Mahwah: Lawrence Erlbaum.

Downey, D. B. (1995). When bigger is not better: Family size, parental resources, and children's educational performance. *American Sociological Review, 60,* 746–61.

Eggebeen, D. J., & Davey, A. (1998). Do safety nets work? The role of anticipated help in times of need. *Journal of Marriage and the Family, 60,* 939–950.

Epstein-Lubow, G., Davis, J. D., Miller, I. W., & Tremont, G. (2008). Persisting burden predicts depressive symptoms in dementia caregivers. *Journal of Geriatric Psychiatry and Neurology, 21,* 198–203.

Family Caregiver Alliance. (2005). Fact Sheet: Selected caregiver statistics. Retrieved from http://www.caregiver.org/caregiver/jsp/content_node.jsp?nodeid=439 (accessed May 21, 2010).

Fingerman, K. L. (1995). Aging mothers' and their adult daughters' perceptions of conflict behaviors. *Psychology and Aging, 10,* 639–649.

Fingerman, K. L. (1996). Sources of tension in the aging mother and adult daughter relationship. *Psychology and Aging, 11,* 591–606.

Fingerman, K. L. (2001). *Aging mothers and their adult daughters: A study in mixed emotions.* New York: Springer.

Fingerman, K. L., & Birditt, K. S. (2010). Adult children and aging parents. In K. W. Schaie (Ed.), *Handbook of the psychology of aging* (7th ed., pp. 219–232). New York: Elsevier.

Fingerman, K. L., Chen, P. C., Hay, E. L., Cichy, K. E., & Lefkowitz, E. S. (2006). Ambivalent reactions in the parent and adult-child relationship. *Journals of Gerontology: Psychological Sciences, 61,* 152–160.

Fingerman, K. L., Cheng, Y. P., Tighe, L., Birditt, K. S., & Zarit, S. (2012). Relationships between young adults and their parents. In A. Booth, S. L. Brown, N. Landale, W. Manning, & S. M. McHale (Eds.), *Early adulthood in a family context* (pp. 59–86). New York: Springer.

Fingerman, K. L., Hay, E. L., & Birditt, K. S. (2004). The best of ties, the worst of ties: Close, problematic, and ambivalent relationships across the lifespan. *Journal of Marriage and Family, 66,* 792–808.

Fingerman, K. L., Hay, E. L., Kamp Dush, C. M., Cichy, K., & Hosterman, S. (2005). Role revisions: Parents' and offspring's perceptions of change and continuity in later life. Manuscript under review.

Fingerman, K. L., Hay, E. L., Kamp Dush, C. M., Cichy, K. E., & Hosterman, S. (2007). Parents' and offspring's perceptions of change and continuity when parents experience the transition to old age. *Advances in Life Course Research, 12,* 275–306 doi: 10.1016/S1040-2608(07)12010-4.

Fingerman, K., Miller, L., Birditt, K., & Zarit, S. (2009). Giving to the good and the needy: Parental support of grown children. *Journal of Marriage and Family, 71,* 1220–1233.

Fingerman, K. L., Pitzer, L. M., Chan, W., Birditt, K. S., Franks, M. M., & Zarit, S. (2010). Who gets what and why: Help middle-aged adults provide to parents and grown children. *Journals of Gerontology: Social Science, 66B,* 87–98.

Fingerman, K. L., Pitzer, L., Lefkowitz, E. S., Birditt, K. S., & Mroczek, D. (2008). Ambivalent relationship qualities between adults and their parents: Implications for both parties' well-being. *Journals of Gerontology: Psychological Sciences, 63,* P362–P371.

Fingerman, K. L., VanderDrift, L. E., Dotterer, A., Birditt, K. S., & Zarit, S. (2011). Support of grown children and aging parents in Black and White families. *Gerontologist, 51,* 441–452.

Fredricksen, K. I., & Sharlach, A. E. (1996). Filial maturity: Analysis and reconceptualization. *Journal of Adult Development, 3,* 183–191.

Ganong, L., & Coleman, M. (2006). Obligations to stepparents acquired in later life: Relationship quality and acuity of needs. *Journals of Gerontology: Social Sciences, 61B,* S80–S88.

Giarrusso, R., Feng, D., & Bengtson, V. L. (2004). The intergenerational stake over 20 years. In M. Silverstein (Ed.), *Annual review of gerontology and geriatrics* (pp. 55–76). New York: Springer.

Gleason, M. E., Iida, M., Bolger, N., & Shrout, P. E. (2003). Daily supportive equity in close relationships. *Personality and Social Psychology Bulletin, 29,* 1036–1045.

Gleason, M. E., Iida, M., Shrout, P. E., & Bolger, N. (2008). Receiving support as a mixed blessing: Evidence for dual effects of support on psychological outcomes. *Journal of Personality and Social Psychology, 94,* 824–838.

Grotevant, H. D., & Cooper, C. R. (1986). Individuation in family relationships: A perspective on individual differences in the development of identity and role-taking skill in adolescence. *Human Development, 29,* 82–100.

Grundy, E., & Henretta, J. C. (2006). Between elderly parents and adult children: A new look at the 'sandwich' generation. *Aging & Society, 26,* 707–722.

Ha, J. H., Hong J., Seltzer M. M., & Greenberg, J. S. (2008). Age and gender differences in the well-being of midlife and aging parents with children with mental health or developmental problems: Report of a national study. *Journal of Health and Social Behavior, 49*, 301–316.

Hamilton, B. E., Martin, J. A., &Ventura, S. J. (2009). Births: Preliminary data for 2007. *National Center for Health Statistics: National Vital Statistics Reports, 57*(12). Retrieved from http://www.cdc.gov/nchs/data/nvsr/nvsr57/nvsr57_12.pdf (accessed June 2, 2010).

Hay, E. L., Fingerman, K. L., & Lefkowitz, E. S. (2005). The experience of worry in the parent and adult offspring relationship. Manuscript submitted for publication.

Hay, E. L., Fingerman, K. L., & Lefkowitz, E. S. (2007). The experience of worry in parent-adult child relationships. *Personal Relationships, 14*, 605–622. doi: 10.1111/j.1475-6811.2007.00174.x

Homans, G. F. (1950). *The human group*. New York: Harcourt, Brace, and World.

Johnson, R. W., & Wiener, J. M. (2006). A profile of frail older Americans and their caregivers. *The Urban Institute: The Retirement Project*. Retrieved from http://www.urban.org/UploadedPDF/311284_older_americans.pdf (accessed June 16, 2010).

Kalmijn, M., & De Vries, J. (2009). Change and stability in parent–child contact in five Western countries. *European Journal of Population, 25*, 257–276.

Kamo, Y. (2000). Racial and ethnic differences in extended family households. *Sociological Perspectives, 43*, 211–229.

Kinsella, K. & He, W. (2009). *An Aging World: 2008*. Retrieved from http://www.census.gov/prod/2009pubs/p95–09–1.pdf (accessed March 22, 2010).

Kohli, M. (2005). Intergenerational transfers and inheritance: A comparative view. In M. Silverstein & K. W. Schaie (Eds.), *Intergenerational relations across time and place: Annual review of gerontology and geriatrics* (pp. 266–289). New York: Springer.

Lang, F. R. (2001). Regulation of social relationships in later adulthood. *Journals of Gerontology: Psychological Sciences, 56B*, P321–P326.

Lang, F. R., & Schutze, Y. (2002) Adult children's supportive behaviors and older parents' subjective well-being: A developmental perspective on intergenerational relationships. *Journal of Social Issues, 58*, 661–680.

Lawton, L., Silverstein, M., & Bengtson, V. (1994). Affection, social contact, and geographic distance between adult children and their parents. *Journal of Marriage and the Family, 56*, 57–68.

Livingston, G. & Cohn, D. (2010). *U.S. birth rate decline linked to recession*. Pew research center demographic trends report. Retrieved from http://pewsocialtrends.org/assets/pdf/753-birth-rates-recession.pdf (accessed July 2, 2010).

Lo Sasso, A. T., & Johnson, R. W. (2002). Does informal care reduce nursing home admissions for the frail elderly? *Inquiry, 29*, 279–297.

Lowenstein, A. (2007). Solidarity-conflict and ambivalence: Testing two conceptual frameworks and their impact on quality of life for older family members. *Journals of Gerontology: Social Sciences, 62*, S100–S107.

Lowenstein, A., Katz, R., & Gur-Yaish, N. (2007). Reciprocity in parent–child exchange and life satisfaction among the elderly: A cross-national perspective. *Journal of Social Issues, 63*, 865–883.

Luescher, K., & Pillemer, K. (1998). Intergenerational ambivalence: A new approach to the study of parent–child relations in later life. *Journal of Marriage and the Family, 60*, 413–425.

Merz, E. M., Consedine, N. S., Schulze, H. J., & Schuengel, C. (2009). Well being of adult children and ageing parents: associations with intergenerational support and relationship quality *Aging and Society, 29*, 783–802.

Milkie, M. A., Bierman, A., & Schieman, S. (2008). How adult children influence older parents' mental health: Integrating stress-process and life course perspectives. *Social Psychology Quarterly, 71*, 86–105.

Nydegger, C. (1991). The development of paternal and filial maturity. In K. Pillemer & K. McCartney (Eds.), *Parent–child relations throughout life* (pp. 93–112). Hillsdale: Erlbaum.

Pillemer, K., & Suitor, J. J. (2002). Explaining mothers' ambivalence toward their adult children. *Journal of Marriage and Family, 64*, 602–613.

Pillemer, K., & Suitor, J. J. (2006). Making choices: A within-family study of caregiver selection. *Gerontologist, 46*, 439–448.

Pillemer, K., Suitor, J. J., Mock, S. E., Sabir, M., Pardo, T., & Sechrist, J. (2007). Capturing the complexity of intergenerational relations: Exploring ambivalence within later-life families. *Journal of Social Issues*, *63*, 775–791.

Pinquart, M. (2001). Correlates of subjective health in older adults: A meta-analysis. *Psychology and Aging*, *16*, 414–426.

Rafaeli, E., Cranford, J. A., Green, A. S., Shrout, P. E., & Bolger, N. (2008). The good and bad of relationships: how social hindrance and social support affect relationship feelings in daily life. *Personality and Social Psychology Bulletin 34*: 1703–1718.

Rossi, A. S., & Rossi, P. H. (1990). *Of human bonding: Parent–child relations across the life-course.* New York: Aldine de Gruyter.

Ryan, A. K., & Willits, F. K. (2007). Family ties, physical health, and psychological well-being. *Journal of Aging and Health*, *19*, 907–920.

Ryff, C. D., Lee, Y. H., Essex, M. J., & Schmutte, P. S. (1994). My children and me: Midlife evaluations of grown children and of self. *Psychology and Aging*, *9*, 195–205.

Savla, J., Almeida, D. M., Davey, A., & Zarit, S. H. (2008). Routine assistance to parents: Effects on daily mood and other stressors. *Journal of Gerontology*, *63*, 154–161.

Schoeni, R. F. (1997). Private interhousehold transfers of money and time: New empirical evidence. *Review of Income and Wealth*, *43*, 423–448.

Schoeni, R. F., Freedman, V. A., & Martin, L. G. (2008). Why is late life disability declining? *Milbank Quarterly*, *86*, 47–89.

Seltzer, M. M., Almeida, D. M., Greenberg, J. S., Savla, J., Stawski, R. S., Hong, J., et al. (2009). Psychological and biological markers of daily lives of midlife parents of children with disabilities. *Journal of Health and Social Behavior*, *50*, 1–15.

Shapiro, A. (2004). Revisiting the generation gap: Exploring the relationships of parent/adult-child dyads. *International Journal of Aging and Human Development*, *58*, 127–146.

Silverstein, M., & Bengtson, V. L. (1991). Do close parent–child relationships reduce the mortality risk of older parents? *Journal of Health and Social Behavior*, *32*, 382–395.

Silverstein, M., & Bengtson, V. L. (1997). Intergenerational solidarity and the structure of adult child-parent relationships in American families. *American Journal of Sociology*, *103*, 429–460.

Silverstein, M., Conroy, S., Wang, H., Gairrusso, R., & Bengtson, V. L. (2002). Reciprocity in parent–child relations over the adult life course. *Journals of Gerontology: Social Sciences*, *57*, S3–S13.

Silverstein, M., Gans, D., & Yang, F. M. (2006). Intergenerational support to aging parents: The role of norms and needs. *Journal of Family Issues*, *27*, 1068–1084.

Simon, R. (1992). Teaching against the grain: Texts for a pedagogy of possibility. New York: Bergin & Garvey.

Suitor, J. J., & Pillemer, K. (2000). Did mom really love you best? Developmental histories, status transitions, and parental favoritism in later life families. *Motivation and Emotion*, *24*, 105–120.

Suitor, J. J., Pillemer, K., & Sechrist, J. (2006). Within-family differences in mothers' support to adult children. *Journals of Gerontology: Social Sciences*, *61B*, S10–S17.

Suitor, J. J., Sechrist, J., & Pillemer, K. (2007a). When mothers have favorites: Conditions under which mothers differentiate among their adult children. *Canadian Journal on Aging*, *26*, 85–100.

Suitor, J. J., Sechrist, J., & Pillemer, K. (2007b). Within-family differences in mothers' support to adult children in Black and White families. *Research on Aging*, *29*, 410–435.

Uchino, B. N. (2004). Social support and physical health. New Haven: Yale University Press.

Umberson, D. (1992). Relationships between adult children and their parents: Psychological consequences for both generations. *Journal of Marriage and the Family*, *54*, 664–674.

Ward, R. A. (2008). Multiple parent-adult child relations and well-being in middle and later life. *Journals of Gerontology: Social Sciences*, *63B*, S239–248.

White, T. M., Townsend, A. L., & Stephens, M. A. P. (2000). Comparisons of African American and White women in the parent care role. *Gerontologist*, *40*, 718–728.

Willson, A. E., Shuey, K. M., & Elder, G. H. (2003). Ambivalence in the relationship of adult children to aging parents and in-laws. *Journal of Marriage and Family*, *65*, 1055–1072.

Wolff, J. L., & Kasper, J. D. (2006). Caregivers of frail elders: Updating a national profile. *Gerontologist*, *46*, 344–356.

Youniss, J., & Smollar, J. (1985). Adolescents' relations with mothers, fathers, and friends. Chicago: University of Chicago Press.

Zarit, S., & Eggebeen, D. J. (2002). Parent–child relationships in adulthood and later years. In M. Bornstein (Ed.), *Handbook of parenting, Vol. 1: Children & parenting* (2nd ed., pp. 135–161). Mahwah,: Erlbaum.

6 The Changing Faces of Fatherhood and Father–Child Relationships

From Fatherhood as Status to Father as Dad

Michael E. Lamb

The role of the father has been the focus of speculation for millennia, with multiple references to fathers and fatherhood in the Old and New Testaments, as well as in countless folk-tales, myths, fables, and books. This is not surprising. Unlike narrowly defined psychologic concepts like "working memory," fatherhood is a concept like "love" that has been invoked, defined, and analyzed from an extraordinarily diverse array of perspectives, with psychologists and other social scientists joining the party very late. Unlike the other chapters in this volume that provide up-to-date reviews of how theory has been used in previous content areas, this chapter takes a more historic approach and directs attention to how we reached present understandings of fatherhood. Although I do not attempt to survey the broad expanse of writing and theorizing about fatherhood and father–child relationships here, my task is undeniably complicated by the fact that each reader "knows" what fatherhood means, and what significance it has for children, families, and for society.

Each of us had a father, many of us are fathers, and many of us live (or have lived) with the fathers of our children; as a result, our implicit theoretical conceptions of fatherhood are profoundly shaped by personal experiences, both good and bad. Against such certainties, any review of the social scientific theories faces an uphill struggle. The goal of this chapter is to review changing societal and scholarly perspectives on and conceptualizations of the ways in which fathers affect children's development, drawing where possible on the thoughtful contributions of Elizabeth and Joseph Pleck (1997; E. Pleck, 2004).

The chapter provides a brief summary of the ways in which social scientists' theories about fathers, father–child relationships, and fatherhood have evolved—often in response to changes in society—over the last century. In brief, I begin by noting that fathers were initially conceptualized as husbands and breadwinners, and proceed to show that when researchers first began to study the determinants of child development, their explanatory models did not include fathers. The emergence of attachment theory in the early 1950s increased the emphasis on mothers and early mother–child relationships, with psychologists only 'discovering' fathers in a new wave of research that began in the 1960s and burgeoned in the 1970s. Whereas the English feminist movement criticized patriarchy and thus put focus on men's status in society and roles in relation to women, it was the emphasis of Scandinavian feminists and social reformers that helped foment interest in paternal behavior and father–child relationships, ushering in conceptions of 'the new father.'

FATHERHOOD AS DEFINED BY STATUS IN THE FAMILY STRUCTURE

One striking feature of successive theoretical constructions of fatherhood is the extent to which the role was defined until the 1970s by a status within the family structure rather than by the relationship with children for which it was named. Thus, sociologists such as Durkheim and Parsons and Bales, like psychoanalysts such as Freud and Jung, and developmental psychologists like Hall, implicitly and explicitly defined fathers in their theories as either heads of the family or as the principal sources of economic support for the family. When Freud first contemplated how fathers might affect their children's development, he did not focus on the interactions they might have shared but on fathers' role as heads of the family and mothers' romantic partners. Jung focused on mythical archetypes. In both cases, the children's interpretation of and desires, for diverse reasons, to emulate their fathers' fearsome behavior as family leaders or heads, were believed to prompt identification and imitation.

It was Philip Wylie (1942), an American author with an interest in psychology and social issues, who first punctured the comfortable assumption that fathers in general radiated confidence and leadership to those around them. As leaders of society and family, Wylie warned in *Generation of vipers*, men (particularly fathers) should portray leadership and strength; in fact, he warned, they had allowed themselves to be emasculated, and their evident failures could surely have adverse effects on current and future generations.

Wylie's sharply written critique is noteworthy, not for his close attention to the (admittedly limited) scholarly literature, but for his recognition that individual behavior and performance may (and in his view, often did) deviate from the societal image. His book may represent the first recognition that masculinity could be viewed as a continuous dimension, not merely as an adjective describing the behavior of adult males. In that respect, he may have inadvertently opened the door to psychologic, as opposed to sociologic, research on fatherhood. On the other hand, neither Wylie nor any contemporary social scientists conceived of what we might call paternal behavior—behavior directed by men to their children that might play a role in facilitating the formation of emotionally and psychologically meaningful relationships.

THE CHILD STUDY MOVEMENT

Systematic research on developmental processes in childhood began before Wylie's popular book, complementing the series of guides for parents (read "mothers") that were published as public health promotion exercises in both the US and the UK: The United States Children's Bureau was established in 1912; it immediately began publishing guides for mothers, that were widely distributed (Grotberg, 1976), even though the content was shaped more by custom and assertion than by research. The Oakland and Berkeley Growth Studies (begun in the early 1930s to study children born in 1921/1922 and 1928/1929, respectively) and Terman's longitudinal 'Study of the Gifted' (focused on 1,528 'gifted' children born in California between 1900 and 1925), have been particularly informative, not least because the extended longitudinal data collection provided a unique insight into the impact of both social and genetic background and experienced events on later development; new scholarly contributions continue to emerge from these studies until the present (Friedman & Martin, 2011). Unfortunately for us, fathers' possible direct influences on their children's development received scant attention in these landmark studies; their occupational and educational backgrounds were used to assess the social class milieu in which children grow up as well as their genotypes, but to the extent that social impact was considered, mothers alone were in the frame.

Wylie's emphasis on men's failure to fulfil their roles as masculine, competent leaders of the family was complemented by the first systematic study of fathers' roles in individual child development, albeit achieved by examining the adjustment and well-being of children whose fathers were absent at war. Pauline Sears' (1951; Sears, Pintler, & Sears, 1946) groundbreaking study was the first to report that children, especially boys, were at risk of psychosocial maladjustment when their fathers were absent from their families, and Sears was the first to suggest that the deficit might be attributed to the disruption of a critical socioemotional relationship. Even though Sears failed to take into account the many other ways in which fathers' absences could affect children's development and adjustment (see below), she deserves considerable credit, not only for recognizing that children might have psychologically significant relationships with their fathers, but also for conducting an empirical study designed to test this assertion. When her husband and colleagues later undertook the first systematic study of the extent to which variations in parental values, disciplinary practices, and sociological factors shaped children's development, they could not, and did not, ignore the possibility that paternal behavior affected children's development (Sears, Maccoby, & Levin, 1957).

Building on Robert (e.g., 1947) and Pauline (e.g., 1951) Sears' previous research using projective doll play to explore parent–child relationships, Paul Mussen and his colleagues conducted a series of studies in the 1950s and early 1960s focused specifically on the extent to which psychological characteristics of the father 'affected' children's development (e.g., Mussen, 1961; Mussen & Distler, 1959, 1960; Mussen & Rutherford, 1963). Not surprisingly, given contemporary concerns with sex-role development (as reflected in Wylie's book), he focused on paternal (and filial) masculinity, and the findings are often viewed as sources of partial support for the theoretical proposition that paternal masculinity promotes filial masculinity, especially when the relationship between the two is warm. Ironically, Mussen and his colleagues assumed that the fathers were masculine and obtained most of their information about the father-child relationships, not by observing or questioning the men and children, but by questioning the mothers, and the measures of filial masculinity employed by Mussen and his colleagues were roundly and convincingly criticized by Pleck (1983) in a masterful book, *The myth of masculinity*. These deficiencies notwithstanding, Mussen's studies were influential and paved the way for the first books by a psychologist purporting to document the formative significance of father-child relationships (Lynn, 1969, 1974). Not surprisingly, it emphasized the importance of having fathers who were competent, take-charge, masculine husbands.

The 1960s and 1970s saw clinical psychologists undertake and publish a growing number of studies informed by the theoretical assumption that fathers' deficiencies were pathogenic (see reviews by Biller, 1971, 1974). Perhaps reflective of the time, the focus was typically still on the father's role in the family—as reflected in his power relative to that of his spouse, and in the extent to which he was viewed as an assertive, even authoritarian, figure in the family. Echoing Wylie's critique, the image of the disappointingly ineffective father was portrayed poignantly in the classic film, *Rebel without a cause* (1955) and humorously by popular cartoon characters such as Dagwood Bumstead in America and Andy Capp in Britain. Characteristics of specific father-child relationships, and personality features other than the faces of masculinity—power, control, and assertiveness—were not accorded much attention by researchers, resulting in a sociologically driven view of fatherhood, even in psychological theories.

The tendency of social scientists to focus on men's roles in relation to women rather than in relation to children doubtless reflected the culture of the time. The widespread devastation caused by World War II gave way to massive industrial and social reconstruction, not only in the United Kingdom and Europe, but also in North America. Women who had assumed key roles in industry during the war were unceremoniously pushed out of the workplace to make way for millions of demobilized soldiers; women were urged to focus their attention on home and hearth, raising a new generation (the baby boom generation) within the supportive cocoons created by breadwinning husbands. The resulting social transformation came to be portrayed as a return to the traditional family way of life even though the social and family circumstances were rather novel, and were certainly not "traditional." More than ever, fathers were urged to embrace their responsibilities as breadwinners and heads of households, but attainment of economic success came at a price. Many men had to work long hours, often endured extended commutes to work from the suburban homes increasingly sought by upwardly mobile young and growing families, and attempted to accommodate the nascent consumerism that was to gather strength over the succeeding decades by working harder and longer. In that context, fathers were not rewarded for spending time with their children— that was women's work. Men's time was better spent working or pursuing recreation in the company of workmates.

MOTHERHOOD AND MATRICENTRICISM

The Second World War also left in its wake huge numbers of displaced and orphaned children, and the attempts by psychologists and psychiatrists to understand the lessons and implications of these depredations fostered the development of *attachment theory* in response to the widely-shared conclusion that maternal deprivation had devastating effects on the psychosocial development of young children.

Bowlby's groundbreaking attachment theory very much reflected the times when it came to fathers. As Bowlby wrote in his first book:

> "… fathers have their uses even in infancy. Not only do they provide for their wives to enable them to devote themselves unrestrictedly to the care of the infant and toddler, but, by providing love and companionship, they support the mother emotionally and help her maintain that harmonious contented mood in the atmosphere of which her infant thrives. In what follows, therefore, while continued reference will be made to the mother-child relation, little will be said of the father-child relation; his value as the economic and emotional support of the mother will be assumed."
>
> (Bowlby, 1953, pp. 15–16)

Whereas the first half of the 20th century was marked by increasing emphasis on the exogenous socio-emotional processes shaping child development and adjustment, therefore, it was also a period of increasing matricentricity, with the emphasis on maternal preeminence mutually reinforced by a focus on the crucial importance of the very earliest experiences—those taking place during the first months and years of life, when maternal instincts underscored the 'natural' significance of mother-child interactions. As Bowlby explained, fathers were important parts of the social fabric supporting mothers; research in clinical contexts showed that fathers who did not provide their wives and families with strong, confident, masculine leadership risked undermining the children's psychological well-being as well. Strikingly absent from the debate was reference to the quality of the relationships between fathers and their children, and there was no recognition of the possibility that men might directly affect their children's development by loving, caring for, guiding, educating, speaking to, or even maltreating them. Fathers were largely, as I wrote in 1975, "forgotten contributors to child development" (Lamb, 1975).

The core ideas of attachment theory had been circulating since Bowlby's (1951) book-length World Health Organization-commissioned report on maternal deprivation (*Maternal care and mental health*). However, attachment theory was first outlined formally in *Child care and the growth of love* (1953) published two years later. For a decade between the mid-1950s and 1960s, Bowlby's Tavistock Clinic in London, England, became a forum for debate, discussion, and the formulation of developmental theory. Sceptical about the near total emphasis on mother-child relationships by Bowlby and his colleagues, a German-born psychologist, Rudolf Schaffer, questioned mothers in Scotland about young children's reactions to separations from various people between the times they were 1 and 18 months of age. Although few of the Scottish fathers were involved in the care of their infants, mothers reported that most infants viewed them fondly, beginning around the middle of the first year to cry when they departed as they did when similarly separated from their mothers.

To Schaffer and Emerson (1964), it looked as though these infants had formed attachments to their fathers. Likewise, Pedersen and Robson (1969) found that 75% of the American mothers they questioned reported that their infants responded positively and enthusiastically when their fathers returned from work, with the intensity of greeting by boys particularly correlated with the frequency of paternal caretaking, paternal patience with infant fussing, and the intensity of father-infant play. Among daughters, however, intensity of greeting was correlated only with reported paternal 'apprehension' about girls' well-being. Both studies suggested that infants were emotionally aware of their fathers: could this mean that psychologically significant relationships were developing?

THE DISCOVERY OF PATERNAL BEHAVIOR AND FATHER-CHILD RELATIONSHIPS

The 1970s witnessed growing signs of scepticism about the fundamental theoretical presumptions of developmental psychology, a field then in its ascendancy. Following the publication of the first volume of Bowlby's trilogy on attachment and loss in 1969, attachment theory had become the dominant framework from which intimate social relationships were understood. An early member of the group around Bowlby in London, Mary Ainsworth subsequently conducted a study in Uganda (Ainsworth, 1967) before taking a post in the United States where she became the major American proponent of attachment theory. Somewhat ironically, it was one of her undergraduate students at Johns Hopkins University who subsequently undertook, as a Harvard Ph.D. thesis, the first experimental study in which attachments to mothers and fathers were systematically compared. Kotelchuck's (1972) thesis and its subsequent publication (Kotelchuck, 1976) challenged the notion that babies do not form attachments to their fathers just as Schaffer and Pederson had done.

Kotelchuck (1976) reported that 12-, 15-, 18-, and 21-month-old infants predictably protested when left alone by either parent, explored little while the parents were absent, and greeted them positively when they returned. Few infants protested separation from either parent when the other parent remained with them. A majority of the infants were more concerned about separation from their mothers, but 25% preferred their fathers and 20% showed no preference for either parent. Later research confirmed, not surprisingly, that infants and toddlers also protested being left by either parent in nursery school settings (Field, Gewirtz, Cohen, Garcia, Greenberg, & Collins, 1984). Somewhat unexpectedly, however, Guatemalan babies who experienced a great deal of interaction with their fathers started to protest separation later (not earlier) than those whose fathers were uninvolved (Lester, Kotelchuck, Spelke, Sellers, & Klein, 1974) and the phase during which protest occurred was briefer when involvement was greater (Kotelchuck, 1976; Spelke Zelazo, Kagan, & Kotelchuck, 1973).

The counterintuitive correlations just described suggest that the intensity of separation protest may not index the intensity of attachment. On the other hand, low paternal involvement in caretaking was associated with reduced interaction and proximity seeking in the laboratory (Spelke et al., 1973), and when paternal involvement increased at home, there was a concomitant increase in the amount of father-infant interaction in the laboratory (Zelazo et al., 1977). Measures of separation protest were unaffected. Feldman and Ingham (1975), Lamb (1976b), and Willemsen, Flaherty, Heaton, and Ritchey (1974) all reported no preferences for either parent in different laboratory procedures focused on responses to separation and reunion by American infants. Distress did not discriminate between mothers and fathers in a study by Cohen and Campos (1974) either, but on measures such as the frequency of approach, speed of approach, time in proximity, and use of parents as "secure bases" from which to interact with strangers, 10-, 13-, and 16-month-old infants showed preferences for their mothers over their fathers, as well as clear preferences for fathers over strangers. Likewise, Ban and Lewis (1974) reported that one-year-olds touched, stayed near, and vocalized to mothers more than fathers in 15-minute free-play sessions, whereas no comparable preferences were evident among 2-year-olds. Taken together, then, a number of studies in the 1970s showed that infants formed attachments to both parents, questioning the core theoretical view that infants only formed meaningful relationships with their mothers.

Incredulous, like Schaffer and Kotelchuck, at the widespread assumption that most babies would not form meaningful relationships with other members of their families, I spent a year working in Baltimore with a mildly disapproving Mary Ainsworth before undertaking a series of studies using both a modification of Ainsworth's 'strange situation' laboratory procedure (Ainsworth & Wittig, 1969) as well as naturalistic observations in the home modelled after the methods adopted by Ainsworth in her Baltimore longitudinal study (Ainsworth, Bell, & Stayton, 1972, 1974).

Previous studies had not ascertained exactly how early in their lives infants formed attachments to their fathers, whereas infant-mother relationships were believed to emerge during the crucial period between 6 and 9 months of age (Bowlby, 1969). The lengthy home observations I thus undertook revealed that 7-, 8-, 12-, and 13-month-old infants in traditional Euro-American families showed no preference for either parent over the other on attachment behavior measures (those showing a desire to be near or in contact with the adult) although all showed preferences for the parents over relatively unfamiliar adult visitors (Lamb, 1977c). Similar patterns were evident in a later study of 8- and 16-month-old infants on Israeli kibbutzim (Sagi, Lamb, Shoham, Dvir, & Lewkowicz, 1985). Patterns of separation protest and greeting at home also showed no preferences for either parent in the North American study but the situation changed during the second year of life when many of the infants began to show preferences for their fathers.

By this time, it was clear that babies formed attachments to both parents at the same time, but the existence of preferences for mothers over fathers remained controversial. According to attachment theory (Bowlby, 1969), preferences among attachment figures may not be evident when infants do not need comfort or protection from attachment figures, but infants should focus their attachment behavior more narrowly on primary attachment figures when distressed. My experimental studies showed that, when infants were distressed, they displayed more attachment behaviors, as expected, and that they organized their behavior similarly around whichever parent was present (Lamb, 1976a, 1976c). When both parents were present, however, distressed 12- and 18-month-olds turned to their mothers preferentially (Lamb, 1976a, 1976c), whereas 8- and 21-month-olds showed no comparable preferences (Lamb, 1976b). Especially between 10 and 20 months of age, therefore, mothers appeared to be more reliable sources of comfort and security, even though fathers were more desirable partners for playful interaction at home (Clarke-Stewart, 1978; Lamb, 1977a, 1977c).

In a longitudinal study of less involved and highly involved Swedish fathers and their partners, Lamb, Frodi, Hwang, and Frodi (1983) found that 8- and 16-month-olds showed clear preferences for their mothers on measures of both attachment and affiliative (e.g., smiling and happy vocalizing) behavior, regardless of the fathers' relative involvement in childcare. One reason for this unexpected result may have been that these Swedish fathers were not especially active as playmates; Lamb et al. speculated that playfulness may serve to enhance the salience of fathers, and that in the absence of such cues infants develop clear-cut preferences for their primary caretakers. Frascarolo-Moutinot (1994) later reported that Swiss fathers and mothers were both used as secure bases and sources of security, but only when the fathers were unusually involved in a variety of everyday activities with their infants. By contrast, Swiss infants with traditional (i.e., relatively uninvolved in childcare) fathers clearly obtained more comfort and security, even at home, from their mothers than from their fathers. Increased paternal involvement thus does seem to strengthen infant-father attachment but when mothers assume primary responsibility for childcare, they are likely to be the preferred attachment figures, presumably because the children have had more opportunities to experience their mothers' supportive and responsive care. Most infants, however, clearly have 'enough' interactions with both parents to form attachments to their fathers as well and the conclusion that most fathers developed meaningful relationships with their children quickly became accepted among developmental psychologists.

DO FATHERS AFFECT CHILD DEVELOPMENT?

At the time, formative developmental processes were the principal concern, and thus, having established that infants and young children did form attachment relationships to their fathers, researchers were keen to establish what significance these newly recognized relationships might have. The central theoretical question they asked, therefore, was whether father- child relationships directly affected children's development and adjustment. Those of us who addressed this question initially sought to differentiate between maternal and paternal contributions (to determine whether fathers made unique contributions to children's development) and so conducted descriptive observational accounts of the interactions between young children and their parents. This shift to focus on the quality of interactions between fathers and children further underscored the extent to which the former focus on fathers' status had yielded almost entirely to a focus on fathers' socio-affective relationships with their children.

In the home observation study described earlier, I sought to describe the infants' and toddlers' interactions with both of their parents, finding that, at all ages, children played with their fathers more than with their mothers, enjoyed father-child play more, and played differently with their two parents: more robustly with fathers, more soothingly with mothers (Lamb, 1976a, 1976b, 1977c). Similar observations were made by several other researchers (Belsky, 1979; Clarke-Stewart, 1978; Crawley & Sherrod, 1984; Dickson, Walker, & Fogel, 1997; Power & Parke, 1979; Teti, Bond, & Gibbs, 1988), although rough physical play seemed to become less prominent as children grew older (Crawley & Sherrod, 1984). Both parents encouraged visual exploration, object manipulation, and attention to relations and effects (Power, 1985; Teti et al., 1988).

Differences in the types of playful interaction pursued by mothers and fathers were evident even in the first trimester of their children's lives. When videotaped in face-to-face interaction with their 2- to 25-week-old infants, for example, fathers tended to provide staccato bursts of both physical and social stimulation, whereas mothers tended to be more rhythmic and to make soft, repetitive, imitative sounds (Yogman, 1981). During visits to hospitalized premature infants, mothers were responsive to social cues, whereas fathers were responsive to gross motor cues and were more likely to play and stimulate their infants (Levy-Shiff, Sharir, & Mogilner, 1989; Marton & Minde, 1980).

Fathers and mothers do not simply play differently; play is often an especially salient component of father-infant relationships. According to Kotelchuck's (1976) informants, mothers spent an average of 85 minutes per day feeding their 6- to 21-month-olds, 55 minutes per day cleaning them, and 140 minutes playing with them. The comparable figures for fathers were 15, 9, and 72 minutes. According to parental diaries (Yarrow, MacTurk, Vietze, McCarthy, Klein, & McQuiston, 1984), similarly, the average father spent 6 and 7.3 hours per week playing with his 6- and 12-month-old, respectively (43 and 44% of the time spent alone with the infant) compared with 17.5 and 16.4 hours by the average mother (16 and 19%, respectively, of the time she spent alone with the infant). Clarke-Stewart (1978) and Rendina and Dickerscheid (1976) also suggested that White American fathers were consistently notable for their involvement in play and their lack of involvement in caretaking, and there were similar observations made of middle-income African-American (Hossain, Field, Pickens, & Malphurs, 1997; Hossain & Roopnarine, 1994) and Hispanic-American (Hossain et al., 1997) fathers. Studies of English, French, Swiss, Italian, and Indian fathers also reported that they were more likely than mothers to play with rather than care for infants and toddlers (Best, House, Barnard, & Spicker, 1994; Frascarolo-Moutinot, 1994: Labrell, 1996; McConachie, 1989; Roopnarine, Talukder, Jain, Joshi, & Srivastav, 1992).

Many studies thus revealed that fathers spent proportionately more time than mothers engaged in playing with their children, and that the play itself tended to be more physically stimulating, unpredictable, and arousing than the play favoured by mothers. Could these differences have any psychological significance? Specifically, I wondered whether these distinctive attributes of father-child relationships helped distinguish them behaviorally from mother-child relationships, thereby providing early models of male-and female-typed behavior that facilitated gender identification and sex-role acquisition in early childhood (Lamb, 1977b).

Decades later, this speculation still attracts some scholarly attention (Paquette, 2004) and is consistent with popular lay narratives that emphasize the crucial role of paternal masculinity (e.g., Blankenhorn, 1995) but the hypothesis has not stood up to scrutiny for a number of reasons, including the facts that:

1. While fathers spend greater proportions of their interactions with children engaged in play, children actually spend more time playing with their mothers because they spend more time with them (e.g., Kotelchuck, 1976; Pleck, 1997; Pleck & Masciadrelli, 2004; Yarrow et al., 1984).
2. Although boisterous play is preferred by fathers in some cultures, including the Anglo-American cultures that have been studied most widely, these sex-differentiated patterns are not characteristic of all cultures studied. For example, Taiwanese fathers reported that they rarely played with their children (Sun & Roopnarine, 1996), and fathers on Israeli kibbutzim did not play with their 8- and 16-month-olds more than mothers did (Sagi, Lamb, Shoham, Dvir, & Lewkowicz, 1985). Likewise, German (Best et al., 1994), Swedish (Lamb, Frodi, Hwang, & Frodi, 1983; Frodi, Lamb, Hwang, & Frodi, 1983; Lamb, Frodi, Hwang, & Frodi, 1982), and Aka (hunter gatherer) (Hewlett, 1987) fathers are not notably more playful than mothers.
3. Children raised in cultures where fathers are not characterized by boisterous playfulness still develop normal sex-appropriate gender identities and conventional sex roles.
4. Regardless of the cultures in which they grow up, children raised without co-residents fathers do not have anomalous gender identities or sex roles, as documented by numerous studies conducted over the last 60 years (see review by Lamb, 2002);
5. There is no evidence that variations in paternal playfulness, boisterousness, or masculinity are associated with any aspects of children's adjustment, although children who have good relationships with, and play with, their fathers tend to develop social skills that facilitate interactions and relationships with peers (see Parke, Dennis, Flyr, Morris, Killian, McDowell, & Wild, 2004, for a review).

Indeed, the growing number of studies, many rooted in or inspired by attachment theory (e.g., Ainsworth, Blehar, Waters, & Wall, 1978), established that the quality and security of both the mother- and father-relationship was principally determined by the parents' sensitivity to the children's signals and needs, and that the harmony of child-parent interaction, of which sensitivity appeared to be an integral aspect or component, appeared to be the reliable predictor of positive developmental outcomes (including secure attachment) while unsatisfactory or disharmonious interaction was a reliable predictor of poorer outcomes (including insecure attachment, see reviews by DeWolff & van Ijzendoorn, 1997; Lamb & Lewis, 2010, 2011; Thompson, 2006; van Ijzendoorn & DeWolff, 1997). The empirical evidence thus supported two propositions: that the quality of children's relationships with their fathers indeed affected child development (with several exemplary studies showing that the impact was independent of any maternal influence) and that the important features of paternal behavior—warmth, commitment, sensitivity—were the same as the important features of maternal behavior. Both relationships shaped children's development, in other words, and there was no evidence that the ways in which mothers and fathers affected children's development differed.

The initial studies of this genre focused on infancy and toddlerhood, but an increasing number have focused more recently on the preschool and middle childhood years, during which fathers were expected by those who doubted their importance in earlier years to attain increased significance. Studies of younger and older children necessarily involve different measures of parental behavior, although the concept of authoritative parenting inspired by Baumrind's research in the late 1960s, with its allusions to the importance of both warmth and rational limit setting, captures the commonalities and points of convergence. Regardless of the methods or specific measures employed, however, two consistent themes emerged from this research: relationships with both parents matter and the ways in which they affect children's development are similar rather than different. The sociologically inspired focus on fathers' status in the family had been superseded almost entirely by a focus on social relationships and affective connections.

DIRECT AND INDIRECT INFLUENCES

Between the mid-1970s and the mid-1990s, much of the emphasis was on the direct influences that parents had on their children's development, but in an oft-overlooked chapter, Lewis and Weinraub (1976) reminded developmentalists of the theoretical possibility that indirect effects could be significant as well with, for example, patterns of dyadic interaction (for example, between mothers and children or fathers and children) changing when a third person joined the interaction. A number of experiments at the time provided support for this position (Lamb, 1975, 1976). More profound examples of indirect influence were highlighted by researchers studying the impact of divorce on children's adjustment; they increasingly focused, not on paternal absence as had earlier researchers (e.g., Biller, 1974, 1976) but on the harmful effects of marital conflict (see review by Kelly, 2000), an observation complemented by a particularly productive programme of experimental research by Cummings and his colleagues (see reviews by Cummings, Goeke-Morey, & Raymond, 2004; Cummings, Merrilees, & George, 2010) on the way interaction between the two parents affected children's behavior and adjustment (see Grych, Oxtoby, & Lynn, this volume). Variations in the obverse of marital conflict, marital harmony, were also shown to affect children's behavior, with a couple of studies suggesting that father's behavior was influenced by maternal behavior more than the reverse (Belsky et al., 1984; Lamb & Elster, 1985). Accordingly, by 1990 it was well established and recognized that indirect influences—those emphasized by Bowlby— were indeed extremely important, but as well as, rather than instead of, direct influences.

This changing view of developmental processes was representative of a broader transition within developmental psychology towards more expansive theoretical models, of which the *dynamic contextual model* articulated by Lerner and his colleagues (e.g., Lerner, Lewin-Bizan, & Warren, 2011) was the best example. Building on Bronfenbrenner's (1975, 1979) critique of the narrow approach to development that had taken hold in the 1960s when psychologists vigorously sought to prove that they were 'real scientists,' the more confident theorists approaching the turn of the century were willing to recognize, and increasingly had at their disposal the statistical and methodological tools needed to demonstrate, the complexity of human development and the component processes of socialization. Indeed, the concept of socialization itself fell from favour because it was associated with, and brought back to mind, an outdated theoretical view of development that portrayed the child as a passive recipient of influences from self-consciously socializing adults (see Bell, 1968, for the seminal critique of this proposition). In the emergent alternative view, children were viewed as active participants in the development process whose genetic endowment (including individual differences in temperament and personality) ensured that they affected both their parents and their mutual interactions and whose increasingly sophisticated cognitive resources permitted complex interpretations of meaningful experience, which in turn mediated the effects of those experiences. It is noteworthy that this dynamic contextual view dominated the recent *Handbook of child psychology* (Damon & Lerner, 2006); *Handbook of lifespan developmental psychology* (Lamb & Freund, 2010); and the latest edition of Bornstein and Lamb's (2011) *Developmental science*. For better or worse, it has become the new orthodoxy.

Within the dominant framework or perspective, the influential social network is seen to include not only the whole family (mother, father, siblings, and extended family members) but also participants in other significant contexts that children frequent, including childcare centers and nurseries, the peer group, the community, and, of course, the school. Significantly, furthermore, the former emphasis on the immutable effects of early experiences had given way to a view, initially promoted by gerontological psychologists like Baltes (1987; Baltes, Lindenberger, & Staudinger, 2006; Baltes, Reese, & Lipsitt, 1980), that development continues across the lifespan and is always the joint product of endogenous (biologic and cognitive) and exogenous (especially social) events and processes.

FEMINISM OLD AND NEW

These dramatic changes in the conceptualization of development have been accompanied, though not obviously affected by, major secular changes in societal conceptualizations of men's and women's roles. The first phase of the women's movement in the English-speaking world had emphasized the costs to women of being identified with family responsibilities and with being excluded from significant involvement in professional roles (Friedan, 1963; Greer, 1970; Rich, 1976; Steinem, 1962, 1963). Accordingly, the first wave of feminist-inspired Anglo-American reformers emphasized equality of access via increased opportunities in the workplace. Long before the 1960s, however, Swedish reformers had recognized that substantial equality for women in the workplace was unattainable in the absence of significant changes in the conceptualization of men's roles both at home and in the workplace (Dahlström, 1962). Starting in Scandinavia, and gradually extending to North America, therefore, there emerged the notion of "the new father," one whose role included direct childcare, a supportive relationship with his partner, and co-responsibility for breadwinning (Lamb & Levine, 1983; Levine, 1976; Russell, 1983). This prompted a wave of concern on the part of researchers and social reformers to document the presumed positive effects of increased paternal involvement. The fact that increased involvement seemed to have positive effects when the fathers' behavior was consistent with the ideology and motivations of both the mothers and fathers, while tending to have minimal or even negative effects when it was not sought but brought about by involuntary paternal unemployment, only seemed to underscore the impact of marital harmony on children's development (Radin & Russell, 1983; Russell, 1982, 1983, 1986, 1999). Similar attempts to show that increased paternal involvement significantly influenced children's development when the parents had separated, also yielded unexpected findings; led by a much-cited meta-analysis by Amato and Gilbreth (1999), researchers concluded that simply having more contact was not particularly meaningful. More important was the extent to which fathers were actively involved in their children's lives. It was the quality of the father–child relationships—the extent to which the fathers were active, warm, engaged, authoritative parents—that affected their children's well-being. Such findings, of course, were consistent with the growing body of evidence regarding the positive effects on child development of warm relationships with authoritative mothers and fathers who had mutually respectful and harmonious relationships with one another (Lamb & Lewis, 2011).

NEW PATTERNS OF FATHERHOOD

Two demographic trends became increasingly evident between the mid-1980s and 1990s. On the one hand, time-use studies revealed slow but measurable changes in the amounts of time and the types of activities in which fathers and children engaged when they lived together (Pleck & Masciadrelli, 2004) while, on the other hand, increasing rates of divorce created a situation in which growing numbers of children had little or no contact with their fathers (Amato & Sobolewski, 2004). Ironically, both of these demographic changes were associated, albeit differently, with another dramatic social trend, the increasing rates of female and maternal employment. Employment gave women the confidence and self-sufficiency to leave failing and unsatisfying marriages, and it put the heat on men in two-parent families, pushing them to pick up some domestic responsibilities, including childcare, to compensate for the major shift in household economics and provisioning brought about by changing female roles, which changed most husbands from breadwinners to co-breadwinners.

Notwithstanding the emotional appeal and popular resonance of such early cultural reference points as the 1979 film *Kramer versus Kramer* and *The world according to Garp* (Irving, 1978), the actual changes in paternal behavior over the last four decades have been slow, small, and evolutionary rather than revolutionary, as documented in careful reviews by Pleck and his colleagues (Hofferth, Pleck, Goldscheider, Curtin, & Hrapczynski, 2012; Pleck, 1997; Pleck & Masciadrelli, 2004). But they *have* changed, and they are continuing to change. In Western developed countries, the perception of fathers as breadwinners and heads of their families has been supplanted by a view of them as parents sharing responsibility with their partners, not only for emotional and financial support of the family, but also for direct involvement on the care, supervision, and guidance of their children. Such views are articulated in responses to surveys and are evident in multiple descriptions of maternal and paternal behavior.

Nowhere are these altered expectations of mothers and fathers clearer than in the growing literature on parenting arrangements after divorce (e.g., Drodz & Kuehnle, 2012). Although most children predominantly live with their mothers post-divorce, the numbers who seldom see their fathers appear to have decreased dramatically, while the numbers who see them regularly have increased in parallel since the late 1970s (Amato, Meyers, & Emery, 2009; Dunn, 2008; Furstenberg, Morgan & Allison, 1987). Policy-makers in many countries have agonized over ways to keep both parents involved post-separation (Dunn, 2008; Fabricius, Braver, Diaz, & Velez, 2010; Parkinson, 2010).

CONCLUSION

From our contemporary vantage point in the second decade of the twenty-first century, it is clear that the concepts of fatherhood and father–child relationships have changed substantially over the last century, and that there is a remarkable contemporary consensus about them. Among social scientists from diverse disciplinary backgrounds, there is universal recognition that fathers substantially affect the well-being of their children, both directly (via their interactions with them) and indirectly (through the impact on significant others in the children's lives). These influences are increasingly seen as potentially positive or negative, with the beneficial effects of warm, sensitive, committed fathers necessarily viewed alongside the harmful effects of uninvolved, rejecting, and violent fathers on their children. Father–child relationships develop early in life, and they continue to shape the adjustment and well-being of both the children and adults concerned over decades, rather than simply over months and years. Within different societies, as within different families, fathers play a variety of roles—as sources of love and care; as guardians, protectors, providers, and teachers; as models of behavior to both emulate and abjure; and as supportive partners to others who have similarly complex roles and responsibilities. Some effects may be as clearly attributable to the specific behaviors as to the effects on family climate. Other behaviors may have sharply different effects in different ideological, religious, or cultural contexts. Maddening as it may seem to those who prefer theoretical simplicity and clarity, fathers do not play a single, significant, universal and unique role in children's lives. Instead, it is clear that they fill several distinct and overlapping roles, with varying degrees of success.

REFERENCES

Ainsworth, M. D. S., Blehar, M. C., Waters, E., & Wall, S. (1978). *Patterns of attachment*. Hillsdale, NJ: Erlbaum.

Ainsworth, M. D. S. (1967). *Infancy in Uganda*. Baltimore: Johns Hopkins University Press.

Ainsworth, M. D. S., Bell, S. M., & Stayton, D. J. (1972). Individual differences in the development of some attachment patterns. *Merrill Palmer Quarterly, 18*, 123–143.

Ainsworth, M. D. S., Bell, S. M., & Stayton, D. J. (1974). Infant-mother attachment and social development: 'Socialization' as a product of reciprocal responsiveness to signals. In M. P. M. Richards (Ed.), *The integration of a child into a social world* (pp. 99–135). Cambridge: Cambridge University Press.

Ainsworth, M. D. S., & Wittig, B. A. (1969). Attachment and exploratory behavior of one-year-olds in a strange situation. In B. M. Foss (Ed.), *Determinants of infant behavior* (Vol. 1, pp. 111–136). London, England: Methuen.

Amato, P. R., & Gilbreth, J. G. (1999). Non-resident fathers and children's well-being: A meta-analysis. *Journal of Marriage & the Family, 61,* 557–573.

Amato, P. R., & Sobolewski, J. M. (2004). The effects of divorce on fathers and children: Nonresidential fathers and stepfathers. In M. Lamb (Ed.), *The role of the father in child development* (4th ed., pp. 341–367). Hoboken, NJ: Wiley.

Amato, P. R., Meyers, C. E., & Emery, R. E. (2009). Changes in nonresident father contact between 1976 and 2002. *Family Relations, 58,* 41–53.

Baltes, P. B. (1987). Theoretical propositions of life-span developmental psychology: On the dynamics between growth and decline. *Developmental Psychology, 23,* 611–626.

Baltes, P. B., Lindenberger, U., & Staudinger, U. M. (2006). Life-span theory in developmental psychology. In R. M. Lerner (Ed.), *Handbook of child psychology, Vol. I Theoretical models of human development* (6th ed., pp. 569–664). Hoboken, NJ: Wiley.

Baltes, P. B., Reese, H. W., & Lipsitt, L. P. (1980). Life-span developmental psychology. *Annual Review of Psychology, 31,* 65–110.

Ban, P., & Lewis, M. (1974). Mothers and fathers, girls and boys: Attachment behavior in the one-year-old. *Merrill-Palmer Quarterly, 20,* 195–204.

Bell, R. Q. (1968). A reinterpretation of the direction of effects in studies of socialization. *Psychological Review, 75,* 81–95.

Belsky, J. (1979). Mother–father–infant interaction: A naturalistic observational study. *Developmental Psychology, 15,* 601–607.

Belsky, J., Gilstrap, B., & Rovine, M. (1984). The Pennsylvania Infant and Family Development Project III: Stability and change in mother-infant and father-infant interaction in a family setting at one, three, and nine months. *Child Development, 55,* 692–705.

Best, D. L., House, A. S., Barnard, A. L., & Spicker, B. S. (1994). Parent–child interactions in France, Germany, and Italy: The effects of gender and culture. *Journal of Cross-Cultural Psychology, 25,* 181–193.

Biller, H. B. (1971). *Father, child and sex-role.* Lexington, MA: Heath.

Biller, H. B. (1974). *Paternal deprivation: Family, school, sexuality, and society.* Lexington, MA: Heath.

Biller, H. B. (1976). The father and personality development: Paternal deprivation and sex-role development. In M. Lamb (Ed.), *The role of the father in child development* (1st ed., pp. 89–156). New York: Wiley.

Blankenhorn, D. (1995). *Fatherless America: Confronting our most urgent social problem.* New York: Basic Books.

Bornstein, M. H., & Lamb, M. E. (2011). *Developmental science* (6th ed.). New York: Psychology Press.

Bowlby, J. (1951). *Maternal care and mental health.* Geneva: WHO.

Bowlby, J. (1953). *Child care and the growth of love.* London, England: Penguin.

Bowlby, J. (1969). *Attachment and loss: Vol. 1. Attachment.* New York: Basic Books.

Bronfenbrenner, U. (1975, April). *Social change: The challenge to research and policy.* Paper presented to the Society for Research in Child Development, Denver.

Bronfenbrenner, U. (1979). *The ecology of human development.* Cambridge, MA: Harvard University Press.

Clarke-Stewart, K. A. (1978). And daddy makes three: The father's impact on mother and young child. *Child Development, 49,* 466–478.

Cohen, L. J., & Campos, J. J. (1974). Father, mother, and stranger as elicitors of attachment behaviors in infancy. *Developmental Psychology, 10,* 146–154.

Crawley, S. B., & Sherrod, R. B. (1984). Parent–infant play during the first year of life. *Infant Behavior and Development, 7,* 65–75.

Cummings, E. M., Goeke-Morey, M. C., & Raymond, J. (2004). Fathers in family context: Effects of marital quality and marital conflict. In M. E. Lamb (Ed.), *The role of the father in child development* (4th ed., pp. 196–221). Chichester, UK/Hoboken, NJ: Wiley.

Cummings, E. M., Merrilees, C. E., George, M. W. (2010). Fathers, marriages, and families: Revisiting and updating the framework for fathering in family context. In M. E. Lamb (Ed.), *The role of father in child development* (5th ed., pp. 154–176). Hoboken, NJ: Wiley.

Dahlström, E. (Ed.) (1962). *Kvinnors liv och arbete* [Women's lives and work]. Stockholm: Studieforbundet Näringsliv och Samhälle.

Damon, W. & Lerner, R. M. (Eds.) (2006). *Handbook of child psychology* (6th ed., 4 Vols). Hoboken, NJ: Wiley.

DeWolff, M. S., & Van Ijzendoorn, M. H. (1997). Sensitivity and attachment: A meta-analysis on parental antecedents of infant attachment. *Child Development, 68*, 571–591.

Dickson, K. L., Walker, H., & Fogel, A. (1997). The relationship between smile type and play type during parent–infant play. *Developmental Psychology, 33*, 925–933.

Drodz, L., & Kuehnle, K. (Eds.) (2012). *Parenting plan evaluations: Applied research for the family court.* New York: Oxford University Press.

Dunn, J. (2008). *Family relationships, children's perspectives.* London, England: One Plus One.

Fabricius, W. V., Braver, S. L., Diaz, P. and Velez, C. E. (2010). Custody and parenting time: Links to family relationships and well-being after divorce. In M. E. Lamb (Ed.) *The Role of the Father in Child Development* (5th ed., pp. 201–240). Hoboken, NJ: Wiley.

Feldman, S. S., & Ingham, M. E. (1975). Attachment behavior: A validation study in two age groups. *Child Development, 46*, 319–330.

Field, T., Gewirtz, J. L., Cohen, D., Garcia, R., Greenberg, R., & Collins, K. (1984). Leave-takings and reunions of infants, toddlers, preschoolers, and their parents. *Child Development, 55*, 628–635.

Frascarolo-Moutinot, F. (1994). Engagement paternal quotidien et relations parents–enfant [Daily paternal involvement and parent–child relationships]. Unpublished doctoral dissertation, Universite de Geneve, Geneve, Switzerland.

Friedan, B. (1963). *The feminine mystique.* New York: Norton.

Friedman, H. S., & Martin, L. R. (2011). *The longevity project.* London, England: Hay House.

Frodi, A. M., Lamb, M. E., Hwang, C. P., & Frodi, M. (1983). Father–mother–infant interaction in traditional and nontraditional Swedish families: A longitudinal study. *Alternative Lifestyles, 5*, 142–163.

Furstenberg, F. F., Morgan, S. P., & Allison, P. D. (1987). Paternal participation and children's well-being after marital dissolution. *American Sociological Review, 52*, 695–701.

Greer, G. (1970). *The female eunuch.* New York: McGraw Hill.

Grotberg, E. (1976). *Two hundred years of children.* Washington, DC: US Department of Health, Education, and Welfare.

Hewlett, B. S. (1987). Intimate fathers: Patterns of paternal holding among Aka pygmies. In M. E. Lamb (Ed.), *The father's role: Cross-cultural perspectives* (pp. 295–330). Hillsdale, NJ: Erlbaum.

Hofferth, S. L., Pleck, J. H., Goldscheider, F., Curtin, S., & Hrapczynski, K. (2012). Changing family structure and men's motivation for parenthood and parenting in the United States. In C. S. Tamis-LeMonda & N. Cabrera (Eds.), *Handbook of father involvement* (2nd ed.). New York: Psychology Press.

Hossain, Z., Field, T., Pickens, J., Malphurs, J., & Del Valle, C. (1997). Fathers' caregiving in low-income African-American and Hispanic American families. *Early Development and Parenting, 6*, 73–82.

Hossain, Z., & Roopnarine, J. L. (1994). African-American fathers' involvement with infants: Relationship to their functional style, support, education, and income. *Infant Behavior and Development, 17*, 175–184.

Irving, J. (1978). *The world according to Garp.* New York: Weidenfeld & Nicolson.

Kelly, J. B. (2000). Children's adjustment in conflicted marriage and divorce: A decade review of research. *Journal of the America Academy of Child and Adolescent Psychiatry, 39*, 963–973.

Kotelchuck, M. (1972). *The nature of the child's tie to his father.* Unpublished doctoral dissertation, Harvard University.

Kotelchuck, M. (1976). The infant's relationship to the father: Experimental evidence. In M. E. Lamb (Ed.), *The role of the father in child development* (pp. 329–344). New York: Wiley.

Labrell, F. (1996). Paternal play with toddlers: Recreation and creation. *European Journal of Psychology of Education, 11*, 43–54.

Lamb, M. E. (1975). Fathers: Forgotten contributors to child development. *Human Development, 18*, 245–266.

Lamb, M. E. (1976a). Effects of stress and cohort on mother- and father–infant interaction. *Developmental Psychology, 12*, 435–443.

Lamb, M. E. (1976b). Interactions between eight-month-old children and their fathers and mothers. In M. E. Lamb (Ed.), *The role of the father in child development* (pp. 307–327). New York: Wiley.

Lamb, M. E. (1976c). Twelve-month-olds and their parents: Interaction in a laboratory playroom. *Developmental Psychology, 12*, 237–244.

Lamb, M. E. (1977a). The development of mother–infant and father–infant attachments in the second year of life. *Developmental Psychology, 13*, 637–648.

Lamb, M. E. (1977b). The development of parental preferences in the first two years of life. *Sex Roles, 3*, 495–497.

Lamb, M. E. (1977c). Father–infant and mother–infant interaction in the first year of life. *Child Development, 48*, 167–181.

Lamb, M. E. (2002). Noncustodial fathers and their children. In C. S. Tamis-LeMonda & N. Cabrera (Eds.), *Handbook of father involvement: Multidisciplinary perspectives* (pp. 169–184). Mahwah, NJ: Erlbaum.

Lamb, M. E., & Elster, A. B. (1985). Adolescent mother–infant–father relationships. *Developmental Psychology, 21*, 768–773.

Lamb, M. E., & Freund, A. (Eds.) (2010). *The handbook of life-span development* (Vol. 2). Hoboken, NJ: Wiley.

Lamb, M. E., Frodi, A. M., Hwang, C. P., & Frodi, M. (1982). Varying degrees of paternal involvement in infant care: Attitudinal and behavioral correlates. In M. E. Lamb (Ed.), *Nontraditional families: Parenting and child development* (pp. 117–137). Hillsdale, NJ: Erlbaum.

Lamb, M. E., Frodi, M., Hwang, C. P., & Frodi, A. M. (1983). Effects of paternal involvement on infant preferences for mothers and fathers. *Child Development, 54*, 450–458.

Lamb, M. E., & Levine, J. A. (1983). The Swedish parental insurance policy: An experiment in social engineering. In M. E. Lamb & A. Sagi (Eds.), *Fatherhood and family policy* (pp. 39–52). Hillsdale, NJ: Erlbaum.

Lamb, M. E., & Lewis, C. (2010). The development and significance of father–child relationships in two-parent families. In M. E. Lamb (Ed.), *The role of the father in child development* (5th ed., pp. 94–153). Chichester, UK/Hoboken, NJ: Wiley.

Lamb, M. E., & Lewis, C. (2011). The role of parent-child relationships in child development. In M. H. Bornstein & M. E. Lamb (Eds.), *Developmental science* (6th ed., pp. 469–518). New York: Psychology Press.

Lerner, R. M., Lewin-Bizan, S., & Warren, A. E. A. (2011). Concepts and theories of human development. In M. H. Bornstein & M. E. Lamb (Eds.), *Developmental science* (6th ed., pp. 3–49). New York: Psychology Press.

Lester, B. M., Kotelchuck, M., Spelke, E., Sellers, M. J., & Klein, R. E. (1974). Separation protest in Guatemalan infants: Cross-cultural and cognitive findings. *Developmental Psychology, 10*, 79–85.

Levine, J. (1976). *Who will raise the children?* Boston, MA: Lippincott.

Levy-Shiff, R., Sharir, H., & Mogilner, M. B. (1989). Mother– and father–preterm infant relationship in the hospital preterm nursery. *Child Development, 60*, 93–102.

Lewis, M., & Weinraub, M. (1976). The father's role in the child's social network. In M. E. Lamb (Ed.), *The role of the father in child development* (pp. 157–184). New York: Wiley.

Lynn, D. B. (1969). *Parental and sex-role identification: A theoretical formulation.* Berkeley, CA: McCutchan.

Lynn, D. B. (1974). *The father: His role in child development.* Monterey, CA: Brooks/Cole.

Marton, P. L., & Minde, K. (1980, April). *Paternal and maternal behavior with premature infants.* Paper presented at the meeting of the American Orthopsychiatric Association, Toronto.

McConachie, H. (1989). Mothers' and fathers' interaction with their young mentally handicapped children. *International Journal of Behavioral Development, 12*, 239–255.

Mussen, P. H. (1961). Some antecedents and consequences of masculine sex-typing in adolescent boys. *Psychological Monographs, 75*.

Mussen P. H., & Distler, L. (1959). Masculinity, identification, and father-son relationships. *Journal of Abnormal and Social Psychology, 59*, 35–356.

Mussen, P. H., & Distler, L. (1960). Child rearing antecedents of masculine identification in kindergarten boys. *Child Development, 31*, 89–100.

Mussen, P. H., & Rutherford, E. (1963). Parent-child relation and parental personality in relation to young children's sex-role preferences. *Child Development, 34*, 589–607.

Paquette, D. (2004). Theorizing the father–child relationship: Mechanisms and developmental outcomes. *Human Development*, *47*, 193–219.

Parke, R. D., Dennis, J., Flyn, M. L., Morris, K. L., Killian, C., McDowell, D. J., & Wild, M. (2004). Fathering and children's peer relationships. In M. E. Lamb (Ed.), *The role of the father in child development* (4th ed., pp. 307–340). Hoboken, NJ: Wiley.

Parkinson, P. (2010). Changing policies regarding separated fathers in Australia. In M. E. Lamb (Ed.), *The role of the father in child development* (5th ed., pp. 578–614). Chichester, UK/Hoboken, NJ: Wiley.

Parsons, T., & Bales, R. F. (1955). *Families, socialization and interaction process*. New York: Free Press.

Pedersen, F. A., & Robson, K. (1969). Father participation in infancy. *American Journal of Orthopsychiatry*, *39*, 466–472.

Pleck, E. (2004). Two dimensions of fatherhood: The good dad-bad dad complex. In M. E. Lamb (Ed.), *The role of the father in child development* (4th ed., pp. 32–57). Chichester, UK/Hoboken, NJ: Wiley.

Pleck, E. H., & Pleck, J. H. (1997). Fatherhood ideals in the United States: Historical dimensions. In M. E. Lamb (Ed.), *The role of the father in child development* (3rd ed.; pp. 33–48, 314–318). Chichester, UK/Hoboken, NJ: Wiley.

Pleck, J. H. (1983). *The myth of masculinity*. Cambridge: MIT Press.

Pleck, J. H. (1997). Paternal involvement: Levels, sources, and consequences. In M. E. Lamb (Ed.), *The role of the father in child development* (3rd ed., pp. 66–103, 325–332). New York: Wiley.

Pleck, J., & Masciadrelli, B. P. (2004). Paternal involvement by U. S. resident fathers: Levels, sources and consequences. In M. E. Lamb (Ed.), *The role of the father in child development* (4th ed., pp. 222–271). Chichester, UK/Hoboken, NJ: Wiley.

Power, T. G. (1985). Mother– and father–infant play: A developmental analysis. *Child Development*, *56*, 1514–1524.

Power, T. G., & Parke, R. D. (1979, March). *Toward a taxonomy of father–infant and mother–infant play patterns*. Paper presented to the Society for Research in Child Development, San Francisco.

Radin, N., & Russell, G. (1983). Increased father participation and child development outcomes. In M. E. Lamb & A. Sagi (Eds.), *Fatherhood and family policy* (pp. 191–218). Hillsdale, NJ: Erlbaum.

Rendina, I., & Dickerscheid, J. D. (1976). Father involvement with first-born infants. *Family Coordinator*, *25*, 373–379.

Rich, A. (1976). *Of woman born*. New York: Virago.

Roopnarine, J. L., Talukder, E., Jain, D., Joshi, P., & Srivastav, P., (1992). Personal well-being, kinship tie, and mother–infant and father–infant interactions in single-wage and dual-wage families in New Delhi, India. *Journal of Marriage and the Family*, *54*, 293–301.

Russell, G. (1982). Shared-caregiving families: An Australian study. In M. E. Lamb (Ed.), *Nontraditional families* (pp. 139–172). Hillsdale, NJ: Erlbaum.

Russell, G. (1983). *The changing role of fathers?* St Lucia: University of Queensland Press.

Russell, G. (1986). Primary caretaking and role sharing fathers. In M. E. Lamb (Ed.), *The father's role: Applied perspectives* (pp. 29–57). New York: Wiley.

Russell, G. (1999). Primary caregiving fathers. In M. E. Lamb (Ed.), *Parenting and child development in nontraditional families* (pp. 57–82). Mahwah, NJ: Erlbaum.

Sagi, A., Lamb, M. E., Shoham, R., Dvir, R., & Lewkowicz, K. S. (1985). Parent–infant interaction in families on Israeli kibbutzim. *International Journal of Behavioral Development*, *8*, 273–284.

Sears, R. R. (1947). Influence of methodological factors of doll play performance. *Child Development*, *18*, 190–197.

Sears, R. R., Maccoby, E. E., & Levin, H. (1957). *Patterns of child rearing*. Evanston, IL: Row Peterson.

Sears, R. R., Pintler, M. H., & Sears, P. S. (1946). The effect of father separation on preschool children's doll play aggression. *Child Development*, *17*, 219–243.

Sears, P. S. (1951). Doll play aggression in normal young children: Influence of sex, age, sibling status, father's absence. *Psychological Monographs*, *65*(6).

Schaffer, H. R., & Emerson, P. E. (1964). *The development of social attachments in infancy*. Monographs of the Society for Research in Child Development, 29.

Spelke, E., Zelazo, P., Kagan, J., & Kotelchuck, M. (1973). Father interaction and separation protest. *Developmental Psychology*, *9*, 83–90.

Steinem, G. (1962). The moral disarmament of Betty Coed. *Esquire 58*(September), 97–103.

Steinem, G. (1963). *The beach book*. New York: Viking.

Sun, L. C., & Roopnarine, J. L. (1996). Mother–infant, father–infant interaction and involvement in childcare and household labor among Taiwanese families. *Infant Behavior and Development*, *19*, 121–129.

Teti, D. M., Bond, L. A., & Gibbs, E. D. (1988). Mothers, fathers, and siblings: A comparison of play styles and their influence upon infant cognitive level. *International Journal of Behavioral Development*, *11*, 415–432.

Thompson, R. A. (2006). Early sociopersonality development. In W. Damon, R. A. Lerner, & N. Eisenberg (Eds.), *Handbook of child development, Vol. 3. Social, emotional, and personality development* (6th ed., pp. 24–98). Hoboken, NJ: Wiley.

Van Ijzendoorn, M. H., & DeWolff, M. S. (1997). In search of the absent father—meta-analyzes of infant–father attachment: A rejoinder to our discussants. *Child Development*, *68*, 604–609.

Willemsen, E., Flaherty, D., Heaton, C., & Ritchey, G. (1974). Attachment behavior of one-year-olds as a function of mother vs father, sex of child, session, and toys. *Genetic Psychology Monographs*, *90*, 305–324.

Wylie, P. (1942). *Generation of vipers*. New York: Farah Strauss.

Yarrow, L. J., MacTurk, R. H., Vietze, P. M., McCarthy, M. E., Klein, R. P., & McQuiston, S. (1984). Developmental course of parental stimulation and its relationship to mastery motivation during infancy. *Developmental Psychology*, *20*, 492–503.

Yogman, M. (1981). Games fathers and mothers play with their infants. *Infant Mental Health Journal*, *2*, 241–248.

Zelazo, P. R., Kotelchuck, M., Barber, L., & David, J. (1977, March). *Fathers and sons: An experimental facilitation of attachment behaviors*. Paper presented at the meeting of the Society for Research in Child Development, New Orleans.

Section II

Dating, Cohabiting, and Marital Relationships

7 The Cohabitation Conundrum

Catherine L. Cohan

The marked increase in premarital cohabitation over the last 50 years in the US is part of a constellation of interrelated changes in family demography along with increased divorce rates, declining rates of marriage, increased age at first marriage, and extramarital childbearing (Bramlett & Mosher, 2002; Kreider, 2005). The children who experienced the surge in divorces among their parents were more likely to cohabit with a romantic partner when they became young adults (Sassler, Cunningham, & Lichter, 2009; Thornton, 1991). As the proportion of unmarried partners living together increased, so has the proportion of children who are born to and live with unmarried partners (Bumpass & Lu, 2000; Kennedy & Bumpass, 2008). In turn, children who live with a cohabiting parent may be more likely to cohabit when they become young adults (Sassler et al., 2009). Thus, in just a few generations, cohabitation has become integral to contemporary romantic relationships.

Attitude changes about cohabitation have followed behavioral changes (Cunningham & Thornton, 2005), and negative appraisals of cohabitation have shifted over time to positive appraisals as cohabitation has become more common (Thornton & Young-DeMarco, 2001). Now that a majority of first marriages are preceded by cohabitation (62%), cohabitation is a normative experience (Kennedy & Bumpass, 2008). It may surprise young adults today that not only was unmarried cohabitation eschewed in the US at one time, but it was even illegal. In 2006, a North Carolina state judge ruled that the law from 1805 forbidding unmarried people from living together was unconstitutional (The Associated Press, 2006). Despite changes in the prevalence of and attitudes toward cohabitation, there has been little change in the social and legal institutionalization of cohabitation in the United States. In contrast to marriage with legal protections and constraints and clear social traditions, there are no parallel norms or cultural scripts for American cohabiting partners to follow. For example, cohabiting individuals do not have good labels for referring to their partners. The terms "spouse" or "boyfriend/girlfriend" do not seem to fit (Manning & Smock, 2005). Because it lacks social norms and legal boundaries, Nock (1995) deemed cohabitation "an incomplete institution." With the exception of child support, cohabiting partners who dissolve their relationship in the US do not have legal rights or responsibilities towards each other (Heimdal & Houseknecht, 2003). In contrast, cohabitors in some other countries have legal rights. For example, Swedish cohabitors have the same child custody rights and joint property rights as married couples. And the Dutch Civil Code (articles 80a–80e) allows cohabitors to opt for a registered partnership or a cohabitation contract, which gives them rights to property, inheritance, and employer benefits.

The robust finding that people are more likely to divorce after living together before marriage compared with people who marry directly has been called "the cohabitation effect." This result seems rather counterintuitive. If people test their compatibility during cohabitation, one would expect that the weak relationships would break up before marriage and the strong ones would make the transition to marriage. If that were the case, cohabiters who transition to marriage should have stronger marriages in terms of stability and adjustment. But the research consistently shows that is not the case. An examination of over 100 studies with American samples spanning 25 years, for this chapter, indicated that not one shows any evidence that marriage preceded by cohabitation is superior in any way to direct entry into marriage. However, public perception does not coincide with the research evidence. A majority (67%) of male and female high school seniors reported that living together is a "good idea" (Thornton & Young-DeMarco, 2001). Similarly, a majority (62%) of young adults ages 20–29 in a representative national sample agreed with the statement "Living together with someone before marriage is a good way to avoid eventual divorce" (Popenoe & Whitehead, 2001). The conundrum of cohabitation is this discrepancy between young adults' positive appraisals of cohabitation and the absence of any evidence in the research literature that cohabitation benefits relationship outcomes.

This chapter will discuss theories that have been used to understand and study cohabitation over the last 25 years and reflect on the rich possibilities for further theory and research. A central theoretical question about cohabitation is whether cohabitation is associated with a higher incidence of divorce and poorer marital functioning because of the selection characteristics of people who cohabit or because of something about the experience of cohabitation. Other theoretical questions about cohabitation include the function and purpose of cohabitation with respect to marriage and the role of commitment at the outset of a cohabiting relationship with respect to later relationship outcomes. Over the same period that cohabitation has become normative in the US, there have been similar trends in other Western countries (Kiernan, 2002). Because variations by country in the social and legal institutionalization of unmarried cohabitation are associated with different personal and relationship outcomes, the European cohabitation research cannot simply be lumped together with cohabitation research on American samples. This chapter will focus primarily on American research. However, the cohabitation research from other countries showing how cohabitation varies by social context is particularly illuminating and will be discussed where relevant. To put the theoretical questions in context, the demography of cohabitation will be presented first.

KEY ISSUES IN COHABITATION

DEMOGRAPHIC TRENDS IN COHABITATION

The short answer to the question of "Who cohabits today?" is a majority of young adults. Cohabitation was fairly uncommon in the Vietnam War era (1965–1974) when it preceded 11% of first marriages. Some 30 years later in the 9/11 era (2002), a majority of first marriages (62%) were preceded by cohabitation (Bumpass & Sweet, 1989; Kennedy & Bumpass, 2008). In the 20 years from 1977 to 1997, the number of cohabiting couples increased almost five-fold from 1.1 million to 4.9 million, which represented 1.5 and 4.8% of US households, respectively (Casper, Cohen, & Simmons, 1999). In the 15 years from 1987 to 2002, the proportion of women who ever cohabited went from 33 to 54% across all ages from 19 to 44, with the highest proportion of women with cohabitation experience in the 30–34 age range (61%). Of unions in 2002 among women ages 19–44, 20% were cohabiting unions, double the rate in 1987 (Kennedy & Bumpass, 2008). Rates of cohabitation are similar for women across race and ethnicity (White non-Hispanic 54%, Black non-Hispanic 57%, Hispanic 52%) and has increased across all education levels (Kennedy & Bumpass, 2008). The length of cohabiting unions is relatively short. After 5 years, nearly half of cohabiting couples have made the transition to marriage (49%), over one-third ended their relationship (37%), and a minority were still cohabiting (14%; Kennedy & Bumpass, 2008).

Trends in cohabitation intersect with trends in age of first marriage. The age at first marriage has increased, and that change is largely accounted for by cohabitation before marriage (Bumpass,

Sweet, & Cherlin, 1991). Cohabiting women who marry typically have a single cohabitation experience and marry the man they are living with. The proportion of women with multiple cohabitation experiences is relatively small (15–20% of cohabitors), and they are disproportionately poor (Lichter & Qian, 2008). Trends in cohabitation also intersect with trends in non-marital childbearing. For the period between 1997 and 2000, one-third of births were to unmarried mothers. However, those mothers were not necessarily unpartnered. Half of the non-marital births were to cohabiting biological parents. In addition to those born into a cohabiting union, some children will live with a cohabiting mother after her marriage dissolves. Current estimates are that half of the children in the US will live with a cohabiting mother for some time before age 16 (Kennedy & Bumpass, 2008).

It is too early to say whether the prevalence of cohabitation will continue to rise or has leveled off. Whereas marriage and divorce rates have been measured fairly systematically for most of the last century, it is only in the last 25 years that demographic trends in cohabitation have been measured with large national samples. Much of the demographic cohabitation research is based on the 1987/1988 National Survey of Families and Households survey and the 1995 and 2002 waves of the National Survey of Family Growth. Each wave of data shows an increase over the previous wave in the proportion of women who ever cohabited, the proportion of first marriages preceded by cohabitation, and the proportion of all unions that are cohabiting unions (Bumpass & Lu, 2000; Bumpass & Sweet, 1989; Kennedy & Bumpass, 2008).

HOW DOES COHABITATION FIT INTO THE PROCESS OF MATE SELECTION?

How cohabitation fits into the cultural script of dating, formal engagement, marriage, and childbearing is different for different cohabitors. Some social commentators have been fearful that cohabitation will replace marriage as a lifelong pair bond without legal sanctification. For its time in the 1970s, the sensational and landmark trial of Marvin *vs.* Marvin in California about property rights for cohabiting partners put a public spotlight on unmarried cohabitation and reinforced the view of cohabitation as a substitute for marriage (Mitchelson, 1980). In addition to being a "substitute for marriage" (high commitment to the relationship, low commitment to the institution of marriage), there are other ways that cohabitation fits into the process of mate selection for different couples: as a "precursor to marriage" (high commitment to the relationship, high commitment to the institution of marriage); as a "trial marriage" (low certainty about the relationship, high commitment to the institution of marriage); or as "coresidential dating" (low certainty about the quality of the relationship, low certainty about the institution of marriage; Casper & Bianchi, 2002).

To evaluate how cohabitation fits into the mate selection process, scholars have examined the extent to which cohabitors resemble married couples or dating couples. Different ways of defining the essential features of romantic relationships have led to somewhat different results in terms of identifying the primary type of American cohabiting couple. First, Casper and Bianchi (2002) focused on marriage intentions, relationship quality, and belief in the institution of marriage and found that the greatest proportion of cohabiting relationships resembled a precursor to marriage (46%), followed by coresidential dating (29%), trial marriage (15%), and a substitute for marriage (10%). Second, to identify the dominant type of cohabiting couple in the US, Heuveline and Timberlake (2004) focused on length of cohabitation, likelihood of marriage, and the presence of children. A single type of cohabitation did not emerge, rather they identified two types. Compared with other industrialized countries, the relatively short duration of cohabitation in their American sample (1.2 years) and the modest proportion ending in marriage (48%) resembled an alternative to being single (i.e., coresidential dating), whereas the presence of children among 20% of the cohabiting couples resembled a stage in the marriage process (i.e., a precursor to marriage). Third, focusing on childbearing and marriage intentions, employment status, educational activities, financial independence, and self-identification, Rindfuss and VandenHeuvel (1990) found that cohabitation in the US more often resembled coresidential dating than a stage in the marriage process or an alternative to marriage. All three studies included the presence or absence of long-term commitment as a way to characterize the type of cohabiting couple. However, variability in other defining features of cohabitation types likely led to somewhat different results. An important substantive conclusion here is that cohabitors are not a homogeneous group and that there is diversity in their purposes for cohabitation. By understanding the heterogeneity among cohabiting couples we can begin to identify which cohabiting couples are at risk for poorer relationship outcomes. As will be discussed below, the research evidence shows that commitment during cohabitation is particularly important for relationship outcomes. For example, there is evidence that whether or not cohabiting individuals have a clear commitment or are making plans for marriage when the cohabitation is initiated bears on the success of a future marriage with the cohabiting partner.

THE "COHABITATION EFFECT": COHABITATION AND MARITAL STABILITY AND ADJUSTMENT

A fundamental research question in the cohabitation literature has been whether the marriages of people who cohabited prior to marriage differ from the marriages of people who did not live together before marriage. The research has been consistent in showing that people who live together before marriage have a higher likelihood of divorce compared with those who marry directly (DeMaris & Rao, 1992; Jose, O'Leary, & Moyer, 2010; Kamp Dush, Cohan, & Amato, 2003; Phillips & Sweeney, 2005; Schoen, 1992; Stanley, Rhoades, Amato, Markman, & Johnson, 2010). This consistency is particularly impressive considering the variation in cohorts, datasets, and analytic methods (Smock, 2000). In addition to greater risk for divorce, premarital cohabitation is associated with poorer marital functioning and well-being on a variety of measures. Compared with those who marry directly, married people who lived together before marriage report lower marital happiness and satisfaction (Brown & Booth, 1996; Kamp Dush et al., 2003; Tach & Halpern-Meekin, 2009); poorer marital conflict resolution and social support behaviors (Cohan & Kleinbaum, 2002); a greater likelihood of marital domestic aggression (Kline et al., 2004); lower commitment to their spouse (Stanley, Whitton, & Markman, 2004); more depressive symptoms, and less life satisfaction (Stafford, Kline, & Rankin, 2004).

THEORETICAL PERSPECTIVES ON THE COHABITATION EFFECT

Theoretical perspectives on the cohabitation effect focus on the demography of cohabitation and on relationship processes.

THE WEEDING HYPOTHESIS

The *weeding hypothesis*, an early perspective on cohabitation, suggests that cohabitation should benefit the search for a marriage partner. More information about a potential spouse should yield a better match (Becker, Landes, & Michael, 1977). To the extent that cohabitation yields more information about a partner, it should result in more successful pairings. Poor matches should break up, or be weeded out, before marriage, whereas the remaining strong matches should be more likely to transition to successful marriages. The research evidence on marital stability following cohabitation does not support the weeding hypothesis.

HYPOTHESES RELATED TO THE POPULATION PREVALENCE OF COHABITATION

Considering that the proportion of young adults who cohabit has increased over time, some researchers have hypothesized that the association between cohabitation and marital outcomes may dissipate with more recent generations as the cohabiting population becomes less "selective" (Schoen, 1992; Teachman, 2003). Several studies have shown no period effects when examining cohabitors from different decades, suggesting that associations between cohabitation and poorer marital outcomes persist even as cohabitation has become more common (Jose et al., 2010; Kamp Dush et al., 2003; Tach & Halpern-Meekin, 2009; Teachman, 2002). An alternative explanation is that the modest time frames examined (e.g., 15 years, Teachman, 2002) may be too short to detect any changes.

Tests of whether the personal or interpersonal effects of cohabitation have changed over time are essentially tests of changes in the prevalence and social acceptance of cohabitation. Two cross-sectional comparative studies of European countries formally examined the degree of prevalence and social acceptance of cohabitation and are particularly illuminating because they examined a range of manifestations of cohabitation across countries. Using data from 16 European countries, Liefbroer and Dourleijn (2006) tested the *diffusion hypothesis* by examining union stability as a function of the prevalence or degree of diffusion of cohabitation in the population. They hypothesized that there will be greater union stability for cohabitors when there are roughly equal proportions of people in the population who cohabit before marriage and who marry directly. By contrast, there will be greater union instability when there is either a small, and therefore select, proportion of people who cohabit or who marry directly. When there are equal proportions of people who cohabit or marry directly, there are fewer selection characteristics that differentiate the groups. When cohabitation is relatively rare in a society, early adopters are likely to be unique (e.g., non-traditional, risk takers). When cohabitation is very common in a society, those who reject the cohabitation norm by marrying directly are also likely to be unique (e.g., highly religious). Liefbroer and Dourleijn (2006) found that union dissolution was higher among cohabitors and married people who previously cohabited compared with people who married directly. But, in support of the diffusion hypothesis, differences in union dissolution rates were smallest when the rates of cohabitation and direct marriage were roughly equal at 50% and were highest when there was either a small proportion of people who cohabited or who married directly.

Greater institutionalization of cohabitation might covary with greater prevalence and acceptance. Soons and Kalmijn (2009) conducted a comparative analysis of 30 European countries to examine whether the subjective well-being of cohabiting and married partners varied according to the degree to which cohabitation has been institutionalized in the society. According to the *institutionalization hypothesis*, greater institutionalization will be associated with fewer differences in well-being between people who are cohabiting or married. They defined institutionalization as "the development and strengthening of social norms that define people's behavior in a social institution" (Soons & Kalmijn, 2009, p. 1143) and quantified institutionalization as the prevalence of cohabitation in the society and survey responses about approval of cohabitation. Soons and Kalmijn hypothesized that less institutionalization of cohabitation would be associated with lower subjective well-being scores presumably because of more disapproval. By contrast, greater institutionalization of cohabitation would be associated with higher well-being presumably because of less uncertainty about how to behave, less selectivity, and more legal rights.

There was wide variation in the prevalence of cohabitation among young adults in Europe ranging from 3% in Ukraine to 53% in Sweden. Approval ratings on a scale of 1–5 ranged from a low of 2.48 in Ukraine to 4.49 in Denmark. After controlling for selection characteristics, there was a smaller gap in subjective well-being between cohabitors and married spouses in countries with greater institutionalization of cohabitation (i.e., higher prevalence and approval of cohabitation), supporting the institutionalization hypothesis. Although selection characteristics and institutionalization accounted for a significant portion of the variance in subjective well-being ratings, they did not eliminate the effect of cohabitation status. Thus, there is some some support for the diffusion and institutionalization hypotheses. The two hypotheses that have received the most attention in attempting to explain the cohabitation effect, the selection hypothesis and the causality hypothesis, will be discussed next in turn.

THE SELECTION HYPOTHESIS

One possible explanation for the cohabitation effect is that sociodemographic selection characteristics account for the association between cohabitation and divorce. Even though people from all walks of life cohabit, cohabitation is selective of people with certain characteristics. People who cohabit are more likely to bring characteristics into a cohabiting relationship that are also risk factors for divorce, such as parental divorce, lower income (Bumpass & Sweet, 1989), younger age, and premarital pregnancy and childbirth (Bennett, Blank, & Bloom, 1988). Recent data show that women with less education are more likely to cohabit, such that 64% of women (ages 19–44) without a high school diploma have ever cohabited compared with 45% of women with a college degree (Kennedy & Bumpass, 2008). In addition to socioeconomic characteristics, people who choose to cohabit also tend to have certain attitudes that may work against long-term relationship maintenance, such as less religiosity (Stanley et al., 2004; Thornton, Axinn, & Hill, 1992), less commitment to marriage, and greater acceptance of divorce (Axinn & Thornton, 1992).

The *selection hypothesis* maintains that it is the personal vulnerabilities and attitudes that covary with both the likelihood of cohabitation and divorce that account for poorer marital outcomes among cohabitors and not the experience of cohabitation itself. According to the selection hypothesis, the association between cohabitation and marital outcomes is spurious, and there should be no significant association between cohabitation and divorce after controlling methodologically or statistically for selection characteristics that are associated with both cohabitation and divorce.

There is some support for the selection hypothesis. However, most studies of cohabitation and marital outcomes control for an array of sociodemographic characteristics (e.g., income, education, parental divorce) and still find a significant effect for cohabitation (*cf.* Lillard, Brien, & White, 1995; Tach & Halpern-Meekin, 2009). That most research cannot "explain away" cohabitation by accounting for sociodemographic characteristics suggests either that researchers have not identified the selection characteristics most relevant to cohabitation and marital adjustment or that the cohabitation effect might have another explanation such as that the experience of cohabitation can cause changes in relationship cognitions or constraints that are associated with poorer relationship outcomes.

An important theoretical development in cohabitation research over the last 10 years has been to identify different types of cohabitors rather than aggregating all cohabitors into a single group, which assumes they are homogeneous. Several recent studies suggest there are particular characteristics that put the marriages of cohabitors at greater risk. First, Tach and Halpern-Meekin (2009) showed that nonmarital births accounted for the association between premarital cohabitation and lower marital happiness, such that women who cohabited and did not have a nonmarital birth had similar marital quality to women who married directly (*cf.* Cohan & Kleinbaum, 2002). Second, there is accumulating evidence that the marriages of people who engage in serial cohabitation (i.e. cohabitation experiences with more than one partner) are significantly more likely to end in divorce than those who cohabit with only one partner (DeMaris & MacDonald, 1993; Jose et al., 2010; Lichter & Qian, 2008; Teachman, 2003). Lichter and Qian (2008) showed that most married women who cohabited before marriage cohabited with their future husbands, but a small proportion (14%) of women lived with two or more partners before marriage. What is particularly interesting is that even after accounting for nonmarital fertility and economic circumstances, women with serial cohabitations were less likely to marry their cohabiting partner and were twice as likely to divorce compared with women who only cohabited with their future husband. Possible explanations for the deleterious relationship consequences of serial cohabitation yet to be investigated, include: poor access to men who are good "marriage material;" higher incidence of chronic mental health or substance use problems; personality characteristics like impulsivity; and negative perceptions of marriage.

Third, there is accumulating evidence that pre-engagement cohabitation is associated with poorer marital adjustment and higher risk of divorce compared with post-engagement cohabitation or direct marriage (Kline et al., 2004; Rhoades, Stanley, & Markman, 2009b; Stanley, Rhoades, Amato, Markman, & Johnson, 2010). This finding is a cornerstone of the *Inertia Theory* of cohabitation to explain the higher rate of divorce among cohabitors compared with people who do not cohabit before marriage and will be discussed in greater detail in the section on Inertia Theory.

To demonstrate that particular personal characteristics predict both entrance into cohabitation and marital disruption, a fundamental aspect of the selection hypothesis is that the selection characteristics must *precede* any cohabitation experience. Some characteristics like parental divorce during childhood will not be altered by the experience of cohabitation. However, some characteristics might be altered by the experience of cohabitation. The timing of the measurement of time-varying characteristics with respect to the start of cohabitation is critical in order to identify them as selection characteristics. For example, some earlier studies of cohabitation experience among married couples showed that lower commitment to the institution of marriage was associated with cohabitation experience (Booth & Johnson, 1988; Thomson & Colella, 1992). Because commitment to the institution of marriage was measured cross-sectionally and after the cohabitation experience, it is not possible to know whether a lower value placed on marriage encouraged some people to cohabit first rather than marry or whether the experience of cohabitation soured people's appraisal of marriage.

Cohan and Kleinbaum (2002) showed that newlywed couples who lived together before marriage exhibited poorer conflict resolution and social support behaviors compared with couples who married directly, net of sociodemographic characteristics associated with cohabitation and marital adjustment, including premarital pregnancy. If cohabitation experience is related to marital communication, then communication may be a mechanism that links cohabitation and marital instability. The problem-solving behavior results indicated that premarital cohabitation was associated with more destructive and divisive communication behaviors during marital problem solving that are less likely to achieve a successful resolution and may, in turn, contribute to marital deterioration over time (Gottman, 1994).

The social support behavior results indicated that spouses who cohabited before marriage were less effective in soliciting support from and providing support to their partners. Over time, ineffective support exchanges may lead to marital conflict about that issue, less cohesion between spouses, or mood problems related to stressful life events. Considering research showing that problem-solving and social support behaviors contribute independently and in concert to marital deterioration (Johnson et al., 2005; Sullivan, Pasch, Johnson, & Bradbury, 2010), poorer communication skills among couples with a cohabitation history may make them vulnerable to marital distress. However, the direction of causality was not clear in this cross-sectional study. Are partners with poorer communication skills more likely to select into cohabiting relationships? Does the experience of being in a cohabiting relationship cause people not to utilize their best communication skills? A longitudinal assessment of communication skills as dating and cohabiting relationships develop could address whether the underlying mechanism is due to selection or causal effects. The prevailing theory that is contrasted with the selection hypothesis, the causality hypothesis, is examined next.

The Causality Hypothesis

Demographic characteristics and attitudes related to relationship formation and stability are associated with cohabitation and marital instability, but they do not consistently account for the cohabitation effect. There is another possible explanation. Factors more proximal to partners' daily transactions may be the mechanisms that link cohabitation to marital instability. There may be unique relationship processes fostered by being in a cohabiting relationship that contribute subsequently to the higher rates of marital distress and instability among cohabitors. Thus, another explanation for the cohabitation effect is that the experience of cohabitation itself causes later marital instability by altering partners' values or cognitions about relationships in a negative direction, increasing the likelihood of being stuck in a weak cohabitating relationship that makes the transition to marriage, lowering spouses' threshold for leaving a marriage, and perhaps affecting communication skills.

Because of the necessity for longitudinal data, particularly assessments before entry into cohabitation, research testing the *causality hypothesis* is difficult to conduct. Thus, there are relatively few studies that provide a strong test of the causality hypothesis; however, support for the causality hypothesis is accruing. Relationship experiences appear to alter attitudes about different types of relationships. Compared with their precohabitation reports, young adults who cohabited reported increased acceptance of divorce and decreased rates of religious participation (Axinn & Thornton, 1992; Thornton et al., 1992). A longer duration of cohabitation was associated with declines over time in interest in marriage and children, and cohabitors whose relationships dissolved reported increased acceptance of divorce (Axinn & Barber, 1997). Similar results were documented by Cunningham and Thornton (2005), who examined longitudinal changes in attitudes toward cohabitation in young adults from age 18 to 31 as a function of relationship transitions in the intervening years. Respondents changed their attitudes in ways that coincided with their actions. People who entered their first cohabitation reported increased positive attitudes toward cohabitation, whereas people who married directly reported less favorable views toward cohabitation. One explanation is that to reduce the cognitive dissonance between their attitudes and behavior (Festinger, 1957), people who are less enthusiastic about cohabitation but engage in cohabitation may change their attitudes to align with their behavior. Consequently, they may degrade their perceptions of marriage and develop more positive perceptions of cohabitation.

McGinnis (2003) asserted that "Cohabitation appears to significantly change the context in which decisions about marriage are made in romantic relationships" (p. 105). She found that cohabiting partners perceived both fewer benefits and fewer costs of marriage compared with partners who were in a steady (non-cohabiting) dating relationship. Another way in which the context of relationship type (cohabiting, married) may affect the relationship is through variation in income sharing and organization. American and Swedish cohabiting couples were more likely than married couples to keep their money separate (Heimdal & Houseknecht, 2003). How couples manage access to the money may have consequences for their union stability. In a sample of Puerto Rican mothers, Oropesa and Landale (2005) also found that cohabiting partners were less likely to pool their incomes in a common pot and were more likely to dissolve their relationship compared with married couples. Furthermore, not pooling their incomes accounted for the higher rate of union dissolution of cohabiting couples compared with married couples. In other words, cohabiting couples who pooled their incomes had similar dissolution rates as married couples who pooled their incomes. Income pooling may have a dual function in relationship dynamics. It may be a consequence of equality, trust, and commitment in the relationship and it may foster even greater feelings of equality, trust, and commitment by signifying interdependence and egalitarianism. With an unclear future, cohabiting couples may be more reluctant to pool finances than married couples. On the one hand, cohabiting partners protect their resources by not pooling their incomes. On the other hand, they may not benefit from the ways that income pooling can strengthen their bond and contribute to relationship maintenance (if that is their goal). It should be noted that although the Oropesa and Landale (2005) study is consistent with the notion that cohabitation establishes a context that pulls for particular relationship dynamics, it was based on cross-sectional data and leaves open the possibility of an alternative explanation that selection characteristics such as trust might covary with both entrance into cohabitation and pooling incomes.

INERTIA THEORY

Inertia theory is a contemporary theory about cohabitation that has its roots in the causal perspective on cohabitation and focuses on two related aspects of cohabitation: (1) how the passage of time and often unintended accumulation of investments in a cohabiting relationship can propel a weak relationship into marriage and (2) how the temporal order of the start of the cohabitation and formal commitment to the relationship are associated with relationship outcomes. "At the start of a coresidential union, a couple decides either to live together—perhaps before marrying—or to marry directly" (Lillard et al., 1995, p. 438). That description of entering a cohabiting relationship reflected the assumption among scholars at the time that couples who embarked upon living together engaged in a deliberate decision-making process.

More recently, researchers have focused specifically on how cohabiting relationships start. More people slide into cohabitation than make an overt and mutual decision to live together (Stanley, Rhoades, & Markman, 2006; Manning & Smock, 2005). *How* people enter a cohabiting relationship may have significant consequences for the outcome of the relationship if the partners later marry. As emerging theory and evidence suggest, the problem with information gathering about the partner during cohabitation is that cohabitation increases the constraints against leaving the relationship (Stanley et al., 2006). This is particularly important in the context of relationships in which partners "slide" into cohabitation.

Qualitative methods have uncovered details about the entrance into cohabitation in ways that survey research has not. The entrance into cohabitation runs the gamut from deliberate to accidental. Manning and Spock's (2005) interviews with 115 young adults showed that half (53%) did not consider entering into cohabitation to be a deliberate process. Instead, entering a cohabiting relationship was often gradual and more of an alternative to living with parents or roommates than as a step toward marriage. As evidence that the start of a cohabiting was often fuzzy, only 10% of the sample could identify the month and year the cohabitation began. Sassler (2004) interviewed 25 cohabiting college students about how they entered into cohabitation. Finances, convenience, and the need for housing were common reasons for cohabitation. Respondents rarely described cohabitation as a trial marriage, which corroborates the survey research on the role of cohabitation in American relationship formation and development (Casper & Bianchi, 2002). Half of the sample reported that their relationship progressed quickly and that they cohabited within 6 months of starting to date. Commitment to the relationship followed after moving in together. A memorable interview that I conducted with a newlywed spouse is consistent with Sassler's finding that entrance into cohabitation can be fast and can precede commitment. When asked about how the relationship began, the wife reported that on the night she met her future husband, who had been living in temporary housing, he stayed the night with her and never left.

Among cohabiting couples who marry, how can the start of their cohabiting relationship affect their future marriage? The qualitative research suggests that many couples begin to live together for convenience or financial reasons early in the relationship before two aspects of relationship development have occurred—the growth of commitment and an understanding of a partner's liabilities (Stanley et al., 2006). For example, a dating couple starts to spend one or two nights together a week at each other's apartments. After spending more and more nights together at their separate apartments, the couple decides to share the boyfriend's apartment after the girlfriend's lease expires or the boyfriend's roommate moves out. Moving in together was not necessarily driven by a mutual decision to advance their commitment to the relationship but to benefit from economies of scale and convenience.

Through the passage of time, mutual investments in the cohabiting relationship develop, often unintentionally. Cohabiting couples may acquire material goods like couches and condos and even more substantial investments like children (Kennedy & Bumpass, 2008). The accumulation of mutual investments is probably less likely to occur for dating couples. These mutual investments formed during cohabitation can propel a shaky cohabitation into marriage. Stanley et al. (2006) have called this situation "relationship inertia" when the investments that develop in a cohabiting relationship are also barriers to leaving the relationship. Despite problems with the relationship, these constraints can encourage some cohabiting couples to marry, couples that might not have married if they dated but did not live together. They hypothesized that "...there is nothing about cohabitation that necessarily increases levels of dedication. Increased constraints may make it more difficult to terminate the relationship, but the partners may or may not feel more dedicated. Thus, some cohabitants could find themselves being less than ideally compatible but likewise find that ending the relationship has become difficult, tipping the scale toward staying together and, for some, marriage" (p. 504).

Consequently, a cohabiting couple with a weak relationship may transition into a weak marriage because the partners may feel pressure from inside and outside the relationship to get married. In the long-run, the constraints that propelled a weak cohabiting relationship into marriage are not strong enough to overcome the weaknesses and sustain it. If the same couple were dating and not living together, they might have broken off the dating relationship before making the transition to a shaky marriage and then divorce (Glenn, 2002; Stanley, Rhoades, & Fincham, 2011).

Rhoades, Stanley, and Markman (2009a) have tested ways in which the experience of cohabitation can cause marital distress. Building on the qualitative work on entrance into cohabitation, they developed a self-report measure to assess reasons for cohabitation and examined how those reasons were associated with relationship functioning. Partners endorsed "spending time together" as a reason for cohabitation most frequently followed by "convenience" and "to test the relationship." Men and women who were cohabiting to spend more time together reported more relationship confidence and dedication. Men and women who were cohabiting to test the relationship endorsed more abandonment anxiety, negative interaction with the partner, more psychological aggression with the partner, and lower relationship adjustment and confidence. Women who reported cohabiting because of convenience endorsed lower religiousness, less relationship confidence and dedication, and more psychological aggression. In sum, cohabitation for the sake of convenience or to test the relationship was indicative of a rockier relationship, whereas cohabitating to spend more time with the partner was indicative of greater commitment to the relationship.

The temporal order of the beginning of a cohabiting relationship and commitment to the partner appears to be a key agent in the marital outcomes of cohabiting couples. Stanley, Rhoades, Markman, and colleagues have conducted three different studies to examine marital outcomes as a function of whether formal commitment to the relationship (i.e., engagement) preceded cohabitation or followed cohabitation. Across two different samples, 43% cohabited before engagement, 16–21% cohabited after engagement, and 36–41% did not cohabit prior to marriage (Kline et al., 2004; Rhoades et al., 2009b). Consistently and after controlling for selection characteristics, couples who cohabited before engagement (before a formal commitment was made) had poorer marital functioning and were more likely to divorce compared with couples who cohabited after engagement or not until marriage. There were few differences in marital outcomes between couples who cohabited after engagement or not until marriage (Kline et al., 2004; Rhoades et al., 2009b; Stanley et al., 2010).

Three studies with similar results provide compelling evidence that the "cohabitation effect" may actually be a "pre-engagement effect" (Stanley et al., 2011) and that sliding into a cohabitation without plans for marriage augurs poorly for marriage (see also Brown & Booth, 1996; Brown, 2000). This finding is particularly important because cohabitation precedes engagement for a significant proportion of cohabiting couples. It appears that relationship problems that were present during cohabitation do not necessarily get resolved before marriage and persist into marriage.

In sum, there is evidence for the selection hypothesis, the causal hypothesis, and inertia theory as explanations for "the cohabitation effect." Some recent evidence suggests that certain selection characteristics such as multiple cohabitation partners or nonmarital childbirth account for poorer outcomes among cohabitors who marry. There is also recent empirical support for the causal hypothesis such that after the experience of cohabitation, attitudes can change in ways that are less supportive of long-term relationship maintenance. Stanley and colleagues' inertia theory also points to how sliding into cohabitation can have the unintended and unanticipated consequence of increasing investments that can lead to marriage, often relationships that started with little information about compatibility or established commitment. They have compelling empirical support that not all marriages of cohabiting couples are vulnerable—just those that cohabit prior to a formal commitment.

Integrating "Competing" Hypotheses

Although the selection and causality hypotheses have been viewed as mutually exclusive, they are not necessarily so and both perspectives are useful (Kamp Dush et al., 2003). The integration of selection and relationship process variables into a mediational model will yield a richer understanding of how cohabitation is associated with marital functioning. For some people, demographic background characteristics may be the proximal cause of entry into cohabitation rather than marriage. Once in a cohabiting relationship, however, processes related to the experience of cohabitation may become the proximal causes of marital dysfunction and instability, and demographic characteristics become more distal influences. Lewis (1997) argued that when trying to understand development, concurrent variables have greater explanatory power than variables from the past. In a meta-analysis of longitudinal studies of marriage, Karney and Bradbury (1995) showed that demographic characteristics and communication skills are related to changes in marital satisfaction and stability over time. However, communication skills, which are more proximal to spouses' daily transactions, account for greater variance in marital outcomes than do demographic factors, which are more distal. Focusing on background characteristics as well as relationship processes will yield a more complete understanding of how cohabitation fits into a broader temporal model of relationship development.

LIMITATIONS OF EXISTING THEORY USE AND DEVELOPING THEORY FOR THE NEXT GENERATION OF COHABITATION RESEARCH

After approximately 25 years, cohabitation research is notable for using rigorous survey methods with large, often longitudinal, samples and for systematically examining key questions such as the demography of cohabitation and the consequences of cohabitation for marriage. Much of the cohabitation literature has been descriptive rather than theoretical. But there are opportunities for developing theory with respect to behavioral and cognitive mechanisms that are unique to cohabiting relationships. Large longitudinal surveys gathered every 5–7 years will continue to be important for documenting changes over time in the demography of cohabitation. However, to make greater substantive progress in understanding cohabitation the next generation of cohabitation research should delve more deeply into relationship dynamics in different types of cohabiting relationships to explain why they have poorer marital outcomes. In other words, how do romantic partners interact with each other under conditions of incongruent or uncertain commitment and different levels of constraint on leaving the relationship? Is relationship satisfaction lower among cohabitors who feel the decision to cohabit is an easily changeable one?

While large-scale survey data have been instrumental in addressing the selection hypothesis of cohabitation, it is less suited to address questions about relationship dynamics. In the last 10 years, several qualitative studies with relatively small samples have focused on reasons for entering a cohabiting relationship and have been instrumental in moving forward theory about relationship dynamics in cohabitation (Manning & Smock, 2005; Sassler, 2004; see also Edin, Kefalas, & Reed, 2004). Next, I outline ways that scholars can inform the development of theory for the next generation of cohabitation research.

COMMITMENT AND RELATIONSHIP BEHAVIOR

Important developments in the next wave of cohabitation research will come from understanding relationship outcomes as a function of the *dyadic, behavioral, and cognitive mechanisms* in cohabiting relationships with different levels of commitment before marriage. If differences in premarital commitment are related to different marital outcomes, how might the different levels of commitment during cohabitation play out in daily interactions in terms of partners' relationship behaviors and cognitions? In other words, what are the behavioral and cognitive mechanisms linking commitment to relationship maintenance behaviors (e.g., income pooling, social support) and subsequently to marital outcomes? Across three samples (one with observed behavior and two with self-reported marital conflict-resolution behavior), Stanley and colleagues showed more negative behavioral interactions among those who cohabited prior to engagement compared with those who cohabited after engagement or not until marriage (Kline et al., 2004; Rhoades et al., 2009b; Stanley et al., 2010). As Stanley and colleagues hypothesized, one possibility is that cohabiting couples with a shaky relationship develop investments in the relationship that propel partners who are not necessarily suited for each other into marriage (relationship inertia).

A second possibility, consistent with the selection hypothesis, is that people with poorer relationship communication skills select into cohabitation prior to formal commitment. This explanation is very challenging to test in terms of the scope and the expense of the study because it requires a longitudinal study of people with assessment before they enter a romantic relationship and then assessment again when they are in a romantic relationship.

A third explanation, which is consistent with the causal hypothesis, is described by the observation that "No one washes a rental car" (Peters & Austin, 1985). People do not exert their best effort or take the greatest responsibility when there is no sense of "ownership." Although originally discussed as a business model, the observation is apt for conceptualizing behavioral mechanisms in cohabiting relationships with an unclear commitment and an uncertain future. When people "slide" into a cohabitation and have no particular expectation that the relationship will last long or turn into marriage, there may be less incentive to devote the significant energy required for maximally constructive conflict resolution and support communication that can foster greater relationship satisfaction, intimacy, and commitment. If so, perhaps less effort exerted on communication during cohabitation prior to engagement carries over into marriage, where poorer communication skills are less likely to resolve conflicts and may generate new conflict and ultimately marital distress and dissolution.

CONSTRAINTS AGAINST LEAVING THE RELATIONSHIP

An important way that cohabitation differs from marriage is the constraints to leaving the relationship. Whereas cohabiting couples may have more constraints than dating couples, they have fewer constraints against leaving the relationship than married couples. The context of the constraints might shape the behaviors of the partners in the relationship. Objectively, both spouses in a marriage are constrained against leaving by their mutual legal commitment. Aside from objective constraints against leaving, spouses possess subjective views about their freedom to leave their marriages or not.

Drawing on social exchange theories (for a review, see Sabatelli & Shehan, 1993), Frye, McNulty, and Karney (2008) examined marital problem-solving behavior as a function of both spouses' perceived constraints against leaving the marriage. They cited previous studies showing that some spouses with high constraints to leaving enacted more adaptive relationship maintenance behaviors whereas other spouses with high constraints (who may feel trapped) behaved more negatively toward their partners. They argued that knowing the perceived constraints of one spouse was not sufficient to explain that spouse's behavior and that dyadic assessment of constraints was necessary. Across three different studies, they found that wives who perceived higher constraints to leaving the marriage behaved less negatively when their husbands perceived lower constraints to leaving the marriage. One interpretation is that wives with higher commitment to the marriage reduced their negative behavior to protect the marriage if they perceived that their husbands could leave. This study provided evidence for the importance of dyadic marital constraints for relationship maintenance behavior.

To understand why marriages preceded by cohabitation have poorer marital outcomes, it will be important to extend this line of inquiry on constraints and relationship behavior. Cohabiting couples do not have the legal constraints that married couples have, and there are often discrepancies between cohabiting partners in their commitment to staying in the relationship for the long term. There are important questions to be examined about cohabitors' perceived constraints to leaving the cohabiting relationship and their relationship maintenance behavior in light of the fact that many cohabiting relationships start without an explicit or clear understanding about the future of the relationship (Kline et al., 2004). Constraints may work differently for cohabiting and married couples. On the one hand, Stanley and colleagues hypothesized that investments (constraints) can propel a weak cohabiting relationship into marriage. On the other hand, Frye et al. (2008) found evidence that wives were less negative when they perceived higher constraints against leaving the marriage than their husbands did.

Relational Uncertainty

A line of communication studies research on the construct of *relational uncertainty* has clear implications for understanding cohabitation and relationship outcomes. Because so many cohabiting relationships begin with ambiguous commitment, a fundamental aspect of those cohabiting relationships is relational uncertainty. Relational uncertainty is defined as "the degree of confidence individuals have in their perceptions of involvement within interpersonal relationships" (Knobloch & Satterlee, 2009, p. 106). Individual, relationship, and situational factors shape relationship uncertainty. In turn, relationship uncertainty tints the cognitive and emotional impact of incoming messages and how responses are communicated. Studies of relational uncertainty have been conducted with dating and married couples, but a literature search revealed no relational uncertainty research with cohabiting couples.

Knobloch and Satterlee (2009) reviewed the relational uncertainty research and showed multiple ways in which greater relational uncertainty impairs communication, such as formulating messages that are less clear, avoiding communication about sensitive topics, attributing more negative intent to the partner's message, more negative appraisals of the partner and relationship, and feeling less confident in one's ability to communicate with their partner. As they point out, couples with the highest levels of relational uncertainty may have the greatest needs for clear, direct, and unbiased communication, but the relational uncertainty may interfere with the success of that communication. Key questions to be addressed in the area of cohabitation are how relational uncertainty differs as a function of the type of cohabiting relationship (e.g., precursor to marriage, coresidential dating, trial marriage) and how variations in relational uncertainty are associated with relationship maintenance, such as conflict resolution, social support behavior, and attributions about the partner and the relationship.

Changeable Decisions and Post-Decision Satisfaction

Many cohabitors prefer cohabitation over marriage because it does not have the legal bonds and entrance into and out of the relationship can be relatively easy (Manning & Smock, 2005). Generally speaking, people prefer decisions that can be changed over decisions that cannot be changed. Interestingly and contrary to their preference for changeable decisions, people are more satisfied with the outcome of a decision when it *cannot* be changed. Further, people underestimate the extent to which the changeability of a decision can affect their satisfaction with the outcome of the decision (Gilbert & Ebert, 2002). When it comes to satisfaction with decisions that cannot be changed, it appears that "buyer's rejoice" is a more common response than "buyer's remorse."

Although tested with consumer decisions, the social psychology of changeable decisions and post-decision satisfaction is relevant to cohabitation and can be integrated with research on motivated partner enhancement and positive illusions in romantic relationships (e.g., Murray, Holmes, Dolderman, & Griffin, 2000; Murray, Holmes, & Griffin, 1996). Some individuals who slide into cohabitation may see their relationship as changeable and prefer it that way. In other words, they can exit the relationship relatively easily if it does not work out. An unintended consequence is that they also may not engage in the cognitive effort to generate satisfaction with a relationship that is viewed as changeable. In contrast, couples who enter a cohabiting relationship after engagement, when the decision is less changeable, may be more satisfied with their partners because they engage in post-decision efforts to bolster their decision by attending to positive aspects of their partners and minimizing the negative aspects. Perceiving that staying with a cohabiting partner is a changeable decision may affect individuals' satisfaction with the partner and their behavior toward the partner.

ATTACHMENT THEORY

Social scientists have focused on cohabitation with respect to relationship outcomes. But relationship outcomes are not the only goals being served with cohabitation. An important area for future research and theoretical development is how cohabiting partners perceive they are benefiting as an individual from cohabitation, such as freedom and flexibility (Edin, 2005; Manning & Smock, 2005; Sassler, 2004). Stanley et al. (2011) posed an interesting hypothesis about how cohabitation might serve personal needs. After several generations of high divorce rates, there may be more young adults with attachment insecurity, i.e., difficulty forming and maintaining close intimate relationships.

Uncertainty and anxiety about relationship stability may contribute to increasing rates of cohabitation because the ambiguity essential to many cohabiting relationships may feel "safer" for those with attachment insecurity. *Attachment theory* has been an active area of close relationships research with respect to the behavior of dating and married couples (e.g., Collins & Feeney, 2004; Hazan & Shaver, 1994). Attachment theory has not been extended yet to cohabitation research except for the work by Rhoades et al. (2009a) showing that partners who were cohabiting in order to test the relationship endorsed higher levels of attachment insecurity. Important questions for future cohabitation research are whether people with attachment insecurity are more likely to enter a cohabiting relationship rather than a dating non-cohabiting relationship or direct marriage or whether the experience of a cohabiting relationship with an uncertain commitment and future causes partners to develop attachment insecurity.

CONCLUSION

Further theoretical development and research on the dynamics of cohabiting relationships and subsequent relationship outcomes are crucial because a significant portion of young adults cohabit and "decisions made during the transition to adulthood have a particularly long-lasting influence on the remainder of the life course because they set individuals on paths that are sometimes difficult to change" (Thornton, Axinn, & Xie, 2007, p. 13). The American research evidence over the last 25 years shows no benefits of cohabitation in terms of the key outcomes that social scientists measure—personal well-being and relationship adjustment, satisfaction, and stability. Contrary to the notion that cohabitation is beneficial to a relationship, it may undermine the success of a future marriage, particularly when it occurs before engagement, involves multiple cohabitation experiences with different partners, or results in the birth of a child prior to marriage.

The next generation of cohabitation researchers needs to do at least two things to elucidate why marriages preceded by cohabitation are more vulnerable. First, they need to delve deeply into the relationship dynamics of cohabiting couples that might be the mechanisms for their relationship outcomes. With the addition of behavior, Rusbult's *investment model*, a variant of *interdependence theory*, might serve as a useful organizing framework because it integrates many of the constructs in the cohabitation research discussed above such as relationship persistence, commitment, relationship satisfaction, and investments (Rusbult, 1983; Rusbult & Van Lange, 2003).

Second, researchers need to test possible mechanisms for relationship outcomes with research methods that have not been used before in the cohabitation literature—experimental designs in the laboratory. The best way to test theories about different relationship mechanisms is with studies that systematically vary the conditions and isolate different mechanisms. For example, we can examine how aspects of relationship maintenance (e.g., liking, cooperation, support, problem solving, forgiveness, devaluing the attractiveness of other potential mates, self-sacrifice) in response to a cooperation or problem-solving task in the laboratory with strangers, roommates, and romantic partners vary under conditions of high and low relational uncertainty, high and low constraints on leaving the relationship, changeable and unchangeable decisions, and high and low expectations for future interactions. Although external validity may be compromised with laboratory experiments, there is a significant advantage in terms of the precision of testing theoretical mechanisms because the high internal validity of experiments allows the researcher to draw conclusions about whether the independent variables cause changes in the dependent variables.

Other advantages of laboratory research are the cost-savings and ability to answer questions in a relatively short amount of time compared with large (and more expensive) surveys and longitudinal designs. It will be fruitful to use all of the methodological tools in the tool box, including survey research, longitudinal designs, qualitative research, and experimental designs, to obtain a more comprehensive understanding of cohabitation and who is at greatest risk for poorer relationship outcomes under which conditions.

REFERENCES

Axinn, W. G., & Barber, J. S. (1997). Non-family living and family formation values in early adulthood. *Journal of Marriage and the Family, 59*, 595–611.

Axinn, W. G., & Thornton, A. (1992). The relationship between cohabitation and divorce: Selectivity or causal influence? *Demography, 29*, 357–374.

Becker, G. S., Landes, E., & Michael, R. T. (1977). An economic analysis of marital instability, *Journal of Political Economy, 85*, 1141–1187.

Bennett, N. G., Blanc, A. K., & Bloom, D. E. (1988). Commitment and the modern union: Assessing the link between premarital cohabitation and subsequent marital stability. *American Sociological Review, 53*, 127–138.

Booth, A., & Johnson, D. (1988). Premarital cohabitation and marital success. *Journal of Family Issues, 9*, 255–272.

Bramlett, M. D., & Mosher, W. D. (2002). Cohabitation, marriage, divorce, and remarriage in the United States. National Center for Health Statistics. *Vital Health Statistics, 23*(22).

Brown, S. L. (2000). Union transitions among cohabitors: The significance of relationship assessments and expectations. *Journal of Marriage and the Family, 62*, 833–846.

Brown, S. L., & Booth, A. (1996). Cohabitation versus marriage: A comparison of relationship quality. *Journal of Marriage and Family, 58*, 668–678.

Bumpass, L., & Lu, H. H. (2000). Trends in cohabitation and implications for children's family contexts in the United States. *Population Studies, 54*, 29–41.

Bumpass, L. L., & Sweet, J. A. (1989). National estimates of cohabitation. *Demography, 26*, 615–625.

Bumpass, L. L., Sweet, J. A., & Cherlin, A. (1991). The role of cohabitation in declining rates of marriage. *Journal of Marriage and the Family, 53*, 913–927.

Casper, L. M., & Bianchi, S. M. (2002). *Continuity and change in the American family.* Thousand Oaks, CA: Sage.

Casper, L. M., Cohen, P. N., & Simmons, T. (1999). How does POSSLQ measure up?: Historical estimates of cohabitation. U. S. Bureau of the Census, *Population Division Working Paper No. 36.*

Cohan, C. L., & Kleinbaum, S. (2002). Toward a greater understanding of the cohabitation effect: Premarital cohabitation and marital communication. *Journal of Marriage and Family, 64*, 180–192.

Collins, N. L., & Feeney, B. C. (2004). Working models of attachment shape perceptions of social support: Evidence from experimental and observational studies. *Journal of Personality and Social Psychology, 87*, 363–383.

Cunningham, M., & Thornton, A. (2005). The influence of union transitions on White adults' attitudes toward cohabitation. *Journal of Marriage and the Family, 67*, 710–720.

DeMaris, A., & MacDonald, W. (1993). Premarital cohabitation and marital instability: A test of the unconventionality hypothesis. *Journal of Marriage and the Family, 55*, 399–407.

DeMaris, A., & Rao, K. V. (1992). Premarital cohabitation and subsequent marital stability in the United States: A reassessment. *Journal of Marriage and the Family, 54*, 178–190.

Edin, K. (2005). *Promises I can keep: Why poor women put motherhood before marriage.* Berkeley, CA: University of California Press.

Edin, K., Kefalas, M. J., & Reed, J. M. (2004). A peek inside the black box: What marriage means for poor unmarried parents. *Journal of Marriage and Family*, *66*, 1007–1014.

Festinger, L. (1957). *A theory of cognitive dissonance*. Evanston, IL: Row and Peterson.

Frye, N. E., McNulty, J. K., & Karney, B. R. (2008). How do constraints on leaving a marriage affect behavior within the marriage? *Journal of Family Psychology*, *22*, 153–161.

Gilbert, D. T., & Ebert, J. E. J. (2002). Decisions and revisions: The affective forecasting of changeable outcomes. *Journal of Personality and Social Psychology*, *82*, 503–514.

Glenn, N. D. (2002). A plea for greater concern about the quality of marital matching. In A. J. Hawkins, L. D. Wardle, & D. O. Coolidge (Eds.), *Revitalizing the institution of marriage for the twenty-first century: An agenda for strengthening marriage* (pp. 45–58). Westport, CT: Praeger.

Gottman, J. M. (1994). *What predicts divorce?: The relationship between marital processes and marital outcomes*. Hillsdale, NJ: Lawrence Erlbaum.

Hazan, C., & Shaver, P. R. (1994). Attachment as an organizational framework for research on close relationships. *Psychological Inquiry*, *5*, 1–22.

Heimdal, K. R., & Houseknecht, S. K. (2003). Cohabiting and married couples' income organization: Approaches in Sweden and the United States. *Journal of Marriage and Family*, *65*, 525–538.

Heuveline, P., & Timberlake, J. M. (2004). The role of cohabitation in family formation: The United States in comparative perspective. *Journal of Marriage and Family*, *66*, 1214–1230.

Johnson, M. D., Cohan, C. L., Davila, J., Lawrence, E., Rogge, R. D., Karney, B. R., Sullivan, K. T., & Bradbury, T. N. (2005). Problem-solving skills and affective expressions as predictors of change in marital satisfaction. *Journal of Consulting and Clinical Psychology*, *73*, 15–27.

Jose, A., O'Leary, K. D., & Moyer, A. (2010). Does premarital cohabitation predict subsequent marital stability and marital quality? A meta-analysis. *Journal of Marriage and Family*, *72*, 105–116.

Kamp Dush, C. M., Cohan, C. L., & Amato, P. R. (2003). The relationship between cohabitation and marital quality and stability: Change across cohorts? *Journal of Marriage and Family*, *65*, 539–549.

Karney, B. R., & Bradbury, T. N. (1995). The longitudinal course of marital quality and stability: A review of theory, method, and research. *Psychological Bulletin*, *118*, 3–34.

Kennedy, S., & Bumpass, L. (2008). Cohabitation and children's living arrangements: New estimates from the United States. *Demographic Research*, *19*, 1663–1692.

Kiernan, K. (2002). Cohabitation in Western Europe: Trends, issues, and implications. In Alan Booth & Ann Crouter (Eds.), *Just living together: Implications of cohabitation on families, children, and social policy* (pp. 3–30). Mahwah, NJ: Lawrence Erlbaum Associates.

Kline, G. H., Stanley, S. M., Markman, H. J., Olmos-Gallo, P. A., St. Peters, M., Whitton, S. W., & Prado, L. M. (2004). Timing is everything: Pre-engagement cohabitation and increased risk for poor marital outcomes. *Journal of Family Psychology*, *18*, 311–318.

Knobloch, L. K., & Satterlee, K. L. (2009). Relational uncertainty: Theory and application. In T. D. Afifi & W. A. Afifi (Eds.), *Uncertainty, information management, and disclosure decisions: Theories and applications* (pp. 106–127). New York: Routledge.

Kreider, R. M. (2005). Number, timing, and duration of marriages and divorces: 2001. *Current Population Reports, P70–97, US Census Bureau*, Washington, DC.

Lewis, M. (1997). *Altering fate: Why the past does not predict the future*. New York: Guilford Press.

Lichter, D. T., & Qian, Z. (2008). Serial cohabitation and the marital life course. *Journal of Marriage and Family*, *70*, 861–878.

Liefbroer, A. C., & Dourleijn, E., (2006). Unmarried cohabitation and union stability: Testing the role of diffusion using data from 16 European countries. *Demography*, *43*, 203–222.

Lillard, L. A., Brien, M. J., & Waite, L. J. (1995). Premarital cohabitation and subsequent marital dissolution: A matter of self-selection? *Demography*, *32*, 437–457.

Manning, W. D., & Smock, P. J. (2005). Measuring and modeling cohabitation: New perspectives from qualitative data. *Journal of Marriage and Family*, *67*, 989–1002.

McGinnis, S. L. (2003). Cohabiting, dating, and perceived costs of marriage: A model of marriage entry. *Journal of Marriage and Family*, *65*, 105–116.

Mitchelson, M. (1980). *Living together*. New York: Simon and Schuster.

Murray, S. L., Holmes, J. G., Dolderman, D., & Griffin, D. W. (2000). What the motivated mind sees: Comparing friends' perspectives to married partners' views of each other. *Journal of Experimental Social Psychology*, *36*, 600–620.

Murray, S. L., Holmes, J. G., & Griffin, D. W. (1996). The benefits of positive illusions: Idealization and the construction of satisfaction in close relationships. *Journal of Personality and Social Psychology, 70,* 79–98.

Nock, S. L. (1995). A comparison of marriages and cohabiting relationships. *Journal of Family Issues, 16,* 53–76.4

Oropesa, R. S., Landale, N. S. (2005). Equal access to income and union dissolution among mainland Puerto Ricans. *Journal of Marriage and Family, 67,* 173–190.

Peters, T. J., & Austin, N. (1985). *A passion for excellence: The leadership difference.* New York: Random House.

Phillips, J. A., & Sweeney, M. M. (2005). Premarital cohabitation amd marital disruption among White, Black, and Mexican American women. *Journal of Marriage and Family, 67,* 296–314.

Popenoe, D., & Whitehead, B. D. (2001). *The state of our unions: The social health of marriage in America.* Piscataway, NJ: The National Marriage Project, Rutgers University.

Rhoades, G. K., Stanley, S. M., & Markman, H. J. (2009a). Couples' reasons for cohabitation: Associations with individual well-being and relationship quality. *Journal of Family Issues, 30,* 233–258.

Rhoades, G. K., Stanley, S. M., & Markman, H. J. (2009b). The pre-engagement cohabitation effect: A replication and extension of previous findings. *Journal of Family Psychology, 23,* 107–111.

Rindfuss, R. R., & VandenHeuvel, A. (1990). Cohabitation: A precursor to marriage or an alternative to being single? *Population and Development Review, 16,* 703–726.

Rusbult, C. E. (1983). A longitudinal test of the investment model: The development (and deterioration) of satisfaction and commitment in heterosexual involvements. *Journal of Personality and Social Psychology, 45,* 101–117.

Rusbult, C. E., & Van Lange, P. A. M. (2003). Interdependence, interaction, and relationships. *Annual Review of Psychology, 54,* 351–375.

Sabatelli, R. M., & Shehan, C. L. (1993). Exchange and resource theories. In P. G. Boss, W. J. Doherty, R. LaRossa, W. R. Schumm, & S. K. Steinmetz (Eds.), *Sourcebook of family theories and methods: A contextual approach* (pp. 385–417). New York: Plenum Press.

Sassler, S. (2004). The process of entering into cohabiting unions. *Journal of Marriage and Family, 66,* 491–505.

Sassler, S., Cunningham, A., & Lichter, D. T. (2009). Intergenerational patterns of union formation and relationship quality. *Journal of Family Issues, 30,* 757–786.

Schoen, R. (1992). First unions and the stability of first marriages. *Journal of Marriage and the Family, 54,* 281–284.

Smock, P. J. (2000). Cohabitation in the United States: An appraisal of research themes, findings, and implications. *Annual Review of Sociology, 26,* 1–20.

Soons, J. P. M., & Kalmijn, M. (2009). Is marriage more than cohabitation? Well-being differences in 30 European countries, *Journal of Marriage and Family, 71,* 1141–1157.

Stafford, L., Kline, S. L., & Rankin, C. (2004). Married individuals, cohabiters, and cohabiters who marry: A longitudinal study of relational and individual well-being. *Journal of Social and Personal Relationships, 21,* 231–248.

Stanley, S. M., Rhoades, G. K., Amato, P. R., Markman, H. J., & Johnson, C. A. (2010). The timing of cohabitation and engagement: Impact on first and second marriages. *Journal of Marriage and Family, 72,* 906–918.

Stanley, S. M., Rhoades, G. K., & Fincham, F. D. (2011). Understanding romantic relationships among emerging adults: The significant roles of cohabitation and ambiguity. In F. D. Fincham & M. Cui (Eds.), *Romantic relationships in emerging adulthood* (pp. 234–251). New York: Cambridge University Press.

Stanley, S. M., Rhoades, G. K., & Markman, H. J. (2006). Sliding versus deciding: Inertia and the premarital cohabitation effect. *Family Relations, 55,* 499–509.

Stanley, S. M., Whitton, S. W., & Markman, H. J. (2004). Maybe I do: Interpersonal commitment and premarital or nonmarital cohabitation. *Journal of Family Issues, 25,* 496–519.

Sullivan, K. T., Pasch, L. A., Johnson, M. D., & Bradbury, T. N. (2010). Social support, problem solving, and the longitudinal course of newlywed marriage. *Journal of Personality and Social Psychology, 98,* 631–644.

Tach, L., & Halpern-Meekin, S. (2009). How does premarital cohabitation affect trajectories of marital quality? *Journal of Marriage and Family, 71,* 298–317.

Teachman, J. D. (2002). Stability across cohorts in divorce risk factors. *Demography, 39,* 331–351.

Teachman, J. D. (2003). Premarital sex, premarital cohabitation, and the risk of subsequent marital dissolution among women. *Journal of Marriage and Family, 65,* 444–455.

The Associated Press (2006, July 20). *Judge Rules N.C. Anti-Cohabitation Law Unconstitutional.*

Thomson, E., & Colella, U. (1992). Cohabitation and marital stability: Quality or commitment? *Journal of Marriage and the Family, 54,* 259–267.

Thornton, A. (1991). Influence of the marital history of parents on the marital and cohabitational experiences of children. *American Journal of Sociology, 96,* 868–894.

Thornton, A., Axinn, W. G., & Hill, D. H. (1992). Reciprocal effects of religiosity, cohabitation, and marriage. *American Journal of Sociology, 98,* 628–651.

Thornton, A., Axinn, W. G., & Xie, Y. (2007). *Marriage and cohabitation.* Chicago: University of Chicago Press.

Thornton, A., & Young-DeMarco, L. (2001). Four decades of trends in attitudes toward family issues in the United States: The 1960s through the 1990s. *Journal of Marriage and Family, 63,* 1009–1037.

8 Same-Sex Relationships

Kendrick A. Rith and Lisa M. Diamond

After decades of invisibility, the unique experiences of lesbian, gay, and bisexual (collectively denoted *sexual-minority*) individuals are finally receiving rigorous scholarly attention. Whereas much early research on this population focused on individual-level dynamics and challenges, such as identity development and mental health, the past several decades have witnessed an explosion of research on their close relationships, especially their romantic ties. These studies have broadened our knowledge of the sexual-minority life course and have advanced our understanding of the processes through which sexual orientation shapes day-to-day interpersonal functioning.

In this chapter, we review some of the dominant theoretical perspectives (both explicit and implicit) that have guided this body of research, highlighting their strengths and limitations, and noting some of the most important emerging advances. First, however, some clarifications are needed. Throughout this chapter we refer to *sexual-minority* individuals and families, as opposed to *gay/lesbian/bisexual* individuals and families. We do this because not all individuals with same-sex romantic relationships identify as lesbian, gay, or bisexual; in fact, the *majority* of such individuals do not (Laumann, Gagnon, Michael, & Michaels, 1994; Mosher, Chandra, & Jones, 2005; Wichstrom & Hegna, 2003). Despite the diversity of these individuals' experiences, one thing they undeniably share is that their same-sex relationships place them squarely outside conventional norms prescribing uniform heterosexuality—hence the term *sexual-minority*, which is now generally used to refer to *any* individual with same-sex attractions or relationships. Whether or not such individuals personally adopt identity labels such as gay, lesbian, or bisexual, their marginalized status in society exposes them to potential stigma, shame, and harassment, while potentially depriving them of social support, public acknowledgment, and social validation for their intimate ties. As we review below, these factors are critically important in understanding potential differences between same-sex and other-sex couples. By using the term *sexual-minority*, we clarify that the most distinctive and important feature of same-sex relationships is not that the participants identify as gay/lesbian/bisexual, but that these ties are pursued in a society that posits only *other-sex* romantic ties as healthy, normative, and desirable.

KEY ISSUES ON SAME-SEX COUPLES

We begin with a brief review of the major topics and findings in research on same-sex couples over the past several decades. This review provides a useful starting point for discussions of theory, largely because it clarifies the *atheoretical* nature of much prior research: Quite simply, the dominant question that has guided research on same-sex romantic relationships has been, "How do they differ from other-sex romantic relationships?" This question has generally been posed as an empirical rather than theoretical one, and conceptual reasons for *expecting* differences have rarely been explicitly articulated. Thankfully, this has changed in recent years (as demonstrated below), yet it is useful to bear in mind that the history of research on same-sex couples has largely been a matter of tallying up their similarities and differences from other-sex couples: Accordingly, we organize our brief review of previous research along these lines.

SIMILARITIES BETWEEN SAME-SEX AND OTHER-SEX COUPLES

Considerable research has found that basic processes of relationship formation, maintenance, and functioning are largely similar between same-sex and other-sex couples. For example, both heterosexuals and sexual minorities report desiring the same qualities in a romantic partner, such as affection, dependability, shared interests, and similar religious beliefs (see review by Peplau & Spalding, 2000). Gender differences in "mate preferences" are also similar—regardless of sexual orientation, men place a higher value on a potential partner's physical attractiveness than do women, whereas women place relatively greater value on personality characteristics (Bailey, Gaulin, Agyei, & Gladue, 1994). Sexual minorities and heterosexuals also meet partners through the same general routes, including work, school, mutual friends, recreational activities, and the internet (Bryant & Demian, 1994; Elze, 2002; Peplau & Beals, 2003). Perhaps the most distinctive feature of relationship formation among sexual-minority populations is a greater tendency to develop romantic relationships with individuals who started out as close same-sex friends (Nardi, 1999; Rose & Zand, 2000). This may simply reflect the fact that in many sexual-minority communities, one's available pool of friends and dating partners is drawn from the same small population.

Few differences have been found between same-sex and other-sex couples' overall relationship satisfaction. For example, a 5-year longitudinal study by Kurdek (1998) found no significant differences between partners in married heterosexual couples and cohabiting same-sex couples in initial levels of relationship satisfaction or change in satisfaction over time. Furthermore, determinants of satisfaction are comparable across same-sex and other-sex couples, such as similarity in background characteristics, values and attitudes (Hall & Greene, 2002; Kurdek & Schnopp-Wyatt, 1997), and overall levels of intimacy, autonomy, fairness, equity, and constructive problem-solving (Kurdek, 1998; Schreurs & Buunk, 1996). As for conflict, same-sex and other-sex couples have been found to argue at similar rates, and about the same topics, such as money, sex, partner criticism, and household tasks (Kurdek, 2006; Metz, Rosser, & Strapko, 1994). Likewise, same-sex couples appear to pursue the same types of strategies for conflict resolution, at similar rates, as do their heterosexual counterparts (e.g., negotiation, compromise, personal attacks, stonewalling) (Kurdek, 1998).

DIFFERENCES BETWEEN SAME-SEX AND OTHER-SEX COUPLES

Nonetheless, a number of salient differences have been found between same-sex and other-sex couples, and these differences provide the most fruitful avenues for theoretically-grounded investigation. Among the most salient differences is relationship stability. Studies have generally found that cohabiting same-sex couples have higher rates of relationship dissolution than do married heterosexual couples, but rates do not differ from those of cohabiting other-sex couples. For example, in a 5-year prospective study, Kurdek (1998) found that 7% of married heterosexual couples broke up, compared with 14% of cohabiting gay couples and 16% of cohabitating lesbian couples. Given that the relationship-related predictors of dissolution are largely similar across same-sex and other-sex couples (i.e., problems with intimacy, equality, and problem-solving strategies), differences in relationship stability appear to be due to differences in barriers to dissolution (Beals, Impett, & Peplau, 2002; Kurdek, 1998), as we address in greater depth below. In short, the institution of marriage provides married heterosexual couples with stronger structural and institutional ties to one another, which accounts for their greater longevity compared with cohabiting other-sex and same-sex couples (Kurdek, 1998; Kurdek & Schmitt, 1986).

Another salient area of difference between same-sex and other-sex couples concerns sexual behavior and exclusivity. Although all long-term couples tend to show a decline in the frequency of sexual behavior over time, this decline appears to be more precipitous in same-sex female couples, and less so among same-sex male couples (reviewed in Peplau, Fingerhut, & Beals, 2004). In explaining this phenomenon, some researchers have emphasized that women (regardless of sexual orientation) are generally socialized to repress or ignore their sexual feelings, and to wait for their partner to initiate sexual activity rather than initiating it on their own (Blumstein & Schwartz, 1983; Nichols, 1988, 1990). Others, however, have noted that perceived differences in sexual frequency may be partly attributable to differences in how sexual behavior is operationalized: Conventional measures that tabulate sexual acts with respect to penetrative activities may fail to adequately capture the full range of sexual expression in female same-sex couples (Frye, 1990; Rothblum, 2000).

As for monogamy, male–male couples consistently report placing less value on sexual exclusivity than do other-sex or female–female couples (Bryant & Demian, 1994). For example, in Blumstein and Schwartz' well-known American Couples Study (1983), only 28% of lesbian partners, 21% of heterosexual wives, and 26% of heterosexual husbands reported engaging in extradyadic sex, compared with 82% of gay men. Notably, extradyadic sexual activity in gay men is often pursued with the full knowledge of both partners, and often in accordance with specified rules governing such behavior (reviewed in Bonello, 2009). However, recent research suggests that norms and expectations regarding monogamy in male–male couples might be undergoing gradual change. A 1994 survey of over 2,500 respondents conducted by the lesbian and gay magazine, *The Advocate* (Lever, 1994), found that even though 48% of gay men reported having extradyadic sex in their relationships, over 70% of the respondents indicated they preferred long-term monogamous relationships over other arrangements.

CURRENT THEORIES OF SAME-SEX RELATIONSHIP FUNCTIONING

SOCIAL STIGMATIZATION AND SEXUAL-MINORITY STRESS

Perhaps the most important defining characteristic of individuals with same-sex attractions and relationships is their marginalized status in contemporary society. Accordingly, one of the most important theories purporting to explain the distinctive dynamics of same-sex relationships is *minority stress theory* (Crocker, Major, & Steele, 1998; Goffman, 1963; Link & Phelan, 2001). This family of theories was originally developed to explain the ramifications of social marginalization on *individual* health and well-being, but as we discuss below, it has increasingly been used to explain *relationship* dynamics and processes. Minority stress theory maintains that the chronic experience, expectation, and/or perception of social stigmatization, prejudice, and discrimination (whether on the basis of sexuality, ethnicity, socioeconomic status, gender, religion, etc.) create a state of chronic stress among socially marginalized individuals that takes a long-term toll on their mental and physical health (Allison, 1998; Clark, Anderson, Clark & Williams, 1999; Link & Phelan, 2001; Meyer, 1995; Mirowsky & Ross, 1989).

Theories of minority stress share a number of key assumptions. First, minority stress is *unique*, such that marginalized individuals experience this form of stress *in addition* to the general stressors of everyday life, thereby increasing their overall stress exposure and hence the amount of energy and resources that they must expend in order to adapt on a day-to-day basis. Second, minority stress is *chronic*, given that it results from relatively stable sociocultural conditions. As a result, socially marginalized individuals face *prolonged* exposure to stress, with few opportunities for recovery. Third, minority stress is *socially based*, originating in social and cultural institutions, norms, and processes that are highly specific to the individual's particular social context, and also beyond his/her direct control.

In 2003, Meyer published an influential article extending minority stress theory to *sexual* minorities, arguing that anti-homosexual stigma played a unique and important role in shaping the health and well-being of individuals with same-sex attractions and relationships. His formulation of sexual-minority stress distinguished between *distal* and *proximal* stressors: Distal stressors include relatively objective forms of marginalization and discrimination, such as straightforward harassment and victimization. In contrast, proximal stressors include those that are more subjective, and depend more heavily on the individual's perceptions and appraisals of the experience (e.g., if a sexual-minority individual does not receive a promotion, it may be difficult to objectively discern whether this was attributable to his/her sexual-minority status). According to Meyer, *both* proximal and distal stressors take a toll on the well-being of sexual-minority individuals. Meyer also posited a number of stress processes that are specifically relevant to sexual minorities: (1) *expectation of rejection*, such that sexual-minority individuals become hypervigilant to cues of rejection in their interactions with others, due to a chronic expectation that their stigmatized sexual-minority status makes them undesirable; (2) *concealment*, in which sexual-minority individuals must chronically contend with the strain of hiding their sexual-minority status (and, in particular, their intimate relationships) in order to avoid harm and rejection; and (3) *internalized homophobia*, such that individuals come to adopt (often without their own conscious awareness) negative views and stereotypes about sexual minorities and their relationships, leading them to hold negative self-views and to struggle with chronic shame and negative emotions.

Importantly, Meyer's model acknowledges that not all sexual minorities face the same exposure to these detrimental processes. Rather, individuals' (and couples') vulnerability to sexual-minority stress depends on the way in which their sexual-minority status is integrated into their overall sense of self. Specifically, Meyer argued that the *prominence, valence*, and *level of integration* of one's sexual-minority identity is important for understanding why some sexual-minority individuals and couples suffer more negative repercussions of minority stress than do others. *Prominence* denotes the degree to which one's sexual-minority identity is prioritized over other salient identities (such as ethnic or religious identity). For instance, one woman in a same-sex couple might view her lesbian identity as a critical feature of her self-concept; her partner, however, might base her self-concept primarily on her profession or her ethnicity. Accordingly, the first woman may be exposed to greater levels of minority stress when she perceives that her intimate relationship is not treated with legitimacy or respect by friends, colleagues, or society at large. *Valence* denotes the degree to which a person views a specific aspect of his/her identity positively or negatively. Research has consistently shown that negative self-concepts are a robust predictor of depressive symptomology (Allen, Woolfolk, Gara, & Apter, 1996), which is why many LGBT-affirmative therapeutic approaches emphasize the process of replacing *negative* societal views of same-sex sexuality and relationships with *positive*, affirming views (Coleman, 1981–1982; Loiacano, 1993; Meyer & Dean, 1998; Rotheram-Borus & Fernandez, 1995). *Identity integration* refers to the degree to which one's sexuality is integrated with other facets of one's identity. Many "coming out" models posit the synthesis of an individual's sexual minority identity with other aspects of self-concept as critical for the overall processes of healthy identity development (see Cass, 1979), as this synthesis allows for a complex, differentiated sense of self in which no single feature is a primary site of vulnerability.

Most of the research on minority stress has focused on its health implications for sexual-minority individuals, and has reliably documented associations between sexual minorities' mental and physical health and their exposure to social stigmatization, marginalization, and victimization (Diaz, Ayala, Bein, Jenne, & Marin, 2001; Kimmel & Mahalik, 2005; Meyer, 1995; 2003; Waldo, 1999). Yet increasingly, researchers have extended the minority stress perspective to explain the distinctive dynamics of same-sex couples (Rostosky, Riggle, Gray, & Hatton, 2007). Hence, even though minority stress began as a theory of intrapsychic functioning, it is increasingly being used to understand and explain *interpersonal* processes and cognitions.

Much of this work has focused on the detrimental implications of *internalized homophobia*, the phenomenon by which sexual-minority individuals gradually internalize societal denigration and stigmatization, developing a negative sense of self and a chronic sense of conflict between their same-sex sexuality and their desire for social validation and affirmation (Herek, 2004). Meyer and Dean (1998) described internalized homophobia as the most insidious form of minority stress because even though it originates with *external* social marginalization, the gradual *internalization* of stigma, negativity, and stereotyping makes these stressors impossible to escape. Hence, even in the absence of objective forms of social stigma and rejection, individuals with high levels of internalized homophobia continue to suffer from feelings of illegitimacy and shame, expectations of rejection, and low self-esteem.

Internalized homophobia has been linked to a number of negative mental health outcomes, such as depression, risky sexual behavior, eating disorders, and suicidality (Meyer & Dean, 1998; Meyer, 1995, 2003; Remafedi, French, Story, Resnick, & Blum, 1998; Williamson & Hartley, 1998). Notably, it is also associated with same-sex relationship quality: sexual-minority men with higher levels of internalized homophobia are less likely to participate in romantic relationships (Meyer & Dean, 1998), and their romantic relationships are shorter and more conflict-ridden (Meyer & Dean, 1998; Ross & Rosser, 1996). In addition, sexual-minority individuals with high levels of internalized homophobia report more problems in their *non*-romantic relationships (i.e., ties to friends, family members, and colleagues), suggesting that internalized shame and negativity might impair their interpersonal functioning more generally (Balsam & Szymanski, 2005; Otis, Rostosky, Riggle, & Hamrin, 2006). Investigating the processes by which stigmatization gradually "gets under the skin" to erode individuals' well-being and relationship functioning is a priority for future research on same-sex couples.

One particularly elegant line of research has taken advantage of the "natural experiment" provided by statewide ballot initiatives outlawing same-sex marriage to investigate how sexual-minority individuals and their relationships are affected by living in communities that take active, visible steps to deny legitimacy to their partnerships (Balsam & Szymanski, 2005; Otis, Rostosky, Riggle, & Hamrin, 2006). These studies have found that sexual-minority individuals living in states that passed laws against same-sex marriage experienced significantly higher levels of psychological distress, consistent with minority stress theory (Rostosky, Riggle, Horne, & Miller, 2009) and also heightened fears about the status of their relationships (Rostosky, Riggle, Horne, Denton & Huellemeier, 2010) than partners in same-sex couples in other states. Furthermore, studies have found that sexual-minority stress can "spill over" from one partner to another, potentially magnifying the negative repercussions for the couple as a whole (Kurdek, 2000; Rostosky & Riggle, 2002).

Importantly, there is also evidence that in some couples, the *reverse* can happen, such that well-functioning same-sex relationships can buffer partners from the stress of social stigmatization. For example, Fingerhut (2010) found that the association between internalized homophobia and psychosocial adjustment was attenuated among California same-sex couples who had pursued some form of legal or symbolic recognition for their relationship. Similarly, Riggle, Rostosky, and Horne (2010) found that same-sex couples in legally recognized relationships reported significantly less psychological distress than those in committed—but not legally recognized—relationships. This does not, however, suggest that formal recognition for same-sex relationships would provide a "magic buffer" against the stress of social stigmatization. In their study of same-sex couples who entered into civil unions in Vermont, Todosijevic and colleagues (2005) found that many of these couples continued to struggle with familial rejection of their relationship. Similarly, Eskridge and Spedale (2006) noted that same-sex married couples in Denmark and other Scandinavian countries (which have significantly more accepting attitudes toward same-sex sexuality than does the US) continue to confront daily prejudice and social rejection. Clearly, much work remains to be done in identifying the dynamic, reciprocal linkages between minority stress and couple functioning, and the mechanisms underlying these linkages, yet minority stress theory is clearly one of the most important and generative theoretical approaches to the study of same-sex relationships.

Before leaving minority stress theory, it is important to note that researchers have increasingly begun to investigate the "flip side" of stigma and marginalization—*social support*—as an important moderator of minority stress. Specifically, sexual-minority individuals who have access to friends, family members, and colleagues who specifically support their sexuality *and* who affirm and validate their same-sex relationships appear to be less vulnerable to mental health problems (Grossman, D'Augelli, & Hershberger, 2000; Waller, 2001; Zea, Reisen, & Poppen, 1999) as well as relationship problems and pessimism (Blair & Holmberg, 2008; Lehmiller & Agnew, 2006; Murphy, 1989; Rostosky, Korfhage, Duhigg, Stern, Bennet, & Riggle, 2004). Unfortunately, however, many sexual-minority individuals face difficulties obtaining such support, especially from family members (Kurdek, 2004). Interestingly, in some cases family disapproval of one's same-sex relationships appears to *strengthen* the tie between partners (LaSala, 1998), in what has been called the "Romeo & Juliet effect" (Driscoll, Davis, & Lipetz, 1972), by drawing them together against a common obstacle, forcing them to develop adaptive coping strategies, and prompting them to develop strong "chosen families" of supportive friends (Weston, 1991). Clearly, future research on the push and pull between marginalization and support, the manner in which they are perceived and experienced by sexual-minority individuals and couples, and their diverse effects on couple functioning are likely to remain a critical topic for future research.

GENDER-ROLE THEORY

Another theoretical framework that has guided research on same-sex couples focuses on *gender roles*, and specifically how "combining" men with men and women with women produces relationship dynamics that differ from those of heterosexual couples. Gender differences in interpersonal attitudes, cognitions, and behaviors have long been fruitful topics of relationship research, and same-sex couples provide unique opportunities to examine how broadly gender-related patterns operate. In particular, studying same-sex couples makes it possible to test two implicit models of relationship functioning against one another. The first model presumes that same-sex couples mimic the gender dynamics of heterosexual couples by having one partner adopt "the male role" while the other adopts the "the female role" (i.e., one person does most of the housework, whereas the other earns more money; one person places relatively greater emphasis on emotional than sexual intimacy, whereas the other will show the opposite pattern).

The alternative model is one of "gender magnification." According to this model, sexual-minority individuals maintain the very same gender role to which they have been socialized (just like heterosexuals). Accordingly, male–male couples end up with a "double dose" of male-typical behaviors and female–female couples end up with a "double dose" of female-typical behaviors. Evidence resoundingly supports the latter model, and perhaps most interestingly, it further suggests that there are *advantages* to gender-related similarity in same-sex couples. Specifically, such similarity appears to facilitate smoother day-to-day communication, support, and negotiation (Gottman, Levenson, Swanson et al., 2003; Roisman et al., 2008; Stacey & Biblarz, 2001). Such similarity in day-to-day experiences also seems to facilitate relationship functioning. For example, one study found that lesbian women suffering from PMS (premenstrual syndrome) reported high levels of responsiveness, understanding, open communication, and responsibility-sharing by their female partners. This is notably different from reports of *heterosexual* women, who typically report that their male partners fail to understand, support, or validate their PMS symptoms (Ussher & Perz, 2008).

Although both male–male and female–female couples appear to benefit from gender similarity in day-to-day functioning and communication, female–female couples appear to have an additional advantage due to women's relationally-oriented socialization (Choderow, 1978; Jordan, 1987). Women are encouraged from an early age to seek and prioritize high levels of connectedness and intimacy within their close interpersonal ties (Cross & Madson, 1997). As a result, they tend to surpass men with respect to interpersonal sensitivity, empathy, emotional awareness, and emotional expressivity, especially in their romantic relationships (Barrett, Lane, Sechrest, &

Schwartz, 2000; Guerrero, Jones, & Boburka, 2006; Stevens, Minotte, & Mannon, 2007; Thomas & Fletcher, 2003). Because of this, women are better skilled and more comfortable with "emotion work" in relationships compared with men (Duncombe & Marsden, 1998; Erickson, 2005; Minnotte, Pedersen, Mannon & Kiger, 2010), and more successful in achieving relational "mutuality" (Jordan, 1991). In contrast, men are socialized to emphasize autonomy, independence, and self-reliance, which can interfere with intimacy and expressiveness in romantic relationships (reviewed in Green, Bettinger, & Zacks, 1996).

Consequently, lesbian couples tend to exhibit more emotional connectedness, cohesion, and intimacy than gay male or heterosexual couples (Green et al., 1996; Kurdek, 1998; Zacks, Green, & Marrow, 1988). In addition, they exhibit greater capacity for mutual empathy (Ussher & Perz, 2008), more egalitarianism, as well as more flexibility in shared decision-making (Eldridge & Gilbert, 1990; Green et al., 1996; Matthews, Tartaro, & Hughes, 2003), and greater adaptability in dealing with emotional needs and household tasks (Connolly, 2006; Connolly & Sicola, 2006). Observational research has found that lesbian couples show more effective patterns of conflict resolution characterized by more positive emotional tone and more effective negotiation (Gottman, Levenson, Gross et al., 2003; Metz, Rosser, & Strapko, 1994; Roisman et al., 2008). Interestingly, investigators initially critiqued the heightened connectedness of female-female couples as evidence of problematic "fusion" or "merger" (Burch, 1986; Hill, 1999; Kresten & Bepko, 1980). More recent work suggests that female–female couples manage to *balance* emotional expressiveness and sharing with boundary-setting and autonomy, suggesting successful resolution between the competing demands of individual emotion regulation and dyadic empathy and emotional sensitivity (Ackbar & Senn, 2010; Ussher & Perz, 2008).

Importantly, there is more evidence for interpersonal *strengths* in female–female couples than for interpersonal *deficits* in male-male couples. Initially, researchers expected that because men are socialized to value independence and autonomy over connectedness and intimacy, male–male couples would be characterized by distance and disengagement (Kresten & Bepko, 1980). Yet, this does not appear to be the case. Most studies detect no differences (or trivial differences) between levels of support, intimacy, cohesion, and satisfaction between male–male and male–female couples (Kurdek, 2004, 2006; Means-Christensen, Snyder, & Negy, 2003), and in many cases male–male relationship functioning appears to *surpass* that of male–female couples (Green et al., 1996; Kurdek, 2006).

The one area in which male-male couples *do* appear distinctive is sexual exclusivity: As noted earlier, male–male couples are more likely than either male–female or female–female couples to report engaging in extradyadic sexual activity, usually with the explicit knowledge of their partner (see also Bonello, 2009; Solomon et al., 2004). This is commonly attributed to the fact that men are socialized to separate sex from love more easily than are women, making it possible for two men in a committed relationship to mutually agree that extradyadic sexual activity does not threaten their emotional commitment to one another (reviewed in Bonello, 2009). Such couples explicitly distinguish *emotional* monogamy from *sexual* monogamy (Adam, 2006; LaSala, 2004), and often negotiate guidelines to ensure that extradyadic sex does not lead to romantic attachment (for example, forbidding one another from having extradyadic sex with the same person more than once). A number of studies have compared relationship functioning and satisfaction in sexually monogamous versus non-monogamous male–male couples, and have found no significant differences in satisfaction or stability (reviewed in Bonello, 2009). The exceptions were couples that had difficulty communicating effectively about their respective needs and desires, especially desires to renegotiate the "rules" around their arrangement, and couples in which one partner explicitly violated the rules (Bonello, 2009). Overall, the literature on non-monogamy demonstrates the importance of treating salient differences between same-sex and heterosexual couples *not* as evidence of dysfunction, but instead as potentially adaptive strengths.

THEORIES OF GENDER AND POWER

Another topic of interest with regard to gender roles in same-sex couples concerns power and equality. In heterosexual couples, gender remains the principal indicator of who has greater power (manifested in domains ranging from decision-making, influence strategies, household labor, and problem-solving), and in couples characterized by power inequality, the male partner usually has the upper hand (Gillespie, 1971; Scanzoni, 1982), even in dating couples (Felmlee, 1994; Peplau & Campbell, 1989). In same-sex couples, gender is necessarily less related to power for the obvious reason that both partners are of the same sex (see review by Peplau & Spalding, 2000). Furthermore, same-sex couples have been found to place a higher priority on establishing equity in their relationships than do heterosexual couples, and the majority describes the ideal balance of power in their relationships as "exactly equal" (Peplau & Cochran, 1980). When power imbalances do exist, however, they tend to vary across different domains, rather than showing a consistent pattern. This is perhaps most evident with respect to household responsibilities: Directly contrary to the notion that one partner in a same-sex relationship takes the classically "female" role and one partner takes the "male" role in these domains, research suggests that same-sex couples develop largely idiosyncratic arrangements, allowing their respective interests and desires to shape daily practice (Huston & Schwartz, 2002). Accordingly, it is not uncommon for same-sex partners to mix and match female-typed and male-typed tasks and roles. The end result appears to be that same-sex couples show more equitable distributions of household labor than do heterosexual couples (Kurdek, 1993; Patterson, 1995).

This is not to suggest, of course, that same-sex couples are uniformly successful in avoiding power differentials. Peplau and Cochran (1980) found that although most same-sex couples wanted completely equitable relationships, not all of them were able to achieve this goal. Although figures vary from study to study, over half of male–male couples and approximately 40% of female–female couples report power discrepancies in their relationships (Harry & DeVall, 1978; Peplau & Cochran, 1980; Reilly & Lynch, 1990). Such discrepancies are often linked to income disparities (Caldwell & Peplau, 1984; Harry & DeVall, 1978; Reilly & Lynch, 1990), especially in male–male couples (Blumstein & Schwartz, 1983). Research on influence strategies is also instructive. Historically, research in this area has differentiated between "weak," female-typed strategies (such as withdrawal or the expression of negative emotions) and "strong" male-typed strategies (such as bargaining, bullying, reasoning, or interrupting the other person). However, research comparing heterosexual couples to same-sex couples suggests that gender differences in the use of weak versus strong strategies have more to do with power than with gender (Falbo & Peplau, 1980; Howard, Blumstein, & Schwartz, 1986). Specifically, individuals who *perceive themselves* as more powerful tend to use stronger strategies such as bargaining or bullying, regardless of gender or sexual orientation, whereas individuals who perceive themselves as less powerful tend to use weaker strategies such as withdrawal (Kollock, Blumstein, & Schwartz, 1986). Furthermore, Howard and colleagues (1986) found that for some influence strategies, the gender of one's *partner* proved more important than one's own gender: Specifically, manipulation and supplication (i.e., making pleas and appeals) were most common among individuals with *male* partners, regardless of the individual's gender.

Clearly, research on how each partner's gender—and gender socialization—shapes same-sex relationship dynamics has important implications for understanding such dynamics in *all* couples. Yet future investigations of such topics must be paired with more systematic assessments of individual differences *other than* gender in order to more clearly specify the mechanisms through which gender-related effects operate. For example, how might individual difference dimensions such as locus of control (Kurdek, 2000; Schmitt & Kurdek, 1987), attachment style (Gaines & Henderson, 2002), rejection sensitivity (Downey & Feldman, 1996), and affective states such as anxiety and depression (Kurdek, 1998; Oetjen & Rothblum, 2000; Schmitt & Kurdek, 1987) mediate or moderate the effects of gender composition on couple functioning? Future research along these lines will enable researchers to explain not only differences *among* female–female, male–male, and male–female couples, but to identify and explain differences *within* each relationship type.

THEORIES OF COMMITMENT: INVESTMENTS, REWARDS, AND BARRIERS

Research on the stability of same-sex relationships (relative to married and cohabiting heterosexual couples) has drawn from a variety of theories purporting to predict and explain relationship commitment, most notably Levinger's pioneering work (1965) that viewed commitment—or "cohesiveness"—as a function of three fundamental interpersonal "forces:" *present attractions*, *alternative attractions*, and *barriers*. Present attractions included the psychological and material benefits associated with one's current relationship, whereas alternative attractions included the benefits that could be gained by leaving the relationship (potentially—although not necessarily—for another partner). Barriers include obstacles to leaving the relationship, which include everything from inconvenience to financial hardship to social stigmatization to love. Johnson (1999) similarly emphasized the multifaceted nature of commitment, distinguishing motives such as "love" from motives such as "social disapproval." In his model, however, he used these motives to conceptualize three distinct types of commitment: Personal commitment (maintaining a relationship because one finds it enjoyable and satisfying), moral commitment (maintaining a relationship because of perceived moral or ethical obligations), and structural or "constraint" commitment (maintaining a relationship because it is too costly or too difficult to leave). Although Johnson's tripartite model might at first appear simplistic, he actually perceived each type of commitment as multidimensional and multifaceted. Moral commitment, for example, incorporated not only an individual's potential religious beliefs about the sanctity of marriage vows, but also a sense of ethical obligation to one's partner, especially if the partner was perceived to have made notable sacrifices over the years for the relationship. Structural commitment included concrete barriers to dissolution (e.g., complex or expensive divorce proceedings) as well as *perceived* obstacles (e.g., fears of social ostracization).

Several studies (Beals et al., 2002; Kurdek, 1992, 2000) have successfully applied these theoretical models to same-sex relationships, finding that the basic determinants of relationship stability are the same for same-sex couples as for heterosexual couples: specifically, the combination of *attractors* to the relationship, such as love and satisfaction, with psychological and structural *barriers to dissolution*, such as the lack of desirable alternatives, legal marriage, children, joint property, and so forth. (which is directly consistent with Rusbult's (1983) influential *investment model*). The lack of social-legal recognition for same-sex relationships means that same-sex couples automatically have fewer barriers to relationship dissolution than do married heterosexual couples, and this is consistent with the fact that their breakup rates are higher than those of married couples, but comparable to those of unmarried cohabiting heterosexuals (Kurdek, 1998).

Further evidence of the importance of structural barriers to dissolution comes from a number of recent studies that have directly compared same-sex cohabiting couples in "civil unions" to same-sex cohabiting couples *without* civil unions, and also to the married heterosexual siblings of civil union couples (Solomon, Rothblum, & Balsam, 2004, 2005; Todosijevic, Rothblum, & Solomon, 2005). These couples started out quite similar to each other on overall satisfaction or functioning, yet a 3-year follow-up assessment found that the same-sex couples in civil unions were less likely to have broken up than same-sex couples who had not pursued civil unions (Balsam, Beauchaine, Rothblum, & Solomon, 2008), supporting the notion that barriers to dissolution play a key role in influencing couples' attitudes about, and motivations to deal with, hurdles in their relationships (Kurdek, 1998).

Along the same lines, partners in same-sex couples report that formalizing their relationships makes them feel more "real" (Lannutti, 2007) and enhances their sense of commitment, even if they had already been committed to one another beforehand (Alderson, 2004). Perhaps for this reason, Solomon and colleagues (2005) found that 54% of same-sex couples reported increased love and commitment to one another after having had a civil union. One question that awaits future longitudinal research is whether other methods of legally acknowledging and formalizing same-sex relationships, such as naming one another as insurance beneficiaries and/or legal heirs, purchasing property together, giving one another power of attorney, designating one another as medical proxies, legally taking the same last name, or merging finances (Badgett, 1998; Beals, Impett, & Peplau, 2002; Suter & Oswald, 2003), have the same repercussions for couple functioning, commitment, and stability as more "official" forms of recognition, such as civil unions and domestic partnerships.

LIMITATIONS OF CURRENT THEORETICAL MODELS

Perhaps the greatest limitation of current theory is that it has more often been used to *explain* existing findings than to *drive* research and identify meaningful and testable hypotheses. To some extent, this reflects the fact (noted earlier) that initial research on same-sex couples tended to focus on identifying similarities with and differences from other-sex couples. This line of research can be traced back to the early 1970s, shortly after homosexuality was no longer considered a mental illness in the Diagnostic and Statistical Manual of Mental Disorders. The next several decades saw a surge of "liberal humanistic" research characterized by the underlying assumption that homosexuality is a natural and healthy variation of human sexuality and that gay and lesbian individuals are fundamentally similar to heterosexuals, except for the gender of their sexual/romantic partners (reviewed and critiqued by Kitzinger, 1987). Whereas same-sex relationships had historically been pathologized as inauthentic, exploitative, and destructive (reviewed by Hart & Richardson, 1981), research dating from the 1980s began with the premise of fundamental *isomorphism* between same-sex and other-sex relationships. The primary research task, then, was not to explain "same-sex relationships", as if they were a fundamentally unique type of relationship, but instead to systematically tabulate specific areas of similarity and difference between same-sex and other-sex dyads (e.g., see Kurdek, 1993, 1998, 2000, 2004, 2006).

This presumption of fundamental isomorphism between same-sex and other-sex couples is certainly an improvement over the historical assumption of homosexual pathology, but researchers have increasingly noted that it, too, entails important theoretical shortcomings, most notably the fact that heterosexual couples are implicitly posited as the standard for normal, healthy functioning (Bonello & Cross, 2010; Kitzinger & Coyle, 1995). According to this implicit standard, same-sex couples appear healthy and "normal" when they *resemble* other-sex couples, whereas *differences* between same-sex and other-sex couples are "problems" to be explained. Even when such differences are attributed to factors such as minority stress instead of inherent homosexual pathology, the underlying message is *different means deviant*.

Perhaps the most salient example concerns extradyadic sexual activity. As noted earlier, male–male couples often make explicit arrangements permitting extradyadic sexual activity. On one hand, this might be viewed as an extremely sophisticated and adaptive way to deal with common relationship problems such as jealousy, sexual temptation, discrepancies in sex drive, and the challenges of maintaining long-term commitment in the face of "ups" and "downs" in sexual activity. Yet not a single empirical study of this topic (at least to our knowledge) has considered whether the thoughtful, planful approach to extradyadic sex taken by male–male couples might actually represent a *better and healthier* "norm" for relationship functioning than the traditional sexual monogamy expected within heterosexual marriage. To be clear, we are not suggesting that this is the case, we are simply highlighting that *the question is never posed*. Hence, the "presumed isomorphism" approach that continues to dominate research on same-sex relationships constrains the theories that we develop and test about relationship functioning.

The best solution to this problem may be for researchers to conduct *less* research directly comparing same-sex and other-sex couples, and more research investigating *within-group variation* among same-sex couples. Although extant research on differences between same-sex and other-sex couples has provided an important empirical foundation, the next generation of theoretically-grounded research on same-sex relationship should substantively chart the full range of *variation* in relationship norms and patterns, and should seek to explain the causes and consequences of this variation. This, of course, requires that researchers recruit increasingly diverse and representative samples of same-sex couples. One example of the importance of diversity concerns minority stress: minority stress theory suggests that the cumulative stress exposure of *ethnic-minority* same-sex couples should be substantially greater than that of White same-sex couples, given that ethnic-minority same-sex couples must contend with marginalization on the basis of their sexuality *and* marginalization based on their ethnicity. Minority stress theories would also predict that couples with traditionally conservative religious traditions should suffer compounded effects of minority stress, as well as couples living in isolated geographic regions where they lack social support for their relationship. As of now, such clear-cut, theory-driven predictions have not been tested, largely owing to the difficulty of recruiting diverse samples of same-sex couples. A chronic problem in this area of research is that the construct of interest—social marginalization on the basis of sexual orientation—directly influences the *visibility and accessibility* of the population of interest, and also their willingness to participate in research (especially among those who may face multiple forms of marginalization).

Recall that we began this chapter by noting that the majority of individuals with same-sex attractions and relationships do not openly identify as lesbian/gay/bisexual. Individuals facing extreme levels of minority stress might be the *most* likely to desist from identifying as lesbian/gay/bisexual, making them extremely difficult to sample or study. Hence, researchers interested in conducting rigorous, scientifically meaningful tests of the ramifications of minority stress for same-sex couples' functioning must use creative strategies to capture "hidden" populations of same-sex couples that may face particularly distinctive minority stress experiences. Whereas much previous research recruited participants through newspapers and community centers, future research testing minority stress theories should take advantage of the internet to study individuals who might be actively hiding their same-sex relationships, and who might be facing extremely high levels of day-to-day homophobia and stigmatization. Up until now, this hidden population of "same-sex couples at risk" has gone largely ignored, for straightforward methodological reasons. Yet in order for theory-based research on same-sex couples to thrive and to yield meaningful new insights, we must devote greater attention to sampling, and to ensuring that we recruit as diverse and representative sample of same-sex couples as possible.

Longitudinal research is also critical, given that individuals' exposure to social marginalization (and their capacities to *cope* with such marginalization) undergo notable change over the lifespan. Existing research on same-sex couples is replete with anecdotal accounts of couples who experienced notable changes in the quality of their relationship after moving to geographical regions that were more or less accepting of their relationship; if such changes are, in fact, attributable to changes in exposure to minority stress, then we must conduct *prospective* studies of same-sex couples to rigorously test this possibility. Another reason for the importance of prospective research is the evidence for variability in sexual attraction, behavior, and identity over the lifespan (Diamond, 2008). Contrary to the widespread notion that the typical gay/lesbian individual experiences exclusive attractions for the same-sex, and will do so continuously over the lifespan, a variety of random representative studies indicate that the vast majority of individuals with same-sex attractions also experience other-sex attractions, even if only sporadically, and that they have engaged in *both* same-sex and other-sex relationships (reviewed in Diamond, 2008). Hence, an individual's current participation in a same-sex *or* other-sex relationship is no guarantee that he or she will continue to pursue this type of relationship in the future. Importantly, abrupt changes from same-sex to other-sex relationships (or vice versa) do not signal corresponding changes in sexual orientation; rather, alternating between same-sex and other-sex relationship may simply reflect the fact that more individuals experience sexual attractions to *both* sexes (even those that "lean" strongly in one direction or another) than experience *exclusive* same-sex attractions. We know little about (and there is little theory to help us to predict) whether individuals "translate" patterns of relationship cognition and behavior from same-sex to other-sex relationships and vice versa.

NEW THEORETICAL ADVANCES

As noted earlier, Meyer's (2003) minority stress model was originally derived to explain mental health in sexual-minority *individuals*, and it does not specifically address the potentially unique impact of minority stress on *dyadic* processes relevant to same-sex couples (Butterworth, 2010; Peplau & Fingerhut, 2007). Accordingly, one intriguing direction for future research and theory development involves the integration of Meyer's minority stress framework with existing, well-validated models of how stress exposure influences *couple* functioning, such as Karney and Bradbury's (1995) *vulnerability-stress-adaptation (VSA) model of marriage* (Butterworth, 2012). The VSA model of marriage provides a framework for conceptualizing how relationship satisfaction and stability is influenced by the combined effects of: (1) each partner's *enduring vulnerabilities*, such as personality traits, family history, and education; (2) exposure to *stressful events*, such as financial strain, chronic illness, etc.; and (3) the couple's *adaptive and maladaptive interpersonal processes*, such as social support provision and conflict resolution.

Butterworth (2012) has argued that the VSA model provides a promising framework for understanding how the social marginalization faced by sexual minorities might influence not only their mental well-being, but their *relationship* functioning. It further suggests that some same-sex couples may be more "at risk" for relationship problems than others (e.g., those that face particularly high levels of social marginalization; couples with particularly poor interpersonal strategies for coping with stress and day-to-day conflict; and couples in which one or both partners struggle with enduring vulnerabilities such as anxiety, depression, attachment insecurity). Future research that substantively *integrates* insights from Meyer's model with existing theoretical models of stress exposure in heterosexual couples is a critical direction for future scholarship.

Another key direction for future theory development concerns questions of *mechanism*, as noted by Meyer himself (2003). Whereas Meyer's original minority stress model posited that stress serves as the key mediator between one's minority status and his/her mental health outcomes (i.e., minority status → stress → psychopathology), Hatzenbuehler (2009) recently proposed an alternative formulation, based in transactional definitions of stress (Monroe, 2008), which grants a much larger role to sexual-minority individuals' *responses* to stress. In Hatzenbuehler's model, sexual-minorities' chronic exposure to social stress may overburden their coping and emotion regulation capacities, in turn impairing a range of social, interpersonal, and cognitive processes. These deficits may in turn confer elevated risk for pathology. Hence, whereas Meyer's model focused on the pathway from sexual-minority status to mental health, positing stress exposure as the key mediator, Hatzenbuehler's model focuses on the pathway from *stress* to mental health, positing impairments in social–interpersonal–cognitive processes as the mediator. Hence, Hatzenbuehler's model places significantly greater emphasis than did Meyer's original model on sexual-minority individuals' *responses* to chronic stress, thereby granting a greater role for psychological than social factors in predicting *which* sexual-minority individuals may face risks for mental health challenges. Although this model (like minority stress models more generally) focuses on individual well-being rather than couple functioning, it also holds tremendous promise for understanding links between minority stress exposure and relationship satisfaction and stability in same-sex couples. In particular, Hatzenbuehler's emphasis on variability in sexual-minority individuals' responses to stress may help to explain why two members of a same-sex couple, with relatively comparable levels of exposure to minority stress, may end up showing substantially different ramifications at the level of interpersonal behavior and mental health.

Finally, one promising recent advance involves reconceptualizing appropriate comparison groups for same-sex couples, when attempting to investigate specific effects of social marginalization. Historically, researchers have compared same-sex couples to cohabiting heterosexual couples with similar demographic characteristics. Yet, Rothblum and her colleagues (Rothblum & Factor, 2001; Solomon, Rothblum, & Balsam, 2004) have pioneered the approach of comparing sexual-minority individuals to their heterosexual *siblings* in order to identify specific effects of sexual-minority status on psychological and social outcomes. The advantage of using siblings as a comparison group is that they have similar demographic backgrounds, religious backgrounds, family rearing environments, personalities, and even genetic histories. This allows researchers to rule out numerous relevant confounds when interpreting differences between sexual-minority and heterosexual individuals, and identifies a range of fascinating questions regarding the interpretation of both similarities and differences.

Although this approach has largely been employed as a methodological strategy for improving the quality of empirical research on sexual-minority individuals and their relationships, we think it opens up promising *theoretical* possibilities as well, in particular for understanding the specific pathways through which siblings with similar family environments end up developing divergent patterns of relationship formation and functioning in adulthood. Relatively little research has focused on the sibling relationships of sexual-minority individuals more generally, and we think that greater attention to similarities and differences between the romantic relationships of sexual-minority individuals and the romantic relationships of their siblings may open up new directions for theorizing about the dynamic processes through which individuals' personal attributes (temperament, social skills, sexual orientation) *interact* with their family backgrounds (including the quality of their ties to both parents and siblings) to shape the types of romantic ties they seek and achieve in adulthood.

Another domain in which theoretical advances are underway concerns investigation of the implications of different types of same-sex relationship formalization (e.g., legal marriage, domestic partnership, civil unions) on couple functioning. As noted earlier, studies have found that the availability of legal formalization appears to promote satisfaction and commitment in same-sex couples (Solomon, Rothblum, & Balsam, 2004; Solomon et al., 2005; Todosijevic, Rothblum, & Solomon, 2005), and yet the mechanisms underlying these effects (as well as potential moderators) require greater study. Studies have increasingly investigated intriguing differences between *symbolic* and *legal* strategies for formalizing same-sex ties: Fingerhut (2010) found that couples who had formalized their relationships symbolically (through commitment ceremonies or weddings with no legal bearing) reported greater life satisfaction and relationship satisfaction, whereas those who formalized their relationships legally (through registered domestic partnerships) reported greater investments in their relationship (which is known to promote relationship stability and commitment, Rusbult, 1983). This suggests that symbolic formalization has particularly strong implications for personal and moral aspects of commitment (consistent with findings regarding the wearing of rings and the changing of last names, Suter & Daas, 2007; Suter & Oswald, 2003), whereas legal formalization has relatively stronger implications for structural aspects of commitment (Johnson, 1999). Some same-sex couples, however, desist from symbolic formalization, claiming that rituals such as commitment ceremonies lack meaning if they do not have legal standing (Reczek, Elliott, & Umberson, 2009).

Both symbolic and legal formalization, however, appear to play a role in reducing what Green (2008) has called "relational ambiguity," or the lack of standard cultural "rules" by which partners can gauge the progress and future status of their relationship, as well as their own responsibilities and duties at different stages of development. Green notes that heterosexual marriage comes with a set of cultural expectations that partners can rely upon to guide their behavior, such as cohabitation, pooled property and finances, and caring for one another (and one another's extended families) in times of illness. Without the clear demarcation of *marriage*, same-sex couples must make such decisions on a case-by-case basis, and must openly and repeatedly revisit questions—and conflicts— about whether their relationship is "serious" or "long-term" enough to warrant certain commitments and sacrifices (such as giving up a job opportunity, allowing elderly parents to share the household, etc.). In some cases, same-sex couples cannot even identify a reliable marker of when their relationship *began* (Reczek et al., 2009). Hence, pursuing either symbolic or legal formalization may help to decrease relational ambiguity and create a set of shared expectations about the status and future of the relationship. Integrating these insights into current theories of commitment has the potential to advance our understanding of both same-sex and other-sex couples, and the processes by which they solidify and maintain their bonds.

FUTURE DIRECTIONS AND IMPLICATIONS

As noted earlier, much of the work comparing same-sex to other-sex couples has treated relationship functioning and relationship satisfaction as primary outcomes, consistent with theoretical approaches such as the VSA model that examine how individual and contextual factors contribute to relationship functioning. Yet there are numerous theoretical approaches, such as social-psychological models of social support and developmental models of attachment over the lifespan (reviewed in Diamond, Fagundes, & Butterworth, 2010), which treat the functioning of close relationships as *predictors* of individual well-being and stress-susceptibility, rather than *outcomes* of such factors. Such models yield a new and different set of research questions regarding links between sexual-minority individuals' exposure to minority stress and the quality of their intimate same-sex relationships. Specifically, instead of asking, "How does minority stress potentially impair same-sex relationship functioning?" we might instead ask, "How does the experience of a warm, nurturant, emotionally satisfying same-sex relationship buffer sexual-minority individuals from future experiences of minority stress, reducing their internalized homophobia and enhancing their self acceptance?" After all, given that sexual-minority individuals are stigmatized because of their same-sex relationships, and given that same-sex relationships have been historically stereotyped as unsatisfying, immature, and pathological (reviewed in Diamond, 2006), it is possible that satisfying same-sex relationships might prove particularly influential on sexual-minority individuals' future self-concepts and resilience. By the same token, dysfunctional same-sex relationships might not simply "result" from cumulative minority stress and internalized homophobia, they might actually *lead* to greater stress vulnerability and greater internalized homophobia.

The two theoretical models just described, with their reversed causal arrows, are not mutually exclusive. It is possible (and perhaps likely) that experiences of stress/support and same-sex relationship quality influence one another reciprocally over time. Yet it is possible that for some individuals, at some stages of life (or some stages of the coming out process), the strength of influence is stronger in one direction than the other. Systematically investigating this possibility, using longitudinal research, would not only make important contributions to our understanding of stress, support, and relationship quality, but would also promote the continued development and application of rigorous social-psychological theory in the domain of same-sex relationships.

In pursuing such directions for theory and research, it behooves us to recall Kitzinger's (1987) influential critique of the first wave of "gay-affirmative" research in the 1970s and 1980s. She pointed out that the *lack* of significant mental health differences between gay/lesbian and heterosexual individuals might have appeared to represent the triumph of scientific objectivity over social prejudice, but in fact simultaneously functioned to *reinforce* the social disenfranchisement of sexual-minority individuals by implicitly predicating their social acceptability on patterns of thought, feeling, and behavior that were "just like" those of heterosexuals. Her analysis demonstrated the importance of vigilantly monitoring the multiple sociocultural and political forces inescapably shaping the context in which scholarship on sexual-minority relationships is conducted and interpreted. We must continually check and revisit our explicit and implicit theories of sexuality and relationships in order to appropriately represent how these phenomena develop, unfold, and interact within the life courses of diverse sexual-minority individuals. The end result of such efforts will be a deeper understanding of intimate relationships in the context of same-sex sexuality *and* a deeper understanding of same-sex sexuality in the context of intimate relationships.

Another important and interesting direction for future theory and research on same-sex couples concerns the impact of *childbearing* on relationship functioning, and the impact of couples' implicit ideologies about gender, power, and "natural" parenthood on their caregiving practices. These topics are ripe for investigation given that increasing numbers of same-sex couples are rearing children together (a phenomenon that has been dubbed the "gay baby boom," by Johnson & O'Connor, 2002) Census data reveal that 24% of same-sex couples have a child under 18 in the home (this figure is larger—34%—among female–female couples, Gates & Ost, 2004). In previous generations, such children usually resulted from one partner's previous heterosexual marriage, but this pattern has been changing. An increasing number of same-sex couples are having children together through adoption, artificial insemination, and surrogacy (reviewed in Diamond & Butterworth, 2008). Considerable research has been conducted to test for differences between the parenting of same-sex and other-sex couples, as well as differences in their children's social and psychological outcomes. Thus far, studies reveal few differences, and those which *have* emerged tend to favor same-sex couples, for example demonstrating that they often show *higher* levels of parental involvement, time spent with children, warmth, affection, shared decision-making, shared childcare, and overall satisfaction with parenting than heterosexual couples (Dunne, 2000; Fulcher, Sutfin, & Patterson, 2008; Golombok et al., 2003; Patterson, Sutfin, & Fulcher, 2004). These differences are typically attributed to the fact that same-sex parents are often characterized by particularly strong motives to have and care for children, given the social and legal obstacles that they must navigate in order to do so (Bergman, Rubio, Green, & Padron, 2010; Bos, Van Balen, & Van den Boom, 2003).

Yet, some of the most interesting and theoretically rich areas for future research concern same-sex couples' struggles to apply *or* subvert conventional ideologies about gender, power, and "natural" parenthood in the process of negotiating their new roles as parents. For example, studies of female–female households have consistently found that the mother who gave birth to the child tends to take on a stronger parenting role and to develop a closer tie to the child, despite the fact that most same-sex parents *seek* to develop completely egalitarian parenting roles and practices (Bos, Van Balen, & Van den Boom, 2007; Dundas & Kaufman, 2000; Goldberg & Perry-Jenkins, 2007; Johnson & O'Connor, 2002). Biblarz and Savci (2010) argued that these trends suggest that lesbians are just as vulnerable as are heterosexuals to the societal ideology of "biologism," which implicitly posits biological parents as more "authentic" parents. Numerous studies demonstrate that nonbiological mothers in same-sex couples often fail to be acknowledged as "real" mothers by their friends, families, and society at large (reviewed in Bergen, Suter, & Daas, 2006). Although such findings are usually cited as evidence of the unique challenges faced by same-sex parents, they have broader implications for family theory that have yet to be fully explored. Specifically, they speak directly to long-standing debates over the degree to which couples structure their respective roles and responsibilities according to rational trade-offs and negotiations (i.e., which partner has more time, which partner is the better cook or Little League coach) versus implicit (and sometimes downright irrational) gender ideologies. Over 20 years ago, Brines (1994) published an influential article seeking to explain the oft-documented, paradoxical finding that husbands who were being economically supported by their wives did less housework than husbands who were primary bread-winners. She argued that the performance or non-performance of housework was functioning, for the economically dependent men, as a form of "symbolic exchange," allowing them to compensate for their failure to uphold a conventional masculine *economic* role by adopting a highly traditional masculine role with respect to household labor. Numerous studies since that time have explored how housework and childcare provide potent sites for couples to enact—both consciously and unconsciously—ideologies and expectations about gender, and the circumstances that moderate this enactment (for a few recent examples, see Gaunt, 2006; Johnson, 2010; Katz-Wise, Priess, & Hyde, 2010; Koivunen, Rothaupt, & Wolfgram, 2009; Thebaud, 2010).

Hence, rather than assuming that gender is not an issue when it comes to the household and parenting arrangements of same-sex couples, future research would profit by taking more seriously psychological and sociological theories—such as symbolic exchange—that emphasize the ways in which men and women find themselves reproducing conventional gender roles in the context of marriage and childrearing even when those roles prove inefficient, or even (in the case of politically-minded same-sex couples) when they are actively *resisted*. We have the potential to build richer theories from studying cases in which same-sex couples do or do not find themselves reproducing conventional gender roles, especially in the time-intensive and emotionally-charged context of parenting. Given that a common critique of same-sex parents is that they provide "too much" modeling of one gender and "not enough" of another, close examination of the circumstances that shape same-sex couples' gender "performances," and the flexibility of these performances over time, has much to contribute to our understanding of gender roles more generally, and not simply in the context of same-sex couples.

CONCLUSION

Perhaps the most important conclusion to be drawn from the existing body of research on same-sex couples, and the most important guiding principle for future theory and research, is that this population of individuals and couples is just as diverse as the population of heterosexual individuals and couples. Accordingly, theoretical development will be enhanced to the extent that we move beyond simply testing for differences between sexual-minority and heterosexual individuals, and instead investigate the specific interpersonal *processes and mechanisms* through which an individual's status as a sexual minority shapes the formation, functioning, and long-term development of his/her closest interpersonal ties. Also we must remember that interpersonal experiences are embedded in highly specific sociocultural and interpersonal contexts, and these contexts must be analyzed to accurately discern how and why particular subsets of sexual minorities have relationship experiences with distinctive psychological and social implications.

REFERENCES

Ackbar, S., & Senn, C. Y. (2010). What's the confusion about fusion? Differentiating positive and negative closeness in lesbian relationships. *Journal of Marital and Family Therapy, 36*, 416–430.

Adam, B. D. (2006). Relationship innovation in male couples. *Sexualities, 9*, 5–26.

Alderson, K. G. (2004). A phenomenological investigation of same-sex marriage. *Canadian Journal of Human Sexuality, 13*, 107–122.

Allen, L. A., Woolfolk, R. L., Gara, M. A., & Apter, J. T. (1996). Possible selves in major depression. *Journal of Nervous and Mental Disease, 184*, 739–745.

Allison, K. W. (1998). Stress and oppressed social category membership. In J. K. Swim & C. Stangor (Eds.), *Prejudice: The target's perspective* (pp. 145–170). San Diego, CA: Academic Press.

Badgett, M. V. L. (1998). The economic well-being of lesbian, gay, and bisexual adults' families. In C. Patterson & A. R. D' Augelli (Eds.), *Lesbian, gay, and bisexual identities in families: Psychological Perspectives* (pp. 231–248). New York: Oxford University Press.

Bailey, J. M., Gaulin, S., Agyei, Y., & Gladue, B. (1994). Effects of gender and sexual orientation on evolutionarily relevant aspects of human mating psychology. *Journal of Personality and Social Psychology, 66*, 1081–1093.

Balsam, K. F., Beauchaine, T. P., Rothblum, E. D., & Solomon, S. E. (2008). Three-year follow-up of same-sex couples who had civil unions in Vermont, same-sex couples not in civil unions, and heterosexual married couples. *Developmental Psychology, 44*, 102–116.

Balsam, K. F., & Szymanski, D. M. (2005). Relationship quality and domestic violence in women's same-sex relationships: The role of minority stress. *Psychology of Women Quarterly, 29*, 258–269.

Barrett, L. F., Lane, R. D., Sechrest, L., & Schwartz, G. E. (2000). Sex differences in emotional awareness. *Personality and Social Psychology Bulletin, 26*, 1027–1035.

Beals, K. P., Impett, E. A., & Peplau, L. A. (2002). Lesbians in love: Why some relationships endure and others end. *Journal of Lesbian Studies, 6*, 53–63.

Bergen, K. M., Suter, E. A., & Daas, K. L. (2006). 'About as solid as a fish net': Symbolic construction of a legitimate parental identity for nonbiological lesbian mothers. *Journal of Family Communication, 6*, 201–220.

Bergman, K., Rubio, R. J., Green, R.-J., & Padron, E. (2010). Gay men who become fathers via surrogacy: The transition to parenthood. *Journal of GLBT Family Studies, 6*, 111–141.

Biblarz, T. J., & Savci, E. (2010). Lesbian, gay, bisexual, and transgender families. *Journal of Marriage & the Family*, *72*, 480–497.

Blair, K. L., & Holmberg, D. (2008). Perceived social network support and well-being in same-sex versus mixed-sex romantic relationships. *Journal of Social and Personal Relationships*, *25*, 769–791.

Blumstein, P., & Schwartz, P. (1983). *American couples: Money, work, sex*. New York: Morrow.

Bonello, K. (2009). Gay monogamy and extra-dyadic sex: A critical review of the theoretical and empirical literature. *Counselling Psychology Review*, *24*, 51–65.

Bonello, K., & Cross, M. C. (2010). Gay monogamy: I love you but I can't have sex with only you. *Journal of Homosexuality*, *57*, 117–139.

Bos, H. M. W., Van Balen, F., & Van den Boom, D. C. (2003). Planned lesbian families: Their desire and motivation to have children. *Human Reproduction*, *18*, 2216–2224.

Bos, H. M. W., van Balen, F., & van den Boom, D. C. (2007). Child adjustment and parenting in planned lesbian-parent families. *American Journal of Orthopsychiatry*, *77*, 38–48.

Brines, J. (1994). Economic dependency, gender, and the division of labor at home. *American Journal of Sociology*, *100*, 652–688.

Bryant, A. S., & Demian. (1994). Relationship characteristics of American gay and lesbian couples: Findings from a national survey. *Journal of Gay and Lesbian Social Services*, *1*, 101–117.

Burch, B. (1986). Psychotherapy and the dynamics of merger and lesbian couples. In T. S. Stein & C. J. Cohen (Eds.), *Contemporary perspectives on psychotherapy with lesbians and gay men* (pp. 57–72). New York: Plenum.

Butterworth, M. (2012). Social marginalization, interpersonal behavior, and relationship outcomes: A preliminary test of an integrative framework for same-sex and other-sex couples. Unpublished manuscript, University of Utah.

Caldwell, M. A., & Peplau, L. A. (1984). The balance of power in lesbian relationships. *Sex Roles*, *10*, 587–599.

Cass, V. (1979). Homosexual identity formation: A theoretical model. *Journal of Homosexuality*, *4*, 219–235.

Choderow, N. (1978). *The reproduction of mothering*. Berkeley, CA: University of California Press.

Clark, R., Anderson, N. B., Clark, V. R., & Williams, D. R. (1999). Racism as a stressor for African Americans: A biopsychosocial model. *American Psychologist*, *54*, 805–816.

Coleman, E. (1981–1982). The developmental stages of the coming out process. *Journal of Homosexuality*, *7*, 31–43.

Connolly, C. M. (2006). A feminist perspective of resilience in lesbian couples. *Journal of Feminist Family Therapy*, *18*, 137–162.

Connolly, C. M., & Sicola, M. K. (2006). Listening to lesbian couples: Communication competence in long-term relationships. In J. J. Bigner (Ed.), *An introduction to GLBT family studies* (pp. 271–296). New York: Haworth Press.

Crocker, J., Major, B., & Steele, C. (1998). Social stigma. In D. Gilbert, S. T. Fiske, & G. Lindzey (Eds.), *The handbook of social psychology* (4th ed., pp. 504–553). Boston, MA: McGraw Hill.

Cross, S. E., & Madson, L. (1997). Models of the self: Self-construals and gender. *Psychological Bulletin*, *122*, 5–37.

Diamond, L. M. (2006). The same-sex intimate relationships of sexual minorities. In D. Perlman & A. L. Vangelisti (Eds.), *The Cambridge handbook of personal relationships* (pp. 293–312). New York: Cambridge University Press.

Diamond, L. M. (2008). *Sexual fluidity: Understanding women's love and desire*. Cambridge, MA: Harvard University Press.

Diamond, L. M., & Butterworth, M. R. (2008). The close relationships of sexual minorities: Partners, family, and friends. In M. C. Smith & T. G. Reio (Eds.), *Handbook of research on adult development and learning* (pp. 350–377). Mahway, NJ: Lawrence Erlbaum.

Diamond, L. M., Fagundes, C. P., & Butterworth, M. R. (2010). Intimate relationships across the lifespan. In M. E. Lamb, L. White & A. Freund (Eds.), *Handbook of Lifespan Development*, Vol. 2 (pp. 379–433). New York: Wiley.

Diaz, R. M., Ayala, G., Bein, E., Jenne, J., & Marin, B. V. (2001). The impact of homophobia, poverty, and racism on the mental health of Latino gay men. *American Journal of Public Health*, *91*, 927–932.

Downey, G., & Feldman, S. I. (1996). Implications of rejection sensitivity for intimate relationships. *Journal of Personality and Social Psychology*, *70*, 1327–1343.

Driscoll, R., Davis, K., & Lipetz, M. E. (1972). Parental interference and romantic love. *Journal of Personality and Social Psychology, 24,* 1–10.

Duncombe, J., & Marsden, D. (1998). Stepford wives and hollow men? Doing emotion work, doing gender and authenticity in heterosexual relationships. In G. Bendelow & S. Williams (Eds.), *Emotions in social life: Critical themes and contemporary issues* (pp. 34–47). London, England: Routledge.

Dundas, S., & Kaufman, M. (2000). The Toronto Lesbian Family Study. *Journal of Homosexuality, 40,* 65–79.

Dunne, A. (2000). Opting into motherhood: Lesbians blurring the boundaries and transforming the meaning of parenthood and kinship. *Gender & Society, 14,* 11–35.

Eldridge, N. S., & Gilbert, L. A. (1990). Correlates of relationship satisfaction in lesbian couples. *Psychology of Women Quarterly, 14,* 43–62.

Elze, D. E. (2002). Against all odds: The dating experiences of adolescent lesbian and bisexual women. *Journal of Lesbian Studies, 6,* 17–29.

Erickson, R. J. (2005). Why emotion work matters: Sex, gender, and the division of household labor. *Journal of Marriage and the Family, 67,* 337–351.

Eskridge, W. N., & Spedale, D. R. (2006). *Gay marriage: For better or for worse? What we've learned from the evidence.* New York: Oxford University Press.

Falbo, T., & Peplau, L. A. (1980). Power strategies in intimate relationships. *Journal of Personality and Social Psychology, 38,* 618–628.

Felmlee, D. H. (1994). Who's on top? Power in romantic relationships. *Sex Roles, 31,* 275–295.

Fingerhut, A. W. (2010). Relationship formalization and individual and relationship well-being among same-sex couples. *Journal of Social and Personal Relationships, 27,* 956–969.

Frye, M. (1990). Lesbian "sex". In J. Allen (Ed.), *Lesbian philosophies and cultures.* Albany, NY: State University of New York Press.

Fulcher, M., Sutfin, E., & Patterson, C. (2008). Individual differences in gender development: Associations with parental sexual orientation, attitudes, and division of labor. *Sex Roles, 58,* 330–341.

Gaines, S. O., Jr., & Henderson, M. C. (2002). Impact of attachment style on responses to accommodative dilemmas among same-sex couples. *Personal Relationships, 9,* 89–93.

Gates, G. J., & Ost, J. (2004). *The gay and lesbian atlas.* Washington, DC: Urban Institute.

Gaunt, R. (2006). Biological essentialism, gender ideologies, and role attitudes: What determines parents' involvement in child care. *Sex Roles, 55,* 523–533.

Gillespie, D. L. (1971). Who has the power? The marital struggle. *Journal of Marriage and the Family, 33,* 445–458.

Goffman, E. (1963). *Stigma: Notes on the management of spoiled identity.* New York: Touchstone.

Goldberg, A. E., & Perry-Jenkins, M. (2007). The division of labor and perceptions of parental roles: Lesbian couples across the transition to parenthood. *Journal of Social and Personal Relationships, 24,* 297–318.

Golombok, S., Perry, B., Burston, A., Murray, C., Mooney-Somers, J., Stevens, M., et al. (2003). Children with lesbian parents: A community study. *Developmental Psychology, 39,* 20–33.

Gottman, J. M., Levenson, R. W., Gross, J. J., Frederickson, B. L., McCoy, K., Rosenthal, L., et al. (2003). Correlates of gay and lesbian couples' relationship satisfaction and relationship dissolution. *Journal of Homosexuality, 45,* 23–43.

Gottman, J. M., Levenson, R. W., Swanson C., Swanson, K., Tyson, R., & Yoshimoto, D. (2003) Observing gay, lesbian and heterosexual couples' relationships: Mathematical modeling of conflict interaction. *Journal of Homosexuality, 45,* 65–91.

Green, R. J. (2008). Gay and lesbian couples: Successful coping with minority stress. In M. McGoldrick & K. V. Hardy (Eds.), *Re-visioning family therapy: Race, culture, and gender in clinical practice* (2nd ed., pp. 300–310). New York: Guilford Press.

Green, R. J., Bettinger, M., & Zacks, E. (1996). Are lesbian couples fused and gay male couples disengaged?: Questioning gender straightjackets. In J. Laird & R.-J. Green (Eds.), *Lesbians and gays in couples and families: A handbook for therapists* (pp. 185–230). San Francisco, CA: Jossey-Bass.

Grossman, A. H., D'Augelli, A. R., & Hershberger, S. L. (2000). Social support networks of lesbian, gay, and bisexual adults 60 years of age and older. *Journal of Gerontology, 55,* 171–179.

Guerrero, L. K., Jones, S. M., & Boburka, R. R. (2006). Sex differences in emotional communication. An K. Dindia & D. J. Canary (Eds.), *Sex differences and similarities in communication,* (2nd ed., pp. 241–261). Fahwah, NJ: Lawrence Erlbaum.

Hall, R. L., & Greene, B. (2002). Not any one thing: The complex legacy of social class on African American lesbian relationships. *Journal of Lesbian Studies, 6,* 65–74.

Harry, J., & DeVall, W. B. (1978). *The Social Organization of Gay Males.* New York: Praeger.

Hart, J., & Richardson, D. (1981). *The theory and practice of homosexuality.* London, England: Routledge & Kegan Paul.

Hatzenbuehler, M. L. (2009). How does sexual-minority stigma "get under the skin"? A psychological mediation framework. *Psychological Bulletin, 135,* 707–730.

Herek, G. M. (2004). Beyond "homophobia": Thinking about sexual prejudice and stigma in the twenty-first century. *Sexuality Research & Social Policy, 1,* 6–24.

Hill, C. A. (1999). Fusion and conflict in lesbian relationships? *Feminism and Psychology, 9,* 179–185.

Howard, J. A., Blumstein, P., & Schwartz, P. (1986). Sex, power, and influence tactics in intimate relationships. *Journal of Personality and Social Psychology, 51,* 102–109.

Huston, M., & Schwartz, P. (2002). Gendered dynamics in the romantic relationships of lesbians and gay men. In A. E. Hunter (Ed.), *Readings in the psychology of gender: Exploring our differences and commonalities* (pp. 167–178). Needham Heights, MA: Allyn & Bacon.

Johnson, J. A. (2010). Using gender: The personal, interpersonal, and emotional strategies of domestic labor. *Sociological Spectrum, 30,* 695–724.

Johnson, S. M., & O'Connor, E. (2002). *The gay baby boom: The psychology of gay parenthood.* New York: New York University Press.

Johnson, M. P. (1999). Personal, moral, and structural commitment to relationships: Experiences of choice and constraint. In J. M. Adams & W. H. Jones (Eds.), *Handbook of interpersonal commitment and relationship stability* (pp. 73–87). Dordrecht, the Netherlands: Kluwer Academic.

Jordan, J. V. (1987). *Clarity in connection: Empathic knowing, desire and sexuality.* Wellsley, MA: Stone Center, Wellsley College.

Jordan, J. V. (1991). The meaning of mutuality. In A. G. Kaplan, J. B. Miller, I. Stiver & J. Surrey (Eds.), *Women's growth in connection: Writings from the Stone Center* (pp. 81–96). New York: Guilford.

Karney, B. R., & Bradbury, T. N. (1995). The longitudinal course of marriage and marital instability: A review of theory, method, and research. *Psychological Bulletin, 118,* 3–34.

Katz-Wise, S. L., Priess, H. A., & Hyde, J. S. (2010). Gender-role attitudes and behavior across the transition to parenthood. *Developmental Psychology, 46,* 18–28.

Kimmel, S. B., & Mahalik, J. R. (2005). Body image concerns of gay men: The roles of minority stress and conformity to masculine norms. *Journal of Consulting and Clinical Psychology, 73,* 1185–1190.

Kitzinger, C. (1987). *The social construction of lesbianism.* London, England: Sage.

Kitzinger, C., & Coyle, A. (1995). Lesbian and gay couples: Speaking of difference. *The Psychologist, 8,* 64–69.

Koivunen, J. M., Rothaupt, J. W., & Wolfgram, S. M. (2009). Gender dynamics and role adjustment during the transition to parenthood: *Current perspectives. The Family Journal, 17,* 323–328.

Kollock, P., Blumstein, P., & Schwartz, P. (1986). Sex and power in interaction: Conversational privileges and duties. *American Sociological Review, 50,* 34–46.

Kresten, J., & Bepko, C. S. (1980). The problem of fusion in lesbian relationships. *Family Process, 19,* 277–289.

Kurdek, L. A. (1992). Relationship stability and relationship satisfaction in cohabiting gay and lesbian couples: A prospective longitudinal test of the contextual and interdependence models. *Journal of Social and Personal Relationships, 9,* 125–142.

Kurdek, L. A. (1993). The allocation of household labor in gay, lesbian, and heterosexual married couples. *Journal of Social Issues, 49,* 127–139.

Kurdek, L. A. (1998). Relationship outcomes and their predictors: Longitudinal evidence from heterosexual married, gay cohabiting, and lesbian cohabiting couples. *Journal of Marriage and the Family, 60,* 553–568.

Kurdek, L. A. (2000). Attractions and constraints as determinants of relationship commitment: Longitudinal evidence from gay, lesbian, and heterosexual couples. *Personal Relationships, 7,* 245–262.

Kurdek, L. A. (2004). Are gay and lesbian cohabiting couples really different from heterosexual married couples? *Journal of Marriage & Family, 66,* 880–900.

Kurdek, L. A. (2006). Differences between partners from heterosexual, gay, and lesbian cohabiting couples. *Journal of Marriage and Family, 68,* 509–528.

Kurdek, L. A., & Schmitt, J. P. (1986). Relationship quality of partners in heterosexual married, heterosexual cohabiting, and gay and lesbian relationships. *Journal of Personality and Social Psychology*, *51*, 711–720.

Kurdek, L. A., & Schnopp-Wyatt, D. (1997). Predicting relationship commitment and relationship stability from both partners' relationship values: Evidence from heterosexual dating couples. *Personality and Social Psychology Bulletin*, 23, 1111–1119.

Lannutti, P. J. (2007). The influence of same-sex marriage on the understanding of same-sex relationships. *Journal of Homosexuality*, *53*, 135–157.

LaSala, M. C. (1998). Coupled gay men, parents, and in-laws: Intergenerational disapproval and the need for a thick skin. *Families in Society*, *79*, 585–595.

LaSala, M. C. (2004). Extradyadic sex and gay male couples: Comparing monogamous and nonmonogamous relationships. *Families in Society*, *85*, 405–412.

Laumann, E. O., Gagnon, J. H., Michael, R. T., & Michaels, S. (1994). *The social organization of sexuality: Sexual practices in the United States*. Chicago: University of Chicago Press.

Lehmiller, J. J., & Agnew, C. R. (2006). Marginalized relationships: The impact of social disapproval on romantic relationship commitment. *Personality and Social Psychology Bulletin*, *32*, 40–51.

Lever, J. (1994, August 23). Sexual revelations. *The Advocate*, 17–24.

Levinger, G. (1965). Marital cohesiveness and dissolution: An integrative review. *Journal of Marriage & the Family*, *27*, 19–28.

Link, B. G., & Phelan, J. C. (2001). Conceptualizing stigma. *Annual Review of Sociology, 27*, 363–385.

Loiacano, D. K. (1993). Gay identity among Black Americans: Racism, homophobia, and the need for validation. In L. D. Garnets & D. C. Kimmel (Eds.), *Psychological perspectives on lesbian and gay male experiences* (pp. 364–375). New York: Columbia University Press.

Matthews, A. K., Tartaro, J., & Hughes, T. L. (2003). A comparative study of lesbian and heterosexual women in committed relationships. *Journal of Lesbian Studies*, *7*, 101–114.

Means-Christensen, A. J., Snyder, D. K., & Negy, C. (2003). Assessing nontraditional couples: Validity of the Marital Satisfaction Inventory-Revised with gay, lesbian, and cohabiting heterosexual couples. *Journal of Marital and Family Therapy*, *29*, 69–83.

Metz, M. E., Rosser, B. R. S., & Strapko, N. (1994). Differences in conflict-resolution styles among heterosexual, gay, and lesbian couples. *Journal of Sex Research*, *31*, 293–308.

Meyer, I. H. (1995). Minority stress and mental health in gay men. *Journal of Health and Social Behavior*, *36*, 38–56.

Meyer, I. H. (2003). Prejudice, social stress, and mental health in lesbian, gay, and bisexual populations: Conceptual issues and research evidence. *Psychological Bulletin*, *129*, 674–697.

Meyer, I. H., & Dean, L. (1998). Internalized homophobia, intimacy, and sexual behavior among gay and bisexual men. In G. M. Herek (Ed.), *Stigma and sexual orientation: Understanding prejudice against lesbians, gay men, and bisexuals* (pp. 160–186). Thousand Oaks, CA: Sage.

Minnotte, K. L., Pedersen, D. E., Mannon, S. E., & Kiger, G. (2010). Tending to the emotions of children: Predicting parental performance of emotion work with children. *Marriage & Family Review*, *46*, 224–241.

Mirowsky, J., & Ross, C. E. (1989). *Social causes of psychological distress*. Hawthorne, NY: Aldine De Gruyter.

Monroe, S. M. (2008). Modern approaches to conceptualizing and measuring human life stress. *Annual Review of Clinical Psychology*, *4*, 33–52.

Mosher, W. D., Chandra, A., & Jones, J. (2005). *Sexual behavior and selected health measures: Men and women 15–44 years of age, United States, 2002*. Advance data from vital and health statistics, No. 362. Hyattsville, MD: National Center for Health Statistics.

Murphy, B. C. (1989). Lesbian couples and their parents: The effects of perceived parental attitudes on the couple. *Journal of Counseling and Development*, *68*, 46–51.

Nardi, P. M. (1999). *Gay men's friendships*. Chicago: University of Chicago Press.

Nichols, M. (1988). Low sexual desire in lesbian couples. In S. R. Leiblum & R. C. Rosen (Eds.), *Sexual desire disorders* (pp. 387–412). New York: Guilford.

Nichols, M. (1990). Lesbian relationships: Implications for the study of sexuality and gender. In J. C. Gonsiorek & J. D. Weinrich (Eds.), *Homosexuality: Research implications for public policy* (pp. 350–364). Newbury Park, CA: Sage.

Oetjen, H., & Rothblum, E. D. (2000). When lesbians aren't gay: Factors affecting depression among lesbians. *Journal of Homosexuality*, *39*, 49–73.

Otis, M. D., Rostosky, S. S., Riggle, E. D. B., & Hamrin, R. (2006). Stress and relationship quality in same-sex couples. *Journal of Social and Personal Relationships*, *23*, 81–99.

Patterson, C. J. (1995). Families of the baby boom: Parents' division of labor and children's adjustment. *Developmental Psychology*, *31*, 115–123.

Patterson, C. J., Sutfin, E. L., & Fulcher, M. (2004). Division of labor among lesbian and heterosexual parenting couples: Correlates of specialized versus shared patterns. *Journal of Adult Development*, *11*, 179–189.

Peplau, L. A., & Spalding, L. R. (2000). The close relationships of lesbians, gay men and bisexuals. In C. Hendrick, & S. S. Hendrick (Ed.) *Close relationships: A sourcebook* (pp. 111–124). Thousand Oaks, CA: Sage

Peplau, L. A., & Campbell, S. M. (1989). Power in dating and marriage. In J. Freeman (Ed.), *Women: A feminist perspective* (4th ed.). Palo Alto, CA: Mayfield.

Peplau, L. A., & Cochran, S. D. (1980, September). *Sex differences in values concerning love relationships*. Paper presented at the American Psychological Association, Montreal, Canada.

Peplau, L. A., & Fingerhut, A. W. (2007). The close relationships of lesbians and gay men. *Annual Review of Psychology*, *58*, 405–424.

Peplau, L. A., Fingerhut A. W., & Beals K. P. (2004). Sexuality in the relationships of lesbians and gay men. In J. Harvey, A. Wenzel, S. Sprecher (Ed.) *Handbook of Sexuality in Close Relationships* (pp. 350–369). Mahwah, NJ: Erlbaum.

Peplau, L. A., & Beals, K. P. (2003). The family lives of lesbians and gay men. In A. L. Vangelisti (Ed.), *Handbook of family communication* (pp. 233–248). Mahwah, NJ: Erlbaum.

Reczek, C., Elliott, S., & Umberson, D. (2009). Commitment without marriage: Union formation among long-term same-sex couples. *Journal of Family Issues*, *30*, 738–756.

Reilly, M. E. & Lynch, J. M. (1990). Power-sharing in lesbian partnerships. *Journal of Homosexuality*, *19*, 1–30

Remafedi, G., French, S., Story, M., Resnick, M. D., & Blum, R. (1998). The relationship between suicide risk and sexual orientation: Results of a population-based study. *American Journal of Public Health*, *88*, 57–60.

Riggle, E. D. B., Rostosky, S. S., & Horne, S. G. (2010). Psychological distress, well-being, and legal recognition in same-sex couple relationships. *Journal of Family Psychology*, *24*, 82–86.

Roisman, G. I., Clausell, E., Holland, A., Fortuna, K., & Elieff, C. (2008). Adult romantic relationships as contexts of human development: A multimethod comparison of same-sex couples with opposite-sex dating, engaged, and married dyads. *Developmental Psychology*, *44*, 91–101.

Rose, S., & Zand, D. (2000). Lesbian dating and courtship from young adulthood to midlife. *Journal of Lesbian Studies*, *6*, 85–109.

Ross, M. W., & Rosser, B. R. S. (1996). Measurement and correlates of internalized homophobia: A factor analytic study. *Journal of Clinical Psychology*, *52*, 15–21.

Rostosky, S. S., & Riggle, E. D. B. (2002). 'Out' at work: The relation of actor and partner workplace policy and internalized homophobia to disclosure status. *Journal of Counseling Psychology*, *49*, 411–419.

Rostosky, S. S., Korfhage, B. A., Duhigg, J. M., Stern, A. J., Bennett, L., & Riggle, E. D. B. (2004). Same-sex couple perceptions of family support: A consensual qualitative study. *Family Process*, *43*, 43–57.

Rostosky, S. S., Riggle, E. D. B., Gray, B. E., & Hatton, R. L. (2007). Minority stress experiences in committed same-sex couple relationships. *Professional Psychology: Research and Practice*, *38*, 392–400.

Rostosky, S. S., Riggle, E. D. B., Horne, S. G., & Miller, A. D. (2009). Marriage amendments and psychological distress in lesbian, gay, and bisexual (LGB) adults. *Journal of Counseling Psychology*, *56*, 56–66.

Rostosky, S. S., Riggle, E. D. B., Horne, S. G., Denton, F. N., & Huellemeier, J. D. (2010). Lesbian, gay, and bisexual individuals' psychological reactions to amendments denying access to civil marriage. *American Journal of Orthopsychiatry*, *80*, 302–310.

Rothblum, E. D. (2000). Sexual orientation and sex in women's lives: Conceptual and methodological issues. *Journal of Social Issues*, *56*, 193–204.

Rothblum, E. D., & Factor, R. J. (2001). Lesbians and their sisters as a control group: Demographic and mental health factors. *Psychological Science*, *12*, 63–69.

Rotheram-Borus, M. J., & Fernandez, M. I. (1995). Sexual orientation and developmental challenges experienced by gay and lesbian youths. *Suicide and Life-Threatening Behavior, 25(Supplement)*, 26–34.

Rusbult, C. E. (1983). A longitudinal test of the investment model: The development (and deterioration) of satisfaction and commitment in heterosexual involvements. *Journal of Personality and Social Psychology, 45*, 101–117.

Scanzoni, J. (1982). *Sexual bargaining: Power politics in the American marriage* (2nd ed.). Chicago: University of Chicago Press.

Schmitt, J. P., & Kurdek, L. A. (1987). Personality correlates of positive identity and relationship involvement in gay men. *Journal of Homosexuality, 13*, 101–109.

Schreurs, K. M. G., & Buunk, B. P. (1996). Closeness, autonomy, equity and relationship satisfaction in lesbian couples. *Psychology of Women Quarterly, 20*, 577–592

Solomon, S. E., Rothblum, E. D., & Balsam, K. F. (2004). Pioneers in partnership: Lesbian and gay male couples in civil unions compared with those not in civil unions and married heterosexual siblings. *Journal of Family Psychology, 18*, 275–286.

Solomon, S. E., Rothblum, E. D., & Balsam, K. F. (2005). Money, housework, sex, and conflict: Same-sex couples in civil unions, those not in civil unions, and heterosexual married siblings. *Sex Roles, 52*, 561–575.

Stacey, J., & Biblarz, T. J. (2001). How does the sexual orientation of parents matter? *American Sociological Review, 66*, 159–183.

Stevens, D. P., Minnotte, K. L., Mannon, S. E., & Kiger, G. (2007). Family work performance and satisfaction: Gender ideology, relative resources, and emotion work. *Marriage & Family Review, 40*, 47–74.

Suter, E. A., & Daas, K. L. (2007). Negotiating heteronormativity dialectically: Lesbian couples' display of symbols in culture. *Western Journal of Communication, 71*, 177–195.

Suter, E. A., & Oswald, R. F. (2003). Do lesbians change their last names in the context of a committed relationship? *Journal of Lesbian Studies, 7*, 71–83.

Thebaud, S. (2010). Masculinity, bargaining, and breadwinning: Understanding men's housework in the cultural context of paid work. *Gender & Society, 24*, 330–354.

Thomas, G., & Fletcher, G. J. O. (2003). Mind-reading accuracy in intimate relationships: Assessing the roles of the relationship, the target, and the judge. *Journal of Personality and Social Psychology, 85*, 1079–1094.

Todosijevic, J., Rothblum, E. D., & Solomon, S. E. (2005). Relationship satisfaction, affectivity, and gay-specific stressors in same-sex couples joined in civil unions. *Psychology of Women Quarterly, 29*, 158–166.

Ussher, J. M., & Perz, J. (2008). Empathy, egalitarianism and emotion work in the relational negotiation of PMS: The experience of women in lesbian relationships. *Feminism & Psychology, 18*, 87–111.

Waldo, C. R. (1999). Working in a majority context: A structural model of heterosexism as minority stress in the workplace. *Journal of Counseling Psychology, 46*, 218–232.

Waller, M. A. (2001). Gay men with AIDS: Perceptions of social support and adaptational outcome. *Journal of Homosexuality, 41*, 99–117.

Weston, K. (1991). *Families we choose: Lesbians, gays, kinship*. New York: Columbia University Press.

Wichstrom, L., & Hegna, K. (2003). Sexual orientation and suicide attempt: A longitudinal study of the general Norwegian adolescent population. *Journal of Abnormal Psychology, 112*, 144–151.

Williamson, I., & Hartley, P. (1998). British research into the increased vulnerability of young gay men to eating disturbance and body dissatisfaction. *European Eating Disorders Review, 6*, 60–70.

Zacks, E., Green, R.-J., & Marrow, J. (1988). Comparing lesbian and heterosexual couples on the Circumplex Model: An initial investigation. *Family Process, 27*, 471–484.

Zea, M. C., Reisen, C. A., & Poppen, P. J. (1999). Psychological well being among Latino lesbians and gay men. *Cultural Diversity and Ethnic Minority Psychology, 5*, 371–379.

9 Understanding Marital Distress
Polarization Processes

Brian R. Baucom and David C. Atkins[1]

Well-functioning marriages[2] can be seen in spouses' ability to adapt to and tolerate each other's differences, work together to create and preserve intimacy, and flexibly respond to and resolve conflict. In contrast, spouses in distressed marriages frequently do not engage in these collaborative processes, but rather think, interact, and experience one another in ways that make intimacy more difficult to achieve and that intensify existing conflict. We refer to escalating behavioral, cognitive, and emotional processes in distressed marriages as *polarization processes*. This chapter argues that polarization processes exacerbate marital distress that occurs as a result of individual differences becoming more pronounced, conflict becoming more entrenched, and spouses becoming less tolerant of each other. Moreover, polarization processes are influenced by intrapersonal, interpersonal, and intergenerational risk factors.

Unlike most of the other chapters in this volume, because of the vastness of the marital literature, this chapter focuses on a circumscribed, yet extremely important, topic within the literature on marriage—polarization processes—rather than on marriage in general. The chapter begins with an overview of polarization processes, reviews theoretical approaches and supporting empirical literatures that have been used to study aspects of the polarization model, and closes with suggestions for ways to advance the study of polarization processes in future research.

KEY ISSUES ON POLARIZATION PROCESSES

Polarization is a dynamic process between partners that magnifies and exaggerates sources of marital distress (Figure 9.1). It occurs when attempts to resolve problems, create change, or seek emotional connection are unsuccessful and result in partners feeling increasingly hopeless, dissatisfied, and separate from one another over time (McGinn, McFarland, & Christensen, 2009). Thus, the end result of polarization is that fundamental tasks and goals for building and preserving a healthy marriage are interrupted. The polarization process comprises behaviors, cognitions, and emotions that promote dysfunctional relating between partners.

This conceptualization of the polarization process was originally described by Jacobson and Christensen (1998) as a core component in the development of relationship distress. Their polarization

---

[1] Preparation of this manuscript was supported by a grant from the National Institute of Child Health and Human Development (HD060410) awarded to Brian R. Baucom at the University of Southern California.

[2] As we write this chapter, the sociopolitical definition of marriage is in rapid flux. In this chapter, we use the term marriage to refer broadly to committed, intimate relationships composed of two adults who share a sense of history, who experience emotional bonding with one another, and who meet the needs of one another as well as of their intimate relationship independent of the gender composition of the couple (Anderson & Sabatelli, 2010).

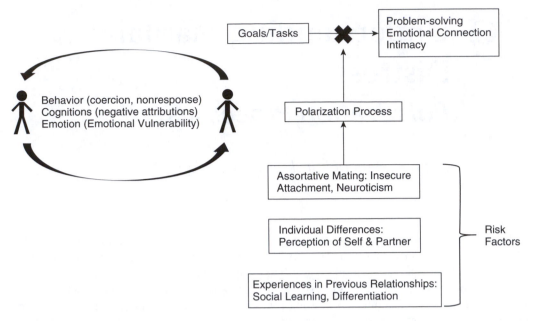

FIGURE 9.1   Polarization model.

model integrates elements of several well established etiological models of relationship distress including emotional vulnerabilities from *attachment theory* (Bowlby, 1969) and *family systems models* (e.g., Bowen, 1978), individual differences and emotional reactivity from personality models (Huston, 1998), and dysfunctional behavioral cycles and attributions from *behavioral and cognitive behavioral models* (Epstein & Baucom, D., 1993; Fletcher & Fincham, 1991). We briefly note how satisfied couples avoid becoming immersed in polarization processes before considering the behaviors, cognitions, and emotions that make up the polarization process and the risk factors that influence polarization.

Spouses in satisfied marriages typically respond in pro-relationship ways that not only avoid engagement in polarizing processes but also promote numerous aspects of relationship functioning such as commitment, conflict resolution, trust, and relationship satisfaction (Agnew, Van Lange, Rusbult, & Langston, 1998; Arriaga & Rusbult, 1998; Wieselquist, Rusbult, Foster, & Agnew, 1999). Though there is evidence that satisfied spouses engage in higher rates of overall positive behaviors than do distressed spouses (e.g., Gottman & Levenson, 1992) and that declines in overall positive behaviors are associated with increased risk for marital distress and divorce (Huston, Caughlin, Houts, Smith, & George, 2001; Markman, Rhoades, Stanley, Ragan, & Whitton, 2010), the ability to respond in a pro-social manner to objectionable partner behaviors is a particularly important mechanism for avoiding polarization (Margolin & Wampold, 1981; Rusbult, Verette, Whitney, Slovik, & Lipkus, 1991). Rusbult and colleagues (1991) termed these responses *accommodation behaviors*. These behaviors include loyalty (i.e., being patient, empathic, or supportive in response to criticism from a partner; Rusbult et al., 1991), editing (i.e., resisting the impulse to respond negatively when a partner has behaved badly; Gottman, Notarius, Gonso, & Markman, 1976), and forgiveness (e.g., Fincham, 2000). Accommodation behaviors protect relationships from polarization not only by reducing the likelihood of engagement in the polarizing behavioral cycles described below but also by reducing the likelihood of cognitive polarization, such as vilifying one another for perceived shortcomings (Agnew et al., 1998; Arriaga & Rusbult, 1998).

POLARIZATION PROCESSES

Polarizing behaviors, which Jacobson and Christensen (1998) refer to as the mutual trap, are best conceptualized as cyclical transactions between spouses; most often they take the form either of coercive behaviors or of rejecting and invalidating responses to vulnerable disclosures. Coercion is frequent during conflict, while rejection and invalidation are commonly seen when partners attempt to create intimacy or to seek support. Independent of the specific behavioral form polarizing behaviors take, their function is consistent. They are concomitant with high levels of behavioral reactance, aversive emotional reactivity, and cognitive rigidity (Baucom, B., McFarland, & Christensen, 2010b; Baucom, B., Atkins, Eldridge, McFarland, Sevier, & Christensen, 2011; Caughlin & Vangelisti, 2000; Kirby, Baucom, D., & Peterman, 2005) and are characterized by frequent empathic failure (i.e., difficulty recognizing or accurately perceiving the emotional state of the other; Verhofstadt, Buysse, Ickes, Davis, & Devoldre, 2008). Much of the frustration and hopelessness experienced by spouses when engaging in polarizing behaviors can be understood as natural but unintended by-products of the behaviors themselves.

Coercion refers to the use of aversive behavior by one spouse in an attempt to change the other spouse's behavior (Patterson, 1982). Coercive behaviors typically play out in one of two polarizing cycles: (1) negative reciprocity, or (2) the demand–withdraw interaction pattern. Negative reciprocity describes a feedback loop of negative behavior, in which coercive change attempts by one partner lead to negative responses from the other. In the demand–withdraw interaction pattern, one partner (the demander) nags, criticizes or complains in an attempt to create change, while the other partner (the withdrawer) refuses to discuss change, changes the topic of conversation, or simply ends the interaction in an attempt to maintain the status quo. *Coercion theory* suggests that when coercive attempts to create change are at least occasionally successful, both partners' behavior tends to become more extreme, or polarized, through a process of intermittent reinforcement (e.g., Baucom, B., et al., 2010b). For example, if a demander nags his partner until she gives in and makes a requested change, the demander is positively reinforced by getting what he wants and the withdrawer is negatively reinforced by no longer having to endure the aversive nagging. This process strengthens the likelihood of more intense and prolonged demanding and withdrawing in the future. The behavioral reactance endemic to these polarizing cycles of behavior has led to them being described as ironic processes (e.g., Rohrbaugh et al., 2001), and is also likely to be a key contributor to the frustrated, stuck, and misunderstood feelings of many polarized spouses.

Though polarizing behavior has been most commonly examined during conflict between spouses, there is growing empirical evidence that failed attempts to initiate intimacy or to seek support are additional forms of behavioral polarization. We refer jointly to both of these forms of behavior as non-responsive polarizing behaviors. In a typical failed attempt at creating intimacy or seeking support, one spouse makes an attempt to emotionally connect with his or her partner (e.g., makes a vulnerable disclosure or attempts to initiate intimate physical contact), and the behavioral response of the partner results in the disclosing spouse feeling unloved, uncared for, and/or rejected. Repeated occurrences of this cycle result in decreased trust and increased risk for the development of insecure attachment between spouses (Cutrona et al., 2005), as well as for engaging in coercive, polarizing behaviors during conflict (Gottman & Driver, 2005).

Similar polarization patterns can be seen in attributions for individual differences, conflict, and emotional experiences. Partners often come to vilify one another, viewing each other in uncompassionate ways, and understanding differences as failings in the other. Emotional vulnerabilities triggered during polarizing behavioral cycles are often associated with intense, negative feelings that are overwhelming and strongly aversive for many spouses (i.e., flooding; Gottman, 1993). Polarized spouses frequently have difficulty regulating these strong emotions and lash out with "hard" expressions against their spouse (Doohan, Carrere, & Riggs, 2010; Gottman, 1993; Larson, Blick, Jackson, & Holman, 2010; O'Leary, Smith Slep, & O'Leary, 2007). Hard expressions present the self as strong and tough, and include blame, contempt, and hostility. Because they are attacking, these expressions usually lead to separation and misunderstanding rather than to empathic understanding of the emotional vulnerability being intensely experienced. Attributing blame for enduring conflict to the other spouse adds fuel to already high levels of motivation to get the other spouse to change aspects of his or her personality and behavior that are assumed to be causing the distress and further increases risk for future polarization (Caughlin & Vangelisti, 2000; Sagrestano, Christensen, & Heavey, 1998). We now consider risk factors that contribute to the likelihood of spouses engaging in polarization.

RISK FACTORS FOR POLARIZATION

Christensen and Jacobson (2000) suggest that the seeds of polarization are sown in the earliest stages of a relationship. Sources of initial attraction between partners frequently become sources of distress with the passage of time. For example, complementary differences between partners are often exciting during courtship; however, over time, differences can shift from sources of attraction and bonding to sources of conflict and distance between partners. Additionally, differences that tap into partners' emotional vulnerabilities are common threats to marital satisfaction from the very beginning of a relationship.

Research on assortative mating offers empirical support for the potential of sources of attraction to serve as risk factors for eventual polarization. *Assortative mating* is the phenomena of people tending to select partners who are more similar to themselves than would be expected by chance. Though some findings are inconsistent, there is empirical support for the frequent occurrence of assortative mating across a wide range of variables including intelligence, cognitive style, personality, attitudes, interests, beliefs, and emotional experience (e.g., Glicksohn & Golan, 2001; Luo & Klohnen, 2005; McRae et al., 2008; Watson et al., 2004).

From the viewpoint of polarization, what is most striking is that patterns of assortative mating are just as common for personality attributes and styles that confer risk for polarization and marital distress as they are for those that predict positive marital outcomes. Insecure attachment and neuroticism are two examples of traits that are often shared between partners and that can contribute to polarization. Attachment style refers to the cognitive-affective schema that an individual develops based on his or her unique interpersonal experiences and uses to direct social interaction and to understand relationships (Collins, Cooper, Albino, & Allard, 2002). There is general agreement that individuals can be classified as securely or insecurely attached.

Securely attached individuals are "comfortable with intimacy, willing to depend on others for support, and confident that they are loved and valued by others" (Collins et al., 2002, p. 969). Insecure attachment is more variable and can take multiple forms.[3] For example, individuals with an anxious attachment style tend to have "an exaggerated desire for closeness, coupled with a heightened concern about being rejected and unloved." Alternatively, individuals with an avoidant attachment style "value self-reliance and are uncomfortable with intimacy and interdependence" (Collins et al., 2002, p. 969)." Securely attached individuals are significantly more likely to select securely attached mates and insecurely attached individuals tend to become involved with insecurely attached partners (e.g., Collins et al., 2002; Collins & Read, 1990) and partners who are higher in neuroticism (Collins et al., 2002).

Neuroticism refers to an individual's tendency to experience negative affect, with more highly neurotic individuals being more likely to experience negative affect than less neurotic individuals. Consistent with assortative mating findings for attachment, positive correlations have also been found between spouses' levels of neuroticism across cultures and age cohorts (e.g., McRae et al., 2008).

---

[3] There has been some controversy about whether attachment is a categorical trait, or whether individuals vary along dimensions of attachment. Moreover, there have been different proposals for the number of different attachment styles. For a review, see Ravitz, Maunder, Hunter, Sthankiya, and Lancee (2010).

Both partners' insecure attachment styles and higher levels of neuroticism are strongly linked with negative marital outcomes (e.g., Dyrenforth, Kashy, Donnellan, & Lucas, 2010; Luo et al., 2008; Mondor, McDuff, Lussier, & Wright, 2011) and increase the likelihood that the couple will engage in polarizing behavioral cycles (e.g., Buss, 1992; Collins et al., 2002; Caughlin & Vangelisti, 2000; Pasch, Bradbury, & Davila, 1997).

Another risk factor for polarization is found in the individual differences that inevitably exist between spouses. Even though there is strong evidence of assortative mating across a wide range of variables, the effect sizes of these associations tend to be small to moderate (McRae et al., 2008). This means that while individuals may be more similar than would be expected by chance, there are also notable differences between partners (DeCuyper, De Bolle, & de Fruyt, 2011; Huston & Houts, 1998). Individual differences between partners can be initial sources of attraction when they offer opportunities for broadening perspectives, having novel experiences, and expanding capabilities (i.e., self-expansion; Aron & Aron, 1997). Difference based opportunities for self-expansion are particularly attractive for people who have a high level of reward seeking motivation (Mattingly, McIntyre, & Lewandowski, 2011) and when differences pose a low level of threat to the relationship (Aron, Steele, Kashdan, & Perez, 2006).

Regardless of whether individual differences were an initial source of attraction or not, they are potent risk factors for marital distress by increasing the likelihood of polarization. Individual differences have not been consistently found to have a direct effect on marital distress. Some studies link greater differences between spouses to lower levels of concurrent marital satisfaction (e.g., Gonzaga, Campos, & Bradbury, 2007; Luo et al., 2008), but other studies find that greater differences are associated with higher levels of marital satisfaction over time, to depend on age (Shiota & Levenson, 2007), or to be unrelated to marital satisfaction (e.g., Gattis, Berns, Simpson, & Christensen, 2004). Rather, individual differences between spouses appear to impact marital distress indirectly through their effect on how spouses view one another and interact with one another.

More pronounced individual differences are associated with more divergent perspectives on spouses' qualities and attributes and an increased likelihood of engaging in polarizing interaction patterns. For example, higher levels of self-verification, which refers to agreement between partners about an individual's attributes, are associated with higher levels of intimacy, authenticity, trust, behavioral commitment, and relationship satisfaction (Burke & Stets, 1999; Swann, De La Ronde, & Hixon, 1994). Likewise, agreement between spouses' about one spouse's personality is more robustly and more consistently associated with higher levels of marital satisfaction than is either spouse feeling that the two spouses' personalities are similar (Decuyper et al., 2011). Importantly, perceptual accuracy (agreement between spouses' judgments) is also significantly associated with actual similarity (similarity of spouses' personalities); partners tend to describe each other in more divergent ways when their personalities are actually more different from one another. With regard to polarizing interaction patterns, a number of specific individual differences between spouses, such as differences in neuroticism and desired level of closeness (Caughlin & Vangelisti, 2000; Christensen & Shenk, 1991), are associated with more frequent and more intense engagement in polarizing behaviors.

Finally, there are many additional intrapersonal factors that contribute to spouses' tendencies to engage in or to refrain from engaging in polarizing behavior. One particularly important additional set of factors is social learning experiences in earlier significant relationships (e.g., family of origin experiences and prior romantic relationships). There is ample evidence that children who grow up in homes where parents engage in destructive marital communication behaviors and in less nurturant parenting behaviors tend to engage in higher levels of destructive marital communication behaviors with their own spouses (Conger, Cui, Bryant, & Elder, 2000; Story, Karney, Lawrence, & Bradbury, 2004). Likewise, levels of polarizing behavior appear to be stable across first and second marriages (Sandin Allen, Baucom, Burnett, Epstein, & Rankin-Esquer, 2001). As is true of many other behaviors, repeated exposure to polarizing behavior in significant interpersonal contexts appears to increase the likelihood that spouses will engage in polarizing behaviors in their own marriages.

In summary, the polarization process describes a behavioral, affective, and cognitive cycle in which unsuccessful attempts to quell relationship distress and to enhance intimacy backfire and result in spouses engaging in more extreme forms of behavior over time and feeling increasingly hopeless, separate, and deeply dissatisfied. Vulnerabilities, such as differences that fed initial attractions, spouses' individual personalities, and spouses' social learning experiences in previous romantic relationships and family of origin, confer risk for engaging in polarizing behavioral cycles. In turn, polarizing behavioral cycles are frequently associated with high levels of emotional reactance, high levels of blame, and low levels of acceptance for individual differences between partners, which increase the likelihood of both further polarization and diminished satisfaction over time.

UNIQUE AND OVERLAPPING ASPECTS OF THE POLARIZATION MODEL

Before reviewing theoretical perspectives that lend support to the polarization model, it is important to consider how this model is similar to and different from other models of relationship distress. There is strong similarity with other models on foundational assumptions, such as the importance of emotion, behavior, and cognition (e.g., *cognitive behavioral models*—Epstein & Baucom, D., 2002; Bradbury & Fincham, 1990; Markman, Stanley, & Blumberg, 1994; the *vulnerability-stress-adaptation model*—Karney & Bradbury, 1995; and the *cascade model of marital dissolution*—Gottman, 1993). Conceptual overlap with these other models likely reflects the collaborative and synergistic work of many researchers during the 1980s and 1990s on such dominant areas of inquiry as attributions, behavioral sequences, and emotional reactivity. Despite considerable content overlap across these models, each also has unique conceptual aspects that differentiate it from the others.

The polarization model can be distinguished from these more general models of relationship distress in two primary ways. First, the polarization process itself is the specific aspect of marital distress that is associated with the intensification of conflict producing behaviors, cognitions, and emotional experiences. There are many other aspects of the development of marital distress that are not described by the polarization process. Second, the risk factors described by the polarization model: (1) incorporate mechanisms that describe how forces that initially bring spouses together can eventually drive partners apart; (2) explicitly include interpersonal variables across multiple generations and relationships that impinge on current marital functioning; and (3) provide proximal pathways (e.g., triggered emotional vulnerabilities), by which relatively static intrapersonal variables (e.g., family of origin experiences, neuroticism, and insecure attachment) increase the likelihood of engaging in specific behavioral cycles that contribute to the escalation of marital distress. Thus, the polarization model is a more narrowly circumscribed conceptual model that describes a particular set of marital distress producing processes and related risk factors than many of the other etiological models of marital distress cited above.

REVIEW AND CRITIQUE OF THEORETICAL PERSPECTIVES ON POLARIZATION

The importance of the polarization process for the development of marital distress finds support from a number of theoretical perspectives. No one single theory has been applied to the study of all elements that comprise the polarization model; rather, individual components have been empirically examined in isolation or jointly in small number. The resulting set of findings creates a patchwork quilt of support for the ideas presented above. We focus our selective review on a collection of theories that combine to offer a wide range of perspectives and that have been empirically evaluated. Theoretical perspectives on key elements of each aspect of the polarization model (polarizing behaviors, polarizing cognitions, and emotional vulnerability) are presented below, and references for additional information on theories discussed in brief or omitted due to space limitations are included where possible.

THEORETICAL PERSPECTIVES ON POLARIZING BEHAVIORAL CYCLES

Demand/Withdraw Interaction Pattern

The majority of the theoretical work on and empirical inquiry into polarizing behavioral cycles has concentrated on the demand/withdraw interaction pattern. The most enduring focus of this research has been to account for variability in demanding and withdrawing behavior between spouses. Variability in demanding and withdrawing behaviors appears to come from an interaction between two primary sources: gender and which spouse has determined the topic of discussion. In general, women tend to *demand* more than men, men tend to *withdraw* more than women, and all spouses tend to demand more and withdraw less when discussing topics they have identified relative to discussing topics their partners' have identified. Additionally, gender and topic interact such that gender differences are more pronounced during discussion of topics determined by women than during discussion of topics determined by men. During wife selected topics, wives demand significantly more than husbands and husbands withdraw significantly more than wives (e.g., Heavey, Layne, & Christensen, 1993; Vogel & Karney, 2003); however, during husband selected topics, some studies find husband demand/wife withdraw to occur at significantly higher levels than wife demand/husband withdraw (e.g., Klinetob & Smith, 1996), although other studies find no significant differences between spouses' behavior (e.g., Vogel & Karney, 2003).

Several different theoretical models have been advanced and evaluated to account for these patterns of demanding and withdrawing behaviors. The *escape conditioning model* (Gottman & Levenson, 1988) emphasizes the importance of emotional reactivity for gender differences in demanding and withdrawing behavior. This model suggests that men's tendency to withdraw more than women is linked to men's tendency to experience higher levels of aversive arousal during interpersonal conflict (i.e., to be more emotionally reactive) than women[4]; withdrawing may be an effective way to reduce aversive arousal. Tests of the escape conditioning model consistently find associations between higher levels of overall demand/withdraw behavior and higher levels of aversive arousal for both spouses using a variety of methods for measuring arousal including physiology (e.g., Kiecolt-Glaser et al., 1996); vocally encoded arousal (Baucom, B., et al., 2011); and self-report (Verhofstadt, Buysse, De Clercq, & Goodwin, 2005). Similar consistency is seen in associations between arousal and withdrawing behavior where most studies fail to link withdrawing behavior to arousal (e.g., Baucom, B., et al., 2011; Kiecolt-Glaser et al., 1996). One exception to this general pattern comes from the work of Denton, Burleson, Hobbs, Von Stein, & Rodroguez (2001), who link higher levels of withdrawing behavior to greater systolic blood pressure reactivity.

Despite the failure of most studies to link arousal to withdrawing behavior, the escape conditioning model continues to figure prominently in examination of demand/withdraw behavior. Two recent studies suggest refinements to the model, which may help to account for previous null findings. In partial support of the escape condition model, Verhofstadt and colleagues (2005) find husbands to report lower levels of arousal after conversations in which they withdrew more and demanded less but wives reported higher levels of arousal after conversations in which they withdrew more and demanded less; these results suggest that the escape conditioning model may be more applicable to men than to women.

In contrast to the hypothesis of the escape conditioning model, Baucom, B., et al. (2011) find demanders to exhibit higher levels of aversive arousal than withdrawers and suggest that this finding

---

[4] Subsequent studies to Gottman and Levenson (1988) have produced conflicting results regarding whether men or women are more emotionally reactive during interpersonal conflict. For example, Kiecolt-Glaser and Newton (2001) conclude that women are more reactive to interpersonal stressors than men. This inconsistency in findings paired with recent findings documenting that gay male and lesbian couples engage in demand-withdraw behaviors in similar ways to heterosexual couples (B. Baucom et al., 2010b; Holley, Sturm, & Levenson, 2010) suggests that the escape conditioning model may be more appropriately thought of as an individual differences model (i.e., spouses are different in their reactivity to relationship conflict) than a gender differences model.

may be explained by considering the specific emotions associated with demanding and withdrawing behaviors. Demanding is most likely to occur in the context of approach oriented emotions like anger and frustration while withdrawing is most likely to occur in the context of avoidance oriented emotions like anxiety and fear. Additional work is needed to further examine gender differences in the applicability of the escape conditioning model and to empirically examine links between different emotions and demanding and withdrawing behaviors.

Though it retains a focus on individual differences between spouses, the *gender role socialization model* (e.g., Sagrestano, L. M., Heavey, C. L., & Christensen, A., 2006) takes an alternative perspective from the escape conditioning model. This model suggests that women's tendency to demand may be related to socialization experiences that reinforce the importance of having a communal orientation and engaging in relationship maintaining behaviors (alternatively referred to as femininity or expressivity), while men's propensity to withdraw may be related to socialization experiences that encourage independence and autonomy (alternatively referred to as masculinity or instrumentality; Bem, 1974; Helmreich, Spence, & Wilhelm, 1981). There is mixed empirical support for the gender role socialization model.

In consistent support of the model, numerous studies link higher levels of desired closeness to higher levels of demanding behavior (e.g., Christensen, 1987). Results are less consistent when socialization experiences are operationalized in terms of gender stereotyped personality characteristics (e.g., femininity and masculinity). Walczynski (1997) links higher levels of femininity to higher levels of demanding, but Caughlin and Huston (2002) link higher levels of femininity to lower levels of self demand/partner withdraw. This collection of findings provides general support for this model and indicates that proximal measures of socialization experiences with particular relevance for marriages, such as level of desired closeness, are more strongly linked to demand/withdraw behavior than are more general measures of socialization experiences, such as overall masculinity and femininity.

Finally, the *conflict structure model* (Heavey et al., 1993) emphasizes the importance of interdependence between *requestor* and *requestee* for the demand/withdraw interaction pattern. When the requestor is seeking change it frequently cannot occur without the agreement and participation of the requestee. This interdependent nature of the desired change establishes a structure where the requestor is more likely to demand and the requestee is more likely to withdraw. Recent work by Eldridge and colleagues (Eldridge, Sevier, Jones, Atkins, & Christensen, 2007) both confirms this model and suggests the need to consider which spouse is the agent of change to better understand variability in demanding and withdrawing behaviors across interaction contexts. Eldridge et al. (2007) find that spouses tend to withdraw more and demand less than their partners when they (the spouse) are the agent of change independent of which spouse is seeking change. Though interdependence of demanding and withdrawing behaviors is clearly an important aspect of this polarizing behavioral cycle (e.g., Baucom, B., et al., 2010b), interdependence of desired change does not fully account for gender differences in demanding and withdrawing behaviors.

In summary, demand/withdraw behavior has been studied from several theoretical perspectives including the escape conditioning model, the gender role socialization model, and the conflict structure model. The escape conditioning, gender role socialization, and conflict structure models have all received mixed empirical support and no one theory is able to fully account for variability in demanding and withdrawing behaviors. Recent developments suggest that continued investigation of moderators of the escape conditioning model (specifically gender and specific emotions) may help to further understand how proximal correlates of triggered emotional vulnerabilities (i.e., aversive emotional arousal) are related to demanding and withdrawing behavior.

Intimacy

Theoretical development of and empirical inquiry into intimacy and social support processes have largely been driven by motivations other than understanding how these processes are related to polarization. Much of the existing literature on intimacy and social support examines the importance of these two processes for overall relationship functioning with a particular emphasis on positive relationship processes and as a mechanism for coping with stress and crisis. However, the *interpersonal process model of intimacy* (Reis & Shaver, 1988; Reis & Patrick, 1996) and the *relationship enhancement model of social support* (Cutrona, Russell, & Gardner, 2005) have direct relevance for understanding polarization and additionally suggest specific mechanisms by which intimacy and social support processes may contribute to the development of polarization.

The interpersonal process model of intimacy suggests that intimacy is a transactional process between partners that occurs when one partner discloses a personally relevant thought or feeling and receives a response from the partner that feels validating, caring, and understanding (Reis & Shaver, 1988). A spouse's needs, goals, and motivations are assumed to impact his or her behavior and to act as a filter for interpreting the other's behavior. Specific behaviors are not assumed to have the same meaning for all couples but rather to vary in the extent to which they are experienced as meeting underlying needs and goals. Highly responsive behaviors that meet needs and goals are more likely to result in intimacy than are less responsive behaviors. A number of studies provide strong empirical support for this model. For example, higher levels of self- and partner disclosure are associated with higher levels of intimacy and perceived partner responsiveness partially mediates the effects of both self- and partner disclosure on intimacy for both husbands and wives (Dorian & Cordova, 2001, as cited in Dorian & Cordova, 2004; Laurenceau, Barrett, & Pietromonaco, 1998; Laurenceau, Barrett, & Rovine, 2005).

The relationship enhancement model (Cutrona et al., 2005) of social support is conceptually similar to the interpersonal process model of intimacy in many respects. The relationship enhancement model suggests that supportive behaviors are beneficial to the extent that they are perceived to be consistently available from a spouse who is motivated by kindness, love, and commitment. Behaviors perceived in this way are considered to provide adequate and sensitive support (Cutrona, Shaffer, Wesner, & Gardner, 2007; Lawrence, et al., 2008), which is very similar to the concept of partner responsiveness in the interpersonal process model of intimacy. Supportive behavior results in increased levels of trust in and secure attachment to the partner, reflected in an enhanced expectation that the partner will be responsive to future needs. These changes ultimately impact relationship satisfaction and stability through changes in both behavior, such as decreased reassurance seeking, and cognition, such as a decreased likelihood of making blaming attributions for negative partner behaviors.

Despite the considerable overlap of the two models, there are two important conceptual differences. The first is the intent of the models to explain how couples cope with distress versus how couples create intimacy. The relationship enhancement model was originally developed to investigate the impact of social support processes on relational and physical health and, as a result, is more focused on couple interaction within the context of intra- and interpersonal distress. In contrast, the interpersonal process model of intimacy is a more general model that can be equally applied to interactions within the context of distress (i.e., those that involve a disclosure about a vulnerable topic) as well as those within the context of flourishing (i.e., those that involve disclosure about feelings of love for the spouse). The second main conceptual difference is what kind of behaviors the two models consider to be relevant. The interpersonal process model of intimacy considers emotional disclosure to be substantially more important than informational disclosure (Laurenceau et al., 2005). In contrast, the relationship enhancement model considers information and emotional disclosures to be of similar importance.

The importance of these theoretical models for the polarization process comes from consideration of interactions where personally relevant disclosure or support seeking behavior is responded to in a manner that is not perceived as validating, caring, and understanding. Theorists (e.g., Wile, 1993) have suggested and researchers have documented that unsuccessful attempts at initiating intimate interactions are associated with an increased likelihood of engaging in coercive polarization processes, such as the demand/withdraw interaction pattern, during conflict (Gottman & Driver, 2005; Laurenceau et al., 2005). These findings are consistent with the well documented association between greater desired closeness and increased levels of demand/withdraw behavior during conflict. The experience of closeness with one's partner is a defining characteristic of intimate interactions; thus, it is likely that partners who desire, but have difficulty achieving, closeness and intimacy are also more likely to engage in coercive patterns during conflict. In a similar fashion, insensitive and inadequate provision of social support is associated with a stronger tendency to engage in negative reciprocity (Pasch et al., 1997).

Findings linking failed attempts to create intimacy or to seek support to an increased likelihood of engaging in coercive behavioral cycles help to explicate specific paths by which potentially positive processes can contribute to polarization. One limitation of this line of research is that positive behavioral processes and coercive behavioral processes have largely been examined in isolation. The few studies that have examined both are inconsistent in their conclusions with some studies finding both positive and coercive processes to be associated with concurrent (Pasch & Bradbury, 1998) and longitudinal relationship functioning (Sullivan, Pasch, Johnson, & Bradbury, 2010), but other studies finding significant associations only between coercive processes and longitudinal relationship functioning (Markman et al., 2010). Additionally, there have yet to be studies of associations between positive and coercive processes within the context of the same interaction. One intuitive hypothesis about the linkage between positive and coercive processes that can be derived from polarization theory is that a failed attempt at creating intimacy or seeking social support may immediately precede coercive behavior. For example, if one partner wants to be close with the other but is unsuccessful in gaining the desired closeness, it is plausible that the partner desiring closeness may feel hurt by a perceived rebuke or sleight and continue to push for closeness using "hard" expressions that include anger, blame, and are attacking of the other spouse (e.g., "What is wrong with you?" or "Why are you so selfish?"; Sanford, 2007) that lead into conflict with high levels of coercion. These couples may be qualitatively different from couples that typically engage in coercive behavior without first experiencing a failed attempt at creating intimacy or seeking social support.

THEORETICAL PERSPECTIVES ON POLARIZING COGNITIVE PROCESSES

A final element of polarization that has been subjected to theoretical development and empirical examination is the way that spouses understand the causes of relationship conflict and the impact of individual differences on relationship functioning. *Attribution theory* (e.g., Bradbury & Fincham, 1990; Epstein & Baucom, D., 2002; Fincham, 2001) has been the dominant theoretical framework for examining cognitive processes related to marital distress for the previous two decades.

Findings from research on marital attributions support three key tenets of the polarization model. First, a growing body of evidence suggests that longitudinal associations between attributions and relationship satisfaction are bidirectional. This finding is consistent with the idea of vilification presented above and the general idea of polarization as a cyclical and escalating process. When spouses come to see one another as being responsible for negative behavior, independent of the perceived cause of the negative behavior, spouses become less satisfied, and when spouses are less satisfied, they tend to see each other in increasingly conflict-promoting ways (Fincham & Bradbury, 1993; Fincham, Harold, & Gano-Phillips, 2000; Karney & Bradbury, 2000). Second, though not all studies link attributions to behavior (e.g., Bradbury, Beach, Fincham, & Nelson, 1996), higher levels of conflict-promoting attributions are associated with higher levels of both coercive polarizing cycles (Bradbury & Fincham, 1992) and failed attempts at initiating and maintaining intimacy (Kirby et al., 2005). Third, vulnerabilities associated with an increased tendency to engage in polarizing behavior (i.e., neuroticism) are also associated with an increased likelihood of making conflict-promoting attributions (Karney, Bradbury, Fincham, & Sullivan, 1994; McNulty, 2008).

As other authors have noted (e.g., Fincham, 2001), one limitation of existing research on attribution theory is that attributions for the occurrence of actual behaviors have yet to receive substantial empirical attention. The current state of knowledge is largely based on attributions for partner behaviors in general; very little is currently known about attributions for specific behaviors during the course of conflict, intimacy initiation, or support seeking. One exception is the work of Clements and Holtzworth-Munroe (2008), who find that violent male and female spouses make more aggressive attributions than non-violent distressed and non-violent non-distressed spouses for specific behaviors during interaction. Their methodology could be used to examine attributions for polarizing behavioral cycles and may be of particular value in examining polarizing cycles that involve withdrawal. As Fincham (2001) notes, attributions are more common for acts of commission (e.g., a criticism, demand, or vulnerable disclosure) than acts of omission (e.g., withdrawal, non-response, or side-stepping), and the role of attributions in polarizing behavioral cycles may therefore vary depending on both partners' behaviors.

THEORETICAL PERSPECTIVES ON EMOTIONAL VULNERABILITY AS A RISK FACTOR FOR POLARIZING PROCESSES

In this section, we focus on two of the aspects of emotional vulnerabilities, personality and family of origin experiences. Attachment theory, described above, offers a valuable perspective for conceptualizing the importance of both personality and family of origin experiences for polarization. Another theoretical perspective that offers important insight into the role of personality for polarization comes from the work of Huston and colleagues (Huston & Houts, 1998; Huston, Caughlin, Houts, Smith, & George, 2001), who evaluated two competing models for explaining the impact of personality on marital functioning over time.

The *disillusionment model* (Huston, 1994) suggests that spouses attempt to conceal problematic characteristics and make unsustainable efforts to ignore incompatibilities during courtship but that these efforts quickly subside after marriage. The *perpetual problems model* (Huston, 1994) alternatively proposes that aspects of spouses' personalities that contribute to marital distress are evident from the earliest stages of a relationship and that spouses develop emotional and cognitive reactions to these aspects of personality that remain relatively stable over the course of the marriage.

Data collected over the first 13 years of marriage lend strong support to both the perpetual problems model and the disillusionment model, but suggest that the two models do not apply equally to all couples. The perpetual problems model appears to best differentiate couples who remain married and are satisfied from couples who remain married but are dissatisfied. For example, in married, satisfied couples, spouses view their partners' personalities more positively during the engagement period than do spouses in married, dissatisfied couples. The disillusionment model is better able to distinguish couples who divorce from those who remain married. For example, declines in positive views of partners' personalities and increases in negative views of partners' personalities are significantly larger in couples that divorced than in couples that remained married. These findings document two different routes by which personality is related to polarization and suggest that the timing of the onset of polarization is significant for the long-term viability of a marriage. Relationships in which polarization emerges after marriage appear particularly fragile and likely to end in divorce, whereas in relationships that show some polarization during engagement, relationship stability appears more likely even when in the context of marital dissatisfaction.

In addition to a strong emphasis on attachment, research on the impact of family of origin experiences on adult relationship functioning has largely focused on the impact of parental divorce. The impact of experiencing parental divorce for polarization is most likely to be indirect and mediated through more proximal variables, such as attachment (e.g., Hazan & Shaver, 1992), behavior (e.g., Story et al., 2004), and attributions (e.g., Grych & Fincham, 1992), discussed elsewhere in this chapter. Clearer theoretical implications and more immediate ties between family of origin experiences and polarization come from Gubbins, Perosa, and Bartle-Haring's (2010) examination of the association between differentiation, derived from Bowen's (1978) *family system theory*, and emotional reactivity during conflict. Differentiation refers to one's sense of self as separate versus overlapping from others; more specifically, differentiation refers to one's ability to use emotional and cognitive resources for directing and regulating behavior as well as to one's ability to balance separation from and connectedness with others. Highly differentiated spouses are able to "maintain a sense of self during intense interactions, to remain calm, problem solve, and compromise…, are comfortable both with intimacy and autonomy," whereas less differentiated spouses are "over-whelmed by emotions and either engage in emotional cutoff or seek fusion with others" (Gubbins et al., 2010, p. 384). In a sample of 169 married couples, higher levels of differentiation were associ-ated with significantly lower levels of emotional reactivity during conflict (Gubbins et al., 2010). Lower levels of differentiation may therefore be associated with greater likelihood of polarization. One unique contribution of this finding comes from the inclusion of one's ability to "maintain a sense of self during intense interactions" (Gubbins et al., 2010, p. 384) in the concept of differentia-tion. Flooding (i.e., feeling emotionally overwhelmed and out of control during conflict; Gottman, 1993) is a specific form of extreme emotional reactivity that may coincide with loss of a sense of self during intense conflict. Sense of self is an interesting and underexplored concept that may yield new insights into the emotional reactivity component of polarization in future research.

LIMITATIONS OF EXISTING THEORY USAGE AND SUGGESTIONS FOR FUTURE THEORETICAL DEVELOPMENTS AND RESEARCH ON POLARIZATION

As described in the preceding section, a wide range of theories have been profitably applied to the study of processes in the polarization model. One striking characteristic about much of this work is that while emotion figures prominently in many theoretical models and is oftentimes mentioned as a hypothesized mechanism of action, few studies have explicitly examined emotional processes in the polarization process. One clear exception to this general pattern is work based on the escape conditioning model (Gottman & Levenson, 1988) but theoretical limitations of and mixed empirical support for this model restrict its ability to account for the full range of polarizing behavioral, emo-tional, and cognitive processes. Emotion, therefore, remains a profitable area for future research and theoretical development. Of the numerous potential processes in the field of emotion, empathy holds particular promise for future study and theoretical development related to polarization.

Empathy is a complex phenomenon that has been defined by scholars and researchers in numerous ways. Consistent with previous definitions of the term (see Batson, 2009, for a review), we use empathy to refer to the process by which spouses experience, perceive, and interpret the internal emotional and cognitive states of one another. It is important to distinguish the process of empathy from an empathic response, which is the behavioral outcome of the process of empathy. An attuned empathic response not only expresses an accurate interpretation of the internal state of the other spouse but also is delivered in a manner that conveys an emotional understanding, pro-motes constructive problem-solving, and enhances intimacy. In contrast, a non-empathic response fails to communicate an emotional understanding, maintains conflict, or inhibits intimacy. Both the process of empathy and the expression of empathic understanding (or lack thereof) are likely to play important roles in polarizing processes.

The *perception action model of empathy* (PAM; Preston & de Waal, 2002) and the *empathic accuracy model* (Ickes & Simpson, 1997) provide conceptual foundations for developing theory that relates empathy to the polarization process. PAM is a broad and comprehensive intrapersonal model of empathy that describes the physiological substrates of empathy and that identifies individual factors that increase risk for inaccurate interpretation and non-empathic response. The empathic accuracy model is an interpersonal model that describes how relationship variables influence the likelihood of accurate interpretation. Though these two models were developed to describe distinct aspects of empathy, they contain several points of conceptual overlap that are also highly consistent with core ideas in the polarization model. We briefly review both models below and note similarities with the polarization model, describe novel hypotheses derived from both models, and conclude by identifying priority areas for future theoretical development.

PAM suggests that empathy consists of three primary aspects, physiological activation and neural representation, automatic cognitive processing, and effortful cognitive processing. The initial phase of empathy occurs when attending to the emotional state of another individual (referred to as the object) activates a cascade of neural representations and corresponding physiological states that are similar to the emotional state being observed by the perceiver. It is similar to the concepts of *emotional transmission* (e.g., Larson & Almeida, 1999); *emotional contagion* (e.g., Hatfield, Cacioppo, & Rapson, 1992); and *coregulation* (e.g., Saxbe & Repetti, 2010). This cascade of responses results in the perceiver experiencing a similar emotional state as the object. Empathy occurs when the perceiver is able to recognize that part of his or her emotional state is in response to the object's emotional state (Hoffman, 2000) and is therefore able to accurately interpret the internal state of the object.

It is important to note that this cascade of response does not necessarily lead to empathy but can alternatively lead to personal distress. Personal distress occurs when the perceiver is not able to differentiate his or her own emotions from his or her partner's emotions, which is likely to be the case during intense conflict and when experiencing flooding. It is also interesting to note that the idea of distinguishing the emotional state of the self and partner is similar to the concept of sense of self in differentiation discussed above. Personal distress is thought to lead to efforts to reduce one's own level of aversive arousal (e.g., the escape conditioning model), whereas empathy is thought to lead to efforts to reduce the other spouse's aversive arousal or emotional need (i.e., attuned responses; Batson, Fultz, & Schoenrade, 1987). Empirical support for PAM is rapidly mounting in animal models as well as in research on psychological disorders and neurological conditions (e.g., autism and frontal lobe damage) where difficulty with empathy is a defining feature (see Preston, 2007, for a review).

Whereas PAM describes intrapersonal aspects of empathy, the empathic accuracy model describes how relationship variables impact empathy and suggests how empathic inaccuracy may be related to the developmental course of polarizing processes. The empathic accuracy model was originally developed to understand how correctly inferring a partner's internal state (which reflects a high level of empathic accuracy) can alternatively be beneficial for, detrimental for, or unrelated to marital functioning. The possibility that empathic accuracy can be detrimental for marital functioning is counter-intuitive; indeed, much research is based on the notion that accurately inferring another's internal state promotes better communication and enhances overall marital satisfaction (e.g., Noller & Ruzzene, 1991). However, empirical support for this supposition is mixed with studies finding higher levels of empathic accuracy to be related to both higher and lower levels of relationship satisfaction (see Ickes & Simpson, 1997, for a review).

The empathic accuracy model suggests that one important determinant of the variability in these findings is the degree of relationship threat experienced during interaction. In support of this idea, Ickes and colleagues (e.g., Simpson, Orina, & Ickes, 2003) link higher levels of empathic accuracy to short-term declines in closeness during threatening interactions and find that empathic inaccuracy during threatening interactions is a protective factor against relationship instability. Conversely, higher levels of empathic accuracy during less threatening interactions are consistently linked with better marital functioning and with increased likelihood of engaging in accommodation behaviors (Bissonnette, Rusbult, & Kilpatrick, 1997).

A final important consideration for extending the empathic accuracy model to the polarization process comes from findings demonstrating that levels of empathic accuracy are unstable over time and that the impact of empathic accuracy on marital functioning appears to decline over time. Longitudinal studies of within-subject empathic accuracy generally find little to no association in empathic accuracy over time (e.g., Bissonnette et al., 1997; Thomas, Fletcher, & Lange, 1995, as cited in Thomas & Fletcher, 1997) and find the association between empathic accuracy and relationship functioning to wane over time. For example, Bissonnette et al. (1997) link empathic accuracy to marital functioning only for couples within their first year of marriage; however, even couples who demonstrated an early association between empathic accuracy and marital functioning fail to evidence a significant link between the two variables once they have been married for 2 or more years.

This collection of findings suggests that correctly inferring a partner's internal state is particularly important during the early years of marriage. However, processes that are protective of nascent relationships may ultimately lead to the development of cognitive and behavioral polarization. Ickes and Simpson (1997) suggest early empathic inaccuracy may protect relationships by allowing spouses to maintain positive views of one another and of their relationship and by allowing the couple to become conflict-habituated before confronting particularly threatening issues. However, the long-term benefits of such a process clearly necessitate a couple becoming conflict-habituated which is not the case for couples who become polarized. Rather, it is likely that early empathic inaccuracy contributes to the onset of polarization by contributing to the development of habitual patterns of polarizing behavior based on misunderstanding between partners in situations that involve significant relationship threat.

These findings are convergent with those from the disillusionment model (Huston & Houts, 1998) described earlier. Spouses who initially had highly positive views of one another and who showed subsequent declines in these views were more likely to divorce than were spouses who showed smaller declines in how positively they viewed one another. Likewise, early empathic inaccuracy may contribute to initial maintenance of positive views of a spouse but also set the stage for strong subsequent polarization which may in turn lead to divorce.

These models of empathy can also be extended to non-responsive behavioral polarization. Intimacy initiation attempts and support seeking behaviors are likely to involve low to moderate levels of relationship threat. There are clearly times when seeking support could be highly threatening to a marriage (such as in the context of a life-threatening illness or after losing a job) but these examples are likely exceptions rather than the rule. The empathic accuracy model suggests that high levels of empathic accuracy are likely to promote better relationship functioning during these interactions, and PAM suggests that improved relationship functioning may occur at least in part because higher levels of empathic accuracy give the support providing spouse better insight into what the support seeking spouse needs. These extrapolations dovetail nicely with the concept of support adequacy common to current models of social support. Support adequacy (e.g., Dehle, Larsen, & Landers, 2001) refers to the extent to which provided support matches the needs of the support seeking spouse (i.e., is the partner providing the kind of support that the support seeking spouse wants?). Support adequacy is thought to play a more central role in determining the impact of the support on the receiver than is the quantity or particular type of support provided (Lawrence et al., 2008). Initial support for this hypothesis comes from the work of Verhofstadt and colleagues (2008), who find that higher levels of emotional similarity (a form of attuned emotional responding and a precursor to empathic accuracy) are associated with higher levels of adequate support provision.

In sum, PAM and the empathic accuracy model suggest that the end result of empathy, namely whether one spouse correctly understands the internal state of the other spouse, is impacted both by intrapersonal variables (i.e., personal distress) and by relationship variables (i.e., relationship threat). A simultaneously high level of both variables defines an emotional state similar to what the polarization model refers to as a triggered emotional vulnerability. These models also allow for tentative links to be drawn between empathic misunderstanding, behavioral polarization, and cognition polarization that would benefit from future research.

Combining these two models allows for specification of at least two specific and testable hypotheses regarding the role of empathy in both coercive and nonresponsive polarizing behavior. The first hypothesis examines the role of attending to a partner's emotional state. Empathic inaccuracy could occur either by not attending to the emotional state of the spouse or by failure to attend to the full range of the spouse's emotional state. This latter possibility is particularly likely in polarized marriages. As discussed above, expression of emotional vulnerability is assumed to play a key role in both coercive and non-responsive polarizing cycles, but emotional vulnerability in polarized marriages tends to be communicated using hard expressions that present the self as strong, that are attacking of the partner, and that minimize direct expression of the felt emotional vulnerability. Even if spouses are attempting to attend to one another's emotional states, emotional vulnerability (such as sadness, loneliness, or disappointment) expressed within the context of anger, outrage, or bitterness may make it difficult for partners to attend to both the partner's vulnerable emotional state and the more salient anger. Thus, the lower the ratio of vulnerable disclosure to angry recrimination, the greater the likelihood of empathic inaccuracy and behavioral and cognitive polarization.

The second hypothesis involves partners' attributions for their own emotional states. When spouses attend to their partners' emotional state but do not understand that they are experiencing what their partner is experiencing, personal distress is likely to result and empathic accuracy is likely to be low. When spouses are unaware that at least part of their emotional state is occurring in response to their partner's emotional state during conflict, flooding (Gottman, 1993) is particularly like to occur. Conflict is inherently upsetting and arousing for most spouses. If spouses experience additional arousal within the context of an already upsetting situation, it may contribute to a feeling of being overwhelmed or flooded. Indirect support for this possibility comes from findings showing that individual vulnerabilities that increase the risk for flooding also increase the likelihood of empathic inaccuracy (Ditzen et al., 2009; Rodrigues, Saslow, Garcia, John, & Keltner, 2009).

Some of our recent work provides additional indirect support for this hypothesis. We examined within and between spouse associations in vocally encoded emotional arousal during the problem-solving interactions of chronically and stably distressed treatment-seeking couples using a series of dynamic linear models based on the work of Boker and Laurenceau (2005). These models showed significant covariation between spouses' level of arousal (i.e., when one spouse was more highly aroused, the other was also likely to be more highly aroused) and that when one spouse is more highly aroused, the partner has greater difficulty maintaining an optimum level of arousal (Baucom, B., Atkins, & Christensen, 2010a). These results indicate that distressed spouses have greater difficulty maintaining a comfortable level of arousal when they are already highly aroused and are pulled into an emotional resonance with their highly aroused partners. Though vocally encoded arousal was not linked to empathy or to coercive or nonresponsive polarizing behaviors in these models, other research has linked higher levels of arousal to higher levels of demand/withdraw behavior in these same couples (e.g., Baucom, B., et al., 2011).

The role of attributions for emotional state also holds promise for understanding factors that contribute to the co-occurrence of coercive and nonresponsive behavioral cycles in polarized marriages. Spouses who are likely to get flooded by emotion during conflict may also be distressed by emotional similarity experienced during intimacy initiation and support seeking. If a spouse has difficulty recognizing that some of his or her own emotional state is in reaction to the partner's emotional state during conflict, it is also possible that this spouse would be distressed by his or her own emotional response to a partner's vulnerable disclosure. These spouses may deliberately attempt to attend to their partner's emotional needs but have considerable difficulty tolerating the emotion they experience while doing so. Alternatively, difficulty tolerating emotional arousal experienced during positive interaction with a spouse may also contribute to the push/pull behavior typified by the behavior of polarized couples. The same difficulty with tolerating emotion may also make it difficult for spouses to tolerate heightened levels of emotional arousal experienced while receiving social support or during intimate moments. It is possible that a spouse could make a vulnerable disclosure and receive an attentive response from the partner, but still wind up experiencing distress if that spouse has difficulty tolerating the subsequent level of emotional arousal.

In addition to empirical examination of hypotheses directly derived from PAM and the empathic accuracy model, theoretical refinement is needed to further clarify the role of empathy in the polarization model. Below, we identify three areas of need for theoretical development with a focus on the role of the relationship in the occurrence of empathy. A first area for theoretical refinement is related to the equifinality of empathic inaccuracy. As Ickes and Simpson (1997) suggest, there are many relational processes that may influence one's spouse tendency to incorrectly infer the emotional state of the other in addition to the degree of perceived relationship threat. Behavioral interdependence, epitomized in polarized behavioral cycles such as demand/withdraw and negative escalation, is hypothesized to be one such obstacle to empathic accuracy in intimate relationships (Sillars, 1985). However, the polarization model suggests that behavioral interdependence is at least partially the product of empathic inaccuracy. This tautology leads to three possibilities: (1) empathic inaccuracy and polarizing behavioral cycles may develop in parallel; (2) polarizing behavioral cycles may contribute to the onset of empathic inaccuracy; or (3) empathic inaccuracy may contribute to the onset of polarizing behavioral cycles. The nature of the association between empathic inaccuracy and polarizing behavioral cycles is likely to vary across couples, but none of the existing theoretical models suggest risk factors or mechanisms that help to explain why some couples demonstrate one particular path of development nor do they conceptualize the implications of the different paths for polarization and relationship functioning.

A second area for theoretical refinement is incorporation of the dynamic nature of behavioral exchange during interaction. The polarization model assumes that each spouse's behavior and emotional state are simultaneously reactions to the other spouse as well as precursors of the other spouse's behavioral and emotional response. Reformulating the linear, sequential structure described by PAM and the empathic accuracy model as a dynamic, iterative process would increase the flexibility of the models and likely increase the ability of these models to account for within-couple variation in empathy and empathic responding both over the course of an interaction as well as over longer periods of time.

A final area that warrants additional theoretical development is the links among empathy, empathic accuracy, and behavioral responses. Neither PAM nor the empathic accuracy model suggest how empathic accuracy is embedded in the behavioral responses of spouses nor do they suggest what types of behavioral responses are likely to be functional or dysfunctional. Empathic responses are likely to be idiosyncratic in nature, and it is probable that they will be most easily clustered into attuned empathic responses and mis-attuned, non-empathic responses by considering their functional outcomes. Support adequacy is an example of this type of classification scheme. Support adequacy defines the functionality of supportive behaviors by considering how closely they are aligned to the kind of support that is desired. This definition is flexible enough to allow both the support giving spouse and the support seeking spouse to vary considerably over time (different behaviors can be considered either functional or dysfunctional on different occasions) while also being grounded in a consistent metric (how close is the support given to the support desired).

CONCLUSION

The polarization process describes how coercive and non-responsive behavioral cycles, vilifying attributions, and emotional reactivity become more extreme over time. The polarization model elucidates intrapersonal (e.g., neuroticism, insecure attachment), interpersonal (e.g., assortative mating and individual differences), and intergenerational (social learning and differentiation) risk factors for engaging in the polarizing process. Substantial empirical evidence supports many of the theoretical assumptions of the polarization model, and a large body of theoretical and empirical work has been dedicated to understanding polarizing processes. Recent developments in the study of nonresponsive polarizing cycles are particularly noteworthy as they identify new avenues for exploration and provide novel frameworks for expanding our understanding of a broader range of polarizing behavioral cycles. Future work on the nature of the associations between nonresponsive and coercive cycles is particularly needed. Likewise, exploration of emotional polarizing processes is ripe for additional empirical and theoretical development. Empathic failure is theoretically implicated as a core element of polarization processes, and the Perception Action Model of empathy and the empathic accuracy model appear to offer great potential for developing theory and testing specific hypotheses about the role of empathy in polarization processes.

The value of refining and incorporating empathy models into the polarization model comes not only from the additional theoretical complexity and breadth they offer but also from the fact that they may help identify targets for clinical intervention. For example, linking difficulty tolerating emotional arousal to coercive and nonresponsive cycles suggests that exposure may be a valuable form of intervention for polarized spouses (Christensen, Atkins, Baucom, B., & Yi, 2010). Likewise, identifying individual dispositions, relational processes, and areas of conflict that contribute to empathic inaccuracy may help define target mechanisms for disrupting this unique form of cognitive distortion that tends to be a blind-spot for many spouses. It is a fascinating contradiction that the longer spouses have been married, the less they appear to use actual behavior to interpret the internal states of their partners during interaction yet the greater their confidence in the accuracy of their interpretation (e.g., Sillars & Scott, 1983). In contrast to spouse's exquisite awareness of other polarizing processes that are frequently amongst stated reasons for seeking couple therapy, spouses appear to have very little insight into how well they are able to understand one another's internal experience. Continued refinement of the polarization model along these lines holds promise for more clearly identifying the causal factors driving the entrenched tug-of-war in many distressed marriages and for suggesting targets for intervention that are likely to be effective in helping distressed couples assume more collaborative and less polarizing stances.

REFERENCES

Agnew, C. R., Van Lange, P. A. M., Rusbult, C. E., & Langston, C. A. (1998). Cognitive interdependence: Commitment and the mental representation of close relationships. *Journal of Personality and Social Psychology, 74*, 939–954.

Anderson, S. A., & Sabatelli R. M. (2010). *Family interaction: A multigenerational developmental perspective.* Boston: Allyn & Bacon.

Aron, A., & Aron, E. N. (1997). Self-expansion motivation and including the other in the self. In S. Duck (Ed.), *Handbook of personal relationships: Theory, research, and interventions* (2nd ed., pp. 251–270). London, England: Wiley.

Aron, A., Steele, J. L., Kashdan, T. B., & Perez, M. (2006). When similar do not attract: Tests of a prediction from the self-expansion model. *Personal Relationships, 13*, 387–396.

Arriaga, X. B., & Rusbult, C. E. (1998). Standing in my partner's shows: Partner perspective taking and reactions to accommodative dilemmas. *Personality and Social Psychology Bulletin, 24*, 927–948.

Batson, C. D. (2009). These things called empathy: Eight related but distinct phenomena. In J. Decety & W. Ickes (Eds.), *The social neuroscience of empathy* (pp. 3–16). Cambridge, MA: MIT Press.

Batson, C.D., Fultz, J., & Schoenrade, P.A. (1987). Distress and empathy: Two qualitatively different motivational consequences. *Journal of Personality, 55*, 19–39. doi: 10.1111/j.1467-6494.1987.tb00426.x

Baucom, B., Atkins, D., & Christensen, A. (2010a). *Changes in vocally encoded emotional arousal in two behavioral couple therapies.* Poster presented at the triannual meeting of the World Congress of Behavioral and Cognitive Therapies, Boston, MA.

Baucom, B., McFarland, P., & Christensen, A. (2010b). Gender, topic, and time in observed demand/withdraw interaction in cross- and same-sex couples. *Journal of Family Psychology, 24*, 233–242.

Baucom, B. R., Atkins, D., Eldridge, K., McFarland, P., Sevier, M., & Christensen, A. (2011). The language of demand/withdraw: Verbal and vocal expressions in dyadic interaction. *Journal of Family Psychology, 25*, 570–580.

Bissonnette, V. L., Rusbult, C. E., & Kilpatrick, S. D. (1997). Empathic accuracy and marital conflict resolution. In W. Ickes (Ed.), *Empathic accuracy* (pp. 251–281). New York: The Guilford Press.

Bem, S. L. (1974). The measurement of psychological androgyny. *Journal of Consulting and Clinical Psychology, 42*, 155–162.

Boker, S. & Laurenceau, JP. (2005). Dynamical systems modeling: An application to the regulation of intimacy and disclosure in marriage. In T. Walls & J. Schafer (Eds.), *Models for intensive longitudinal data*, Oxford, England: Oxford University Press.

Bowen, M. (1978). *Family therapy in clinical practice.* New York: Jason Aronson.

Bowlby, J. (1969). *Attachment and loss. Vol. I. Attachment.* New York: Basic Books.

Bradbury, T. B., Beach, S. R. H., Fincham, F. D., & Nelson, G. M. (1996). Attributions and behavior in functional and dysfunctional marriages. *Journal of Consulting and Clinical Psychology*, *64*, 569–576.

Bradbury, T. N., & Fincham, F. D. (1990). Attributions in marriage: Review and critique. *Psychological Bulletin*, *107*, 3–33.

Bradbury, T. N., & Fincham, F. D. (1992). Attributions and behavior in marital interaction. *Journal of Personality and Social Psychology*, *63*, 613–628.

Burke, P. J., & Stets, J. E. (1999). Trust and commitment through self-verification. *Social Psychology Quarterly*, *62*, 347–360.

Buss, D. M. (1992). Manipulation in close relationships: Five personality factors in interactional context. *Journal of Personality*, *59*, 663–688.

Caughlin, J. P., & Huston, T. L. (2002). A contextual analysis of the association between demand/withdraw and marital satisfaction. *Personal Relationships*, *9*, 95–119.

Caughlin, J. P., & Vangelisti, A. L. (2000). An individual difference explanation of why married couples engage in the demand/withdraw pattern of conflict. *Journal of Social and Personal Relationships*, *17*, 523–551.

Christensen, A. (1987). Detection of conflict patterns in couples. In K. Hahlweg & M. J. Goldstein (Eds.), *Understanding major mental disorder: The contribution of family interaction research* (pp. 250–265). New York: Family Process Press.

Christensen, A., & Jacobson, N. (2000). *Reconcilable differences*. New York: Guilford Press.

Christensen, A., & Shenk, J. L. (1991). Communication, conflict, and psychological distance in nondistressed, clinic, and divorcing couples. *Journal of Consulting and Clinical Psychology*, *59*, 458–463.

Christensen, A., Atkins, D., Baucom, B., & Yi, J. (2010). Couple and individual adjustment for 5 years following a randomized clinical trial comparing traditional versus integrative behavioral couple therapy. *Journal of Consulting and Clinical Psychology*, *78*, 225–235.

Clements, K., & Holtzworth-Munroe, A. (2008). Aggressive cognitions of violent versus nonviolent spouses. *Cognitive Therapy Research*, *32*, 351–369.

Collins, N. L., Cooper, M. L., Albino, A., & Allard, L. (2002). Psychosocial vulnerability from adolescence to adulthood: A prospective study of attachment style differences in relationship functioning and partner choice. *Journal of Personality*, *70*, 965–1008.

Collins, N. L., & Read, S. J. (1990). Adult attachment, working models, and relationship quality in dating couples. *Journal of Personality and Social Psychology*, *58*, 644–663.

Conger, R. D., Cui, M., Bryant, C. M., & Elder, G. H., Jr. (2000). Competence in early adult romantic relationships: A developmental perspective on family influences. *Journal of Personality and Social Psychology*, *79*, 224–237.

Cutrona, C. E., Russell, D. W., & Gardner, K. A. (2005). The relationship enhancement model of social support. In T. A. Revenson, K. Kayser, & G. Bodenmann (Eds.), *Couples coping with stress* (pp. 3–23). Washington, DC: American Psychological Association.

Cutrona, C., Shaffer, P., Wesner, K., & Gardner, K. (2007). Optimally matching support and perceived spousal sensitivity. *Journal of Family Psychology*, *21*, 754–758.

DeCuyper, M., De Bolle, M., & de Fruyt, F. (2011). Personality similarity, perceptual accuracy, and relationship satisfaction in dating and married couples. *Personal Relationships*, *19*(1), 128–145.

Dehle, C., Larsen, D., & Landers, J. (2001). Social support in marriage. *American Journal of Family Therapy*, *29*, 307–324.

Denton, W. H., Burleson, B. R., Hobbs, B. V., Von Stein, M. & Rodroguez, C. P. (2001). Cardiovascular reactivity and initiate/avoid patterns of marital communication: A test of Gottman's psychophysiologic model of marital interaction. *Journal of Behavioral Medicine*, *24*, 401–421.

Ditzen, B., Schaer, M., Gabriel, B., Bodenmann, G., Elhert, U., & Heinrichs, M. (2009). Intranasal oxytocin increases positive communication and reduces cortisol levels during couple conflict. *Biological Psychiatry*, *65*, 728–731.

Doohan, E. A. M., Carrere, S., & Riggs, M. L. (2010). Using relational stories to predict the trajectory toward marital dissolution: The oral history interview and spousal feelings of flooding, loneliness, and depression. *Journal of Family Communication*, *10*, 57–77.

Dorian, M. & Cordova, J. V. (2001, November). *Observing intimacy in marriage: Testing a behavioral theory of intimacy*. Poster presented at the 35th Annual American Association of Behavior Therapy, Philadelphia, PA.

Dorian, M. & Cordova, J. V. (2004). Observing intimacy in couples' interactions. In P. K. Kering & D. Baucom (Eds.), *Couple observational coding systems*. Mahwah, NJ: Lawrence Erlbaum Associates.

Dyrenforth, P. S., Kashy, D. A., Donnellan, M. B., & Lucas, R. E. (2010). Predicting relationship and life satisfaction from personality in nationally representative samples from three countries: The relative importance of actor, partner, and similarity effects. *Journal of Personality and Social Psychology*, *99*, 690–702.

Eldridge, K. A., Sevier, M. Jones, J., Atkins, D. C. & Christensen, A. (2007). Demand-withdraw communication in severely distressed, moderately distressed, and nondistressed couples: Rigidity and polarity during relationship and personal problem discussions. *Journal of Family Psychology*, *21*, 218–226. doi: 10.1037/0893-3200.21.2.218

Epstein, N. & Baucom, D.H. (1993). Cognitive factors in marital disturbance. In P. C. Kendall & K. S. Dobson (Eds.), *Psychopathology and cognition* (pp. 351–385). New York: Academic Press.

Epstein, N., & Baucom, D. H. (2002). *Enhanced cognitive-behavioral therapy for couples: A contextual approach*. Washington, DC: American Psychological Association.

Fincham, F. D. (2000). The kiss of the porcupines: From attributing responsibility to forgiving. *Personal Relationships*, *7*, 1–23.

Fincham, F. D. (2001). Attributions in close relationships: From balkanization to integration. In G. J.O. Fletcher and M. S. Clark (Eds.), *Blackwell handbook of social psychology: interpersonal processes* (pp. 3–31). Malden, MA: Blackwell.

Fincham, F. D., & Bradbury, T. N. (1993). Marital satisfaction, depression, and attributions: A longitudinal analysis. *Journal of Personality and Social Psychology*, *64*, 442–452.

Fincham, F. D., Harold, G., & Gano-Phillips, S. (2000). The longitudinal association between attributions and marital satisfaction: Direction of effects and role of efficacy expectations. *Journal of Family Psychology*, *14*, 267–285.

Fletcher, G. J., & Fincham, F. D. (1991). Attribution processes in close relationships. In G. J. Fletcher & F. D. Fincham (Ed.), *Cognition in close relationships* (pp. 7–35). Hillsdale, NJ: Erlbaum.

Gattis, K. S., Berns, S., Simpson, L. E., & Christensen, A. (2004). Birds of a feather or strange birds? Ties among personality dimensions, similarity, and marital quality. *Journal of Family Psychology*, *18*, 564–574.

Glicksohn, J., & Golan, H. (2001). Personality, cognitive style and assortative mating. *Personality and Individual Differences*, *30*, 1199–1209.

Gonzaga, G. C., Campos, B., & Bradbury, T. (2007). Similarity, convergence, and relationship satisfaction in dating and married couples. *Journal of Personality and Social Psychology*, *93*, 34–48.

Gottman, J. (1993). The roles of conflict engagement, escalation, and avoidance in marital interaction: A longitudinal view of five types of couples. *Journal of Consulting and Clinical Psychology*, *61*, 6–15.

Gottman, J., & Driver, J. (2005). Dysfunctional marital conflict and everyday marital interaction. *Journal of Divorce & Remarriage*, *43*, 63–77.

Gottman, J. M., & Levenson, R. W. (1988). The social psychophysiology of marriage. In P. Noller & M. A. Fitzpatrick (Eds.), *Perspectives on marital interaction* (pp. 182–200). Clevedon, England: Multilingual Matters.

Gottman, J., & Levenson, R. (1992). Marital processes predictive of later dissolution: Behavior, physiology, and health. *Journal of Personality and Social Psychology*, *63*, 221–233.

Gottman, J. M., Notarius, C., Gonso, J., & Markman, H. (1976). *A couple's guide to communication*. Champaign, IL: Research Press.

Grych, J. H., & Fincham, F. D. (1992). Marital dissolution and family adjustment: An attributional analysis. In T. L. Orbuch (Ed.), *Close relationship loss: Theoretical approaches* (pp. 157–173). New York: Springer-Verlag.

Gubbins, C. A., Perosa, L. M., & Bartle-Haring, S. (2010). Relationships between married couples' self-differentiation/individuation and Gottman's model of marital interactions. *Contemporary Family Therapy*, *32*, 83–395.

Hatfield, E., Cacioppo, J. T. & Rapson, R. L. (1992) Primitive emotional contagion. In M. S. Clark (Ed), *Emotion and social behavior* (pp. 151–177). Thousand Oaks, CA: Sage Publications.

Hazan, C., & Shaver, P. R. (1992). Broken attachments. In T. L. Orbuch (Ed.), *Close Relationship Loss: Theoretical Approaches* (pp. 90–108). Hillsdale, NJ: Lawrence Erlbaum Associates, Inc.

Heavey, C. L., Layne, C., & Christensen, A. (1993). Gender and conflict structure in marital interaction: A replication and extension. *Journal of Consulting and Clinical Psychology*, *61*, 16–27.

Helmreich, R. L., Spence, J. T., & Wilhelm, J. A. (1981). A psychometric analysis of the Personal Attributes Questionnaire. *Sex Roles*, *7*, 1097–1108.

Hoffman, M. L. (2000). *Empathy and moral development: Implications for caring and justice*. Cambridge, MA: Cambridge University Press.

Holley, S., Sturm, V. E., & Levenson, R. W. (2010). Exploring the basis for gender differences in the demand-withdraw pattern. *Journal of Homosexuality*, *57*, 666–684.

Huston, T. L. (1994). Courtship antecedents of marital satisfaction and love. In R. Erber & R. Gilmore (Eds.), *Theoretical frameworks for personal relationships* (pp. 43–65). Hillsdale, NJ: Erlbaum.

Huston, T. L., & Houts, R. M. (1998). The psychological infrastructure of courtship and marriage: The role of personality and compatibility in romantic relationships. In T. N. Bradbury (Ed.), *The developmental course of marital dysfunction* (pp. 114–151). Cambridge, MA: Cambridge University Press.

Huston, T. L., Caughlin, J. P., Houts, R. M., Smith, S. E., & George, L. J. (2001). The connubial crucible: Newlywed years as predictors of marital delight, distress, and divorce. *Journal of Personality and Social Psychology*, *80*, 237–252.

Ickes, W., & Simpson, J. A. (1997). Managing empathic accuracy in close relationships. In W. Ickes (Ed.), *Empathic Accuracy* (pp. 218–250). New York: The Guilford Press.

Jacobson, N. S., & Christensen, A. (1998). *Acceptance and change in couple therapy: A therapist's guide to transforming relationships*. New York: Norton.

Karney, B. R., & Bradbury, T. N. (1995). The longitudinal course of marital quality and stability: A review of theory, methods, and research. *Psychological Bulletin*, *118*, 3–34.

Karney, B. R., & Bradbury, T. N. (2000). Attributions in marriage: State or trait? A growth curve analysis. *Journal of Personality and Social Psychology*, *78*, 295–309.

Karney, B. R., Bradbury, T. N., Fincham, F. D., & Sullivan, K. T. (1994). The role of negative affectivity in the association between attributions and marital satisfaction. *Journal of Personality and Social Psychology*, *66*, 413–424.

Kirby, J. S., Baucom, D. H., & Peterman, M. A. (2005). An investigation of unmet intimacy needs in marital relationships. *Journal of Marital and Family Therapy*, *31*, 313–325.

Kiecolt-Glaser, J. K., & Newton, T. L. (2001). Marriage and health: His and hers. *Psychological Bulletin*, *127* (4), 472–503.

Kiecolt-Glaser, J. K., Newton, T., Cacioppo, J. T., MacCallum, R. C., Glaser, R., Malarkey, W. B. (1996). Marital conflict and endocrine function: Are men really more physiologically affected than women? *Journal of Consulting and Clinical Psychology*, *64*, 324–332.

Klinetob, N. A., & Smith, D. A. (1996). Demand-withdraw communication in marital interaction: Tests of interpersonal contingency and gender role hypotheses. *Journal of Marriage and the Family*, *58*, 945–957.

Larson, R. W., & Almeida, D. M. (1999). Emotional transmission in the daily lives of families: A new paradigm for studying family processes. *Journal of Marriage and Family*, *61*, 5–20.

Larson, J. H., Blick, R. W., Jackson, J. B., & Holman, T. B. (2010). Partner traits that predict relationship satisfaction for neurotic individuals in premarital relationships. *Journal of Sex and Marital Therapy*, *36*, 430–444.

Laurenceau, J. P., Barrett, L. F., & Pietromonaco, P. R. (1998). Intimacy as an interpersonal process: The importance of self-disclosure, partner disclosure, and perceived partner responsiveness in interpersonal exchanges. *Journal of Personality and Social Psychology*, *74*, 1238–1251.

Laurenceau, J. P. Barrett, L. F., & Rovine, M. J. (2005). The interpersonal process model of intimacy in marriage: A daily-diary and multilevel modeling approach. *Journal of Family Psychology*, *19*, 314–323.

Lawrence, E., Bunde, M., Barry, R., Brock, R. L., Sullivan, K. T., Pasch, L. A., et al. (2008). Partner support and marital satisfaction: Support amount, adequacy, provision and solicitation. *Personal Relationships*, *15*, 445–463.

Luo, S., & Klohnen, E. C. (2005). Assortative mating and marital quality in newlyweds: A couple-centered approach. *Journal of Personality and Social Psychology*, *88*, 304–326.

Luo, S., Chen, H., Yue, G., Zhang, G., Zhaoyang, R., & Xu, D. (2008). Predicting marital satisfaction from self, partner, and couple characteristics: Is it me, you, or us? *Journal of Personality*, *76*, 1231–1265.

Markman, H., Stanley, S., & Blumberg, S. L. (1994). *Fighting for your marriage*. San Francisco, CA: Jossey-Bass.

Markman, H. J., Rhoades, G. K., Stanley, S. M., Ragan, E., & Whitton, S. (2010). The premarital communication roots of marital distress: The first five years of marriage. *Journal of Family Psychology*, *24*, 289–298.

Margolin, G., & Wampold, B. (1981). Sequential analysis of conflict and accord in distressed and nondistressed marital partners. *Journal of Consulting and Clinical Psychology*, 49, 554–567.

Mattingly, B. A., McIntyre, K. P., & Lewandowski, G. W. (2011). Approach motivation and the expansion of self in close relationships. *Personal Relationships*, 19, 113–127.

McGinn, M.M., McFarland, P.T., & Christensen, A. (2009). Antecedents and consequences of demand/withdraw. *Journal of Family Psychology, 23,* 749–757. doi: 10.1037/a0016185

McNulty, J. (2008). Neuroticism and interpersonal negativity: The independent contributions of perceptions and behaviors. *Personality and Social Psychology Bulletin*, 34, 1439–1450.

McRae, R. R., Martin, T. A., Hrebickova, M., Urbanek, T., Boomsma, D. I., Willemsen, G., & Costa, P. T. Costa, P. T., Jr. (2008). Personality trait similarity between spouses in four cultures. *Journal of Personality*, 76, 1137–1163.

Mondor, J., McDuff, P., Lussier, Y., & Wright, J. (2011). Couples in therapy: Actor-partner analyses of the relationships between adult romantic attachment and marital satisfaction. *American Journal of Family Therapy*, 39, 112–123.

Noller, P., & Ruzzene, M. (1991). Communication in marriage: The influence of affect and cognition. In G. J. O. Fletcher & F. Fincham (Eds.), *Cognition in close relationships* (pp. 203–223). Hillsdale, NJ: Erlbaum.

O'Leary, K. D., Smith Slep, A. M, O'Leary, S. G. (2007). Multivariate models of men's and women's partner aggression. *Journal of Consulting and Clinical Psychology*, 75, 752–764. doi: 10.1037/0022-006X.75.5.752

Pasch, L., & Bradbury, T. (1998). Social support, conflict, and the development of marital dysfunction. *Journal of Consulting and Clinical Psychology*, 66, 219–230.

Pasch, L. A., Bradbury, T. N., & Davila, J. (1997). Gender, negative affectivity, and observed social support behavior in marital interaction. *Personal Relationships*, 4, 361–378.

Patterson, G. R. (1982). *Coercive family process*. Eugene, OR: Castalia.

Preston, S. D., & de Waal, F. B. M. (2002). Empathy: Its ultimate and proximal bases. *Behavioral and Brain Sciences*, 25, 1–72.

Preston, S. D. (2007). A perception-action model for empathy. In T. F. D. Farrow & P. Woodruff (Eds.), *Empathy in mental illness* (pp. 428–447). Cambridge, MA: Cambridge University Press.

Ravitz, P., Maunder, R., Hunter, J., Sthankiya, B., & Lancee, W. (2010). Adult attachment measures: A 25-year review. *Journal of Psychosomatic Research*, 69, 419–432.

Reis, H.T., & Patrick, B.C. (1996). Attachment and intimacy: Component processes. In E.T. Higgins & A.W. Kruglanski (Eds.), *Social psychology: Handbook of basic principle* (pp. 523–563). New York: Guilford Press.

Reis, H.T., & Shaver, P. (1988). Intimacy as an interpersonal process. In S. Duck, D.F. Hale., S.E. Hobfoll, W. Ickes, & B.M. Montgomery (Eds.), *Handbook of personal relationships: Theory, reserach, and interventions* (pp. 367–389). Oxford, England: John Wiley & Sons.

Rodrigues, S. M., Saslow, L. R., Garcia, N., John, O. P., & Keltner, D. (2009). Oxytocin receptor genetic variation relates to empathy and stress reactivity in humans. *Proceedings of the National Academy of Sciences of the United States of America*, 106, 21437–21411.

Rohrbaugh, M. J., Shoham, V., Trost, S. Muramoto, M., Cate, R. M. & Leischow, S. (2001). Couple dynamics of change-resistant smoking: Toward a family consultation model. *Family Process*, 40, 15–31.

Rusbult, C. E., Verette, J., Whitney, G. A., Slovik, L. F., & Lipkus, I. (1991). Accommodation processes in close relationships: Theory and preliminary empirical evidence. *Journal of Personality and Social Psychology*, 60, 53–78.

Sagrestano, L., Christensen, A., & Heavey, C. (1998). Social influence techniques during marital conflict. *Personal Relationships*, 5, 75–89.

Sagrestano, L. M., Heavey, C. L., & Christensen, A. (2006). Individual differences versus social structural approaches to explaining demand-withdraw and social influence behaviors. In K. Dindia & D. J. Canary (Eds.), *Sex differences and similarities in communication* (pp. 379–395). Mahweh, NJ: Erlbaum.

Sandin Allen, E., Baucom, D. H., Burnett, C. K., Epstein, N., & Rankin-Esquer, L. A. (2001). Decision-making power, autonomy, and communication in remarried spouses compare with first-married spouses. *Family Relations*, 50, 326–334.

Sanford, K. (2007). The couple's emotion rating form: Psychometric properties and theoretical associations. Psychological Assessment, 19, 411–421.

Saxbe, D., & Repetti, R. L. (2010). For better or for worse? Coregulation of couples' cortisol levels and mood states. *Journal of Personality and Social Psychology, 98*, 92–103.

Shiota, M. N. & Levenson, R. W. (2007). Birds of a feather don't always fly farthest: Similarity in big five personality predicts more negative marital satisfaction trajectories in long-term marriages. *Psychology and Aging, 22*, 666–675.

Sillars, A.L. (1985). Interpersonal perception in relationships. In W. Ickes (Ed.), *Compatible and Incompatible Relationships* (pp. 277–305). New York: Springer-Verlag.

Sillars, A. L., & Scott, M. D. (1983). Interpersonal perception between intimates: An integrative review. *Human Communication Research, 10*, 153–176.

Simpson, J. A., Orina, M. M., & Ickes, W. (2003). When accuracy hurts, and when it helps: A test of the empathic accuracy model in marital interactions. *Journal of Personality and Social Psychology, 85*, 881–893.

Story, L. B., Karney, B. R., Lawrence, E., & Bradbury, T. N. (2004). Interpersonal mediators in the intergenerational transmission of marital dysfunction. *Journal of Family Psychology, 18*, 519–529.

Sullivan, K., Pasch, L., Johnson, M., & Bradbury, T. (2010). Social support, problem solving, and the l ongitudinal course of newlywed marriage. *Journal of Personality and Social Psychology, 98*, 631–644.

Swann, W. B., Jr., De La Ronde, C., & Hixon, J. G. (1994). Authenticity and positivity strivings in marriage and courtship. *Journal of Personality and Social Psychology, 66*, 857–869.

Thomas, G., & Fletcher, G. J.O. (1997). Empathic accuracy in close relationships. In W. Ickes (Ed.), *Empathic accuracy* (pp. 195–217). New York: Guilford Press.

Verhofstadt, V., Buysse, A., De Clercq, A., & Goodwin, R. (2005). Emotional arousal and negative affect in marital conflict: The influence of gender, conflict structure, and demand-withdrawal. *European Journal of Social Psychology, 35*, 449–467.

Verhofstadt, V., Buysse, A., Ickes, W., Davis, M., & Devoldre, I. (2008). Support provision in marriage: The role of emotional similarity and empathic accuracy. *Emotion, 8*, 792–802.

Vogel, D. L., & Karney, B. R. (2003). Demands and withdrawal in newlyweds: Elaborating on the social structure hypothesis. *Journal of Social and Personal Relationships, 19*, 685–701.

Walczynski, P. (1997). *Power, personality, and conflictual interaction: An exploration of demand/withdraw interaction in same-sex and cross-sex couples.* Unpublished doctoral dissertation, University of California, Los Angeles.

Watson, D., Klohnen, E. C., Casillas, A., Simms, E. N., Haig, J. & Berry, D. S. (2004). Match makers and deal breakers: analyses of assortative mating in newlywed couples. *Journal of Personality, 72*, 1029–1068.

Wieselquist, J., Rusbult, C. E., Foster, C. A., & Agnew, C. R. (1999). Commitment, pro-relationship behavior, and trust in close relationships. *Journal of Personality and Social Psychology, 77*, 942–966.

Wile, D. (1993). *After the fight*. New York: Guilford Press.

Section III

Conflict and Aggression in Families

10 Understanding Conflict in Families

Theoretical Frameworks and Future Directions

Darby E. Saxbe, Aubrey J. Rodriguez, and Gayla Margolin[1]

To be in a family is to experience conflict: it is an unavoidable feature of family life. However, families vary tremendously in how they handle conflict. Episodes of conflict can be productive, helping to facilitate communication, or they can be damaging, destructive, and even dangerous. For researchers and clinicians who focus on families, theories of why conflicts develop, how they unfold, and how families resolve them (or fail to resolve them) warrant close attention.

Conflict within families has been defined similarly to conflict within other interpersonal relational contexts. Specifically, conflict is a perceived incompatibility in goals (Deutsch, 1973; Margolin, 1988), although the phenomenology of conflict is a complex mixture of cognitive, affective, and behavioral elements. Within families, conflict may be inevitable due to the longevity and depth of the bonds, and to the role of the family as the primary environment for socialization and provision of instrumental, affective, and informational support. A family's ability to fulfill all of its roles at any given point, and particularly over time, will be conditioned by its flexibility and adaptability. As individuals and relationships within a family develop, new goals and needs emerge. Conflict is the process by which families adapt to and negotiate emerging and disparate goals; thus, frequent conflict within the family environment is normative.

Empirical research attests to the prevalence of conflict within families; in community samples, the average frequency of marital conflict has been estimated at a few large disagreements per month (Kirchler, Rodler, Holzl, & Meier, 2001; McGonagle, Kessler, & Schilling, 1992). During adolescence, parent–child conflicts may occur on a weekly or even daily basis (Laursen, 1993; Montemayor, 1986) with conflict between mothers and daughters lasting about 15 minutes and conflicts with sons lasting about 6 minutes (Patterson & Forgatch, 2005). Conflict seems to be most frequent within the sibling relationship, occurring up to several times per hour (Lollis, Ross, & Leroux, 1996). The frequency of conflicts tends to decrease over time, suggesting that conflicts revolve primarily around transient needs and tasks of individual and family development. For example, parent–child conflict and sibling conflict tend to decrease after adolescence (Laursen, Coy, & Collins, 1998; Stocker, Lanthier, & Furman, 1997). In addition, marital conflict appears to decrease over time (Johnson, White, Edwards, & Booth, 1986; Sillars & Wilmot, 1989; Carstensen, Gottman, & Levenson, 1995), as couples move beyond negotiating roles and responsibilities related to child-bearing and rearing.

---

[1] The preparation of this chapter was funded in part by NIH-NICHD NRSA award 1F32HD063255–0 (Saxbe, PI) and NIH-NICHD grant R01-HD046807 (Margolin, PI).

In the next section, we offer a brief description of key issues in the study of conflict, including conflict properties and processes. We then turn to consider theories used to understand family conflict. Some limitations and suggestions for future theoretical development are outlined before we offer our concluding comments.

KEY ISSUES IN THE STUDY OF CONFLICT

CONFLICT PROPERTIES

Although family conflict is universal, much is at stake in terms of individual and relational development, and mismanagement of conflict may result in negative psychosocial effects. Although the incidence and frequency of conflict has not been found to produce increased individual or relational risk, some global characteristics of conflict have been linked to poorer outcomes. Characteristics that have received the most empirical attention include conflict severity, degree of resolution, and content.

Severity

Conflict severity, often operationalized as the extent to which verbal or physical aggression is involved, has been linked to child abuse, power assertive parenting, child externalizing and internalizing problems, child post-traumatic stress symptoms, and child aggression (Doumas, Margolin, & John, 1994; Duman & Margolin, 2007; El-Shiekh, Cummings, Kouros, Elmore-Staton, & Buckhalt, 2008; Margolin & Gordis, 2003; Margolin & John, 1997).

Degree of Resolution

In addition, the degree to which conflict is resolved seems an important dimension; marital conflicts that are both hostile and end in disengagement rather than negotiation of a solution have been linked to poorer family outcomes than hostile but engaged interactions (Katz & Gottman, 1997; Katz & Woodin, 2002). By contrast, children who perceive resolutions of marital conflicts have more adaptive emotional responses to the conflict (Cummings, Ballard, El-Shiekh, & Lake, 1991; Kerig, 1996). However, resolution of conflicts has been challenging to assess, as it appears that a majority of couples engage in serial arguments, in which conflicts recur over time and become well-rehearsed (Gottman & Levenson, 1999; Roloff & Johnson, 2002). The effect of these recurring conflicts on family adjustment is not well understood.

Content

Although the content of disagreements generally has been presumed to be less important than the processes of conflict, marital arguments surrounding issues of trust strike more at the core of the relationship than arguments surrounding the details of daily life, such as household management. Moreover, marital arguments surrounding child issues in contrast to couple-specific issues have been linked to greater emotional reactivity in children (Grych & Fincham, 1990; Jouriles et al., 1991).

CONFLICT PROCESSES

Demand–Withdraw

Careful empirical observations of how conflict unfolds over time have revealed patterns that sustain and escalate conflict. One such dyadic conflict pattern is the demand–withdraw interaction pattern (Christensen & Heavey, 1990), which is a cycle characterized by repeated requests for change from the individual in the demanding role, and attempts to escape or avoid the discussion from the individual in the withdrawing role. Originally described in marital partners, and associated with gender roles and socialization (Heavey, Layne, & Christensen, 1993; Klinetob & Smith, 1996), the demand–withdraw interaction pattern has been more strongly linked to marital dissatisfaction than are overall levels of negativity (Caughlin & Huston, 2002). The demand–withdraw pattern within marital relationships exerts some influence on child outcomes; marital conflict involving overt expressions of hostility was associated with elevated externalizing problems in youth, whereas withdrawal or disengagement was associated with increased youth internalizing symptoms (Katz & Gottman, 1993). Other investigators have found direct effects for marital withdrawal, and indirect effects for marital hostility on child adjustment (Sturge-Apple, Davies, & Cummings, 2006). Demand–withdraw interaction within the parent–adolescent relationship has also been linked with poor individual and relational outcomes, including substance use and low self-esteem (Caughlin & Malis, 2004).

Reciprocity and Negativity

Negative reciprocity, another transactional conflict process (Epstein, Baucom, & Rankin, 1993; Gottman, Markman, & Notarius, 1977; Margolin & Wampold, 1981), describes the extent to which dyad members respond to their partner's negative behavior or affect with further negativity. The defining characteristic of negative reciprocity is the participants' difficulty in exiting or recovering from the conflict once it has begun. Negative reciprocity discriminates distressed marriages from nondistressed marriages; whereas distressed and non-distressed couples show similar rates of reciprocation of positive behavior, distressed couples demonstrate higher rates of negative reciprocity (Burman, Margolin & John, 1993).

Nonetheless, it is not a foregone conclusion that negativity takes a toll on family relationships. Some researchers (e.g., Gottman, 1993, 1994; Johnson et al., 2005) have suggested that couples may be able to endure and thrive despite high levels of negativity if sufficient positivity exists within the relationship. According to Gottman (1994), a 5:1 ratio of positive to negative experiences may provide such a buffering effect, suggesting that affective intensity may be less powerful than affective balance in predicting dyadic satisfaction.

Mutual Coercion

A related risky conflict interaction is the pattern of mutual coercion.

In coercive conflict, dyads engage in a pattern of negative escalation that creates increasingly aversive conditions until one partner yields, thereby reinforcing the coercive cycle (Patterson & Forgatch, 2005). Individuals in coercive family relationships learn over time that ramping up the negativity of an interaction is the most effective way to terminate the conflict. Within a marital conflict interaction, coercive processes may manifest in physically aggressive behaviors, or psychological threats (e.g., to end the marriage). Children contribute to coercive processes by increasing the volume and intensity of tantrums, particularly in public places. Coercive patterns have been implicated in the development of youth antisocial behaviors (Patterson, DeBaryshe, & Ramsey, 1989), but can also apply to other family and individual outcomes.

Consequences of Conflict

It is widely accepted that the family is a highly interdependent system, as *family systems theory* posits. Thus, when two family members have a conflict, a third person may be persuaded to enter into an alliance or to support one or both of the conflictual parties. Alternatively, with most families characterized by a high level of emotional attunement, a third-party family member may be quite aware of others' emotional distress and, for the sake of everyone involved, may be quite motivated to interrupt an ongoing conflict. Nonetheless, despite good intentions, inept attempts to disrupt conflict processes may actually exacerbate conflict or create different sources of conflict and might heighten rather than reduce the overall level of family stress. Thus, unresolved family conflicts have the potential not only to persist but also to expand in scope to include more people and encompass more issues. Empirical research has established that third parties often join in dyadic conflict interactions, that they are equally likely to attempt to stop or to further the conflict, and that their involvement affects both the process and the outcome of the conflict (Vuchinich, Emery, & Cassidy, 1988).

High levels of aggressive, destructive family conflict have well-documented, deleterious effects on children's well-being (Repetti, Taylor, & Seeman, 2002). The impact on children has been attributed to their attempts to resolve the family conflict or their sense of being responsible for family conflict. Moreover, some conflicts between adult family members disrupt parents' implementation of good parenting practices including involvement, monitoring, and effective problem-solving, with obvious consequences for the children. Family conflict may be especially meaningful to children's development, even more so than other types of family functioning; for example, marital conflict has been linked more consistently with child problems than other dimensions of the marital relationship, such as lack of warmth and spouses' dissatisfaction with the marriage (Grych & Fincham, 1990). Although many studies of family conflict behavior have focused on either marital or on parent–child conflict, studying family aggression across multiple domains may uncover additive effects (Margolin, Vickerman, Oliver, & Gordis, 2010). For example, an index of family aggression that included both marital and parent–child conflict behavior had a dose–response relationship (i.e., the greater the exposure to aggression, the greater the risk of negative outcomes) with youth outcomes including academic failure, depression, and somatic complaints (Margolin et al., 2010).

OVERVIEW OF THEORIES USED TO UNDERSTAND FAMILY CONFLICT

In the following sections, we discuss a number of theories that address how conflicts arise, how they progress, and how they impact families. Although there are multiple ways to organize the many theories that explicate family conflict, we chose to structure this chapter around two main types of theories: theories that primarily involve processes internal to the family (e.g., the transmission of emotion from one family member to another) and theories that primarily involve processes external to the family (e.g., the family's adaptation to the cultural or socioeconomic environment). In the first section, we consider theories describing the transmission of negative emotion from one domain to another within a person (e.g., spillover theory), from person to person (e.g., crossover theory or emotion transmission theory), and from family subsystem to family subsystem (focusing specifically on theories on the impact of marital conflict on children, such as cognitive–contextual theory and the emotional security hypothesis). In the second section, we discuss theories that describe the influence of external processes on family conflict, including ecological systems theory and theories of families' adaptation to external stressors, and review literature on the influence of culture, socioeconomic status/poverty, work, and military service on family conflict and well-being.

INTERNAL PROCESSES

Family conflicts are more likely to develop when individual family members are experiencing negative mood states, such as feelings of stress, irritation, anger, or frustration. Individuals in high-conflict families may also be more reactive to each others' negative mood states, exacerbating rather than modulating shifts in negative emotion and therefore furthering the progression of aversive conflict (e.g., Levenson & Gottman, 1983). In the following sections, we describe theories that help to explain how negative affect is transferred within and across family members, leading to both the initiation and the perpetuation of family conflict.

Within-Person Spillover

Spillover theory (Crouter, 1984; Piotrkowski, 1979; Repetti, 1989) describes how cognitions and emotions from one domain (such as the workplace) transfer to another domain, like the home. Spillover theory was developed by researchers interested in work–family conflict who were seeking to describe how experiences at work inform experiences at home, but the term 'spillover' can be applied to any transfer of thoughts and feelings from one domain to another (e.g., from home to school or from home to work). Spillover can be both positive and negative; for example, winning a promotion at work might inspire a mother's good humor with family members later in the day. However, the research on spillover that is most relevant to family conflict has focused on the spillover of negative emotions from the workplace into the home.

Several daily diary studies have found that an individual's negative social interactions at work, such as disagreements with coworkers, may affect his or her behavior at home, leading to short-term increases in family conflict (e.g., Bolger, DeLongis, Kessler, & Wethington, 1989; Story & Repetti, 2006). Another daily diary study found that husbands were actually *less* likely to engage in angry marital behaviors after a more stressful day at work (Schulz, Cowan, Cowan, & Brennan, 2004), but this effect was specific to husbands reporting high levels of marital satisfaction. That same study found wives to be more socially withdrawn after a busier workday; other studies have found similar evidence for withdrawal among wives following higher workload days (Story & Repetti, 2006).

Within-person spillover processes can also influence the likelihood of parent–child conflict. For example, mothers of infants reporting a negative social climate at work showed subsequent differences in parenting: they interacted in ways that were more negative and less sensitive during free play (Costigan, Cox, & Cauce, 2003). Interestingly, that same study also found the quality of paternal parenting to be diminished by mothers' negative social climate at work. Repetti and Wood (1997) found that after a higher workload day, more aversive interactions occurred between mothers and their preschool-age children; however, this effect only emerged for mothers reporting more symptoms of psychological distress.

Not only can spillover contribute to family conflict, but family conflict may reciprocally affect within-person spillover processes. Story and Repetti (2006) found that patterns of work-family spillover differed for high-conflict and low-conflict families. Individuals in families who reported more overall conflict were consistently more reactive to short-term daily job stressors, and both husbands and wives in those families were more likely to express anger and to withdraw from marital interaction on evenings following difficult workdays. A contentious family climate may make it more difficult for family members to return to equilibrium after challenging experiences, while spillover may, in turn, contribute to chronic family conflict.

In conclusion, research on the within-person spillover theoretical framework has confirmed that negative emotions can transfer across domains and can contribute to family conflict, especially when individuals or family systems are already vulnerable to stress.

Crossover and Emotion Transmission

In addition to the spillover of negative emotions from other domains, conflicts can also be viewed from a *crossover theoretical perspective*; the spillover of negative affect and stress from one family member to the other (Westman, 2001). A literature on "emotion transmission" within families (Larson & Almeida, 1999) has sought to map out the pathways by which one family member's mood or stress state affects other family members. Research in this area has been enhanced by methodological advances in experience-sampling and daily diary studies, as well as analytic approaches, such as multilevel modeling, that can estimate both within- and between-person change. A number of studies have found that short-term changes in the emotions and behaviors of one family member predict changes in the emotions and behaviors of other family members. While positive emotions can be transmitted within families, negative emotions may be more "contagious," and there is more evidence for the transmission of negative than positive emotions within families (Larson & Almeida, 1999).

Emotion transmission research has explored processes of sending and receiving emotions within families. One finding has been that emotion transmission processes are not always reciprocal or circular within families, and that some family members may be more likely to send while others are more likely to receive emotions. The distribution of power within families may affect the direction of transmission. For example, husbands' emotions appear to affect wives' emotions more than vice versa (Bolger et al., 1989; Larson & Richards, 1994), while negative affect appears to transmit more readily from parents to children than vice versa (Cummings & Davies, 1994; Larson & Almeida, 1999). For example, a diary study found that within distressed families, conflict from the marital relationship affected conflict in parent–child and sibling relationships (Christensen & Margolin, 1988; Margolin, Christensen, & John, 1996).

The above study found more transmission between family subsystems in distressed than in non-distressed families, and other researchers (e.g., Gottman, 1979) echo that finding. It appears that individual and relationship distress may heighten reactivity to negative emotions within the families: individuals who are more depressed and anxious may be more likely to transmit negative emotions to others, and may be more reactive to ambiguous or mildly negative statements from others (Larson & Gillman, 1999; Repetti & Wood, 1997).

Most of the research on spillover processes within families has focused on affective states, but there is also evidence that families coregulate on a physiological level; one study found that momentary levels of the stress hormone cortisol were correlated within couples over several days, and that these correlations were stronger when couples reported greater marital distress (Saxbe & Repetti, 2010). Therefore, just as more distressed families appear to show stronger transmission of negative affect, they might also show stronger transmission of physiological arousal and stress states.

Spillover of Conflict from One Family Subsystem to Another

Family systems theory views the family as an interconnected system, such that conflict in one domain may lead to changes in other domains. For example, marital conflict may affect the parent–child relationship, such that a child might feel pressured to ally with one parent and become "parentified" (Broszormenyi-Nagy & Spark, 1973). Alternatively, parents might transfer their marital tensions onto a child with problematic behavior, creating an "identified patient" who can become the focus of any family discontent (Minuchin et al., 1975).

There is evidence, as mentioned above, that conflict in one family subsystem (e.g., the marital dyad) can have repercussions for other subsystems (e.g., the parent–child and sibling relationships). Researchers have invoked both the "spillover hypothesis"—the idea that marital conflict spills over to negatively affect other family relationships—and the "compensatory hypothesis," which posits that parents can buffer their children from marital conflict through positive parent–child relationships (Erel & Burman, 1995). A meta-analysis of 68 studies (Erel & Burman, 1995) found clear support for the spillover hypothesis, suggesting that marital discord is linked with more negative relationships between parents and children. Several researchers have developed theories that elaborate on the impact of marital conflict on children's well-being, based on how children appraise and understand both the conflict and their own ability to handle the conflict.

Cognitive–Contextual Theory

The *cognitive–contextual theory* (Grych & Fincham, 1990) proposes that children's appraisals of marital conflict mediate the effects of conflict on their well-being. Children's appraisal, or understanding of the conflict, depends on multiple factors, including the child's age and emotional development, contextual factors (such as the child's previous experience of conflict, the perceived emotional climate of the family, proximal factors such as the child's mood that day, and the child's temperament), and characteristics of the conflict itself (e.g., the content of the conflict, the intensity of the conflict, and whether the conflict is resolved). Appraisals include both *primary processing*—e.g., whether the conflict is threatening or relevant to the child in the short term—and *secondary processing*, or the child's attempt to understand why the conflict occurred and whether he or she feels able to cope with it. For example, as part of secondary processing, the child may make judgments about who is to blame for the conflict; children who blame themselves may suffer self-esteem problems, while children who blame their parents may experience guilt or confusion. Children also have efficacy expectations about their ability to cope with the conflict, which are shaped by their social competence, self-esteem, age, and affective arousal to the conflict, among other factors.

Emotional Security Hypothesis

The *emotional security hypothesis* (Davies & Cummings, 1994) builds on the cognitive–contextual theory and also draws from *attachment theory*. Like the cognitive–contextual theory, it focuses on the factors that mediate the impact of marital conflict on children, emphasizing the meaning that children place on marital conflict. Conflict is posited to be more negative for children if it threatens their emotional security, which includes several component processes: (1) children's own emotion regulation (the level of emotional arousal children feel during and after conflict, and their ability to cope with that arousal); (2) children's attempts to regulate conflict by trying to affect parents' behavior (intervening in arguments, attempting to distract or comfort parents); and (3) children's internal representations of their parents and themselves. This model has received empirical support (Cummings, Davies & Campbell, 2000; Davies, Harold, Goeke-Morey, & Cummings, 2002).

EXTERNAL PROCESSES

In addition to the process of internal adaptation to the affective environment within the family, family systems and subsystems also must adapt to stressors within their environments. Negotiating a response to environmental stressors often provokes or exacerbates conflict within the family system. Some family theories posit distal mechanisms or contextual conditions that affect family conflict, whereas other theories attempt to describe how stress is managed in proximal processes. Among the models of distal influence, Bronfenbrenner's *ecological systems theory* (1979) nests the family system (i.e., the *microsystem*) in other spheres of environmental influence. For example, the mesosystem includes the communication between different microsystems, e.g., a child's teachers and parents, while the exosystem and the macrosystem describe larger influences beyond the family, such as the community (*exosystem*) and the values and expectations of the culture (*macrosystem*). According to this model, conflict may occur within the family system as a result of clashes between ecological spheres, as well as the spillover of stress from sphere to sphere. Bronfenbrenner's later articulation (1986, 1995) of the *bioecological model* incorporates the influences of biology/genes as well as a chronosystem, which accounts for the influence of historical time; this iteration thus incorporates research from the *family life course perspective* (discussed below). Another theory focuses specifically upon developmental time: *family life cycle theory* (Mattesich & Hill, 1987) is essentially a stage theory, which suggests the normative tasks and challenges that may produce conflict as a family system—and each of its individual members—develops. For example, during the period of time known as the transition to parenthood, *partners* in a couple must renegotiate their roles, responsibilities, priorities, and attachment to care and provide for a new baby; the theory suggests that conflict during this period will often center on the negotiation of these shifts.

At a more molecular level, theories alternately called *family stress, crisis, or resilience theories*, represented by the ABCX (Hill, 1949), double ABCX (McCubbin & Patterson, 1982), and family stress (Conger & Elder, 1994) models have also been utilized to describe the process by which families adjust to stressors in the environment; principal components of these models include the process of stressor appraisal, existence and utilization of resources, crisis (i.e., a condition of disruption and disorganization), and the pileup of stressors over time and, potentially, from multiple sources. For example, the *ABCX theory* describes how the response of a family ("X") to a family crisis ("A") might be affected by internal family resources and social supports ("B") and by family appraisals (e.g. perceptions of self-efficacy; "C"). Families that lack "B" and "C" protective factors—e.g., families that are isolated or impoverished, and whose members feel hopeless—are at heightened risk for the adverse consequences of "A" events. The double ABCX theory extends this model to include post-crisis factors (e.g., coping mechanisms) and accounts for the accumulation or piling up of multiple stressors affecting the family.

Relatedly, the newer *vulnerability–stress–adaptation model* (Karney & Bradbury, 1995) describes factors related to individual, subsystem, and system-level vulnerability, aspects of the stressor and stressor appraisal, and processes of family adaptation. In this model, conflict is one of the central mechanisms at the subsystem and system levels by which families adapt to, cope with, or combat external stressors. The following sections on culture, socioeconomic status, work, and military service provide examples of distal influences and proximal processes by which external stressors spill over into or exacerbate conflict within the family system.

Culture

Culture provides an important context that can moderate the processes and outcomes of family conflict (Markus & Lin, 1999; Yau & Smetana, 2003). Some researchers view culture as a static family attribute and assess the impacts of broad aspects of culture such as individualism–collectivism and "familism" (an orientation in which the needs of the family as a group supersede the needs of individual family members) on the expression and outcomes of conflict. For example, families with stronger familistic values may appraise conflict within the parent–child relationship as more threatening than those with weaker familistic values (Hernandez, Garcia, & Flynn, 2010). Cultural differences in values that shape parenting and marital roles and dynamics may also affect whether conflict will occur and the forms it may take. For example, low levels of respect for authority were linked to more intense mother–daughter conflict among African-American and Latina pairs than among European-American pairs when the daughters were in middle childhood (Dixon, Graber, & Brooks-Gunn, 2008).

However, culture is rarely best understood as an invariant characteristic, as families and individuals often transition between cultures, through geographic relocation (immigration), subjective identification with ethnic identities and subcultures, and assimilation and acculturation processes. Each of these dynamic cultural processes may incur stress and evoke conflict within the family. The process of immigration often imposes great strain on family members as well as family relationships, due to the pile-up of economic, cultural, social, and political stressors. Additionally, consistent with the *family life course perspective*, the timing of immigration during the family life cycle may greatly influence the experiences of recent immigrant families (Pyke, 2005). Recent work on ethnic identity development suggests that the successful exploration of both heritage and dominant cultures and the achievement of ethnic identity have been associated with better family relations and youth adjustment (Phinney, Chavira, & Williamson, 1992). Yet, little is known about the effects of ethnic identity exploration on family relations and the incidence and intensity of family conflict.

In addition, individual family members often assimilate or acculturate to their new surroundings to different degrees and at different rates, with notable generational differences. The presence of an acculturation gap in families has been linked to alienation and conflict, and subsequent adjustment problems (Lee, Cho, Kim, & Ngo, 2000; Tseng & Fuligni, 2000). A study of US-born Asian-Indian adolescents and their families (Farver, Darang, & Bhadha, 2002) found higher levels of family conflict when parents were less accepting of the host culture than their children (i.e., when the acculturation gap was large); smaller acculturation gaps were associated with less conflict and better youth adjustment. Similarly, Smokowski and Bacallao (2006) found that parent–child conflict mediated the relation between acculturation stress and acculturation status on US-born Latino adolescents' aggressive behaviors. However, greater identification with the host culture or smaller acculturation gaps have not been uniformly linked to lower conflict and better adjustment in families (e.g., Lau et al., 2005; Smokowski, Rose, & Bacallao, 2008), highlighting the need for further research to clarify these effects and potential moderators.

Socioeconomic Status/Poverty

Low incomes and low socioeconomic status are additional contextual factors to consider in assessing family functioning broadly, and in relation to family conflict in particular. Economic hardship has been linked to difficulties within family relationships, and is a risk factor for poor marital quality, divorce, and child internalizing and externalizing behavior (Amato, Booth, Johnson, & Rogers, 2007; Karney, Story, & Bradbury, 2005). In line with the family life course perspective and other developmental theories, early work by Elder (1974) described the influence of timing of economic hardship on family outcomes in his studies of families following the Great Depression. For example, adolescent boys demonstrated better adjustment, largely due to their ability to seek employment and to decreased time with the family. Later research prompted the development of Conger and Elder's (1994) *family stress model*, which, like the crisis models described above, suggests that an imbalance between financial demands and resources leads to deterioration in family relationships and results in instability; this model has received considerable empirical support (Conger, Conger, & Martin, 2010). In this literature, acute economic stress was linked to parental distress and depression, which spilled over into negative and conflictual interactions with spouses and children, which were linked to subsequent poor marital and youth outcomes (Conger et al., 1993; Conger, Ge, Elder, Lorenz, & Simons, 1994; Robila & Krishnakumar, 2006). Similar findings have emerged among families experiencing more chronic forms of poverty (Hammack, Robinson, Crawford, & Li, 2004; Magnuson & Duncan, 2002; Nievar & Luster, 2006; Scaramella, Neppl, Ontai, & Conger, 2008). In support of the centrality of stressor appraisal in the family stress model, perception of economic strain—in addition to increases in family conflict—was found to mediate the relation between SES and adolescent outcomes (Wadsworth & Compas, 2002).

Work–Family Conflict

In the remainder of this section, we highlight two further contexts in which theoretical frameworks on conflict have been examined: work–family conflict and military service.

We have already discussed the work–family spillover hypothesis and how it affects the families' internal processes, but researchers have also examined the intersection between work and family spheres at the level of the mesosystem, for example in terms of workplace and work role demands on family life. Long work hours, shiftwork, dangerous or stressful jobs (e.g., police officers), conflict with coworkers, employee–supervisor relations, and workplace policies can all affect family dynamics (Barnett, Gareis, & Brennan, 2008; Dikkers et al., 2007; Haines, Marchand, & Harvey, 2006; Bianchi & Milkie, 2010). In addition, normative stressors suggested by the family life course perspective (e.g., providing childcare for preschool children; Erickson, Martinengo, & Hill, 2010) may affect parents' adaptability to work stress and their ability to balance work and family demands. In this way, the influence of the workplace may either independently incite conflict, or may contribute to the pileup of stressors and existing conflicts that taxes families' abilities to cope with these stressors. For example, work role overload has been linked with increased conflict, poor marital quality, and less positive involvement with children for mothers and fathers (Cinamon, Wiesel, & Tzuk, 2007; Crouter, Bumpus, Head, & McHale, 2001; Crouter, Perry-Jenkins, Huston, & Crawford, 1989; Hart & Kelley, 2006; Higgins, Duxbury, & Irving, 1992; Kinnunen, Gerris, & Vermulst, 1996; Stewart & Barling, 1996). Increasing work demands may diminish time, energy, and psychological resources that family role fulfillment also requires; subjective experience of strain may also cross over to other family members by emotion transmission, or through aggressive or undermining behaviors (Small & Riley, 1990; Westman, Keenan, Roziner, & Benyamini, 2008).

Notably, conflict within the family can also spill over into the work domain, suggesting that relations between strain in work and family roles may be reciprocal and cyclical (Byron, 2005; Ford, Heinen, & Langkamer, 2007). Finally, in line with *resilience theory*, the appraisal of work and family demands is also an important factor, as workers' appraisals of work and family demands may determine whether increased demands in either sphere are stressors or opportunities (see Grzywacz & Bass, 2003; Bianchi & Milkie, 2010).

Military Service

Military families provide an example of how accumulated, intersecting stressors affect family life, in that families with a military service-member parent are affected by each of the environmental stressors addressed in the foregoing sections. Cultural concerns are prominent, because the military is a distinct subculture, with norms dictating conduct, values, and priorities. In addition, military families are often required to relocate, requiring adaptation and acculturation to new international or regional customs. Related to socioeconomic status, the military provides a class structure that is reified and displayed in rank insignias and pay scales; although military families may enjoy stability in income, the implications of rank and status (e.g., commissioned versus enlisted personnel) may profoundly affect families (Wiens & Boss, 2006). Finally, the military is a workplace for the service-member, and work–family conflict is common, especially given the demanding nature of the institution (Segal, 1986). Thus, the literatures already discussed may shed light on the role of these external stressors on conflict within military families.

However, in addition to these sources of stress, the experience of military families is also marked by stresses related to the cycle of deployment, and extended periods of service-member absence. The theoretical perspective most often applied to understanding the effects of deployment on families, *ambiguous loss theory* (Boss, 2004; Wiens & Boss, 2006), has its roots in family stress theories (Boss & Greenberg, 1984). According to ambiguous loss theories, the combination of physical absence and psychological presence of the service-member will lead to ambiguity in family boundaries and a vacancy in family roles. Thus, families with a deployed parent will be likely to experience conflict when defining new roles during deployment, as well as when relinquishing those roles upon the service-member's return (Mmari, Roche, Sudhinaraset, & Blum, 2009; Sayers, Farrow, Ross, & Oslin, 2009). The existing research has supported the phenomena of role shifts and ambiguity regarding the loss of the parent among children and adolescents in military families (Huebner, Mancini, Wilcox, Grass, & Grass, 2007; Faber, Willerton, Clymer, MacDermid, & Weiss, 2008). In addition, research has described links between the civilian parent distress and child distress in military families during parental deployment (Kelley, 1994; Cozza, Chun, & Polo, 2005; Flake, Davis, Johnson, & Middleton, 2009; Chandra et al., 2010), which may indicate the presence of spillover due to the civilian parent's role strain.

LIMITATIONS AND SUGGESTIONS FOR FUTURE RESEARCH AND THEORETICAL DEVELOPMENT

In the above sections, we reviewed a number of theories related to family conflict, ranging from theories of within-person processes (e.g. spillover) to theories that describe families in the context of their communities and culture (e.g., ecological systems theory). However, despite the multitude of theories pertaining to family conflict, many studies that describe conflict and discord within the family are not primarily theory-driven. Indeed, as Karney and Bradbury (1995) conclude in their review of marital research, although there has been a proliferation of studies on marriage over the past half-century, the field has gotten broader (testing the influence of more variables on marital outcomes) rather than deeper (replicating and building on prior studies to develop a thorough explanation of marital processes). Karney and Bradbury argue that research on marriage has been driven more by an interest in specific outcomes (e.g., divorce, adjustment) than by an interest in the processes that produce those outcomes (e.g., how marital stability and satisfaction change over time). Analogous critiques can be applied to research specific to family conflict as well, emphasizing the need for theory development in this area. Whereas the impact of aversive family conflict on the health and development of individual family members is well-understood, there is less understanding of how family members interact to both create and resolve family conflicts, of the variety of ways in which family conflicts can unfold, or of the factors that protect some family members from the negative effects of aversive conflict while negatively affecting others. Greater understanding of process-level variables and of factors that moderate the initiation, the progression, and the impact of family conflict is warranted.

Understanding the Family as an Interconnected System

Though families are widely understood to be complex, holistic, interdependent systems in which individuals and relationships develop, defining and understanding conflict as a system-level process has proven challenging. Research on the features and processes of family conflict has been marked by dynamic tension between conceptual and methodological concerns. As a result, family conflict has been primarily operationalized and studied at the dyadic level, and interdependence has been examined by relating dyadic processes to outcomes within other subsystems. For example, marital conflict—the most well-understood type of family conflict—has been assessed in relation to outcomes and processes within participating individuals (e.g., the spouses), observing individuals (e.g., individual children), subsystems with overlapping membership (e.g., parent–child and coparenting relationships), and subsystems with non-overlapping membership (e.g., the sibling relationship). Although this approach has yielded many useful insights, there is evidence that many family conflicts are not primarily dyadic, but can have triadic, quadratic, or even more complex combinations of multiple perspectives (Vuchinich et al., 1988). Despite its influence on the work of clinical practitioners, the family systems view of the family as interdependent has not translated into a comprehensive body of research mapping the multitude of possible interconnections between and among family members and subsystems. Advances in statistical modeling that can represent interdependence between multiple parties, such as multilevel modeling, can help facilitate research in this area.

Additionally, fairly little research has examined the processes by which stress in one family system affect stress in another. Erel and Burman's (1995) meta-analysis shows significant, but modest connections between conflict in the marital relationship and parent–child conflict. It is possible that families show variability in the degree to which family subsystems interact. What differentiates the families characterized by high versus low spillover across family subsystems? We need more comprehensive models of how marital conflict, parent–child conflict, and sibling conflict reciprocally influence each other. There is also limited understanding of how external events that affect one family subsystem reverberate to the rest of the family. For example, how might the challenges of a special needs child affect the internal dynamics of a marriage, or how might a marital stressor, such as infidelity, affect trust and communication in the parent–child relationship? Research that takes a systemic perspective on the family can help address those questions.

Understanding Interconnections between Internal and External Processes

The structure of our review itself points to another area in which more theoretical integration is needed: in reconciling theories of internal family dynamics, such as spillover, emotion transmission, and interconnections between family subsystems (summarized in the first part of our review) with theories that make sense of the external factors that impinge on families (summarized in the second). Individual differences, socioeconomic resources, community supports, and cultural values can all influence how families communicate and connect, while processes internal to the family—such as the strength and direction of emotion transmission—can affect families' responses to circumstances like poverty or military deployment. Greater attention to moderators is needed in both cases to provide more complete theoretical understanding. For example, family stress theories that incorporate a focus on family members' appraisals of a stressor could be elaborated to include information about the crossover of positive and negative appraisals within the family. Similarly, theories that explain how family conflict affects children (e.g. cognitive–contextual theory and the emotional security hypothesis) could be broadened to incorporate accounts of how cultural differences in family structure affect these processes. In cultures where extended family networks take on more childrearing responsibility, for example, parental marital conflict may be experienced by children as less threatening to their well-being.

Incorporating genetics into Family Research

The term "gene-environment interaction" implies that genetic make-up and early environment are separable and affect individual development in different ways. However, most families consist of genetically related individuals, making it challenging for researchers to tease these influences apart. Parenting styles and children's genetically-predisposed temperaments can interact to produce parent–child conflict, for example, but parenting styles themselves are influenced by genetics. For example, children who are aggressive and impulsive may have parents with similar traits who are quick to use corporal punishment, thus exacerbating the children's oppositional behavior (Jaffee, Belsky, Harrington, Caspi, & Moffitt, 2006). Yet, much family research and theory views personality on an individual level. Theoretical models of family conflict that consider individual difference factors can be improved by acknowledging the effect of genes and the fact that genetic variation within families is non-random (that is, family members tend to be genetically similar). For example, personality characteristics have been posited to affect children's responses to marital conflict. One well-documented finding is that children's intelligence can be a protective factor in coping with marital conflict (e.g., Katz & Gottman, 1997). However, given the heritability of intelligence, it is possible that parents' intelligence, rather than children's intelligence, is protective: perhaps more intelligent parents exhibit different kinds of conflict behaviors or are better able to explain episodes of conflict to their children. Similarly, children may show biological vulnerabilities that make them more vulnerable to family conflict, such as greater physiological reactivity (Davies & Cummings, 1994; El-Sheikh & Whitson, 2006). Yet, children who tend to show a stronger physiological response to conflict might share that trait with parents who are also more reactive, changing the ways that family conflict unfolds in their families. Models that include genetic processes and account for the possible genetic interconnections between family members can help untangle these issues, as can research on twins, siblings, and adopted and foster children.

Developing Models of Resilience

More information is needed on how families develop resilience to internal and external stressors to enrich theoretical accounts of resilience. The same stressor, such as the death of a child or the illness of a parent, can make some families and some individual family members stronger but create unremitting tension and conflict in others. For example, a wife's diagnosis of breast cancer has been found to affect both her own psychosocial functioning and that of her partner (Baucom et al., 2009). Whereas most spouses show decreased negative affect over time following cancer treatment, a sizable number of couples show continued distress even after treatment has been completed (Omne-Ponten, Holmberg, Bergstrom, Sjoden, & Burns, 1993). Similarly, the death of a child has been linked with long-term declines in parents' individual and marital well-being, but variability appears to exist, such that some parents are able to draw meaning from the experience and show posttraumatic growth (Rogers, Floyd, Seltzer, Greenberg, & Hong, 2008). Which attitudes and assumptions do family members bring to external crises as well as internal stresses that minimize rather than maximize conflict? *Social cognitive theory*, which posits that individuals' cognitions, affect, and motivations influence their responses to environmental stressors (Bandura, 1986), offers a useful framework for studying the role of family processes in challenging situations.

Understanding Longitudinal Processes

Families are dynamic systems, changing from year to year and from generation to generation. Yet, many theories of family conflict treat the family as a fairly static entity that responds to internal and external events in fixed ways. Just as more longitudinal studies of marital and family processes are needed (Karney & Bradbury, 1995), so too are more longitudinal studies of family conflict. Do different risk factors for family conflict exist at different stages in the life of the family, and does family conflict have different implications at different times? For example, are there 'critical windows' where families might experience more conflict—e.g., at the transition to parenthood, the addition of a sibling, or youths' onset of puberty? Are there other times of relative calm?

How do children's appraisals of family conflict change over time? For example, children may benefit from witnessing family conflict if the conflict is resolved productively (Davies & Cummings, 1994). However, very young children might have less ability to distinguish between productive and destructive conflict. Similarly, high levels of parent–child conflict might be more or less problematic at different ages and stages in the life of the family; in adolescence, conflict can be a positive sign of individuation, but parent–adolescent conflict in the context of a stressful life event, like military deployment or marital dissolution, might be problematic. What are the stress points in families, and the sources of both continuities and discontinuities in the trajectory of family conflict over time?

Longitudinal research can also help to elucidate intergenerational processes, further refining conceptual models of risk and resilience. Why do some individuals who grow up in conflictual families perpetuate patterns of conflict with their own spouse and children, whereas others develop very different patterns from the family-of-origin? How does a history of parental-marital conflict shape marital functioning in subsequent generations?

Understanding Family Conflict in Non-Traditional Families

This chapter has made frequent reference to the family systems perspective, which maps relationships among individual family members and family subsystems. However, family systems theory evolved from work with traditional two-parent families, in which marriage preceded the birth of a child. Marital dissolution, single-parenthood, remarriage, and step-parenthood can all change the composition of family subsystems and the boundaries between different subsystems, and provide new potential sources of conflict. For example, family systems theorists tend to view alliances between parents and children that threaten the marital dyad as problematic. However, in blended families, the parent–child dyad might precede the formation of the new marital dyad, making questions of alliance and boundaries more complex. In both the marital and in the parent–child domains, the role of the new step-parent can be difficult to define. Aspects of marital and parent–child relationship functioning that tend to be almost universally beneficial in non-divorced families, such as positive marital interactions and authoritative parenting styles, have been linked to problematic outcomes in blended families (Hetherington & Clingempeel, 1992), suggesting that it can be challenging for even the best-intentioned step-parent to occupy an appropriate role within the family. Similarly, sibling dynamics can change with marital transitions, both because the existing relationship between siblings is altered and because of the introduction of new step-siblings into the family. However, relatively little is known about sibling relationships in the wake of divorce and remarriage (Hetherington & Clingempeel, 1992), and little is also known about the interconnections between different family subsystems in the wake of family reorganization. Given that divorce affects a significant proportion of American families, and has been associated with negative consequences for both adults and children (Amato, 2000), models of family conflict geared towards understanding nontraditional families are needed.

Applying Research to Practice

Although many family researchers draw from theories that were originally developed in clinical contexts, such as family systems theory, the more recent literature on family interactions has not had as much impact on interventions, leading to a growing divide between research and practice. There are many empirically supported couples' therapies, such as Cognitive Behavioral Couples Therapy (Baucom & Epstein, 1990) and Integrative Behavioral Couples Therapy (Christensen, Jacobson, & Babcock, 1995), but relatively few empirically supported therapies that focus specifically on family functioning. In fact, Black and Lebow (2010) liken the divide between research and practice in family psychology to a couple's behavior in a failing marriage, characterized by poor communication, a perceived lack of shared values and goals, and competing worldviews. Several family-oriented therapies have received empirical support, such as social learning approaches; interventions to treat and prevent antisocial behavior problems in children (Dishion & Kavanagh, 2003; Forgatch & Patterson, 2010); multisystemic therapy (MST), an intensive treatment targeted to juvenile offenders (Henggeler & Schaefer, 2010); and multidimensional family therapy (MDFT), a family-based treatment aimed at youth with substance abuse and behavior problems (Liddle, 2002). Family theories have the potential to help bridge the divide between research and practice by highlighting additional intervention opportunities that focus on family-level processes, such as emotion transmission between family members or spillover between family subsystems. There is evidence that family-level interventions, whether they target marital dynamics, parent–child dynamics, or both, improve children's psychosocial function and reduce their risk for psychopathology (Cowan & Cowan, 2002). However, this area needs not just more integration of research and practice, but also a more nuanced understanding of the family-level mechanisms that make certain interventions effective. For example, a family that engages in aggressive conflict behavior might exacerbate a child's behavior problems through threats to the child's emotional security. Targeting both the child's appraisals of the conflict behavior and the conflict behavior itself might lead to a more successful intervention than one that focuses only on the child's cognitions.

CONCLUSION

We believe that the state of theory and research on family processes is currently at an exciting juncture—particularly with new data collection techniques and new statistical methods allowing us greater access to the everyday processes in families' lives. These methods thus allow us to test specific theories that reflect change in families and to develop richer theories. For example, electronic daily diaries and experience sampling allow us to capture everyday patterns of spillover and crossover within families in real time, and also shed light on other family-level and situational variables that might affect spillover and crossover processes. These data collection procedures go along with statistical advances that allow for the modeling of greater complexity—e.g., multilevel modeling approaches that adjust for interdependence within dyads, triads, and groups—are ideal for examining family systems theories, theories of spillover and emotion transmission, and other theories of family conflict. Advances in genetic research and in the sampling and analysis of biomarkers, such as cortisol and salivary alpha-amylase, can also extend findings on families' emotions into the realm of physiology and health. This has the potential to enrich theories of family conflict. In short, advanced methods contribute to theory development, for example through elucidating how pathways through which everyday family life affects health and well-being, and contributing to the creation of more sophisticated theoretical models.

Research has demonstrated that families are dynamic, interconnected systems. The interplay between family members and family subsystems can sometimes manifest itself as conflict. It is important for theory development to capture this richness. The next generation of researchers can address which factors strengthen or weaken families' interconnectedness, and in what contexts interconnectedness acts as a source of resilience or as a source of vulnerability. Research into family processes has been marked by the assumption that conflict is destructive, albeit occasionally seen as a prompt towards growth and emotional closeness. In our view, conflict is a multidimensional process that can emerge in healthy as well as in dysfunctional family environments. Researchers have much to gain from studying the variegated ways in which conflict can unfold and the meaning that it holds for the family. Future theories of family conflict will benefit from the development of richer, more complex, and more multidimensional accounts of families in conflict.

REFERENCES

Amato, P. R. (2000). The consequences of divorce for adults and children. *Journal of Marriage and Family*, *62*, 1269–1287.

Amato, P. R., Booth, A., Johnson, D. R., & Rogers, S. J. (2007). *Alone together: How marriage in America is changing*. Cambridge, MA: Harvard University Press.

Bandura, A. (1986). *Social foundations of thought and action: A social cognitive theory*. Englewood Cliffs, NJ: Prentice Hall.

Barnett, R. C., Gareis, K. C., & Brennan, R. T. (2008). Wives' shift work schedules and husbands' and wives' well-being in dual-earner couples with children: A within-couple analysis. *Journal of Family Issues*, *29*, 396–422.

Baucom, D. H., Porter, L. S., Kirby, J. S., Gremore, T. M., Wiesenthal, N., Aldridge, W.... Keefe, F. J. (2009). A couple-based intervention for female breast cancer. *Psycho-Oncology*, *18*, 276–283.

Baucom, D. H., & Epstein, N. (1990). *Cognitive-behavioral marital therapy*. New York: Brunner/Mazel.

Bianchi, S. M. & Milkie, M. A. (2010). Work and family research in the first decade of the 21st century. *Journal of Marriage and Family*, *72*, 705–725.

Black, D. A. & Lebow, J. (2010) Systemic research controversies and challenges. In J. H. Bray and M. Stanton (Eds.), *The Wiley-Blackwell handbook of family psychology*. Oxford, England: Blackwell.

Bolger, N., DeLongis, A., Kessler, R. C., & Wethington, E. (1989). The contagion of stress across multiple roles. *Journal of Marriage and the Family*, *51*, 175–183.

Boss, P. (2004). Ambiguous loss research, theory, and practice: Reflections after 9/11. *Journal of Marriage and Family*, *66*, 551–566.

Boss, P., and Greenberg, J. (1984). Family boundary ambiguity: A new variable in family stress theory. *Family Process*, *23*, 535–546.

Bronfenbrenner, U. (1979). *The ecology of human development: Experiments by nature and design*. Cambridge, MA: Harvard University Press.

Bronfenbrenner, U. (1986). Ecology of the family as a context of human development: Research perspectives. *Developmental Psychology*, *22*, 723–742.

Bronfenbrenner, U. (1995). Developmental ecology through space and time: A future perspective. In P. Moen, G. H. Elder, & K. Luscher (Eds.), *Examining lives in context: Perspectives on the ecology of human development* (pp. 619–647). Washington, DC: American Psychological Association.

Broszormenyi-Nagy, I., & Spark, G. M. (1973). *Invisible loyalties: Reciprocity in intergenerational family therapy*. Hagerstown, MD: Harper & Row.

Burman, B., Margolin, G., & John, R. S. (1993). America's angriest home videos: Behavioral contingencies observed in home reenactments of marital conflict. *Journal of Consulting and Clinical Psychology*. *61*, 28–39.

Byron, K. (2005). A meta-analytic review of work–family conflict and its antecedents. *Journal of Vocational Behavior*, *67*, 169–198.

Carstensen, L. L., Gottman, J. M., & Levenson, R. W. (1995). Emotional behavior in long-term marriage. *Psychology and Aging*, *10*, 140–149.

Caughlin, J. P., & Huston, T. L. (2002). A contextual analysis of the association between demand/withdraw and marital satisfaction. *Personal Relationships*, *9*, 95–119.

Caughlin, J. P. & Malis, R. S. (2004). Demand/withdraw communication between parents and adolescents: Connections with self-esteem and substance use. *Journal of Social and Personal Relationships*, *21*, 125–148.

Chandra, A., Lara-Cinisomo, S., Jaycox, L. H., Tanielian, T., Burns, R. M., Ruder, T., & Han, B. (2010). Children on the homefront: The experience of children from military families. *Pediatrics*, *125*, 13–22.

Christensen, A., & Heavey, C. L. (1990). Gender, power and marital conflict. *Journal of Personality and Social Psychology*, *59*, 73–85.

Christensen, A., Jacobson, N. S., & Babcock, J. C. (1995). Integrative behavioral couples therapy. In N. S. Jacobson 8c A. S. Gurman (Eds.), *Clinical handbook of couples therapy* (2nd ed., pp. 31–64). New York: Guilford Press.

Christensen, A., & Margolin, G. (1988). Conflict and alliance in distressed and nondistressed families. In R. Hinde & J. Stevenson-Hinde (Eds.), *Relationships within families: Mutual influences* (pp. 263–282). Oxford, England: Oxford University Press.

Cinamon, R. G., Wiesel, A. & Tzuk, K. (2007). Work–family conflict within the family: Crossover effects, perceived parent–child interaction quality, parental self-efficacy, and life role attributions. *Journal of Career Development*, *34*, 79–100.

Conger, R. D., Conger, K. J., Elder, G. H., Jr., Lorenz, F. O., Simons, R. L., & Whitbeck, L. B. (1993). Family economic stress and adjustment of early adolescent girls. *Developmental Psychology*, *29*, 206–219.

Conger, R. D., Conger, K. J., & Martin, M. J. (2010). Socioeconomic status, family processes, and individual development. *Journal of Marriage and Family, 72*, 685–704.

Conger, R. D., & Elder, G. H., Jr. (Eds.). (1994). *Families in troubled times: Adapting to change in rural America*. Hawthorne, NY: Aldine de Gruyter.

Conger, R. D., Ge, X., Elder, G. H. Jr., Lorenz, F. O., & Simons, R. L. (1994). Economic stress, coercive family process, and developmental problems of adolescents. *Child Development, 65*, 541–561.

Costigan, C. L., Cox, M. J., & Cauce, A. M. (2003). Work-parenting linkages among dual-earner couples at the transition to parenthood. *Journal of Family Psychology, 17*, 397–408.

Cowan, P. A., & Cowan, C. P. (2002). Interventions as tests of family systems theories: Marital and family relationships in children's development, and psychopathology. *Development and Psychopathology. Special issue on interventions as tests of theories, 14*, 731–760.

Cozza, S. J., Chun, R. S., & Polo, S. A. (2005). Military families and children during Operation Iraqi Freedom. *Psychiatric Quarterly, 76*, 371–378.

Crouter, A. C. (1984). Spillover from family to work: The neglected side of the work-family interface. *Human Relations, 37*, 425–442.

Crouter, A. C., Bumpus, M. F., Head, M. R., & McHale, S. M. (2001). Implications of overwork and overload for the quality of men's family relationships. *Journal of Marriage and Family, 63*, 404–416.

Crouter, A. C., Perry-Jenkins, M., Huston, T. L., & Crawford, D. W. (1989). The influence of work-induced psychological states on behavior at home. *Basic and Applied Social Psychology, 10*, 273–292.

Cummings, E. M., Ballard, M., El-Shiekh, M., & Lake, M. (1991). Resolution and children's responses to interadult anger. *Developmental Psychology, 27*, 462–470.

Cummings, E. M., & Davies, P. T. (1994). *Children and marital conflict: The impact of family dispute and resolution*. New York: Guilford Press.

Cummings, E. M., Davies, P. T., & Campbell, S. B. (2000). *Developmental psychopathology and family process: Theory, research, and clinical implications*. New York: Guilford Press.

Davies, P. T., & Cummings, M. E. (1994). Marital conflict and child adjustment: An emotional security hypothesis. *Psychological Bulletin, 116*, 387–411.

Davies, P. T., Harold, G. T., Goeke-Morey, M., Cummings, E. M. (2002). Children's emotional security and interparental conflict. *Monographs of the Society for Research in Child Development, 67*, 1–129.

Deutsch, M. (1973). *The resolution of conflict: Constructive and destructive processes*. New Haven, CT: Yale University Press.

Dikkers, J. S. E., Geurts, S. A. E., Kompier, M. A. J., Taris, T. W., Houtman, I. L. D., & van den Heuvel, F. (2007). Does workload cause work-home interference or is it the other way around? *Stress and Health, 23*, 303–314.

Dishion, T. J., & Kavanagh, K. (2003). *Intervening with adolescent problem behavior: A family-centered approach*. New York: Guilford Press.

Dixon, S. V., Graber, J. A., & Brooks-Gunn, J. (2008). The roles of respect for parental authority and parenting practices in parent–child conflict among African American, Latino, and European American families. *Journal of Family Psychology, 22*, 1–10.

Doumas, D., Margolin, G., & John, R. S. (1994). The intergenerational transmission of aggression across three generations. *Journal of Family Violence, 9*, 157–175.

Duman, S., & Margolin, G. (2007). Parents' aggressive influences and children's aggressive problem solutions with peers. *Journal of Clinical Child and Adolescent Psychology, 36*, 42–55.

Elder, G. (1974). *Children of the Great Depression: Social change in life experience*. Chicago: University of Chicago Press.

El-Shiekh, M., Cummings, E. M., Kouros, C. D., Elmore-Staton, L., & Buckhalt, J. (2008). Marital psychological and physical aggression and children's mental and physical health: Direct, mediated, and moderated effects. *Journal of Consulting and Clinical Psychology, 76*, 138–148.

El-Shiekh, M., & Whitson, S. A. (2006). Longitudinal relations between marital conflict and child adjustment: vagal regulation as a protective factor. *Journal of Family Psychology, 20*, 30–39.

Epstein, N., Baucom, D. H., & Rankin, L. A. (1993). Treatment of marital conflict: A cognitive-behavioral approach. *Clinical Psychology Review, 13*, 45–57.

Erel, O. & Burman, B. (1995) Interrelatedness of marital relations and parent-child relations: A meta-analytic review. *Psychological Bulletin, 118*, 108–132.

Erickson, J. J., Martinengo, G., & Hill, E. J. (2010). Putting work and family experiences in context: Differences by family life stage. *Human Relations*, *63*, 955–979.

Faber, A. J., Willerton, E., Clymer, E., MacDermid, S. M., & Weiss, H. M. (2008). Ambiguous absence, ambiguous presence: A qualitative study of military reserve families in wartime. *Journal of Family Psychology*, *22*, 222–230.

Farver, J. M., Darang, S. K., & Bhadha, B. R. (2002). East meets west: Ethnic identity, acculturation, and conflict in Asian Indian families. *Journal of Family Psychology*, *16*, 338–350.

Flake, E. M., Davis, B. E., Johnson, P. L. & Middleton, L. S. (2009). The psychosocial effects of deployment on military children. *Journal of Developmental Behavioral Pediatrics*, *30*, 271–278.

Ford, M. T., Heinen, B. A., & Langkamer, K. L. (2007). Work and family satisfaction and conflict: A meta-analysis of cross-domain relations. *Journal of Applied Psychology*, *92*, 57–80.

Forgatch, M. S., & Patterson, G. R. (2010). Parent Management Training – Oregon Model: An intervention for antisocial behavior in children and adolescents. In J. R. Weisz & A. E. Kazdin (Eds.), *Evidence-based psychotherapies for children and adolescents* (2nd ed., pp. 159–178). New York: Guilford Press.

Gottman, J. M. (1979). *Marital interaction: empirical investigations*. New York: Academic Press.

Gottman, J. M. (1993). The roles of conflict engagement, escalation, and avoidance in marital interaction: A longitudinal view of five types of couples. *Journal of Consulting and Clinical Psychology*, *61*, 6–15.

Gottman, J. M. (1994). *What predicts divorce? The relationships between marital processes and marital outcomes*. Hillsdale, NJ: Lawrence Erlbaum.

Gottman, J. M. & Levenson, R. W. (1999). How stable is marital interaction over time? *Family Process*, *38*, 159–165.

Gottman, J., Markman, H., & Notarius, C. (1977). The topography of marital conflict: A sequential analysis of verbal and nonverbal behavior. *Journal of Marriage and the Family*, *39*, 461–477.

Grych, J. H., & Fincham, F. D. (1990). Marital conflict and children's adjustment: A cognitive-contextual framework. *Psychological Bulletin*, *108*, 267–290.

Grzywacz, J. G., & Bass, B. L. (2003). Work, family, and mental health: Testing different models of work-family fit. *Journal of Marriage and Family*, *65*, 248–262.

Haines, V. Y., Marchand, A., & Harvey, S. (2006). Crossover of workplace aggression experiences in dual-earner couples. *Journal of Occupational Health Psychology*, *11*, 305–314.

Hammack, P. L., Robinson, W. L., Crawford, I., & Li, S. T. (2004). Poverty and depressed mood among urban African-American adolescents: A family stress perspective. *Journal of Child and Family Studies*, *13*, 309–323.

Hart, M. S., & Kelley, M. L. (2006). Fathers' and mothers' work and family issues as related to internalizing and externalizing behavior of children attending day care. *Journal of Family Issues*, *27*, 252–270.

Heavey, C. L., Layne, C., & Christensen, A. (1993). Gender and conflict structure in marital interactions: A replication and extension. *Journal of Consulting and Clinical Psychology*, *61*, 16–27.

Henggeler, S. W., & Schaeffer, C. (2010). Treating serious antisocial behavior using multisystemic therapy. In J. R. Weisz & A. E. Kazdin (Eds.), *Evidence-based psychotherapies for children and adolescents* (2nd ed., pp. 159–178). New York: Guilford Press.

Hetherington, E. M., & Clingempeel, W. G. (1992). Coping with marital transitions: A family systems perspective. *Monographs of the Society for Research in Child Development*, *57*. Chicago: University of Chicago Press.

Hernandez, B., Garcia, J. I. R., & Flynn, M. (2010). The role of familism in the relation between parent-child discord and psychological distress among emerging adults of Mexican descent. *Journal of Family Psychology*, *24*, 105–114.

Higgins, C., Duxbury, L. E., & Irving, R. H. (1992). Work-family conflict in the dual-career family. *Organizational Behavior and Human Decision Processes*, *51*, 51–75.

Hill, R. (1949). *Families under stress: Adjustment to the crises of war separation and reunion*. New York: Harper & Brothers.

Huebner, A. J., Mancini, J. A., Wilcox, R. M., Grass, S. R., & Grass, G. A. (2007). Parental deployment and youth in military families: Exploring uncertainty and ambiguous loss. *Family Relations*, *56*, 112–122.

Jaffee, S. R., Belsky, J., Harrington, H., Caspi, A., & Moffitt, T. E. (2006). When parents have a history of conduct disorder: How is the caregiving environment affected? *Journal of Abnormal Psychology*, 115, 309–319.

Johnson, D. R., White, L. K., Edwards, J. N., & Booth, A. (1986). Dimensions of marital quality. *Journal of Family Issues*, 7, 31–49.

Johnson, M. D., Cohan, C. L., Davila, J., Lawrence, E., Rogge, R. D., Karney... Bradbury, T. N. (2005). Problem-solving skills and affective expressions as predictors of change in marital satisfaction. *Journal of Consulting and Clinical Psychology*, 73, 15–27.

Jouriles, E. N., Murphy, C., Farris, A. M., Smith, D. A., Richters, J. E., & Waters, E. (1991). Marital adjustment, parental disagreements about child rearing and behavior problems in boys: Increasing the specificity of the marital assessment. *Child Development*, 62, 1424–1433.

Karney, B. R., & Bradbury, T. N. (1995). The longitudinal course of marital quality and stability: A review of theory, method, and research. *Psychological Bulletin*, 118, 3–34.

Karney, B. R., Story, L. B., & Bradbury, T. N. (2005). Marriages in context: Interactions between chronic and acute stress among newlyweds. In T. A. Revenson, K. Kayser, & G. Bodenmann (Eds.), *Emerging perspective on couples' coping with stress* (pp. 13–32). Washington, DC: American Psychological Association.

Katz, L. F., & Gottman, J. M. (1997). Buffering children from marital conflict and dissolution. *Journal of Clinical Child Psychology*, 26, 157–171.

Katz, L. F., & Gottman, J. M. (1993). Patterns of marital conflict predict children's internalizing and externalizing behaviors. *Developmental Psychology*, 29, 940–950.

Katz, L. F., & Woodin, E. M. (2002). Hostility, hostile detachment, and conflict engagement in marriages: Effects on child and family functioning. *Child Development*, 73, 636–651.

Kelley, M. L. (1994). The effects of military-induced separation on family factors and child behavior. *American Journal of Orthopsychiatry*, 64, 103–111.

Kerig, P. K. (1996). Assessing the links between interparental conflict and child adjustment: The conflicts and problem-solving scales. *Journal of Family Psychology*, 10, 454–473.

Kinnunen, U., Gerris, J., & Vermulst, A. (1996). Work experiences and family functioning among employed fathers with children of school age. *Family Relations*, 45, 449–455.

Kirchler, E., Rodler, C., Holzl, E., & Meier, K. (2001). *Conflict and decision-making in close relationships: Love, money, and daily routines*. Philadelphia: Psychology Press.

Klinetob, N. A., & Smith, D. A. (1996). Demand-withdraw communication in marital interaction: Tests of interpersonal contingency and gender role hypotheses. *Journal of Marriage and the Family*, 58, 945–957.

Larson, R., & Almeida, D. M. (1999). Emotional transmission in the daily lives of families: A new paradigm for studying family processes. *Journal of Marriage and the Family*, 61, 5–20.

Larson, R. W., & Gillman, S. (1999). Transmission of emotions in the daily interactions of single-mother families. *Journal of Marriage and the Family*, 61, 21–37.

Larson, R. W., & Richards, M. H. (1994). *Divergent realities: The emotional lives of mothers, fathers, and adolescents*. New York: Basic Books.

Lau, A. S., McCabe, K. M., Yeh, M., Garland, A. F., Wood, P. A., & Hough, R. L. (2005). The acculturation gap-distress hypothesis among high-risk Mexican American families. *Journal of Family Psychology*, 19, 367–375.

Laursen, B. (1993). The perceived impact of conflict on adolescent relationships. *Merrill-Palmer Quarterly*, 39, 535–550.

Laursen, B., Coy, K. C., & Collins, W. A. (1998). Reconsidering changes in parent-child conflict across adolescence: A meta-analysis. *Child Development*, 69, 817–832.

Lee, R. M., Choe, J., Kim, G., & Ngo, V. (2000). Construction of the Asian American family conflicts scale. *Journal of Counseling Psychology*, 47, 211–222.

Levenson, R. W., & Gottman, J. M. (1983). Marital interaction: physiological linkage and affective exchange. *Journal of Personality and Social Psychology*, 45, 587–97.

Liddle, H. A. (2002). *Multidimensional Family Therapy (MDFT) for adolescent cannabis users*. Rockville, MD7 Center for Substance Abuse Treatment, Substance Abuse and Mental Health Services Administration.

Lollis, S., Ross, H., & Leroux, L. (1996). An observational study of parents' socialization or moral orientation during sibling conflicts. *Merrill Palmer Quarterly*, *42*, 475–494.

Magnuson, K. A. & Duncan, G. J. (2002). Parents in poverty. In M. H. Bornstein (Ed.) *Handbook of parenting*. Vol. 4 *Social conditions and applied parenting* (pp. 95–121). Mahwah, NJ: Lawrence Erlbaum.

Margolin, G. (1988). Marital conflict is not marital conflict is not marital conflict. In R. de V. Peters and R. McMahon (Eds.), *Social learning and systems approaches to marriage and the family* (pp. 193–216). New York: Brunner/Mazel.

Margolin, G., Christensen A., & John, R. S. (1996). The continuance and spill-over of everyday tensions in distressed and nondistressed families. *Journal of Family Psychology*, *10*, 304–321.

Margolin, G., & Gordis, E. B. (2003). Co-occurrence between marital aggression and parents' child abuse potential: The impact of cumulative stress. *Violence and Victims*, *18*, 243–258.

Margolin, G., & John, R. S. (1997). Children's exposure to marital aggression: Direct and mediated effects. In G. J. Kantor & J. L. Jasinski (Eds.), *Out of darkness: contemporary perspectives on family violence* (pp. 90–104). Thousand Oaks, CA: Sage.

Margolin, G., Vickerman, K. A., Oliver, P. H., Gordis, E. B. (2010). Violence exposure in multiple interpersonal domains: Cumulative and differential effects. *Journal of Adolescent Health*, *47*, 198–205.

Margolin, G., & Wampold, B. F. (1981). A sequential analysis of conflict and accord in distressed and nondistressed marital partners. *Journal of Consulting and Clinical Psychology*, *49*, 554–567.

Markus, H. R., & Lin, L. R. (1999). Conflictways: Cultural diversity in the meanings and practices of conflict. In D. A. Prentice & D. T. Miller (Eds.), *Cultural divides: understanding and overcoming group conflict* (pp. 302–333). New York: Russell Sage.

Mattesich P, Hill R (1987) Life cycle and family development. In: Sussman MB, Steinbmetz SK (Eds.) *Handbook of Marriage and the Family*. New York: Plenum, 437–465.

McCubbin, H. I., & Patterson, J. M. (1982). Family adaptation to crises. In H. I. McCubbin, A. E. Cauble, & J. M. Patterson (Eds.), *Family stress, coping, and social support* (pp. 26–47). Springfield, IL: Charles C Thomas.

McGonagle, K. A., Kessler, R. C., & Schilling, E. A. (1992). The frequency and determinants of marital disagreements in a community sample. *Journal of Social and Personal Relationships*, *9*, 507–524.

Minuchin, S., Baker, L., Rosman, B., Liebman, B., Milman, L., Todd, T. C. (1975). A Conceptual Model of Psychosomatic Illness in Children: Family Organization and Family Therapy. *Archives of General Psychiatry*, *32*, 1031–1038.

Mmari, K, Roche, K. M., Sudhinaraset, M. & Blum, R. (2009). When a parent goes off to war: Exploring the issues faced by adolescents and their families. *Youth and Society*, *40*, 455–475.

Montemayor, R. (1986). Family variation in parent-adolescent storm and stress. *Journal of Adolescent Research*, *1*, 15–31.

Nievar, M. A., & Luster, T. (2006). Developmental processes in African American families: An application of Mcloyd's theoretical model. *Journal of Marriage and Family*, *68*, 320–331.

Omne-Ponten, M., Holmberg, L., Bergstrom, R., Sjoden, P., & Burns, T. (1993). Psychosocial adjustment among husbands of women treated for breast cancer: Mastectomy vs. breast conserving surgery. *European Journal of Cancer*, *29A*, 1393–1397.

Patterson, G. R., DeBaryshe, B., & Ramsey, E. (1989). A developmental perspective on antisocial behavior. *American Psychologist*, *44*, 329–335.

Patterson, G. R., & Forgatch, M. S. (2005). *Parents and adolescents living together: Part I. The basics*. Champaign, IL: Research Press.

Phinney, J., Chavira, V., & Williamson, L. (1992). Acculturation attitudes and self-esteem among high school and college students. *Youth and Society*, *23*, 299–312.

Piotrkowski, C. S. (1979). *Work and the family system*. New York: Free Press.

Pyke, K. (2005). "Generational deserters" and "black sheep": acculturative differences among siblings in Asian immigrant families. *Journal of Family Issues*, *26*, 491–517.

Repetti, R. L. (1989). Effects of daily workload on subsequent behavior during marital interaction: The roles of social withdrawal and spouse support. *Journal of Personality and Social Psychology*, *57*, 651–659.

Repetti, R. L., Taylor, S. E., & Seeman, T. E. (2002). Risky families: Family social environments and the mental and physical health of offspring. *Psychological Bulletin*, *128*, 330–366.

Repetti, R. L., & Wood, J. (1997). Effects of daily stress at work on mothers' interactions with preschoolers. *Journal of Family Psychology*, *11*, 90–108.

Robila, M., & Krishnakumar, A. (2006). Economic pressure and children's psychological functioning. *Journal of Child and Family Studies*, *15*, 435–443.

Rogers, C. H., Floyd, F. J., Seltzer, M. M., Greenberg, J., & Hong, J. (2008). Long-term effects of the death of a child on parents' adjustment in midlife. *Journal of Family Psychology*, *22*, 203–211.

Roloff, M. E. & Johnson, K. L. (2002). Serial arguing over the relational life course: Antecedents and consequences. In A. L. Vangelisti, H. T. Reis, & M. A. Fitzpatrick (Eds.), *Stability and change in relationships: advances in personal relationships* (pp. 107–128). New York: Cambridge University Press.

Saxbe, D. E., & Repetti, R. L. (2010). For Better or Worse? Coregulation of Couples' Cortisol Levels and Mood States. *Journal of Personality and Social Psychology*, *98*, 92–103. 10.1037/a0016959.

Sayers, S. L., Farrow, V. A., Ross, J., & Oslin, D. W. (2009). Family problems among recently returned military veterans referred for a mental health evaluation. *Journal of Clinical Psychiatry*, *70*, 163–170.

Scaramella, L. V., Neppl, T. K., Ontai, L. I., & Conger, R. D. (2008). Consequences of socioeconomic disadvantage across three generations: Parenting behavior and child externalizing problems. *Journal of Family Psychology*, *22*, 725–733.

Schulz, M. S., Cowan, P. A., Cowan, C. P., & Brennan, R. T. (2004). Coming home upset: Gender, marital satisfaction, and the daily spillover of workday experience into couple interactions. *Journal of Family Psychology*, *18*, 250–263.

Segal, M. W. (1986). The military and the family as greedy institutions. *Armed Forces and Society*, *13*, 9–38.

Sillars, A. L., & Wilmot, W. W. (1989). Marital communication across the life span. In J. F. Nussbaum (Ed.), *Life-span communication: Normative issues* (pp. 225–253). Hillsdale, NJ: Lawrence Erlbaum.

Small, S. A., & Riley, D. (1990). Toward a multidimensional assessment of work spillover into family life. *Journal of Marriage and the Family*, *52*, 51–61.

Smith, D. K., & Chamberlain, P. (2010). Multidimensional treatment foster care for adolescents: Processes and outcomes. In J. R. Weisz & A. E. Kazdin (Eds.), *Evidence-based psychotherapies for children and adolescents* (2nd ed., pp. 159–178). New York: Guilford Press.

Smokowski, P. R. & Bacallao, M. L. (2006). Acculturation and aggression in Latino adolescents: A structural model focusing on cultural risk factors and assets. *Journal of Abnormal Child Psychology*, *34*, 659–673.

Smokowski, P. R., Rose, R. & Bacallao, M. L. (2008). Acculturation and Latino family processes: How cultural involvement, biculturalism, and acculturation gaps influence family dynamics. *Family Relations*, *57*, 295–308.

Stewart, W., & Barling, J. (1996). Fathers' work experiences effect children's behaviors via job-related affect and parenting behaviors. *Journal of Organizational Behavior*, *77*, 221–232.

Stocker, C. M., Lanthier, R. P., & Furman, W. (1997). Sibling relationships in early adulthood. *Journal of Family Psychology*, *11*, 210–221.

Story, L. B., & Repetti, R. L. (2006). Daily occupational stressors and marital behavior. *Journal of Family Psychology*, *20*, 690–700.

Sturge-Apple, M. L., Davies, P. T., & Cummings, E. M. (2006). Hostility and withdrawal in marital conflict: Effects on parental emotional unavailability and inconsistent discipline. *Journal of Family Psychology*, *20*, 227–238.

Tseng, V., & Fuligni, A. J. (2000). Parent-adolescent language use and relationships among immigrant families with East Asian, Filipino, and Latin American backgrounds. *Journal of Marriage and the Family*, *62*, 465–476.

Vuchinich, S., Emery, R. E., & Cassidy, J. (1988). Family members as third parties in dyadic family conflict: Strategies, alliances, and outcomes. *Child Development*, *59*, 1293–1302.

Wadsworth, M. E. & Compas, B. E. (2002). Coping with family conflict and economic strain: The adolescent perspective. *Journal of Research on Adolescence*, *12*, 243–274.

Westman, M. (2001). Stress and strain crossover. *Human Relations*, *54*, 717–752.

Westman, M., Keenan, G., Roziner, I., & Benyamini, Y. (2008). The crossover of perceived health between spouses. *Journal of Occupational Health Psychology*, *13*, 168–180.

Wiens, T. W., & Boss, P. (2006). Maintaining family resiliency before, during, and after military separation. In C. A. Castro, A. B. Adler, & C. A. Britt, (Eds.), *Military life: The psychology of serving in peace and combat*. Bridgeport, CT: Praeger Security International.

Yau, J. & Smetana, J. (2003). Adolescent-parent conflict in Hong Kong and Shenzhen: A comparison of youth in two cultural contexts. *International Journal of Behavioral Development, 27*, 201–211.

11 Theories of Intimate Partner Violence

*Richard E. Heyman, Heather M. Foran,
and Jesse L. Wilkinson*[1]

"There is nothing more practical than a good theory," wrote social psychologist Kurt Lewin (1952, p. 169). Theory organizes disparate facts and ideas into a coherent, testable set of premises that can guide research and interventions. Theory, particularly feminist theory, was instrumental in raising awareness about "wife battering" (now referred to by the more inclusive term intimate partner violence, IPV), passing laws to criminalize it, establishing infrastructures to protect women and to prosecute and rehabilitate the men who assault them, and researching its causes and treatments. However, good scientific theories to which Lewin refers are not just practical because they are useful in the real world but also because they are testable; that is, "good theories" are refutable and refineable. Thus, there is a corollary to Lewin's maxim, implied repeatedly through the history of science (e.g., Kuhn, 1970): there is little more impeding than a practical but reified theory. That is, the capacity of a theory to do good is a function of its fit to the phenomenon and reification prevents refining the theory as science generates new findings.

In this chapter, we will first provide a quick overview of the scope and impact of IPV and the controversy over how to define and measure the phenomenon of interest. We will then review the theoretical approaches that currently receive the largest attention (i.e., Feminist, Behavioral, Cognitive Behavioral, Attachment, Neurobiological, and Integrative theories) and will briefly mention other notable approaches. Finally, we will recognize limitations and make recommendations for future theoretical progress in IPV research.

KEY ISSUES IN INTIMATE PARTNER VIOLENCE

PREVALENCE AND IMPACT

Physical IPV, when defined as any physical assault (from pushing to using weapons), has a yearly prevalence of approximately 15% of couples in nationally representative studies from the US (e.g., Straus & Gelles, 1990; Schafer, Caetano, & Clark, 1998) and 12–20% in similar studies in England, Greece, Germany, Portugal, Spain (e.g., Machado, Gonçalves, Matos & Dias, 2007; Medina-Ariza & Barberet, 2003; Ruiz-Pérez & Plazaola-Castaño, 2005; Stathopoulou, 2004). Physical IPV is associated with increased risk for physical injury and seeking medical attention (Coker et al., 2002; Morse, 1995; Stets & Straus, 1990), and with increased risk for current poor health and having a chronic disease that developed after the IPV started (Coker et al., 2002). IPV

---

[1] Richard Heyman's preparation of this chapter was supported by the National Institute on Dental and Craniofacial Research, National Institute of Heath, Grant R21DE01953701A1.

victimization is associated with higher rates of depressive symptoms (e.g., Magdol, Moffitt, Caspi, & Silva, 1998), post-traumatic stress disorder (PTSD; e.g., Jones, Hughes, & Unterstaller, 2001), substance dependence (e.g., Magdol et al., 1998), and fear (Morse, 1995; Tjaden & Thoennes, 2000).

Exposure to IPV also impacts children in affected households, three-quarters of whom see or hear it (Mahoney, Donnelly, Boxer, & Lewis, 2003; O'Brien, John, Margolin, & Erel, 1994). A meta-analysis of 118 studies about children exposed to parental IPV found that on a host of outcomes (internalizing problems, externalizing problems, social problems, academic problems, negative affect/distress, negative cognitions), exposed children fared significantly worse than non-exposed children ($d = -0.34$; Kitzmann, Gaylord, Holt, & Kenny, 2003).

Defining and Measuring IPV

The operationalization of partner abuse has, over the years, provoked some exceptionally bitter debate (see Straus, 1990). The most widely used measure within the field, the Conflict Tactics Scale (CTS; Straus, 1979), asked about a series of psychologically and physically aggressive acts that increase in severity. Although successful in obtaining what, at the time, were surprisingly high self-reports of physically assaultive behaviors (e.g., Straus, Gelles, & Steinmetz, 1980), the CTS has been criticized repeatedly as being gender insensitive by ignoring the impact and context of the assaultive acts as well as who initiated the acts and what the intention/motivation of the actor was (e.g., Kimmel, 2002; White, Smith, Koss, & Figueredo, 2000). In the US, a major difficulty in the field since its inception is the commonplace conflation of assault and impact under the label "battering." This conflation is what is behind the widely disseminated factoid that "a woman is beaten every 15 seconds" in the US (e.g., Feminist.com, 2011)—true only if pushes and grabs are examples of beatings. On the one hand, these high prevalences are good for lobbying; on the other hand, the majority of these "batterers" in the US do not use assault to exert power/control over the victim, do not escalate in severity over time, and do not cause injury and fear (e.g., Johnson & Ferraro, 2000). Furthermore, at least half of these "batterers" are women. In sum, applying words that imply impact and context (e.g., battering) to results derived from measures that purposefully split off assault from impact/context (e.g., the CTS) resulted in confusion and internal conflict, not to mention willful misinterpretation by those asserting that the women's movement has gone too far (see DeKeseredy, 2000).

The Center for Disease Control and Prevention's IPV Uniform Definitions (Saltzman, Fanslow, McMahon, & Shelley, 1999) were a major, high profile step toward requiring that IPV meet two criteria: an act of a particular type (physical or sexual) *and* an impact (injury, harm, or death). Although framed in gender-neutral language, it reflected the gendered reality that women are the predominant victims of maltreatment (e.g., Tjaden & Thoennes, 2000). The same act plus impact approach (although with somewhat different operationalizations) has been used with high reliability in field usage (Heyman & Slep, 2006, 2009) and in risk and protective factor research (Foran, Heyman, Slep, Snarr, & U.S. Air Force Family Advocacy Program, 2011; Slep, Foran, Heyman, & Snarr, 2010 Slep, Foran, Heyman, & U.S. Air Force Family Advocacy Program, 2011).

Typologies and Trajectories

One question that has caused considerable controversy in theories about IPV is whether it is a homogenous phenomenon or whether there are different "types" of perpetrators. Two typologies that have received considerable attention are those of Johnson (2008) and Holtzworth-Munroe and Stuart (1994).

For some time, scholars (e.g., Straus, 1990) have noted that those studying (a) women in shelters and men in court-mandated treatment and (b) individuals in the general population and couples presenting for therapy were describing different ends of the proverbial elephant, but debate regarding appropriate conceptualization/treatment of maltreatment remained. Despite innumerable attempts at conceptual, empirical, and clinical rapprochement, it was not until Johnson's (1995, 2008) formulation of two subsets of violence ("situational couple violence" and "intimate terrorism," to use his current labels), that true accommodation appeared possible. Johnson and Leone (2005, p. 324) summarized the distinction between the types: "Intimate terrorism is violence that is embedded in a general pattern of control; situational couple violence is not." Empirical support for Johnson's hypotheses that the two types have different causes, contexts, frequencies, and sequelae is growing (e.g., Graham-Kevan & Archer, 2003; Johnson & Leone, 2005; Smith, Thornton, & DeVellis, 2002), although it has never been put to a true empirical test via taxometric analyses (e.g., Meehl, 1995).

Holtzworth-Munroe and Stuart (1994) conducted a review of existing typologies for male perpetrators of IPV and proposed three types: *family only*, *dysphoric/borderline*, and *violent/antisocial*. *Family only* perpetrators were proposed to engage in less severe violence, be less likely to engage in psychological or sexual abuse, and have less accompanying psychopathology; *dysphoric/borderline* perpetrators were proposed to have attachment-related difficulties, to engage in moderate violence that may include psychological or sexual abuse, and to potentially have a history of criminal behavior; and *violent/antisocial* perpetrators were proposed to engage in moderate to severe violence, have higher extrafamilial aggression, have more severe histories of criminal behavior, and have a higher propensity for antisocial personality disorder and substance abuse. In a follow-up cluster analysis study testing the 1994 typologies (Holtzworth-Munroe, Meehan, Herron, Rehman, & Stuart, 2000), a fourth category emerged, which fell between *family only* and *violent/antisocial* that the authors labeled *low-level antisocial*. Presumably if these categories accurately represented qualitatively distinct subtypes of violent men, they should be stable across time (Cavanaugh & Gelles, 2005); however, Holtzworth-Munroe, Meehan, Herron, Rehman, and Stuart (2003) found the group membership to be less stable than anticipated. In a longitudinal examination of the typology, Holtzworth-Munroe et al. (2000) found violence desistance in all groups, even (unexpectedly) in the most chronically violent *violent/antisocial* group. On follow-up, few distinctions emerged between the *violent/antisocial* and *dysphoric/borderline* types (Holtzworth-Munroe et al., 2000) and other studies (Delsol, Margolin, & John, 2003; Sartin 2005) have found this ambiguity as well.

Yet, as will be discussed later in this chapter, very little work in the IPV area is informed by developmental psychopathology research. That is, most theoreticians start with an aggressive person in a romantic relationship and hypothesize about the social or psychological reasons for that behavior. Some researchers have had the opportunity, however, to investigate the lifelong trajectories of aggressive individuals, with IPV as one of the outcomes. Moffitt and colleagues' program (summarized in Moffitt, 2007) has been the most extensive. They found that children who are high on aggression in early childhood are at high risk for life-long mental disorders. Moffitt (2007) described two subgroups of highly aggressive boys: "life course persistent" antisocial individuals (7% of the population) and "desisters" (21% of the population). At age 26, "life course persistent" males were the most elevated on violent crime (including IPV and child abuse) and a host of other serious problems (e.g., antisocial personality disorder, psychopathy, depressive symptoms; Moffitt, Caspi, Harrington, & Milne, 2002). The "desisters" (i.e., were similar to the life course persistent as boys but not very delinquent as adolescents) were not a success story, as they likely desisted because of isolating, internalizing mental health problems (e.g., at age 26 they were elevated on social phobia, panic disorder with agoraphobia, depressive disorders), were socially isolated, had difficulty making friends, had financial and work problems, and were low-level chronic offenders (Moffitt et al., 2002). The remainder of the population either abstained from antisocial acts (11%), was low (47%), or committed "adolescent-limited" acts (14%). The "adolescent limited" group, although committing antisocial acts as teens, differed from the life course group by tending to commit property offenses (rather than violent ones) and to commit acts of lower levels of frequency and intensity.

We introduce the *life course perspective* because it highlights two important points for theoreticians. First, for children on the "life course persistent" trajectory, violence in intimate relationships is another expression of consistent, persistent aggressive antisocial behavior. Their use of aggression to exert power and control over people in their environments is so pervasive that it cannot be construed as only being grounded in male–female power dynamics. Second, adolescence raises two challenges for children on a "normal" trajectory. The key challenge is that intimate relationships are a main source of violence in the lives of adolescents and emerging adults, with about half of adolescents in US samples reporting dating physical violence—reviewed by Glass et al., 2003—and between 29–57% of US engaged couples reporting physical violence during the year prior to marriage (e.g., Lawrence & Bradbury, 2001, 2007; McLaughlin, Leonard, & Senchak, 1992; O'Leary et al., 1989). Although IPV in these relationships is often non-impactful, it can have serious (often unintended) consequences and can become part of the behavioral repertoire. Another challenge is that those in the "adolescent limited" group can get snared in antisocial behavior, especially if involved in substance abuse/dependence. The resulting exposure to deviant peers and the correctional system, impact on occupational prospects, and substance problems are all risk factors for IPV.

THEORIES EXPLAINING IPV

FEMINIST THEORY

Feminist theory emphasizes males' use of violence against their female partners, the goal of which is to establish and maintain the power and control over them that men have traditionally exerted over women (e.g., Dobash & Dobash, 1979). Although gender, power, and control are unifying themes, the feminist perspective is not a simple one. Acts of IPV are viewed as occurring within the multifaceted historical, cultural, and sociopolitical contexts through which gender differentials are exhibited, enforced, and propagated (e.g., through media messages or in the workplace through unequal wages and other forms of discrimination). On one hand, these entrenched institutional themes of male dominance are central to instilling individuals' beliefs about gender and expectations about family structure and marriage; on the other hand, they prevent women from having autonomy and escaping the cycle of abuse. Even the label "IPV" is contentious, as feminists argue that it obfuscates the centrality of gender that is inherent to the phenomenon.

Perhaps the most influential and widely used feminist model of domestic violence is the *Power and Control Wheel* (Pence & Paymar, 1993), developed from focus groups of battered women in 1984 by the Domestic Abuse Intervention Project in Duluth, Minnesota. The wheel provides a framework for describing the larger cycle of abuse by which men deliberately victimize women. It shows that physical and sexual violence, the corporal forms of IPV, are often embedded in more elaborate patterns of power and control. Behavioral control tactics characteristic of abusive relationships are shown as the spokes of the wheel: threat, intimidation, coercion, emotional abuse, economic abuse, isolation, minimization and denial, use of children as a weapon of emotional abuse against the partner (e.g., disparaging partner to children, threatening to harm children as a means of emotionally wounding partner), and use of male privilege (Pence & Paymar, 1993). These tactics contribute to the development of a complex and inescapable web of abusive treatment: one form of abuse (e.g., economic abuse; e.g., a man preventing his partner from working) may lead to other forms of abuse (e.g., emotional abuse, such as the same man saying his partner is "a parasite" because she does not earn money). Since it was developed, the model has been widely used in social service training, batterer intervention programs, and scientific research; it has also guided the initial formulation and revision of IPV policy and law. The Power and Control Wheel has been instrumental in expanding past views of domestic violence as a private, family matter toward its view as a complex societal issue of substantial public health magnitude (Graffunder, Noonan, Cox, & Wheaton, 2004).

Feminist theory, as the intellectual force behind the women's movement of the 1960s and 1970s, reshaped the world—most notably in high income countries (e.g., U.S. Violence Against Women Act, implemented in 1995), but also in international action (e.g., United Nations Division for the

Advancement of Women)—by empowering women (and some sympathetic men) to establish shelters for victimized women, change public opinion about the morality of IPV, lobby for the enactment of laws to protect IPV victims, and develop therapeutic interventions for both perpetrators and victims (Koss & White, 2008). These developments were largely informed by the voices of women who have experienced battering and come into contact with social services such as shelters, law-enforcement agencies, or hospitals. Research mostly involved victim-centered, qualitative studies that explored the contextual complexities that victims of IPV face (e.g., economic dependency, children, religious disapproval regarding separation), refuting psychodynamic conceptualizations such as female masochism or simplistic and victim-blaming solutions such as "Why doesn't she just leave?" (Yllö, 1993; Yllö & Bograd, 1988).

Interventions for perpetrators derived from Feminist theory—the ones that are by far the most commonly used and that are mandated in almost all states—use psychoeducation heavily, believing that IPV is an individual choice, albeit one that is widely-supported by societal attitudes. By challenging these individual beliefs that support women's subjugation (combined with the threat of legal sanctions), the goal for batterers' intervention programs is that men will choose to stop using IPV and instead treat their partners in a respectful, egalitarian way (Pence & Paymar, 1993).

BEHAVIORAL THEORIES

Behavioral theories rely on observable behavior (as a reaction to Freudian introspection). They posit that the causes of behavior lie in the accumulated experience of environmental reinforcements or punishments for behavior (rather than in internal processes), and emphasize targeted (rather than complex) phenomena for study/intervention (Domjan, 2003). Although behavioral theories, by definition, focus on explaining the function of behavior for individuals (i.e., idiographic examinations), most implementations (for both IPV and other problems) use invariant applications that presuppose the adaptive nature of nonaggressive competing responses.

Operant behavioral theories focus on four basic learning principles revolving around reinforcement and punishment. Although often overlooked, it is critical to understand that labeling responses as "reinforcing" or "punishing" can only be done retrospectively. That is, the terms only apply to whether the specific stimulus→response pairing results in future increases or decreases in the frequency of behavior. For example, there is no such thing as a universal "punishment"—a response (such as slapping) may decrease the occurrence of the stimulus behavior (such as insulting) in some people, but increase it or have no effect on others.

Positive reinforcement involves the contingent application of a reward following a behavior, increasing the likelihood that the behavior will be performed. Negative reinforcement involves the contingent removal of an aversive stimulus following a behavior, increasing the likelihood that the behavior will be performed. Punishment involves the contingent provision of an aversive consequence following a behavior, decreasing the likelihood that the behavior will be performed. Finally, omission (negative punishment) involves the contingent removal of a reward following a behavior, decreasing the likelihood that the behavior will be performed.

Four other principles—applications of the above learning principles—factor into most behavioral interventions in this field: extinction (i.e., failure to reinforce a previously reinforced aggressive behavior, decreasing the likelihood that the aggressive behavior will be performed), setting events (i.e., events that affect the likelihood of behavior by temporarily changing the value of the consequence), stimulus control (i.e., removing or changing antecedents or settings associated with aggressive behavior, decreasing the likelihood that the aggressive behavior will be performed), and overlearning (i.e., cognitive, affective, and behavioral patterns become routinized and, over time, do not require much mindfulness, or even conscious awareness, to execute them).

The most developed theoretical application of behavioral principles is by Bell and Naugle (2008). Like the *General Aggression Model* by Anderson and Bushman (2002) discussed below, Bell and Naugle proposed a "contextual framework" for researching and understanding IPV rather than a testable, overarching (i.e., *nomethetic*) model. Proposing a framework for organizing possible influencing variables is in keeping with an operant approach, which focuses on the costs and rewards of aggressive behavior and modifying the contingencies so that: (a) aggressive behavior is either not reinforced or is punished, and (b) non-aggressive behavior is either reinforced or is not punished. Because of their specificity, operant approaches tend to be idiographic, and their effectiveness is often tested via single subject experiments. The hallmark of operant approaches is functional analysis, defined as "(1) The identification of important, controllable, causal functional relations applicable to specified behaviors for an individual...; [and] (2) The experimental manipulation of hypothesized controlling variables as a method of determining functional relations" (Haynes & O'Brien, 2000, p. 302). Functional analysis is the practical application of behavioral theory, as it tries to: (a) identify the antecedents, consequences, and settings that reward violent behavior, and (b) change these environmental factors so that nonaggression, rather than aggression, is rewarded.

Bell and Naugle's (2008) framework includes five elements that influence IPV: (1) antecedents, both distal/static (e.g., genes, childhood victimization) and proximal (e.g., interpersonal conflict); (2) discriminative stimuli (e.g., location; presence/absence of children); (3) verbal rules/beliefs (e.g., about violence, relationships); (4) motivating factors (e.g., alcohol use; emotional distress); and (5) behavioral repertoire (e.g., communication and anger management skills). As a behavioral model, the framework emphasizes the consequences of IPV and whether they increase (e.g., escape argument, partner compliance) or decrease (e.g., partner leaving relationship) the likelihood of IPV reoccurring. Because of the operant approach, no assumptions are made that any outcome is a universal reinforcer or punisher, nor that any precursor variable universally increases or decreases the likelihood that IPV will be initiated. Other applications of behavioral theory to understanding IPV can be found in Myers (1995) and Peterson and Calhoun (1995).

In treatment contexts, a behavioral functional analysis may be useful not only because it suggests which behaviors may be maintaining IPV but also because it allows the interventionist to hypothesize, teach, and reinforce what behaviorists call "functionally equivalent behaviors"—behaviors that may serve the same function as IPV but that are not harmful to the partner or the relationship. Time out (partners agreeing ahead of time that it is acceptable to request to pause the conflict to allow for separating, calming down, thinking about constructive approaches, and resuming the discussion) may for many people be a functionally equivalent behavior to replace what typically occurs (e.g., physically aggressive, coerced exits from conflict).

Finally, treatments grounded in behavioral principles that have been used for other clinical problems may find uses with IPV. For example, exposure and response prevention (ERP), a treatment of choice with anxiety disorders (Franklin, Abramowitz, Kozak, Leavitt, & Foa, 2000), has recently been used to intervene with people with anger control problems (some of whom are aggressive). ERP generally is believed to work through habituation to the eliciting stimulus (e.g., anxiety-elicitors for those with Obsessive Compulsive Disorder and anger elicitors for those with aggression problems) and through the prevention of negative reinforcement. Participants are exposed to anger provocations, but are prevented from responding with anger or aggression. Tafrate and Kassinove (1998) found that ERP resulted in moderate effect sizes for the reduction of anger, whereas ERP with coping self-statements resulted in large effect sizes. Because this study—the only empirical test of this approach—did not use a clinical population and did not measure aggression as an outcome, it is too early to know if this approach is an effective form of aggression treatment.

Coercion Theory

Perhaps the most developed and influential behavioral model of dyadic conflict is Patterson and colleagues' *coercion theory* (Patterson, 1982), which explains how, via negative reinforcement, negative escalation sequences can be reinforcing for both partners, despite their unpleasant and destructive qualities. Coercion theory posits that people learn coercive behavior through the ways in which conflicts are resolved. Over time, if Partner A responds to Partner B's escalating aversive behavior by giving in (thus ceasing his/her own aversive behavior), Partner B learns to escalate to get his/her way. Importantly, both partners' behaviors are maintained through reinforcement. Partner B is negatively reinforced for escalating (via Partner A shutting up) and may be positively reinforced as well (via Partner A doing what Partner B was asking for in the argument). Partner A is negatively reinforced for giving in (via the termination of Partner B's aversive behavior). Over time, these conflicts serve as learning trials. Of course, Partner B does not always win. Sometimes, Partner B backs down in response to the Partner A's aversive escalation. Thus, once a coercive process takes hold, both members of the dyad are faced with an unfortunate choice: (a) give in and lose the battle, or (b) win via out-escalating the other. This process leads to ever darker, bitter battles. In Patterson's (1976) exquisite phrasing, each partner is both the "victim and architect of a coercive system." (p. 1)

Social exchange theory

Social exchange theory (e.g., Thibaut & Kelley, 1959) is a behavioral theory that emphasizes the cost–benefit analyses that underlie behavior in interactive contexts. Social exchange theory has been used both to describe: (a) the moment by moment behavioral choices of individuals and (b) the summary decisions people make about their relationships and their desires to continue them. In the latter regard, the theory hypothesizes that an individual's satisfaction with a relationship derives from a comparison of the outcomes (i.e., benefits minus costs) to an internalized "comparison level" of what relationships have to offer (i.e., outcomes minus the comparison level). However, dissatisfied individuals may not leave, because that decision involves the comparison level of alternatives. That is, one individual might believe that alternative relationships (or no relationship) would provide higher outcomes and thus might leave, whereas another with a similar degree of satisfaction may stay because even though she estimates that a relationship should, in general, provide better outcomes than this, she thinks that the alternatives would be even worse (perhaps because she perceives she is less desirable because she has young children or is older).

The *investment model* (Rusbult, 1980) built on social exchange theory, posits that relationship commitment (and thus, decisions to leave) depends on three factors: satisfaction (i.e., rewards and costs in the current intimate relationship), alternatives (i.e., rewards and costs in possible alternatives), and investments (i.e., psychological and/or material resources tied to the relationship). In support of the investment model, victimized women's higher commitment levels are predicted by higher levels of satisfaction, greater perceived investments, and fewer alternatives (Rhatigan & Axsom, 2006; Rusbult & Martz, 1995; Truman-Schram et al., 2000). Rusbult and Martz (1995), studying women from a shelter, found that commitment at initial assessment predicted decisions to stay or leave up to the one-year follow-up. Additionally, Rhatigan and Street (2005) reported evidence that the investment model predicted IPV victimized and non-victimized women's decisions to stay or leave. These investment model findings indicate that IPV victimized women's commitments to their intimate relationships are consistent with reward/cost models rather than due to passivity or psychoanalytic notions of masochism.

COGNITIVE-BEHAVIORAL THEORIES

Social Learning Theory

Social learning theory (e.g., Bandura, 1977, 1986) is an extension of behavioral theories and postulates that behavior is influenced by cognitive/affect, behavioral, and environmental factors. Two key concepts that differentiate social learning from behavioral theories are modeling and predictive knowledge.

Through his experiments, including the famous aggression experiment with the "Bobo" doll (Bandura, Ross, & Ross, 1961), Bandura established that not all learning need occur through trial and error (as in operant learning) or the pairing of conditioned and unconditioned stimuli (as in classical conditioning). Learning can also be accomplished vicariously (i.e., by watching stimulus→response chains enacted by others). The importance of modeling in the acquisition of aggressive and anxious behavior is well established (see Huesmann, 1997; Mineka & Ben Hamida, 1998, for recent reviews), as are a number of elements of the model that increase learning (e.g., similarity of the model to the observer, whether the model struggles to perform the behavior or does so effortlessly; see Chance, 1994). Three important sources of modeling impact IPV according to social learning theories. First, children often witness or are exposed to the aftermath of IPV between their parents or parental figures (such as intimate partners of divorced/unmarried parents). Second, children directly experience aggression at the hands of their parents, through which use of might to exert domination is modeled. Finally, models of violence and coercion abound in popular culture and unhealthy community environments.

Via predictive knowledge, people formulate estimations of the outcomes of behavioral enactment that moderate their performance of target behaviors. Efficacy expectancies (i.e., predictions about whether one has the ability/means to carry out a target behavior, sometimes referred to as self-efficacy) and outcome expectancies (i.e., predictions about what the likely consequences would be from carrying out the target behavior) are two leading examples. Both factor into social learning theories of IPV. People rely on behaviors they think they have the capacity to enact and thus enhancing: (a) skills to use non-coercive and non-IPV and (b) efficacy expectancies for these nonviolent options are at the heart of social learning-based interventions. Outcome expectancies are in essence the same cost–benefit estimations postulated by social exchange theory—what do I gain and lose, what does my partner gain and lose, what is his/her probable response, and what are the environmental consequences (e.g., from children, neighbors, police) to the behavior? Social learning theory does not propose that this calculus is always done explicitly (i.e., with full conscious awareness); rather, such predictive capacity (based on operant and vicarious experience) is the basis for implementing one set of behaviors versus another.

Social Information Processing

Operant behavioral theories (e.g., Skinner, 1963) focus on stimulus→response relationships, but disregard the gap between stimulus and response as unobservable and thus (at the time) unstudyable. *Social information processing theory* (McFall, 1982) focuses on the "→" in the stimulus→response chain, positing five components of competent social responding: encoding of social cues, interpretation of social cues, response search, response evaluation, and enactment. The first two components are receptive: encoding involves the appraisal of social behavior and interpretation involves the infusion of meaning to those cues. The other three components involve behavioral activation: evocation of response options, generation of outcome expectancies for these behaviors, and performance of the selected behavior.

Dodge (1993) posits that people who frequently aggress make interpretations (often incorrect) of hostile intent when others transgress (often unintentionally) against them. There is some evidence that men who commit IPV may have information processing deficits that nonviolent men do not (Holtzworth-Munroe, 1992). For example, men who commit IPV and are in distressed relationships have been shown to be more likely than both non-IPV but relationship distressed men and non-IPV, nondistressed men to attribute negative intent to their female partners' behavior, particularly in those situations involving jealousy, rejection, or potential public embarrassment (Holtzworth-Munroe, 1994). There is also some evidence for the implication of information processing on the intergenerational transmission of IPV. Experiencing or witnessing familial abuse as a child may lead to PTSD symptoms, which may deleteriously influence information processing (e.g., hypervigilance to perceptions of threat may cause an increased propensity for blaming attributions), ultimately causing vulnerability to abuse perpetration in adult intimate relationships (Taft, Schumm, Marshall, Panuzio, & Holtzworth-Munroe, 2008). However, directionality cannot be assumed and prospective research is needed to elucidate the relationship among PTSD, information processing, and abuse perpetration.

ATTACHMENT/PSYCHODYNAMIC THEORY

Attachment theory (e.g., Ainsworth, Blehar, Waters, & Wall, 1978; Bowlby, 1969) focuses on the primacy of the caregiver–caretaker relationship in establishing individuals' representations of interpersonal relations. These representations or "styles" are internalized first via interactions with the primary caregiver (typically the mother) and are generally classified as secure and non-secure, with the latter type falling into three patterns: dismissing (e.g., appears indifferent to both separation and reunion with attachment figure), preoccupied (e.g., clingy and anxious about separation with attachment figure), and fearful (e.g., fearful upon separation, ambivalent upon reunion with attachment figure—both approaching and avoiding contact).

Because attachment styles are generally viewed to remain fairly stable throughout the lifespan, they have been theorized to affect adult close relationships (e.g., romantic partners). Thus, the theory has also been used to understand characteristics that may increase a person's propensity for perpetrating IPV. Research has shown that fearful attachment styles in male perpetrators are strongly related to self-reported domination/isolation and emotional abuse (Dutton, Saunders, Starzomski, & Bartholomew, 1994; Stosny, 1995); preoccupied men showed this pattern also, but to a lesser extent.

The most prominent elaboration of the association between insecure attachment and IPV is Dutton's description of borderline personality organization (BPO), which describes individuals with "abusive personalities" who simultaneously desire intimacy and intensely fear abandonment and rejection from their partners. This combination is thought to lead to outbursts of aggression when the perpetrator feels particularly vulnerable or threatened in the relationship. It is important to note that individuals with BPO are hypothesized to be violent specifically within the family—their private and public identities may differ. Dutton proposes that BPO is a result of early maltreatment in the family and thus may have implications for the intergenerational transmission of IPV. Although Dutton (1995) has reported initial support for the theory, few other investigators have evaluated it, and a recent literature review (Bolen, 2000) concluded that empirical support for attachment theory is inconsistent.

NEUROBIOLOGICAL THEORIES OF TRAUMA

The neurobiological conditioning perspective, similar to several of the other theories already reviewed, gives past negative experiences a central etiological role in understanding current aggressive behaviors. This perspective explicates how one may biologically be at heightened risk for engaging in partner violence due to the impact of traumatic experiences on physiological reactions and cognitive processing. Evolutionarily functional, innate, and organized behavioral patterns exist to respond to danger (e.g., fight/flight response) and can be shaped through environmental interaction. Although humans, like all animals, are born with perceptual and behavioral systems to scan for and respond to danger, these systems are plastic and responsive to environmental influences. LeDoux (2002) posited two information pathways, a danger related pathway from the thalamus to the amygdala and a slower, non-threat-based pathway from the cortex to the amygdala. The former, although adaptive in the face of real environmental dangers, can become primed to such an extent via traumatic experience that hyperarousal and hypervigilance result. The latter, although a more accurate gauge of true threat, is not evolutionarily advantageous in danger-rich environments. Thus, through exposure to a dangerous, traumatic environment, neural connections can be formed and strengthened that favor attention to danger-cues in social information processing. As summarized by Crittenden (1998, p. 19). "Experience with fear-eliciting stimuli lead to potentiated response states in which the individual is hypervigilant with regard to stimuli indicative of danger, responds more rapidly to such stimuli, and responds with great amplitude…. The more intense and frequent the danger that is experienced early in life and throughout life, the more rapid, protective, affect laden and preconscious will be the response…" Thus, immersion in violent, noxious family or community environments may put individuals at higher risk for angry and violent reactions to environmental provocations (or perceived provocations), increasing the likelihood of IPV.

Reflecting the cross-cutting nature of this framework, evidence supporting this theory has been observed at several levels. Studies examining victims of trauma have found an increased fear response as measured neurobiologically (brain imaging studies), physiologically (heart rate, galvanic skin response), behaviorally (reaction time), cognitively (attention to danger cues, information processing), and affectively (expression and intensity of emotion). Hence, in individuals with a history of this type of theorized conditioning, the heightened responsivity may increase the likelihood of reacting with aggressive behavior to real or perceived danger cues.

DEVELOPMENTAL IMPLICATIONS

Development of a hypervigilant physiological response to real or perceived danger cues can occur throughout the lifespan following exposure to traumatic experiences (Repetti, Taylor, & Seeman, 2002). A childhood history of trauma (e.g., child maltreatment) and living with parents who are unpredictable, chaotic, and affectively labile may lead to increased likelihood of developing a hypervigilant physiological response to danger cues, and this may persist throughout the lifespan. This physiological conditioning is not limited to children, but can occur at any age. Evidence for differential physiological reactivity following traumatic experiences in adulthood has been demonstrated in combat veterans (e.g., Butler, 1990), rape victims, and other adult trauma victims (e.g., Foa, Riggs, & Gershuny, 1995). Thus, trauma can have both psychological (e.g., attributional biases toward negative intent; Dodge, 1993) and physiological effects (hypervigilant physiological responses) that potentiate IPV.

INTEGRATIVE APPROACHES

We have thus far reviewed several theories of IPV, some of which intersect and others that are more disparate. Clearly, the range of theories suggests that IPV is a multi-determined phenomenon and one perspective is not sufficient alone. In recent years, to account for the range of risk factors identified for IPV, the field has moved towards more integrative theories of IPV. Dutton's *ecological theory* and Finkel's *self-regulation theory* are two examples of attempts to take a broad integrative theoretical framework.

SELF-REGULATION THEORY

Finkel's (2007) recent review organizes risk factors into two categories: those that impel one toward IPV and those that inhibit IPV. His model posits that only when both: (a) strong impelling forces and (b) weak inhibiting forces are present in a situation will someone be at high risk for perpetration of IPV. This review summarizes literature and/or posits risk factors for strong violence-impelling forces at different levels of influence, including distal (e.g., witnessing parental IPV), dispositional (e.g., trait anger), relational (e.g., jealousy), and situational (e.g., blameful attributions). He also posits weak violence-inhibiting forces at the same levels of influence. The impelling and inhibiting heuristic is useful in organizing: (a) risk factors research for IPV and (b) intervention research into weakening factors that impel violence and into strengthening factors that inhibit activated violent impulses.

ECOLOGICAL THEORY

Similar to Finkel's self-regulation theory, ecological theories of IPV hypothesize that violence is related to both proximal and distal factors. An ecological theory of IPV has been widely used as a framework for integrating the risk factors of IPV and organizes risk factors into four levels—individual (ontogenic), relationship (microsystem), community (exosystem), and societal (macrosystem). Ecological theories of IPV suggests there is an interplay between risk factors within and between levels and that more distal factors are less strongly related to IPV (Dutton, 1995; Heise, 1998; Stith, Smith, Penn, Ward, & Tritt, 2004). Individual level risk factors include demographic characteristics, history of child maltreatment, substance abuse, and personality traits. Relationship level risk factors include marital conflict and parenting problems. Community level risk factors include work stress, neighborhood violence, and community cohesion. Societal level risk factors include gender inequalities, poverty, and cultural norms. Ecological theory provides a practical heuristic for integrating risk and protective factor research on IPV and has been adapted for this purpose by major violence research organizations (e.g., Centers for Disease Control and Prevention, 2012; Dahlberg & Krug (2002).

LIMITATIONS OF HOW THEORY HAS BEEN USED AND SUGGESTIONS FOR FUTURE THEORETICAL DEVELOPMENT

Whether they recognize it or not, both men and women—especially in high-income countries that have made enormous strides in women's rights and protections since the 1960s—owe an enormous debt to feminist theory and its practical implications. By helping knock down de jure and de facto societal elements that tolerated IPV and other forms of violence against women, feminist theory helped empower half the population and engender expectations of equal rights, opportunities, and safety. The economic and intellectual energy and social enlightenment and egalitarianism that accompanied empowering half the population had transformative effects (e.g., Graffunder, Noonan, Cox, & Wheaton, 2004; Koss & White, 2008), notwithstanding inequities in political, economic, and social power that remain across the globe (e.g., Kristof & WuDunn, 2009).

However, within the IPV area, the social successes of feminist theory have led to a theoretically stunted field, as the dominant theoretical stance, enshrined in the legal requirements for treatment of IPV perpetrators across the US, is that IPV is solely about "power and control." Given the multifactorial nature of determinants of human behavior and the heterogeneity of those who perpetrate or are victimized by IPV (often the same people), no simplistic, single cause model—including feminist "power and control" theories that control intervention (e.g., Dutton & Corvo, 2006)—is likely to be supported scientifically.

Lest it seem as if IPV's theoretical insularity is unique, one of the greatest family scientists of the twentieth century, Gerald Patterson, noted a similar unfolding in the less politically-contentious area of child antisocial behavior. Patterson (2005) wrote that, in his area, there were three significant areas of theory and intervention regarding the causes of child aggression: social information processing, emotion down-regulation, and behavioral contingencies. He concluded, "Historically, each of the three positions engaged in a wholehearted pursuit of the null hypothesis and largely ignored the literature in the other three areas. Each of them repeatedly proved that their explanation for aggression was better than no theory at all" (Patterson, 2005, p. 28)

Patterson's (2005) pungent point has three major implications. First, all social science theoreticians need to approach their task with a deep sense of humility. Although it is true that proving that one's theory is better than no theory at all is an accomplishment, no theory accounts for more than a relatively small percentage of the variance. An exceedingly crude map might be better than no map, but it should not be confused for a comprehensive, well-tested one.

Second, theoreticians and researchers are commonly so focused on the developments and implications in their one small theoretical area (e.g., behavioral approaches to IPV) that they are unaware of advances in other related areas within their own narrow field (e.g., developmental approaches to IPV), to literature in a slightly broader field (e.g., human aggression), or to other areas that could be informative (e.g., gene X environment interactions).

Third, several areas making crude maps can be stitched together to form an even better (but admittedly still crude) map. This idea has been the clarion call of recent IPV theoretical works (e.g., Bell & Naugle, 2008; Bogat, Levendosky, & von Eye, 2005; Rhatigan et al., 2005; Sellers, Cochran, & Branch, 2005; Whitaker et al., 2006; Wilkinson & Hamerschlag, 2005)

ANDERSON AND BUSHMAN'S GENERAL AGGRESSION MODEL

The most satisfying example of theoretical and research integration for aggression (though not for IPV specifically) is Anderson and Bushman's (2002) *general aggression model* (GAM). The literature on human and animal aggression is quite well developed, involves many of the theories previously described, and likely has tremendous bearing on IPV.

Overall, the GAM attempts to explain the person X social environment interactions that result in aggression. The theory maps the inputs (personal and situational) that affect each actor's "routes" (i.e., the internal states of affect, cognition, and arousal) that affect outcomes (social information processes and behavior—either thoughtful or impulsive), which serve as the social stimuli to the other actors, whose responses then serve as the input for another iteration through the GAM's processes.

Biological Factors

Anderson and Bushman (2002, p. 35) treat biological factors in a footnote, noting that "we believe that genetic and other biological factors operate via influences on learning, decision-making, arousal, and affective processes." Although this non-reductionistic approach (see Dutton et al., 1994) may be accurate, it is unsatisfying as it leaves the GAM going into great detail integrating literatures on behavioral and psychological processes while refusing to do a similar job for biological factors that cannot solely be mapped via psychological processes. This theoretical blind spot may decrease the translational implications of the anger and aggression literature.

Two literatures on gene X environment interactions and neural differences in emotional processing exemplify the need to incorporate biological factors into a comprehensive model of aggression. In the gene X environment interaction area, Bakermans-Kranenburg and van Ijzendoorn (2006) found that harsh/insensitive parenting was associated with elevated aggressive behavior only when the child had a dopamine D4 receptor polymorphism; further, children with this genetic marker exposed to harsh/insensitive parenting, compared to those not so exposed, had a six times higher risk of elevated levels of externalizing behavior. Suomi and colleagues (e.g., Suomi, 2005) have found gene–environment interactions affecting aggression in polymorphisms of the serotonin transport gene (5-HTT) in rhesus monkeys, and Verona, Joiner, Johnson, and Bender (2006) found gene–environment interaction effects on a laboratory analogue aggression task for men (but not for women). Suomi's extensive program of research has led him to conclude that gene by environment interactions that influence aggression and other key social behaviors "are ubiquitous and can occur at a variety of points throughout development" (Suomi, 2005, p. 24). Identifying important gene by environment interactions would deepen our understanding of important pathways toward IPV for subgroups of individuals.

In the neural study of emotion, Harmon-Jones' (2003; Harmon-Jones & Allen, 1998) motivational direction hypothesis posits that anger provoking events elicit asymmetrical left versus right frontal cortical activity because of the approach-motivational properties of anger, even though other negative emotions tend to elicit right frontal asymmetries. Further, anger results in more left versus right frontal activity when participants believe that they will be about to respond to provocations (e.g., Harmon-Jones & Allen, 1998; Harmon-Jones & Sigelman, 2001; Lazarus, 1991). Moreover, there are large individual differences in frontal asymmetries. In sum, Anderson and Bushman's model has routes for affect and arousal and incorporating the burgeoning literature on the determinants of individual differences in these pathways will be an important supplement to any comprehensive model of aggression.

Inputs

The GAM discusses person and situational factors. Person factors include traits, sex/gender, beliefs (including efficacy and outcome expectancies), attitudes, values, long-term goals, and scripts. Situation factors include aggressive cues, provocation ("perhaps the most important single cause of human aggression," p. 37), frustration, pain and discomfort, alcohol/drugs/caffeine, and incentives/perceived benefits. Setting events would also be included here.

Routes

Anderson and Bushman (2002) described the three linked phenomenological states: cognitions (e.g., hostile thoughts, scripts/attributional biases), affect (mood/emotion, expressive motor responses) and arousal.

Outcomes

In the GAM, outcomes are the cognitive and behavioral products of the inputs and routes. First are immediate (automatic) appraisals (comprising affective, goal, and intention elements). What happens next is key to aggression. If the person has available resources (e.g., time, cognitive capacity) and if the immediate appraisal is flagged as both important and non-congruent with goals, then the person will engage in a more effortful cognitive reappraisal. If available resources are lacking—including if well-practiced, potentiated behavioral action are faster than inhibitory forces—impulsive actions are enacted (which may be aggressive or nonaggressive depending on the product of the immediate appraisal.)

Other Important Considerations

Anderson and Bushman (2002) also discuss how, over time, social cognitions and behaviors develop into personality processes. These processes are automatized and potentiated, thus requiring less cognitive or behavioral effort to evoke aggression.

CONCLUSION

The consistent conclusion of those reviewing and proposing theories of IPV is that they need: (a) to be more comprehensive; (b) to acknowledge, embrace, and explain the heterogeneity of IPV causes, severities, and directionalities; and (c) to be more ecological, recognizing the intraindividual, couple, subcultural, and societal forces that influence IPV. Given the tens of thousands of studies on human aggression, it is clear that single factor explanations are woefully inadequate and that, at best, our current theories are better than no theory, but fall far short of predicting a satisfying portion of the variance in aggression occurrence and severity. Rather than insist on how much we know and maintain that interventions based on our hubris should be legally prescribed for all perpetrators, all in the field of human aggression, and IPV in particular, must recognize that we know very little compared with what we need to know and that the safety and psychological and physical health of the large number of adults and children impacted by noxious and violent home environments require improved comprehensive theories and translational research.

REFERENCES

Ainsworth, M. D., Blehar, M. C, Waters, E. & Wall, S. (1978). *Patterns of attachment: A psychological study of the strange situation*. Hillside, NJ: Erlbaum.

Anderson, C. A., & Bushman, B. J. (2002). Human aggression. *Annual Review of Psychology, 53*, 27–51. doi: 10.1146/annurev.psych.53.100901.135231.

Bakermans-Kranenburg, M. J., & van IJzendoorn, M. H. (2006). Gene-Environment interaction of the dopamine D4 receptor (DRD4) and observed maternal insensitivity predicting externalizing behavior in preschoolers. *Developmental Psychobiology, 48*, 406–409. doi: 10.1002/dev.20152.

Bandura, A. (1986). *Social foundations of thought and action: A social and cognitive theory*. Englewood Cliffs, NJ: Prentice Hall.

Bandura, A. (1977). *Social learning theory*. Englewood Cliffs, NJ: Prentice Hall.

Bandura, A., Ross, D., & Ross, S. A. (1961). Transmission of aggression through imitation of aggressive models. *Journal of Abnormal and Social Psychology*, *63*, 575–582. doi: 10.1037/h0045925.

Bell, K. M., & Naugle, A. E. (2008). Intimate partner violence theoretical considerations: Moving towards a contextual framework. *Clinical Psychology Review*, *28*, 1096–1107. doi:10.1016/j.cpr.2008.03.003.

Bogat, G. A., Levendosky, A. A., & von Eye, A. (2005). The future of research on intimate partner violence: Person-oriented and variable-oriented perspectives. *American Journal of Community Psychology*, *36*, 49−70. doi: 10.1007/s10464-005-6232-7.

Bolen, R. M. (2000). Validity of attachment theory. *Trauma, Violence and Abuse*, *1*, 128–153. doi: 10.1177/1524838000001002002.

Bowlby, J. (1969). *Attachment and loss*. New York: Basic Books.

Butler, R. W., Braff, D. L., Rausch, J., Jenkins, M. A., Sprock, J., & Geyer, M. A. (1990) Physiological evidence of exaggerated startle response in a subgroup of Vietnam veterans with combat-related posttraumatic stress disorder. *American Journal of Psychiatry*, *147*, 1308–1312.

Cavanaugh, M. M., & Gelles, R. J. (2005). The utility of male domestic violence offender typologies: New directions for research, policy, and practice. *Journal of Interpersonal Violence*, *20*, 155−166. doi: 10.1177/0886260504268763.

Centers for Disease Control and Prevention (2012). Understanding Intimate Partner Violence: Fact Sheet 2012. Atlanta, GA. Retrieved from http://www.cdc.gov/violenceprevention/pdf/IPV_factsheet-a.pdf.

Chance, P. (1994). *Learning and behavior*. Pacific Grove, CA: Brooks/Cole.

Coker, A. L., Davis, K. E., Arias, I., Desai, S., Sanderson, M., Brandt, H. M., & Smith, P. H. (2002). Physical and mental health effects of intimate partner violence for men and women. *American Journal of Preventive Medicine*, *23*, 260–268. doi: 10.1016/S0749-3797(02)00514-7

Crittenden, P. M. (1998) Dangerous behavior and dangerous contexts: A 35-year perspective on research on the developmental effects of child physical abuse. In P. K. Trickett & C. J. Schellenbach (Eds.), *Violence against children in the family and in the community* (pp. 11–38). Washington, DC: American Psychological Association. doi: 10.1037/10292-001.

Dahlberg, L. K., & Krug, E. G. (2002). Violence, a global public health problem. In E. G. Krug, R. Lozano, L. K. Dahlberg, A. B. Zwi, & J. A. Mercy (Eds.), *World Report on Violence and Health* (pp. 1–56). Geneva, Switzerland: World Health Organization.

Delsol, C., Margolin, G., & John, R. S. (2003). A typology of maritally violent men and correlates of violence in a community sample. *Journal of Marriage and Family*, *65*, 635−651. DOI: 10.1111/j.1741-3737.2003.00635.x

DeKeseredy, W. S. (2000). Current controversies on defining nonlethal violence against women in intimate heterosexual relationships: Empirical implications. *Violence Against Women*, *6*, 728–746. doi: 10.1177/10778010022182128

Dobash, R. E., & Dobash, R. P. (1979). *Violence against wives*. New York: Free Press.

Dodge, K. (1993). Social-cognitive mechanisms in the development of conduct disorder and depression. *Annual Review of Psychology*, *44*, 559–584. doi: 10.1146/annurev.ps.44.020193.003015

Domjan, M. (2003). *The principles of learning and behavior* (5th ed.). Belmont, CA: Thomson/Wadsworth.

Dutton, D. G. (1995). Trauma symptoms and PTSD-like profiles in perpetrators of intimate abuse. *Journal of Traumatic Stress*, *8*, 299–316. doi: 10.1002/jts.2490080210.

Dutton, D. G., & Corvo, K. (2006). Transforming a flawed policy: A call to revive psychology and science in domestic violence research and practice. *Aggression and Violent Behavior*, *11*, 457–483. doi: 10.1016/j.avb.2006.01.007.

Dutton, D. G., Saunders, K., Starzomski, A., & Bartholomew, K. (1994). Intimacy, anger and insecure attachment as precursors of abuse in intimate relationships. *Journal of Applied Social Psychology*, *24*, 1367−1386. doi: 10.1111/j.1559-1816.1994.tb01554.x.

Feminist.com (2011). Facts about violence. Retrieved from http://www.feminist.com/antiviolence/facts.html.

Finkel, E. J. (2007). Impelling and inhibiting forces in the perpetration of intimate partner violence. *Review of General Psychology*, *11*, 193–207. doi: 10.1037/1089-2680.11.2.193.

Foa, E. B., Riggs, D. S., & Gershuny, B. S. (1995). Arousal, numbing, and intrusion: Symptom structure of PTSD following assault. *American Journal of Psychiatry*, *152*, 116–120.

Foran, H., Heyman, R. E., Slep, A. M. S., Snarr, J. D., & U.S. Air Force Family Advocacy Program (2011). *Hazardous alcohol use and intimate partner violence in the military: Understanding protective factors.* Manuscript submitted for publication. doi: 10.1037/a0027688.

Franklin, M. E., Abramowitz, J. S., Levitt, J. T., Kozak, M. J., & Foa, E. B. (2000). Effectiveness of exposure and ritual prevention for obsessive–compulsive disorder: Randomized compared with nonrandomized samples. *Journal of Consulting and Clinical Psychology, 68,* 594–602. doi: 10.1037/0022-006X.68.4.594.

Glass, N., Fredland, N., Campbell, J., Yonas, M., Sharps, P., & Kub, J. (2003). Adolescent dating violence: prevalence, risk factors, health outcomes, and implications for clinic practice. *Journal of Obstetric, Gynecologic, & Neonatal Nursing, 33,* 227–238. doi: 10.1177/0884217503252033.

Graffunder, C. M., Noonan, R. K., Cox, P., & Wheaton, J. (2004). Through a public health lens. Preventing violence against women: An update from the U.S. Centers for Disease Control and Prevention. *Journal of Women's Health, 13,* 5–16. doi:10.1089/154099904322836401.

Graham-Kevan, N., & Archer, J. (2003). Physical aggression and control in heterosexual relationships: The effect of sampling. *Violence & Victims, 18,* 181–196. doi: 10.1891/vivi.2003.18.2.181.

Harmon-Jones, E. (2003). Anger and the behavior approach system. *Personality and Individual Differences, I,* 995–1005.

Harmon-Jones, E., & Allen, J. J. B. (1998). Anger and frontal brain activity: EEG asymmetry consistent with approach motivation despite negative affective valence. *Journal of Personality and Social Psychology, 74,* 1310–1316. doi: 10.1037/0022-3514.74.5.1310.

Harmon-Jones, E., & Sigelman, J. (2001). State anger and prefrontal brain activity: Evidence that insult related relative left prefrontal activation is associated with experienced anger and aggression. *Journal of Personality and Social Psychology, 80,* 797–803. doi: 10.1037/0022-3514.80.5.797.

Haynes, S. N., & O'Brien, W. H. (2000). *Principles and practice of behavioral assessment.* New York: Kluwer.

Heise, L. L. (1998). Violence against women: An integrated, ecological framework. *Violence Against Women, 4,* 262–290. doi: 10.1177/1077801298004003002.

Heyman, R. E., & Slep, A. M. S. (2006). Creating and field-testing diagnostic criteria for partner and child maltreatment. *Journal of Family Psychology, 20,* 397–408. doi: 10.1037/0893-3200.20.3.397.

Heyman, R. E. & Slep, A. M. S. (2009). Reliability of family maltreatment diagnostic criteria: 41 site dissemination field trial. *Journal of Family Psychology, 23,* 905–910. Doi: 10.1037/a0017011.

Holtzworth-Munroe, A. (1992). Social skill deficits in maritally violent men: Interpreting the data using a social information processing model. *Clinical Psychology Review, 12,* 605–617. doi:10.1016/0272-7358(92)90134-T.

Holtzworth-Munroe, A., & Stuart, G. L. (1994). Typologies of male batterers: Three subtypes and the differences among them. *Psychological Bulletin, 116,* 476–497. Doi: 10.1037/0033-2909.116.3.476.

Holtzworth-Munroe, A., Meehan, J. C., Herron, K., Rehman, U., & Stuart, G. L. (2000). Testing the Holtzworth-Munroe and Stuart (1994) batterer typology. *Journal of Consulting and Clinical Psychology, 68,* 1000–1019. doi: 10.1037/0022-006X.68.6.1000.

Holtzworth-Munroe, A., Meehan, J. C., Herron, K., Rehman, U., & Stuart, G. L. (2003). Do subtypes of maritally violent men continue to differ over time? *Journal of Consulting and Clinical Psychology, 71,* 728–740. Doi: 10.1037/0022-006X.71.4.728.

Huesmann, L. R. (1997). Observational learning of violent behavior: Social and biosocial processes (pp. 69–88). In A. Raine, P. A. Brennen, D. P. Farrington, & S. A. Mednick (Eds.), *Biosocial bases of violence.* London, England: Plenum.

Johnson, M. P. (1995). Patriarchal terrorism and common couple violence: Two forms of violence against women. *Journal of Marriage and the Family, 57,* 283–294.

Johnson, M. P. (2008). *A typology of domestic violence: Intimate terrorism, violent resistance, and situational couple violence.* Boston: Northeastern University Press.

Johnson, M. P., & Ferraro, K. J. (2000). Research on domestic violence in the 1990s: Making distinctions. *Journal of Marriage and Family, 62,* 948–963. doi: 10.1111/j.1741-3737.2000.00948.x.

Jones, L., Hughes, M., & Unterstaller, U. (2001). Post-traumatic stress disorder (PTSD) in victims of domestic violence: A review of the research. *Trauma, Violence, & Abuse, 2,* 99–119. doi: 10.1177/1524838001002002001.

Johnson, M. P., & Leone, J. M. (2005). The differential effects on intimate terrorism and situational couple issues. *Journal of Family Issues, 26,* 322–349. Doi: 10.1177/0192513X04270345.

Kimmel, M. S. (2002). "Gender symmetry" in domestic violence: A substantive and methodological research review. *Violence Against Women, 8,* 1332–1363. Doi: 10.1177/107780102237407.

Kitzmann, K., Gaylord, N. K., Holt, A. R., & Kenny, E. D. (2003). Child witnesses to domestic violence: A meta-analytic review. *Journal of Consulting and Clinical Psychology, 71*, 339–352. doi: 10.1037/0022-006X.71.2.339.

Koss, M. P., & White, J. W. (2008), National and global agendas on violence against women: Historical perspective and consensus. *American Journal of Orthopsychiatry, 78*, 386–393. doi: 10.1037/a0014347.

Kristoff, N. D., & WuDunn, S. (2009). *Half the sky: Turning oppression into opportunity for women worldwide*. New York: Knopf.

Krug E. G., Dahlberg, L. L., Mercy, J. A., Zwi, A. B., & Loranzo, R.(2002). *World report on violence and health*. Geneva: World Health Organization. doi:10.1016/S0140-6736(02)11133-0.

Kuhn, T. S. (1970). *The structure of scientific revolutions* (2nd ed.). Chicago: University of Chicago Press.

Lawrence, E., & Bradbury, T. N. (2001). Physical aggression and marital dysfunction: A longitudinal analysis. *Journal of Family Psychology, 15*, 135–154. doi: 10.1037/0893-3200.15.1.135.

Lawrence, E, & Bradbury, T. N. (2007). Trajectories of change in physical aggression and marital satisfaction. *Journal of Family Psychology, 21*, 236–247. doi: 10.1037/0893-3200.21.2.236.

Lazarus, R. S. (1991). *Emotion and adaptation*. New York: Oxford University Press.

LeDoux, J. (2002). *Synaptic self: how our brains become who we are*. New York: Viking.

Lewin, K. (1952). *Field theory in social science: Selected theoretical papers by Kurt Lewin*. London, England: Tavistock.

Machado, C., Goncalves, M., Matos, M., & Dias, A. R. (2007). Child and partner abuse: Self-reported prevalence and attitudes in the north of Portugal. *Child Abuse & Neglect, 31*, 657–670. doi:10.1016/j.chiabu.2006.11.002,

Mahoney, A., Donnelly, W. O., Boxer, P., & Lewis, T. (2003). Marital and severe parent-to adolescent physical aggression in clinic-referred families: Mother and adolescent reports on co-occurrence and links to child behavior problems. *Journal of Family Psychology, 17*, 3–19. doi: 10.1037/0893-3200.17.1.3.

Magdol, L., Moffitt, T. E., Caspi, A., & Silva, P. A. (1998). Hitting without a license: Testing explanations for differences in partner abuse between young adult daters and cohabitors. *Journal of Marriage and the Family, 60*, 41–55. doi:10.2307/353440.

McLaughlin, I. G., Leonard, K. E., & Senchak, M. (1992). Prevalences and distribution of premarital aggression among couples applying for a marriage license. *Journal of Family Violence, 7*, 309–319. doi: 10.1007/BF00994621.

McFall, R. M. (1982). A review and reformulation of the concept of social skills. *Behavioral Assessment, 4*, 1–33. doi: 10.1007/BF01321377.

Medina-Ariza, J., & Barberet, R. (2003). Intimate partner violence in Spain. Findings from a national survey. *Violence against Women, 9*, 302–322. doi: 10.1177/1077801202250073.

Meehl, P. E. (1995). Bootstraps taxometrics: Solving the classification problem in psychopathology. *American Psychologist, 50*, 266–275. doi: 10.1037/0003-066X.50.4.266.

Mineka, S. & Ben Hamida, S. (1998). Observational and nonconscious learning. In W. O'Donohue (Ed.), *Learning and behavior therapy* (pp. 421–439). Boston: Allyn and Bacon.

Morse, B. J. (1995). Beyond the Conflict Tactics Scales: Assessing gender differences in partner violence. *Violence and Victims, 10*, 251–272.

Moffitt, T. E. (2007). A review of research on the taxonomy of life-course persistent and adolescence-limited offending. In D. Flannery, A. Vazonsyi, & I. Waldman (Eds.) *The Cambridge handbook of violent behavior*. New York: Cambridge University Press.

Moffitt, T. E., Caspi, A., Harrington, H., & Milne, B. J. (2002). Males on the life-course persistent and adolescence-limited antisocial pathways: Follow-up at age 26 years. *Development and Psychopathology, 14*, 179–207. doi: 10.1017/S0954579402001104.

Myers, D. L. (1995). Eliminating the battering of women by men: Some considerations for behavior analysis. *Journal of Applied Behavior Analysis, 28*, 493–507. doi: 10.1901/jaba.1995.28-493.

O'Brien, M., John, R. S., Margolin, G., & Erel, O. (1994). Reliability and diagnostic efficacy of parents' reports regarding children's exposure to marital aggression. *Violence and Victims, 9*, 45–62. doi: 10.1037/0022-006X.57.2.263.

O'Leary K. D., Barling J., Arias I., Rosenbaum A., Malone J., & Tyree A. (1989). Prevalence and stability of spousal aggression. *Journal of Consulting and Clinical Psychology, 57*, 263–268. doi: 10.1037/0022-006X.57.2.263

Patterson, G. R. (2005). The next generation of PMTO models. *Behavior Therapist, 28*, 25–32.

Patterson, G. R. (1982). *Coercive family processes*. Eugene, OR: Castilla Press.

Patterson, G. R. (1976). The aggressive child: Victim and architect of a coercive system. In L. A. Hamerlynck, E. J. Mash, & L. C. Handy (Eds.) *Behavior modification and families: I. Theory and research* (pp. 1–30). New York, NY: Brunner & Mazel.

Pence, E., & Paymar, M. (1993). *Education groups for men who batter: The Duluth model*. New York: Springer.

Peterson L., & Calhoun K. (1995). On advancing behavior analysis in the treatment and prevention of battering—Commentary on Myers. *Journal of Applied Behavior Analysis*. *28*, 509–514. doi: 10.1037/0022-006X.57.2.263.

Repetti, R., Taylor, S., & Seeman, T. (2002). Risky families: Family social environments and the mental and physical health of offspring. *Psychological Bulletin*, *128*, 330–366. doi: 10.1037/0033-2909.128.2.330.

Rhatigan, D. L., & Axsom, D. A. (2006). Using the investment model to understand battered women's commitment to abusive relationships. *Journal of Family Violence*, *21*, 153–162. doi: 10.1007/s10896-005-9013-z.

Rhatigan, D. L., Moore, T. M., & Street, A. E. (2005). Reflections on partner violence: Twenty years of research and beyond. *Journal of Interpersonal Violence*, *20*, 82–88. doi: 10.1177/0886260504268599.

Rhatigan, D. L. & Street, A. E. (2005). The impact of intimate partner violence on decisions to leave dating relationships: A test of the investment model. *Journal of Interpersonal Violence*, *20*, 1580–1597. doi: 10.1177/0886260505280344.

Ruiz-Pérez, I., Plazaola-Castaño, J. (2005). Intimate partner violence and mental health consequences in women attending family practice in Spain. *Psychosomatic Medicine*, *67*, 791–797. doi: 10.1097/01.psy.0000181269.11979.cd.

Rusbult, C. E. (1980). Commitment and satisfaction in romantic associations: A test of the investment model. *Journal of Experimental Social Psychology*, *45*, 101–117. doi:10.1016/0022-1031(80)90007-4.

Rusbult, C. E., & Martz, J. M. (1995). Remaining in an abusive relationship: An investment model analysis of nonvoluntary dependence. *Personality and Social Psychology Bulletin*, *21*, 558–571. doi: 10.1177/0146167295216002.

Saltzman, L. E., Fanslow, J. L., McMahon, P. M., & Shelley, G. A. (1999). *Intimate partner violence surveillance: Uniform definitions and recommended data elements* (Version 1.0). Atlanta, GA: Center for Disease Control and Prevention.

Sartin, R. M. (2005). Characteristics associated with domestic violence perpetration: An examination of factors related to treatment response and the utility of a batterer typology. *Dissertation Abstracts International. Section B: The Sciences and Engineering*, *65*(8-B), 4303.

Schafer, J., Caetano, R., & Clark, C. L. (1998). Rates of intimate partner violence in the United States. *American Journal of Public Health*, *88*, 1702–1704. doi:10.2105/AJPH.88.11.1702.

Sellers, C. S., Cochran, J. K., & Branch, K. A. (2005). Social learning theory and partner violence: A research note. *Deviant Behavior*, *26*, 379–395. doi:10.1080/016396290931669.

Skinner, B. F. (1963). Operant behavior. *American Psychologist*, *18*, 503–515.

Slep, A. M. S., Foran, H. M., Heyman, R. E., & Snarr, J. (2010). Unique risk and protective factors for partner aggression in a large-scale Air Force survey. *Journal of Community Health*, *35*, 375–383. doi: 10.1007/s10900-010-9264-3.

Slep, A. M. S., Foran, H. M., Heyman, R. E., Snarr, J. D., & USAF Family Advocacy Program (2011). Risk factors for clinically significant intimate partner violence among active duty members. *Journal of Marriage and Family,* *73*, 486–501.

Smith, P. H., Thornton, G. E., & DeVellis, R. (2002). A population-based study of the prevalence and distinctiveness of battering, physical assault, and sexual assault in intimate relationships. *Violence Against Women*, *8*, 1208–1232. doi: 10.1177/107780102320562691.

Stathopoulou, G. (2004). Greece. In K. Malley-Morrison (Ed.), *International perspectives on family violence and abuse: A cognitive ecological approach* (pp. 131–149). Mahwah, NJ: Erlbaum.

Stets, J. E., & Straus, M. A. (1990). Gender differences in reporting marital violence and its medical and psychological consequences. In M. A. Straus and R. J. Gelles, (Eds.), *Physical violence in American families* (pp. 151–165). New Brunswick, NJ: Transaction Publishers.

Stith, S. M., Smith, D. B., Penn, C. E., Ward, D. B., & Tritt, D. (2004). Intimate partner physical abuse perpetration and victimization risk factors: A meta-analytic review. *Aggression and Violent Behavior*, *10*, 65–98. doi: 10.1016/j.avb.2003.09.001.

Straus, M. A. (1979). Measuring intrafamily conflict and violence: The Conflict Tactics (CT) Scale. *Journal of Marriage and the Family*, *41*, 75–88. doi: 10.2307/351733.

Straus, M. A., & Gelles, R. J. (1990). *Physical violence in American families: Risk factors and adaptation to violence in 8,145 families*. New Brunswick, NJ: Transaction Publishers.

Straus, M. A., Gelles, R. J., & Steinmetz, S. K. (1980). *Behind closed doors*. Newbury Park, CA: Sage.

Stosny, S. (1995). Treating attachment abuse: A compassion approach. New York: Springer.

Suomi, S. J. (2005). Genetic and environmental factors influencing the expression of impulsive aggression and serotonergic functioning in rhesus monkeys. In R. E. Tremblay, W. W. Hartup, & J. Archer (Eds.), *Developmental origins of aggression* (pp. 63–82). New York: Guilford Press.

Tafrate, R. C., & Kassinove, H. (1998). Anger control in men: Barb exposure with rational, irrational, and irrelevant self-statements. *Journal of Cognitive Psychotherapy, 12*, 187–211.

Taft, C. T., Schumm, J. A., Marshall, A. D., Panuzio, J., & Holtzworth-Munroe, A. (2008). Family-of-origin maltreatment, posttraumatic stress disorder symptoms, social information processing deficits, and relationship abuse perpetration. *Journal of Abnormal Psychology, 117*, 637–646. doi: 10.1037/0021-843X.117.3.637.

Thibaut, J. W., and Kelley, H. H. (1959). *The social psychology of groups*. New York: Wiley.

Tjaden, P., & Thoennes, N. (2000). Prevalence and consequences of male-to-female and female-to-male intimate partner violence as measured by the national violence against women survey. *Violence Against Women, 6*, 142–161.

Truman-Schram, D. M., Cann, A., Calhoun, L., & Vanwallendael, L. (2000). Leaving an abusive dating relationship: An investment model comparison of women who stay versus women who leave. *Journal of Social and Clinical Psychology, 19*, 161–183. doi: 10.1521/jscp.2000.19.2.161.

Verona, E., Joiner, T.E., Johnson, F., & Bender, T.W. (2006). Gender specific gene-environment interactions on laboratory-assessed aggression. *Biological Psychology, 71*(1), 33–41.

Whitaker, D. J., Morrison, S., Lindquist, C., Hawkins, S. R., O'Neil, J. A., Nesius, A. M., et al. (2006). A critical review of interventions for the primary prevention of perpetration of partner violence. *Aggression and Violent Behavior, 11*, 151–166.

White, J. W., Smith, P. H., Koss, M. P., & Figueredo, A. J. (2000). Intimate partner aggression: What have we learned? Comment on Archer (2000). *Psychological Bulletin, 126*, 690–696. doi: 10.1037/0033-2909. 126.5.690.

Wilkinson, D. L., & Hamerschlag, S. J. (2005). Situational determinants in intimate partner violence. *Aggression and Violent Behavior, 10*, 333–361. doi: 10.1177/10778010022181769.

Yllö, K., & Bograd, M. (Eds.). (1988). *Feminist perspectives on wife abuse*. Newbury Park, CA: Sage.

Yllö, K. A. (1993). Through a feminist lens: Gender, power, and violence. In R. J. Gelles and D. R. Loseke (Eds.), *Current controversies on family violence*. Newbury Park, CA: Sage.

12 Theories of Child Abuse

Tamara Del Vecchio, Ann C. Eckardt Erlanger, and Amy M. Smith Slep

Lore in the field of child maltreatment suggests that the start of child protection from abuse began in the 1870s with the case of Mary Ellen. A child who was abused by her caregivers, Mary Ellen was removed from the home through work with the Society for the Prevention of Cruelty to Animals. The New York Society for the Prevention of Cruelty to Children was created as a consequence of the public outrage and negative media coverage (Pfohl, 1977). Almost 100 years later, prompted by the seminal book *The Battered Child* (Helfer & Kempe, 1968), the field began progressing at a rapid rate with the establishment of mandated reporting (1960s; Besharov, 1983) and the child welfare system (1970s; Child Abuse Prevention and Treatment Act, CAPTA, 1974).

Our knowledge of the impact of child maltreatment has expanded tremendously, as has our understanding of the factors that place parents at risk for perpetration. Although rates of child maltreatment in the US are high, at approximately 1 million per year, prevalence rates do appear to be decreasing (Sedlak et al., 2010). Furthermore, our repertoire of efficacious interventions for the prevention (e.g., Olds, Henderson, Chamberlin, & Tatelbaum, 1986) and treatment (e.g., Kolko, 1996; Lutzker, 1984) of child maltreatment perpetration has grown substantially over the last several years. However, several critical gaps remain.

Perhaps the most fundamental is a lack of consensus regarding definitions of child maltreatment. Without such definitions, scholars, researchers, and clinicians are all placed at a disadvantage and left unsure on how to best consider data from various sources and methodologies. Additionally, theoretical development has slowed. Some deceleration is an outcome of the natural progression and maturing of a field. However, the slowing also reflects shifts in research focus, driven, in part, by a change in priorities among funding agencies to emphasize intervention and impact on victims. Despite the current state of research, the foundations to move forward, address gaps, and significantly advance theory in the next decade are strong.

In this chapter, we will present the key findings and results in child abuse and neglect and review theoretical frameworks for conceptualizing child maltreatment. The chapter will include limitations of these theories and possible future theoretical directions for understanding child maltreatment.

KEY FINDINGS IN CHILD MALTREATMENT

"Child maltreatment" is a broad term and typically includes both abuse (i.e., acts of commission) and neglect (i.e., acts of omission). Furthermore, abuse is often categorized as physical, emotional or psychological, or sexual. Neglect ranges from extreme deprivation to failures to ensure adequate education and medical care. Throughout this chapter, we will use child maltreatment as the umbrella term that includes all forms of maltreatment, and will specify neglect or specific types of abuse as relevant for describing specific theories or research findings.

In less than 50 years, the issue of child maltreatment in the US has undergone remarkable shifts. The last 10 years has seen a tremendous maturing of our societal perspective on, as well as our empirical understanding of the treatment of maltreatment. Here, we briefly review several recent key findings that are shaping the future of child maltreatment research.

DEFINING AND MEASURING CHILD MALTREATMENT

Defining child maltreatment in a manner that allows consistent decisions in fieldwork and research settings has been largely elusive. Although the rate of research on child maltreatment has slowed, the last 10 years has seen considerable progress on this front. Heyman and Slep (2006, 2009; Slep & Heyman, 2006) developed and tested operationalized definitions of child maltreatment for the United States Air Force Family Advocacy Program. Criteria were developed for types of abuse (physical, emotional, sexual) and neglect of children. Each set of criteria includes acts committed by the offender and the impact (actual or potential) on the victim. In a series of field trials and a dissemination trial, when implemented by decision-making boards in the military, percent agreement with master reviewers (experienced clinicians trained in the criteria serving as the "gold standard") improved from 50% to over 90%. In addition to the criteria, clinical assessment interviews and self-report questionnaires were developed to support consistent operationalizations of maltreatment in both clinical and research settings. Interestingly, the implementation of these definitions, which were perceived by stakeholders in the community (e.g., committee members, clinicians, leaders) as unbiased and fair to the alleged perpetrators and victims (Slep & Heyman, 2006), was associated with a significant reduction in recidivism among alleged and substantiated perpetrators as compared with recidivism under the prior definitions (Snarr, Heyman, Slep, Malik, & USAF Family Advocacy Program, 2011).

This work is now being extended in an effort to establish systems for reliably classifying the severity of maltreatment and to apply these definitions in civilian child protective systems. If consistent definitions of maltreatment were reliably applied in both community and research-based efforts, this would result in more reliable decision-making processes for families, more accurate data, and better generalizability of research findings to community and clinical systems.

RATES OF CHILD MALTREATMENT

One of the most provocative recent findings has been the apparent declining rate of child maltreatment, the first decline since it began being rigorously tracked. Even though rates of child maltreatment are decreasing, large numbers of children are still maltreated. An estimated 1,256,600 children were maltreated during 2005–2006 (17.1 per 1,000 children), according to the Fourth National Incidence Study of Child Abuse and Neglect (NIS–4; Sedlak et al., 2010). In a representative sample of youth in the US, as many as 60.6% reported being victimized or witnessing victimization; 10% of these children had been maltreated (Finkelhor, Turner, Ormrod, & Hamby, 2009).

Still, there is converging evidence that child maltreatment is on the decline. NIS–4 results indicated a statistically significant decline in the frequency of child sexual abuse, with a marginal decrease in child physical abuse and child emotional abuse (Sedlak et al., 2010). During the 1990s, substantiated cases of child sexual abuse by child protective agencies decreased by 39% (Jones, Finkelhor, & Kopiec, 2001). Between 1993 and 2004, child maltreatment and child victimization as assessed in the National Victimization Survey (a nationally representative survey of children and adolescents) declined by 40–70%, after a peak in 1993 (Finkelhor & Jones, 2006). The evidence suggests that the frequency of physical and sexual maltreatment has declined, with a possible decline in child neglect masked due to changes in reporting (Jones, Finkelhor, & Halter, 2006).

There are several possible influences on this decline in child maltreatment. During the 1980s and 1990s, substantial funding and attention were devoted to child sexual abuse prevention and intervention (both community and criminal justice based). Perhaps these activities were effective public health measures (Jones & Finkelhor, 2003). Additional economic changes and increased use of psychiatric medication by would-be perpetrators might also contribute to the decline in physical and sexual maltreatment. Moreover, the decline could be reflective of a change in awareness of and decreasing tolerance of physical and sexual abuse of children.

OUTCOMES

Over the last several years, two important and disparate conclusions have emerged from research on the impact of maltreatment. First, the effects of maltreatment can be substantially broader than the emotional, behavioral, and social effects that were initially the focus of research. The Adverse Childhood Experiences (ACEs) study from 1995 through 1997 by the Centers for Disease Control and Prevention (CDC) utilized a sample of 17,000 participants to examine the physical outcomes of a negative childhood (Felitti, Vincent, Anda, Robert, & Nordenberg, 1998). ACEs, which include child maltreatment, along with family dysfunction, have been found to influence physical health. For example, ACEs increase the risk of liver disease; this relation is strongly mediated by substance abuse and dangerous sexual activities (Dong, Dube, Felitti, Giles, & Anda, 2003).

Physical differences in the brain are associated with child maltreatment victimization. Parental verbal abuse (a behavior that can be considered child emotional maltreatment) is related to a change in neurological functioning, specifically white matter tracts. In a sample of young adults, it was found that those exposed to parental verbal abuse had altered neural pathways related to language and psychopathology (e.g., anxiety, depression); (Choi, Jeong, Rohan, Polcari, & Teicher, 2009). The corpus callosum is also affected by child maltreatment. Psychiatric patients who were maltreated (abused or neglected) had a smaller corpus callosum when compared with healthy controls (by 17%) and other psychiatric patients who were not maltreated (11%). Furthermore, it appeared that neglect, as compared with other forms of maltreatment, played the biggest role in reduced corpus callosum area (15–18% difference; Teicher et al., 2004). In an interesting series of studies examining the impact of emotional neglect, operationalized as children who spent time in orphanages and then were adopted into nurturing homes, the children with a history of institutionalization had deficits in inhibition, visual memory, attention, and visually mediated learning. Yet, these children scored at appropriate developmental thresholds on comparative tasks with auditory and executive processes (Pollak et al., 2010). In other work, severe neglect history in institutionalized children appeared to increase levels of stress hormones (cortisol) with extended elevations after mother–child interactions (Fries, Shirtcliff, & Pollak, 2008) even after years in responsive environments. These results indicate that even within the context of a close relationship, these children can experience prolonged problematic hormone regulation and neurological impacts of maltreatment (DeBellis, et al., 1994; DeBellis, Lefter, Trickett, & Putnam, 1994; Ito, et al., 1993).

Although the majority of child maltreatment research focuses on negative results and excludes resilient outcomes, there is also evidence to show that children can experience maltreatment with no apparent negative effects, and perhaps fair better than might be expected. In categorizing abused and neglected individuals, McGloin and Widom (2001) defined resiliency through the following areas: employment, education, socialization, psychiatric health, and absence of homelessness, substance abuse, and criminality. Using these categories, 22% of victims of child maltreatment were classified as resilient. Looking at gender difference, females were labeled as more resilient than males (i.e., females met more resiliency criteria as outlined in the above categorizes) (McGloin & Widom, 2001).

Even in maltreatment traditionally thought of as more severe (child sexual abuse), there appear to be a significant number of resilient outcomes. Meta-analytic evidence pertaining to college students who were sexually abused as children shows that they, on average, are slightly less well adjusted in terms of psychological functioning and social adjustment when compared with college students without a sexual abuse history. However, child sexual abuse explained less than 1% of the variance; poor family environment was a much better predictor of adjustment than sexual abuse itself (Rind, Tromovitch, & Bauserman, 1998). Parental support and level of stress resulting from abuse predict better outcomes among sexually abused females (Spaccarelli & Kim, 1995).

So, what role does the onset of maltreatment play in later challenges? Although child maltreatment has been linked with an array of problematic outcomes, much of this literature suffers from significant methodological limitations. Often, comparison groups of children differ from maltreated groups in a number of ways other than merely maltreatment. Types of child maltreatment covary (Edwards, Holden, Felitti, & Anda, 2003) and child maltreatment covaries with a wide variety of other problematic parenting behaviors (Brown, Cohen, Johnson, & Salzinger, 1998), as well as a myriad of other family (e.g., intimate partner violence, Appel & Holden, 1998; Slep & O'Leary, 2005) and more macro-level factors (e.g., poverty, Coulton, Korbin, Su, & Chow, 1995) that relate to problematic child outcomes. As research on the impact of maltreatment moves forward, it will be important to continue to try to tease apart the role of maltreatment as part of this stew of adverse contexts and experiences for children.

THEORETICAL CONCEPTUALIZATIONS OF CHILD MALTREATMENT

BEHAVIORAL THEORIES

Behavioral theories have had a strong influence on conceptualizations of child maltreatment, serving as the basis for several more specific theoretical arguments. Behavioral theories emphasize reinforcement, positive or negative, in the development of aggressive behavior. Positive reinforcement involves the introduction of a reward contingent upon aggressive behavior serving to increase the likelihood of future aggression. Negative reinforcement increases the likelihood that aggression will occur in the future by a removal of an aversive stimulus contingent upon aggression.

Coercion theory (Patterson 1982; Reid, Patterson, & Snyder, 2002) suggests positive and negative reinforcement that occur in dyadic conflict result in a learned pattern of aggressive escalation. A parent and child in a conflict escalate with increasingly noxious behaviors, until one person capitulates. The person who "wins" is negatively reinforced for escalating through the removal of the aversive conflict behavior and often positively reinforced through the attainment of a reward such as earning privileges or gaining compliance. The person who "loses" is negatively reinforced via the other's cessation of aversive behavior. Physically abusive behavior patterns can occur as a result of the escalation process that crests with aggressive discipline and is reinforced due to its variable effectiveness at "winning." Moreover, consistent with coercion theory, abusive mothers are also more inconsistent and likely to provide positive consequences for their child's aversive behavior than non-abusive mothers (Oldershaw, Walters, & Hall, 1986). Patterson (1976) established that the most likely antecedent for aversive behavior is the aversive behavior displayed by another family member. As such, the "victim" in these conflictual interactions is also the "architect" of the aggressive exchanges by supplying reinforcement to the aggressor. Through this process, abusive parents and their children may develop dysfunctional patterns for parent–child interactions that encourage conflict and aggression and the escalation of that aggression to injurious forms of discipline. Moreover, children learn maladaptive behavior patterns that contribute to externalizing behavior problems (Snyder, 2002) and may develop a proclivity to aggression resulting in an intergenerational cycle of child maltreatment (Swick & Williams, 2006).

Social learning theory (e.g., Bandura, 1977; 1986), an extension of behavioral theory, posits that behavioral change occurs through vicarious, or observed, reinforcement. In their oft-cited study on imitative learning of aggressive behavior, Bandura, Ross, and Ross (1961) demonstrated that aggressive behavior could be learned through the observation of aggressive actors without the need for direct reinforcement. Thus, observational learning of aggressive behaviors bypasses the need for learning of aggression through directly experienced consequences. Modeling as a mechanism for learning of aggressive behavior is well established (see Huesmann, 1997; Mineka & Hamida, 1998, for reviews).

The intergenerational transmission hypothesis asserts that children grow up to repeat what they experienced and saw as children with their own children. Social learning is most often presumed as a primary mechanism for the intergenerational transmission of child maltreatment. Social learning theory, as applied to the intergenerational transmission hypothesis, postulates that abusive behavior is learned through the witnessing of abusive parenting and subsequent modeling of an abusive parent. Parents who used severe physically aggressive techniques were more likely to report witnessing partner aggression in childhood (Straus, 1994; Straus & Smith, 1990). Moreover, numerous studies have found relations between parent abuse history and the occurrence and severity of child abuse perpetration (Ethier, Couture, & Lacharite, 2004; Gelles & Straus, 1987; Gil, 1971; Heyman & Slep, 2002; Kaufman & Zigler, 1993; Stith, et al., 2009). Heyman and Ezzell (2005) estimate that intergenerational transmission of child physical abuse occurs in one-third of the cases. Although fewer than 1% of parents without a child physical abuse history maltreat their own children within the first few years of life, only about 7% of parents with abuse history maltreat (Browne 1995; Dixon, Brown, & Hamilton-Giachritsis, 2009). Thus, even though abuse history remains a significant risk factor, it does not follow that abused children will necessarily be abusive parents (Heyman & Ezzell, 2005)

Child sexual abuse perpetrators are also more likely to be abused as children, physically (d =0.49) and sexually (d =0.70; Whitaker et al., 2008). On average, 28% of sex offenders have a child sexual abuse history, with higher rates among male victims of male offenders (Starzyk & Marshall, 2003). Koyabashi, Sales, Becker, Figueredo, and Kaplan (1995) suggest that male offending has a greater impact on victims and may result in sexual confusion for male victims. Although not directly evaluated, modeling of inappropriate sexual behavior may be the mechanism through which child sexual abuse is transmitted to new perpetrators. As with physical abuse, however, although a history of victimization is more often found among sexual abuse perpetrators than people who do not perpetrate sexual abuse, the vast majority of sexual abuse victims will not go on to become perpetrators.

COGNITIVE MODELS

Social information processing models of abusive behavior emphasize the role of cognitive processes, such as schemas, executive functioning deficits, and attributions and appraisals as predictors of abusive parenting (Azar, Reitz, & Goslin, 2008). Parenting schemas, or mental scripts, develop from past experiences, influenced by family experiences and cultural norms. Schemas represent people's views of themselves as parents, the parenting role in general, and expectations for children; and are proposed to mediate the relation between child behavior and abusive parental responses. New information, such as a specific instance of child behavior, is then filtered through these schemas. This results in selective attention to schema-consistent cues in parent–child interactions. Once activated, schemas can influence simultaneous cognitive, affective, and behavioral responses.

Adaptive schemas are flexible and can be modified through trial-and-error learning (Azar, Nix, & Makin-Byrd, 2005). Contingent, responsive parenting requires the ability to modify responding based on the needs of the particular situation (Azar &Weinzierl, 2005). In contrast, abusive parents rely on schemas that are rigid and negative affect laden (Azar, Nix, & Makin-Byrd, 2005; Milner, 2000; Nayak & Milner, 1998). These rigid cognitive schemas may reflect deficits in executive functioning; that is, cognitive flexibility. Consistent with this model, several studies have indicated that abusive parents are more likely to underestimate task demands and overestimate their children's developmental abilities, resulting in unrealistic expectations (Azar & Rohrbeck, 1986; Spinetta, 1978; Twentyman & Plotkin, 1982). When the child naturally disconfirms expectations, parents are angered and respond in an overly harsh manner.

Within the social information processing framework, parents' negative perceptions and evaluations of child behavior and positive outcome expectancies for abusive behavior are thought to contribute to abusive responding (Milner 1993; Milner, 2000). Compared with non-abusive parents, abusive parents are more likely to endorse negative attributions for child behavior, appraise child behavior more negatively, and have unrealistic expectations for child behavior. For example, Bauer and Twentyman (1985) asked mothers to respond to hypothetical vignettes and found that abusing mothers were the most likely to view their child as acting intentionally to annoy them. Moreover, Larrance and Twentyman (1983) report that physically abusive parents make more internal and stable attributions for negative child behavior and external, unstable attributions for positive child behavior. Chilamkurti and Milner (1993) found that mothers at high-risk for child abuse evaluated minor child transgressions as more wrong and endorsed more power assertive disciplinary techniques than low-risk mothers. In one of the few studies to incorporate observational measures of child behavior, Reid et al. (2002) found that even though abusive parents reported significantly more aggression and hyperactivity than non-abusive parents, independent observers did not identify differences in the mean rate of aversive behavior or severity of conduct problems. Sexual abuse perpetrators overestimate children's sexual development and are more likely to misinterpret children's behaviors as sexual advances (Ward & Keenan, 1999).

Parents at-risk for abuse may evidence positive outcome expectancies for abusive behavior; high-risk mothers perceive the use of power assertive discipline by others as more appropriate than their counterparts (Chilamkurti & Milner, 1993). Results regarding attitudes about physical discipline are mixed. Slep and O'Leary (2007) found that these attitudes uniquely contribute to aggressive parenting in the context of a multivariate prediction model. In contrast, Stith and colleagues (2009) found non-significant effect sizes for the association between approval of corporal punishment and child physical abuse. Perhaps the inconsistent findings are due to interactive effects. Crouch and Behl (2001) found that the association between stress and child physical abuse risk was moderated by the parents' level of belief in the value of corporal punishment; the relation was stronger for those who value corporal punishment. In addition, sexual abuse perpetrators are more likely to rationalize their behaviors and report that children benefit from the sexual behavior or actively sought out sexual contact (Stermac & Segal, 1989).

Abuse as a Function of Stress and Anger

The roles of stress and anger in etiological models of child maltreatment have garnered considerable attention in the literature (Dopke & Milner, 2000; Gaudin, Polansky, Kilpatrick, & Shilton, 1993; Whipple & Webster-Stratton, 1991; Williamson, Bourduin, & Howe, 1991). Abusive and high-risk parents report more stressful life events and more parenting stress than non-abusive parents (Coohey & Braun, 1997; Crouch & Behl, 2001; Dopke & Milner, 2000; Mash, Johnston, & Kovitz, 1983; Rodriguez & Green, 1997; Rosenberg & Reppucci, 1983; Stith et al., 2009). The number of stressful life events is also associated with child sexual abuse, as mothers of sexually abused children report a greater number of stressful life events compared with mothers of non-abused children (Pianta, Egeland, & Erikson, 1989).

Clearly, however, not all parents who encounter stress abuse their children. In a prospective study of low-income mothers, Egeland, Breitenbucher, and Rosenberg (1980) examined differences between stressed mothers who abused their children and stressed mothers who did not abuse their children. Although the mothers did not differ in type of life stress events experienced, abusive mothers reported more aggression and defensiveness, and less seeking of support in reaction to the stress. Moreover, abusive mothers, compared with non-abusive mothers, are more likely to report loneliness (Milner & Robertson, 1990; Spinetta, 1978). Although the availability of supportive resources does not distinguish abusive from non-abusive parents (Chaffin, Kelleher, & Hollenberg, 1996), abusive parents report receiving less social support (Corse, Schmid &Trickett, 1990; Pianta, Egeland, & Erikson, 1989).

Thus, current theory suggests that stress is not a *sufficient* condition for child maltreatment perpetration. Pianta (1984) argues that abusive parents have poor coping skills and are more likely to cope in negative ways, such as drinking and hostility, resulting in an increased risk for child-directed violence. When stress cannot be coped with effectively, parents are more likely to develop negative perceptions of child behavior and engage in abusive or neglectful behaviors (Belsky, 1993). Hillson and Kuiper (1994) suggest that specific coping strategies are associated with specific abuse types. Neglectful parents are more likely to engage in behavioral or mental disengagement characterized by a withdrawal of caregiver behaviors or the use of mental distractors to avoid the stressor. In contrast, physically abusive parents are more likely to engage in rumination and venting of negative emotions. The coping pattern may change over time as automatic coping responses are developed. Moreover, physically abusive and neglecting parents show deficits in problem-solving skills related to childrearing and childcare (Azar, Robinson, Hekimian, & Twentyman, 1984; Dawson, de Armas, McGrath, & Kelly, 1986). Hansen, Pallotta, Tishelman, Conaway, and MacMillan (1989) compared physically abusive and neglectful parents to clinic and community parents and found that although abusive parents were deficient in problem-solving ability, problem-solving skill deficits were not significantly associated with child behavior problems. In addition, even though clinic parents and abusive parents reported similar levels of child behavior problems, clinic parents generated more solutions and more effective solutions than did the abusive parents. Thus, abusive parenting may reflect deficits in coping and the ability to determine and select effective solutions to childrearing problems.

Anger is associated with child abuse risk and abusive status (Ammerman, 1990; Dopke & Milner, 2000; Rodriguez & Green, 1997). Aversive childrearing events occur with great frequency during early childhood (e.g., temper tantrums, defiance) and elicit anger, annoyance, and frustration. Angry emotional responses to children may result in an overwhelming flood of negative emotions and selection of over-learned, schema-consistent, dysfunctional parenting techniques (Gottman, Katz, & Hooven, 1996). Moreover, abusive mothers' evidence increased sensitivity to child negative affect. Milner, Halsey, and Fultz (1995) found that high-risk, compared with low-risk mothers reported more negative affectivity (e.g., distress, hostility) to infant cries. In addition, when presented with videotaped infant cries, abusive mothers' evidence increased physiological reactivity (e.g. heart rate, skin conductance, and diastolic blood pressure) (Frodi & Lamb, 1980). Abusive parents also report feeling more angry or annoyed in response to children's behavior in general, and specifically with regard to social or moral transgressions, than non-abusive parents (Bauer & Twentyman 1985; Dopke & Milner, 2000; Spinetta, 1978; Trickett & Kuczynski, 1986). A recent meta-analytic review by Stith et al. (2009) examining 155 studies found that parent anger consistently predicted both child physical abuse and neglect.

PSYCHOPATHOLOGY

The *psychopathological model* of child maltreatment focuses on the perpetrator's mental health as an etiological factor. Although several disorders have been implicated as predictors of child physical abuse and neglect perpetration, two disorders have consistently evidenced associations with perpetration: depression and substance abuse. A large body of research documents the relation between depression and child physical abuse and neglect (Cummings & Cicchetti, 1990; Downey & Coyne, 1990; Gil, 1971; Kinard, 1982; Scott, 1992; Stith et al., 2009). Using wave II data from National Institute for Mental Health's Epidemiologic Catchment Area Survey, Chaffin, et al. (1996) found that major depression was a significant predictor of the onset of physical abuse, controlling for substance use and demographic variables. Although depression was also found to significantly predict neglect univariately, the strength of the relation decreased to non-significant levels when substance use and demographic variables were included as predictors.

Data from the Epidemiologic Catchment Area Survey also indicated that substance use predicted the onset of child physical abuse and neglect (Chaffin, et al., 1996). In addition, Murphy, et al. (1991) examined the prevalence of substance abuse in a sample of cases of serious child abuse or neglect brought before a juvenile court. The presence of parental substance abuse in at least one of the parents was indicated in 43% of the cases. Among addicted parents, Black and Mayer (1980) found that 41% of their children met criteria for serious neglect, abuse, or both, although all experienced some degree of neglect. In a community sample of over 11,000 individuals, abusive parents were more likely than their matched controls to report substance abuse; the association was independent of levels of depression and social support (Kelleher, Chaffin, Hollenberg, & Fischer, 1994). However, depression and substance use are neither necessary nor specific to child abuse perpetrators.

In a meta-analytic review examining characteristics associated with the perpetration of child sexual abuse, Whitaker and colleagues (2008) identified several psychopathological correlates of maltreatment. Consistent with the findings for child physical abuse and neglect, substance abuse was a significant predictor of perpetration. However, the associations with depression and maltreatment were less consistent; studies evidenced positive and negative effects. In addition, Whitaker et al. identified a relation between anxiety symptoms and antisocial personality disorder and child sexual abuse perpetration.

FAMILY ENVIRONMENT

Indicators of "high-risk" family environments, such as early motherhood, poverty, and a low level of education, influence the capacity to parent and have been implicated in the etiology of child physical abuse and neglect. Parenting age is associated with a number of risk factors including low level of education, higher levels of stress, less social support, and coercive discipline practices (Brooks-Gunn & Chase-Lansdale, 1995; Ketterlinus, Lamb, & Nitz, 1991; Stevens-Simon, Nelligan, & Kelly, 2001). Young mothers are at a slightly increased risk for physical abuse behaviors and neglect (Dixon, Brown, & Hamilton-Giachritsis, 2009; Stith, et al., 2009; Wolfner & Gelles, 1993). Although several studies have found that age was negatively related to the severity of physical abuse (Connelly & Straus, 1992; Gil, 1971), using Epidemiological Catchment Area data, Chaffin et al. (1996) failed to find a significant association between parents' age and whether or not severe physical abuse was perpetrated. The relation between parent age and child neglect is unclear with several studies indicating no effect (Schumacher, Slep & Heyman, 2001; Stith et al., 2009). Moreover, Allen and Pothast (1994) found no significant age difference between sexual abusers and non-abusers.

Income level has been consistently found to be negatively associated with child physical abuse (Chaffin, et al., 1996; Garbarino, 1976; Straus, Gelles, & Steinmetz, 1980; Gil, 1971; Sedlak, 1997; Wolfner & Gelles, 1993) and neglect (Brown, et al., 1998; Pelton, 1994). In addition to occurrence, severity of abuse may be associated with poverty; severe injuries have been found to be more likely among low-income families (Gelles, 1992; Gil, 1971; Kruttschnitt, McLeod, & Dornfeld, 1994; Sedlak & Broadhurst, 1996). However, both the Epidemiological Catchment Area and the National Family Violence Survey failed to find an association between severity of perpetration and income level (Chaffin, et al., 1996; Ross, 1996). Perhaps the inconsistent findings may be due to type of child maltreatment evaluated: neglect, physical abuse, or sexual abuse. For example, using 1990 Census data and Child Protective Services data, Drake and Pandey (1995) found that neighborhood poverty was most strongly associated with neglect as compared with other forms of abuse. In addition, in a meta-analytic review of 155 studies, Stith et al. (2009) found that unemployment was moderately related to child neglect, but only minimally related to child physical abuse.

Demographic factors, such as age and socioeconomic status, are unlikely to be direct determinants of abuse status. Instead, the association between poverty and abuse status is likely to be indirect, mediated by stress associated with poverty (Pianta, 1984). Furthermore, poverty is correlated with educational level, single parent status, and psychopathology, and each is associated with child maltreatment status (Allen & Pothast, 1994; Gil, 1971; Milner & Chilamkurti, 1991). Poverty is associated with a low level of education, and educational level predicts child maltreatment risk when controlling for income level (Rodriguez, 2008). Lower income families also tend to have more children and having multiple children under 18 increases the risk for child physical abuse and neglect perpetration (Gil, 1971). Single parent status is also associated with both the incidence and chronicity of child maltreatment (Ethier, et al., 2004; Sedlak & Broadhurst, 1996), although severity of perpetration and single parent status are not significantly related (Chaffin, et al., 1996; Connelly & Straus, 1992).

Mothers who work full-time are less likely to report physical abuse perpetration (Gelles & Hargreaves, 1990). Black, Heyman, and Slep (2001) suggest that perhaps time spent with children is a better predictor of perpetration than employment status in itself. Although variables indexing social disadvantage, such as poverty and a low level of education, are associated with abuse perpetration, child maltreatment is not exclusively a lower SES condition. Lower income parents are more likely to come in contact with Child Protective Services and, as a result, the association between poverty and child maltreatment perpetration may also be an artifact of sampling biases (Gil, 1971). In contrast to physical abuse and neglect, income and educational level are not related to child sexual abuse (Finkelhor & Baron, 1986; Putnam, 2003).

ECOLOGICAL MODEL

Perhaps the most widely accepted etiological model of child maltreatment is a multidimensional integration of diverse factors operating at more proximal and more distal levels of influence. Parent characteristic models are greatly limited by the failure to identify variables that account for a large portion of the variance. Based on Bronfenbrenner's perspective (1979), the *ecological model of child maltreatment* suggests that the environment influences parents at multiple levels of the ecological system (Belsky, 1980). The systems represent levels of influence from the most proximal (i.e., ontogenic—psychopathology, family of origin influences) to the most distal (i.e., cultural norms). Relations are not necessarily unidirectional (e.g., Cicchetti & Lynch, 1993; Wolfe, 1987). For example, abusive parenting contributes to child behavior problems and likely is a source of parental stress, and these negative sequelae affect other systems such as work and school performance (Swick & Williams, 2006).

Within an ecological framework, child maltreatment is thought to occur as a function of the society, community and family ecology supporting or undermining the quality of parent–child interactions. The empirical literature has identified risk and protective factors that exist at all levels of the ecology (see Black, et al., 2001; Stith et al., 2009, for reviews). Ecological theories suggest that more proximal factors, such as parental psychopathology, have the most direct effect on parent–child interaction and abuse, and that the effects of more distal factors are often mediated through their impact on more proximal factors. In other words, the presence of risk factors (e.g., neighborhood stressors) directly results in negative outcomes or increases the likelihood of exposure to additional risk factors. Negative interactions that can occur between person and environment may result in multiple challenges (e.g., Felitti, et al., 1998) and poor outcomes (e.g., Choi, et al., 2009). In contrast, protective factors buffer against the effects of the risk factors, and can compensate for other, even proximal, risk factors, resulting in more successful outcomes (Cicchetti, 2004). Thus, it is not only the number of risk factors at each level of the ecology that determines the likelihood of child maltreatment, but also the balance among the factors; if risk factors outweigh protective factors, the risk for child maltreatment is increased. However, there is little data to suggest which risk factors are most important or how risk factors interact to increase overall risk.

LIMITATIONS OF EXISTING THEORY USAGE

In this section, we briefly highlight some of the main limitations to how theory has been developed and applied to the study of child maltreatment.

Lack of Operational Definitions

Perhaps one of the biggest limitations in the field of child maltreatment is the lack of consistent, operational definitions. As a consequence of the absence of uniform criteria, unreliable data collected by community-based systems poorly inform policy makers and can contribute to erroneous conclusions about the etiology of child maltreatment. Ambiguous thresholds for maltreatment can result in unfair decision-making at the family level. For example, two hypothetical child neglect cases with virtually the same set of circumstance might result in radically different outcomes—one case might be substantiated (i.e., officially documented as an incident of child maltreatment or "founded") and the other unsubstantiated (i.e., officially dismissed as below threshold or lacking evidence or "unfounded"). This sends profoundly inconsistent messages to both the perpetrator and the victim about society's view of their behaviors and experiences. Further, the use of assessment approaches that are not specifically designed to collect information necessary to make reliable substantiation decisions make it challenging for researchers to compare outcomes and progress the field in a targeted way.

Application of uniform definitions will greatly facilitate the integration of research across different samples and with different methodologies, thereby speeding the rate at which theories can be refined. Moreover, varying assessment methods could be considered strengths if better incorporated into the study outcomes. For example, Stockhammer, Salzinger, Feldman, and Mojica's (2001) examination of Child Protective Services records and parent report suggests that agency records provide more reliable information about proximal factors, such as specific incidents of maltreatment, and parent reports provide more accurate information about distal factors, such as family context.

Mixed Abuse Types

There are fundamental gaps in our understanding of the relations among different types of abuse. Most child welfare contexts do not carefully assess for all forms of maltreatment, with most systems preferring to pursue the most salient type in an incident or family. Researchers typically categorize families either through often-limited child protective service records, or based on the assessment of a single type of maltreatment intended to be the focus of the research. In addition, measures of specific forms of abuse and neglect are lacking. Therefore, we have little information about the distinctiveness of abuse types (i.e., how overlapping versus distinct physical and emotional abuse are or how often neglect and abuse co-occur). In addition, aggregating maltreatment types muddles our models of abuse perpetration. Differences in child maltreatment are found at a fundamental level; namely, most physical and emotional abuse, as well as neglect, occurs at the hands of a parent or caregiver, while much sexual abuse occurs at the hands of other adults in the child's circle (e.g., Finkelhor, 1984). Conflating abuse types also makes it difficult to assess differential predictors. For example, theories of sexual abuse emphasize general characteristic of families of sexual abuse victims in contrast to perpetrator-specific variables. Low prevalence rates of child sexual abuse and the tendency for studies on risk factors for child abuse to combine all forms of maltreatment make it difficult to identify specific predictors of sexual abuse. These gaps in our knowledge contribute to limitations in our theories and methodological issues in our research.

Theories of child maltreatment will be able to better specify testable mechanisms when they identify whether theories of maltreatment are specific to maltreatment type or generalize across types, that is, physical abuse only, physical abuse and neglect, or all types of maltreatment including sexual abuse. Theories specific to abuse type, or that allow for generalization across types, would result in stronger etiological theories that can be refined through scientific investigations. In addition, understanding under which circumstances variables indicate significant risk or protection would inform theoretical advancements and interventions for populations that often present with complex typologies.

THEORY TESTING

Several additional limitations exist in child maltreatment theory as it currently exists. First, despite the fact that transactional, ecological conceptualizations of child maltreatment have been in the literature for over 20 years, the field has not moved much beyond fairly broad, non-specific conceptualizations. Understandably, examining ecological models of child maltreatment is difficult; the necessary studies would be large, and likely be the product of interdisciplinary research teams using a wide variety of methods to adequately capture different types of variables. Although studies would be expensive and time consuming, they are necessary if we are going to move beyond theoretical heuristic frameworks to testable ecological models that identify specific predictors and interrelations among predictors. In contrast, much of the recent risk factor research was not developed to test etiological theories directly. Thus, although such efforts contribute to the knowledge base, results can only offer support for model components rather than clarifying underlying mechanisms. It is no longer sufficient to explore constituent parts of child maltreatment models.

Second, development is often unaddressed by theories of child maltreatment. This is an important gap. Risk of abuse varies by age for overall harm, physical abuse, sexual abuse, emotional abuse, emotional neglect, and educational neglect (Sedlak et al., 2010). It is likely that at least some of the processes that contribute to abuse play out differently with infants as compared with adolescents. Specifying mechanisms that change over the course of children's development, as has been done with respect to the role of parenting in the etiology of conduct disorder, for example (e.g., Forgatch & Patterson, 2010), would be an important advance. Additionally, theories of intergenerational transmission could likely gain increased predictive power if the role of development in determining the impact of exposure to family of origin violence were included.

Third, existing theories are more developed with respect to risk mechanisms than protective effects. Although broad conceptualizations of child maltreatment all acknowledge the importance of protective factors, theories are silent with respect to where in the causal chain specific protective factors are hypothesized to operate. Mistakenly, protective factors are often conceptualized as a lack of risk factors instead of separate variables that influence child maltreatment in the presence of vulnerabilities. Although specific protective factors are often unidentified, resiliency studies and models (e.g., McGloin & Widom, 2001; Spaccarelli & Kim, 1995) suggest that internal and external protective factors can result in a synergistic effect, bolstering a child's functioning in the face of maltreatment. It is critical that theories of child maltreatment explain not only the occurrence of maltreatment, but also non-occurrence in the context of risk.

Fourth, there are few longitudinal studies of maltreating parenting, with only a few notable exceptions (e.g., Chaffin, et al., 1996; Erickson, Egeland, & Pianta, 1989), studying families early enough that they can truly test theories of onset of maltreatment as compared with the maintenance of maltreatment. No longitudinal studies speak to the onset of sexual abuse perpetration. This limits the field's ability to disentangle mechanisms that are truly etiological from those that might contribute to the recurrence or severity of maltreatment. Thus, most theories do not distinguish these two causal processes, yet important differences might exist between them.

Finally, theories of child maltreatment, especially those that are informed by work with families involved with child protective services, need to account for the disproportionate detection of child maltreatment by systems (e.g., child welfare) in addition to the rates of child maltreatment itself. For example, poverty is a risk factor for all forms of child maltreatment. However, it is likely also a risk factor for being detected for child maltreatment and becoming involved in the child welfare system. People with few financial resources often live in close quarters, and neighbors are more likely to overhear episodes of abuse and notice neglect than people who live in affluent neighborhoods. Low income families are also involved with many more service providers, most of whom are mandated reporters, and see them more frequently than high income families. These sorts of factors could contribute to easier detection of maltreatment in low income as compared with high-income families resulting in higher apparent rates of child maltreatment among lower income families as compared with families who are at lower risk for detection. This conflation of maltreatment risk and detection risk could result in the apparent inflation of the contribution of poverty to child maltreatment. It may be inappropriate to generalize the risk factors derived from and theories developed on families involved in the child welfare system to rest of the population. In fact, more representative samples find smaller effect sizes for the link between income and abuse (e.g., Slep & O'Leary, 2007). Disentangling these issues will enable greater precision and specificity in our theories.

SUGGESTIONS FOR THEORETICAL ADVANCES

The child maltreatment literature has a substantial research base; however, progress in the field has slowed considerably. As reviewed earlier, this change in progress can be attributed to several factors. To move forward, we need to begin to do more integrative research that cuts across focal theories and develops well-specified, but testable, integrative and comprehensive theories.

Theories in other areas (e.g., negative emotion and aggression) have informed theories of child maltreatment to some degree, but there continues to be room for improvement. Theories of anger, emotion regulation, coping, general aggression, as well as theories of other forms of family violence all can be brought to bear on child maltreatment theory. The literature clearly demonstrates that emotional and physical abuse of children is associated with emotional and physical abuse of partners (O'Leary, Slep, & O'Leary, 2000). Theories that can account for unique and shared predictors of the co-occurrence of aggression are overdue and will inform our understanding of both child and partner abuse. In the first study to investigate whether different risk profiles characterize different types of aggressors, Slep and O'Leary (2009) sampled males and females, including those who were physically aggressive only with their children or their partners, or aggressive toward both children and partners. Individuals who were aggressive toward only their partners or only their children had distinct risk profiles, with highest levels of risk on the role-specific variable sets. Role-specific variables were risk factors tied to the specific relationship. They included factors such as jealousy and partner-blaming attributions in the couple dyad and parenting style and child-blaming attributions in the parent–child dyad. With the exception of men who were physically aggressive only with their children, single role aggressive individuals' risk levels were significantly lower on role-independent (e.g., stress, depressive symptoms, alcohol problems) and unrelated role-specific risk factors than they were on role-related risk factors. Being the first work of this type, it is premature to say that profiles based on whether people perpetrate both child and partner abuse or only one form of abuse might translate not only into different risk profiles, but might also suggest different etiological theories and different interventions. However, identifying distinct patterns of behaviors in aggressive parents and partners would provide additional guidance for childcare workers who address whether there is risk for a child in a maritally violent household. Theories accounting for specific and common risk factors for child maltreatment are in their infancy, but hold promise.

Ecological theory is attractive because it incorporates many risk factors to better represent the complex nature of child maltreatment. Although ecological theory has been popular for years, researchers have typically tested components of the theory separately rather than the theory as a whole. This is a bit counter-intuitive, because the crux of ecological theory is the entire environment, its systems, and the interactions among those systems. However, the study of singular risk factors dominates the literature. Moreover, distal predictors of child maltreatment have been evaluated with a broad stroke and as a result there is little understanding of the mechanisms through which distant variables influence child maltreatment. Slep and O'Leary (2007), using a representative sample, did test an ecological model of parental aggression, finding support for an ecological approach. Risk factors from all ecological levels included in the study were retained in the model, and more distal factors were mediated through more proximal, parent–level variables. This study suggests that the field can begin to integrate disparate, focal theories of abuse and work toward an empirically supported, integrated, ecological model of child maltreatment.

Recent efforts have been made to address the lack of operational definitions. Most maltreatment definitions are not sufficiently operationalized to be reliably applied in clinical settings. By incorporating the best of existing definitions and adding operationalizations when necessary, Heyman and Slep (2006, 2009; Slep & Heyman, 2006) were able to develop definitions that could be reliably applied in both field and research settings. These definitions include both the act committed/omitted and the impact (actual or potential) on the victim. For example, child physical abuse includes two criteria, as well as a few exclusions.

> Criterion A is: "The non-accidental use of physical force on the part of a child's caregiver. Physical force includes, but is not limited to, spanking with hand; dropping; pushing; shoving; slapping; grabbing; poking; hair-pulling; scratching; pinching; restraining; shaking; throwing; biting; kicking; hitting with fist; hitting with a stick, strap, or other object; scalding; burning; poisoning; stabbing; applying force to throat; cutting off air supply; holding under water; using a weapon."
>
> Criterion B is: "Significant impact on the child involving any of the following: (1) More than inconsequential physical injury; (2) Reasonable potential for more than inconsequential physical injury given the inherent dangerousness of the act, the degree of force used and the physical environment in which the acts occurred; (3) More than inconsequential fear reaction." There are three exclusions, (1) "acts committed to protect self from imminent physical harm," which includes three specific criteria [not excerpted here], (2) (a)cts committed to protect child, others, or pet from imminent harm, as evidenced by…" two specific criteria [not excerpted here], and (3) (a)cts committed during developmentally appropriate physical play…"

A full appendix of these definitions has been published (see Slep & Heyman, 2006).

Field trials were conducted to determine the reliability of maltreatment determinations (i.e., substantiation decisions) in the field as compared with those of master reviewers. After changes to assessment, training, and changes to the decision-making committee, agreement between the master reviews and committee members increased from about 50% to over 90% (Heyman & Slep, 2006). Agreement remained at over 90% after widespread dissemination throughout the United States Air Force (Heyman & Slep, 2009). Social workers involved in the maltreatment cases reported finding the new system fair. In an unexpected finding, re-offense was cut in half. At one year, offenders whose incident met substantiation criteria went from 14 to 7%. We believe that this effect occurred through a few key mechanisms. First, alleged perpetrators are imbedded within a system that is aware of and can react to maltreatment findings. When these findings were made in a clearer, more consistent, and fairer manner, the entire process and the substantiation decisions likely take on more weight in the eyes of leadership. Because the Air Force member's supervisors are part of the proceedings, it is easy to imagine that a clearer and fairer system could result in clearer messages about inappropriate behavior being sent to involved families. These findings indicate that reliable criteria, in combination with a system viewed as just, could result in maltreatment prevention (Snarr, et al., 2011) and could better inform research.

CONCLUSION

To move into the next phase of child maltreatment theory, there needs to be a two-fold approach: use of the uniform definitions of child maltreatment and, as a result, the logical integration of tested theories. A significant barrier to the progression of the field is the lack of agreed upon definitions of child maltreatment upon which to base the research frameworks. Without clear and specific definitions, meaningful advances will be challenging and potentially unreliable. Operational definitions are needed to create a consistent system in practical and research settings. The extensive work done with military child welfare systems as discussed earlier could offer a uniform set of criteria (see Heyman & Slep, 2009; Heyman & Slep, 2006; Slep & Heyman, 2004, 2006). However, the investigation of the operational definition of child maltreatment has been limited to military populations. The utility of the criteria and systems have yet to be examined in non-military populations.

Greater integration across theoretical models of child maltreatment would improve our understanding of the etiology and maintenance of child maltreatment. Etiological models of child maltreatment have emphasized individual risk factors, and therefore, they lack the interplay of that person with the environment. This interplay is the central tenet of ecological theory and in general, the move into ecological models has been beneficial. Although ecological models of child maltreatment have been available for several decades, little progress has been made with regard to identification of risk factors specific to child maltreatment types, protective factors, and the interactions among them (e.g., Slep & O'Leary, 2007). Given the flexibility of the ecological model, it lends itself to integration with other theories of violence and maltreatment. All of the more specific theories reviewed in this chapter can be considered within the ecological framework. For example, coercion theory clearly operates at the family level. However, individual risk factors found in other specific theories (e.g., cycle of violence, anger and stress) operate at the ontogenetic level and might influence a parent's risk for engaging in coercive conflict. By carefully considering how specific theories might intersect, we can pose testable ecological models. Looking ahead, operational definitions of child maltreatment and an integration of the vast amount of literature on child maltreatment is essential to move the field forward in all domains to better identify families at-risk for perpetration.

REFERENCES

Allen, C. M., & Pothast, H. L. (1994). Distinguishing characteristics of male and female child sex abusers. *Journal of Offender Rehabilitation, 21*, 73–88.

Ammerman, R. T. (1990). Etiological models of child maltreatment: A behavioral perspective. *Behavior Modification, 14*, 230–254. doi: 10.1177/01454455900143002.

Appel, A. E., & Holden, G. W. (1998). The co-occurrence of spouse and physical child abuse: A review and appraisal. *Journal of Family Psychology, 12*, 578–599. doi: 10.1177/107755902237264.

Azar, S. T., Nix, R. L., & Makin-Byrd, K. N. (2005) Parenting schemas and the process of change. *Journal of Marital and Family Therapy, 31*, 45–58. doi: 10.1111/j.1752-0606.2005.tb01542.x.

Azar, S. T., Reitz, E. B., & Goslin, M. C. (2008). Mothering: Thinking is part of the job description: Application of cognitive views to understanding maladaptive parenting and doing intervention and prevention work. *Journal of Applied Developmental Psychology, 29*, 295–304. doi: 10.1016/j.appdev.2008.04.009.

Azar, S. T., Robinson, D. R., Hekimian, E., & Twentyman, C. T. (1984). Unrealistic expectations and problem-solving ability in maltreating and comparison mothers. *Journal of Consulting and Clinical Psychology, 52*, 687–691. doi: 10.1037/0022-006X.52.4.687.

Azar, S. T., & Rohrbeck, C. A. (1986). Child abuse and unrealistic expectations: Further validation of the Parent Opinion Questionnaire. *Journal of Consulting and Clinical Psychology, 54*, 867–868. doi: 10.1037/0022-006X.54.6.867.

Azar, S. T., & Weinzierl, K. M. (2005). Child maltreatment and childhood injury research: A cognitive behavioral approach. *Journal of Pediatric Psychology, 30*, 598–614. doi: 10.1093/jpepsy/jsi046.

Bandura, A. (1977) Self-efficacy: Toward a unifying theory of behavioral change. *Psychological Review, 84*, 191–215. doi: 10.1037/0033-295X.84.2.191.

Bandura, A. (1986) *Social Foundations of Thought and Action: A Social-Cognitive View.* Englewood Cliffs, NJ: Prentice-Hall. doi: 10.1002/9780470479216.corpsy0836.

Bandura, A., Ross, D., & Ross, S. A. (1961). Transmission of aggression through imitation of aggressive models, *Journal of Abnormal and Social Psychology, 63*, 575–582. doi: 10.1037/h0045925.

Bauer, W. D., & Twentyman, C. T. (1985). Abusing, neglectful, and comparison mothers' responses to child-related and non-child-related stressors. *Journal of Consulting and Clinical Psychology, 53*, 335–343.

Belsky, J. (1980). Child maltreatment: An ecological integration. *American Psychologist, 35*, 320–335. doi: 10.1037/0003-066X.35.4.320.

Belsky, J. (1993). Etiology of child maltreatment: A developmental–ecological analysis. *Psychological Bulletin, 114*, 413–434. doi: 10.1037/0033-2909.114.3.413.

Besharov, D. J. (1983). Child protection: Past progress, present problems and future directions. *Family Law Quarterly, 165*, 151–172. doi: 10.1016/S1359-1789(00)00021-5.

Black, D. A., Heyman, R. E., & Slep, A. M. S. (2001). Risk factors for child physical abuse. *Aggression and Violent Behavior, 6*, 121–188. doi: 10.1016/S1359-1789(00)00021-5.

Black. R., & Mayer, J. (1980). Parents with special problems: Alcohol and opiate addiction. *Child Abuse & Neglect, 4*, 45–54. http://dx.doi.org/10.1016/0145-2134(80)90033-2.

Bronfenbrenner, U. (1979). *The ecology of human development: Experiments by nature and design.* Cambridge, MA: Harvard University Press.

Brooks-Gunn, J., & Chase-Lansdale, L. (1995). Adolescent parenthood. In M. H. Bornstein (Ed.), *Handbook of parenting: Vol.3. Status and social conditions of parenting* (pp. 113– 150). Mahwah, NJ: Erlbaum.

Brown, J., Cohen, P., Johanson, J. G., & Salzinger, S. (1998). A longitudinal analysis of risk factors for child maltreatment: Findings of a 17-year prospective study of officially recorded and self-reported child abuse and neglect. *Child Abuse & Neglect, 22*, 1065–1078. doi: 10.1016/S0145-2134(98)00087-8.

Browne, K. D. (1995). Preventing child maltreatment through community nursing. *Journal of Advanced Nursing, 21*, 57–63. doi: 10.1046/j.1365-2648.1995.21010057.x.

Chaffin, M., Kelleher, K., & Hollenberg, J. (1996). Onset of physical abuse and neglect: Psychiatric, substance abuse, and social risk factors from prospective community data. *Child Abuse & Neglect, 20*, 191–203. doi: 10.1016/S0145-2134(95)00144-1.

Chilamkurti, C., & Milner, J. S. (1993). Perceptions and evaluations of child transgressions and disciplinary techniques in high- and low-risk mothers and their children. *Child Development, 64*, 1801–1814. doi: 10.1111/j.1467-8624.1993.tb04214.x.

Child Abuse Prevention and Treatment Act (CAPTA) of 1974, Pub. L. No. 93–247 (1974).

Choi, J., Jeong, B., Rohan, M., Polcari, A., & Teicher, M. (2009). Preliminary evidence for white matter tract abnormalities in young adults exposed to parental verbal abuse. *Biological Psychiatry, 65*, 227–234. http://dx.doi.org/10.1016/j.biopsych.2008.06.022.

Cicchetti, D. (2004). An odyssey of discovery: Lessons learned through three decades of research on child maltreatment. *American Psychologist, 59*, 731–741. doi: 10.1037/0003-066X.59.8.731.

Cicchetti, D., & Lynch, M. (1993). Toward an ecological/transactional model of community violence and child maltreatment: Consequences for children's development. *Psychiatry, 56*, 96–118.

Connelly, D. C., & Straus, M. A. (1992). Mother's age and risk for physical abuse. *Child Abuse & Neglect, 16*, 709–718. doi:10.1016/0145-2134(92)90107-3.

Coohey, C., & Braun, N. (1997). Toward an integrated framework for understanding child physical abuse. *Child Abuse & Neglect, 21*, 1081–1094. doi: 10.1016/S0145-2134(97)00067-7.

Corse, S. J., Schmid, K., & Trickett, P. K. (1990). Social network characteristics of mothers in abusing and nonabusing families and their relationships to parenting beliefs. *Journal of Community Psychology, 18*, 44–59. doi: 10.1002/1520-6629(199001)18:1<44::AID-JCOP2290180107>3.0.CO;2-F.

Coulton, C. J., Korbin, J. E., Su, M., & Chow, J. (1995). Community level factors and child maltreatment. *Child Development, 66*, 1262–1276. doi: 10.1111/j.1467-8624.1995.tb00934.x.

Crouch, J. L., & Behl, L. E. (2001). Relationships among parental beliefs in corporal punishment, reported stress, and physical child abuse potential. *Child Abuse & Neglect, 25*, 413–419. doi: 10.1016/S0145-2134 (00)00256-8.

Cummings, E. M., & Cicchetti, D. (1990). Attachment, depression, and the transmission of depression. In Greenberg, M. T., Cicchetti, D., and Cummings E. M. (Eds.), *Attachment during the preschool years* (pp. 339–372). Chicago: University of Chicago Press.

Dawson, B., de Armas, A., McGrath, M. L., & Kelly, J. A. (1986). Cognitive problem-solving training to improve the child-care judgment of child neglectful parents. *Journal of Family Violence, 1*, 209–226. doi: 10.1007/BF00978560

DeBellis, M. D., Chrousos, G. P., Dorn, L. D., Burke, L. Helmers, K., Kling, M. A., … Putnam, F. W. (1994). Hypothalamic-pituitary-adrenal axis dysregulation in sexually abused girls. *Journal of Clinical Endocrinology and Metabolism, 78*, 249–255. doi: 10.1210/jc.78.2.249.

DeBellis, M. D., Lefter, L., Trickett, P. K., & Putnam, F. W. (1994). Urinary catecholamine excretion in sexually-abused girls. *Journal of the American Academy of Child and Adolescent Psychiatry, 33*, 320–327. doi: 10.1097/00004583-199403000-00004.

Dixon, L., Brown, K., & Hamilton-Giachritsis, C. (2009) Patterns of risk and protective factors. *Journal of Family Violence, 24*, 111–122. doi: 10.1007/s10896-008-9215-2.

Dong, M., Dube, S. R., Felitti, V. J., Giles, W. H., & Anda, R. F. (2003). Adverse childhood experiences and self-reported liver disease: New insights into the causal pathway. *Archives of Internal Medicine*, *163*, 1949–1956. doi:10.1001/archinte.163.16.1949.

Dopke, C. A., & Milner, J. S. (2000). Impact of child noncompliance on stress appraisals, attributions, and disciplinary choices in mothers at high and low risk for child physical abuse. *Child Abuse & Neglect*, *24*, 493–504. doi: 10.1016/S0145-2134(00)00110-1.

Downey, G., & Coyne, J. (1990). Children of depressed parents. An integrative review. *Psychological Bulletin*, *108*: 50–76. doi: 10.1037/0033-2909.108.1.50.

Drake, B., & Pandey, S. (1995). Understanding the relationship between neighborhood poverty and specific types of child maltreatment. *Child Abuse & Neglect*, *20*, 1003–1018. doi:10.1016/0145-2134(96)00091-9.

Edwards, V. J., Holden, G. W., Felitti, V. J., & Anda, R. F. (2003). Relationship between multiple forms of childhood maltreatment and adult mental health in community respondents: Results from the adverse childhood experiences study. *American Journal of Psychiatry*, *160*, 1453–1460. doi: 10.1176/appi.ajp.160.8.1453.

Egeland, B., Breitenbucher, M. C., & Rosenberg, M. S. (1980). Prospective study of the significance of life stress in the etiology in child abuse. *Journal of Consulting and Clinical Psychology*, *48*, 195–205. doi: 10.1037/0022-006X.48.2.195.

Erickson, M. F., Egeland, B., & Pianta, R. (1989). The effects of maltreatment on the development of young children. In D. Cicchetti and V. Carlson (Eds.), *Child maltreatment: Theory and research on the causes and consequences of child abuse and neglect* (pp. 647–684). New York: Cambridge University Press.

Ethier, L. S., Couture, G., & Lacharite, C. (2004). Risk factors associated with the chronicity of high potential for child abuse and neglect. *Journal of Family Violence*, *19*, 13–24. doi: 10.1023/B:JOFV.0000011579.18333.c9.

Felitti, M., Vincent, J., Anda, M., Robert, F., & Nordenberg, M. (1998). Relationship of childhood abuse and household dysfunction to many of the leading causes of death in adults: The Adverse childhood experiences (ACE) study. *American Journal of Preventive Medicine*, *14*, 245–258. http://dx.doi.org.ezproxy.med.nyu.edu/10.1016/S0749-3797(98)00017-8.

Finkelhor, D. (1984). *Child Sexual Abuse: New Theory and Research*. New York: The Free Press.

Finkelhor, D., & Baron, L. (1986). Risk factors for child sexual abuse. *Journal of Interpersonal Violence*, *1*, 43–71. doi: 10.1177/088626086001001004.

Finkelhor, D. & Jones, L. M. (2006). Why have child maltreatment and child victimization declined? *Journal of Social Issues*, *62*, 685–716. doi:10.1111/j.1540-4560.2006.00483.x.

Finkelhor, D., Turner, H., Ormond, R., & Hamby, S. L. (2009) Violence, abuse, and crime exposure in a national sample of children and youth. *Pediatrics*, *124*, 1411–1423. doi:10.1542/peds.2009-0467.

Forgatch, M. S., & Patterson, G. R. (2010). Parent Management Training – Oregon Model: An intervention for antisocial behavior in children and adolescents. In J. R. Weisz & A. E. Kazdin (Eds.), *Evidence-based psychotherapies for children and adolescent* (2nd ed., pp. 159–177). New York: Guilford Press.

Fries, A. B., Shirtcliff, E. A., & Pollak, S. D. (2008). Neuroendocrine dysregulation following early social deprivation in children. *Developmental Psychobiology*, *50*, 588–599. doi: 10.1002/dev.20319.

Frodi, A. M., & Lamb, M. E. (1980). Child abusers' responses to infant smiles and cries. *Child Development*, *51*, 238–241. doi: 10.2307/1129612.

Garbarino, J. (1976). A preliminary study of some ecological correlates of child abuse: The impact of socioeconomic stress on mothers. *Child Development*, *47*, 178–185. doi: 10.2307/1128297.

Gaudin, J. M., Polansky, N. A., Kilpatrick, A. C., & Shilton, P. (1993). Loneliness, depression, stress, and social supports in neglectful families. *American Journal of Orthopsychiatry*, *63*, 597–605. doi: 10.1037/h0079475.

Gelles, R. J. (1992). Poverty and violence towards children. *American Behavioral Scientist*, *35*, 258–274. doi: 10.1177/0002764292035003005.

Gelles, R. J., & Hargreaves, E. F. (1990). Maternal employment and violence toward children. In M. A. Straus and R. J. Gelles, (Eds.), *Physical violence in American families: Risk factors and adaptation in 8,154 families* (pp. 263–277). New Brunswick, NJ: Transaction Books.

Gelles, R. J., & Straus, M. A. (1987). Is violence toward children increasing? A comparison of 1975 and 1985. National Survey Rates. *Journal of Interpersonal Violence*, *2*, 212–222. doi: 10.1177/088626087002002006.

Gil, D. G. (1971). Violence against children: Physical abuse in the United States. *The American Journal of Nursing*, *71*, 1812–1814.

Gottman, J. M., Katz, L., & Hooven, C. (1996). Parental meta-emotion philosophy and the emotional life of families: Theoretical models and preliminary data. *Journal of Family Psychology*, *10*, 243–268. doi: 10.1037/0893-3200.10.3.243.

Hansen, D., Pallotta, G., Tishelman, A., Conaway, L., & MacMillan, V. (1989). Parental problem-solving skills and child behavior problems: A comparison of physically abusive, neglectful, clinic, and community families. *Journal of Family Violence*, *4*, 353–368. doi: 10.1007/BF00978576.

Helfer, R. E., & Kempe, C. H. (Eds.). (1968). *The battered child*. Chicago: The University of Chicago Press.

Heyman, R. E., & Ezzell, C. E. (2005). Interpersonal violence. In A. P. Giardino & R. Alexander (Eds.) *Child maltreatment: Two-volume set* (pp. 639–658). St Louis, MO: G.W. Medical Publishing.

Heyman, R. E., & Slep, A. M. S. (2002). Do child abuse and interpersonal violence lead to adulthood family violence? *Journal of Marriage and Family*, *64*, 864–870. doi: 10.1111/j.1741-3737.2002.00864.x.

Heyman, R. E., & Slep, A. M. S. (2006). Creating and field-testing diagnostic criteria for partner and child maltreatment. *Journal of Family Psychology*, *20*, 397–408. doi: 10.1037/0893-3200.20.3.397.

Heyman, R. E., & Slep, A. M. S. (2009). Reliability of family maltreatment diagnostic criteria: 41 site dissemination field trial. *Journal of Family Psychology*, *23*, 905–910. doi: 10.1037/a0017011.

Hillson, J. M. C., & Kuiper, N. A. (1994). Stress and coping model of child maltreatment. *Clinical Psychology Review*, *14*, 261–285. doi: 10.1016/0272-7358(94)90025-6.

Huesmann, L. R. (1997). Observational learning of violent behavior: Social and biosocial processes. In A. Raine, P. A. Brennan, et al. (Eds.), *Biosocial bases of violence* (pp. 69–88). New York: Plenum Press.

Ito, Y., Teicher, M. H., Glod, C. A., Harper, D., Magnus, E., & Gelbard, H. A. (1993). Increased prevalence of electrophysiological abnormalities in children with psychological, physical, and sexual abuse. *Journal of Neuropsychiatry and Clinical Neurosciences*, *5*, 401–408.

Jones, L. M., & Finkelhor, D. (2003). Putting together evidence on declining trends in sexual abuse: A complex puzzle. *Child Abuse & Neglect*, *27*, 133–135. doi: 10.1016/S0145-2134(02)00534-3.

Jones, L. M., Finkelhor, D., & Halter, S. (2006). Child maltreatment trends in the 1990s: Why does neglect differ from sexual and physical abuse? *Child Maltreatment*, *11*, 107–120. doi: 10.1177/1077559505284375.

Jones, L. M., Finkelhor, D., & Kopiec, K. (2001). Why is sexual abuse declining? A survey of state child protection administrators. *Child Abuse & Neglect*, *25*, 1139–1158. doi: 10.1016/S0145-2134(01)00263-0.

Kaufman, J., & Zigler, E. (1993). The intergenerational transmission of abuse is overstated. In R. J. Gelles, & D. R. Loseke (Eds.), *Current controversies on family violence* (pp. 209–221). Newbury Park, CA: Sage.

Kelleher, K., Chaffin, M., Hollenberg, J., & Fischer, E. (1994). Alcohol and drug disorders among physically abusive and neglectful parents in a community-based sample. *American Journal of Public Health*, *84*, 1586–1590. doi: 10.2105/AJPH.84.10.1586.

Ketterlinus, R. D., Lamb, M. E., & Nitz, K. (1991). Development and ecological sources of stress among adolescent parents. *Family Relations: Interdisciplinary Journal of Applied Family Studies*, *40*, 435–441.

Kinard, E. M. (1982). Child abuse and depression: Cause or consequences? *Child Welfare*, *7*, 403–413.

Kolko, D. J. (1996). Clinical monitoring of treatment course in child physical abuse: Psychometric characteristics and treatment comparisons. *Child Abuse & Neglect*, *20*, 23–43. doi:10.1016/0145-2134(95)00113-1.

Koyabashi, J., Sales, B. D., Becker, J. V., Figueredo, A. J., & Kaplan, M. S. (1995). Perceived parental deviance, parent–child bonding, child abuse, and child sexual aggression. *Sexual Abuse: A Journal of Research and Treatment*, *7*, 25–44. doi: 10.1177/107906329500700105.

Kruttschnitt, C., McLeod, J. D., & Dornfeld, M. (1994). The economic environment of child abuse. *Social Problems*, *41*, 201–217. doi: 10.2307/3096935.

Larrance, D. T., & Twentyman, C. T. (1983). Maternal attributions and child abuse. *Journal of Abnormal Psychology*, *92*, 449–457. doi: 10.1037/0021-843X.92.4.449.

Lutzker, J. R. (1984). Project 12-Ways: Treating child abuse and neglect from an ecobehavioral perspective. In R. F. Dangel & R. A. Polster (Eds.), *Parent training: Foundations of research and practice* (pp. 260–297). New York: Guilford Press.

Mash, E. J., Johnston, C., & Kovitz, K. (1983). A comparison of the mother–child interactions of physically abused and non-abused children during play and task situations. *Journal of Clinical Child Psychology*, *12*, 337–346. doi:10.1080/15374418309533154.

McGloin, J. M. & Widom, C. S. (2001). Resilience among abused and neglected children grown up. *Development and Psychopathology*, *13*, 1021–1038. doi: 10.1017/S095457940100414X.

Milner, J. S. (1993). Social information processing and physical child abuse. *Clinical Psychology Review*, *13*, 275–294. doi: 10.1016/0272-7358(93)90024-G.

Milner, J. S. (2000). Social information processing and child physical abuse: Theory and research. In D. J. Hersen (Ed.), *Nebraska symposium on motivation* (Vol. 45). *Motivation and child maltreatment* (pp. 39–84). Lincoln, NE: University of Nebraska.

Milner, J. S., & Chilamkurti, C. (1991). Physical child abuse perpetrator characteristics: A review of the literature. *Journal of Interpersonal Violence, 6*, 346–367. doi: 10.1177/088626091006003007.

Milner, J. S., Halsey, L. B., & Fultz, J. (1995). Empathic responsiveness and affective reactivity to infant stimuli in high and low-risk for physical child abuse mothers. *Child Abuse & Neglect, 19*, 767–780. doi: 10.1016/0145-2134(95)00035-7.

Milner, J. S., & Robertson, K. R. (1990). Comparison of physical child abusers, intrafamilial sexual child abusers, and child neglecters. *Journal of Interpersonal Violence, 5*, 37–48. doi: 10.1177/088626090005001003.

Mineka, S., & Hamida, S. (1998). Observational and nonconscious learning. In W. O'Donohue (Ed.), *Learning and behavior therapy* (pp. 421–439). Needham Heights, MA: Allyn and Bacon.

Murphy, J. M., Jellinek, M., Quinn, D., Smith, G., Poitrast, F. G., & Goshko, M. (1991). Substance abuse and serious child mistreatment: Prevalence, risk, and outcome in a court sample. *Child Abuse & Neglect, 15*, 197–211. doi: 10.1016/0145-2134(91)90065-L.

Nayak, M. B., & Milner, J. S. (1998). Neuropsychological functioning: Comparison of mothers at high and low risk for child physical abuse. *Child Abuse & Neglect, 22*, 687–703.

O'Leary, K. D., Slep, A. M. S., & O'Leary, S. G. (2000). Co-occurrence of partner and parent aggression: Research and treatment implications. *Behavior Therapy, 31*, 631–648. doi: 10.1016/S0005-7894(00)80035-0.

Oldershaw, L., Walters, G. C., & Hall, D. K. (1986). Control strategies and noncompliance in abusive mother–child dyads: An observational study. *Child Development, 57*, 722–732. doi: 10.2307/1130349.

Olds, D. L., Henderson, C. R., Chamberlin, R., & Tatelbaum, R. (1986). Preventing child abuse and neglect: A randomized trial of nurse home visitation. *Pediatrics, 78*, 65–79. PMID: 2425334.

Patterson, G. R. (1976). The aggressive child: Victim and architect of a coercive system. In E. J. Mash, L. A. Hamerlynck, & L. C. Handy (Eds.). *Behavior modification and families* (pp. 267–316). New York: Brunner/Mazel.

Patterson, G. R. (1982). *Coercive family process*. Eugene, OR: Castalia.

Pelton, L. (1994). The role of material factors in child abuse and neglect. In G. Melton & F. Barry (Eds.). *Protecting children from abuse and neglect: Foundations for a new national strategy* (pp. 131–181). New York: Guilford Press.

Pfohl, S. J. (1977). The "discovery" of child abuse. *Social Problems, 24*, 310–323.

Pianta, B. (1984). Antecedents of child abuse. *School Psychology International, 5*, 151–160. doi: 10.1177/0143034384053005.

Pianta, R., Egeland, B., & Erikson, M. F. (1989). The antecedents of maltreatment: Results of the Mother–Child Interaction Research Project. In D. Cicchetti & V. Carlson (Eds.), *Child maltreatment: Theory and research on the causes and consequences of child abuse and neglect* (pp. 203–253). New York: Cambridge University Press. doi: 10.1017/CBO9780511665707.008.

Pollak, S. D., Nelson, C. A., Schlaak, M. F., Roeber, B. J., Wewerka, S. S., Wiik, K. L.,... Gunnar, M. R. (2010). Neurodevelopmental effects of early deprivation in postinstitutionalized children. *Child Development, 81*, 224–236. doi: 10.1111/j.1467-8624.2009.01391.x.

Putnam, F. W. (2003). Ten-year research update review: Child sexual abuse. *Journal of the American Academy of Child and Adolescent Psychiatry, 42*, 269–278. doi: 10.1097/00004583-200303000-00006.

Reid, J., Patterson, G. R., & Snyder, J. (2002). *Antisocial behavior in children and adolescents*. Washington, DC: American Psychological Association.

Rind, B., Tromovitch, P., & Bauserman, R. (1998). A meta-analytic examination of assumed properties of child sexual abuse using college samples. *Psychological Bulletin, 124*, 22–53. doi: 10.1037/0033-2909.124.1.22

Rodriguez, C. M. (2008). Ecological predictors of disciplinary style and child abuse potential in a Hispanic and Anglo-American sample. *Journal of Child and Family Studies, 17*, 336–352. doi: 10.1007/s10826-007-9145-2.

Rodriguez, C. M., & Green, A. J. (1997). Parenting stress and anger expression as predictors of child abuse potential. *Child Abuse & Neglect, 21*, 367–377. doi: 10.1016/S0145-2134(96)00177-9.

Rosenberg, M. S., & Reppucci, N. D. (1983). Abusive mothers: Perceptions of their own and their children's behavior. *Journal of Consulting and Clinical Psychology, 51*, 674–682. doi: 10.1037/0022-006X.51.5.674.

Ross, S. M. (1996). Risk of physical abuse to children of spouse abusing parents. *Child Abuse & Neglect, 20*, 589–598. doi: 10.1016/0145-2134(96)00046-4.

Schumacher, J. A., Slep, A. M. S., & Heyman, R. E. (2001). Risk factors for child neglect. *Aggression and Violent Behavior, 6*, 231–254. http://dx.doi.org/10.1016/S1359-1789(00)00024-0.

Scott, D. (1992). Early identification of maternal depression as a strategy in the prevention of child abuse. *Child Abuse and Neglect, 16*, 345–358. doi: 10.1016/0145-2134(92)90044-R.

Sedlak, A. J. (1997). Risk factors for the occurrence of child abuse and neglect. *Journal of Aggression, Maltreatment, and Trauma, 1*, 1490–187. doi:10.1300/J146v01n01_09.

Sedlak, A. J., & Broadhurst, D. D. (1996). Third National Incidence Study of Child Abuse and Neglect: Final report. Washington, DC: US Department of Health and Human Services, Administration for Children and Families, National Center on Child Abuse and Neglect.

Sedlak, A. J., Mettenburg, J., Basena, M., Petta, I., McPherson, K., Greene, A., & Li, S. (2010). *Fourth national incidence study of child abuse and neglect (NIS–4): Report to Congress*. Washington, DC: U. S. Department of Health and Human Services, Administration for Children and Families. Retrieved from http://www.childwelfare.gov/pubs/issue_briefs/cm_prevention.pdf.

Starzyk, K. B., & Marshall, W. L. (2003). Childhood family and personological risk factors for sexual offending. *Aggression and Violent Behavior, 8*, 93–105. http://dx.doi.org/10.1016/S1359-1789(01)00053-2.

Slep, A. M. S. & Heyman, R. E. (2004). Severity of partner and child maltreatment: Reliability of scales used in America's largest child and family protection agency. *Journal of Family Violence, 19*, 95–106. doi: 10.1023/B:JOFV.0000019840.36496.a1.

Slep, A. M. S., & Heyman, R. E. (2006). Creating and field-testing child maltreatment definitions: Improving the reliability of substantiation determinations. *Child Maltreatment, 11*, 397–408. doi:10.1037/0893-3200.20.3.397.

Slep, A. M. S., & O'Leary, S. G. (2005). Parent and partner violence in families with young children: Rates, patterns, and connections. *Journal of Consulting and Clinical Psychology. 73*, 435–444. doi: 10.1037/0022-006X.73.3.435.

Slep, A. M. S., & O'Leary, S. G. (2007). Multivariate models of mothers' and fathers' aggression toward their children. *Journal of Consulting and Clinical Psychology, 75*, 739–751. doi: 10.1037/0022-006X.75.5.739.

Slep, A. M. S., & O'Leary, S. G. (2009). Distinguishing risk profiles among parent-only, partner-only, and dually-perpetrating physical aggressors. *Journal of Family Psychology, 23*, 705–716. doi: 10.1037/a0016474.

Snarr, J. D., Heyman, R. E., Slep, A. M. S., Malik, J., & USAF Family Advocacy Program. (2011). Preventive impacts of reliable family maltreatment criteria. *Journal of Consulting and Clinical Psychology, 79*, 826–833. doi:10.1037/a0025994.

Snyder, J. (2002). Reinforcement and coercion mechanisms in the development of antisocial behavior: Peer relationships. In J. B. Reid, G. R. Patterson, & J. Snyder (Eds.), *Antisocial behavior in children and adolescents: A developmental analysis and model for intervention* (pp. 101–122). Washington, DC: American Psychological Association. doi:10.1037/10468-005.

Spaccarelli, S., & Kim, S. (1995). Resilience criteria and factors associated with resilience in sexually abused girls. *Child Abuse & Neglect, 19*, 1171–1182. doi: 10.1016/0145-2134(95)00077-L.

Spinetta, J. J. (1978). Parental personality factors in child abuse. *Journal of Consulting and Clinical Psychology, 46*, 1409–1414. doi: 10.1037/0022-006X.46.6.1409.

Stermac, L. E., & Segal, Z. V. (1989). Adult sexual contact with children. An examination of cognitive factors. *Behavioural Therapy, 20*, 573– 584. http://dx.doi.org/10.1016/S0005-7894(89)80135-2.

Stevens-Simon, C., Nelligan, D., & Kelly, L. (2001). Adolescents at risk for mistreating their children: 1: Prenatal identification. *Child Abuse & Neglect, 6*, 737–751. doi: 10.1016/S0145-2134(01)00236-8.

Stith, S. M., Liu, T., Davies, L. C., Boykin, E. L., Alder, M. C., Harris, J. M., … Dees, J. E. M. E. G. (2009). Risk factors in child maltreatment: A meta-analytic review of the literature. *Aggression and Violent Behavior, 14*, 13–29. doi: 10.1016/j.avb.2006.03.006.

Stockhammer, T. F., Salzinger, S., Feldman, R. S., & Mojica, E. (2001). Assessment of the effect of physical child abuse within an ecological framework: Measurement issues. *Journal of Community Psychology, 29*, 319–344. doi: 10.1002/jcop.1020.

Straus, M. A. (1994). *Beating the devil out of them: Corporal punishment in American families*. New York: Lexington Books.

Straus, M. A., Gelles, R. J., & Steinmetz, S. K. (1980). *Behind closed doors: Violence in the American family*. Garden City: Doubleday, Anchor Press.

Straus, M. A., & Smith, C. (1990). Family patterns and child abuse. In M. A. Straus & R. J. Gelles (Eds.), *Physical Violence in American families: Risk factors and adaptations to violence in 8,145 Families*. New Brunswick, NJ: Transaction Publishers.

Swick, K. J., & Williams, R. D. (2006). An analysis of Bronfenbrenner's bio-ecological perspective for early childhood educators: Implications for working with families experiencing stress. *Early Childhood Education Journal*, *33*, 371–378. doi: 10.1007/s10643-006-0078-y.

Teicher, M. H., Dumont, N. L., Ito, Y., Vaituzis, C., Giedd, J. N., & Andersen, S. L. (2004). Childhood neglect is associated with reduced corpus callosum area. *Biological Psychiatry*, *56*, 80–85. doi: 10.1016/j.biopsych.2004.03.016.

Trickett, P. K., & Kuczynski, L. (1986). Children's misbehaviors and parental discipline strategies in abusive and nonabusive families. *Development Psychology*, *22*, 115–123. doi: 10.1037/0012-1649.22.1.115.

Twentyman, C. T., & Plotkin, R. C. (1982). Unrealistic expectations of parents who maltreat their children: An educational deficit that pertains to child development. *Journal of Clinical Psychology*, *38*, 497–503. doi: 10.1002/1097-4679(198207)38:3<497::AID-JCLP2270380306>3.0.CO;2-X.

Ward, T., & Keenan, T. (1999). Child Molesters' Implicit Theories. *Journal of Interpersonal Violence, 14*(8), 821–838. doi: 10.1177/088626099014008003.

Whipple, E. E., & Webster-Stratton, C. (1991). The role of parental stress in physically abusive families. *Child Abuse & Neglect*, *15*, 279–291. doi: 10.1016/0145-2134(91)90072-L.

Whitaker, D. J., Le, B., Hanson, R. K., Baker, C. K., McMahon, P. M., Ryan, G., … Donovan, R. (2008). Risk factors for the perpetration of child sexual abuse: A review and meta- analysis. *Child Abuse & Neglect*, *32*, 529–54. doi: 10.1016/j.chiabu.2007.08.005.

Williamson, J. M., Bourduin, C. M., & Howe, B. A. (1991). The ecology of adolescent maltreatment: A multilevel examination of adolescent physical abuse, sexual abuse, and neglect. *Journal of Consulting and Clinical Psychology*, *59*, 449–457. doi: 10.1037/0022-006X.59.3.449.

Wolfe, D. A. (1987). *Child abuse: Implications for child development and psychopathology* (Vol. 10). Newbury Park, CA: Sage.

Wolfner, G. D., & Gelles, R. J. (1993). A profile of violence toward children: A national study. *Child Abuse & Neglect*, *17*, 197–212. doi: 10.1016/0145-2134(93)90040-C.

13 The Effects of Interparental Conflict on Children

John Grych, Claire Oxtoby, and Mark Lynn

Children exposed to hostile and aggressive conflict between their caregivers are at increased risk for a wide range of psychological and physical health problems (for reviews, see Buehler, et al., 1997; Cummings & Davies, 2002). Over the past two decades, tremendous progress has been made in understanding how interparental conflict gives rise to adjustment problems in children. These advances reflect the confluence of several theoretical perspectives that provide a multifaceted description of the processes that underlie the link between conflict and child maladjustment. The conceptual models salient in this area include both broad theoretical frameworks and domain-specific models tailored to the unique context of parental conflict. In this chapter, we highlight the dominant theoretical models that have guided research on the impact of interparental hostility and aggression on children, examine their empirical support, and identify directions for the continued evolution of research in this area. But first, we describe how we define the constructs that the chapter will focus on.

Although research in this area is based primarily on samples of married parents, we will use the term "interparental" rather than "marital" because conflict between a child's caregivers is assumed to be distressing for children whether they are married or not. This assumption has not been tested directly, however, and the question of whether the nature of the caregivers' relationship influences the impact of interparental aggression on children deserves consideration, especially because families with two married parents and their biological children now are in the minority in the US. We will use the term "conflict" to refer to the overt manifestation of disagreements between caregivers, rather than the existence of those disagreements. As discussed below, conflicts become increasingly stressful for children as parental behavior becomes more hostile, demeaning, or threatening, and so we will use the terms conflict and aggression interchangeably. Although verbal aggression occasionally may escalate to low levels of physical aggression in some couples, we will reserve the term "violence" for more severe physical aggression in order to distinguish families exhibiting normative levels of conflict from those characterized by frequent and severe violence.

KEY ISSUES IN STUDYING INTERPARENTAL CONFLICT AND CHILD ADJUSTMENT

All couples have occasional disagreements or differences of opinion, but it is the way that parents manage their disagreements, rather than the existence of discord *per se*, that affects children's risk for maladjustment (e.g., Buehler, et al., 1997; Grych & Fincham, 2001). As couples' behavior becomes increasingly hostile and aggressive, children are more likely to exhibit problems across a range of domains. Research documenting the associations between interparental conflict and child functioning is extensive, and to provide a reasonably concise review of this work we will focus on findings regarding the parameters of the link between conflict and children's functioning, the effects of conflict on children's responses to later interactions, and potential mediators of the association between parental conflict and child adjustment.

ASSOCIATIONS BETWEEN CONFLICT AND CHILD ADJUSTMENT

Early research investigating the impact of interparental conflict on children focused on describing the nature of this association. Most of these studies utilized parental reports of conflict behaviors ranging from civil discussion to physical violence, and broad indicators of child adjustment problems. Buehler and her colleagues (1997) summarized this work in a meta-analytic review of 68 empirical studies. They reported a mean effect size of 0.32 between interparental conflict and child adjustment, which is between a small and moderate effect (Cohen, 1977), and slightly larger than the effect size of divorce on child adjustment (0.29; Amato, 2001). This meta-analysis also examined particular dimensions of interparental conflict. It showed that overt expressions of hostility ($d = 0.35$) are more closely associated with adjustment problems than the frequency with which conflict occurs ($d = 0.19$), and that cooperative, constructive resolution of discord predicts better child adjustment ($d = 0.30$). Associations with internalizing and externalizing problems were of similar magnitude, as were effect sizes for boys and girls. Most studies included in the meta-analysis limited their assessment of child functioning to internalizing and externalizing problems, but other investigations indicate that exposure to higher levels of interparental aggression also is associated with greater aggression in peer relationships (e.g., Marcus, Lindahl, & Malik, 2001) and adolescent dating relationships (e.g., Kinsfogel & Grych, 2004), poorer school achievement (e.g., Harold, Aitken, & Shelton, 2007), and poorer physical health (e.g., El-Sheikh, Cummings, Kouros, Elmore-Staton, & Buckhalt, 2008).

Although compelling, most of these findings reflect concurrent associations and therefore do not prove that exposure to conflict *causes* adjustment problems. In addition, the level of conflict in couples' relationships covaries with other family processes associated with child adjustment, including marital satisfaction, child maltreatment, and divorce, that also could explain the association with maladjustment. Thus, to determine if interparental aggression actually affects children's development, it is critical to investigate whether exposure to conflict is related to increases in maladjustment over time, and if it uniquely predicts child functioning after accounting for other types of family stressors.

There were relatively few longitudinal studies conducted at the time of Buehler and colleagues' (1997) meta-analysis, but the effect size from these studies was slightly but not significantly smaller than for cross-sectional studies ($d = 0.28$). Since then, several longitudinal analyses have been conducted, and they show that exposure to higher levels of interparental conflict predicts increases in adjustment problems over 1–3 years (e.g., Cui, Conger, & Lorenz, 2005; Grych, Harold, & Miles, 2003; Shelton & Harold, 2008; Schoppe-Sullivan, Schermerhorn, & Cummings, 2007). Although temporal associations are not definitive proof of causation, they provide stronger grounds for inferring that interparental conflict has adverse effects on children's development.

Interparental aggression also has been shown to uniquely predict children's adjustment after accounting for the level of satisfaction in the parents' relationship, parent–child conflict, and family structure (divorced vs. intact) (Grych & Fincham, 2001). Further, there is evidence that observing parental conflicts has more deleterious effects than conflict that occurs outside of children's awareness (e.g., Emery, 1982; Hetherington, 1989). Child reports of the level of conflict they have witnessed better predict their adjustment than parental reports of conflict (Grych & Fincham, 1993), and the few studies that have distinguished whether conflict occurs in front of children or not indicates that witnessing parental anger and aggression is more closely related to adjustment problems than conflict that occurs "behind closed doors" (e.g., Hetherington, 1989). These findings underscore the importance of understanding children's experiences of conflict and investigating what happens when they witness a hostile or aggressive parental interaction.

CHILDREN'S RESPONSES TO CONFLICT

In addition to reliably predicting adjustment problems, witnessing interparental hostility and aggression has an impact on how children respond to later conflictual interactions between their caregivers. Unlike other types of violence (e.g., media), which tend to lead to desensitization over time, children exposed to greater interparental aggression tend to exhibit *more* distress and physiological arousal and report *greater* threat in response to conflict over time (e.g., Cummings, Pelligrini, Notarioius, & Cummings, 1989; El-Sheikh, 1994; Garcia, O'Hearn, Margolin, & John, 1997; Grych, 1998). Documentation of this sensitization effect has led to conceptual and empirical efforts to understand what happens when children witness conflict between their caregivers and how their experiences in the moment may lead to broader adjustment problems. Several mechanisms have been proposed to account for sensitization and to explain how children's responses to conflict at the time may undermine their development; because the proposed processes are associated with particular conceptual models, we will briefly summarize data on hypothesized mediators and then discuss them in greater detail in the Theoretical Models section below.

MEDIATORS OF THE RELATION BETWEEN INTERPARENTAL CONFLICT AND CHILD ADJUSTMENT

Initially, it was hypothesized that interparental conflict affected children by undermining the quality of parent–child relationships. Parents in contentious relationships tend to be less attentive to or engaged with their children and to exhibit greater hostility and aggression toward them (for reviews, see Erel & Burman, 1995; Grych, 2002). Studies investigating links among parental conflict, parenting, and adjustment indicate that parenting partially mediates the association between conflict and child adjustment, but that interparental conflict continues to predict child functioning even after parenting difficulties have been taken into account (e.g., Doyle & Markowitz, 2005; Harold & Conger, 1997; Schoppe-Sullivan, Schermerhorn, & Cummings, 2007).

Efforts to understand the effects of witnessing interparental aggression have since expanded to identify a range of potential mediating processes. This research was summarized in a meta-analysis of 71 studies that examined relations among interparental conflict, one or more of the proposed mediators, and children's internalizing and externalizing problems (Rhoades, 2008). The largest number of studies ($n = 50$) have examined cognitive factors, including children's appraisals of threat and self-blame and perceptions of control. Across all cognitive variables, the effect sizes were $r = 0.34$ for internalizing problems and $r = 0.21$ for externalizing problems. A total of 22 studies examined relations between coping behaviors and adjustment. There were a sufficient number of studies to compute effect sizes for two types of behavioral strategies: involvement in parental conflicts was more strongly related to internalizing ($r = 0.29$) than externalizing ($r = 0.15$) problems, whereas avoidance was significantly related only to internalizing problems ($r = 0.26$) (externalizing $r = 0.04$). Eighteen studies assessed children's negative affective responses to conflict, with reported effect sizes of $r = 0.31$ for internalizing problems and $r = 0.15$ with externalizing problems. There were only six studies that assessed physiological processes, and they produced significant but smaller effects: the effect size was $r = 0.14$ for internalizing problems and $r = 0.11$ for externalizing problems. All of the proposed mediators had significantly stronger relations with internalizing than externalizing problems. Cognitions and emotions both had significantly stronger associations with internalizing problems than did behavioral and physiological variables, and cognitive factors had stronger associations with externalizing than the other three types of mediators. Most of the effect sizes were larger for older than younger children, but there was little evidence of reliable differences in effect sizes between boys and girls.

Thus, there is empirical support for several factors proposed to mediate the impact of interparental conflict on children, including cognitive, emotional, behavioral, and physiological constructs. In the next section, we discuss the conceptual models that provide the theoretical basis for understanding how these factors may contribute to adjustment problems in children from highly conflictual homes.

THEORETICAL MODELS OF THE EFFECTS OF INTERPARENTAL CONFLICT ON CHILDREN

SOCIAL LEARNING THEORY

The first conceptual model that was systematically applied to studying the effects of conflict on children was *social learning theory* (Bandura, 1986), which proposes that children who witness their parents engaging in hostile or aggressive behavior learn to be aggressive through modeling and vicarious reinforcement. This type of learning does not simply involve children acquiring and repeating specific behaviors that they observe, but rather the development of knowledge and beliefs about what behavior is appropriate or effective in a particular context. According to this perspective, children exposed to elevated levels of conflict and aggression may come to view aggression as a normative or justifiable way to resolve conflict, express anger, or exert control over another person, particularly if it is seen as effective. These beliefs in turn make it more likely that youths will engage in aggression when they are in similar situations, such as conflicts with peers or dating partners. In addition, the failure to model more constructive strategies for managing conflict and anger may result in children developing a repertoire of behaviors dominated by aggressive behavior.

The correlations reported between parent and child aggression are consistent with a modeling hypothesis, but they do not provide direct or specific evidence that modeling is the mechanism driving children's behavior. As we discuss below, other conceptual approaches offer alternative explanations for why children from highly conflictual homes would be more aggressive toward others. Several studies have tested a more specific modeling hypothesis, that children are more likely to imitate the conflict behavior of the same-sex parent, but they have produced inconsistent findings. For example, whereas Crockenberg and Forgays (1996) found that boys' aggression was more closely related to their fathers' conflict behavior than to their mothers, with the opposite pattern holding for girls, Crockenberg and Langrock (2001) reported no differences in the strength of the associations between children's aggression and their same- and opposite-sex parent. The question of whether aggressive conflict behavior is perceived to be more effective by children from high conflict homes has not been examined directly, but there is substantial evidence that youths exposed to higher levels of interparental discord view aggression in close relationships as more acceptable. Beliefs about the justifiability of aggression in turn have been found to mediate the association between interparental aggression and aggression towards peers (e.g., Marcus, et al., 2001) and dating partners, especially for boys (Foshee, Linder, MacDougall, & Bangidwala, 2001; Kinsfogel & Grych, 2004).

Social learning theory offers a plausible explanation for why children exposed to higher levels of interparental conflict would become more aggressive, and the empirical evidence suggests that children from highly discordant families are more likely to view aggressive behavior as more acceptable and to engage in more aggressive behavior toward others. However, observational learning does not account for the elevated levels of anxiety and depressive symptoms seen in these children, and does not address one of the most salient aspects of witnessing conflict: the level of distress it causes most children. The next perspective focuses explicitly on interparental conflict as a stressor and identifies how children's responses to conflict could lead to a range of adverse developmental outcomes.

STRESS AND COPING THEORY

The negative affect that children typically express when observing their caregivers engaged in angry and aggressive behavior towards each other underscores the stressful nature of this experience (e.g., Cummings, Goeke-Morey, & Papp, 2003; Cummings, Zahn-Waxler, & Radke-Yarrow, 1981). A study of 2,480 ethnically diverse 5th graders found that "having parents fight in front of you" was judged to be the third most distressing event on a list of common childhood stressors (parental separation was #1; fighting *with* parents was #6; Lewis, Siegel, & Lewis, 1984).

Conceptualizing interparental conflict as a stressful event provides a lens for understanding both children's immediate reaction to conflict and its broader effects on their functioning. Decades of research show that the perception of stress engages cognitive, emotional, behavioral, and physiological processes designed to mobilize individuals' resources and respond adaptively. Some of these responses may be effective for coping with parental conflict, but others can have short- and long-term adverse consequences (for a review, see Kerig, 2001).

A variety of *stress and coping theories* have been developed, but the most influential in the present context is Lazarus and Folkman's model (1984; Lazarus, 1991). This theory proposes that individuals' subjective perception of an event, or appraisal, determines the impact of the event. According to this model, when a potentially stressful event occurs, individuals first appraise whether there is something "at stake" for them, or is relevant to their goals. If so, they evaluate their ability to respond effectively to it, and then engage in efforts to manage or cope with the threat. Lazarus and Folkman (1984) identified two primary classes of coping responses: problem-focused, which are efforts to act on and change the stressor, and emotion-focused, which are inwardly-directed efforts to regulate their emotional reactions (and often involve withdrawal from the stressful situation). Lazarus and Folkman's model has been valuable for understanding how adults cope in an array of stressful situations, and Grych and Fincham (1990) drew on it in developing a framework for understanding children's responses to interparental conflict.

Cognitive–Contextual Framework

The *cognitive–contextual framework* (Grych & Fincham, 1990), describes a set of processes proposed to guide children's responses to hostile and aggressive interactions between their caregivers. It holds that when children witness a parental disagreement, they attempt to understand what is happening, why it is happening, and what they can do about it. Conflictual interactions between the parents can be threatening for a number of reasons (also see Crockenberg & Langrock, 2001). Children have a stake in the stability and harmony of family relationships, and conflict can evoke fears of parents hurting each other, separating, or turning their anger toward children. More fundamentally, the expression of anger is salient even to very young children (e.g., Terwogt & Harris, 1993), and so overt hostility by their caregivers is likely to be distressing regardless of children's ability to understand the causes and consequences of the anger. Perceiving threat engages further attempts to understand and respond to the interaction. Aversive or upsetting events generally elicit efforts to understand their causes (e.g., Van den Broek, 1997), and Grych and Fincham (1990) proposed that children are especially sensitive to determining whether they played some role in causing parental conflicts. Self-blame appraisals have been linked both to greater negative affect and increased motivation to intervene in the conflict (e.g., Grych & Fincham, 1993). Children's coping efforts in turn are proposed to be shaped by their attributions, coping efficacy, and emotions.

The appraisal process described in the cognitive–contextual framework is informed by social information processing models as well as Lazarus and Folkman's work, but affect also plays an important role in shaping children's evaluations of conflict (Grych & Cardoza-Fernandes, 2001). Emotions serve a signaling function, alerting and orienting the individual to potential threats or benefits in the environment, and motivating behavior intended to protect or promote the individual's well-being (e.g., Campos, Campos, & Barrett, 1989). Threat appraisals involve both the perception of potential danger and the emotional experience of fear, and attributions of self-blame include both a sense of responsibility for causing or resolving the conflict and feelings of shame and sadness. Thus, the cognitive and affective dimensions of appraisals are inextricably linked and together shape the meaning of the event for children.

The appraisals that children make in a given situation are proposed to be influenced by two factors: the way that conflict is expressed (e.g., level of anger and aggression, content, resolution) and the broader context in which it occurs. Children report greater threat and lower coping efficacy as disagreements get increasingly hostile, and more self-blame when the topic concerns the child or child raising issues (e.g., Grych, 1998; Grych & Fincham, 1993). How the conflict is resolved also is important, and it appears that the degree of negative affect expressed is more salient to children than whether parents actually come to an agreement on the points of contention (e.g., Shifflett-Simpson & Cummings, 1996). Salient aspects of the "context" proposed to shape children's perceptions include their prior exposure to parental discord, the emotional climate of the family, and the quality of parent–child relationships, and all have been shown to predict their appraisals (e.g., DeBoard, Fosco, Raynor, & Grych, 2010; Fosco & Grych, 2007; Grych, 1998). For example, children report greater self-blame in families characterized by high levels of negative affect and low levels of positive affect (Fosco & Grych, 2007) and by more coercive and controlling parent–child relationships (DeBoard, et al., 2010), and less threat when they have a more secure relationship with their parents (DeBoard, et al., 2010). Similarly, the sensitization effect can be understood as a result of children's prior experiences with parental conflict shaping or priming their appraisals when new disagreements arise: children who have witnessed angry, aggressive parental interactions are more likely to expect conflict to escalate, and to report greater threat and negative affect (Grych, 1998; Grych & Cardoza-Fernandes, 2001).

Finally, the cognitive-contextual framework holds that children who experience greater threat and self-blame when conflict occurs are at risk for developing adjustment problems (Grych & Fincham, 1990). When conflict is frequent, these appraisals are predicted to lead to elevated levels of anxiety and depression, and if they result in children becoming involved in their parents' disagreements, greater disruptive and aggressive behavior. Appraisals of threat and self-blame have been supported as pathways through which conflict leads to greater internalizing and externalizing problems in both cross-sectional (e.g., Grych, Fincham, Jouriles, & McDonald, 2000; Fosco & Grych, 2008) and longitudinal studies (e.g., Grych, Harold, & Miles, 2003; Shelton & Harold, 2008). In addition to computing an effect size averaged across different types of cognitions, Rhoades' (2008) meta-analysis summarized findings from 22 studies that examined specific associations between threat and self-blame appraisals and child adjustment (accounting for the level of conflict they had witnessed). These analyses showed that threat and self-blame each had significant, moderate-sized partial effects on internalizing and small but significant associations with externalizing problems. (rs .21–.40).

Emotional Responses to Stress

Although emotions are included in the cognitive-contextual framework, less attention was paid to their role in shaping children's responses than to cognitive factors. Crockenberg and Langrock (2001) developed a model that focused on the specific emotions that children experience during conflict and their implications for immediate responding and longer-term functioning. They argue that the emotions individuals experience in response to a threat reflect the meaning of the situation (also see Mandler, 1975; Stein & Levine, 1987); more specifically, they reflect their evaluation of how the event impacts important goals. For example, fear arises when a goal is threatened but is not yet lost, sadness when the goal is seen as lost, and anger when the potential for loss motivates an active attempt to regain the goal. This model has generated few empirical tests, but Crockenberg and her colleagues conducted two studies that showed that fearful responses to interparental conflict were more closely related to internalizing problems and angry responses were more closely related to externalizing problems (Crockenberg & Forgays, 1996; Crockenberg & Langrock, 2001), Rhoades' meta-analysis included nine studies that assessed associations between emotions and adjustment after accounting for children's exposure to conflict, but did not distinguish among different kinds of emotions. She reported that negative affect had a partial effect size of $r = 0.24$ for internalizing problems and $r = 0.16$ for externalizing problems.

Biological Responses to Stress

Contemporary stress and coping models also place increasing emphasis on the biological underpinnings of the human stress response and their consequences for functioning. Perception of a stressor engages multiple physiological systems, including the hypothalamic–pituitary–adrenal axis (HPA axis), sympathetic (SNS) and parasympathetic branches (PNS) of the autonomic nervous system, and neurotransmitters such as serotonin and norepinephrine, in a coordinated effort to mobilize the individual to respond to the potential threat (e.g., DeBellis, 2001). Several of these processes have been studied in relation to interparental conflict (e.g., HPA, SNS), and this research supports the hypothesis that they may mediate or moderate the effects of conflict on children (e.g., Davies, Sturge-Apple, Cicchetti, & Cummings, 2007; El-Sheik & Whitson, 2006; Katz & Gottman, 1995). Most studies of these biological stress processes have examined them in isolation, though there are emerging efforts to understand more complex associations among them (e.g., El-Sheikh, Erath, Buckhalt, Granger, & Mize, 2008; El-Sheikh, et al., 2009).

The stress and coping perspective thus identifies multiple processes that occur in response to threatening or upsetting events that may explain how children's exposure to interparental conflict leads to sensitization and to broader problems in adjustment. The cognitive–contextual framework places particular emphasis on children's efforts to make sense of angry and aggressive interactions, but their efforts to cope with this stressor involve emotional, behavioral, and physiological processes as well. However, these models are less clear about why interparental conflict is such a significant stressor for children. The next conceptual approach offers an answer.

ATTACHMENT THEORY

Bowlby (1969) argues that infants have a biologically-based need to seek protection and care because of their level of dependency early in life. When caregivers consistently meet their needs, young children develop a secure attachment relationship that promotes the development of self-esteem, autonomy, and emotion regulation. They also develop "internal working models" (see Bretherton & Munholland, 1999) that represent their beliefs and expectations about self and other in close relationships. To the extent that parents are available, sensitive, and responsive to children's needs, they develop the expectation that caregivers are trustworthy and caring and the belief that the self is valued. Bowlby focused primarily on the parent–child relationship as the source for children's "felt security" but noted that other close relationships also could influence the evolution of working models over the course of development. Attachment theory has been expanded in recent years to consider how relationship experiences in childhood and adulthood, including the quality of the relationship between children's parents, can influence attachment security. Waters and Cummings (2000) proposed that witnessing aggression between parents could undermine children's view of parents as sources of security and affect their working models of relationships, and there is empirical support for a link between interparental conflict and children's attachment (El-Sheikh & Elmore-Staton, 2004; Frosch, Mangelsdorf, & McHale, 2000; Laurent, Kim, & Capaldi, 2008; Owen & Cox, 1997).

EMOTIONAL SECURITY THEORY

Davies and Cummings (1994) further extended attachment theory by proposing that children develop a sense of security in the family that is related to but distinct from the quality of the attachment relationships that they have with their parents. In the same way that a caregiver acts as a secure base for the child, the family is conceptualized as a source of comfort, stability, and protection for children. Conflict between caregivers threatens that sense of security, which Davies and Cummings denote as "emotional security" or "security in the family system" to distinguish it from security in parent–child relationships. According to their model, when children's emotional security is threatened, they experience distress and attempt to regain security through several means.

First, they respond with negative emotions, especially fear, which is proposed to facilitate the processing and recall of prior negative events and to increase their attention to potential sources of threat. Second, they may become involved in the conflict in an effort to stop it or reduce their exposure to it by withdrawing. Third, they develop cognitive representations that reflect the potential consequences of conflict for their well-being and for their parents' relationship, which enable them to anticipate future threats and act to prevent or avoid them. These emotional, behavioral, and cognitive processes together are conceptualized as the measurable indicators of emotional security, which is viewed as a hypothetical or latent construct (Davies & Cummings, 1994; Davies, Harold, Goeke-Morey, & Cummings, 2002).

These processes also are proposed to account for sensitization to later conflict episodes and to the increased risk for maladjustment in children from highly conflictual homes. According to emotional security theory, children who frequently are exposed to hostile interactions between their caregivers are primed to detect early signs of conflict and respond with increased negative affect, expectations of further threatening behavior, and attempts to prevent the interactions from escalating. However, repeated activation of this system may deplete the resources that children need to function adaptively in other contexts. In addition, efforts to preserve security may develop into rigid patterns of responding to parental conflict that may be ineffective in responding to other kinds of stressors that require different kinds of responses, leaving them vulnerable to broader adjustment problems as a result (Davies, et al., 2002).

The distinction between security in parent–child relationships and security in the broader family system is supported by modest correlations between self-report measures of each construct, and unique associations of each construct with parenting difficulties and adjustment problems (Davies, et al., 2002). Indicators of emotional security also have been shown to mediate the association between children's exposure to interparental conflict and adjustment problems in both cross-sectional (e.g., Davies & Cummings, 1998) and longitudinal investigations (e.g., Davies, et al., 2002; El-Sheikh, et al., 2008). In most of these studies, the emotional, behavioral, and cognitive indicators of emotional security are combined into a single construct; the few studies that have examined these indicators separately indicate that the emotional and cognitive processes are more closely associated with child adjustment problems than are behavioral responses (e.g., Davies & Cummings, 1998). Research on the emotional security model also has investigated how other aspects of family functioning relate to indicators of emotional security. For example, family cohesion and the quality of parent–child relationships moderated the association between emotional security and children's adjustment; specifically, in families with poorer parent–child relations and lower levels of cohesion, emotional security (in the family system) was more strongly related to child maladjustment than in families reporting more positive relationships and greater cohesion (Davies, et al., 2002).

These latter findings underscore the importance of considering interparental conflict in the broader family context. Social learning, stress and coping, and attachment models all focus primarily on intrapersonal processes as mechanisms for understanding the impact of interparental aggression on children. The final theory that we discuss takes a more "wide angle" view of the family, addressing how characteristics of the family as a whole may influence the impact of parental conflict on children.

FAMILY SYSTEMS THEORY

Family systems theory is an approach to understanding families that encompasses several models with a common set of features (Cox & Paley, 1997, Minuchin, 1985). Family systems perspectives view the family as an organized whole composed of interdependent subsystems; these subsystems, which can be dyads, triads, or larger units, are demarcated by boundaries that define the degree of closeness among the members and between the subsystem and other subsystems. Historically, systems thinking has had a larger impact on psychotherapy than research with families, but in recent years, systems principles have become more prominent in the study of interparental conflict. Next, we discuss how three key principles derived from systems theory—wholism, interdependence, and boundaries—have offered insights into understanding how conflict between caregivers can affect children.

Wholism

The principle of wholism asserts that the functioning of a particular subsystem in the family is influenced by broader patterns of interaction in the family, and that families have qualities that are not reducible to characteristics of individuals or particular relationships. It suggests that other dimensions of family functioning affect how children perceive and respond to conflict, and identifies characteristics that may be particularly relevant in this regard. As noted above, studies of the cognitive-contextual framework and emotional security theory have drawn on this principle in examining children's appraisals of conflict and their emotional security. Specifically, children were more likely to report self-blame for parental conflict when the families' emotional climate was high in negative affect and low in positive affect (Fosco & Grych, 2007) and when children experienced harsh or controlling parenting (DeBoard, et al., 2010). These findings suggest that other interactions and experiences children have in the family color the meaning of parental interactions; specifically, when family relationships are characterized by criticism, invalidation, and negativity, children are more likely to feel at fault for conflicts that arise between their parents. In contrast, children's perceptions of threat were linked only to prior exposure to parental disagreements, suggesting that expectations about the course and outcome of parental conflicts are guided specifically by their experiences with similar conflicts in the past. The finding by Davies and his colleagues (2002) that high levels of cohesion among family members reduced the strength of the relation between children's emotional insecurity and their adjustment problems similarly illustrates how broader patterns of family interaction shape the impact of conflict in the couples' subsystem.

Interdependency

Family systems theory states that individuals and relationships mutually influence each other. This principle has been prominent in understanding the associations between the quality of couples' intimate relationship and their relationships with their children. Many studies have documented the "spillover" of negative affect from the marital to the parent–child relationship (e.g., Davies, Sturge-Apple, & Cummings, 2004; El-Sheikh & Elmore-Staton, 2004; Margolin, Gordis, & Oliver, 2004; Schoppe-Sullivan, Schermerhorn, & Cummings, 2007) in which discord and hostility in the couple's relationship affect how parents treat their children. For example, Lindahl, Malik, Kaczynski, & Simons (2004) showed that the nature of power dynamics in couples' relationships predicted the way that they expressed and resolved conflict. Much less attention has been paid to the reciprocal effect of parenting on marriage, however. The principle of interdependency also suggests that children's behavior in response to conflict will influence couple and family functioning, although this possibility had been neglected until recently. For instance, Schermerhorn, Cummings, DeCarlo, & Davies (2007) have shown that when children exhibit agentic behavior (e.g., trying to stop arguments, comforting parents) in response to parental disagreements, parents reported lower levels of conflict one year later. In contrast, when children expressed dysregulated behavior (e.g., yelling at family members, causing trouble), levels of conflict were higher.

Boundaries

Boundaries define and delineate individuals and subsystems and reflect the degree of closeness in particular relationships as well as closeness and conflict between subsystems. The permeability of boundaries ranges from enmeshed to disengaged, and healthy families are characterized by flexible boundaries that avoid either extreme. In one of the few studies investigating boundaries in relation to interparental conflict, Davies and his colleagues (Davies, Cummings, & Winter, 2004) found that children in both enmeshed and disengaged families exhibited lower levels of emotional security, which partially mediated associations between family boundaries and child adjustment. The concept of boundaries also is relevant to understanding the potential effects of interparental conflict because children are sometimes drawn into their parents' arguments, which violates the boundary between the parental subsystem and the child. This triadic pattern, called triangulation, can result in the formation of cross-generational coalitions in which one parent allies with the child against the other parent, which in turn can lead to problems in children's relationships with both parents.

There is considerable evidence that triangulation is associated with adverse child outcomes (e.g., Buchanan & Waizenhofer, 2001; Fosco & Grych, 2008; Kerig, 1995), and several studies have investigated whether children's appraisals of conflict are linked to their tendency to become drawn into parental disagreements. For example, Gerard, Buehler, Franck, & Anderson (2005) reported that children triangulated into parental disagreements reported greater threat and lower coping efficacy when conflict occurred, and that all three variables had unique associations with internalizing and externalizing problems. Fosco and Grych (2010) recently attempted to untangle the association between triangulation and appraisals in a longitudinal study in which triangulation and appraisals of threat, self-blame, and coping efficacy were measured on two occasions, 9 months apart. They found that higher levels of perceived threat and lower coping efficacy at Time 1 predicted child reports of greater triangulation at Time 2, whereas triangulation at Time 1 predicted higher levels of self-blame at Time 2. In contrast, Shelton and Harold (2008) found that greater self-blame for conflict led to greater child involvement a year later. Although the results from these studies are not entirely consistent, they suggest that integrating constructs from family systems theory with those drawn from the cognitive-contextual framework may provide insight into how intrapersonal and interpersonal processes related to conflict are linked.

SUMMARY

Together, these conceptual models have generated a large literature examining the processes by which exposure to interparental conflict affects children's development. Although the mechanisms that they propose differ, all focus on understanding how children's responses to conflict in the moment can give rise to broader problems in psychological functioning. Most of this work has utilized measures of internalizing and externalizing problems as outcomes, and consequently much more is known about factors that may contribute to adjustment problems than other developmental domains. Despite the progress made in identifying the processes that mediate the effects of interparental conflict on children, there are a number of limitations of this literature. As we describe in the next section, theory and research in this area have had a fairly narrow focus that leaves a number of important questions unanswered.

THEORETICAL LIMITATIONS IN THE STUDY OF THE EFFECTS OF INTERPARENTAL CONFLICT ON CHILDREN

The theories described above have produced a rich description of processes within the person and within the family that shape the impact of interparental aggression on children, but they have paid less attention to the larger context in which families live. In particular, neither the conceptual models nor the studies used to test them adequately represent the diversity in family life in the US in the twenty-first century. Diversity can be characterized on a number of dimensions, and below we discuss two that deserve further integration into the study of interparental conflict.

DIVERSITY IN FAMILY FORMS

Existing family theories of interparental conflict have not adequately addressed the demographic changes that have reshaped contemporary families in the USA. Families with two married parents and their biological children now are in the minority as more individuals postpone marriage or choose not to marry, cohabit, raise children outside of marriage, and continue to divorce at a high rate (e.g., Cherlin, 2010). Most of the theories described in this chapter assume that children live with two parents with whom they have long-established relationships, and it is not clear whether the same processes would apply in nontraditional families. In particular, children's appraisals of and reactions to interparental conflict could differ depending on the nature of their relationships with each parent (or parent figure). A study of family violence supports this possibility. Sullivan, Juras, Bybee, Nguyen, and Allen (2000) found that children living in violent families reported lower self-competence and greater fear when their mother's partner (who perpetrated the violence) was their biological father or stepfather rather than a boyfriend. What is "at stake" in parental disagreements may be influenced by factors such as the length of each caregiver's relationship with the child, their biological and legal status, and each parents' behavior during the conflict. Similarly, whereas responding to a disagreement by taking one parent's side may be maladaptive in an intact family with two biological parents, the same behavior might be quite reasonable if the child has a much more established relationship with one parent than the other.

The increasing number of same-sex couples raising children highlights the lack of attention to gay and lesbian parents in this literature. In addition to better representing these families, studies of same-sex couples provide an opportunity to examine the role of gender in understanding the impact of parental conflict on children. Findings with regard to parent and child gender have been inconsistent to date, and no systematic differences between males and females have been documented. Studying gay and lesbian couples may provide a different perspective for examining how parental gender might affect children's perceptions of conflict. For example, children of same-sex parents tend to hold more egalitarian views of power relations between men and women (e.g., Bos & Sandfort, 2010), which in turn may influence how they interpret aggression between their parents.

DIVERSITY IN ETHNICITY

Despite the growing ethnic diversity of the US population, there is a dearth of research examining how ethnicity may affect the relationship between interparental conflict exposure and child adjustment (see McLoyd, Harper, & Copeland, 2001). Family theories have failed to incorporate the influence of cultural values, practices, and beliefs on processes proposed to influence children's responses to parental conflict. Families from different cultural backgrounds may differ in what they consider normative or acceptable ways to express anger and manage discord, and consequently the meaning and impact of particular behaviors may vary across families. Differences in processes such as acculturation and the involvement of extended family members also may affect how children perceive and respond to interparental conflict. Further, cultural factors may influence how children respond to parental disagreements and manage negative affect. For example, Asian and American Indian children and Latino girls tend to express distress in more internalizing behavior, whereas African American children and Latino boys have a tendency to display greater externalizing behavioral difficulties (Allen & Majidi-Ahi, 1989; Ramirez, 1989).

The few studies that have systematically examined ethnicity have produced inconsistent findings. For example, Lindahl and Malik (1999) found a moderating effect of ethnicity on the relationship among family cohesion, parenting style, and externalizing behavior in boys. For Hispanic families, lax and inconsistent parenting styles were associated with greater externalizing behaviors in boys, whereas for European American and multiracial families, more authoritarian parenting was associated with greater externalizing behaviors. In contrast, El-Sheikh and her colleagues (2008) found no differences in the associations among interparental aggression, emotional security, and adjustment in African American and Anglo children. Exploring the role of culture in family functioning will benefit from the application of theory that explicates how particular beliefs or values may influence parents' and children's behavior, rather than group analyses that assume universality in the processes proposed to explain the effects of conflict on children.

ROLE OF INDIVIDUAL CHARACTERISTICS

Theories in this area have focused primarily on interactions and experiences within the family as sources of variability in children's responses to conflict. They reflect the assumption that children's perceptions, emotions, and behavioral responses to conflict are determined primarily by events that occur in the family. Although these interpersonal processes are important, it is likely that there are stable individual characteristics that make some kinds of emotional and cognitive responses more likely than others. Studies of interparental conflict that have included siblings have shown that they differ in their responses to conflict and associations between conflict and adjustment despite living in what is ostensibly the same environment (e.g., Skopp, McDonald, Manke, & Jouriles, 2005). This work suggests that within-person differences in temperament or personality play a significant role in shaping children's reactions in the moment as well as its broader effects on adjustment. Stable qualities such as temperament, personality, and emotional regulation may help explain why some children are more distressed by parental discord than others, why some children intervene while others withdraw, and why some children develop internalizing versus externalizing problems and others appear unaffected. For example, children who have difficulty regulating their affect and behavior are likely to be more distressed by any stressor, more likely to respond maladaptively, and more likely to develop adjustment problems in high conflict homes. Focusing primarily on family interactions as the source of children's responses may miss information critical for understanding the impact of discord on children.

SUGGESTIONS FOR DEVELOPING A MORE COMPREHENSIVE THEORETICAL UNDERSTANDING OF THE EFFECTS OF INTERPARENTAL CONFLICT ON CHILDREN

The limitations described above highlight the need to develop more comprehensive theoretical models that can account for the potential influence of broader social, cultural, and demographic factors on the intra- and interpersonal processes emphasized by the models discussed in this chapter, as well as stable individual characteristics that may influence how children respond to conflict. In addition, the proliferation of hypothesized mechanisms proposed by these theories raises questions about which are most important for understanding the effects of conflict and how they may be inter-related. Most studies guided by a particular conceptual model have assessed only the processes associated with that model. However, a handful of investigations have explored relations among processes drawn from different theoretical models, and this research provides an initial empirical basis for integrating ideas drawn from different models.

As described above, family systems principles have influenced the development of the cognitive–contextual framework and emotional security theory, and several studies have examined links between specific family systems processes and constructs identified in particular conceptual models (e.g., Davies, et al., 2002; Gerard, et al., 2005; Grych, Raynor, & Fosco, 2004). Although the findings from these studies are not entirely consistent, they indicate that characteristics of the family can influence how children perceive and respond to hostility and aggression between their parents, and that children's appraisals in turn predict whether they are likely to be triangulated into later conflictual episodes. In addition to these efforts to connect intrapersonal processes to interpersonal interactions, there have been two studies that examined constructs drawn from both the cognitive–contextual framework and emotional security theory. These studies faced a methodological challenge: the response processes proposed to occur when children witness conflict are quite similar in the two models and therefore difficult to discriminate at the measurement level. In particular, the cognitive-contextual framework highlights the role of children's appraisals, which are both cognitive and affective in nature, and two of the indicators of emotional insecurity are children's emotional reactions to and cognitions about the conflict. Consequently, the self-report measures typically used to assess these constructs overlap to some extent in their content and lead to similar predictions (Buehler, Lange, & Franck, 2007).

Davies and his colleagues (2002) addressed this issue by removing items from the Threat sub-scale of the Children's Perception of Interparental Conflict scale (CPIC; Grych, Seid, & Fincham, 1992) that they viewed as measuring emotions rather than cognitions (e.g., "When my parents argue, I worry they might split up," "When my parents argue I am afraid that something bad will happen"). Their goal was to emphasize the focus on emotions in the emotional security model, but because the appraisal of threat involves both the perception of danger and the emotional response to that danger, a measure that does not include both is not a valid assessment of children's appraisals. Perhaps not surprisingly, the abbreviated threat scale did not uniquely predict adjustment problems when it was included in the same model as a measure of emotional security that was composed of items tapping emotional, behavioral, and cognitive responses to conflict (SIS; Security in the Interparental Subsystem; Davies, Forman, Rasi, & Stevens, 2002). Only the emotional security latent variable uniquely predicted children's internalizing problems, whereas this construct and self-blame apprais-als uniquely predicted externalizing problems.

Buehler and colleagues (2007) took a different approach to the problem of overlapping content on self-report measures of appraisals and emotional security. They conducted a factor analysis of all the items from the CPIC and SIS to identify factors that were empirically distinct from each other. The best fitting solution included nine non-orthogonal factors: emotional dysregulation, perceived threat to self and family, constructive family representations, coping efficacy, self-blame, avoid-ance, behavioral dysregulation, internalization of feelings, and child involvement in conflict. The intercorrelations among the scales were moderate, but all had unique associations with a latent vari-able of interparental conflict comprised of maternal and paternal self-reports and an observational measure. They then examined which of these factors uniquely predicted internalizing and external-izing problems assessed 1 year later. Internalizing problems were uniquely predicted by self-blame, emotional dysregulation, negative family representations, avoidance, and internalization of feelings, whereas externalizing problems were uniquely associated with threat and self-blame appraisals. Only child involvement in conflict was not related to one of the measures of adjustment. Although the specific scales that emerged in this study require replication in other samples, Buehler and her colleagues' study indicates that it is possible to distinguish between constructs drawn from the cognitive-contextual framework and emotional security theory. However, it also suggests that the scales that emerge empirically may not map precisely on to the processes described in the models.

Finally, Fosco and Grych (2008) tested a mediational model that integrated constructs drawn from three models: perceived threat and self-blame (cognitive-contextual framework), emotional dysregulation (emotional security theory), and triangulation (family systems theory). To avoid confounding measurement of emotions and appraisals, emotions were assessed by having children and their parents rate children's emotional responses to a parental conflict discussion that occurred in the lab and their appraisals were assessed with children's reports on the Threat and Self-Blame subscales from the CPIC. Triangulation was assessed with both parent and child reports, and inter-parental conflict with parent reports, child reports, and observational coding of the conflict discus-sion. Fosco and Grych (2008) compared the fit of the data to three models proposing different relations among appraisals, emotional regulation, and triangulation. A model conceptualizing them as parallel, independent mediators fit the data significantly better than the two alternative models, and better than a model that reversed the direction of effects among the variables. Children's self-blame appraisals and emotional responses were uniquely associated with both internalizing and externalizing problems, threat appraisals uniquely predicted internalizing problems, and triangula-tion predicted externalizing problems.

These empirical studies indicate that constructs derived from multiple conceptual models offer valuable insight into the effects of interparental conflict on children. More specifically, appraisals, emotion regulation, cognitive representations, and triangulation appear to function as independent mediators. Behavioral responses are likely to be important components of a comprehensive model as well, although understanding which behaviors are more or less adaptive in this context will require a more fine-grained analysis than the distinction between involvement and withdrawal highlighted by emotional security theory (e.g., Schermerhorn, et al., 2007). Further, because the effects of particular behaviors will be determined in part by how parents respond to them, family systems constructs like triangulation also are likely to play an important role.

These findings also suggest that it may be feasible to develop a more comprehensive conceptual framework that integrates key aspects of these models. The cognitive–contextual framework and emotional security theory in particular offer complementary perspectives and describe similar processes as occurring when children observe interparental discord. The primary differences between them involve the rationale for why conflict is distressing to children and the interpretation of children's responses to parental disagreements. Both models view conflict between their caregivers as a threat to children, but the cognitive–contextual framework conceptualizes threat more broadly, arguing that conflict can impact a number of important goals, whereas the emotional security model focuses on conflict as a threat to children's sense of security in the family. Threat to the stability of the family may be the most prominent concern in intact families in which children have relatively balanced alliances with each parent, but it is likely that what children perceive to be most threatening will vary in different contexts. For example, in violent families, threats to the health or safety of one or both parents may be most salient to children (e.g., DeBoard & Grych, 2011), in families in which child maltreatment occurs, children may worry about the possibility that parents who are angry with each other will become abusive toward them, and in blended families the relatively greater closeness of children's relationship with one parent may make the security of that relationship more important to them than the stability of the family as a whole.

Both models also describe cognitive, affective, and behavioral aspects of children's responses to parental discord, but the emotional security theory considers them to be indicators of emotional insecurity and attempts to regain security, whereas the cognitive–contextual framework views them as the same processes that occur when children try to cope with any stressful event. Cognition, emotion, and behavior are part of a broader stress response system that has evolved to mobilize adaptive responses to threat and danger, and conceptualizing children's reactions to parental conflict in this way has several advantages. First, it facilitates the comparison of findings from this research with work on children's responses to other types of aversive events. Identifying which processes and sequelae are common across events and which are specific to particular kinds of experiences will improve understanding of the effects of stress and trauma on development and guide the design of cohesive interventions for children exposed to different kinds of aversive experiences. Second, examining response processes separately, rather than treating them as indicators of a single hypothetical construct, offers the opportunity to investigate how they interact and relate to other factors that may shape the impact of conflict on children (e.g., individual differences in personality, cultural beliefs). Finally, conceptualizing children's responses to interparental discord from a stress and coping perspective provides a theoretical basis for seamlessly integrating physiological processes into existing models. Biological factors play a critical role in regulating children's reaction to stress and trauma and have implications for their short-and long-term functioning (e.g., DeBellis, 2001; Susman, 2006). The variables examined in relation to parental conflict thus far (e.g., vagal tone, cortisol) are indicators of biological systems found to be important for understanding the effects of other types of adverse events, including sexual abuse, family violence, and child maltreatment (e.g., DeBellis, 2001; El-Sheikh, et al., 2008; Trickett, Noll, Susman, Shenk, & Putnam, 2010; Watts-English, Fortson, Gibler, Hooper, & DeBellis, 2006); thus, they provide another point at which research on interparental conflict may be integrated with research on other childhood stressors.

CONCLUSION

Significant progress has been made in understanding the impact of exposure to interparental conflict on children. Conceptual models guided by social learning, stress and coping, attachment, and family systems theories have produced a detailed account of intrapersonal and family factors that shape children's responses to conflict. As family forms continue to evolve and diversify, these models will need to change as well. Integrating the processes that have been studied to date into larger, more comprehensive models that take into account the context in which families live as well as stable individual differences that children bring into these interactions will enhance the sophistication of theory and research in this area and increase their usefulness for understanding contemporary families.

REFERENCES

Allen, L., & Majidi-Ahi, S. (1989). Black American children. In J. T. Gibbs and L. N. Huang (Eds.), *Children of color: Psychological interventions with minority youth* (pp. 148–178). San Francisco: Jossey-Bass.

Amato, P. R. (2001). Children of divorce in the 1990s: An update of the Amato and Keith (1991) Meta-analysis. *Journal of Family Psychology, 15*, 355–370.

Bandura, A. (1986). *Social foundations of thought and action: A social–cognitive theory*. Englewood Cliffs, NJ: Prentice-Hall.

Bos, H., & Sandfort, T. (2010). Children's gender identity in lesbian and heterosexual two-parent families. *Sex Roles, 62*, 114–126.

Bowlby, J. (1969). *Attachment and loss,* Vol. 1. *Attachment*. London: Hogarth.

Bretherton, I., & Munholland, K. A. (1999). Internal working models in attachment relationships: A construct revisited. In J. Cassidy & P. Shaver (Eds.), *Handbook of attachment* (pp. 89–111). New York: Guilford Press.

Buchanan, C. M., & Waizenhofer, R. (2001). The impact of interparental conflict on adolescent children: Considerations of family systems and family structure. In A. Booth, A. C. Crouter, & M. Clements (Eds.), *Couples in conflict* (pp. 149–160). Mahwah, NJ: Erlbaum.

Buehler, C., Lange, G., & Franck, K. L. (2007). Adolescents' cognitive and emotional responses to marital hostility. *Child Development, 78*, 775–789.

Buehler, C. Anthony, C. Krishnakumar, A., Stone, G., Gerard, J., & Pemberton, S. (1997). Interparental conflict and youth problem behaviors: A meta-analysis. *Journal of Child and Family Studies, 6*, 233–247.

Campos, J. J., Campos, R. G., & Barrett, K. C. (1989). Emergent themes in the study of emotional development and emotion regulation. *Developmental Psychology, 25*, 394–402.

Cherlin, A. J. (2010). Demographic trends in the United States: A review of research in the 2000s. *Journal of Marriage and Family, 72*, 1–17.

Cohen, J. (1977). *Statistical power for the behavioral sciences*. New York: Academic Press.

Cox, M. J., & Paley, B. (1997). Families as systems. *Annual Review of Psychology, 48*, 243–267.

Crockenberg, S. & Forgays, D. K. (1996). The role of emotion in children's understanding of emotional reactions to marital conflict. *Merrill-Palmer Quarterly, 42*, 22–47.

Crockenberg, S. & Langrock, A. (2001). The role of specific emotions in children's responses to interparental conflict: A test of the model. *Journal of Family Psychology, 15*, 162–182.

Cui, M., Conger, R. D., & Lorenz, F. O. (2005). Predicting change in adolescent adjustment from change in marital problems. *Developmental Psychology, 41*, 812–823.

Cummings, E. M., & Davies, P. T. (2002). Effects of marital conflict on children: Recent advances and emerging themes in process-oriented research. *Journal of Child Psychology and Psychiatry, 43*, 31–63.

Cummings, E. M., Goeke-Morey, M. C., & Papp, L. M. (2003). Children's responses to everyday marital conflict tactics in the home. *Child Development, 74*, 1918–1929.

Cummings, J. S., Pellegrini, D. S., Notarius, C. I., & Cummings, E. M. (1989). Children's responses to angry adult behavior as a function of marital distress and history of interparent hostility. *Child Development, 60*, 1035–1043.

Cummings, E. M., Zahn-Waxler, C., & Radke-Yarrow, M. (1981). Young children's responses to expressions of anger and affection by others in the family. *Child Development, 52*, 1274–1282.

Davies, P. T. & Cummings, E. M. (1998). Exploring children's emotional security as a mediator of the link between marital relations and child adjustment. *Child Development, 69*, 124–139.

Davies, P. T., & Cummings, E. M. (1994). Marital conflict and child adjustment: An emotional security hypothesis. *Psychological Bulletin, 116*, 387–411.

Davies, P. T., Cummings, E. M., & Winter, M. A. (2004). Pathways between profiles of family function-ing, child security in the interparental subsystem, and child psychological problems. *Development and Psychopathology*, *16*, 525–550.

Davies, P. T., Forman, E. M., Rasi, J. A., & Stevens, K. (2002). Children's emotional security in the marital subsystem: Psychometric properties for a new measure. *Child Development, 73*, 544–562.

Davies, P. T., Harold, G. T., Goeke-Morey, M. C., & Cummings, E. M. (2002) Child emotional security and interparental conflict. *Monographs of the Society for Research in Child Development*, *67*, 3.

Davies, P. T., Sturge-Apple, M. L., Cicchetti, D., & Cummings, E. M. (2007). The role of child adrenocortical functioning in pathways between forms of interparental conflict and child maladjustment. *Developmental Psychology*, *43*, 918–930.

Davies, P. T., Sturge-Apple, M. L., & Cummings, E. M. (2004). Interdependencies among interparental discord and parenting styles: The role of adult attributes and relationship characteristics. *Development and Psychopathology*, *16*, 773–797.

DeBellis, M. D. (2001). Developmental traumatology: The psychological development of maltreated children and its implications for research, treatment, and policy. *Development and Psychopathology*, *13*, 539–564.

DeBoard, R. L., Fosco, G. M., Raynor, S. R., & Grych, J. H. (2010). The role of parenting in understanding the association between children's appraisals of interparental conflict and adjustment problems. *Journal of Clinical Child and Adolescent Psychology*, *39*, 163–175.

DeBoard, R. L. & Grych, J. H. (2011). Children's Perceptions of Intimate Partner Violence: Causes, consequences, and coping. *Journal of Family Violence*, *26*, 343–354.

Doyle, A. B. & Markowitz, D. (2005). Parenting, marital conflict, and adjustment from early- to mid-adolescence: Mediated by adolescent attachment style? *Journal of Youth and Adolescence*, *34*, 97–110.

El-Sheikh, M. (1994). Children's emotional and physiological responses to interadult angry behavior: The role of history of interparental hostility. *Journal of Abnormal Child Psychology*, *22*, 661–678.

El-Sheikh, M., Cummings, E. M., Kouros, C. D, Elmore-Staton, L. & Buckhalt, J. (2008). Marital psychologi-cal and physical aggression and children's mental and physical health: Direct, mediated, and moderated effects. *Journal of Consulting and Clinical Psychology*, *76*, 138–148.

El-Sheikh, M. & Elmore-Staton, L. (2004). The link between marital conflict and child adjustment: Parent-child conflict and perceived attachments as mediators, potentiators, and mitigators of risk. *Development and Psychopathology*, *16*, 631–648.

El-Sheikh, M., Erath, S. A., Buckhalt, J. A., Granger D. A., & Mize, J. (2008). Cortisol and children's adjust-ment: The moderating role of sympathetic nervous system activity. *Journal of Child Abnormal Psychol-ogy*, *36*(4), 601–611.

El-Sheikh, M., Kouros, C. D., Erath, S., Cummings, E. M., Keller, P. S., & Elmore-Staton, L. (2009). Marital conflict and children's externalizing behavior: Interactions between parasympathetic and sympathetic nervous system activity. *Monographs of the Society for Research in Child Development*, *74*, 1–101.

El-Sheikh, M., & Whitson, S. A. (2006). Longitudinal relations between marital conflict and child adjustment: Vagal regulation as a protective factor. *Journal of Family Psychology*, *20*, 30–39.

Emery, R. E. (1982). Interparental conflict and the children of discord and divorce. *Psychological Bulletin*, *92*, 310–330.

Erel, O. & Burman, B. (1995). Interrelatedness of marital relations and parent-child relations: A meta-analytic review. *Psychological Bulletin*, *118*, 108–132.

Fosco, G. M. & Grych, J. H. (2007). Emotional expression in the family as a context for children's appraisals of interparental conflict. *Journal of Family Psychology*, *21*, 248–258.

Fosco, G. M. & Grych, J. H. (2008). Emotional, cognitive, and family systems mediators of children's adjustment to interparental conflict. *Journal of Family Psychology*, *22*, 843–854.

Fosco, G. M. & Grych, J. H. (2010). Adolescent Triangulation into Parental Conflicts: Longitudinal Implica-tions for Appraisals and Adolescent-Parent Relations. *Journal of Marriage and the Family, 72,* 254–266.

Foshee, V. A., Linder, F., MacDougall, J. A., & Bangidwala, S. (2001). Gender differences in the longitudinal predictors of adolescent dating violence. *Preventive Medicine*, *32*(2), 128–141.

Frosch, C., Mangelsdorf, S., & McHale, J. (2000). Marital behavior and the security of preschooler-parent attachment relationships: Attachment and adjustment. *Journal of Family Psychology*, *14*, 144–161.

Garcia O'Hearn, H., Margolin, G., & John, R. S. (1997). Mothers' and fathers' reports of children's reactions to naturalistic marital conflict. *Journal of the American Academy of Child and Adolescent Psychiatry*, *36*, 1366–1373.

Gerard, J. M., Buehler, C., Franck, K., & Anderson, O. (2005). In the eyes of the beholder: Cognitive appraisals as mediators of the association between interparental conflict and youth maladjustment. *Journal of Family Psychology*, *19*, 376–384.

Grych, J. H. (1998). Children's appraisals of interparental conflict: Situational and contextual influences. *Journal of Family Psychology*, 12, 437–453.

Grych, J. H. (2002). Marital relationships and parenting. In M. Bornstein (Ed.), *Handbook of parenting* (2nd ed., pp. 203–226). Mahwah, NJ: Erlbaum.

Grych, J. H. & Cardoza-Fernandes, S. (2001). Understanding the impact of interparental conflict on children: The role of social cognitive processes. In J. Grych & F. Fincham (Eds.), *Interparental conflict and child development: Theory, Research, and application* (pp. 157–187). New York: Cambridge University Press.

Grych, J. H., & Fincham, F. D. (1990). Marital conflict and children's adjustment: A cognitive-contextual framework. *Psychological Bulletin*, *108*, 267–290.

Grych, J. H., & Fincham, F. D. (1993). Children's appraisals of marital conflict: Initial investigations of the cognitive-contextual framework. *Child Development*, *64*, 215–230.

Grych, J. H., & Fincham, F. D. (2001). *Interparental conflict and child development: Theory, research, and application*. New York, NY: Cambridge University Press.

Grych, J. H, Fincham, F. D., Jouriles, E. N., & McDonald, R. (2000). Interparental conflict and child adjustment: Testing the mediational role of appraisals in the cognitive-contextual framework. *Child Development*, *71*, 1648–1661.

Grych, J. H, Harold, G. T. & Miles, C. J. (2003). A prospective investigation of appraisals as mediators of the link between interparental conflict and child adjustment. *Child Development*, *74*, 1176–1193.

Grych, J. H., Raynor, S. R., & Fosco, G. M. (2004). Family processes that shape the impact of interparental conflict on adolescents. *Development and Psychopathology*, *16*, 649–665.

Grych, J. H., Seid, M., & Fincham, F. D. (1992). Assessing marital conflict from the child's perspective: The Children's Perception of Interparental Conflict Scale. Child Development, *63*, 558–572.

Harold, G. T. & Conger, R. D. (1997). Marital conflict and adolescent distress: The role of adolescent awareness. *Child Development*, *68*, 333–350.

Harold, G. T., Aitken, J., & Shelton, K. H. (2007). Inter-parental conflict and children's academic attainment: A longitudinal analysis. *Journal of Child Psychology and Psychiatry*, *48*(12), 1223–1232.

Hetherington, E. M. (1989). Coping with family transitions: Winners, losers, and survivors. *Child Development*, *60*, 1–14.

Katz, L. F. & Gottman, J. M. (1995). Vagal tone protects children from marital conflict. *Development and Psychopathology*, *7*, 83–92.

Kerig, P. K. (1995). Triangles in the family circle: Effects of family structure on marriage, parenting and child adjustment. *Journal of Family Psychology*, *9*, 28–43.

Kerig, P. K. (2001). Children's coping with interparental conflict. In J. Grych & F. Fincham (Eds.), *Interparental conflict and child development: Theory, research, and application* (pp. 213–245). New York: Cambridge University Press.

Kinsfogel, K. M. & Grych, J. H. (2004). Interparental conflict and adolescent dating relationships; Integrating cognitive, emotional, and peer influences. *Journal of Family Psychology*, *18*, 505–515.

Laurent, H. K., Kim, H. K., & Capaldi, D. M (2008). Prospective effects of interparental conflict on child attachment security and the moderating role of parents' romantic attachment. *Journal of Family Psychology*, *22*, 377–388.

Lazarus, R. S. (1991). Cognition and motivation in emotion. *American Psychologist*, *46*, 352–367.

Lazarus, R. S., & Folkman, S. (1984). *Stress, appraisal, and coping*. New York: Springer.

Lewis, C. E., Siegel, J. M., & Lewis, M. A. (1984). Feeling bad: Exploring sources of distress among preadolescent children. *American Journal of Public Health*, *74*, 117–122.

Lindahl, K. M., & Malik, N. M (1999). Observations of marital conflict and power: Relations with parenting in the triad. *Journal of Marriage and the Family*, *61*, 320–330.

Lindahl, K. M., Malik, N. M., Kaczynski, K., & Simons, J. S. (2004). Couple power dynamics, systemic family functioning, and child adjustment: A test of a meditational model in a multiethnic sample. *Development and Psychopathology*, *16*, 609–630.

Mandler, G. (1975). *Mind and emotion*. New York: Wiley.

Marcus, N. E., Lindahl, K. M., & Malik, N. M. (2001). Interparental conflict, children's social cognitions, and child aggression: A test of a mediational model. *Journal of Family Psychology*, *15*, 315–333.

Margolin, G., Gordis, E. B., & Oliver, Ph. H. (2004). Links between marital and parent-child interactions: Moderating role of husband-to-wife aggression. *Development and Psychopathology, 16,* 753–771.

McLoyd, V. C., Harper, C. I., & Copeland, N. L. (2001). In J. Grych & F. Fincham (Eds.), *Interparental conflict and child development: Theory, research, and application* (pp. 98–125). New York: Cambridge University Press.

Minuchin, P. (1985). Families and individual development: Provocations from the field of family therapy. *Child Development, 56,* 289–302.

Owen, M., & Cox, M., (1997). Marital conflict and the development of infant–parent attachment relationships. *Journal of Family Psychology, 11,* 152–164.

Ramirez, O. (1989). Mexican-American children and adolescents." In J. T. Gibbs and L. N. Huang (Eds.), *Children of color: Psychological interventions with minority youth* (pp. 223–250). San Francisco: Jossey-Bass.

Rhoades, K. A. (2008). Children's responses to interparental conflict: A meta-analysis of their associations with adjustment. *Child Development, 6,* 1942–1956.

Schermerhorn, A. C., Cummings, E. M., DeCarlo, C. A., & Davies, P. T. (2007). Children's influence in the marital relationship. *Journal of Family Psychology, 21, 259–269.*

Schoppe-Sullivan, S. J., Schermerhorn, A. C., & Cummings, E. M. (2007). Marital conflict and children's adjustment: Evaluation of the parenting process model. *Journal of Marriage and the Family, 69,* 1118–1134.

Shelton, K. H., & Harold, G. T. (2008). Pathways between interparental conflict and adolescent psychological adjustment. *Journal of Early Adolescence, 28,* 555–582.

Shifflett-Simpson, K., & Cummings, E. M. (1996). Mixed message resolution and children's responses to interadult conflict. *Child Development, 67,* 437–448.

Stein, N. L., & Levine, L. (1987). Thinking about feelings: The development and organization of emotional knowledge. In R. Snow & M. Farr (Eds.), *Aptitude, learning, and instruction* (Vol. 3, pp. 165–197). Hillsdale, NJ: Erlbaum.

Skopp, N. A., McDonald, R., Manke, B., & Jouriles, E. N. (2005). Siblings in domestically violent families: Experiences of interparent conflict and adjustment problems. *Journal of Family Psychology, 17,* 324–333.

Sullivan, C. M., Juras, J., Bybee, D., Nguyen, H., & Allen, N. (2000). How children's adjustment is affected by their relationships to their mothers abusers. *Journal of Interpersonal Violence, 15,* 587–602.

Susman, E. J. (2006). Psychobiology of persistent antisocial behavior: Stress, early vulnerabilities and the attenuation hypothesis. *Neuroscience and Biobehavioral Reviews, 30,* 376–389.

Terwogt, M. M., & Harris, P. L. (1993). Understanding of emotion. In M. Bennett (Ed.), *The development of social cognition* (pp. 62–86). New York: Guilford Press.

Trickett, P. K., Noll, J. G., Susman, E. J., Shenk, C. E., & Putnam, F. W. (2010). Attenuation of cortisol across development for victims of sexual abuse. *Development and Psychopathology, 22,* 165–175.

Van den Broek, P. (1997). Discovering the cement of the universe: The development of event comprehension from childhood to adulthood. In P. van den Broek, P. Bauer, & T. Bourg (Eds.), *Developmental spans in event comprehension and representation* (pp. 321–342). Mahwah, NJ: Erlbaum.

Waters, E., & Cummings, E. M. (2000). A secure base from which to explore relationships. *Child Development, 71,* 164–172.

Watts-English, T., Fortson, B. L., Gibler, Hooper, S. R., & DeBellis, M. D. (2006). The psychobiology of maltreatment in childhood. *Journal of Social Issues, 62,* 717–736.

Section IV

Structural Variations and Transitions in Families

14 Transition to Parenting Within Context

Jacqueline D. Shannon, Lisa Baumwell, and Catherine S. Tamis-LeMonda

According to a life course perspective, individuals' lives are constantly changing, and these changes follow trajectories that have developmental implications for the individual (Elder, 1998). One frequently studied transition experienced by most adult couples is the transition to parenthood, which occurs at the birth of a first child. Researchers have termed this the "family stage" in the developmental life cycle (Elder, 1998). When parents commit to the "family stage," they experience high levels of excitement as well as the physical and psychological stresses associated with pregnancy, delivery, and raising a child (Belsky, Ward, & Rovine 1986). Theoretical work on the transition to parenthood suggests that parents' adjustment to this phase influences future parent–child and coparental relationships (Florsheim, Moore, & Edgington, 2003). The demands of parenthood can lead to individual growth, especially when new parents are supported, or the challenges can be overwhelming, having deleterious effects on parent–child relationships and, ultimately, children's development and family relationships (Belsky, 1993).

KEY ISSUES IN THE STUDY OF THE TRANSITION TO PARENTHOOD

Early attachment theorists and clinicians who examined maternal experiences and couple relationships around pregnancy and birth largely emphasized maladjustment and crisis. For example, mothers' initial trimester of pregnancy was classified as a period of "normal crisis," involving both physical and psychological changes (Bibring, 1959). Simultaneously, changes that occurred in families transitioning from a couple to a triad at the birth of their baby were viewed as a "crisis event" for couples (Dyer, 1963; LeMasters, 1957). Others suggest that the addition of a baby forces couples to quickly reorganize their established relationship leading to stress and strain in the relationship and decreased marital satisfaction (LeMasters, 1957).

This early research, however, was primarily based on parents' retrospective accounts of their transition to parenthood. A number of prospective longitudinal studies have since been completed in which couples were followed from before to after they made the transition to parenthood (e.g., C. P. Cowan & Cowan, 1992; Heinicke, 2002). As a result, researchers began to challenge this crisis perspective based on longitudinal data and ecological theories that examined both negative and positive changes reported by new parents (Belsky, Spanier, & Rovine, 1983; C. P. Cowan & Cowan, 1995, 2000).

More recent research makes clear that many couples look forward to the birth of their first baby and report tremendous joy and personal growth in their new role (Palkowitz, 1996). Nonetheless, new parents continue to experience some emotional upheaval (Belsky, 1984; C. P. Cowan &

Cowan, 2000). How many positive and negative experiences they encounter during this transition will depend on multiple factors. For instance, how parents adjust to the needs of their newborn and renegotiate their roles and relationships within the family is critical to future parent–child relationships and children's outcomes (Belsky, 1984).

Extant theories of parenting, including the transition to parenting, have focused on White, middle-class, two-parent families, even though they are now in the minority (Bornstein & Sawyer, 2005). As the US has increased in its diversity, there has been a gradual shift in parenting research to studying families from other circumstances and cultural backgrounds with different family structures. Furthermore, trends over the past several decades have resulted in rising numbers of mothers joining the labor market, changes in the gendered division of household labor, and major changes in family structure (Tamis-LeMonda, Baumwell, & Cabrera, in press). As a result, many fathers and other family members are actively involved in the daily lives of their young children, even in populations facing the social-demographic risks of poverty and father non-residency (see Cabrera et al., 2004; Cabrera, Ryan, Jolley, Shannon, & Tamis-LeMonda, 2008) All of these contextual factors shape the experiences of families during the transition to parenthood.

Theories of parenting, however, have not necessarily been reflective of the changing demographics of the US. Although research guided by traditional theories of parenting have extended our knowledge of the utility of the theory, sometimes these theories have suggested deficiencies in non-normative cultures, rather than ultimately changing the theory in question (Chaudhary, 1999). This is true regarding theories that focus on the universality of becoming a parent ("etic") *or* that use a culturally specific and indigenous approach ("emic"). Etic approaches, in which theories of human behavior are developed in one context and applied to another, are not universally applicable. Similarly, an emic approach to human behavior, in which development is studied within a particular community, has the risk of the cultural group becoming marginalized.

Influential theorists saw the tension between the approaches as a "dilemma" (e.g., Helfrich, 1999), while others (e.g., Pike, 1967) saw the value of both. Etic approaches allow a rough, tentative starting point and typically meet the practical demands of financial and time pressures. Emic approaches help us understand particular attitudes and values of different cultural groups and by studying these cultures, a predictive science of behavior can progress (Pike, 1967). Neither approach is incompatible with the other. Practices of particular cultural groups influence behavior, as does living in a single social context (Hall & Barongan, 2002). Indeed, multicultural psychology has suggested that integrating the two is possible and extant models of how families transition to parenthood would benefit from such an approach.

In this chapter, we first consider three core theoretical perspectives to understand the changes occurring during the transition to parenthood: *attachment theory*, a *family systems perspective*, and an *ecological model*. We focus on specific subsystems within these theories that have critical implications for children's social and emotional development. Next, we discuss how each of these core theories integrate context. Finally, we propose a conceptual framework to study the transition to parenting from a multicultural perspective that uses the complementary strategies of etic- and emic-level explanations.

THEORIES OF THE TRANSITION TO PARENTING

Drawing partially on evolutionary theory, attachment theory assumes that parents instinctually form bonds with their children, that parent–child bonds are similar across families, even though the quality of the bonds may differ (Bowlby, 1969). Attachment theory, which also has roots in psychoanalytic theory, posits that during pregnancy, mothers and fathers begin to fantasize about and prepare for pregnancy (Fonagy, Steele, & Steele, 1991). These early expectations of their relationship with and feelings toward their infants influence the quality of their parenting and interactions with their infants after birth (Bowlby, 1969; Fonagy et al., 1991; Ward & Carlson, 1995; Zeanah, Keener, Anders, & Vieira-Buker, 1987).

In contrast, the family systems perspective goes beyond the parent–child relationship, conceptualizing the family as an organized system consisting of interdependent dyadic and triadic subsystems (e.g., mother–father, parent–child, sibling–sibling, intergenerational forces, stressors that impact the family) that exert bidirectional influences over time (Cox & Paley, 1997; Minuchin, 1985).

In the ecological model, there are multiple interacting systems that affect individuals, and a fuller understanding of parenting rests on consideration of these wider, contextual systems and the levels of influence these systems have on one another and on individual behaviors (Belsky, 1984; Bronfenbrenner & Morris, 1998). Below, we elaborate on how each of these three theories has helped to further our understanding of the transition to parenthood and we conclude with suggestions for a perspective that include contextual and sociocultural influences simultaneously.

ATTACHMENT THEORY

Among the most important social and emotional tasks of an infant's first year of life is the establishment of a primary attachment relationship. Bowlby's (1969) attachment theory identified the importance of infants' early relationships with their primary caregivers beginning at birth and persisting through adulthood. Bowlby (1980) also proposed that infants, from their subjective experiences with their primary caregivers, construct internal working models (IWM) of the self and of others and that internal working models shape emotional, cognitive, and behavioral responses within these attachment relationships. Further, parents appropriate attunement and sensitive responsiveness to their infants form the basis for children's sense of security and trust in others and a belief that they are worthy of that trust (Ainsworth, 1973; Sroufe & Waters, 1977). The bond that parents form with their infants is critical for sensitive parenting (Ainsworth, 1973). Mental abstractions of early attachment relationships organize the individual's behaviors, emotions, and expectations, especially in times of stress and transition, including the transition to parenthood (Bowlby, 1988).

Specifically, attachment theorists claim there is a strong link between individuals' experiences with their parents during infancy and their later capacity to form and maintain other relationships (Main & Goldwyn, 1984). For instance, adults raised by nurturing and responsive parents during infancy are also likely to provide sensitive and responsive caregiving to their infants when they become parents and to give and seek emotional support when they are distressed (Bowlby, 1980; Main, Kaplan, & Cassidy, 1985). In contrast, adults raised by parents who were cold and rejecting of their emotional and physical needs during infancy are likely to provide insensitive care to their infants when they become parents and to distrust and interpret others' actions more negatively including their partners, particularly in times of distress (Bowlby, 1980; Main et al., 1985; Rohner, 1986).

Transitions Across the Prenatal Period: Disbelief to Fantasy

Simultaneously with attachment theory grew psychoanalytic analyses of maternal retrospective reports of their experiences during pregnancy. Prenatal attachment was seen as a process in which a pregnant woman's emotional energy was focused on the fetus (Bibring, 1959; Bibring, Dwyer, Huntington, & Valenstein, 1961). It was assumed that the fetus becomes more human to the woman as her pregnancy progresses, and in time the fetus becomes loved both as an extension of self and as a separate "other." This early relationship was supported by a team of physicians who observed the intense grief expressed by mothers of infants who died during birth (Kennell, Slyter, & Klaus, 1970).

During the initial trimester of pregnancy, a presumed period of 'normal crisis', the mother often has difficulty describing any attributes or functions of her fetus, and has difficulty believing that her baby is really inside her (Bibring, 1959). The mother withdraws into herself and is preoccupied with changes in her own body. However, as the fetus develops, the mother increasingly focuses on her baby as "other." The use of ultrasound during pregnancy provides the mother a visual image of the fetus, which further allows her to view the fetus as a "little" person (Lumley, 1980). The onset of fetal movements during the second trimester of pregnancy, the point of 'quickening,' is when the mother begins to see the developing fetus as a separate individual from her and she becomes attached to her infant—not her pregnancy (Lumley, 1982).

During the final trimester, the woman begins to have a clearer representation of herself as mother and her infant as distinct. The mother begins to recognize the fetal movements and patterns, and bestows on her baby-to-be, a temperament and personality (Mebert & Kalinowski, 1986; Zeanah, Keener, Stewart, & Anders, 1985). She gives meaning to and labels these perceived characteristics, such as "quiet" or "active." Her fantasies about the baby become more specific—who the baby will be like and resemble (Mebert & Kalinowski, 1986). Her responses to the growing fetus can be seen as a very early form of interaction and her perception of the personality of the fetus during pregnancy is related to her behaviors toward her infant (Leifer, 1977). The mother's expectations of her infant's personality influence her perceptions of her behaviors toward the infant, which, in turn, shape her infant's behavior so that information consistent with her expectations will more likely be attended to, acted upon, and reinforced by the mother.

Importance of Parents' Childhood Relationships with Their Own Parents

The attachment system is activated during stressful experiences, and because the transition to parenting is considered to be a stressful event for new parents, it is hypothesized that expectant parents' memories of childhood relationships with their caregiver may be especially salient as they begin to prepare for the birth of their newborn (Bowlby, 1988; C. P. Cowan, Cowan, Heming, & Miller, 1991).

Furthermore, attachment research suggests an intergenerational influence in which the stability and predictability of the infant–mother attachment begins during pregnancy. That is, the mother's representation of her own mother during pregnancy may be related to the pattern of attachment she will develop with her own infant (Fonagy et al., 1991; Ward & Carlson, 1995). For instance, in one study, pregnant mothers' representation of attachment was examined in relation to the quality of their subsequent infant–mother relationships (Fonagy et al., 1991). One-hundred primiparous mothers were administered the Adult Attachment Interview (AAI) during their third trimester of pregnancy, and, the quality of their infants' attachment was measured using the Strange Situation (SS) when their children were 12 months of age. Results indicate that 75% of the time investigators accurately predicted infants who were securely or insecurely attached to their mother based on the mother's classification on the prenatal AAI. This research supports the idea of a strong intergenerational influence of attachment, and further suggests that the mother's current representation of her own mother may be the most significant predictor of the attachment she will develop with her own infant.

The importance of childhood attachments for the quality of parenting in early infancy also applies to fathering. In our own research of 60 Latino and African American, inner-city fathers and their 6- to 11-month-old infants, the fathers' perceptions of their childhood relationships with their own fathers directly contributed to the quality of their parenting, supporting theory and empirical research linking childrearing histories with parent–infant relationships (P. A. Cowan, Cohn, Cowan, & Pearson, 1996; Shannon, Tamis-LeMonda, & Margolin, 2005). Specifically, we found that men's experiences of paternal acceptance, but not maternal acceptance, predicted whether or not fathers were responsive and didactic with their infants, and remained so after considering significant demographic protective factors (i.e., men's resident and marital status, education, and income). These findings, however, contrast with others showing that men's childhood experiences were unrelated to their interactions with their own children (C. P. Cowan & Cowan, 1990; Cox et al., 1985; Volling & Belsky, 1992). However, only Cox and colleagues (1985) included men's childhood experiences with their fathers, rather than solely their mothers, or their fathers and mothers combined as a unit. Our study further supports the value of examining parents' maternal and paternal childhood experiences to more thoroughly understand the complexity of how earlier relationships link to current parenting. Although in this study we include an ethnically diverse group of fathers, attachment theory does not generally include cultural context within their framework.

FAMILY SYSTEMS PERSPECTIVE

Child development research has moved beyond focusing on the parent–child dyad to include the child as part of a family system. Pioneers such as Bowen (1978), interested in the treatment of mental disorders, viewed the family as a fluid, ever changing system made up of a variety of subsystems. Change in one part of the family system is followed by a corresponding change in other parts; systems can function on a continuum from functional to dysfunctional. Six domains are posited to interact in forming the family system: individual characteristics of parents and child, the couple relationship, relationships between parent and child, relationships between siblings, intergenerational relationship patterns, and the stressors and protective factors outside the family (P. A. Cowan, Powell, & Cowan, 1997). Although this model does include familial risks and protective factors, the cultural impact on family functioning is virtually ignored (P. A. Cowan & Cowan, 2002).

The transition to parenthood is considered an important, and for many, rewarding change in the family system. Nonetheless, new parents are faced with several challenges and stressors that threaten family functioning (Belsky, 1984). A heavily researched and influential subsystem on the child during this time is the marital or couple relationship (Lawrence, Cobb, Rothman, Rothman, & Bradbury, 2008).

Couple Relationship

There exists strong empirical evidence that the transition to parenthood negatively affects marital satisfaction (e.g., Elek, Hudson, & Bouffard, 2003; Harwood, McLean, & Durkin, 2007; Shapiro, Gottman, & Carrère, 2000). In fact, some researchers have posited that declines in marital quality after the birth of a child start a downward spiral in which recovery is difficult (e.g., Pacey, 2004). However, others suggest the effect is minor, short-lived, and can even be beneficial (e.g., P. A. Cowan & Cowan, 1988). Clearly, there is great variation in couples' responses to the birth of a child, and the sources of this variation are of theoretical and practical interest.

There is consensus that when prenatal expectations are violated, there are lower levels of marital satisfaction and that partners with higher expectations before the birth of their infants have more declines in marital satisfaction postpartum (Lawrence, Nylen, & Cobb, 2007). In fact, when women overestimated the amount of help they would receive from their partners, marital satisfaction declined (Hackle & Ruble, 1992). The opposite holds true when optimism is met by positive experiences after the birth of an infant: realistic optimism is beneficial to the partner relationship during the transition to parenthood (Harwood et al., 2007).

In many early investigations of marital change during the transition to parenthood, confounding variables such as marriage duration, remarriage, whether the pregnancy was planned, and prenatal and postnatal levels of marital satisfaction, were not controlled. More recent studies—with matched comparison groups of childless couples—show that parenthood negatively affects marital satisfaction, but to varying degrees based on sex (women report more disenchantment than men), partner satisfaction before the birth of the child, and by the degree to which the pregnancy was planned (Lawrence et al., 2008). After the birth of a child, both women and men report dissatisfaction with the amount of time spent together, less contentment with their sexual relationship, more disagreements, and an uneven division of labor in household and infant care (Knauth, 2000; Shapiro et al., 2000).

When dissatisfaction and conflict are high, children are likely affected. Indeed, Satir (1972) argued that couples were the "architects of the family." When mothers and fathers get along, they can work together to protect their children from stress; however, when there is marital conflict, stressors inside and outside the family become exaggerated and children are at risk (P. A. Cowan, Cowan, Ablow, Johnson, & Measelle, 2005).

Extant literature supports the family systems' hypothesis that marital and parent–child relationships are interdependent (Grych, 2002) and that the quality of the relationship of the couple, beginning during the transition to parenting, is related to their relationship to the child and the child's subsequent development (e.g., C. P. Cowan & Cowan, 2000). A meta-analytic review of 68 studies found significant and positive relationships between marital quality (operationally defined as marital satisfaction, marital coalition, and lack of overt conflict) and parent–child relationships (Erel & Burman, 1995; Shannon, Tamis-LeMonda, & Cabrera, 2006). Marital discord negatively affects children's psychological health (Cummings, Goeke-Morey, & Raymond, 2004; Shelton & Harold, 2008); and parent–child interactions (Cabrera, Shannon, Jolley-Mitchell, & West, 2009; C. P. Cowan et al., 1991), children's peer relationships (Parke et al., 2004) either by directly "spilling" over into parent–child relationships or by being mediated by emotional availability (Barth & Parke, 1993).

The importance of relationship satisfaction to parents' interactions with children has been documented in families in White samples (e.g., Belsky, Youngblade, Rovine, & Volling, 1991; Fomby & Cherlin, 2007) and, more currently, with low-income and diverse ethnic groups (Cabrera et al., 2009). In our study of a national sample of Mexican American families, a global measure of couple happiness was predictive of early father engagement with infants, but did not predict mother–infant interactions. Yet, the quality of the marital relationship moderated the association between unwanted pregnancy and parenting activities for both mothers and fathers. When parents were not happy with one another, supportive parenting behaviors decreased (e.g., maternal sensitivity and father involvement), which ultimately put children at risk (Cabrera et al., 2009).

Coparenting

Coparenting refers to how parents coordinate their roles as parents (Feinberg, 2003). More specifically, coparenting includes mothers' and fathers' agreements on childrearing, division of labor, support, and the management of family interactions (McHale, Khazan, Rotman, DeCourcey, & McConnell, 2002). This conceptualization of coparenting is based on self-reports from spouses in heterosexual married couples with a single child (Van Egeren & Hawkins, 2004), although a more inclusive definition has also been proposed: "when at least two individuals are expected by mutual agreement or societal norms to have conjoint responsibility for a particular child's well-being" (Van Egeren & Hawkins, 2004, p. 166). This description of coparenting has more applicability to different types of families from different cultures regardless of the couples' sexual, marital, economic, or caregiving status.

The expectant couple's mental representations and discussions about coparenting begin before the birth of a child and are predictors of subsequent coparenting, even when parenting expectations are not met. As evidence of the centrality of coparenting in marital quality, 62 White families were studied prior to their infants' births, at 6 months after the infants' birth, as well as a follow-up when children were 3 years old. "Coparenting solidarity," "partner support," "undermining coparenting," and "shared parenting" were measured as indicators of "marital quality" (marital behavior and adjustment). Parents' perceptions of support, solidarity, and the perception that the partner is a significant contributor to caregiving were central to marital quality, with fathers relying more on mothers' perceptions of their parenting ability (Van Egeren & Hawkins, 2004).

The importance of coparenting to children's outcomes has also been documented. It is thought to more directly influence the child than marital satisfaction alone (Feinberg, 2003). For instance, supportive coparenting has been related to discipline, more patience, and less exhaustion in parents (Furstenberg, Brooks-Gunn, & Chase-Lansdale, 1989) and higher levels of sensitivity and involvement in fathers (Shannon, Tamis-LeMonda, & Cabrera, 2006). Difficulties in coparenting have been associated with children's emotional and behavioral problems from infancy throughout childhood (Vaughn, Block, & Block, 1988; Van Egeren & Hawkins, 2004).

AN ECOLOGICAL MODEL

Congruent with Bronfenbrenner's (Bronfenbrenner & Morris, 1998) premise that the wider society and culture influences the individual, family systems theory has been augmented by an ecological perspective to include the extrafamilial and contextual networks of individuals; according to this perspective, the child is influenced by the physical, social, and cultural contexts surrounding him or her, within and across time (Bornstein & Sawyer, 2005).

Parenting in Low-Income and Ethnically Diverse Fathers and Mothers

Findings from the Early Head Start studies (Cabrera et al., 2004; Vogel, Boller, Faerber, Shannon, & Tamis-LeMonda, 2003) reveal that between 70 and 85% of low-income fathers regularly participate in their young children's lives in the routines of feeding, diapering, and play. Accordingly, it can be assumed that as fathers engage in these coparenting activities, they provide their children with meaningful experiences that build on and/or complement the interactions children have with their mothers. However, for some, the demands of caring for a new infant can strain the family system and lead to decline in involvement over time and the "magic moment" (Carlson, McLanahan, & England, 2004) can dissipate soon after the infant's birth.

Just as there is scant research on the prenatal behaviors of mothers, there is even less on fathers' supportive behaviors during the prenatal period (Tamis-LeMonda, Yoshikawa, & Kahana-Kalman, 2009). To that end, using data from the Early Head Start National Evaluation Project, we analyzed the interviews of 2,160 low-income mothers to assess the prenatal involvement and accessibility of fathers over a five-year period (Shannon, Cabrera, Tamis-LeMonda, & Lamb, 2009). Among other variables, influential contextual factors such as the mother--father relationship and fathers' ethnicity were also considered in our model, as extant research suggests that these variables predict fathers' commitment to and involvement with their infants and young children over time (Cabrera, Shannon, West, & Brooks-Gum, 2006; Cummings et al., 2004; Tamis-LeMonda et al., 2004).

Father residency and prenatal involvement (accompanying mothers to prenatal doctor visits, discussing pregnancy) predicted fathers' presence in their children's lives up to 5 years later (Shannon et al., 2009). Some 70% of fathers who resided with their partners at birth remained accessible to their children in pre-kindergarten, whereas only 30% of fathers not cohabitating continued to be accessible five years later. Of those fathers who were highly involved prenatally, 65% remained accessible to their 5-year-olds, whereas only 14% of fathers who were not involved with mothers' prenatally were present in the lives of their 5-year-olds. These findings indicate that the father's relationship with the mother and infant during the prenatal period (residency and involvement as proxies) predicts later father involvement with his child. As a group, fathers were moderately to highly involved with their infants prenatally; however, there were some racial and ethnic differences worth noting. Residency was a stronger predictor of White and Latino fathers' continued presence and prenatal involvement was a stronger predictor of African American fathers' accessibility to their children, indicating the need to look at a variety of different family structures across cultural groups.

We also assessed the associations among prenatal father involvement, the quality of the partner relationship, and coparenting of toddlers in 204 low-income Dominican, Mexican, and African American families (Tamis-LeMonda et al., 2009). We found that most fathers were involved with mothers' pregnancies; over 95% of fathers spoke to mothers about the pregnancy and felt the baby move. High levels of father involvement continued when children were 14-months old. The majority of fathers engaged in activities with their children, spent time alone watching their children, and most ate at least one meal with their children and families daily. Also, prenatal involvement and ethnicity influenced later involvement; fathers who were higher on measures of prenatal involvement were more likely to spend time with their 6-month-olds and engaged in more activities with their 14-month-olds as compared to those who were low on prenatal involvement. Mexican men, relative to other ethnic groups, engaged in more hospital visitation during the prenatal period and were more likely to eat meals with their children when children were 14 months. This finding might be due to the higher rates of residency in Mexican men, and "familism" or family-centered concern (Parke et al., 2004).

Notably, the quality of the mother–father relationship immediately after the transition to a new baby (i.e., when infants were 1 month of age) mediated the relationship between prenatal involvement and postnatal involvement (Tamis-LeMonda et al., 2009). Particularly for non-resident fathers, those who maintained positive relationships with mothers were more likely to watch over their infants in their partners' absence and to eat regular meals with them. These findings point to the need for practitioners to employ culturally sensitive prenatal interventions that focus on enhancing the quality of the mother–father relationship, especially for couples not cohabitating.

In a study of fathers' *postpartum* relationships with their partners and children, we inquired into how demographics (e.g., age, education, marital status, income), partner quality, and father engagement related to children's outcomes by *directly* interviewing fathers and observing their interactions with their infants (Shannon et al., 2006). Participants were 74 racially and ethnically diverse, low-income fathers from the Father and Newborn Study (FANS) and their 8- and 16-month-olds. Based on father–child interactions during free play, fathers' responsive and didactic behaviors were associated with infants' mastery and communicative behaviors at both ages. Fathers who rated their relationship as positive and who felt supported by their partners were consistently more engaged with their infants and increased their responsiveness by the time children were 16 months old. Furthermore, fathers' responsiveness was important to infants' social and communicative behaviors.

How does an ethnocultural background affect mothers' expectations during the transition to a new baby? To address this question, we interviewed 369 low-income Chinese, Dominican, Mexican, and African American mothers in New York City hospital maternity wards about their concerns regarding children's development, parenting, family, and resources. Mothers from the four ethnic groups expressed trepidations about resources (e.g., work, childcare) more than child development (e.g., milestones) (Tamis-LeMonda & Kahana-Kalman, 2009). This finding is in contrast to the researched concerns of European American mothers from middle-income backgrounds (e.g., Harwood et al., 2007). Also, mothers who did not reside with their partners talked about resources more frequently than those who resided with fathers, and these concerns make sense in light of the increased economic responsibility that may co-occur with father non-residency.

Ethnicity moderated the effects of father residency on mothers' views about parenting and family. For Latinas, father residency was associated with greater concerns about the family (e.g., family interdependence), whereas African American mothers emphasized family more when fathers did not reside with them. In Latino families, having a baby may reinforce the mother–father bond, especially when partners reside together. In African American families, mothers might be concerned about the family situation in the context of father non-residency. In general, Mexican and Dominican mothers spoke more about family than mothers of other backgrounds, especially the health and well-being of family members and the integration of their newly born infant into the family unit, perhaps reflecting the traditional value of familismo in their postpartum views (Tamis-LeMonda & Kahana-Kalman, 2009). This illustrates the importance of the contextual aspects of the family system in mothers' postpartum concerns, aspirations, and relationships, all of which have implications for children's later development (Heinicke & Guthrie, 1992).

LIMITATIONS OF THEORY IN THE TRANSITION TO PARENTING

The transition to parenthood is considered an exciting, challenging, and stressful time in families. We have considered three core theoretical perspectives to understand the changes occurring during the transition to parenthood: *attachment theory*, a *family systems perspective*, and an *ecological model*. However, in the past decade with changing demographics in the US, it is becoming evident that theories must go beyond the mother–child dyad, traditional family subsystems, and using a general external standard to explain cultural differences during the transition to parenting.

In attachment theory, families from different backgrounds may look deficient when compared to White middle-class families. Decreased normative levels of parent sensitivity and secure behaviors in contextually diverse families have been documented by some researchers (Day, 2011). For example, middle- and working-class, Anglo American mothers from the US encouraged more independence, creativity, and self-confidence in their children, while middle- and working-class mothers in Puerto Rico emphasized childrearing values such as obedience, respect and emotional interdependence on families (Harwood, Miller, & Irizarry, 1995). As a result of these childrearing values, Puerto Rican mothers appeared to be more intrusive to and controlling of their infants than Anglo American mothers. However, Puerto Rican infants of controlling mothers were *not* likely to be insecurely attached. In contrast, Anglo American infants with controlling mothers were likely to be identified as insecure (Carlson & Harwood, 2003).

In general, family systems theory has emphasized how family relationships, assumed comparable in most families, impact the child; family structure and context has received limited attention. For instance, fathers and other coparents have been frequently omitted in family-based approaches (Cabrera, Shannon, & Jolley-Mitchell, in press). Yet, in many of the cultural groups in the US (e.g., Latino, African American, Chinese), a high proportion of grandparents coparent their grandchildren (Goodman & Silverstein, 2006) and the influence of family may vary depending on certain circumstances, such as father residency, immigration experience or acculturation (Cabrera, Shannon, & La Taillade, 2009; Kurrien & Vo, 2004; Tamis-LeMonda & Kahana-Kalman, 2009). Although recent immigrants from Latino countries often rely on the grandparents to take on the role of coparent (Hovey & Magaña, 2000), immigrant parents from Vietnam look to non-family members from their new communities to serve as coparents (Kurrien & Vo, 2004). An emic-tailored family system framework may be enhanced by considering different family structures with multiple caregivers (e.g., mother–grandmother coparents, mother–non-resident fathers) during the transition to parenting.

Within the ecological theoretical model, there is acknowledgment of the embeddedness of families within a variety of formal and informal social support systems as well as the cultures in which they exist, however, concepts that are not universal are sometimes applied to all cultural groups. This may lead to an attribution that variations in culture, language, or socioeconomic status are due to deficiencies in other cultural groups rather than the differences being due to normative developmental processes. It cannot be assumed that "one size fits all" and universal approaches to our theoretical understanding of the transition to parenthood within diverse ethnic and cultural groups may require emic adaptations for optimal use.

In our own research, we have employed both etic and emic approaches in studying the transition to parenthood in diverse cultural groups. We have advanced the field regarding how context influences the "family stage" and children's development. Nonetheless, the question arises about the impact of our research on theoretical development.

SUGGESTIONS FOR FUTURE THEORETICAL DEVELOPMENTS IN UNDERSTANDING THE TRANSITION TO PARENTHOOD

Historically, traditional theories like attachment theory and family systems theory, carry an "imposed etic" in which a European American standard is imposed on our notions about other cultural groups. Emic interpretations provide important culturally based meanings absent when an "imposed etic" is used in studying diverse cultures. Contextual interpretations (the emic approach) are essential in augmenting etic approaches that associate variations in cultural context to variations in behavior. Berry (1999) postulates "derived etics," or similarities among cultures that could be discerned when emic perspectives are used in a number of contexts. This requires theories that are "revolutionary," in which our knowledge of psychological phenomena is negotiated and altered, not just available for generating explanations (Chaudhary, 1999).

A Novel Conceptualization of Coparenting Beginning during the Transition to Parenting

One example of how contextually-based research can influence a traditional theory of the transition to parenting is in the area of coparenting. To date, family-based theories of coparenting have been primarily limited to White, middle-class, traditional two-parent families. Feinberg (2003) noted that "the form of the coparenting relationship is shaped to a large extent by parents' beliefs, values, desires, and expectations, which in turn are shaped by the dominant culture as well as subcultural themes within socioeconomic, ethnic, religious, and racial groups" (p. 98). This implies that there are similar components of coparenting that exist across cultures, which has some support from psychometric evidence (McHale, Kuersten-Hogan, & Rao, 2004).

The appearance of the various components of coparenting may differ by culture. For instance, if there is an expectation that mothers are more nurturing than fathers, then this belief may shift how mothers and fathers engage in triadic play interactions with their infants. Consequently, cross-cultural studies of coparenting during the transition to parenting can "proceed from cultural definitions of shared parenting, instead of importing constructs from the cultures in which coparenting theory and research originated" (McHale et al., 2004, p. 231).

Using an emic approach to coparenting, qualitative research conducted by Caldera and colleagues (2002) suggested that most but not all of Feinberg's (2003) theoretical components of coparenting were evident in the structure of coparenting among Mexican American families. Specifically, they examined how fathers and mothers negotiate and manage parenting issues, within a sample of 14 Mexican American couples (mothers and fathers) who were predominantly first generation immigrants (Caldera, Fitzpatrick, & Wampler, 2002). There were two overarching themes that emerged: one on how parents initially decided to manage coparenting and the second regarding their ongoing process of negotiating, which was divided into six coparenting dimensions. These dimensions were similar to the conceptual models of coparenting presented by Feinberg (2003) and Van Egeren and Hawkins (2004), which were: (1) *joint decision making*: valuing the input of both parents; (2) *support*: providing relief when one parent is experiencing role strain; (3) *cooperation*: the process of mutually agreeing on how to divide tasks; (4) *conflict*: disagreeing with, contradicting and interrupting each other; (5) *coordination of parenting tasks*: emphasis on satisfaction with division of labor; and (6) *compensation*: filling in the "gaps" of the other parent's shortcomings. The latter two coparenting dimensions—coordination and compensation—were distinct from prior conceptual models. A strength of Caldera's qualitative study was that the coparenting beliefs and values identified within this group of Mexican American couples originated from parents' own words and perspectives, rather than having their views guided by a theory based on non-Latino, White samples. This emic and "derived etic" approach to coparenting should be incorporated into a family systems' interpretation that is done longitudinally, beginning during the transition to parenting.

CONCLUSION

The transition to parenthood and becoming a family can be a rewarding and growth producing experience. Increasing numbers of infants live in families that include: non-resident fathers (Cabrera et al., 2004; Carlson et al., 2004); biological parents and step-parents (Hetherington & Stanley-Hagan, 2002); adoptive parents (Brodzinsky & Pinderhughes, 2002); and grandparents (Smith & Drew, 2002). Theorists, researchers, and practitioners need to attend to the relationships in all varieties of families, to make them more satisfying and less conflicted, in order to benefit the family as a whole system (P. A. Cowan, Cowan, & Knox, 2010). This requires adopting a new framework in which families are nested within broader cultural, socioeconomic, and family backgrounds. The unique hopes, aspirations, and experiences of diverse families at the transition to having a new baby need to be addressed by contextually sensitive theories and research (Tamis-LeMonda et al., 2009).

REFERENCES

Ainsworth, M. D. (1973). The development of infant-mother attachment. In B. Caldwell & H. Ricciuti (Eds.), *Review of child development research* (Vol. 3, pp. 1–94). Chicago: University of Chicago Press.

Barth, J. M., & Parke, R. D. (1993). Parent-child relationship influences on children's transition to school. *Merrill-Palmer Quarterly, 39*, 173–195.

Belsky, J. (1984). The determinants of parenting: A process model. *Child Development, 55*, 83–96.

Belsky, J. (1993). Etiology of child maltreatment: A developmental-ecological analysis. *Psychological Bulletin, 114*, 413–434.

Belsky, J., Ward, M., & Rovine, M. (1986). Prenatal expectations, postnatal experiences, and the transition to parenthood. In R. Ashmore & D. Brodzinsky (Eds.), *Perspectives on the family* (pp. 111–146). Hillsdale, NJ: Erlbaum.

Belsky, J., Spanier, G. B., & Rovine, M. (1983). Stability and change in marriage across the transition to parenthood. *Journal of Marriage and the Family, 45*, 567–577.

Belsky, J., Youngblade, L., Rovine, M., & Volling, B. (1991). Patterns of marital change and parent-child interaction. *Journal of Marriage and the Family, 53*, 487–498.

Berry, J. W. (1999). Emics and etics: A symbiotic conception. *Culture and Psychology, 5*, 165–171.

Bibring, G. L. (1959). Some considerations of the psychological processes in pregnancy. *Psychoanalytic Study of the Child, 14*, 113–121.

Bibring, G. L., Dwyer, T. F., Huntington, D. S., & Valenstein, A. F. (1961). A study of the psychological processes in pregnancy and of the earliest mother-child relationship. *Psychoanalytic Study of the Child, 16*, 9–72.

Bornstein M. H., & Sawyer J. (2005). Family systems. In K. McCartney and D. Phillips (Eds), *Blackwell handbook on early childhood development* (pp. 381–398). Malden, MA: Blackwell.

Bowen, M. (1978). *Family therapy in clinical practice*. New York: Jason Aronson.

Bowlby, J. (1969). *Attachment and loss: Vol. 1: Attachment*. New York: Basic Books.

Bowlby, J. (1980). *Attachment and loss: Vol. 3: Loss*. New York: Basic Books.

Bowlby, J. (1988). *A secure base*. New York: Basic Books.

Brodzinsky, D.M. & Pinderhughes, E. (2002). Parenting and child development in adoptive families. In M. Bornstein (Ed.), *Handbook of parenting, Vol. 1: Children and parenting* (2nd ed., pp. 279–311). Hillsdale, NJ: Erlbaum.

Bronfenbrenner, U., & Morris, P. A. (1998). The ecology of developmental processes. In W. Damon & R. M. Lerner (Eds.), *Handbook of child psychology, 1. Theoretical models of human development* (5th ed., pp. 993–1028). New York: Wiley.

Cabrera, N., Ryan, R., Jolley, S., Shannon, J. D., & Tamis-LeMonda, C. (2008). Low-income nonresident father involvement with their toddlers: Variation by fathers' ethnicity, resources, and mother-father relationship. *Journal of Family Psychology, 22*, 643–647.

Cabrera, N., Ryan, R., Shannon, J. D., Brooks-Gunn, J., Vogel, C., Raikes, H. et al. (2004). Low-income fathers' involvement in their toddlers' lives: Biological fathers from the Early Head Start research and evaluation study. *Fathering: A Journal of Theory, Research, and Practice about Men as Fathers, 2*, 5–30.

Cabrera, N., Shannon, J. D., Jolley-Mitchell, S., & West, J. (2009). Mexican American mothers and fathers' prenatal attitudes and father prenatal involvement: Links to mother-infant interaction and father engagement. *Journal of Sex Roles, 60*, 510–526.

Cabrera, N., Shannon, J. D., & Jolley-Mitchell, S. (in press). Coparenting in Latino families. In S. C. Chuang & C. S. Tamis-LeMonda (Eds.), *Gender roles in immigrant families*. New York: Springer.

Cabrera, N., Shannon, J. D., & La Taillade, J. J. (2009). Predictors of co-parenting in Mexican American families and direct effects on parenting and child social emotional development. *Journal of Infant Mental Health, 30*, 523–548.

Cabrera, N. J., Shannon, J. D., West, J., & Brooks-Gum, J. (2006). Parental interactions with Latino infants: Variation by country of origin and English proficiency. *Child Development, 77*, 1190–1207.

Caldera, Y. M., Fitzpatrick, J., & Wampler, K. S. (2002). Coparenting in intact Mexican American families: Mothers' and fathers' perceptions. In J. M. Contreras, K. A. Kerns, & A. Neal-Barnett (Eds.), *Latino children and families in the United States: Current research and future directions* (pp. 107–131). Westport, CT: Praeger.

Carlson, V., & Harwood, R. (2003). Attachment, culture, and the caregiving system: Cultural patterning of everyday experiences among Anglo and Puerto Rican Mother-infant pairs. *Infant Mental Health Journal, 24*, 53–73.

Carlson, M., McLanahan, S., & England, P. (2004). Union formation in fragile families. *Demography 41*, 237–261.

Chaudhary, N. (1999). Diversity, definitions, and dilemmas: A commentary on Helfrich's principle of triarchic resonance. *Culture and Psychology, 5*, 155–163.

Cowan, C. P., & Cowan, P. A. (1990). Becoming a family: Research and intervention. In I. E. Sigel & G. H. Brody (Eds.), *Methods of family research: Biographies of research projects: Vol. 1. Normal families* (pp. 1–51). Hillsdale, NJ: Erlbaum.

Cowan, C. P., & Cowan, P. A. (1992). *When partners become parents: The big life change for couples*. New York: Basic Books.

Cowan, C. P., & Cowan, P. A. (1995). Interventions to ease the transition to parenthood. *Family Relations, 44*, 412–423.

Cowan, C. P., Cowan, P. A., Heming, G. & Miller, N. B. (1991). Becoming a family: Marriage, parenting and child development. In P. A. Cowan & M. Hetherington (Eds.), *Family transitions* (pp. 79–110). Hillsdale, NJ: Erlbaum.

Cowan, P. A., Cohn, D. A., Cowan, C. P., & Pearson, J. (1996). Parents' attachment histories and children's externalizing and internalizing behaviors: Exploring family models of linkage. *Journal of Consulting and Clinical Psychology, 64*, 53–63.

Cowan, P. A., & Cowan, C. P. (1988). Changes in marriage during the transition to parenthood: Must we blame the baby? In G. Y. Michaels and W. A. Goldberg (Eds.), *The transition to parenthood: Current theory and research* (pp. 114–154). New York: Cambridge University Press.

Cowan, P. A., & Cowan, C. P. (2002). Interventions as tests of family systems theories: Marital and family relationships in children's development, and psychopathology. *Development and Psychopathology. Special issue on Interventions as tests of theories, 14*, 731–760.

Cowan, P. A., Cowan, C. P., Ablow, J., Johnson, V., & Measelle, J. (2005). *The family context of parenting in children's adaptation to elementary school*. Mahwah, NJ: Erlbaum.

Cowan, P. A., Cowan, C. P., & Knox, V. (2010). Marriage and fatherhood programs. *Future of Children, 20*, 205–230.

Cowan, P. A., Powell, D., & Cowan, C. P. (1997). Parenting interventions: A family systems perspective. In I. E. Sigel & K. A. Renninger (Eds.), *Handbook of Child Psychology, Vol. 4: Child psychology in practice,* (5th ed., pp. 3–72). New York: Wiley.

Cox, M. J., Owen, M. T., Lewis, J. M., Riedel, C., Scalf-McIver, L., & Suster, A. (1985). Intergenerational influences of the parent-infant relationship in the transition to parenthood. *Journal of Family Issues, 6*, 543–564.

Cox, M. J., & Paley, B. (1997). Families as systems. *Annual Review of Psychology, 48*, 243–267.

Cummings, E. M., Goeke-Morey, M. C., & Raymond, J. L. (2004). Fathers in family context: Effects of marital quality and marital conflict. In M. E. Lamb (Ed.), *The role of the father in child development,* (4th ed., pp. 196–221). Hoboken, NJ: Wiley.

Day, C. A. (2011). Parenting children in high-risk environments: An examination of maternal sensitivity in poverty. In D. W Davis & M. C. Logsdon (Eds.), *Maternal sensitivity: A scientific foundation for practice* (pp. 195–214). New York: Nova.

Dyer, E. D. (1963). Parenthood as crisis: a re-study. *Marriage and Family Living, 25*, 196–201.

Elder, G. H. (1998). The life course and human development. In R. M. Lerner (Ed.) and W. Damon (Gen. Ed.), *Handbook of child psychology, Vol. 1: Theoretical models of human development,* (5th ed., pp. 939–991). New York: Wiley.

Elek, S. M., Brage Hudson, D., & Bouffard, C. (2003). Marital and parenting satisfaction and infant care self-efficacy during the transition to parenthood: The effect of infant sex. *Issues in Comprehensive Pediatric Nursing, 26*, 45–57.

Erel, O., & Burman, B. (1995). Interrelatedness of marital relations and parent-child relations: A meta-analytic review. *Psychological Bulletin, 118*, 108–132.

Feinberg, M. E. (2003). The internal structure and ecological context of coparenting: A framework for research and intervention. *Parenting: Science and Practice, 3*, 95–131.

Florsheim, P., Moore, D., & Edgington, C. (2003). Romantic relations among adolescent parents. In P. Florsheim (Ed.), *Adolescent romantic relations and sexual behaviour: Theory, research, and practical implications* (pp. 297–324). Mahwah, NJ: Erlbaum.

Fomby, P., & Cherlin, A. J. (2007). Family instability and child well-being. *American Sociological Review, 72*, 181–204.

Fonagy, P., Steele, H., & Steele, M. (1991). Maternal representations of attachment during pregnancy predict the organization of infant-mother attachment at one year of age. *Child Development, 62*, 891–905.

Furstenberg, F. F., Brooks-Gunn, J., and Chase-Lansdale, L. (1989). Teenage pregnancy and childbearing. *American Psychologist, 44*, 313–320.

Goodman, C. C., & Silverstein, M. (2006). Grandmothers raising grandchildren: Ethnic and racial differences in well-being among custodial and co-parenting families. *Journal of Family Issues, 11*, 1605–1626.

Grych, J. H. (2002). Marital relationships and parenting. In M. H. Bornstein MH (Ed.). *Handbook of parenting, Vol. 4: Social conditions and applied parenting* (pp. 203–226). Mahwah, NJ: Erlbaum.

Hackle, L. S., & Ruble, D. N. (1992). Changes in the marital relationship after the first baby is born: predicting the impact of expectancy disconfirmation. *Journal of Personality and Social Psychology, 62,* 944–957.

Hall, G. C. N., & Barongan, C. (2002). *Multicultural psychology*. Upper Saddle River, NJ: Prentice Hall.

Harwood, K., McLean, N., & Durkin, K. (2007). First-time mothers' expectations of parenthood: What happens when optimistic expectations are not matched by later experiences? *Developmental Psychology, 43*, 1–12.

Harwood, R., Miller, J., & Irizarry, N. (1995). *Culture and attachment: Perceptions of the child in context*. New York: Guilford Press.

Heinicke, C. M. (2002). *The transition to parenting*. Mahwah, NJ: Erlbaum.

Heinicke, C. M., & Guthrie, D. (1992). Stability and change in husband-wife adaptation and the development of the positive parent-child relationship. *Infant Behavior and Development, 15*, 109–127.

Helfrich, H. (1999). Beyond the dilemma of cross-cultural psychology: Resolving the dilemma between etic and emic approaches. *Culture and Psychology, 5*, 131–153.

Hetherington, E. M., & Stanley-Hagan, M. (2002). Parenting in divorced and remarried families. In M. H. Bornstein (Ed.), *Handbook of parenting. Vol. 3: Being and becoming a parent* (pp. 287–316). Mahwah, NJ: Lawrence Erlbaum.

Hovey, J. D., & Magaña, C. (2000). Acculturative stress, anxiety, and depression among Mexican immigrant farm workers in the Midwest United States. *Journal of Immigrant Health, 2*, 119–131.

Kennell, J. H., Slyter, H., & Klaus, M. H. (1970). The mourning response of parents to the death of a newborn infant. *New England Journal of Medicine, 283*, 344–349.

Knauth, D. G. (2000). Predictors of parental sense of competence for the couple during the transition to parenthood. *Research in Nursing and Health, 23,* 496–509.

Kurrien, R., & Vo, E. D. (2004). Who's in charge?: Coparenting in South and Southeast Asian families. *Journal of Adult Development, 11*, 207–219.

Lawrence, E., Cobb, R. J., Rothman, A. D., Rothman, M. T., & Bradbury, T. N. (2008). Marital Satisfaction across the transition to parenthood. *Journal of Family Psychology, 22*, 41–50.

Lawrence, E., Nylen, K., & Cobb, R.J. (2007). Prenatal expectations and marital satisfaction over the transition to parenthood. *Journal of Family Psychology 21*, 155–164.

Leifer, M. (1977). Psychological changes accompanying pregnancy and motherhood. *Genetic Psychology Monographs, 95*, 55–96.

LeMasters, E. E. (1957). Parenthood as crisis. *Marriage and Family Living, 19*, 352–355.

Lumley, J. M. (1980). Through a glass darkly: Ultrasound and prenatal bonding. *Birth, 17*, 214–217.

Lumley, J. M. (1982). Attitudes to the fetus among primigravidae. *Australian Pediatric Journal, 18*, 106–109.

Main, M. & Goldwyn, R. (1984). Predicting rejection of her infant from mother's representation of her own experience: Implications for the abused-abusing intergenerational cycle. *Child Abuse and Neglect, 8*, 203–217.

Main, M., Kaplan, N., & Cassidy, J. (1985). Security in infancy, childhood, and adulthood: A move to the level of representation. *Monographs of the Society for Research in Child Development, 50*, 66–104.

McHale, J., Khazan, I., Erera, P., Rotman, T., DeCourcey, W., & McConnell, M. (2002). Coparenting in diverse family systems. In M. H. Bornstein (Ed.), *Handbook of parenting, Vol. 3: Being and becoming a parent* (pp. 75–107). Mahwah NJ: Erlbaum.

McHale, J. P., Kuersten-Hogan, R., & Rao, N. (2004). Growing points for coparenting theory and research. *Journal of Adult Development, 11*, 221–234.

Mebert, C. & Kalinowski, M. (1986). Parents' expectations and perceptions of infant temperament: "pregnancy status" differences. *Infant Behaviour and Development, 9*, 321–334.

Minuchin, P. (1985). Families and individual development: Provocations from the field of family therapy. *Child Development, 56*, 289–302.

Pacey, S. (2004). Couples and the first baby: Responding to new parents' sexual and relationship problems. *Sexual and Relationship Therapy, 19*, 223–246.

Palkowitz, R. (1996). Parenting as a generator of adult development: Conceptual issues and implications. *Journal of Social and Personal Relationships, 13*, 571–592.

Parke, R. D., Coltrane, S., Duffy, S., Buriel, R., Dennis, J., Powers, J. et al. (2004). Economic stress, parenting, and child adjustment in Mexican American and European American families. *Child Development, 75,* 1632–1656.

Pike, K. L. (1967). *Language in relation to a unified theory of the structure of human behavior.* The Hague: Mouton.

Rohner, R. P. (1986). *The warmth dimension: Foundations of parental acceptance-rejection theory.* Thousand Oaks, CA: Sage.

Satir, V. (1972). *Peoplemaking: Because you want to be a better parent.* Palo Alto, CA: Science and Behavior Books, Inc.

Shannon, J. D., Cabrera, N., Tamis-LeMonda, C. S., & Lamb, M. E. (2009). Who stays and who leaves? Father accessibility across children's first five years. *Parenting: Science and Practice, 9,* 78–100.

Shannon, J. D., Tamis-LeMonda, C. S., & Cabrera, N. (2006). Fathering in infancy: Mutuality and stability between 6 and 14 months. *Parenting: Science and Practice, 6,* 167–188.

Shannon, J. D., Tamis-LeMonda, C. S., & Margolin, A. (2005). Father involvement in infancy: Influences of past and current relationships. *Infancy, 8,* 21–41.

Shapiro, A. F., Gottman, J. M. & Carrère, S. (2000). The baby and the marriage: Identifying factors that buffer against decline in marital satisfaction after the baby arrives. *Journal of Family Psychology, 14,* 59–70.

Shelton, K. H. & Harold, G. T. (2008). Interparental conflict, negative parenting, and children's adjustment: Bridging links between parents' depression and children's psychological distress. *Journal of Family Psychology, 22,* 712–724.

Smith, P. K., & Drew, L. M. (2002). Grandparenthood. In M. H. Bornstein (Ed.), *Handbook of parenting, Vol. 3: Being and becoming a parent* (pp. 141–169). Mahwah, NJ: Erlbaum.

Sroufe, L. A., & Waters, E. (1977). Attachment as an organizational construct. *Child Development, 48,* 1184–1199.

Tamis-LeMonda, C. S., Baumwell, L., & Cabrera, N. J. (in press). Fathers' role in children's language development. In N. J. Cabrera & C. S. Tamis-LeMonda (Eds.), *Handbook of father involvement: Multi-disciplinary perspectives* (2nd ed.). New York: Taylor & Francis.

Tamis-LeMonda, C. S., & Kahana-Kalman, R. (2009). Mothers' views at the transition to a new baby: Variation across ethnic groups. *Parenting: Science and Practice, 9,* 36–55.

Tamis-LeMonda, C. S., Shannon, J. D., Cabrera, N., & Lamb, M. E. (2004). Fathers and mothers at play with their 2- and 3-year olds: Contributions to language and cognitive development. *Child Development, 75,* 1806–1820.

Tamis-LeMonda, C. S., Yoshikawa, H., & Kahana-Kalman, R. (2009). Father involvement in immigrant and ethnically diverse families from the prenatal period to the second year: Prediction and mediating mechanisms. *Sex Roles, 60,* 496–509.

Van Egeren, L. A., & Hawkins, D. P. (2004). Coming to terms with coparenting: Implications of definition and measurement. *Journal of Adult Development, 11,* 165–178.

Vaughn, B. E., Block, J. H., & Block, J. (1988). Parental agreement on child-rearing during early childhood and the psychological characteristics of adolescents. *Child Development, 59,* 1029–1033.

Vogel, C. A., Boller, K., Faerber, J., Shannon, J. D., & Tamis-LeMonda, C. S. (2003). *Understanding fathering: The early head start of fathers of newborns.* Mathematica Policy Research Publication, No. 8517, pp. A. 1–A. 10.

Volling, B. L., & Belsky, J. (1992). Infant, father, and marital antecedents of infant-father attachment security in dual-earner and single-earner families. *International Journal of Behavioral Development, 15,* 83–100.

Ward, M. J., & Carlson, E. (1995). Associations among adult attachment representations, maternal sensitivity, and infant-mother attachment in a sample of adolescent mothers. *Child Development, 66,* 69–79.

Zeanah, C. H., Keener, M. A., Anders, T. F. & Vieira-Buker, C. (1987). Adolescent mothers' perceptions of their infants before and after birth. *American Journal of Orthopsychiatry, 57,* 351–360.

Zeanah, C. H., Keener, M. A., Stewart, L., & Anders, T. F. (1985). Prenatal perceptions of infant personality: A preliminary investigation. *Journal of the American Academy of Child Psychiatry, 24,* 204–210.

15 Theoretical Approaches to Studying Divorce

David H. Demo and Cheryl Buehler

Divorce continues to be widely studied among family scholars with nearly 2,000 studies on the topic published in the last decade (Amato, 2010). Although the divorce rate in the US appears to have declined from its peak around 1980, 2% of all marriages end in divorce each year and demographic projections suggest that between 43 and 46% of current marriages will end in divorce (Schoen & Canudas-Romo, 2006; Schoen & Standish, 2001). Marriages and cohabiting relationships in the US are also more likely to be dissolved than relationships in other Western nations. Comparatively, American women are more likely to marry; they marry and cohabit for the first time at an earlier age; and their marriages are more likely to end in divorce (Cherlin, 2009). Within the first 5 years of marriage, more than one-fifth of American marriages end in divorce, twice the rate in other Western nations (Cherlin, 2009).

In this chapter, we examine whether the theoretical lens that family scholars use in studying divorce affects the explanations offered for: (a) the correlates and consequences of divorce; (b) variation in the divorce experience; and (c) mediating and moderating influences. We begin by reviewing key topics and findings in the divorce literature, then describe common and less-often utilized theoretical approaches to the study of divorce. We conclude by identifying limitations in how theory has (and has not) been applied, and we offer some suggestions for how theory might be used more profitably.

KEY TOPICS, ISSUES, AND FINDINGS

Considerable attention has been devoted to understanding five aspects of the divorce process: (a) antecedents or precursors of divorce; (b) effects of divorce on adult adjustment; (c) effects on parenting behaviors and parent–child relationships; (d) implications for larger family systems; and (e) consequences for child and adolescent adjustment.

Precursors of Divorce

An important component of the contemporary cultural context for intimate relationships and living arrangements in the US is a prevailing set of values and beliefs defined by expressive individualism (Bellah, Madsen, Sullivan, Swidler, & Tipton, 1985; Cherlin, 2009). According to this view, adults place a high value on personal growth and fulfillment; they continually monitor their wishes and needs; and when changes are needed, they exit relationships and start new ones. At the same time, many people hold very high and often unrealistic expectations for marital relationships, creating a context in which many marriages are terminated due to lofty expectations, unmet needs, and the desire to pursue alternative relationships. An individualistic cultural orientation to divorce tends to be accompanied by higher divorce rates (Toth & Kemmelmeier, 2009).

The probability that a marriage will end in divorce is also influenced by sociodemographic and life course factors. For example, divorce is more likely for marriages characterized by lower levels of family income and education, young age at marriage, pre-engagement cohabitation, and premarital childbearing (Amato, 2010; Rhoades, Stanley, & Markman, 2009). Other life course experiences associated with a higher probability of divorce include parental divorce, insecure adult attachment orientations, living or working where there are numerous alternatives to the current relationship, and marriages in which partners are less religious (Crowell, Treboux, & Brockmeyer, 2009; Rodrigues, Hall, & Fincham, 2006; South, Trent, & Shen, 2001).

Several relational variables also predict elevated rates of marital dissolution. Formerly married individuals report that a lack of communication, not feeling loved or appreciated, and extramarital sexual involvement were important reasons for their divorce (Amato & Previti, 2003). In fact, extramarital affairs are the leading cause of divorce across 160 cultures (Betzig, 1989). Hurtful and abusive interactions such as criticism, belligerence, and stonewalling undermine positive affect and marital satisfaction, which, in turn, increase the chances of divorce (Gottman & Levenson, 2000). There is also a strong association between aggression and relationship dissolution (Huesmann, Dubow, & Boxer, 2009; Lawrence, Ro, Barry, & Bunde, 2006). Although negative interactions and high levels of hostile conflict erode marital happiness and increase chances of divorce, low-distress marriages are still vulnerable to divorce if the partners exhibit a low level of commitment (Amato & Hohmann-Marriott, 2007).

Personality and mental health problems that increase the likelihood of divorce include neuroticism, antisocial behavior, substance abuse, negative affect, psychiatric disorders, and low levels of agreeableness (Amato & Previti, 2003; Hertenstein, Hansel, Butts, & Hile, 2009; Rodrigues et al., 2006). Formerly married adults often cite incompatibility, growing apart, and experiencing personality problems as major reasons why they divorced (Amato & Previti, 2003).

Adult Adjustment

Divorce consists of multiple, interrelated processes that require spouses who are dissolving their marriages to separate from each other emotionally, psychologically, socially, legally, and financially (Bohannon, 1968). As these processes unfold, usually over a period of years, adults experience a series of stressors and losses. Common losses include valued identities (e.g., wife, husband), sharp declines in financial resources and standard of living (especially for women), and loss of social attachment and emotional support (especially for men) (Gadalla, 2009). As a result, in comparison to their married counterparts, divorced adults report higher rates of unhappiness, depression and anxiety, physical health problems, and alcohol and substance use (Afifi, Boman, Fleisher, & Sareen, 2009; Dube et al., 2009; Hughes & Waite, 2009; Kposowa, 2009; Sbarra, Law, Lee, & Mason, 2009; Sbarra & Nietert, 2009). Among both African Americans and Whites, women are more likely to exhibit symptoms of psychological distress following divorce and men are more prone to alcohol use and dependence (Barrett, 2003; Williams, Takeuchi, & Adair, 1992).

An important research question receiving recent attention from divorce scholars is the trajectory characterizing adult well-being in the years preceding and following divorce. Specifically, is diminished well-being a consequence of legal divorce and its associated stressors (*the divorce causation hypothesis*), or does maladjustment precede (and even contribute to) marital dissolution (*the divorce selection hypothesis*)? A related question is the duration of post-divorce adjustment problems and opportunities for growth and maturation following divorce. Although the evidence is not entirely consistent, studies indicate that adult adjustment problems typically precede physical separation and divorce, and last for 2–3 years following divorce, after which symptoms diminish (Hetherington & Kelly, 2002). Although a minority of divorced adults (10–15%) suffer long-term emotional pain and chronic strain, the more common profile is one of short-term disturbances followed by significant improvements and personal growth (Hetherington & Kelly, 2002; Kitson, 1992).

EFFECTS OF DIVORCE ON PARENTING BEHAVIORS AND PARENT–CHILD RELATIONSHIPS

Approximately 1.1 million American children per year experience their parents' divorce (Kreider, 2007). Following divorce, residential parents (typically mothers) are less involved with their children and less consistent in disciplining. Compared with mothers in first marriages, divorced mothers spend less time with children, talk with them less often, communicate with and monitor their children less effectively, and exhibit reduced levels of warmth, support, and control (Demo & Acock, 1994; Hetherington & Kelly, 2002; McLanahan & Sandefur, 1994; Simons & Associates, 1996). Differences in parenting behaviors between divorced mothers and mothers in first marriages tend to be small, however, and many disappear with appropriate controls. Differences also seem to characterize parenting early in the separation and divorce process rather than later in post-divorce functioning (Beelmann & Schmidt-Denter, 2009). Although parents' relationships with children and adolescents are characterized by heightened disagreement, verbal aggression, and conflict following divorce, most adolescents in divorced families report close relationships and little conflict with their parents (Buchanan, Maccoby, & Dornbusch, 1996).

In the aftermath of divorce, most fathers become non-residential parents and their contact with children diminishes. There is substantial variation, however, in the frequency and nature of the interaction. Evidence from nationally representative surveys indicates that among children living apart from their fathers, approximately 20% did not see their fathers at all in the previous year and an additional 25% saw their fathers less than once per month (King, 1994; Stewart, 1999). Thus, paternal involvement is absent or quite low for nearly half of children with non-residential fathers. On the other hand, the same surveys documented that more than 25% of children in these living arrangements saw their fathers at least weekly and more than 30% spent long periods of time with their fathers. For their part, many non-residential fathers report feeling shut out of their children's lives by the legal system and residential mothers, by competing obligations, and by feeling confused, frustrated, disrespected and devalued as parents (Braver, Shapiro, & Goodman, 2006; Guzzo, 2009; Hetherington & Kelly, 2002). Compared with children and adolescents, young adults report having a desire for greater involvement with their non-residential parents (Schwartz & Finley, 2009).

FAMILY SYSTEMIC EFFECTS

As the process of marital decline unfolds, other relationships in the family system are affected and family routines are disrupted. Studies have documented less effective parenting behaviors, lower levels of parental involvement, more distant parent–child relationships, higher levels of parent–child conflict and abuse, and changes in relations with extended kin years prior to marital dissolution (Amato & Booth, 1996; Sun, 2001). Economic decline, downward mobility, and financial hardship exacerbate existing tensions in divorcing families, particularly mother-headed families (Gadalla, 2009; Sayer, 2006).

Following separation and legal dissolution, former spouses forge new relationships as coparents, children may move back and forth between households, and a process of family disorganization and reorganization ensues across generations, households, and extended families. Former spouses exhibit many different types of coparenting relationships (Miller, 2009), and in most families interparental hostility tends to diminish over time. Hetherington and Kelly (2002) observed that, 6 years post-divorce, the largest group (half her sample) parented independently (parallel parenting), roughly one-quarter were cooperative in their coparenting, and one-quarter remained highly conflicted with one another. Relationships among extended kin are also realigned following divorce, as children's contact with paternal grandparents and other relatives declines, while their contact with maternal relatives increases (Furstenberg & Cherlin, 1991). Compared with married adults, divorced adults generally have reduced interaction with kin and they have fewer married friends and more unmarried friends (Sprecher, Felmlee, Schmeeckle, & Shu, 2006).

CHILD AND ADOLESCENT ADJUSTMENT

Perhaps the most widely studied aspect of divorce is its consequences for children's well-being. The cumulative evidence suggests a range of short-term social, emotional, behavioral, and academic adjustment problems (Amato, 2010; Demo & Fine, 2010; Lansford, 2009). In comparison to children of continuously married parents, children whose parents divorced experience more internalizing behaviors (anxiety and depression) and externalizing problems (aggression, delinquency, alcohol and drug use); they initiate sexual activity at earlier ages, have sex more frequently, and have higher rates of teenage childbearing; and they perform worse on measures of academic performance and educational attainment (Amato, 2010; Kushner, 2009; Lansford, 2009; Sun & Li, 2009). However, there is wide variation in children's adjustment both within and across family structures (Demo & Fine, 2010; Lansford, 2009), and effect sizes are typically small (Amato, 2001).

A smaller but accumulating body of longitudinal data document lower child well-being years before physical separation and legal dissolution. Compared with children and adolescents whose parents remained married over the course of study, those living with married parents who would later divorce had lower self-esteem and academic achievement, greater anxiety and depression, and more behavior problems (Strohschein, 2005; Sun, 2001; Sun & Li, 2001). The available evidence suggests that deficits in child and adolescent well-being exist at least 2–3 years prior to parental divorce and persist for 2–3 years following divorce, although there is substantial variation across outcomes and in children's rate of change over time (Demo & Fine, 2010; Strohschein, 2005; Sun & Li, 2009). Children are quite resilient following parental divorce, with 80% functioning within normal ranges of adjustment several years post-divorce, compared with approximately 90% of children with continuously married parents (Hetherington & Kelly, 2002). By early adulthood, 90% of those who experienced parental divorce exhibit well-being comparable to their peers with continuously married parents (Amato, 2003).

Explanations for diminished child and adolescent well-being during the period leading up to and following parental divorce focus on several key mediating influences: heightened interparental and parent–child conflict, parental maladjustment, reduced parenting effectiveness, low levels of non-residential parent involvement, and declining financial resources (Barber & Demo, 2006; Breivik, Olweus, & Endresen, 2009). We will discuss the broader theoretical relevance and implications of these variables in the next section, but each of these variables, operating individually and collectively, can be viewed as risk factors that are stressful to children as they navigate the divorce process.

THEORIES USED IN STUDYING DIVORCE

Theory has been used in multiple ways in divorce research. A common practice is to use a theory (or set of theories) as a lens, viewpoint, or guiding framework to select certain constructs to operationalize and then examine empirically. Abend (2008) describes this application of theory as providing researchers with "a *Weltanschauung*, or an overall perspective from which one sees and interprets the world" (p. 180). Theory thus provides an a priori framework, approach, perspective, or paradigm. This is the most common way in which theory has been used to guide divorce research. For example, divorce scholars often borrow concepts from a *life course perspective* (sometimes in combination with other perspectives) such as linked lives or trajectories. An alternative way of thinking about and using theory is that it provides "a logically connected system of general propositions between two or more variables" (Abend, 2008, p. 177). Some studies of divorce are based on more systematic uses of theory in which theoretical propositions are explicitly deduced, explicated, and tested.

In this section we describe theories that have been widely used in studying divorce. Most often these theories have been used to frame the study focus or to interpret the findings (i.e., using theory as a lens). Only a minority of studies used theories to deduce hypotheses. We believe using theory deductively would strengthen divorce research and facilitate theory construction, so we have illustrated this process below. After identifying a given theory used across several studies on divorce, we then proceeded to use that theory to deduce sample theoretical propositions. We made these deductions to provide examples of how theories that often have been used only as orienting lenses can also be used to deduce hypotheses. We hope this exercise provides inspiration and guidance for future divorce research that will use theory more deliberately and in a more enriched manner.

To identify theories used in current divorce scholarship, we reviewed the *Handbook of divorce and relationship dissolution* (Fine & Harvey, 2006) and we conducted a systematic review of recent journal publications. Articles published between January, 2009 and February, 2010 were identified in PsychInfo using the keyword descriptor *divorce*. This search resulted in 180 articles. We excluded 51 articles that were based on samples from outside of the US because of broad variation in legal, cultural, and religious contexts that we perceived to be beyond the scope of this review. We also excluded another 32 articles for which the topic of divorce was tangential. Examples of excluded articles include a case study of a girl's emotional flooding during trauma (Anderson, 2009), young stepchildren's perceptions of the remarriage ceremony (Baxter et al., 2009), and the effects of early psychosocial stress on mate selection (Koehler & Chisholm, 2009).

Thus a total of 97 recent papers on divorce were examined for their use of theory. Both qualitative and quantitative research is represented, as well as narrative literature reviews and essays that address cultural, demographic, legal, and practice issues. As we describe below, at least five trends are evident: (a) a bare majority of studies used theory explicitly; (b) both grand and middle-range theory have been used; (c) both research and practice have been guided by theory; (d) theories from a variety of disciplines have been used; and (e) use of particular theories varies somewhat depending on whether divorce is the dependent or independent variable in the study.

Theory was used explicitly in 55 of the 97 papers (56.7%). Of the remaining 42 studies, eight (8.2% of total) suggested to us the use of implied theory by using central theoretical constructs in their study justification or description of hypotheses, primarily constructs from stress and coping or risk and resilience perspectives.

PRECURSORS OF DIVORCE

We use the term precursor to mean theory and research focused on constructs that most likely precede divorce. A variety of theories have guided the examination of divorce precursors, including social exchange theory, the cascade process model of divorce, and a variety of middle-range models created to study divorce antecedents. According to *social exchange theory*, humans are rational, utilitarian beings who are motivated to maximize their rewards and minimize their costs. They also are motivated to consider alternatives to their current situation when their reward-to-cost ratio falls below their expectations (i.e., comparison level). Married individuals consider their choices and weigh the rewards and costs of staying in the current relationship with the rewards and costs of an alternative relationship or status such as being single (Levinger, 1982). Research has tested the proposition that divorce propensity is associated with the ratio of relationship attractions to relationship termination barriers (Hilton & Anderson, 2009; Previti & Amato, 2003). Other studies have examined the link between accumulated assets (benefits) and perceived barriers (costs) of leaving long-term marriages (Dew, 2009; Hilton & Anderson, 2009). The theoretical rationale is that leaving a relationship with a surplus of benefits would only be considered when there are feasible and more attractive life choice alternatives characterizing the decision field.

Another recent framework guiding research on precursors of divorce is Gottman's (1993) *cascade process model*. This theory depicts marital dissolution as a cascading process that involves the unfolding of negative marital behaviors (i.e., criticism, contempt, defensiveness, withdrawal) that lead to lower marital satisfaction, thoughts and considerations of separation, and ultimately separation and divorce. This process is amplified by a cognitive shift to the marriage as futile.

A number of propositions are suggested by *family process or family systems theories*. For example, child behavior problems, adult perceived parenting efficacy, and parenting effectiveness are hypothesized to affect divorce proneness, suggesting both spillover and crossover effects (Hetherington & Kelly, 2002; Moore & Buehler, 2011). Spillover effects characterize within-person processes (e.g., fathers' parenting effectiveness related to personal divorce proneness). Crossover effects characterize within-couple processes (e.g., fathers' parenting effectiveness related to wives' divorce proneness). Theoretically, scapegoating or triangulating children into parents' marital tensions are associated with lower divorce propensity because parents displace the relational anxiety and unhappiness onto another family member, stabilizing the marital dyad.

A wide variety of middle-range models have also been developed to identify specific precursors of divorce. Trauma investigators have hypothesized a positive association between the accumulation of major negative life events during childhood (e.g., poverty, child abuse, parental depression, witnessing intimate partner violence) and the propensity for divorce during adulthood. Using a *trauma perspective*, Cohan et al. (2009) hypothesized that experiencing or living near large-scale disasters elevates emotional insecurity and mental health problems, weakens marital solidarity, and increases chances of divorce, and found evidence that divorce rates increased in geographically proximal areas following a human-made disaster.

Informed by *social exchange theory*, *behavioral theory*, *attachment theory*, and *crisis theory*, Karney and Bradbury (1995) developed the *vulnerability-stress-adaptation model* of marriage. According to this view, enduring vulnerabilities (e.g., poor role models in the family of origin, individual traits such as neuroticism) shape marital interactions (which they call adaptive processes, including dyadic coping, communication, and conflict management). Stressful events also shape marital interactions, which, over time, influence perceptions of marital quality. Marital quality is posited to be inversely associated with probability of divorce.

Middle-range models developed to explain the intergenerational transmission of divorce suggest a positive association between parental divorce and one's own likelihood of divorce. This association is stronger when both partners' parents have divorced than when only one partner's parents have divorced (Amato & Rogers, 1997). These models suggest a number of mediating mechanisms, including negative coparenting relationships, triangulation, and lower commitment to the institution of marriage. Other models emphasize homogamy, suggesting the hypothesis that interracial couples (Zhang & Van Hook, 2009) and couples in which one person graduated college and the spouse did not attend college will have higher divorce rates than other couples (Kalmijn, 1998; Kalmijn & Flap, 2001). These associations may be mediated by discrepancies in shared values and poor conflict management processes.

ADULT ADJUSTMENT

Theory and research on adult well-being following divorce has lagged far behind work on other aspects of divorce. Surprisingly, much of the research on post-divorce adult outcomes is atheoretical, at least in the sense of directly applying and testing theoretically derived hypotheses. Despite these trends, two theoretical paradigms that have guided work in this area are the life course perspective and stress and coping perspectives, sometimes in combination with each other.

A *life course perspective* emphasizes that family transitions and developmental pathways are socially organized and imbued with socially constructed meaning (Elder, 1991). Because society attaches a strong value to marriage, changing from married to separated or divorced should be associated with mental and physical health problems, and lower levels of emotional well-being (a crisis hypothesis). These associations should be stronger for individuals who have lower levels of informal and formal social support than for those with higher social support. In addition, the timing of life events matters from this theoretical perspective, such that the timing of divorce shifts family trajectories. Further, the concept of human agency suggests that the deleterious consequences of marital dissolution should be lessened for individuals who desired a divorce compared with those who did not desire a divorce.

Although, as previously noted, the mean "recovery" time following divorce is roughly 2–3 years (Hetherington & Kelly, 2002); some studies find reduced well-being up to 5–6 years post-divorce (Waite, Luo, & Lewin, 2009). Staying divorced is associated with lower levels of emotional well-being (and greater stress) compared with those who remained married (state and status effects hypotheses). A life course perspective has guided studies suggesting that it is critical to consider physical health over time post-divorce, in addition to mental health and psychological well-being (Hughes & Waite, 2009).

A life course perspective also posits heterogeneity in the trajectories characterizing post-divorce well-being. Studies illustrate three patterns: a small proportion of individuals (15–20%) whose well-being improves following divorce; a majority of individuals whose well-being dips following divorce and returns to baseline levels within 3 years; and a minority of individuals (20–25%) whose well-being declines post-divorce and does not recover within three years. Re-marriage is an important variable to control, and this pattern of heterogeneity might be supported for some outcomes and not for others (Amato, 2010).

Continuities in the life course are associated with selection into stressful events, but these selection effects into divorce account for less of the variance in adults' negative well-being following divorce than do the effects of the transition (Amato, 2010). Consistent with a life course perspective in which functioning before and after a divorce are examined, the level of pre-divorce marital distress is associated positively with psychological well-being post-divorce (Amato & Hohmann-Marriott, 2007).

Viewed from a *stress and coping perspective*, the divorce process is a stressor that alters family routines, roles, boundaries, and processes (Boss, 2002). Consistent with this view, empirical evidence indicates that as early as 3–7 years prior to divorce, married men and women who would later divorce reported greater distress, poorer mental health, elevated alcohol use, and more severe psychophysiological symptoms than their counterparts who remained married (Demo & Fine, 2010; Wade & Pevalin, 2004). However, many studies also report further declines in adult mental health during the first 2–3 years following divorce, suggesting that both selection and causation processes contribute to adult maladjustment (Amato, 2010).

The number of negative divorce-related changes (e.g., loss of income, loss of valued extended kin, moving) is associated inversely with adults' psychological well-being post-divorce (Buehler & Langenbrunner, 1987), especially when changes are concentrated within a short time frame (Pearlin, Schieman, Fazio, & Meersman, 2005).

Social support and integration may moderate the association between divorce-related change and adult well-being. The association is weaker when individuals have support and are socially integrated, because this provides companionship, ties to social networks and resources, and facilitates account-making. Further, financial resources partially buffer the deleterious association between experiencing divorce and mothers' mental health (Varner & Mandara, 2009).

PARENTING BEHAVIORS AND PARENT–CHILD RELATIONSHIPS

Family process or family systems theory views parenting as the most proximal process of family functioning and proposes that harsh, inconsistent, psychologically intrusive parenting is associated inversely with the quality of parent–child relationships post-divorce (Krishnakumar & Buehler, 2000). Supportive, warm parenting that includes monitoring is associated positively with the quality of parent–child relationships post-divorce. Further, family process models posit that child well-being post-divorce is associated with the quality of parent–child relationships post-divorce. Economic adversity, parental distress (primarily self-distress via spillover), and interparental hostility are inversely associated with the quality of post-divorce parenting. These associations may be buffered by parents' feelings of parental competence that have been generated through previous experiences of effective parenting and children's positive responsiveness to parental influence attempts.

Attachment theory as formulated by Bowlby (1969, 1973) and others (Ainsworth, Blehar, Waters, & Wall, 1978) describes the importance of parent–child bonds formed through patterns of interaction and internal working models of attachment during infancy. The theory suggests that parental divorce disrupts parent–child relationships and creates a context for relationship difficulties during adolescence and young adulthood (e.g., rejection sensitivity in dating relationships). This association may be partially mediated by insecure parent–child relationships (Carranza, Kilmann, & Vendemia, 2009), although it is not clear, theoretically, whether this mediating effect should be stronger for residential or non-residential parent–child relationships (Schwartz & Finley, 2009). We believe attachment theory also could be used to examine the larger family system following divorce given a basic proposition that secure bonds with other adults such as grandparents are associated with child well-being (Henderson, Hayslip, Sanders, & Louden, 2009).

Ecological theory's emphasis on multiple interlocking systems that influence behavior and development suggests a number of broader contexts in which parenting behaviors are situated. For example, it predicts that positive kin influence facilitates frequent non-residential parental involvement post-divorce, and positive peer influence should be associated with increased post-divorce non-residential parental involvement. Similarly, work–family conflict should be associated inversely with the quality of parenting post-divorce, and this association should be stronger for residential parents than for non-residential parents. This theoretical perspective also suggests that policies regarding how financial support affects binuclear and trinuclear family functioning should be addressed.

Other theories have received less attention but offer promising frameworks for explaining parenting and parent–child relationships in the years preceding and following divorce. *Self-determination* theory posits that parenting behaviors that promote children's autonomy, competence, and relatedness are central (Friendly & Grolnick, 2009). These parenting behaviors should be examined during and after the divorce transition. A *risk and resilience framework* suggests that good parent–child relationships following marital dissolution buffer the negative association between divorce-related changes and child well-being. Integrating risk and resilience, life course, and ecological perspectives, the *divorce variation and fluidity model* (Demo & Fine, 2010) suggests that parenting quality is positively associated with a quicker return to children's baseline well-being following parental divorce.

FAMILY SYSTEM FUNCTIONING

Family systems theory directs attention to the larger family unit, the interconnections among subsystems, family boundaries, and changes in family routines and relationships following stressor events. Applied to divorcing families, family systems theory is particularly useful for understanding binuclear family systems (Ahrons & Wallisch, 1987), coparenting arrangements, and relationships with extended kin. Parents' personal well-being is positively associated with the quality of post-divorce coparenting. The theory posits that adjustment is a first-order realignment that involves positive changes in communication, decision-making, and sharing emotional support, and adaptation is a second-order shifting in family roles, rules, relationships, rituals, and routines. Redefinitions in family identity facilitate second-order adaptations.

A more recently developed framework is the *forgiveness intervention model* (Bonach, 2009). The model suggests that forgiveness evolves during the divorce transition, varying across the crisis, transition, and readjustment phases. Forgiveness involves exploring the demise of the marriage, letting go of anger, adjusting to a new coparenting relationship, and interacting in a civil manner.

The model proposes that forgiveness and family differentiation should be associated with more effective coparenting following divorce (Bonach, 2009).

CHILD AND ADOLESCENT ADJUSTMENT

The aspect of divorce that has garnered the most theoretically based empirical attention is the consequences of marital dissolution for children's and adolescents' development and well-being. Most of this work has been guided by a variety of separate but interrelated family systems theories (family process, risk and resilience, stress and coping) and attachment perspectives.

Generally, *family process/family systems theories* suggest that experiencing divorce negatively affects parents' economic well-being and their own well-being (physical and psychological health), which, in turn, influence their coparenting relationship and their individual parenting behaviors. Parents' financial and personal well-being are posited to exert both direct effects on parenting and partial indirect effects through coparenting. Amato (2000) developed a similar framework and labeled it the *divorce-stress-adjustment model*. According to family process models, child well-being post-divorce is affected by: (a) their well-being before the divorce; (b) their parents' financial well-being (both residential and non-residential parents'); (c) both parents' personal well-being; (d) interparental hostility; (e) being triangulated into parents' disputes; (f) their parents' coparenting relationship, and most proximally, (g) parenting behaviors and relationships with both parents. In each case, the relationship with the residential parent, as well as his or her well-being and parenting behaviors, are hypothesized to exert stronger effects than those of non-residential parents (Lansford, 2009). It is worth noting that very few, if any, scholars have distinguished between and simultaneously examined spillover (e.g., one parent's well-being to their own parenting) and cross-over effects (one parent's well-being to the other parent's parenting). This is an important direction for future work, as is the need to examine *how* (mediators) and *under what conditions* (moderators) each of these variables influences children's well-being following parental divorce (Amato, 2010). Theoretical and empirical attention to these issues will assist in developing middle-range models that help explain variability and fluidity over time (Demo & Fine, 2010).

A *risk and resilience framework* shares some assumptions with family systems theories. This model has been widely used (both implicitly and explicitly) to guide examinations of children's well-being following marital dissolution (Demo, Aquilino, & Fine, 2005). It directs attention to risk and protective factors that are helpful in explaining why some children fare better than others in response to family disruption and reformation (Hetherington, 1999). Specifically, risk factors include child maladjustment prior to divorce (Hetherington, Bridges, & Insabella, 1998), heightened interparental conflict, reduced involvement with the non-residential parent, maladjustment of the residential parent, economic hardship, and the accumulation of other stressful, divorce-related life changes (e.g., moving, losing friends, changing schools and teachers) (Amato, 1993). Conversely, children's sense of hope, their ability to elicit social support, and close, supportive relationships with extended kin (e.g., grandparents) are proposed to facilitate their well-being following parental divorce. Children's positive self-belief systems (e.g., perceived efficacy) are also posited to be protective (Wolchik, Schenck, & Sandler, 2009).

Stress and coping models share key assumptions, concepts, and propositions with family systems theories discussed earlier. This perspective suggests that experiencing parental divorce and child abuse (i.e., two significant childhood stressors) should be associated with poorer mental health than divorce on its own (Afifi et al., 2009). This proposition is also informed by the *stress vulnerability model* (Hooley & Hiller, 2001), which posits that vulnerability accrues from the accumulation of environmental stressors. A potentially promising application of this model is that it can be used to deduce hypotheses that are specific to divorce-related stressors as well as hypotheses that pose interactions between divorce status and other significant stressors (e.g., child abuse, parental depression, poverty).

Incorporating propositions from a number of theories, *family instability theory* offers an inte-grated framework for understanding the consequences of multiple structural transitions on children (Demo et al., 2005; Fomby & Cherlin, 2007). Children who experience multiple structural transi-tions during childhood have more behavior problems and lower academic achievement than those with fewer transitions (Sun & Li, 2009). Variability and fluidity characterize these responses, with some children improving over time. This theory integrates deleterious effects stemming from elevated stress (suggested by stress and coping models), inconsistent parenting (emphasized by family process/systems theories), cumulative disadvantage (posited by a life course perspective, described below), selection (suggested by biosocial and life course theories), and bidirectionality (implied by family systems theories).

A central concept in a life course framework is cumulative disadvantage (Elder, 1998). Many children who have experienced parental divorce have endured a series of stressful experiences throughout their childhood, including marital distress and parent–child conflict prior to family disruption, continuing conflict post-disruption, parental maladjustment, reduced parenting effec-tiveness, and declining standard of living (Demo & Fine, 2010). In this view, one mechanism by which children suffer deleterious consequences is persisting and cumulative disadvantage rather than the experience of parental divorce *per se*. There has been some support for this, but many stud-ies that have controlled for selection fairly well have found some remaining negative effects of the divorce experience (Amato, 2010).

As noted earlier, attachment theory emphasizes the enduring consequences of parent–child relationships and the bonds formed between parents and children. Applied to child and adolescent adjustment following parental divorce, attachment explanations focus on disruptions to those bonds. Parental divorce is associated with relational insecurity during young childhood and rejection sensitivity during adolescence. Children's secure attachment with a parent buffers the inverse asso-ciation between divorce-related change and children's well-being post-divorce. Positive attachment relations with kin are also protective in that they buffer children from divorce-related change, including negative parenting (Henderson et al., 2009). Importantly, attachment has been a central focus recently for defining best interest in custody evaluations, applying the proposition that chil-dren are better off living with the parent with whom the attachment bond is strongest (Garber, 2009; Huurre, Lintonen, Kaprio, Pilkonen, & Marttunen, 2010; Lee, Kaufman, & George, 2009; Ludolph, 2009).

A *biosocial perspective* suggests that children's preexisting vulnerabilities, pubertal development and timing, and their physiological stress reactivity may exacerbate the negative association between divorce-related stressors and child well-being (Boyce & Ellis, 2005). Alternatively, a genetic trans-mission argument indicates that some of the negative effects observed for children's well-being following divorce are due to genetic transmission rather than environmental "trauma" or "stressors." Amato (2010) reviewed literatures on adult twins and adopted siblings and reported little support for genetic inheritance as an explanation for child outcomes including health problems, antisocial behavior, substance abuse, life satisfaction, and internalizing problems. Another largely unexplored possibility is that there might be gene-by-environment interactions that inhibit children's post-divorce adjustment (Horwitz & Neiderhiser, 2011).

Finally, two theories worthy of further consideration are *self-determination theory* and *resource deprivation theory*. Self-determination theory is based on the idea that parent–child relationships during the process of family disruption and reorganization need to be adapted to meet children's basic psychological needs for autonomy, competence, and relatedness (Friendly & Grolnick, 2009). Resource deprivation or social capital theories assert that reduced levels of parental financial, human, and social resources should be associated with poorer child academic outcomes post-divorce (Sun & Li, 2009). Although few divorce researchers have used these middle-range theories to deduce testable hypotheses, we believe each has much to offer for the examination of child well-being because of the centrality of constructs and propositions focused on child needs and parental resources.

LIMITATIONS OF HOW THEORY HAS BEEN USED IN STUDYING DIVORCE

Our review of recent divorce scholarship suggests three general observations. First, theory is often being used only as a lens or guiding framework. In many empirical studies, a theory, perspective, or model is explicitly identified as the framework that guides the investigation, but there is no attempt to systematically derive and test hypotheses. Second, many theories have been applied selectively and even haphazardly. Third, much more attention has been directed to post-divorce than pre-divorce processes and circumstances.

Using Theory Only as a Lens

We are not the first to lament divorce scholars' inattention to hypothesis-testing and theoretical development. In developing their cognitive–behavioral model to explain how physical aggression leads to relationship distress and dissolution, Lawrence et al. (2006) concluded that "conceptual frameworks for evaluating and integrating these findings remain to be developed (p. 263)." Similarly, Adamsons and Pasley (2006) stated that "Much of the research regarding coparenting following divorce has been atheoretical, as researchers have derived hypotheses from prior empirical literature rather than from theoretical frameworks" (p. 244).

Developing theoretical explanations for aspects of the divorce process is difficult and time-consuming. Yet this work is vital to achieving a fuller understanding of the antecedents, correlates, and consequences of divorce for family members and society. We suggest that an important direction for further work is the development of good middle-range models that explicitly articulate the source of propositions, including extant research and/or theories. For example, a model integrating social capital theories of parenting, self-determination theory, and life course timing issues would have many applications.

Selective or Haphazard Use of Theory

A number of prominent family theories have not been adequately applied to the study of divorce. For example, conspicuously absent from our review of recently published empirical work on divorce is the application of symbolic interactionist, feminist, and communication theories. Emerging theoretical approaches such as biosocial theory (e.g., D'Onofrio & Lahey, 2010) have also received inadequate attention.

In applying established theories, scholars often select specific concepts or propositions to the neglect of other key components of the theory. One illustration is that although family systems theories are frequently used to guide empirical investigations of divorce, the overwhelming focus is on maladjustment (as discussed below), and we rarely see examinations of factors that promote growth in the divorce literature.

Inattention to Pre-Divorce Processes

Although there has been increased recognition of divorce as a process that begins years prior to physical separation and legal divorce, theoretical explanations continue to emphasize how family routines, interactions, relationships, and family members' well-being are influenced in the post-disruption and reformation periods. We suspect this is the result of a prevailing focus on divorce as a stressor event (that triggers outcomes which researchers examine) rather than a life course process. A more balanced perspective that directs attention to early stages of marital decline, pre-disruption parenting behaviors and parent–child dynamics, changing relationships with kin, and pre-disruption to post-disruption trajectories characterizing child, adolescent, and parent well-being will enrich our understanding of divorce.

One of the challenges in conceptualizing early stages of the divorce process, formulating concepts and propositions, and framing research questions is defining when, in fact, the divorce process starts.

Clearly, marital duration prior to divorce is a key variable, and there is substantial variation in relevant family processes (e.g., marital happiness, marital conflict, parental support, parent–child conflict) both prior to and during the early stages of marital breakdown, complicating efforts to specify the amount or nature of marital (or family) dysfunction that predicts divorce. Isolating a specific date when a divorce process began is not likely to be productive or meaningful for most marriages (although identification of specific precipitating events, and therefore dates, may be possible for some marriages that end in divorce). A more fruitful strategy, however, may be to intensify efforts to gather comprehensive data, both retrospectively and prospectively, on a range of pre-disruption family and individual phenomena and inductively develop theories to be tested.

SUGGESTIONS FOR THEORETICALLY INFORMED DIVORCE RESEARCH

In this section, we offer some suggestions for better use of theory in studying divorce. We begin by noting that changes in household composition and family relationships accompanying divorce are more profound and complex than our current theories suggest. For example, family systems theories propose the utility of framing interconnections as binuclear family systems. But with the changing demography of families (including serial cohabitation, multipartnered fertility, and high rates of divorce, re-marriage, and re-divorce), many families experience multiple structural transitions. Theoretical development is thus needed to understand trinuclear and quadranuclear family structures. One idea for examining such families is to apply a *social network analysis* approach and modify it to family network analysis. For example, consider a child who has five parents across three households: the child's residential (biological) mother and her second husband (the child's stepfather), the child's non-residential (biological) father and his cohabiting partner, and the biological father's ex-wife from his second marriage (and child's stepmother). Understanding how divorce and other family transitions have influenced the child's adjustment requires a careful examination of family relationships within and across these households as well as analysis of extrafamilial contexts such as peer, neighborhood, school, and community influences.

A related challenge is to refine existing theories, or develop new theoretical frameworks, for viewing multiple families over time as a child moves into and out of parenting arrangements, and parent figures move into and out of the household over time. Examining changes in household and family membership and niches will require family scholars to distinguish more carefully and consistently between and among units of analysis (e.g., individual, household, family). Developing and testing middle-range models may help us to more fully understand whether divorce is unique as a structural transition, or how it is similar to and different from other transitions such as the dissolution of a cohabiting relationship.

Existing theories also need to be used more broadly to study aspects of divorce. As one example, *identity theory* has been widely used in other areas of family studies, but it has been underutilized in studying divorce-related family processes and consequences. An obvious application would be the examination of fathers' identities as they are reorganized and reconstructed in the aftermath of divorce; many fathers see less of their children post-disruption and they feel disenfranchised as parents (Braver et al., 2006). Mothers' identities are reorganized during this process, too, with many single mothers feeling they now must "do it all," fulfilling expectations associated with bread-winning, nurturing, disciplining, and household labor. *Exchange theory* is another example of an underutilized theory for understanding aspects of divorce such as non-residential fathering.

Finally, we suggest that greater attention needs to be devoted to conceptualizing and empirically investigating adult well-being following divorce. Recognizing the importance for researchers and policy-makers to understand the consequences of parental divorce for children and adolescents, it is surprising that there is much less research on adult well-being following marital dissolution, particularly because one important predictor of child well-being is parental well-being. Up to now the focus has been on divorce as a traumatic or short-term stressor (crisis) rather than a long-term (chronic) stressor. But more recent studies suggest that we need to use longitudinal research, account for selection effects and focus on a variety of outcomes. For example, there is a resurging interest in physical health and yet there is little theory that includes the psychobiological aspects of stress reactivity.

A promising new development is that an increased range of theoretical orientations is being applied to the study of divorce, perhaps partly as a result of investigators from multiple disciplines moving into this research arena. Historically a focus of scholars within the fields of sociology, demography, family studies, developmental psychology, social psychology, and communication, there has been growing interest in divorce among researchers in community psychology, trauma studies, psychiatry, epidemiology, health, and medicine. Expanding our theoretical lens should prove valuable in helping us to understand the complexity of the divorce process, its antecedents, correlates, and consequences.

To complement the wide lens afforded by multidisciplinary perspectives, however, we need theoretical models that provide specificity and precision. One challenge will be for broad frameworks such as life course theory or models such as the vulnerability-stress-adaptation model (Karney & Bradbury, 1995) or the divorce variation and fluidity model (Demo & Fine, 2010) to be applied with specificity. Identifying propositions and testing hypotheses will facilitate our ability to develop and refine our theoretical accounts of divorce. Empirically, quantitative researchers need to examine variability (such as standard deviations) rather than simply group means (upon which many statistical analyses are based) as one way of gaining insights on aspects of both complexity and precision. Amato (2010) calls for more attention to variability in adjustment and heterogeneity of outcomes, specifically research using "multiplicative terms to assess moderation effects (Divorce × Risk or Protective Factors)" (p. 662). Qualitative inquiries can illuminate variability and complexity by exploring extreme or negative cases that do not fit prevailing themes (George & Bennett, 2005). Mixed-method studies with a within-group design would be particularly valuable in learning about variability within divorcing and post-disruption families.

CONCLUSION

How can theory guide future analyses? A fuller understanding of divorce requires that a broad range of theories be applied and tested more consistently, explicitly, and systematically. In conceptualizing the divorce process, considerably more thought needs to be given to questions such as when it starts, what it includes, and how different members of the family experience the divorce. For example, is marital conflict a cause of divorce or is it part of the divorce process (Amato, 2010)? Is there one divorce process that characterizes a family's experience, or do multiple realities require that we conceptualize separate divorce processes for wives, husbands, children, and adolescents? Formulating and answering such fundamental questions requires that we both expand and sharpen our theoretical tools for studying divorce.

REFERENCES

Abend, G. (2008). The meaning of 'theory.' *Sociological Theory*, *26*, 173–199.

Adamsons, K., & Pasley, K. (2006). Coparenting following divorce and relationship dissolution. In M. A. Fine & J. H. Harvey (Eds.), *Handbook of divorce and relationship dissolution* (pp. 241–261). Mahwah, NJ: Erlbaum.

Afifi, T., Boman, J., Fleisher, W., & Sareen, J. (2009). The relationship between child abuse, parental divorce, and lifetime mental disorders and suicidality in a nationally representative adult sample. *Child Abuse and Neglect*, *33*, 139–147.

Ahrons, C. R., & Wallisch, L. S. (1987). The relationship between former spouses. In D. Perlman & S. W. Duck (Eds.), *Intimate relationships: Development, dynamics, and deterioration* (pp. 269–296). Newbury Park, CA: Sage.

Ainsworth, M. D. S., Blehar, M. C., Waters, E., & Wall, S. (1978). *Patterns of attachment*. Hillsdale, NJ: Erlbaum.

Amato, P. R. (1993). Children's adjustment to divorce: Theories, hypotheses, and empirical support. *Journal of Marriage and the Family, 55*, 23–38.

Amato, P. R. (2000). The consequences of divorce for adults and children. *Journal of Marriage and the Family, 62*, 1269–1287.

Amato, P. R. (2001). Children of divorce in the 1990s: An update of the Amato and Keith (1991) meta-analysis. *Journal of Family Psychology, 15*, 355–370.

Amato, P. R. (2003). Reconciling divergent perspectives: Judith Wallerstein, quantitative family research, and children of divorce. *Family Relations, 52*, 332–339.

Amato, P. R. (2010). Research on divorce: Continuing trends and new developments. *Journal of Marriage and Family, 72*, 650–666.

Amato, P. R., & Booth, A. (1996). A prospective study of parental divorce and parent–child relationships. *Journal of Marriage and the Family, 58*, 356–365.

Amato, P. R., & Hohmann-Marriott, B. (2007). A comparison of high and low-distress marriages that end in divorce. *Journal of Marriage and Family, 69*, 621–638.

Amato, P. R., & Previti, D. (2003). People's reasons for divorcing: Gender, social class, the life course, and adjustment. *Journal of Family Issues, 24*, 602–626.

Amato, P. R., & Rogers, S. J. (1997). A longitudinal study of marital problems and subsequent divorce. *Journal of Marriage and the Family, 59*, 612–624.

Anderson, M. (2009). Flooding and renewal: A girl's process of stabilization and renewal. *Journal of Sandplay Therapy, 18*, 83–104.

Barber, B. L., & Demo, D. H. (2006). The kids are alright (at least, most of them): Links between divorce and dissolution and child well-being. In M. A. Fine & J. H. Harvey (Eds.), *Handbook of divorce and relationship dissolution* (pp. 289–311). Mahwah, NJ: Erlbaum.

Barrett, A. (2003). Race differences in the mental health effects of divorce: A reexamination incorporating temporal dimensions of the dissolution process. *Journal of Family Issues, 24*, 995–1019.

Baxter, L., Braithwaite, D., Kellas, J., LeClair-Underberg, C., Normand, E., Routsong, T., & Thatcher, M. (2009). Empty ritual: Young-adult stepchildren's perceptions of the re-marriage ceremony. *Journal of Social and Personal Relationships, 26*, 467–487.

Beelmann, W., & Schmidt-Denter, U. (2009). Mother-child interaction following marital separation: A Longitudinal observational study. *European Psychologist, 14*, 307–319.

Bellah, R., Madsen, R., Sullivan, W. M., Swidler, A., & Tipton, S. M. (1985). *Habits of the heart: Individualism and commitment in America*. Berkeley, CA: University of California Press.

Betzig, L. (1989). Causes of conjugal dissolution: A cross-cultural study. *Current Anthropology, 30*, 654–676.

Bohannon, P. (1968). The six stations of divorce. In P. Bohannon (Ed.), *Divorce and after* (pp. 33–62). Garden City, NY: Doubleday.

Bonach, K. (2009). Empirical support for the application of the Forgiveness Intervention Model to post-divorce coparenting. *Journal of Divorce and Remarriage, 50*, 38–54.

Boss, P. G. (2002). *Family stress management: A contextual approach* (2nd ed.). Thousand Oaks, CA: Sage.

Bowlby, J. (1969). *Attachment and loss. Vol. I: Attachment*. New York: Basic.

Bowlby, J. (1973). *Attachment and loss. Vol. II: Separation*. New York: Basic.

Boyce, W. T., & Ellis, B. J. (2005). Biological sensitivity to context: I. An evolutionary-developmental theory of the origins and functions of stress reactivity. *Development and Psychopathology, 17*, 271–301.

Braver, S. L., Shapiro, J. R., & Goodman, M. R. (2006). Consequences of divorce for parents. In M. A. Fine & J. H. Harvey (Eds.), *Handbook of divorce and relationship dissolution* (pp. 313–337). Mahwah, NJ: Erlbaum.

Breivik, K., Olweus, D., & Endresen, I. (2009). Does the quality of parent–child relationships mediate the increased risk for antisocial behavior and substance abuse among adolescents in single-mother and single-father families? *Journal of Divorce and Remarriage, 50*, 400–426.

Buchanan, C. M., Maccoby, E. E., & Dornbusch, S. M. (1996). *Adolescents after divorce*. Cambridge, MA: Harvard University Press.

Buehler, C., & Langenbrunner, M. (1987). Divorce-related stressors: occurrence, disruptiveness, and area of life change. *Journal of Divorce, 11*, 25–50.

Carranza, L., Kilmann, P., & Vendemia, J. (2009). Links between parent characteristics and attachment variables for college students of parental divorce. *Adolescence, 44*, 253–271.

Cherlin, A. J. (2009). *The marriage go-round: The state of marriage and the family in America today*. New York: Vintage.

Cohan, C., Cole, S., & Schoen, R. (2009). Divorce following the September 11 terrorist attacks. *Journal of Social and Personal Relationships*, *26*, 512–530.

Crowell, J., Treboux, D., & Brockmeyer, S. (2009). Parental divorce and adult children's attachment representations and marital status. *Attachment and Human Development*, *11*, 87–101.

D'Onofrio, B. M., & Lahey, B. B. (2010). Biosocial influences on family: A decade review. *Journal of Marriage and Family*, *72*, 762–782.

Demo, D. H., & Acock, A. (1994). *Family diversity and well-being*. Thousand Oaks, CA: Sage.

Demo, D. H., Aquilino, W. S., & Fine, M. A. (2005). Family composition and family transitions. In V. L. Bengtson, A. C. Acock, K. A. Allen, P. Dilworth-Anderson, & D. M. Klein (Eds.), *Sourcebook of family theory and research* (pp. 119–134). Thousand Oaks, CA: Sage.

Demo, D. H., & Fine, M. A. (2010). *Beyond the average divorce*. Thousand Oaks, CA: Sage.

Dew, J. (2009). The gendered meanings of assets for divorce. *Journal of Family and Economic Issues*, *30*, 20–31.

Dube, S., Fairweather, D., Pearson,W., Felitti, V., Anda, R., & Croft, J. (2009). Cumulative childhood stress and autoimmune diseases in adults. *Psychosomatic Medicine*, *71*, 243–250.

Elder, G. H. Jr. (1991). Life course. In E. F. Borgotta and M. L. Borgotta (Eds.), *The encyclopedia of sociology* (pp. 281–311). New York: Macmillan.

Elder, G. H., Jr. (1998). The life course as developmental theory. *Child Development*, *69*, 1–12.

Fine, M. A., & Harvey, J. H. (2006). *Handbook of divorce and relationship dissolution*. Mahwah, NJ: Erlbaum.

Fomby, P., & Cherlin, A. J. (2007). Family instability and child well-being. *American Sociological Review*, *72*, 181–204.

Friendly, R., & Grolnick, W. (2009). Child adjustment to familial dissolution: An Examination of parental factors using a self-determination theory framework. *Journal of Divorce and Re-marriage*, *50*, 66–80.

Furstenberg, F. F. Jr., & Cherlin, A. J. (1991). *Divided families: What happens to children when parents part*. Cambridge, MA: Harvard University Press.

Gadalla, T. (2009). Impact of marital dissolution on men's and women's incomes: A longitudinal study. *Journal of Divorce and Re-marriage*, *50*, 55–65.

Garber, B. (2009). Attachment methodology in custody evaluation: Four hurdles standing between developmental theory and forensic application. *Journal of Child Custody*, *6*, 38–61.

George, A. L., & Bennett, A. (2005). *Case studies and theory development in the social sciences*. Boston, MA: MIT Press.

Gottman, J. (1993). A theory of marital dissolution and stability. *Journal of Family Psychology*, *7*, 57–75.

Gottman, J. M., & Levenson, R. W. (2000). The timing of divorce: Predicting when a couple will divorce over a 14-year period. *Journal of Marriage and the Family*, *62*, 737–745.

Guzzo, K. (2009). Men's visitation with non-residential children: Do characteristics of coresidential and non-residential children matter? *Journal of Family Issues*, *30*, 921–944.

Henderson, C., Hayslip, B., Sanders, L., & Louden, L. (2009). Grandmother-grandchild relationship quality predicts psychosocial adjustment among youth from divorced families. *Journal of Family Issues*, *30*, 1245–1264.

Hertenstein, M., Hansel, C., Butts, A., & Hile, S. (2009). Smile intensity in photographs predicts divorce later in life. *Motivation and Emotion*, *33*, 99–105.

Hetherington, E. M. (1999). Introduction and overview. In E. M. Hetherington (Ed.), *Coping with divorce, single parenting, and remarriage* (pp. vii–x). Mahwah, NJ: Erlbaum.

Hetherington, E. M., Bridges, M., & Insabella, G. M. (1998). What matters? What does not? Five perspectives on the association between marital transitions and children's adjustment. *American Psychologist*, *53*, 167–184.

Hetherington, E. M., & Kelly, J. (2002). *For better or for worse: Divorce reconsidered*. New York: Norton.

Hilton, J., & Anderson, T. (2009). Characteristics of women with children who divorce in midlife compared with those who remained married. *Journal of Divorce and Re-marriage*, *50*, 309–329.

Hooley, J. M., & Hiller, J. B. (2001). Family relationships and major mental disorder: Risk factors and preventive strategies. In B. Sarason & S. Duck (Eds.), *Personal relationships: Implications for clinical and community psychology* (pp. 61–87). West Sussex, England: Wiley.

Horwitz, B. N., & Neiderhiser, J. M. (2011). Gene-environment interplay, family relationships, and child adjustment. *Journal of Marriage and Family*, *73*, 804–816.

Huesmann, L., Dubow, E., & Boxer, P. (2009). Continuity of aggression from childhood to early adulthood as a predictor of life outcomes: Implications for the adolescent-limited and life-course-persistent models. *Aggressive Behavior*, *35*, 136–149.

Hughes, M., & Waite, L. (2009). Marital biography and health at mid-life. *Journal of Health and Social Behavior*, *50*, 344–358.

Huurre, T., Lintonen, T., Kaprio, J., Pilkonen, M., & Marttunen, M. (2010). Adolescent risk factors for excessive alcohol use at age 32 years, a 16-year prospective follow-up study. *Social Psychiatry and Psychiatric Epidemiology*, *45*, 125–134.

Kalmijn, M. (1998). Intermarriage and homogamy: Causes, patterns, trends. *Annual Review of Sociology*, *24*, 395–421.

Kalmijn, M., & Flap, H. (2001). Assortative meeting and mating: Unintended consequences of organized settings for partner choices. *Social Forces*, *79*, 1289–1312.

Karney, B. R., & Bradbury, T. (1995). The longitudinal course of marital quality and stability: A review of theory, method, and research. *Psychological Bulletin*, *118*, 3–34.

King, V. (1994). Nonresident father involvement and child well-being: Can dads make a difference? *Journal of Family Issues*, *15*, 78–96.

Kitson, G. C. (1992). *Portrait of divorce: Adjustment to marital breakdown*. New York: Guilford Press.

Koehler, N., & Chisholm, J. (2009). Doe early psychosocial stress affect mate choice? *Human Nature*, *20*, 52–66.

Kposowa, A. (2009). Psychiatrist availability, social disintegration, and suicide deaths in U.S. counties, 1990–1995. *Journal of Community Psychology*, *37*, 73–87.

Kreider, R. M. (2007). *Living arrangements of children: 2004*. Current Population Reports, P70–114. Washington, DC: U.S. Census Bureau.

Krishnakumar, A., & Buehler, C. (2000). Interparental conflict and parenting practices: A meta-analysis. *Family Relations*, *49*, 25–44.

Kushner, M. (2009). A dual model for completing parenting plans postseparation. *Journal of Divorce and Re-marriage*, *50*, 330–340.

Lansford, J. (2009). Parental divorce and children's adjustment. *Perspectives on Psychological Science*, *4*, 140–152.

Lawrence, E., Ro, E., Barry, R., & Bunde, M. (2006). Mechanisms of distress and dissolution in physically aggressive romantic relationships. In M. A. Fine & J. H. Harvey (Eds.), *Handbook of divorce and relationship dissolution* (pp. 263–286). Mahwah, NJ: Erlbaum.

Lee, S., Kaufman, R., & George, C. (2009). Disorganized attachment in young children: Manifestations, etiology, and implications for child custody. *Journal of Child Custody*, *6*, 62–90.

Levinger. (1982). A social exchange view on the dissolution of pair relationships. In F. I. Nye (Ed.), *Family relationships: Rewards and costs* (pp. 97–122). Beverly Hills, CA: Sage.

Ludolph, P. (2009). Answered and unanswered questions in attachment theory with implications for children of divorce. *Journal of Child Custody*, *6*, 8–24.

McLanahan, S., & Sandefur, G. (1994). *Growing up with a single parent: What hurts, what helps*. Cambridge, MA: Harvard University Press.

Miller, A. (2009). Face concerns and facework strategies in maintaining post-divorce coparenting and dating relationships. *Southern Communication Journal*, *74*, 157–173.

Moore, M. J., & Buehler, C. (2011). Parents' divorce proneness: The influence of adolescent problem behaviors and parental efficacy. *Journal of Social and Personal Relationships*, *28*, 634–652.

Pearlin, L. I., Schieman, S., Fazio, E. M., & Meersman, S. C. (2005). Stress, health, and the life course: Some conceptual perspectives. *Journal of Health and Social Behavior*, *46*, 205–219.

Previti, D., & Amato, P. R. (2003). Why stay married? Rewards, barriers, and marital stability. *Journal of Marriage and Family*, *65*, 561–573.

Rhoades, G., Stanley, S., & Markman, H. (2009). The pre-engagement cohabitation effect: A Replication and extension of previous findings. *Journal of Family Psychology*, *23*, 107–111.

Rodrigues, A. E., Hall, J. H., & Fincham, F. D. (2006). What predicts divorce and relationship dissolution? In M. A. Fine & J. H. Harvey (Eds.), *Handbook of divorce and relationship dissolution* (pp. 85–112). Mahwah, NJ: Erlbaum.

Sayer, L. C. (2006). Economic aspects of divorce and relationship dissolution. In M. A. Fine & J. H. Harvey (Eds.), *Handbook of divorce and relationship dissolution* (pp. 385–406). Mahwah, NJ: Erlbaum.

Sbarra, D., Law, R., Lee, L., & Mason, A. (2009). Marital dissolution and blood pressure reactivity: Evidence for the specificity of emotional intrusion-hyperarousal and task-rated emotional difficulty. *Psychosomatic Medicine*, *71*, 532–540.

Sbarra, D., & Nietert, P. (2009). Divorce and death: Forty years of the Charleston heart study. *Psychological Science*, *20*, 107–113.

Schoen, R., & Canudas-Romo, V. (2006). Timing effects on divorce: 20th century experience in the United States. *Journal of Marriage and Family*, *68*, 749–758.

Schoen, R., & Standish, N. (2001). The retrenchment of marriage: Results from marital status life tables for the United States. *Population and Development Review*, *27*, 553–563.

Schwartz, S., & Finley, G. (2009). Mothering, fathering, and divorce: The Influence of divorce on reports of and desires for maternal and paternal involvement. *Family Court Review*, *47*, 506–522.

Simons, R. L., & Associates. (1996). *Understanding differences between divorced and intact families*. Thousand Oaks, CA: Sage.

South, S. J., Trent, K., & Shen, Y. (2001). Changing partners: Toward a macrostructural-opportunity theory of marital dissolution. *Journal of Marriage and Family*, *63*, 743–754.

Sprecher, S., Felmlee, D., Schmeeckle, M., & Shu, X. (2006). No breakup occurs on an island: Social networks and relationship dissolution. In M. A. Fine & J. H. Harvey (Eds.), *Handbook of divorce and relationship dissolution* (pp. 457–478). Mahwah, NJ: Erlbaum.

Stewart, S. D. (1999). Nonresident mothers' and fathers' social contact with children. *Journal of Marriage and the Family*, *61*, 894–907.

Strohschein, L. (2005). Parental divorce and child mental health trajectories. *Journal of Marriage and Family*, *67*, 1286–1300.

Sun, Y. (2001). Family environment and adolescents' well-being before and after parents' marital disruption: A longitudinal analysis. *Journal of Marriage and Family*, *63*, 697–713.

Sun, Y., & Li, Y. (2001). Marital disruption, parental investment, and children's academic achievement: A prospective analysis. *Journal of Family Issues*, *22*, 27–62.

Sun, Y., & Li, Y. (2009). Post-divorce family stability and changes in adolescents' academic performance: A Growth-curve model. *Journal of Family Issues*, *30*, 1527–1555.

Toth, K., & Kemmelmeier, M. (2009). Divorce attitudes around the world: Distinguishing the impact of culture on evaluations and attitude structure. *Cross-Cultural Research*, *43*, 280–297.

Varner, F., & Mandara, J. (2009). Marital transitions and changes in African American mothers' depressive symptoms: The Buffering role of financial resources. *Journal of Family Psychology*, *23*, 839–847.

Wade, T. J., & Pevalin, D. J. (2004). Marital transitions and mental health. *Journal of Health and Social Behavior*, *45*, 155–170.

Waite, L., Luo, Y., & Lewin, A. (2009). Marital happiness and marital stability: Consequences for psychological well-being. *Social Science Research*, *38*, 201–212.

Williams, D. R., Takeuchi, D. T., & Adair, R. K. (1992). Marital status and psychiatric disorders among Blacks and Whites. *Journal of Health and Social Behavior*, *33*, 140–157.

Wolchik, S., Schenck, C., & Sandler, I. (2009). Promoting resilience in youth from divorced families: Lessons learned from experimental trials of the New Beginnings program. *Journal of Personality*, *77*, 1833–1868.

Zhang, Y., & Van Hook, J. (2009). Marital dissolution among interracial couples. *Journal of Marriage and Family*, *71*, 95–107.

16 Theory Use in Stepfamily Research

Alan C. Taylor, Mihaela Robila, and Bethany Fisackerly

Stepfamilies result from the union of two adults in which at least one partner has a child from a previous relationship (Ganong & Coleman, 2004). With over 40% of marriages ending in divorce, the US has one of the highest divorce rates in post-industrialized societies (Demo & Fine, 2010). With a high propensity for marriage, the US also stands as a nation with relatively high rates of re-marriage; consequently, stepfamilies are more common in the US than in other country (Teachman & Tedrow, 2008). In fact, nearly 50% of marriages are a remarriage for at least one partner. However, 60% of second marriages and 73% of third marriages end in divorce (US Bureau of the Census, 2006). The high divorce rates among couples in stepfamilies have increased both scholars' and the general public's interest in the patterns that characterize successful relationships among stepparents, stepchildren, and stepsiblings.

Given increased interest in the scholarly literature regarding how stepfamilies function, and the importance of theory use in this research effort, the overall goal of this chapter is to review theories that have been used in examining stepfamily relationships. First, we identify what is currently known about stepfamily relationships and review several important issues relevant to stepfamilies today. We also present findings from our explicit theory-use review of the empirical stepfamily research literature from 2000–2010. Next, we discuss specific theories that have been successfully used within the stepfamily literature, as well as ones that address issues involving these relationships. We conclude by examining limitations of currently used theoretical perspectives and identify potential theoretical paths that may prove worthy of pursuit to advance the stepfamily literature.

KEY ISSUES IN THE STUDY OF THE STEPFAMILIES

Data from the mid-1990s suggest that more than two-thirds of women and three-quarters of men re-marry after divorce (69 and 78%, respectively), while only 5% of women and 12% of men re-marry after a spouse's death (Schoen & Standish, 2001). There are three types of stepfamilies: stepfather families (8.4% of US married couples of childbearing age), stepmother families (1.4% of all US married couples), and families in which both parents are stepparents (0.8% of all married couples of childbearing age) (Robertson et al., 2006). Data from the 2004 Survey of Income and Program Participation suggest that 7.2% of children under age 18 (5.3 million) in the US were living with a biological parent and a married or cohabiting stepparent. Living with a stepfather continued to be significantly more common than living with a stepmother (one in five of these children were living with a biological father and stepmother) (Kreider, 2008).

The literature on stepfamilies has been increasing in the last two decades. Coleman, Ganong, and Fine's (2000) review of the 1990s indicated that this decade registered a significant increase in stepfamily research compared with previous ones in terms of quality and complexity of the studies. Scholars used better samples, and methodology that was more sensitive to stepfamily complexity during the 1990s. One such example was the utilization of longitudinal designs in stepfamily research. However, as Coleman et al. (2000) indicated, many unknowns regarding remarriages and stepfamilies remained. The review of scholarly work on stepfamilies for the following decade (2000–2009) by Sweeney (2010) highlighted the considerable diversity and complexity of remarried families and stepfamilies. Sweeney (2010) indicated that "The past decade's research leaves us with a new appreciation for the diverse structures, processes, and outcomes associated with remarriage and stepfamilies. Much remains unknown, however, and updated data and new analyses are sorely needed" (p. 680).

Forming a stepfamily and growing up in a stepfamily bring opportunities and challenges for adults and children alike. The opportunities for stepfamilies include increased social and financial resources, in addition to increased emotional closeness, bonds, and companionship (e.g., Hofferth & Anderson, 2003). However, most of the literature on stepfamilies has focused on their challenges. Among these challenges is the ambiguous status of stepfamilies. For example, some scholars may be unclear themselves of the definition of the entire stepfamily system and who is included in their empirical investigations, especially when there are resident and non-resident stepparents and stepchildren. Ambiguity can also be felt among the stepfamily members themselves, as the definitions of stepparent–stepchild roles, boundaries, and expectations can often be unclear (Mahoney, 2006). Research continues to emphasize comparisons between youth living with a stepparent and those living with two biological parents, underlining the deficits associated with stepfamilies rather than providing an examination of the factors that promote positive stepfamily outcomes (Sweeney, 2010). Furthermore, despite the increased prevalence of stepfamilies in contemporary society, family policies have been slow to address their needs, and this lack of legal recognition may undermine the roles and responsibilities of stepparents (Jones, 2003).

In a critical review of contemporary research on stepfamilies, Portrie and Hill (2005) indicated that a central theme throughout the literature refers to the benefits of open communication on stepfamilies' well-being, the conformity of stepchildren to a new or reorganized system, and the acceptance of, or openness to, parental monitoring levels compared with two parent biological families. This suggests that stepfamilies that openly communicate and address struggles dealing with role identity, relationships, and new family development are able to transition into the new family more smoothly than those who fail to communicate openly. Other relevant issues family scholars need to consider in researching and working with stepfamilies include examining all of the various relationship interactions in the stepfamily system (Lansford, Ceballo, Abbey, & Stewart, 2001), parental monitoring of stepchildren's behavior (Fisher, Leve, O'Leary, & Leve, 2003), boundary management (Yuan & Hamilton, 2006), the extent of parental involvement among all parental figures connected to the stepfamily (Yuan & Hamilton, 2006), and communication strategies among various subsystems within the stepfamily (Golish, 2003). The demographic changes in family forms indicate that the majority of children growing up now are likely to encounter multiple parental figures. In addition, they will be part of complex and changing kinship networks, and thus they must negotiate changing relations within them (Cherlin & Furstenberg, 1994).

The importance of using a theoretical framework when conducting research on family issues has been underscored (e.g., Cheal, 1991; Klein & White, 1996). Theorizing is "the process of systematically formulating and organizing ideas to understand a particular phenomenon" (Boss, Doherty, LaRossa, Schumm, & Steinmetz, 1993). Referring to the linkage between theory and research in family science, Lavee and Dollahite (1991) indicated that it is necessary to make theory a more explicit part of empirical science. In their review of empirical articles involving stepfamilies with adolescents from 1990–1999, Robila and Taylor (2001) found that less than half used explicit theory to guide their research activities. In our most recent review of the empirical research on stepfamilies, from 2000–2010, we found that a large number of researchers are still not using an explicit theoretical foundation in their research inquiries, methodologies, or their subsequent discussions and implications.

Although the use of theoretical perspectives can fortify research and strengthen our understanding of stepfamily dynamics, research is only as strong as the theoretical foundation upon which it is built. The increased research on stepfamilies during recent decades, and the recognition of the important role family theories play in organizing research findings, provides a fine opportunity to examine theory use in the stepfamily literature.

OVERVIEW OF THEORIES USED TO STUDY STEPFAMILIES

To identify the theories used in current stepfamily scholarship, we conducted a systematic review of journal publications available between the years 2000–2010 using PsychInfo, Social Services Abstracts, SocINDEX, Social Work Abstracts, and Sociological Abstracts. For search purposes, several keywords were inputted, including: stepfamily, stepmother, stepfather, stepchild, parenting, and relationship. We also examined the reference list for each article to identify additional studies not found during our initial search. The time period selected (2000–2010) was chosen in an effort to cover all appropriate research published since the completion of a previous review of explicit theory use in stepfamily and adolescent research from 1990–1999 (Robila & Taylor, 2001). Over 125 journal articles were found on stepfamilies and they included both qualitative and quantitative articles. Several articles were discarded from the pool due to their non-empirical nature (reviews of stepfamily literature or conceptual papers). Finally, we only selected articles that empirically examined stepfamilies and the relationships within them. We excluded several articles in which stepfamilies were not the primary population of investigation.

Data from 102 articles found within peer-reviewed scholarly journals were used for this review. Stepfamily research articles were identified as using theory when one or more theoretical perspectives were explicitly named by the authors. The terms, "theory," "perspective," "hypothesis," "framework," and "approach" were used to identify an author's inclusion of a theoretical framework. Additionally, the term "model" was used to indicate theory usage as long as the model was judged to be theoretical and not statistical in nature. Contrary to the methods used by Lavee and Dollahite (1991) and Hawley and Geske (2000), this review did not examine implicit theory usage. We believe it is the researchers' responsibility to be explicit in describing which theory or theories they used in their research, as each theoretical perspective or paradigm has its own unique assumptions and philosophies.

Each article was examined by two members of the review team, and any discrepancies in identified theories were discussed by team members until a final consensus was made. After analyses of the articles were complete, we then grouped similar theories under the same category for further study. Theories not immediately recognizable (e.g. deficit comparison approach or community connections perspective) were examined using a constant comparative method to discover any common themes or assumptions that could associate them with a larger macro-theory (Bengston, Acock, Allen, Dilworth-Anderson, & Klein, 2005). Theories that could not be consolidated into another category, and were only used once, were labeled as "other". Of the 160 uniquely named theories explicitly mentioned, only 29 ultimately fell into this other category.

Of the 102 stepfamily articles reviewed for this analysis, 76% ($n = 78$) used at least one explicit theory. Furthermore, of these 78 articles using explicit theory, 54% ($n = 42$) used more than one theory in the beginning/introduction and/or discussion sections of their articles. It was not uncommon to find researchers incorporating 3–4 different theories into a single article.

Systems theory was identified as the most widely used theory in stepfamily research during 2000–2010, as 17 of the articles explicitly mentioned it. Social capital theories/social exchange (12) were the next most prevalently used theories, followed by evolutionary theories (10), symbolic interactionism (10), attachment theories (8), and parenting theories (8).

FAMILY SYSTEMS

In recent decades, *family systems theory* has become a theoretical hallmark for scholars interested in understanding the interplay of stepfamily relationships (Afifi, 2008; Bray & Berger, 1993). Its basic tenets have provided researchers with a foundation to examine how stepfamily members' behaviors influence one another and the stepfamily as a whole. The notions of boundaries, rules, and norms, which define appropriate behaviors and membership within and outside of the family (Broderick, 1994), have become a focus of much of the stepfamily literature (Stewart, 2005).

Family systems theory (Bowen 1971, 1972) examines the family in terms of various subsystems, each of which can impact other subsystems and the overall family system. For example, a stepfamily may have a marital subsystem, a stepsibling subsystem, a biological sibling subsystem, and a biological parent–child subsystem. This theory proposes that a three person relationship, particularly if two of the family members "triangulate" the third (see below), is a more unstable unit than a two person relationship. Individuals are consistently interacting and mutually influencing one another, as opposed to a unidirectional influence of one person or relationship to another. Another core concept is that both stability and change in families are expected over time (Minuchin, 1985, 1988). Family members will engage in typical reaction patterns to one another and these reaction patterns are relatively stable over time. However, these patterns may change as new challenges for the family emerge to which the family must adapt. Obviously for newly established stepfamilies, the goal is building and maintaining family system stability. However, with multiple systems converging into newly formed systems, it may take months or years to gain some sense of stability.

Over the past 20 years, scholars have examined stepfamilies by incorporating various systemic concepts and assumptions. Researchers have used the theory to explain the ways in which forming a new family system through remarriage may have influences on other aspects of the family. For instance, two biologically unrelated children living together because of marriage between parents have a new stepsibling relationship. Changes within that sibling relationship can impact the relationships between one of the children and his or her biological parent. Thus, the sibling subsystem is likely to affect the parent–child relationship (Baham, Weimer, Braver, & Fabricius, 2008).

In addition, scholars have documented the difficulties that ensue when triangulation, or loyalty conflicts result from a covert coalition in which two family members unite against another family member. These triangulations commonly exist in newly-formed stepfamilies (Baxter, Braithwaite, & Bryant 2006; Coleman, Fine, Ganong, Downs, & Pauk, 2001). Researchers have noted the challenges that result when the boundaries between custodial parents and children become blurred after a divorce and children become their parents' social support system (emotional parentification) and/or take on additional roles and household tasks that were once assumed by the parent (instrumental parentification) (Alexander, 2003; Biblarz & Gottainer, 2000; Jurkovic, Thirkeild, & Morrell, 2001). In particular, scholars have noted the difficulties stepfathers experience when attempting to enter a family in which cohesive and relatively impermeable boundaries have been created around the custodial mother and her children (Baxter et al., 2006; Coleman et al., 2001; Golish, 2003).

In a more recent study, Gosselin (2010) examined how psychosocial adjustment for individual members within stepmother families is influenced by dynamics within the stepfamily system. By using a systems perspective, stepmother families were viewed as multiperson systems with several interrelated subsystems, where individual and interpersonal factors interact, and where reciprocity plays an important role.

SOCIAL CAPITAL/SOCIAL EXCHANGE

Through our review of the stepfamily research, we found there are several similar theories that examine the needs and preferences for resources desired by stepfamily members. *Social capital theory* has concepts, principles, and philosophies similar to related theories, such as *social exchange theory, equity theory, alternative social capital theory, resource dilution, resource limitation*, and *normative resource theory*. Many authors using these theories acknowledged that relationships within stepfamilies are affected by the way limited resources (e.g. financial, temporal, emotional) are distributed between and among members (Stewart, 2002; Willetts & Maroules, 2004, 2005). In particular, investigating the role that resources and the exchange of these resources play can be seen as a way to better understand and describe stepfamily interactions. Using this perspective, relationships can be understood as reciprocal interactions in which individuals are motivated by self interest to increase the rewards and decrease the costs of affiliation (Ingoldsby, Smith, & Miller, 2004). Each individual is believed to have resources and needs that dictate investment into other members of the family system.

The social capital perspective stresses that blended families must integrate several new family members and a new partner into the family network. These new relationships require time and energy to develop and can place a burden on the family's social capital. This integration may affect the amount of time parents are engaged in positive interactions with children (Coleman et al., 2000) or even lead to behavior problems in children (Kim, Hetherington, & Reiss, 1999).

Coleman (1988) identified four properties of social relations and organizations (both within and outside of families) that facilitate increased social capital: (a) intergenerational closure, (b) stability, (c) dependence, and (d) shared ideology. For Coleman, "intergenerational closure is marked by individuals who see each other daily, have expectations towards each other and develop norms about each others' behavior" (p. 106). As a consequence, when families share a sense of *intergenerational closure*, the result is an environment where one's behaviors have effective sanctions that serve to guide and monitor individual behavior. As a result, children of well-established intergenerationally closed families develop a strong sense of trust, obligation, and high expectations for themselves and other family members, and, thus, act accordingly.

Stability within a social structure also serves as a means of developing sanctioned group norms. As a family maintains its stability and the more developed the group norms, expectations, and obligations become, the higher the level of social capital. *Dependence* on one another within a family assumes that the more members can rely upon one another for aid, the greater the quantity of social capital generated. Family members then begin to develop a shared sense of belonging and reliance on one another over time, which also increases their sense of obligation. Finally, *shared ideology* means that social capital is created when a group of individuals behave in ways that are not only in the interest of themselves, but in the interest of the group (Coleman, 1990).

Stewart (2002) examined how the presence of stepchildren affects childbearing intentions among newly married couples and found that stepchildren had no impact on fertility. From a social capital perspective, their findings suggest that stepchildren may not be able to provide the full social benefits associated with firstborn children. Although social capital theory was used in this article to explain how biological children are preferable to stepfathers than are stepchildren, Lamb (2007) found that in cases of sterility, social capital theory may explain the benefits of stepfather adoption. "The alternative social capital hypothesis posits that sterility may be associated with greater odds of stepfather adoption when men are unable to have the total number of biological children they desire" (p. 1167).

When relationships are perceived as inequitable, tensions may arise between members of a group (Ingoldsby et al., 2004). Henry and McCue (2009) used social capital theory to explain how unbalanced decision-making power within relationships in stepfamilies may cause increases in distress and anger. Using the normative resource model, Felker, Fromme, Arnaut, and Stoll (2002) analyzed how power within families is related to the resources that each partner brings to the marriage. The application of social capital theory in research on stepfamilies provides scholars with a framework for understanding how the availability and distribution of resources may impact the way relationships are formed and governed within the family.

A final example of an effective use of social capital theory comes from MacDonald and DeMaris' (2002) research on the quality of the stepfather–stepchild relationship. They found that when the biological father has little or no parenting input, the stepfather's demand for conformity had a positive effect on the quality of the stepfather–stepchild relationship. However, when the biological father has a great deal of parenting input, the effect of the stepfather's demand for conformity varies depending on the level of interaction between the stepchild and the biological father. When interaction is infrequent, the effect is positive, but as the interaction increases, the effect becomes increasingly negative. These findings fit well with the expectations of social capital theory. Overall, stepchildren who appear to have the most social capital, namely those whose biological fathers frequently interact with them and have a large amount of parenting input, are those whose relationships with their stepfathers are most likely to be poor when the stepfather strongly demands conformity.

EVOLUTIONARY THEORY

Grounded in Darwin's theory of natural selection, *evolutionary theory* posits that the family plays an important role in the survival of individuals (Ingoldsby et al., 2004). Individuals contribute to future generations by producing offspring with their genetic information and by providing for the reproduction and survival of close relatives (Emlen, 1995). Evolutionary theorists (Barkow, Cosmides, & Tooby, 1992; Irons, 1979) contend that both psychological processes and behavioral mechanisms evident in humans today have evolved because they were adaptive for our ancestors. This view of development has been applied to understanding stepfamily relationships and thus has many implications for the dynamics of sibling or parent–child relations within them. For example, Popenoe (1994) claims that stepfathers take less active roles in parenting than biological residential fathers, because they are not invested in the survival of unrelated children. Applying this reasoning, perhaps children from blended families have less invested stepparents (in particular stepfathers) who are more likely to treat siblings differently. This could foster sibling rivalry, given that differential treatment from parents has been found to affect stepsibling relationships. In short, stepfamily relationships tend to be less conflictual when parents do not favor one child over the other, but rather respond warmly and sensitively to all of their children (Boyle, Jenkins, & Georgiades, 2004; Brody, 1998).

Several studies over the past 20 years used an evolutionary perspective to understand parental investment in stepchildren. For example, Hofferth and Anderson (2003) used the evolutionary perspective to suggest why biological parents may have a larger investment in their children than stepparents: "From an evolutionary perspective, investment in biological children increases the ability of the next generation to reproduce and continue the genetic family line" (p. 214). King (2007) hypothesized that nonresidential biological fathers will be more invested in their children than will stepfathers because of the primacy of biology. Likewise, Gunnoe and Hetherington (2004) used evolutionary theory to understand the greater investment on the part of mothers, who are biologically limited with the number of children they can reproduce, as opposed to fathers who are capable of producing unlimited numbers of children.

SYMBOLIC INTERACTIONISM

In recent decades, there have been a number of stepfamily researchers who have used *symbolic interactionism* as a core theoretical perspective to guide their work (Gallardo & Mellon-Gallardo, 2007). Symbolic interactionism posits that the primary task of life is to create relationships with others through the exchange of symbols (Mead, 1934). These perspectives all necessitate a belief that human beings actively work to create meaning through symbols and interactions with others (LaRossa & Reitzes, 1993). Individuals are driven to find significance in the surrounding environment and self-concepts will develop through both societal/cultural processes and interactions with others. In other words, through interaction, we create and negotiate relationships with others. The interaction is constructed through the use of symbols. Symbols are represented through language and as a consequence, communication. A result of communication is the expectation that we can label and classify objects, people, and relationships. These classifications are used to create scripts for interactions with others and expectations for the roles people fulfill (Stryker, 1968).

Adolescents in remarried family households respond to their perceptions of their parent and stepparent (Henry, Nichols, Robinson, & Neal, 2005). A family integration challenge for remarried family households with adolescents is establishing clear roles for parents and stepparents (Coleman et al., 2000). Due to the lack of clear social norms regarding stepparent roles, each remarried family household faces the challenges of defining when and how stepparents are to engage in appropriate "parent behaviors." Symbolic interaction provides a means to understand the specific parent–stepparent behaviors in remarried family households that promote adolescent social competence, including empathic concern (Henry et al., 2005)

When examining stepfathers from a symbolic interactional perspective, these men often subjectively and practically manage their stepfather identities and family circumstances. According to Marsiglio and Hinojosa (2007), stepfathers are active agents in responding to cultural images of stepfatherhood and co-parenting. Men negotiate and produce gendered effects in their lives through interactions with their parents, partners' children, and biological fathers.

Meanings associated with family and stepfamily are socially constructed within the larger culture (Ganong & Coleman, 1997) and negotiated by individual family members through their daily routines and relationship work. In the US, prevailing mainstream norms paint family structure as nuclear, with the man being central to the family. Such norms are reinforced through social policies and institutional practices limiting stepparents' rights and obligations toward stepchildren whom they have not legally adopted (Fine, 1995; Mason, Harrison-Jay, Svare, & Wolfinger, 2002).

Using symbolic interactionism, identity theorists highlight the cognitive schemes enabling stepfamily members to define their situations and to make behavioral decisions (Stryker & Burke, 2000). Scholars have found it significant that stepfathers can be committed to their relationship roles and can accept the psychological centrality of these roles to themselves and their families (Stryker & Serpe, 1994). Others find it important that stepfathers can manage their relational behavior and role perceptions in order to match their standard about what it means to be a stepfather (Marsiglio, 2004).

The lives and experiences of women in stepfamilies have been underinvestigated. Mills (1984) suggests that women have overtly and covertly undermined stepfathers' roles as disciplinarians in the lives of children. According to Hays (1996), Mills ignored the powerful societal messages a mother receives regarding her role in her child's life, namely the message that she is to protect her children against perceived threat, regardless of its source.

Women are active in constructing and recreating their role experiences; however, these experiences are also influenced by the context in which they live and the interactions they have with others (Goffman, 1959). Stepfamily members are continually in the process of both taking and making roles in their everyday relationships with others. This process requires one to regularly revise and adapt in response to changing situations. *Symbolic interactionism* allows researchers to examine how a stepparent or stepchild might adapt or redefine the roles they take on and the meanings they assign them. In addition, this theory provides the researcher with insight as to others' perceptions when a role is assigned or achieved by another family member.

ATTACHMENT THEORY

Another theory researchers use when examining stepfamily relationships is *attachment theory*. Two primary features of a secure attachment are the perceived availability of the parent and the child's reliance on the parent during times of stress (Bowlby, 1969). When children feel secure and accepted in their parental relationships, they feel less threatened by stressful events (Gunnar, 2000) and generally have more positive developmental and behavioral outcomes (Bretherton & Munholland, 1999). By extension, it is reasonable to assume that perceived importance to parents (i.e., parental mattering) creates a sense of relatedness and security about one's social position with regard to significant others, which in turn positively influences adjustment (Marshall, 2001, 2004). As children of stepfamilies typically have two father figures and/or two mother figures, it is imperative to determine how each of these parental figures influences children's psychological adjustment, in addition to their relationship attachments (Schenck et al., 2009).

Planitz and Feeney (2009) used attachment theory to conceptualize how beliefs about stepfamily functioning are affected by previous relationships. If individuals have experienced events that cause them to have negative views of stepfamily functioning, they will be less inclined to respond positively to family conflict. The authors emphasize that "the impact of negative expectations of relationships has been expounded in depth by attachment theorists who have noted that the expectations embodied in negative working models of attachment tend to be self-fulfilling" (p. 94). In other words, if stepfamily members expect their relationships to not meet their needs or even fail, these relationships may prove less likely to succeed.

Attachment theory can also be useful in understanding why certain types of stepparent–stepchild relationships form. For instance, Ceglian and Gardner (2000) used this perspective to predict that attachment style (which develops through experience with previous relationships) will be influential in determining the emotional tone of stepmother–stepchild bonds. A negative attachment style predicts the development of hostile behaviors from stepmothers to the children of their partners. Attachment theory also provides an explanation for how stepfamily relationships can have a powerful impact on children's psychosocial development. "Although traditionally focused on the mother–child relationship, attachment theory also suggests that children can form multiple attachment relationships across development and that each of these relationships may influence children's psychological adjustment either directly or interactively" (Schenck et al., 2009, p. 84). For instance, Schenck and colleagues discovered that when adolescent stepchildren perceived themselves as being important to nonresidential biological fathers, they were at less risk for internalizing problems. Likewise, when these stepchildren believed that their stepfathers were invested in their lives they had lower levels of parent-reported, teacher-reported, and self-reported externalizing problems. By applying an attachment perspective to this study, the researchers were able to conceptualize why relationships with fathers has such a monumental impact on emotional adjustment.

CONFLICT THEORY

According to *conflict theories*, conflict is natural, normal, and inevitable in social relationships (Farrington & Chertok, 1993; Sprey, 1979; White & Klein, 2008). Not only is conflict considered to be endemic, it is also seen as functional and necessary to the survival of family relationships. Due to conflict being both inevitable and endemic, the primary concern is to understand how family members manage conflict. Familial conflict can be defined as a disagreement or altercation among family members over limited resources, contentious means, incompatible goals, or a blend of these (White & Klein, 2008). According to Sprey (1979), conflict is better understood as a process, as opposed to an isolated single behavioral event. While the behavior might be observable, conflict itself does not always express itself visually. Conflict can exist internally as with an individual who is frustrated, discouraged, or distraught with a family member's decision or action.

According to Coleman, et al. (2001), conflict is very different within stepfamilies, as opposed to first-marriage families, because of their unique circumstances. For example, the parent–child bonds precede the marital bonds in stepfamilies, forcing stepparents to face already established family patterns, rituals, rules, and norms. Integrating new rules and rituals, while trying to maintain existing ones, can cause significant conflict among family members. In addition, within stepfamilies, there are often nonresidential parents, who may make the stepparent feel like an extraneous adult with often ambiguous roles in the stepfamily. Conflicts may erupt between a residential biological parent and a nonresident biological parent when seeking to establish consistent rules and maintain similar parenting styles for biological children residing at different home environments. Finally, there can be abrupt and sudden changes in the living arrangements when a stepparent enters the family.

Conflicts may arise when stepchildren move to a new home, where established rules and expectations already exist.

The terms *competition, power, management, consensus,* and *resolution* are concepts used regularly within conflict theory that can readily be applied to stepfamily members and their families. Competition refers to the idea that family members are continually seeking gains (White & Klein, 2008). Conflict then arises when one family member gains more from another when competing for the same resource. In stepfamilies, stepchildren might likely compete among each other and with a stepparent for time, attention, and resources. A new couple having stepchildren may also experience conflict when they compete for time and energy to build and strengthen their own relationship, while their stepchildren might fight against allowing them access to those resources.

Power is the ability to control the direction or course of the action of others. Within stepfamilies, a parent and stepparent might struggle over establishing rules and decision-making as they relate to parenting their children. According to Metts and Cupach (1995), a biological residential parent may feel that a non-residential ex-partner is exerting too much power over their children and within their family. The residential parent may exert significant energy to limit the power and authority an ex-partner has in the family. If the ex-partner pushes back, then conflict will typically emerge. In addition, stepchildren may also resist any parental power a stepparent tries to exhibit in a newly formed stepfamily (Burrell & Mitchell, 1993).

The terms management, consensus, and resolution are interrelated and often discussed together (White & Klein, 2008). Conflict management requires the recognition that there are two competing perspectives; there are scarce resources and each group or person wants to have an opportunity to access those resources. Management results after the conflict has emerged and sufficient negotiating and bargaining has brought about an acceptable compromise. It is important to note that management does not eliminate conflict, but it establishes guidelines and agreements for conflict to keep from escalating. Consensus means agreement and is the preferable outcome of negotiation. It is the awareness among family members that conflict can be managed to the satisfaction of all party members or that the conflict can be completely resolved (White & Klein, 2008). According to Ingoldsby et al. (2004), resolution refers to both the process of a given conflict's ending and the nature of the end state. When conflict is resolved, disputing family members no longer see the issue as competition for scarce resources. There is no more conflict and the resolution is the outcome of the matter.

Although there has been relatively little research on conflict within stepfamilies, specifically using conflict theory, Coleman and colleagues (2001) found that there are several distinct issues over which stepfamily disagreements arise. Collectively, the stepfamilies in their study experienced strife over resources, loyalty conflicts, control over and responsibility for children, and/or disputes with extended family members and nonresidential parents. All of these conflicts can be classified as instances when boundary negotiation resulted in an outcome unsatisfactory to at least one family member.

STRESS AND RESILIENCY THEORIES

Due to the high levels of stress experienced by stepfamily members (Johnson, Wright, Gilchrist, Lane, & Haigh, 2006), *stress theories* have been found to be useful to researchers as well. Stress theory centers on the idea that stressful life events produce role strain, reduce self-esteem and mastery, and ultimately, lead to more negative social and psychological outcomes. In regard to blended families, the stressors associated with stepfamily formation may be amplified for youth who live with half and/or step siblings (Ganong & Coleman, 1994) and are adjusting to a new stepparent style of managing the household and family (Coleman et al., 2000). Some research has indicated that, after statistically controlling for socioeconomic and background characteristics, living in a blended family is still often associated with significantly more negative outcomes for youth (Ginther & Pollack, 2004).

The concept of family resiliency is another valuable framework in understanding stepfamilies (Von Eye & Schuster, 2000). By using resilience-based approaches, key interactional processes can be identified and fortified that enable families to withstand and rebound from crises and challenges (Walsh, 2003). At the most basic level, resilience refers to the positive adaptation patterns in the context of significant risk and adversity (Masten & Powell, 2003). Resiliency combines the interaction of risk factors—stressful events or adverse environmental conditions that increase the vulnerability of individuals—and the presence of personal, familial, and community protective factors that buffer and protect against those vulnerabilities (Norman, 2000). According to McCubbin and McCubbin (1988), family resilience refers to the dimensions, characteristics, and features of families that help them to be both resistant to disruption in the face of change and adaptive in the face of crisis situations.

Although resiliency models have been conceptualized in a number of ways using the *ABC-X model* (Hill, 1949), the *Double ABC-X Model*, and the *FAAR* (Family Adjustment and Adaptation Model) (McCubbin & Patterson, 1983), one of the most recent theoretical developments has been the *Resiliency Model of Family Stress, Adjustment and Adaptation* (McCubbin, Thompson, & McCubbin, 1996). This model consists of two related phases of a family's response to stress. First, the adjustment phase describes the family's pre-crisis functioning and the influence of protective or resistant factors. Second, upon the advent of a family crisis, the family enters into the adaption phase. This phase involves the functioning of recovery factors, referring to the family's ability to adapt in a family crisis situation.

According to Greeff and Du Toit (2009), several resiliency-associated factors have been found among stepfamilies when confronted with crisis or stressful situations. One factor was having supportive family members and an internal support system. When family members feel that they can turn to one another during stressful times, they are more likely to be successful in overcoming adversity. The researchers also found that stepfamilies that communicated successfully fostered resilience by encouraging open emotional expression and collaboration in problem-solving. A strong marital relationship was also important in having a resilient stepfamily. When a married couple was united and happy, the stepfamily was reported as being more resilient.

PARENTING THEORIES

In stepfamily research, parenting theories refer to several distinct perspectives that address how stepparents interact and socialize their children. For example, within *parent socialization theory*, parenting is viewed as the sum of behaviors parents use to prepare their children for adult roles. Parents monitor and set limits on the behaviors of their children (Heatherington, Bridges & Insabella, 1998). Overall, the research on stepfamilies has acknowledged the impact stepparents (biological, non-biological, residential, and non-residential) can have on the development of stepchildren. For instance, the 'cruel stepmother model' featured in Ceglian and Gardner's (2000) research on marital adjustment is applicable to understanding intensely negative interactions within only stepmother–stepchild relationships. Likewise, the substitution or serial parenting hypothesis suggests that children can only have one involved father at a time; thus, an involved stepfather may be able to fill the gap left by an uninvolved biological father (Yuan & Hamilton, 2006).

Many parenting theories focus on the dynamics and relationship quality between stepchildren and stepparents; however, other theories examine how these interactions are both controlled and influenced by the opinions of biological parents. The *maternal gatekeeping* theory used by Adamsons, O'Brien, and Pasley (2007) suggests that mothers retain primary control over children's socialization; thus, paternal involvement (including both the biological and stepfather) will be influenced by maternal allowances. Within the context of stepfamilies, both nonresidential biological father and stepfather involvement in the lives of stepchildren will be influenced by the mother's power. Similarly, the "mother as manager" perspective posits that mothers have direct control over the amount of interaction between biological and stepfathers, a power she may use deliberately (Yuan & Hamilton, 2006).

Although other "macro" theories have been used to some extent within stepfamily research (e.g., *social learning theory*, *biosocial theory*, *feminist perspective*, *ecological theory*), several researchers have employed contextual-specific micro-theories in their research. In our review of stepfamily studies from 2000–2010, 29 such theories (38% of the total number of theoretical perspectives explicitly used) could not be definitively classified into any broader theoretical category. Examples of these theories include: the *routine activities model of crime victimization*, the *community connections perspective*, the *normative–adaptation perspective*, *coercion theory*, and the *deficit comparison approach*. Though as a group, micro-theories made up the largest individual category of theory classification, it is interesting to note that only five journal articles used a micro-theory without reference to any other theoretical perspective.

LIMITATIONS OF HOW THEORY HAS BEEN USED IN STUDYING STEPFAMILIES

Our review of recent stepfamily scholarship suggests a few general observations. First, researchers are using theory more often today than in previous years. In addition, scholars are using a wide range of theories as opposed to focusing on just a select few. Second, as opposed to creating or extending new theories, researchers seem to select a theory to serve their immediate investigative purposes and to satisfy an expectation of theory use in empirical research production.

As mentioned earlier, the most commonly used theoretical perspectives in stepfamily research between 2000–2010 were grounded in systems theory, social capital theory/social exchange, the evolutionary perspective, symbolic interactionism, attachment theory, and parenting models. In 2001, Robila and Taylor identified a list of family theories and perspectives deemed suitable for discussing the experiences of stepfamilies, yet which were absent in the adolescent stepfamily research of the 1990s. This list included social exchange theory, human ecology theory, the life course perspective, communication theory, and symbolic interactionism. It is encouraging to find that all five of these theories were explicitly mentioned in articles examined for the present study.

Although scholars may argue that the use of any theoretical perspective is preferable to no explicit theory, using less well-known 'micro-theories' may be counterproductive in research. One benefit of using explicit theoretical perspectives is that authors can use the theoretical and conceptual assumptions of that framework to both clarify a study's concepts and to apply the findings within the greater body of literature. For example, a researcher may use stress theory to define and specifically apply the concept of boundary ambiguity among stepchildren as a research variable, while at the same time further build upon our general understanding of boundary ambiguity in the field of family studies. However, when the theoretical perspective is so context-specific, or unknown, that the reader has no previous knowledge of its content (i.e. routine activities model of crime victimization), the author does not reap the benefit of that theoretical application. Also disconcerting is the liberal use of the term 'theory' in the literature. Our review methodology dictated that an author's use of specific terms (e.g., theory, framework, perspective) would signal the use of a theory within stepfamily research. However, upon further examination it became clear that many of these 'theories' were merely the authors' attempt at describing another scholar's approach to understanding the material. Using terminology in this manner implies a very broad and even ambiguous understanding of the concept of a theoretical framework. Just because some authors imply the use a theory in their work does not necessarily mean that they are using theory correctly or even using theory at a level that implies a strong research-theory connection.

Compared with the findings of similar studies published in the past 20 years, it is encouraging that our review of the 2000–2010 stepfamily literature found an increase in the percentage of authors using explicit theory in their research. Seventy-six per cent of the empirical articles examined used at least one theory somewhere in the article and half of these articles applied theoretical perspectives in both the introduction and discussion sections. This is a 35% increase over the percentage of stepfamily articles using theory in the previous decade (Robila & Taylor, 2001), although it should be noted that this earlier study focused only on stepfamilies with adolescents while the current research focused on the broader stepfamily literature. Our 2000–2010 stepfamily theory review revealed a 15% increase of explicit theory use in journal articles when compared with the findings of Taylor and Bagdi (2005). In examining all 673 research articles published in the *Journal of Marriage and the Family* between 1990 and 1999, they found that only 61% of authors made explicit reference to theories. Both of these comparisons are a positive sign that theory use in stepfamily research is more prevalent today than in decades past.

Given the aforementioned benefits of explicit theory use, it is not entirely clear why some stepfamily scholars choose not to include a theoretical discussion in their research. Lavee and Dollahite (1991) suggest several reasons that might explain this practice. First, it is quite possible that scholars are so focused on developing research methodologies and interpreting data that they may not give the necessary attention to a discussion of the theoretical implications of their work. Second, some scholars may avoid theoretical discussions due to their lack of experience and understanding of theoretical concepts, principles, and assumptions. Unfortunately, as discussed by Taylor and Bagdi (2005), some editors of professional journals may not place enough value or emphasis on the need for theoretical application in empirical articles. Third, space constraints in journals may lead to strict length requirements, which when coupled with stringent content requirements, may cause scholars to devalue the importance of a theoretical foundation. Journal editors and peer-reviewers have the power to insist on theory inclusion.

In addition, it is possible that stepfamily scholars simply do not place as high a value on a clear theoretical foundation as they do on a well thought out methodology. Our review suggests that many scholars may not feel confident in their understanding or use of theoretical frameworks. The widely ambiguous use of "theory" and its inappropriate application has flooded the field with a large array of models and classifications that are not necessarily sufficient theoretical perspectives. Well-established or sound theories should not only enable researchers to interpret their data in the broader context of family studies, but also guide the development of research questions and hypotheses (Bengston et al., 2005). Our present research identified that 38% of theories used by stepfamily scholars could not be sufficiently tied to any other recognizable theoretical framework. The research suggests that an absence of theoretical discussion may be due in part to a dilution of theoretical understanding that has caused some scholars to hesitate before explicitly using theory. These scholars may find theoretical discussion too confining or restrictive, which may cause them to avoid deeper theoretical discussions and implications altogether.

SUGGESTIONS FOR BETTER USE OF THEORY IN STUDYING STEPFAMILIES

There are several directions stepfamily researchers might consider in order for our understanding of blended family relationships to grow. As family scholars continue to discover relationship phenomena among stepfamilies, we hope that a new theoretical view can also be presented alongside the data, so that the information may be better understood. In her decade review of the stepfamily literature, Sweeney (2010) suggested that family scholars address several areas in order for research to move forward. With these suggestions, we also attempt to connect ways that new or refined theories can emerge with these needed directions.

First, it is suggested that stepfamily researchers move away from the regularly used comparison deficit approaches and focus on positive stepfamily outcomes. Doing so will require the collection of an extensive large-scale stepfamily process data set. A longitudinal dataset would be preferred. This process would be an excellent opportunity for stepfamily scholars to gather data that would not only inform the field, but build and test new theoretical ideas.

Second, more attention is needed to examine specific processes (i.e. discipline decisions, decision-making, and the timing of stepfamily formation) underlying the observed costs and benefits associated with living in stepfamilies. For example, which circumstances and personal attributes are most likely to be valued by adults and children of various family structures? Exchange or Resiliency theory may be expanded to try to gain a better vision of these selectivity processes.

Third, more theoretical development specific to stepfamilies must emerge as a result of our wide acceptance and acknowledgment that stepfamilies are unique with respect to their structures, processes, and outcomes. Although researchers have recently come to understand and document sources of stepfamily heterogeneity, particularly with respect to cohabiting stepfamilies, more conceptual and theoretical investigation is needed to further enhance our understanding of the diversity of stepfamily experiences. More attention is needed to understand stepfamily relationships that extend over multiple households or involve part-time household membership. Also, stepmother families and children's relationships with nonresident mothers and resident biological fathers need to be studied further. New research is also needed to diversify our knowledge of stepfamily experiences across groups defined by age, gender, race, ethnicity, or social class.

Surprisingly, we found only a handful of studies (Weaver & Coleman, 2005, 2010) that used the feminist perspective during our 2000–2010 review. Perhaps a greater emphasis and usage of *feminist theory* or a *gender theoretical approach* may be useful when investigating these types of households, especially in stepmother-led households. These perspectives will allow scholars to strengthen their understanding of personal impressions and reactions to the familial processes women or children experience within stepfamily relationships.

Another direction family scholars need to strengthen is the research in the area of gay and lesbian stepfamilies. In particular, we need to better understand the effects of others' reactions regarding gay or lesbian stepfamilies on those within the family relationship. Recently, Robitaille and Saint-Jacques (2009) examined these relationships using *social stigma theory*, which was employed to understand the process through which stigmatization occurs, as well as its consequences. This theory helped identify possible interventions to provide help for young people involved in GLBT stepfamily situations, diminish negative consequences of stigmatization, and aid in developing less stigmatizing environments. The use of social stigma theory within this context was an innovative way to employ a sociologically-based theory in the "stepfamily" field. There are other avenues scholars can explore in order to better understand the dynamics within same-sex stepfamily relationships.

Finally, existing theories may need to be used more broadly than before to study stepfamily relationships. New theoretical concepts, specific to stepfamilies, may need to be introduced and examined when describing stepfamily relationships and their processes. For example, future family scholars may attempt to introduce stepfamily-specific concepts to the area of conflict theory, a theoretical framework that has been widely accepted in the family field for decades. While using this theory as a foundation, existing concepts could be formulated to address specific types of stepfamily conflict. Often familiar and applied concepts such as structure, resources, negotiation, and consensus could be reframed and labeled to specifically describe conflict within stepfamily relationships. The development and design of a "Stepfamily Conflict Cycle Model" might be developed. Within the model, newly defined concepts specific to blended families, such as stepfamily resources, stepfamily negotiations, and stepfamily conflict processes might be developed in order for the stepfamily literature to move forward with formalized theory specific to blended family relationships. Developing and presenting clearly defined concepts specific to stepsibling conflict, and stepparent–stepchild conflict could help clarify the dynamic conflictual processes within stepfamilies.

CONCLUSION

One direction for theory development, in regard to studying stepfamilies, is to glean knowledge from disciplines outside of the traditional family field. Incorporating and applying theories used effectively in other disciplines could lead to new understanding of stepfamily dynamics and relationships. For example, Schrodt (2006a,b) introduced *schema theory* as an innovative way of examining stepchildren's perceptions of the stepparent–stepchild relationship and closeness. According to schema theory, people are active processors of information from their environments, and schematic thinking derives from the need to organize thinking for the purpose of cognitive economy (Fiske & Taylor, 1991). While having some related philosophical underpinnings to symbolic interactionism, schema theory posits that shared schematic concepts permit individuals to communicate and exchange ideas easily (Wicks, 1992). Schema theory could potentially reveal ways in which stepchildren interpret their stepfamily experiences, including those with stepparents, and develop new schematic concepts of family relationships through communication. Stepfamily members, particularly stepchildren, actively process information related to their experiences and these cognitions are instrumental in their communication and adjustment within their stepfamily situations.

We believe the recent theoretical, research and methodological advancements of Schrodt are exciting and add to the stepfamily literature. His efforts are an example of how one takes a relatively new theoretical perspective that has been used effectively in another field and then applies it to phenomena in the family field. His two recent measures have extended our view of social schema theory by identifying the underlying dimensions of the personal schemata stepchildren hold about their stepparent. In addition, scholars might be able to start to combine the dimensions and theoretical foundations of schema theory with another established family theory (such as symbolic interactionism or biosocial theory) to develop a new theoretical perspective that could further examine and explain stepfamily relationships in a completely new way. There are many opportunities awaiting family scholars who are searching for a new theory that will help us better understand stepfamily interactions and processes, if they allow themselves to think creatively.

REFERENCES

Adamsons, K., O'Brien, M., & Pasley, K. (2007). An ecological approach to father involvement in biological and stepfather families. *Fathering*, *5*, 129–147.

Afifi, T. D. (2008). Communication in stepfamilies: Stressors and resilience. In J. Pryor (Ed.), *The international handbook of stepfamilies: Policy and practice in legal, research, and clinical environments* (pp. 299–320). Hoboken, NJ: John Wiley & Sons.

Alexander, P. C. (2003). Parent-child role reversal: Development of a measure and test of an attachment theory model. *Journal of Systemic Therapies*, *22*, 31–43.

Baham, M. E., Weimer, A. A., Braver, S. L., & Fabricius, W. V. (2008). Sibling relationships in blended families. In J. Pryor (Ed.), *The international handbook of stepfamilies: Policy and practice in legal, research, and clinical environments* (pp. 175–207). Hoboken, NJ: John Wiley & Sons.

Barkow, J., Cosmides, L., & Tooby, J. (Eds.). (1992). *The adapted mind: Evolutionary psychology and the generation of culture*. New York: Oxford University Press.

Baxter, L. A., Braithwaite, D. O., & Bryant, L. E. (2006). Types of communication triads perceived by young-adult stepchildren in established stepfamilies. *Communication Studies*, *57*, 381–400.

Bengston, V., Acock, A., Allen, K., Dilworth-Anderson, P., & Klein, D. (2005). Theory and theorizing in family research: Puzzle building and puzzle solving. In V. Bengston, A. Acock, K. Allen, P. Dilworth-Anderson, & D. Klein (Eds.), *Sourcebook of family theory and research* (pp. 3–33). Thousand Oaks, CA: Sage.

Biblarz, T. J., & Gottainer, G. (2000). Family structure and children's success: A comparison of widowed and divorced single-mother families. *Journal of Marriage and the Family*, *54*, 570–581.

Boss, P. G., Doherty, W. J., LaRossa, R., Schumm, W. R., & Steinmetz, S. K. (1993). *Sourcebook of family theories and methods: A contextual approach*. New York: Plenum Press.

Bowen, M. (1971). Family therapy and family group therapy. In H. Kaplan & B. Sadock (Eds.), *Comprehensive group psychotherapy* (pp. 384–421). Baltimore, MD: Williams & Wilkins.

Bowen, M. (1972). Family therapy and family group therapy. In H. Kaplan & B. Sadock (Eds.), *Group treatment of mental illness* (pp. 145–181). New York: Aronson.

Bowlby, J. (1969). *Attachment and loss: Volume 1: Attachment*. New York: Basic Books.

Boyle, M. H., Jenkins, J. M., & Georgiades, K. (2004). Differential-maternal parenting behavior: Estimating within- and between-family effects on children. *Child Development*, *75*, 1457–1476.

Bray, J. H., & Berger, S. H. (1993). Developmental issues in Stepfamilies Research Project: Family relationships and parent-child interactions. *Journal of Family Psychology*, *7*, 76–90.

Bretherton, I., & Munholland, K. A. (1999). Internal working models in attachment relationships: A construct revisited. In J. Cassidy & P. R. Shaver (Eds.), *Handbook of attachment: Theory, research, and clinical applications* (pp. 89–111). New York: Guilford Press.

Broderick, C. (1994). *Understanding family process*. Newbury Park, CA: Sage.

Brody, G. H. (1998). Sibling relationship quality: Its causes and consequences. *Annual Review of Psychology*, *49*, 1–24.

Burr, W. (1995). Using theories in family science. In R. Day, K. Gilbert, B. Settles, & W. Burr (Eds.), *Research and theory in family science* (pp. 73–91). Pacific Grove, CA: Brooks/Cole.

Burrell, N. A., & Mitchell, A. K. (1993, May). *The definitional impact on conflict styles as stepfamilies reorganize*. Paper presented at the 43rd annual conference of the International Communication Association, Washington, D.C.

Ceglian, C., & Gardner, S. (2000). Attachment style and the 'wicked stepmother' spiral. *Journal of Divorce and Remarriage*, *34*, 111–129.

Cheal, D. (1991). *Family and the state of theory*. Toronto, Canada: University of Toronto Press.

Cherlin, A. J., & Furstenberg, F. F. (1994). Stepfamilies in the United States: A reconsideration. *Annual Review of Sociology*, *20*, 359–381.

Coleman, J. S. (1988). Social capital in the creation of human capital. *American Journal of Sociology*, *94*, S95-S120.

Coleman, J. S. (1990). *Foundations of social theory*. Cambridge, MA: Harvard University Press.

Coleman, M., Fine, M. A., Ganong, L. H., Downs, K. J. M., & Pauk, N. (2001). When you're not the Brady bunch: Identifying perceived conflicts and resolution strategies in stepfamilies. *Personal Relationships*, *8*, 55–73.

Coleman, M., & Ganong, L. (1990). Remarriage and stepfamily research in the 1980s: Increased interest in an old family form. *Journal of Marriage and the Family*, *52*, 925–940.

Coleman, M., Ganong, L., & Fine, M. (2000). Reinvestigating remarriage: Another decade of progress. *Journal of Marriage and the Family*, *62*, 1288–1307.

Chibucos, T. R., Leite, R. W., & Weis, D. L. (2005). *Readings in family theory*. Thousand Oaks, CA: Sage.

Demo, D. H., & Fine, M. A. (2010). *Beyond the average divorce*. Thousand Oaks, CA: Sage.

Emlen, S. (1995). An evolutionary theory of the family. *Proceedings of the National Academy of Sciences of the United States of America*, *92*, 8092–8099.

Farrington, K., & Chertok, E. (1993). Social conflict theories of the family. In P. G. Boss, W. J. Doherty, R. LaRossa, W. R. Shumm, & S. K. Steinmetz (Eds.), *Sourcebook of family theories and methods: A contextual approach* (pp. 357–381). New York: Plenum Press.

Felker, J., Fromme, D., Arnaut, G., & Stoll, B. (2002). A qualitative analysis of stepfamilies: The stepparent. *Journal of Divorce and Remarriage*, *38*, 125–142.

Fine, M. A. (1995). The clarity and content of the stepparent role: A review of literature. *Journal of Divorce and Remarriage*, *24*, 19–34.

Fisher, P. A., Leve, L. D., O'Leary, C. C., & Leve, C. (2003). Parental monitoring of children's behavior: Variation across stepmother, stepfather, and two-parent biological families. *Family Relations*, *52*(1), 45–62.

Fiske, S. T. & Taylor, S. E. (1991). *Social cognition*. New York: McGraw-Hill.

Ganong, L. H., & Coleman, M. (1994). *Remarried family relationships*. Thousand Oaks, CA: Sage.

Ganong, L. H., & Coleman, M. (1997). How society views stepfamilies. *Marriage and Family Review*, *26*, 85–106.

Ganong, L. H., & Coleman, M. (2004). *Stepfamily relationships: Development, dynamics, and interventions*. New York: Kluwer Academic/Plenum.

Gallardo, H., & Mellon-Gallardo, D. (2007). Stepmothering and identity: A co-constructed narrative. *Journal of Divorce and Remarriage*, *48*, 125–139.

Ginther, D. K., & Pollack, R. A. (2004). Family structure and children's educational outcomes: Blended families, stylized facts, and descriptive regressions. *Demography*, *41*, 671–696.

Golish, T. (2003). Stepfamily communication strengths: Understanding the ties that bind. *Human Communication Research*, *29*, 41–80.

Goffman, E. (1959). *Presentation of self in everyday life*. New York: Doubleday.

Gosselin, J. (2010). Individual and family factors related to psychosocial adjustment in stepmother families with adolescents. *Journal of Divorce and Remarriage*, *51*, 108–123.

Greeff, A. P., & Du Toit, C. (2009). Resilience in remarried families. *The American Journal of Family Therapy*, *37*, 114–126.

Gunnar, M. R. (2000). Early adversity and the development of stress reactivity and regulation In. C. A. Nelson Plotsky (Ed.), *The effects of adversity on neurobehavioral development: The Minnesota Symposia on child psychology* (Vol. 31, pp. 163–200). Mahwah, NJ: Erlbaum.

Gunnoe, M., & Hetherington, E. (2004). Stepchildren's perceptions of noncustodial mothers and noncustodial fathers: Differences in socioemotional involvement and associations with adolescent adjustment problems. *Journal of Family Psychology*, *18*, 555–563.

Hawley, D., & Geske, S. (2000). The use of theory in family therapy research: A content analysis of family therapy journals. *Journal of Marital & Family Therapy*, *26*, 17–22.

Hays, S. (1996). *The cultural contradictions of motherhood*. New Haven, CT: Yale University Press.

Henry, C., Nichols, J., Robinson, L., & Neal, R. (2005). Parent and stepparent support and psychological control in remarried families and adolescent empathic concern. *Journal of Divorce and Remarriage*, *43*, 29–46.

Henry, P., & McCue, J. (2009). The experience of nonresidential stepmothers. *Journal of Divorce and Remarriage*, *50*, 185–205.

Heatherington, E. M., Bridges, M., & Insabella, G. M. (1998). What matters? What does not? Five perspectives on the association between marital transitions and children's adjustment. *American Psychologist*, *53*, 167–184.

Hill, R. (1949). *Families under stress*. New York: Harper & Brothers.

Hofferth, S., & Anderson, K. (2003). Are all dads equal? Biology versus marriage as a basis for paternal investment. *Journal of Marriage and Family*, *65*, 213–232.

Ingoldsby, B., Smith, S., & Miller, J. (2004). *Exploring family theories*. Los Angelos, CA: Roxbury.

Irons, W. G. (1979). Natural selection, adaptation, and human social behavior. In N. Chagnon & W. Irons (Eds.), *Evolutionary biology and human social behavior* (pp. 4–39). North Scituate, MA: Duxbury Press.

Johnson, A. J., Wright, K. B., Gilchrist, E., Lane, L., & Haigh, M. M. (2006, November). Factors that predict stress levels for residential and nonresidential stepmothers: The influence of social support, role clarity, and household and childcare responsibilities. Paper presented at the 92nd annual National Communication Association Conference, San Antonio, TX.

Jones, A. C. (2003). Restructuring the stepfamily: Old myths, new stories. *Social Work*, *48*(2), 228–236.

Jurkovic, G. J., Thirkeild, A., & Morrell, R. (2001). Parentification of adult children of divorce: A multidimensional analysis. *Journal of Youth and Adolescence*, *30*, 245–258.

Kim, J. E., Hetherington, E. M., & Reiss, D. (1999). Associations among family relationships, antisocial peers, and adolescents' externalizing behaviors: Gender and family type differences. *Child Development*, *70*, 1209–1230.

King, V. (2007). When children have two mothers: Relationships with nonresident mothers, stepmothers, and fathers. *Journal of Marriage and Family*, *69*, 1178–1193.

Klein, D. M., & White, J. M. (1996). *Family theories: An introduction*. Thousand Oaks, CA: Sage.

Kreider, R. M. (2008). *Living arrangements of children: 2004*. Current Population Reports, (pp. 70–114). Washington, DC: US Census Bureau.

Lamb, K. A. (2007). I want to be just like their real dad: Factors associated with stepfather adoption. *Journal of Family Issues*, *28*, 1162–1188.

Lansford, J. E., Ceballo, R., Abbey, A., & Stewart, A. J. (2001). Does the family structure matter? A comparison of adoptive, two-parent biological, single-mother, stepfather, and stepmother households. *Journal of Marriage and Family*, *63*, 840–852.

LaRossa, R., & Reitzes, D. (1993). Symbolic interactionism and family studies. In P. Boss, W. Doherty, R. LaRossa, W. Schumm, & S. Steinmetz (Eds.), *Sourcebook of family theories and methods: A contextual approach* (pp. 135–163). New York: Plenum.

Lavee, Y., & Dollahite, D. C. (1991). The linkage between theory and research in family science. *Journal of Marriage and the Family*, *53*, 361–373.

MacDonald, W. L., & DeMaris, A. (2002). Stepfather-stepchild relationship quality. *Journal of Family Issues*, *23*, 121–137.

Mahoney, M. M. (2006). Stepparents as third parties in relation to their stepchildren. *Family Law Quarterly*, *40*, 81–108.

Marshall, S. K. (2001). Do I matter? Construct validation of adolescents' perceived mattering to parents and friends. *Journal of Adolescence*, 24, 473–490.

Marshall, S. K. (2004). Relative contributions of perceived mattering to parents and friends in predicting adolescents' psychological well-being. *Perceptual and Motor Skills*, 99, 591–601.

Marsiglio, W. (2004). When stepfathers claim stepchildren: A conceptual analysis. *Journal of Marriage and Family*, 66, 22–39.

Marsiglio, W., & Hinojosa, R. (2007). Managing the multifather family: Stepfathers as father allies. *Journal of Marriage and Family*, 69, 845–862.

Mason, M. A., Harrison-Jay, S., Svare, G. M., & Wolfinger, N. H. (2002). Stepparents: De facto parents or legal strangers? *Journal of Family Issues*, 23, 507–522.

Masten, A. S., & Powell, J. L. (2003). A resilience framework for research, policy and practice. In S. Luthar (Ed.), *Resilience and vulnerability adaptation in the context of childhood adversities* (pp. 1–25). Cambridge, UK: Cambridge University Press.

McCubbin, H. I., & McCubbin, M. A. (1988). Typologies of resilient families: Emerging roles of social class and ethnicity. *Family Relations*, 37, 247–254.

McCubbin, H. I., & Patterson, J. M. (1983). The family stress process: The double ABCX model of adjustment and adaptation. In H. McCubbin, M. Sussman, & J. Patterson (Eds.), *Social stress and the family: Advances and developments in family stress theory and research* (pp. 7–38). New York: Haworth.

McCubbin, H. I., Thompson, A. I., & McCubbin, M. A. (1996). *Family assessment: Resiliency, coping and adaptation – inventories for research and practice*. Madison, WI: University of Wisconsin.

Mead, G. H. (1934). *Mind, self, and society*. In C. W. Morris, (Ed.). Chicago: University of Chicago Press.

Metts, S., & Cupach, W. R. (1995). Postdivorce relations. In M. A. Fitzpatrick & A. L. Vangelisti (Eds.), *Explaining family interactions* (pp. 232–251). Thousand Oaks, CA: Sage.

Mills, D. M. (1984). A model for stepfamily development. *Family Relations*, 33, 365–372.

Minuchin, P. (1985). Families and individual development: Provocations from the field of family therapy. *Child Development*, 56, 289–302.

Minuchin, P. (1988). Relationships within the family: A systems perspective on development. In R. A. Hinde & J. Stevenson-Hinde (Eds.), *Relationships within families: Mutual influences* (pp. 7–26). Oxford, IN: Clarendon.

Norman, E. (2000). *Resiliency enhancement: Putting the strength perspective into social work practice*. New York: Columbia University Press.

Planitz, J. M., & Feeney, J. A. (2009). Are stepsiblings bad, stepmothers wicked, and stepfather evil? An assessment of Australian stepfamily stereotypes. *Journal of Family Studies*, 15, 82–97.

Popenoe, D. (1994). The evolution of marriage and the problem of stepfamilies: A biosocial perspective. In A. Booth & J. Dunn (Eds.), *Stepfamilies: Who benefits? Who does not?* (pp. 3–27). Hillsdale, NJ: Erlbaum.

Portrie, T., & Hill, N. R. (2005). Blended families: A critical review of the current research. *The Family Journal*, 13, 445–451.

Robertson, A., Adler-Baeder, F., Collins, A., DeMarco, D., Fein, D. & Schramm, D. (2006). *Meeting the needs of married, low-income stepfamily couples in marriage education services*. Cambridge, MA: Abt Associates.

Robila, M., & Taylor, A. (2001). The recent use of theory within stepparent and adolescent relationship research. *Journal of Divorce and Remarriage*, 35, 81–92.

Robitaille, C. & Saint-Jacques, M. C. (2009). Social stigma and the situation of young people in lesbian and gay stepfamilies. *Journal of Homosexuality*, 56, 421–442.

Schenck, C., Braver, S., Wolchik, S., Saenz, D., Cookston, J., & Fabricius, W. (2009). Relations between mattering to step- and non-residential fathers and adolescent mental health. *Fathering*, 7, 70–90.

Schoen, R., & Standish, N. (2001). The retrenchment of marriage: Results from marital status life tables for the United States, 1995. *Population and Development Review*, 27, 553–563.

Schrodt, P. (2006a). Development and validation of the Stepfamily Life Index. *Journal of Social and Personal Relationships*, 23, 427–444.

Schrodt, P. (2006b). The Stepparent Relationship Index: Development, validation, and associations with step-children's perceptions of stepparent communication competence and closeness. *Personal Relationships*, 13, 167–182.

Sprey, J. (1979). Conflict theory and the study of marriage and the family. In W. R. Burr, R. Hill, F. I. Nye, & I. Reiss (Eds.), *Contemporary theories about the family* (Vol. 2, pp. 130–159). New York: Free Press.

Stewart, S. D. (2002). The effect of stepchildren on childbearing intentions and births. *Demography*, *39*, 181–197.

Stewart, S. (2005). Boundary ambiguity in stepfamilies. *Journal of Family Issues*, *26*(7), 1002–1029.

Stryker, S. (1968). Identity salience and role performance: The relevance of symbolic interaction theory for family research. *Journal of Marriage and the Family*, *30*, 558–564.

Stryker, S., & Burke, P. (2000). The past, present and future of an identity theory. *Social Psychology Quarterly*, *63*, 284–297.

Stryker, S., & Serpe, R. T. (1994). Identity salience and psychological centrality: Equivalent, overlapping, or complementary concepts. *Social Psychological Quarterly*, *57*, 16–35.

Sweeney, M. M. (2010). Remarriage and stepfamilies: Strategic sites for family scholarship in the 21st century. *Journal of Marriage and the Family*, *72*(3), 667–684.

Taylor, A., & Bagdi, A. (2005). The lack of explicit theory in family research: A case analysis of the Journal of Marriage and the Family, 1990–1999. In V. Bengston, A. Acock, K. Allen, P. Dilworth-Anderson, & D. Klein (Eds.), *Sourcebook of family theory and research* (pp. 22–25). Thousand Oaks, CA: Sage.

Teachman, J., & Tedrow, L. (2008). The demography of stepfamilies in the United States. In J. Pryor (Ed.), *The international handbook of stepfamilies: Policy and practice in legal, research, and clinical environments* (pp. 3 – 29). Hoboken, NJ: Wiley.

U.S. Bureau of the Census. (2006). Statistical abstract of the United States (122nd ed.). Washington, DC: US Government Printing Office. Retrieved from http://www.census.gov.

Von Eye, A., & Schuster, C. (2000). The odds of resilience. *Child Development*, *71*(3), 563–566.

Walsh, F. (2003). Family resilience: A framework for clinical practice. *Family Process*, *41*(1), 1–18.

Weaver, S. E., & Coleman, M. (2005). A mothering but not a mother role: A grounded theory study of the non-residential stepmother role. *Journal of Social and Personal Relationships*, *22*, 477–497.

Weaver, S. E., & Coleman, M. (2010). Caught in the middle: Mothers in stepfamilies. *Journal of Social and Personal Relationships*, *27*, 305–326.

White J. M., & Klein, D. M. (2008). *Family theories*. Thousand Oaks: Sage.

Wicks, R. H. (1992). Schema theory and measurement in mass communication research: Theoretical and methodological issues in news information processing. In S. A. Deetz (Ed.), *Communication yearbook 15* (pp. 115–145). Newbury Park, CA: Sage.

Willetts, M. C., & Maroules, N. G. (2004). Does Remarriage Matter? The well-being of adolescents living with cohabiting versus remarried mothers. *Journal of Divorce and Remarriage*, *41*, 115–133.

Willetts, M. C., & Maroules, N. G. (2005). Parental reports of adolescent well-being: Does marital status matter? *Journal of Divorce and Remarriage*, *43*, 129–148.

Yuan, A., & Hamilton, H. (2006). Stepfather involvement and adolescent well-being: Do mothers and nonresidential fathers matter? *Journal of Family Issues*, *27*, 1191–1213.

Section V

Demographic Variations in Families

17 Becoming Gendered
Theories of Gendering Processes in Early Life

Julia T. Wood

A baby is born. In most cases, it conforms physically to one of two recognized sex categories in Western cultures: female or male. But what will the baby's gender be and how will the child develop that gender? This chapter focuses on how individuals learn gender or how they become gendered beings. The first section of the paper distinguishes between sex and gender. The second section reviews key findings related to sex-linked behavior, with emphasis on demonstrated differences between women and men's social behavior. The third section of the chapter presents four theories that shed light on how individuals learn gender in the early years with emphasis on learning within families. The final section of the chapter identifies limitations of the theories covered in this chapter and offers suggestions for theoretical advances

DISTINCTIONS BETWEEN GENDER AND SEX

Although the terms *sex* and *gender* are routinely treated as interchangeable, they are distinct concepts and the difference between them is important. Sex is a biological characteristic whereas gender is socially constructed, sustained, changed, and performed. Before elaborating this distinction, it is important to note that the line between sex and gender is not as clear as it might seem. In most cases, sex categorization and gender identity are both clear and consistent, that is, biological females develop into primarily feminine individuals and biological males develop into primarily masculine individuals. Yet this general consistency should not eclipse the considerable inconsistencies that exist within and between sex and gender. Intersexed individuals have biological characteristics of both sexes, and transgender[1] individuals have the biological characteristics of one sex yet do not identify with that sex. In less striking cases, male-bodied individuals may be more feminine than most male-bodied individuals and female-bodied individuals may be more masculine than most female-bodied individuals. With this understanding that the line between sex and gender is sometimes blurred, we can now elaborate the conceptual distinction between sex and gender.

---

[1] I use the term *transgender* to refer to individuals who identify with or as a sex other than the one into they were classified at birth. Regardless of whether these individuals have had hormonal treatment or surgery, the term *transgender* is preferred by a majority of members of this community.

SEX

Sex is a designation based on external genitalia (clitoris and vagina in females; penis and testes in males) and internal genitalia (ovaries and uterus in females; prostate gland in males). In most cases, sex is determined by one of the 23 pairs of human chromosomes. The typical sex chromosomal composition is XY for males and XX for females. Yet there are variations such as XO, XXX, XXY and XYY (Blackless et al., 2000; Dreger, 1998). In very rare cases, individuals may have some XY and some XX cells (Gorman & Cole, 2004). During gestation, fetuses are bathed in hormones that spur development of sex organs. Usually fetuses with a Y chromosome are bathed in progesterone, and fetuses without a Y chromosome receive less progesterone. When this is not the case—a fetus is exposed to or deprived of hormones that affect sex differentiation—sex organs consistent with the chromosomal makeup may not develop (Pinsky, Erickson, & Schimke, 1999). In sum, sex is biological category that, although unambiguous and straightforward for many people, admits considerable variation.

GENDER

Gender is a social, symbolic construction that reflects the meanings a society associates with biological sex. Gender varies across cultures and over time within specific cultures. An individual's sex is designated by society without any effort by the individual unless the individual decides to challenge the sex assigned to her or him. Unlike sex, individuals must do something to acquire gender.

Gender, which is also called gender role, involves behaving in ways that society considers feminine or masculine. Individuals express or perform gender in a host of ways: how they speak, dress, and style their hair; squealing at mice and spiders or getting rid of them; wearing floral-based scents or musky, woodsy-based scents; asking or being asked for dates; crossing legs so an ankle is on a knee or one knee is over the other; giving way on walkways or holding ground; having a body mass index below what is healthy or toned abs; and so forth.

But note that the above examples of masculine and feminine behavior reflect twenty-first century Western society. In eighteenth century Western society, femininity would have been performed by wearing corsets, tatting and crocheting, and fainting and requiring vapors to regain consciousness whereas masculinity would have been performed by physical strength and courage, leaving child-rearing to women, and owning and managing land if one was White. Femininity would also have been performed by not voting, holding office, or pursuing professional education. What Westerners consider feminine and masculine today departs significantly from what we considered those to be 300, 200, 100 or even 50 years ago.

In addition to varying over time within a particular society, gender varies across societies. In her classic study of gender in three New Guinea tribes, Margaret Mead (1935/1968) noted three distinct gender patterns. Among the Arapesh, both women and men behaved in ways classified as feminine in Western culture—passive, nurturing, and deferential. Among the Mundugumor, both women and men were aggressive, independent, and competitive. Finally, the Tchambuli had gender roles that inverted those in Western culture—men were delicate and decorative whereas women were aggressive and domineering.

Mead's pioneering research is not the only evidence of gender variation among cultures. In Tahiti, males are mild-tempered and they often express fear or cry (Coltrane, 1996). To become a man in Samoan society, males must submit to the painful process of extensive tattooing from their waists to below their knees (Channell, 2002). Traditionally, a number of native American tribes recognized "two spirit" individuals who preferred to mate with others of their sex, but these people were not considered "gay" or "lesbian" (Gilley, 2006). The Mbuti pygmies in central Africa make little distinction between the sexes in terms of expected and accepted roles and behaviors (Coltrane, 1996), and on Orango Island in West Africa, women choose mates and men cannot refuse

(Callimachi, 2007). In sum, gender is constructed and, for that reason, varies over time and across cultures.

KEY ISSUES IN THE STUDY OF SEX AND GENDER

Sex and gender have been a prominent focus of research for more than 40 years. As a result, we know a good deal about sex-linked behaviors and orientations. This section summarizes research on activity preferences, interaction styles, and relationship orientations that are typical of women and men. Although these patterns have been well documented, they are neither absolute dichotomies nor universal.

FEMALE PATTERNS AND PREFERENCES

Girls and women tend to operate from what is often referred to as a relational orientation (Gilligan, 1982). They are inclined to see relationships as central to their own identities and to invest substantially in relationships. Moreover, they typically view relationships, not as things that are built and then constant in character, but rather as ongoing processes that invite and require continuing investments of thought, feeling, communication, and action.

As a group, women regard communication as central to relationships. Talk is the primary means to learn about others and allow others to learn about oneself (Braithwaite & Kellas, 2006; Cancian & Oliker, 2000; Metts, 2006a,b; Walker, 2004; Wright, 2006). The talk that women engage in tends to be verbally expressive, supportive, and empathic (Guerrero, Jones, & Boburka, 2006; Maccoby, 1998; Mulac, 2006). Yet women's interest in communication is not restricted to the verbal realm. Non-verbally, women are more expressive and responsive than men (Hall, 1998; Henley & Freeman, 1995; Major, Schmidlin, & Williams, 1990). Women tend to orient toward others who are speaking, maintain eye contact, and give nonverbal signals of involvement (Hall, 1998; Wright, 2006).

Women's regard for communication as a way of building and sustaining closeness may explain the finding that both sexes regard talking about relationships as important when there is a problem or conflict, but women are more likely than men to regard talking about a relationship as valuable when there are no problems. Many men do not see the point of talking about a relationship when all is well, but women who view relationships as ongoing processes find it rewarding to do so (Acitelli, 1988; Peretti & Abplanalp, 2004). Women's reliance on communication may also be the reason why women athletes are more likely to talk through tensions with competitors, whereas male athletes are more likely to resort to physical means to settle differences (Sullivan & Short, 2001).

The centrality that many women accord to relationships makes it unsurprising that they tend to assume the role of "relationship expert." More than men, women tend to monitor relationships, analyze interpersonal dynamics, and take responsibility for maintenance and repair work (Canary & Wahba, 2006; Cubbans & Vannoy, 2004; DeMaris, 2007). The maintenance work that women do often includes a "second shift" (DeMaris, 2007; Hochschild with Machung, 2003; Medved, 2009) of homemaking and childcare duties that falls predominantly on women when they return home from their shift in the paid labor market. Although the majority of heterosexual families today have two wage earners, the housework and the care of children, parents, and other relatives continue to be done primarily by women (Baxter, Hewitt, & Western, 2005). Prior to 1995, mothers spent an average of 12 hours a week attending to children. By 2007, mothers with college educations spent an average of 21.2 hours a week, and mothers with less education spent 15.2 hours. Women's greater investment in home maintenance and childcare holds true even when women earn considerably more than their male partners (Baxter et al., 2005; Tichenor, 2005). In fact, men who do not have jobs in the paid labor force and whose female partners work outside the home engage in *less* childcare and home maintenance than men who have jobs in the paid labor force (Dokoupil, 2009).

As a point of comparison, unemployed women spend twice as much time on childcare and house-work as employed women (Dokoupil, 2009).

MALE PATTERNS AND PREFERENCES

Boys and men generally favor what is called an instrumental orientation (Cancian, 1989; Leaper & Ayres, 2007; Wright, 2006), which accords priority to doing things—accomplishing goals, solving problems. Whether the goals are scoring a touchdown, winning an argument, securing a contract, shooting a deer, or resolving a conflict, men tend to focus on actions aimed at bringing about out-comes. Male friends are more likely to build and express affection by reciprocal instrumentality (one friend fixes the other's computer, the other lends the first his car) than by personal disclosures (Chethik, 2001; Inman, 1996; Swain, 1989).

Men tend to use communication to achieve goals including gaining and maintaining their personal status. Verbally this is accomplished through such practices as talking longer than others, making assertions and declarations, using I-references, and interrupting (Mulac, 2006). Non-verbally, men rely on volume, gestures, inflection and touch to assert command over others and situations (Hall, 1998; Henley & Freeman, 1995; Major et al., 1990).

In general, men are less overtly emotionally expressive than women (Guerrero et al., 2006; Wright, 2006). They are less likely than women to make personal disclosures or to talk at length about feelings, particularly with other men (Eisenberg, 2002), and they are less overtly expressive of sympathy and empathy (Eisenberg, 2002; Lynch & Kilmartin, 1999). The consistent finding that men tend not to express emotions overtly does not mean either that men are not emotional or not emotionally expressive. It means only that they less often express their emotions through personal, verbal expression. Men more frequently enact "covert intimacy" (Swain, 1989), especially in friend-ships with other men. Covert intimacy is expressed through friendly competitions, backslaps, and teasing to signal affection.

Men's typically instrumental focus surfaces in their orientation toward relationships. As noted previously, when a relationship seems to be working well and there are no prominent problems, men are less interested in talking about the relationship. This suggests that men, more than women, tend to limit their investments in maintaining relationships, particularly in terms of contributions to the daily work of sustaining families (Cancian & Oliker, 2000; Hochschild with Machung, 2003). Men continue to lag behind women in household chores (Council on Contemporary Families, 2010; DeMaris, 2007). Further, fathers today spend about half as much time with their children as do mothers. That said, today's fathers spend more time with their children than did their own fathers. College-educated fathers spend an average of 9.6 hours a week with their children, and less educated fathers spend an average of 6.8 hours a week with children. That's more than double the amount of time fathers in 1977 spent with children. Fathers under 29 years of age spend more time with chil-dren than older fathers do (Council on Contemporary Families, 2010; Ramey & Ramey, 2009). Many of the sex-linked patterns discussed above can be traced to interaction in the early years during which children are schooled in being masculine or feminine. The next section of this chapter presents theories that explain those learning processes.

THEORIES OF GENDERING

In defining gender earlier, I noted that it does not just happen. Individuals have to do something to become gendered. They have to learn what counts as masculine and feminine and how to perform one or the other or both.

There is no shortage of theories that describe, explain, or predict gender in some fashion. Of these, many are not concerned with the early years of life and familial influences. Biological theory, for example, examines the influence of genetic, hormonal, and other biological features on gender; anthropological theories illuminate differences, sometimes radical, among cultural views of gender.

Because this chapter is concerned with gendering processes in the early years, this section examines four theories that are centrally concerned with the ways in which young children become gendered, that is, how they come to understand what counts as masculine and feminine in their culture and how they learn to embody gender in their self presentations.

At the outset, we should remind ourselves that individual families do not independently invent gender. Rather, families are embedded within larger systems including communities, regions, and cultures, and these larger systems have gender codes or ideologies regarding how women and men should think, feel, act and appear. What families teach children about gender usually reflects the larger culture's views and values, as modified or amended to honor particular familial histories and values. Families, then, tend to serve as socializing agents of the larger culture, inculcating many of its views, values, and expectations in children. The four theories examined in this section assume that cultural ideologies of gender precede individual families.

SOCIAL LEARNING THEORY

Social learning theory was developed by a number of scholars working in different disciplines. Among these, Walter Mischel (1966), Julian Rotter (1954), and Albert Bandura (1986, 2001, 2002) made particularly notable contributions to the theory. In its earliest formulation, social learning theory claimed that individuals learn through two main processes: observation and reinforcement. The first process, observation, occurs as children watch those around them, including those that appear through media systems. Children often imitate or model behaviors they observe in their caregivers and others (Kunkel, Hummert, & Dennis, 2006; Maccoby, 1998; Morrow, 2006). In somewhat traditional families, children perhaps see their mothers cooking, wearing skirts, and crying when upset; they may witness their fathers working on cars, shaving, and comforting women who are crying. According to social learning theory, children may regard the mothers and fathers as representing and modeling appropriate behavior. Having observed parents and others, children then try to imitate what they have observed. A young girl who wears a skirt, cooks on her play stove, and cries is likely to be greeted with approval or at least acceptance. However, a young boy who engages in those same three behaviors is likely to face less hospitable responses.

This leads to the second key concept in social learning theory: consequences in the form of rewards and punishments, which also often come from primary caregivers. The young boy who dons a skirt and cries may be punished with ridicule, scolding, directive advice, or physical penalties. This undesired and unpleasant response decreases the likelihood that he will continue to engage in behaviors that garner the negative response. If punishments are either strong enough initially or repeated consistently, the behaviors may be extinguished. On the other hand, the young girl who received positive responses to the behaviors is likely to repeat them because doing so results in pleasurable outcomes for her—a parent's smile or comfort, praise, a cookie. Repeated over time, these positive reinforcements encourage the young girl to continue behaving in ways considered feminine.

Parents, particularly middle-class parents, continue to follow many conventional gender scripts in terms of what they encourage and discourage in children. They tend to reward assertion and aggression in sons more than in daughters and to reward social skills in daughters more than in sons (Morrow, 2006). Parents also reward sons for being competitive and independent and reward daughters for being cooperative, helpful, and nurturing (Archer & Coyne, 2005; Leaper, Anderson, & Sanders, 1998). An additional way that parents encourage their children to develop gender identities is through the assignment of chores. Girls are more often assigned indoor chores that encourage attention to cleanliness and taking care of others, and coordinating with or accommodating others. Boys are more likely to be assigned outdoor chores that cultivate independent action that does not require significant coordination with others (Babcock & Laschever, 2003; Canary & Emmers-Sommer, 1997).

Along with parents, media are powerful agents of gender socialization. Children who are exposed to media that feature boys being rewarded for aggression and girls being rewarded for deference are likely to imitate the characters and conform to gender-stereotypical behavior (Jamieson & Romer, 2008). However, when children are exposed to media that present counter-stereotypical gender roles, they may develop less restricted notions of what is masculine and feminine. Children who watch a program in which a man takes care of children learn that caregiving is consistent with men and masculinity (Romer, 2008).

Peers also influence development of gender. Girls who are born with a condition known as congenital adrenal hyperplasia have higher testosterone levels than is usual for girls. As infants and young children, girls with this condition demonstrate atypical interest in trucks, toy weapons, and rough play. Yet when they interact with girls their own age, the peers socialize them to like toys more usually associated with girls and to play games more typical of girls (Blum, 1997, 1998). From childhood through adulthood, peer cultures socialize and regulate gender, encouraging males and females to conform to current ideals and expectations (Rudman & Glick, 2008). Men face greater pressures from family and peers to conform to prevailing expectations of masculinity than women do to conform to prevailing expectations of femininity (Cross, 2008; Kimmel, 2008; Messner, 2007).

Although in its original formulation, social learning theory drew conspicuously on behaviorist psychology and the stimulus-response model, more contemporary articulations of the theory have increasing recognized motives, agency, and cognitive processes such as expectancy that are entwined in learning gender and other behaviors. Particularly important in more recent iterations of the theory is the inclusion of self-efficacy, which is one's confidence that she or he can credibly perform the behavior required to achieve a goal such as parental approval or peer acceptance (Bandura, 1986; Bandura, Barbaranelli, Caprara, & Pastorelli, 2001). Later versions of the theory are often referred to as social cognitive theory, which is the name Bandura preferred (1986), perhaps to distinguish his work from the less sophisticated stimulus response formulation that claimed the name of social learning theory.

Cognitive Developmental Theory

Cognitive developmental theory compliments social learning theory. Both focus on how children learn from those around them in the process of developing identity, including gender identity. Both also assume that social interaction precedes development of identity and social consciousness.

Yet cognitive developmental theory's focus is on developmental stages in the progression from infancy to maturity (moral and cognitive maturity specifically) (Gilligan, 1982; Kohlberg, 1958; Piaget, 1932/1965). Of particular relevance to the question of how children become gendered is the stage at which children develop gender constancy, a concept that was introduced by Kohlberg (1966). Infants as young as 7 months can distinguish between the sexes, but they do not have gender constancy, which is the realization that a person's sex is stable and will stay the same throughout his or her life.[2] Kohlberg theorized that children are not motivated to learn how to behave in gender-appropriate ways until they understand that their sex is permanent, which he believed occurred around the age of 7. Later research indicates the age at which gender constancy is secured may be considerably earlier—perhaps by age 3 (Dubois, Serbin, & Derbyshire, 1998; Miller-Day & Fisher, 2006; Warin, 2000).

Once gender constancy is established, children have an internal motivation to learn how to be competent in being and performing the sex into which they are categorized (Levy, 1998). In other words, they are motivated to learn how their gender is socially construed and how to embody that construal. At this stage, boys and girls devote themselves to identifying behaviors and attitudes that others consider masculine and feminine and to learning to enact them. They look for cues about what girls do, wear, and say and what boys do, wear, and say (Martin & Ruble, 2004). Same-sex

---

[2] Obviously, the claim that sex is unchangeable throughout life has been roundly challenged by individuals who have sex-reassignment surgery and subsequently been granted legal status as members of a sex other than the one assigned to them at birth.

models become extremely important as gauges by which young children figure out what behaviors, attitudes, and feelings go with their gender. For many young girls, mothers are the primary source of information about femininity. Likewise, little boys study their fathers and other important males in their world to learn what counts as masculine. Some researchers believe the continuing pattern whereby women do a majority of housework and men resist doing it is shaped by children's observation of the sex-based division of labor in their families of origin (Maccoby, 1998; West & Zimmerman, 1987).

The process of finding gender role models and imitating them is not limited to childhood. Pervading the turbulent teen years is the quest to learn how to be and do femininity and masculinity: how to kiss, what girls and boys should and should not do; how to apply make-up or flex biceps; how to dance (and whether to follow or lead!); how to be a girlfriend or boyfriend; how to treat women and men (Burn, 1996; Franzoi & Koehler, 1998; Mihalic & Elliot, 1997).

Parental modeling is influential in how male and female children develop emotional expressiveness. Mothers talk more about feelings than fathers, and mothers talk more about feelings with daughters than sons (Galvin, 2006; Segrin & Flora, 2005). Although fathers talk less to children than mothers, fathers talk more with daughters than sons and engage in more activities with sons than daughters (Buerkel-Rothfuss, Fink, & Buerkel, 1995; Galvin, 2006). In interacting with children, mothers model nurturing by taking care of children—providing comfort, security, and affection. They tend to interact face-to-face with children and engage in extensive eye contact (Trudeau, 1996). Fathers focus more than mothers on playing with children than taking care of them and fathers exceed mothers in encouraging children, particularly sons, to achieve, take risks, and stretch themselves (Popenoe, 1996; Stacey, 1996). These different patterns of parental interaction may cultivate more robust emotional vocabularies in girls than boys, which may increase girls' and women's confidence and competence in emotional expressiveness.

In concert, social learning theory and cognitive developmental theory present solid descriptions and explanations of the processes by which children learn gender in families. They also provide the basis for predictions of factors that will influence learning gender.

PERFORMANCE THEORY

Performance theory has many and varied strands, but the one relevant to gender socialization has been most articulately advanced by Judith Butler (1993a,b; 2004). According to Butler, there is nothing "natural" or "normal" about gender. Rather, it is something we made up and, as such, we have to continually work to make it real. We do so by performing gender through dress, gestures, and other practices. Butler's point of view is well captured in the statement that gender is not something individuals *have*; it is something they *do*. However, performance of gender is never a solo act, but rather a profoundly social performance. Often individuals perform gender and others affirm their performances. A woman engages in conversational maintenance, asking a man about his day and thoughts, and he responds by talking about happenings in his physical and mental life. A beautifully dressed and coiffed woman enters a room and men give approving glances. Yet, even if others are not present, both in preparing for her entry and in entering the room the performing individual is engaging in stylized femininity as ensconced in cultural life.

The idea that gender is performative blends well with psychological theories' emphasis on developing competence in imitating gender role models. As children become aware that they are gendered, they are motivated to develop competence at performing their gender. They observe and imitate role models. However, rote imitation is not the end point of becoming gendered. The process of imitating a number of specific behaviors that have been observed is presumed eventually to result in deeper understandings of gender that allow individuals to perform gender convincingly in situations in which they have not observed others.

An offshoot of performance theory is gender production theory (De Ruijter, Treas, & Cohen, 2005), which contends that individuals perform (or refuse to perform) household tasks and childcare to communicate their gendered identities (West & Zimmerman, 1987). That is, women are said to perform domestic labor as a way of demonstrating their femininity and caring (DeVault, 1990; Wood, 2011), while men engage in resistance and refuse to perform household labor as a way to enact masculinity (Natalier, 2003).

Also, individuals' experiences and expectations can undermine efforts to distribute labor equally. Because girls and young women are socialized to perform more traditionally "feminine" tasks such as laundry, dishwashing, and bedmaking, typically they enter shared households with greater skills and higher standards for performance than do men. These attributes lead them to criticize the less skillful performance of their partners and to redo or take over tasks "so they are done right" (Wiesmann, Boeije, van Doorne-Huiskes, & den Dulk, 2008). Such behavior tends to undermine men's contributions or is used to justify their failure to contribute to domestic labor.

What psychological and performance theories[3] do not and cannot do is critique the existing embodiments of gender that are taught to children or the differences in what is taught to children in different demographic groups. For that, critical theories are needed. Standpoint theory goes beyond description, explanation, and prediction. As a critical theory, it focuses on structures and practices by which societies classify people into groups and then accord more or less privilege to different groups. Critical theorists are particularly interested in identifying how dominant groups manage to privilege their interests and perspectives and impose them on less powerful groups. At the same time, critical theorists want to understand how oppressed groups become empowered and, in some cases, change dominant patterns and perhaps the ideologies that underlie them. In this sense, critical theories have political edge.

STANDPOINT THEORY

The underpinnings of standpoint theory can be traced to Georg Wilhelm Friedrich Hegel and Karl Marx. In his philosophical work, Hegel (1807) observed that all members of society recognize the system of slavery but its character is perceived quite distinctly by those who are slaves and those who are masters. Marx's (1975, 1977) contribution to what has come to be known as standpoint theory was to insist that the material work people do profoundly shapes consciousness and identity. These two ideas form the crux of standpoint theory, which claims that membership in groups such as those designated by race, class, and gender, shapes what individuals experience and how they learn to interpret their experiences.[4]

The premise of standpoint theory relevant to this chapter is that social location matters. Individuals learn to perceive the world and themselves from the perspective of their social group and the activities in which its members routinely engage. Thus, Sara Ruddick (1989) argues that the demands of mothering—the concrete activities of taking care of a wholly dependent infant—are the genesis of what she calls "maternal thinking" which comprises the values, priorities, sensitivities, and skills needed to care for young children. Ruddick's argument is that what many mothers do is not a matter of "maternal instinct," but is the result of being in situations that require the development of particular priorities, skills, and so forth. Consistent with Ruddick's point is Barbara Risman's (1989)

---

[3] Butler, of course, is a major critical theorist who has done cutting-edge work in queer theory and queer performative theory, which focus on performance's capacity to "queer" or challenge and thereby potentially destabilize conventional cultural categories such as "man," "woman," "straight," and "gay." The aspect of Butler's theorizing relevant to this chapter, however, is her attention to the necessity of expressing or performing gender to make it real and to keep it stabilized in cultural life. To learn more about the critical possibilities of performance theory, see Jaggar (2008) and Shepard (2008).

[4] The aspect of standpoint theory relevant to this chapter is the role of social location in shaping identity. Social location, however, is not equivalent to standpoint. A standpoint requires an oppositional stance that grows out of political awareness of the conditions that create and sustain social hierarchies. Being female (social location) does not guarantee a feminist standpoint and being black does not guarantee an anti-racist standpoint. For a fuller discussion of standpoint theory, see Harding (1991) and Wood (2005).

research on single fathers. Placed in the role of being the sole caregiver for young children, many single fathers become more nurturing, patient, and emotionally expressive than men in general.

Because children's play continues to be primarily sex segregated (Martin, 1997; Martin & Ruble, 2004), as children play in groups, they learn much about their gendered social locations. While boys and girls play some of the same games, they also engage in sex-distinct kinds of play. Young boys tend to favor competitive games such as war, cops and robbers, king of the hill, and any type of ball. Young girls, although increasingly engaging in sports, are more likely than boys to play house, dress up, tea party, and school (Clark, 1998; Maccoby, 1998; Maltz & Borker, 1982; McGuffey & Rich, 2004). Girls tend to play in pairs or in small groups whereas boys typically prefer games that involve larger groups (Benenson, Del Bianco, Philippoussis, & Apostoleris, 1997). These distinct sets of games cultivate different priorities and skills. The different sized groups lead games more typical of girls to be more personal and intimate than those favored by boys. Competitive games encourage those who play them to think about goals or outcomes, to develop strategies for winning, and to do things, physical things. The games more often favored by girls encourage very different skills such as working cooperatively with others because if you do not, they may not play with you, and the game stops. Games typical of young girls also encourage talking more than physical activity because talking is how you negotiate and enact the roles and activities involved in house, school, and tea party (Goodwin, 2006). The process of relating is more emphasized than a particular outcome.

Through activities such as sex-segregated games and being mommy's helper or daddy's helper, many boys and girls are socialized into gendered social communities (Labov, 1972; Langer, 1953, 1979; Wood, 2012). This socialization schools children in ways of interacting (cooperative or competitive) and priorities or emphases (process or outcome; talking or doing; relationships or instrumental accomplishments). The lessons learned on the childhood playground show up in the inclinations of many adult women and men. In general, women regard communication as the primary way to establish relationships; they tend to build egalitarian relationships; they see it as important to support and respond to others; and they take responsibility for maintaining conversations and relationships (Eisenberg, 2002; Fishman, 1978; Hudson, 2001; Johnson, 1996; Mulac, 2006; Taylor, 2002). In general, men see doing things with and for others as a primary way to establish relationships; they focus more on establishing and maintaining status; they are more direct, assertive, and commanding; they are more instrumental; and they are less emotionally verbally responsive (Eisenberg, 2002; Leaper & Ayres, 2007; Mulac, 2006).

Gender, of course, is not the only social location individuals occupy. They are also members of groups defined by race, socio-economic class, religion and so forth. These different social locations are not additive, but interactive. That is, race and class shape what gender means so that African American girls may occupy a social location different in some ways from that of European American girls and working class and upper class Hispanics may be socialized in different communities (Zinn, Hondagneu-Sotelo, & Messner, 2007).

The four theories discussed above—social learning, cognitive developmental, performance, and standpoint—provide much insight into the processes by which infants become gendered. The theories are complementary and, in concert, give a solid overall understanding of the typical ways individuals develop gender. Yet there are issues these theories do not address and types of gender development they do not describe, explain or predict. The next section of the chapter discusses limitations of these theories and directions for future theorizing about gendering processes.

THEORETICAL LIMITATIONS AND ADVANCEMENTS

The theories discussed in the preceding section are most accurately thought of as theories of how individuals learn gender. It would be more precise to describe them as theories that describe and explain how individuals who adopt conventional genders learn to do so. What these theories do not explain is why some children do not adopt conventional gender identities, despite having adequate models of conventional gender to observe and imitate, sufficient rewards and punishments, and requisite performance capacities.

Consider the case of David Reimer (Butler, 2004; Colapinto, 2006). As an 8-month-old infant, David developed phimosis, a condition in which the foreskin of the penis interferes with urination. During the surgery to correct the problem, the surgeon erred tragically and amputated David's penis. Based on doctors' advice, the parents renamed their child Brenda, removed the testicles, and began giving hormones to induce female characteristics. David/Brenda's parents were considerably more aware than most of gender socializing and more intent on rewarding feminine behaviors and negatively responding to masculine behaviors. Despite the parents' efforts to socialize their child as a girl, s/he gravitated toward masculine activities and preferences. David/Brenda liked trucks and guns, ripped off dresses, and insisted on standing to urinate. Here is a case in which a child well before the age of gender constancy is reassigned to a different gender. If socialization and learning and role models of conventional gender were all that are required to develop gender, why did David/Brenda not become feminine?

Although David Reimer's case is illustrative, it is also highly unusual. There are many examples of less extreme cases demonstrating variation in gender identification and expression (Denny, 2004; Pardo, 2008). Transsexuals do not identify with the sex they were assigned at birth. Biological males understand themselves as female and biological females understand themselves as male. Although an accurate estimate of the number of transsexuals is difficult, one widely accepted estimate is 0.25–1% of the population in the US (Olyslager & Conway, 2007). In addition, there are many people who are, in varying degrees, gender nonconforming. Assuming most of these individuals had relatively conventional gender models available and were rewarded for behaviors consistent with their assigned gender and punished for behaviors inconsistent with their assigned gender, the theories discussed in this chapter do not fully account for these individuals' gender identity and their challenges to conventional categories of gender. Those theories also cannot account for how gender nonconforming individuals find models if, in fact, they rely on models to construct their identities and behavioral repertoire.

Existing theories have also given too little attention to families that are not intact, two parent, and heterosexual. We have inadequate knowledge of gendering processes in families that do not fit this model. For example, gay and lesbian parents provide children with two models of the same sex and, in some cases, the same gender. Single parent families continue to increase in the US. Despite these demographics, we have limited research on how having a single parent or two parents of the same sex affects a child's gender development. Particularly in single parent families that do not include a live in or frequently present partner of a different sex, children do not have male and female role models within the family. We need to know how, if at all, this influences children's gender development.

Also understudied are families in which one or both parents are gender nonconforming. Existing psychological theories' emphasis on observation of models and imitation assumes the models conform to conventional gender identities. But what if they do not? Obviously, transgender parents would be of interest as would intentional communities of support that function as extended families for some transgender people. Also of interest are families in which parents' gender nonconformity is less absolute. The recession that began in 2008 has forced more men than women out of paid labor. A number of those men have had to assume primary responsibility for home and children while their wives earned incomes to support the family. In such families, children are exposed to a father and mother in roles different from those of many men and women, respectively. Are children in these families more likely than children in traditional families to see cooking, cleaning, and caring for children as consistent with masculinity?

Like academic departments, these theories too often operate as independent silos. Each theory's efforts to shore up its status sometimes result in refusal to mingle with other theories. But this sort of territoriality has costs. Each theory loses out on refinements and the possibility of a more robust integrative theory by not being in dialogue with other theories. It is likely that a rich understanding of gender development and identity requires expansive, integrative theories that can incorporate the full range of factors that influence how humans understand and express their gender.

CONCLUSION

A priority for future theorizing is the development of theories better able to account for the range of sexual and gender identities with which humans identify. We should not settle for separate theories accounting for transgender and gender nonconforming individuals because that continues to center the gender binary as normative and even "right" and, by direct extension, to marginalize individuals who do not fit neatly and completely into either the male or female box.

REFERENCES

Acitelli, L. (1988). When spouses talk to each other about their relationship. *Journal of Social and Personal Relationships, 5*, 185–199.

Archer, J., & Coyne, S. M. (2005). An integrated review of indirect, relational, and social aggression. *Personality and Social Review, 9*, 212–230.

Babcock, L., & Laschever, S. (2003). *Women don't ask: Negotiation and the gender divide*. Princeton, NJ: Princeton University Press.

Bandura, A. (1986). *Social foundations of thought and action: A social cognitive theory*. Englewood Cliffs, NJ: Prentice-Hall.

Bandura, A. (2001). Social cognitive theory: An agentic view. *Annual Review of Psychology, 52*, 1–26.

Bandura, A. (2002). Social cognitive theory of mass communication. In J. Bryant & D. Zillmann (Eds.), *Media effects: Advances in theory and research* (2nd ed., pp. 121–153). Mahwah, NJ: Erlbaum.

Bandura, A., Barbaranelli, C., Caprara,G., & Pastorelli, C. (2001). Self-efficacy beliefs as shapers of children's aspirations and career trajectories. *Child Development, 72*, 187–206.

Baxter, J., Hewitt, B., & Western, M. (2005). Post-familial families and the domestic division of labor. *Journal of Comparative Family Studies, 36*, 583–600.

Benenson, J., Del Bianco, R., Philippoussis, M., & Apostoleris, N. (1997). Girls' expression of their own perspectives in the presence of varying numbers of boys. *International Journal of Behavioral Development, 21*, 389–405.

Blackless, M., Charuvastra, A., Derryek, A., Fausto-Sterling, A., Lauzanne, K., & Lee, E. (2000). How sexually dimorphic are we? Review and synthesis. *American Journal of Human Biology, 12*, 151–166.

Blum, D. (1997). *Sex on the brain: The biological differences between women and men*. New York: Penguin.

Blum, D. (1998, September/October). The gender blur: Where does biology end and society take over? *Utne Reader*, 45–48.

Buerkel-Rothfuss, N. L., Fink, D. S., & Buerkel, R. (1995). Communication in the father-child dyad: The intergenerational transmission process. In T. J. Socha & G. H. Stamp (Eds.), *Parents, children, and communication: Frontiers of theory and research* (pp. 63–85). Mahwah, NJ: Erlbaum.

Braithwaite, D., & Kellas, J. (2006). Shopping for and with friends: Everyday communication at the shopping mall. In J. T. Wood & S. W. Duck (Eds.), *Composing relationships: Communication in everyday life* (pp. 86–95). Belmont, CA: Thomson/Wadsworth.

Burn, J. (1996). *The social psychology of gender*. New York: McGraw-Hill.

Butler, J. (1993a). *Bodies that matter: On the discursive limits of "sex."* New York: Routledge.

Butler, J. (1993b). *Gender trouble: Feminism and the subversion of identity*. New York: Routledge.

Butler, J. (2004). *Undoing gender*. New York: Routledge.

Callimachi, R. (2007, February 5). Here, women woo, men wait. *Raleigh News & Observer*, p. 10A.

Canary, D. J., & Emmers-Sommer, T. M., with Faulkner, S. (Eds.) (1997). *Sex and gender differences in personal relationships*. New York: Guilford Press.

Canary, D., & Wahba, J. (2006). Do women work harder than men at maintaining relationships? In K. Dindia & D. Canary (Eds.), *Sex differences and similarities in communication* (2nd ed., pp. 359–377). Mahwah, NJ: Erlbaum.

Cancian, F. (1989). Love and the rise of capitalism. In B. Risman & P. Schwartz (Eds.), *Gender and intimate relationships* (pp. 12–25). Belmont, CA: Wadsworth.

Cancian, F., & Oliker, S. (2000). *Caring and gender*. Thousand Oaks, CA: Sage.

Channell, C. (2002, May). The Tatau: A bridge to manhood. *Faces: People, Places and Culture*, pp. 18–22.

Chethik, N. (2001). *FatherLoss: How sons of all ages come to terms with the deaths of their dads*. New York: Hyperion.

Clark, R. A. (1998). A comparison of topics and objectives in a cross section of young men's and women's everyday conversations. In D. J. Canary & K. Dindia (Eds.), *Sex differences and similarities in communication: Critical essays and empirical investigations of sex and gender in interaction* (pp. 303–319). Mahwah, NJ: Erlbaum.

Coltrane, S. (1996). *Family man: Fatherhood, housework, and gender equity*. New York: Oxford University Press.

Colapinto, J. (2006). *As nature made him*. New York: HarperPerennial.

Council on Contemporary Families (2010). Unconventional wisdom. Retrieved from http://www.contemporaryfamilies.org/all/unconventional-wisdom-issue-3.html?q=unconventional+wisdom (accessed April 14, 2010).

Cross, G. (2008). *Men to boys: The making of modern immaturity*. New York: Columbia University Press.

DeMaris, A. (2007). The role of relationship inequity in marital disruption. *Journal of Social and Personal Relationships, 24*, 177–195.

Denny, D. (2004). Changing models of transsexualism. In U. Lelei & J. Drescher (Eds.), *Transgender subjectivities: A Clinician's guide* (pp. 24–40). Binghamton: Haworth Press.

De Ruijter, E., Treas, J. K., & Cohen, P. N. (2005). Outsourcing the gender factory: Living arrangements and service expenditures on female and male tasks. *Social Forces, 84*, 305–322.

DeVault, M. (1990). Conflict over housework: A problem that (still) has no name. In L. Kreisberg (Ed.), *Research in social movements, conflict, and change*. Greenwich, CT: JAI Press.

Dokoupil, T. (2009, March 2). Men will be men. *Newsweek*, p. 50.

Dreger, A. (1998). "Ambiguous sex"—or ambivalent medicine? Ethical issues in the treatment of intersexuality. *Hastings Center Report, 28*, 24–35.

Dubois, D., Serbin, L., & Derbyshire, A. (1998). Toddlers' intermodal and verbal knowledge about gender. *Merrill-Palmer Quarterly, 44*, 338–351.

Eisenberg, N. (2002). Empathy-related emotional responses, altruism, and their socialization. In R. Davidson & A. Harrington (Eds.), *Visions of compassion: Western scientists and Tibetan Buddhists examine human nature* (pp. 131–164). London: Oxford University Press.

Fishman, P. M. (1978). Interaction: The work women do. *Social Problems, 25*, 397–406.

Franzoi, S. L., & Koehler, V. (1998). Age and gender differences in body attitudes: A comparison of young and elderly adults. *International Journal of Aging and Human Development, 47*, 1–10.

Gilley, B. J. (2006). *Becoming two-spirit: Gay identity and social acceptance in Indian country*. Lincoln, NE: University of Nebraska Press.

Gilligan, C. (1982). *In a different voice: Psychological theory and women's development*. Cambridge, MA: Harvard University Press.

Goodwin, M. H. (2006). *The hidden life of girls*. Maiden, MA: Blackwell.

Gorman, C., & Cole, C. (2004, March 1). Between the sexes. *Newsweek*, pp. 54–56.

Guerrero, L., Jones, S., & Boburka, R. (2006). Sex differences in emotional communication. In K. Dindia & D. Canary (Eds.), *Sex differences and similarities in communication* (pp. 242–261). Mahwah, MJ: Erlbaum.

Harding, S. (1991). *Whose science? Whose knowledge: Thinking from women's lives*. Ithaca, NY: Cornell University Press.

Hegel, G. W. F. (1807). *Phenomenology of mind*. J. B. Baillie (Trans.), Germany: Wurzburg & Bamburg.

Hochschild, A. (with Machung, A.). (2003). *The second shift: Working parents and the revolution at home* (Rev. ed.). New York: Viking/Penguin Press.

Hudson, B. (2001). *African American female speech communities: Varieties of talk*. Westport, CT: Bergin & Garvey/Greenwood Press.

Inman, C. (1996). Friendships between men: Closeness in the doing. In J. T. Wood (Ed.), *Gendered relationships: A reader* (pp. 95–110). Mountain View, CA: Mayfield.

Jagger, G. (2008). *Judith Butler: Sexual politics, social change and the power of performance*. New York: Routledge.

Jamieson, P. E., & Romer, D. (Eds.). (2008). *The changing portrayal of adolescents in the media since 1950.* New York: Oxford University Press.

Johnson, F. (1996). Friendships among women: Closeness in dialogue. In J. T. Wood (Ed.), *Gendered relationships: A reader* (pp. 79–94). Mountain View, CA: Mayfield.

Kimmell, M. (2008). *Guyland: The perilous world where boys become men.* New York: Macmillan.

Kohlberg, L. (1958). The development of modes of thinking and moral choice in the years 10 to 16. Unpublished doctoral dissertation, University of Chicago.

Kohlberg, L. (1966). A cognitive-developmental analysis of children's sex-role concepts and attitudes. In E. E. Maccoby (Ed.), *The development of sex role differences* (pp. 82–173). Stanford, CA: Stanford University Press.

Kunkel, A., Hummert, M., & Dennis, M. (2006). Social learning theory: Modeling and communication in the family context. In D. Braithwaite & L. Baxter (Eds.), *Engaging theories in family communication* (pp. 260–275). Thousand Oaks, CA: Sage.

Labov, W. (1972). *Sociolinguistic patterns.* Philadelphia, PA: University of Pennsylvania Press.

Langer, S. K. (1953). *Feeling and form: A theory of art.* New York: Scribner's.

Langer, S. K. (1979). *Philosophy in a new key: A study in the symbolism of reason, rite and art* (3rd ed.). Cambridge, MA: Harvard University Press.

Leaper, C., Anderson, K., & Sanders, P. (1998). Moderators of gender effects on parents' talk to their children: A meta-analysis. *Developmental Psychology, 34,* 3–27.

Leaper, C., & Ayres, M. (2007). A meta-analytic review of gender variations in adults' language use: Talkativeness, affiliative speech, and assertive speech. *Personality & Social Psychology Review, 11,* 328–363.

Levy, G. D. (1998). Effects of gender constancy and figure's height and sex on young children's gender-type attributions. *Journal of General Psychology, 125,* 65–89.

Lynch, J., & Kilmartin, C. (1999). *The pain behind the mask: Overcoming masculine depression.* Binghamton, NY: Haworth Press.

Maccoby, E. E. (1998). *The two sexes: Growing up apart, coming together.* Cambridge, MA: Belknap Press of the Harvard University Press.

Maltz, D. N., & Borker, R. (1982). A cultural approach to male-female miscommunication. In J. J. Gumperz (Ed.), *Language and social identity* (pp. 196–216). Cambridge, UK: Cambridge University Press.

Martin, C., & Ruble, D. (2004). Children's search for gender cues: Cognitive perspectives on gender development. *Current Directions in Psychological Science, 13,* 67–70.

Marx, K. (1975). *Capital.* B. Fowles (Trans.), Vol. 1. New York: Vintage.

Marx, K. (1977). *Early writings.* Q. Hoare (Ed.). New York: Vintage.

McGuffey, S., & Rich, L. (2004). Playing in the gender transgression zone: Race, class, and hegemonic masculinity in middle childhood. In J. Spade & C. Valentine (Eds.), *The kaleidoscope of gender: Prisms, patterns, and possibilities* (pp. 172–183). Belmont, CA: Wadsworth.

Mead, M. (1935/1968). *Sex and temperament in three primitive societies.* New York: Dell.

Medved, C. E. (2009). Crossing and transforming occupational and household gendered divisions of labor. *Communication Yearbook, 33,* 301–341.

Messner, M. (2007). Masculinities and athletic careers. In M. Andersen & P. H. Collins (Eds.), *Race, class, gender: An anthology* (6th ed., pp. 172–184). Belmont, CA: Thomson.

Metts, S. (2006a). Gendered communication in dating relationships. In B. Dow & J. T. Wood (Eds.), *Handbook of Gender & Communication* (pp. 25–40). Thousand Oaks, CA: Sage.

Metts, S. (2006b). Hanging out and doing lunch: Enacting friendship closeness. In J. T. Wood & S. W. Duck (Eds.), *Composing relationships: Communication in everyday life* (pp. 76–85). Belmont, CA: Thomson/Wadsworth.

Mihalic, S., & Elliot, D. (1997). A social learning theory model of marital violence. *Journal of Family Violence, 12,* 21–47.

Miller-Day, M. & Fisher, C. (2006). Communication in mother-adult daughter relationships. In K. Floyd & M. Morman (Eds.) *Widening the family circle: New research on family communication* (pp. 15–38). Newbury Park, CA: Sage.

Mischel, W. (1966). A social learning view of sex differences in behavior. In E. E. Maccoby (Ed.), *The development of sex differences* (pp. 93–106). Stanford, CA: Stanford University Press.

Morrow, V. (2006). Understanding gender differences in context: Implications for young children's everyday lives. *Children and Society, 20,* 92–104.

Mulac, A. (2006). The gender-linked language effect: Do language differences really make a difference? In K. Dindia & D. Canary (Eds.), *Sex differences and similarities in communication* (pp. 219–239). Mahwah, NJ: Erlbaum.

Natalier, K. (2003). 'I'm not his wife': Doing gender and doing housework in the absence of women. *Journal of Sociology, 39*, 253–269.

Olyslager, F., & Conway, L. (2007, September 6). On the calculation of the prevalence of transsexualism. Retrieved from: http://ai.eecs.umich.edu/people/conway/TS/Prevalence/Reports/Prevalence%20of%20 Transsexualism.pdf.

Pardo, T. (2008). Growing up transgender: Research and theory. *Research Facts and Findings*. ACT: Center for Youth Excellence. New York: Cornell University Press.

Peretti, P. O., & Abplanalp, R. R. Jr. (2004). Chemistry in the college dating process: Structure and function. *Social Behavior and Personality, 32*, 147–154.

Piaget, J. (1932/1965). *The moral judgment of the child*. New York: Free Press.

Pinsky, L., Erickson, R., & Schimke, R. (Eds.). (1999). *Genetic disorders of human sexual development*. New York: Oxford University Press.

Popenoe, D. (1996). *Life without father*. New York: Free Press.

Ramey, G., & Ramey, V. A. (2009, August). The rug rat race. NBER Working Paper No. w15284. Retrieved from http://ssrn.com/abstract=1459585 (accessed April 6, 2010).

Risman, B. J. (1989). Can men mother? Life as a single father. In B. J. Risman & P. Schwartz (Eds.), *Gender in intimate relationships* (pp. 155–164). Belmont, CA: Wadsworth.

Romer, D. (2008). Introduction: Mass media and the socialization of adolescents since World War II. In P. E. Jamieson & D. Romer (Eds.), *The changing portrayal of adolescents in the media since 1950* (pp. 3–24). New York: Oxford University Press.

Rotter, J. (1954). *Social learning and clinical psychology*. New York: Prentice-Hall.

Ruddick, S. (1989). *Maternal thinking: Toward a politics of peace*. Boston, MA: Beacon.

Rudman, L. A., & Glick, P. (2008). *The social psychology of gender*. New York: Guilford Press.

Segrin, C., & Flora, F. J. (2005). *Family communication*. Mahwah, NJ: Erlbaum.

Shepard, B. (2008). *Queer political performance and protest*. New York: Routledge.

Stacey, J. (1996). *In the name of the father: Rethinking family values in a postmodern age*. Boston, MA: Beacon.

Sullivan, P. J., & Short, S. E. (2001, June). Furthering the construct of effective communication: A second version of the Scale for Effective Communication in Team Sports. Paper presented at the North American Society for the Psychology of Sport and Physical Activity (NASPSPA), St Louis, MO.

Swain, S. (1989). Covert intimacy: Closeness in men's friendships. In B. J. Risman & P. Schwartz (Eds.), *Gender and intimate relationships* (pp. 71–86). Belmont, CA: Wadsworth.

Taylor, S. (2002). *The tending instinct: How nurturing is essential for who we are and how we live*. New York: Times Books.

Tichenor, V. (2005). Maintaining men's dominance: Negotiating identity and power when she earns more. *Sex Roles, 53*, 191–205.

Trudeau, M. (1996, June 4). *Morning edition*. Public Broadcasting System.

Turner, C. S. (2002). Women of color in the academe: Living with multiple marginality. *The Journal of Higher Education, 73*, 74–93.

Walker, K. (2004). Men, women, and friendship: What they say, what they do. In J. Spade & C. Valentine (Eds.), *The kaleidoscope of gender: Prisms, patterns, and possibilities* (pp. 403–413). Belmont, CA: Thomson/Wadsworth.

Warin, J. (2000). The attainment of self-consistency through gender in young children. *Sex Roles, 3/4*, 209–231.

West, C., & Zimmerman, D. H. (1987). Doing gender. *Gender and Society, 1*, 125–151.

Wiesmann, S., Boeije, H, van Doorne-Huiskes, A, & den Dulk, L. (2008). 'Not worth mentioning': The implicit and explicit nature of decision-making about the division of paid and domestic work. *Community, Work & Family, 11*(4), 341–363.

Wood, J. T. (2005). Feminist standpoint theory and muted group theory: Commonalities and divergences. *Women & Language, 28*, 61–64.

Wood, J. T. (2011). Which ruler? Theorizing the division of domestic labor. *Journal of Family Communication*.

Wood, J. T. (2012). *Gendered Lives* (10th ed.). Boston, MA: Wadsworth-Cengage.

Wright, P. H. (2006). Toward an expanded orientation to the comparative study of women's and men's same-sex friendships. In K. Dindia & D. Canary (Eds.), *Sex differences and similarities in communication* (pp. 37–57). Mahwah, NJ: Erlbaum.

Zinn, M., Hondagneu-Sotelo, P., & Messner, M. (2007). Sex and gender through the prism of difference. In M. Andersen & P. H. Collins (Eds.), *Race, class, gender: An anthology* (6th ed., pp. 147–156). Belmont, CA: Thomson-Wadsworth.

18 Theoretical Perspectives on Acculturation and Immigration

Susan S. Chuang and Robert P. Moreno

Immigration is a global phenomenon, with nearly 200 million immigrants and refugees worldwide since the beginning of the millennium (United Nations, 2005). Canada and the US have the second and third highest proportion of foreign-born populations in the world, respectively, after Australia. Recent population trends reveal that between 2001 and 2006, the Canadian immigrant population increased from 17.9 to 19.8%, the highest increase in 75 years. This is four times the growth rate of native Canadians (3.3%) (Statistics Canada, 2006). A similar pattern is found in the US. In the last decade, the foreign born population increased from 7.9 to 11.1% of the total US population (U.S. Census Bureau, 2006). Consequently, the ethnocultural profiles of these countries have become increasingly multiethnic and multicultural.

Despite the changing demographic landscape, the vast majority of research on the development of children and families draws upon non-immigrants samples. As a result, our conceptual and theoretical frameworks derived from homogenous, non-migrant populations may be ill-suited to guide our thinking as we strive to understand the development of immigrant families and children in our respective societies. By turning our attention to immigrant families, we are forced to re-examine prevailing models of development (predicated on homogeneity and contextual stability) and consider developmental trajectories that are situated (by definition) in a context of change and diversity. Thus, developmental outcomes must be viewed as a function of the dynamic interplay between the resources and liabilities inherent in children, families, and their sociocultural contexts.

Perhaps as a result of the above observations, the roles of culture, immigration, and cultural change on family functioning have recently moved to the forefront of many research agendas (see; Chuang & Gielen, 2009; Chuang & Moreno, 2008, 2011; Chuang & Tamis-LeMonda, 2009). In our work, we view culture as a set of shared values, beliefs, and practices, which include the dynamically structured relationships affecting the course of development. Culture is not an objective reality, but rather it is a shared understanding among individuals, affecting their attitudes, judgments, emotions, and practices. In this sense, culture is not static but fluid and dynamic, dependent upon societal and group factors (Chuang, 2009; Super & Harkness, 2002). Thus, understanding the various pathways of immigration is important as cultural cognitions (acculturation, collectivism, individualism) moderate the effectiveness of parenting and family functioning, which, in turn, influence child development (Bornstein & Cote, 2004).

This chapter begins with an overview of immigration patterns and the various issues such as socioeconomic status and demographic risk factors that must be considered in understanding immigrant families. We then discuss some of the key historical concepts and frameworks that have guided our current field of immigration, followed by contemporary theories. A particular focus will be on the context of immigrant families and their cultural contexts, placing this section within the world-views on cultural orientation. The acculturation processes and parent–child discrepancies will be explored and the extent to which they impact child development. Some attention to the gendered experiences of acculturation and parenting will follow. We conclude by discussing some of the limitations of this field and provide suggestions for theory development and advancing our under-standing of immigration and families.

KEY ISSUES IN THE STUDY OF ACCULTURATION AND IMMIGRATION

Migration to a new country is driven by a variety of circumstances, including the financial needs of the family (e.g., poverty, need to seek employment), dangerous and destructive living conditions (refugees), the desire for political and individual freedom, or, because of potential opportunities for growth and prosperity for their children and themselves. In the majority of cases, international migration involves families that moved from poorer countries to wealthier ones (Chuang & Gielen, 2009). These circumstances influence the degree to which individuals and their families can suc-cessfully adjust and settle, affecting their health and well-being (see Guarnaccia, 1997).

Before researchers begin to disentangle the complexities of immigration and how individuals and families adjust and settle into their new homelands, it is imperative that researchers situate these trends of newcomers within the broader immigrant context. A closer look at immigration patterns reveals radical shifts over the last century in relation to the countries' ethnoprofiles. Although both Canada and the US have been major immigrant-receiving countries for many decades, their policy approaches to cultural diversity have changed significantly over the years but differ in each coun-try's political spheres (Schmidt, 2007). For example, the Canadian growth and diversity in the 1960s were due to the changes of the Immigration Act of 1952, which resulted in immigration poli-cies being developed on the principles of family reunification and labor market contribution. Consequently, Canada accepted individuals from all nations if they met immigration regulations. One of the primary motivations for Canada's immigration reform was the government's realization that the growth of Canada's middle-class, highly skilled population offsprings was not sufficient (Green, 2003; Ray, 2005). Thus, new immigration policies strategically and selectively targeted highly educated immigrants (e.g., physicians, engineers, teachers) who accounted for 54% of all newcomers, 27% were accepted under the family class umbrella (e.g., family reunification), 11% were refugees, and 6% were business class immigrants (declared assets of over a million dollars) (Citizenship and Immigration Canada, 2007). By 2010, the target goal was to have 65% of all new immigrants holding post-secondary education degrees.

Due to these policy changes, immigrants arrived from many countries with diverse cultural back-grounds. For example, before 1971, the majority of Canadian immigrants were of European origin (81%). To date, the population has become increasingly more multiethnic and multicultural with representation of over 200 ethnic groups, with 57% of newcomers from Asian countries. Moreover, newcomers, on average, have higher birth rates than do native, Caucasian families (Statistics Canada, 2006). Thus, the immigrant population and their children are growing at a faster rate than are their native Canadian counterparts. With this increase in foreign-born Canadians, the govern-ment has put in place a nationwide infrastructure that specifically provides free services and programs for new immigrants (almost 1000 settlements serving agencies across Canada) (see; Chuang, Rasmi, & Friesen, 2011; Schmidt, 2007).

Similar to Canada, the US significantly revised its immigration policies; the Act of 1965 that was an extension of the Civil Rights movement. This Act eliminated the highly discriminatory national-origins quota system, with priority given to those with US relatives or with special skills and credentials. This led the way to a significant influx of family reunification (facilitating immigration from Latin America) and employment preferences (facilitating immigration from Asia)

(Martin & Midgely, 2003). The last decade revealed a foreign-born population increase of 3% of the total population. Currently, 20% of the US population is foreign born. In 2000, only 14% of children in immigrant families were of European or Canadian descent. Rather, the majority of families (86%) emigrated from Latin America (62%), Asia (22%), or Africa (2%). Births increased by 47% in immigrant families, compared with a 7% increase in US-born families. To date, one in five children is from an immigrant family (Hernandez, Denton, & MacCartney, 2008). In contrast to Canada, the US federal government has almost no formal policies on facilitating immigrants' successful adjustment into the US, but rather focuses its attention on "gate-keeping." During this time, however, there was a surge in unauthorized international migrants, entering the country illegally. It has been estimated that in 2004, approximately 29% of the foreign-born population were unauthorized. This unexpected surge has led to anti-immigration rhetoric and political mobilization in the US (Schmidt, 2007).

Regions and countries of origin, as well as race/ethnicity, also need consideration in better understanding how immigration impacts children, youth, and families. With their changes in immigration policies, both Canada and the US have substantial numbers of visible minority groups, especially Asians and Latinos. Recent population trends reveal that Asians and Latinos are among the fastest growing groups in both of these countries. For example, from 2001 to 2006, 1.1 million immigrants arrived in Canada, of which 58% were from Asian countries, including the Middle East. Immigrants from the People's Republic of China accounted for 14% of the recent immigrant population (Statistics Canada, 2006). For the US by 1990, 84% of the immigrant population came from Asia and Latin America (U.S. Census Bureau, 1992).

Other demographic factors that may place immigrant children and families at risk are social and economic inequalities. As Hernandez (2004) stated, low socioeconomic status is one of the best-documented indicators of negative consequences for one's health. Specifically, parents' levels of education influence their parental values and practices in socializing their children, and because such parents are more likely to have lower paying jobs, their families have less access to services and programs (e.g., healthcare in the US school materials). In the US immigrant fathers were almost four times more likely to not have graduated from high school than were native fathers (40% versus 12%), which had a generational effect. Specifically, parents who completed fewer years of schooling were more likely to have children also completing fewer years of schooling as well, which consequently led to lower paying jobs when they reached adulthood (e.g., Sewell, Hauser, & Wolf, 1980). The generational effect may, in part, be due to parents' levels of comfort in interacting with teachers and the educational system, and not having the academic knowledge to help their children in their homework (Hernandez & Charney, 1998; Kao, 1999; Rumbaut, 1999). Thus, immigrant families are more likely to be at greater risk of living in poverty than native-born families. For example, recent Canadian immigrants are younger, more likely to be visible minorities, and experience lower income in their first several years in Canada compared to native-born Canadians (Palameta, 2004). In the US more than one-third of the children in immigrant families (34%) are poor, compared to the official poverty rate of 21% (taking into account the local costs of housing, food, transportation, basic necessities, and federal taxes) (Hernandez et al., 2008).

Other family contexts that need to be considered include living arrangements, with specific focus on who is in the home (e.g., extended family, siblings, non-relatives) and their levels of education and employment. Briefly, researchers such as McLanahan and Sandefur (1994) reported that children who live with two parents are, to some extent, at an advantage in their academic success than children in single-parent households. According to Hernandez et al. (2008), immigrant American children were more likely to live in two-parent households than were their native counterparts (84% versus 76%).

Another dimension of family context that should be considered is number of siblings. Immigrant families are more likely to have four or more children than native families (19% versus 14%). Siblings can serve as both an advantage and disadvantage to immigrant families. On the negative side, time and resources of parents are limited, and children tend to experience less academic success and less schooling than children with fewer siblings (Blake, 1989; Hernandez, 1986). However, older siblings can serve as protectors and companions for their younger siblings, and share their available resources. Other family members to consider are the extended family, including grandparents, other relatives, and non-relatives. In comparison to White native families, immigrant families are up to four times more likely to have a live-in grandparent. These additional household members can provide essential childcare, nurturance, and financial support (Hernandez et al., 2008). However, more household members may lead to overcrowding, defined as individuals living with more than one person per room. These housing conditions may make it difficult for children to study and do their homework, and some have found negative consequences for children's behavioral adjustment and psychological health (see Evans, Saegert, & Harris, 2001). Unfortunately, immigrant families are four times more likely to live in overcrowded housing than were native-born families (47% versus 11%) (Hernandez et al., 2008). These factors are among many that researchers need to be mindful of as they attempt to disentangle the effects of immigration on the development of children and their families.

THEORETICAL PERSPECTIVES ON ACCULTURATION AND ADAPTATION

The study of immigrants' transition and adaptation to a new land has been a topic of study for decades. A full discussion is beyond the scope of this chapter (see Berry, 1980; Rudmin, 2009; Sam & Berry, 2006; Van Oudenhoven, 2006). However, it will be useful to first begin with a brief discussion of some of the major historical concepts and theoretical frameworks that have guided and continue to guide researchers.

HISTORICAL CONCEPTIONS OF ACCULTURATION AND ASSIMILATION

Fundamental to the study of immigrant families is the notion of change and adjustment. Regardless of the reasons for immigrating, families, by definition, engage in a process of migration and adaptation (positively or negatively) to their new surroundings. Broadly, acculturation involves change at both individual and societal levels. Attitudes, values, beliefs, and behaviors developed in one cultural milieu must, to some extent, accommodate to a new context. According to Redfield, Linton, and Herskovits (1936):

> Acculturation comprehends those phenomena which result when groups of individuals having different cultures come into continuous first-hand contact, with subsequent changes in the original culture patterns of either or both groups ... under this definition acculturation is to be distinguished from culture change, of which it is but one aspect, and assimilation, which is at times a phase of acculturation (pp. 149–152).

Although Redfield et al. (1936) noted that acculturation change involved individuals from both cultural groups, it has long been perceived as a unidimensional process (Gordon, 1964). Immigrants who retained their culture of origin are at one end of the spectrum, whereas those who replaced their original values, beliefs, and customs for those of the receiving culture are at the other end. From this perspective, the midpoint was to be a temporary point of transition. In fact, a prolonged state of marginality was viewed as psychologically dysfunctional (Stonequest, 1961). The term "marginal man" was used to describe someone who was trying to live in two diverse cultures but is competent in neither. Thus, acculturation, short of full assimilation, was believed to be detrimental.

This belief that assimilation was the key to a successful adaptation process was illustrated in Ruesch, Jacobson, and Loeb's (1948) analysis of acculturation and mental health:

> Crime, suicide, and mental disease are examples of abnormal behavior which commonly are correlated with foreign nativist and ethnic background. Recent neurotic behavior and

psychosomatic conditions have been found to be in part expressions of maladjustment due to culture change (p. 1).

Unfortunately, assimilationist frameworks emerged as the dominate perspective by which research-ers understood the normative pathway for immigrants in the US and elsewhere. Implicit in these assimilationist ideologies was the notion that mainstream culture (middle-class European American) was superior to the various ethnic minority cultures of origin (Buriel & Ment, 1997). The need for immigrants to assimilate was obvious (the betterment of themselves) and failure to assimilate into the host culture or any problems experienced as a result of the acculturation process were attributed to the immigrant group themselves (Bourhis, Moïse, Perreault, & Senécal, 1997).

Remnants of this assumption that immigrants should somehow have impaired health due to migration are still evident in today's research in the guise of the "immigrant paradox" (see Rudmin, 2009, for a review). When immigrants fare better than their non-immigrant counterparts, such as being in better physical health, researchers view this finding as a "paradox" and against "common sense." Such assumptions discount the strengths and uniqueness of families who draw upon their individual, familial, and cultural capabilities to deal with stressful or challenging situations.

ECOLOGICAL AND MULTIDIMENSIONAL PERSPECTIVES ON ACCULTURATION

Arguing against the view that acculturation is an individual phenomenon that necessitates a simple replacement of one's customs, values, and beliefs for those of the new host culture, researchers re-conceptualized acculturation as a multiple dimensional process, both in terms of the contextual influence involved in immigrant's adaptation, as well as the nature of the acculturation process itself.

Ecological Perspectives

The most widely used ecological models or frameworks relevant to the study of immigrant families and children have stemmed from cross-cultural and developmental psychology. Both perspectives hold that human activity and development can only be understood within its ecological context. From cross-cultural psychology, Berry offers his ecocultural framework (Berry, Poortinga, Segall, & Dasen, 2002; Berry, 2008). As do others (Bronfenbrenner 1979; Whiting, 1974), he argues that the collective and individual can only be understood within its context. However he contrasts his framework with other ecological approaches that have tended to view culture as relatively stable (Bennett, 1976). Rather, Berry argues that human activity (and its development) is largely a process of adaptation as it adjusts and accommodates to ecological, sociopolitical, and other cultural forces (as in the case of immigration). As ecological circumstances change, cultures change, and therefore, are in a constant state of flux and continually concerned with "creation, metamorphosis, and re-creation" (Berry, 2008, p. 28).

From this perspective, family is a major conduit for cultural transmission. The family links children's behavioral development to the broader sociocultural context. This link occurs through enculturation and socialization. Enculturation refers to the overall adoption values, norms, behav-iors, and ultimately their incorporation into society through a tacit process of children being immersed and surrounded by their culture. Socialization, on the other hand, is a more explicit process involving deliberate teaching and encouragement so that particular characteristics, skills, and behaviors are acquired. In the case of immigrant families these processes become more complex as these families have (to varying degrees) a "foot" in more than one culture. Moreover, a complete understanding of the adaptation process (and the family's role in the process) requires an account of the challenges and resources afforded by the cultural institutions (work, schools, communities, etc.) and the surrounding sociopolitical features, prior to, and after relocation. Only then will we be able to have any understanding how families enter into, and deal with the process of acculturation following their settlement in our societies (Berry, 2008).

From the area of developmental psychology, the most widely used framework is Bronfenbrenner's *bioecological model* (1979, 1986; Bronfenbrenner & Morris, 2006). The model explicitly describes the various social systems that interact directly and indirectly with the individual. The microsystem is the immediate and direct dyad relationships with the individual (family unit), which has received the most attention in the family acculturation research (Chun, 2006). The interconnections between the microsystems are the mesosystems (e.g., peers, schools, families). Exosystems are relationships that indirectly influence the individual (e.g., governmental policies on immigration) and macrosystems reflect the group's social, political, cultural values, norms, and beliefs. Lastly is the chronosystem, that takes into consideration the time of development (e.g., those immigrating before Canada's Multiculturalism Act faced different challenges than recent immigrants). It is Bronfenbrenner's (1979, 1986) explicit stress of the importance of understanding individuals in their social and cultural contexts that have prevailed over time. Thus, the "immigration context" is an added layer to the complexities of family dynamics and functioning. More often than not, researchers are more mindful that culture, acculturation, and other social factors need to be taken into consideration when examining families.

The use of an ecological framework in conjunction with acculturation models allows us to better explore the multiple intersections and overlapping contexts (e.g., family, peers, schools, communities) that determine the well-being of immigrant families. Family functioning becomes much more complex in culturally unfamiliar environments as children and youth become exposed to new mesosystems or extra-familial ecologies (e.g., schools, peer groups) whereas parents are also exposed to other institutions that indirectly affect children such as governmental policies, workforce (exosystems). Moreover, for immigrants, the family becomes another part of the child's social system and culture as a major socialization agent that influences the child's acculturation orientation (Nauck, 2001). At a microsystem level (dyadic approach), family systems models (e.g., Hoffman, 1981; Tamis-LeMonda, 2004) stress that parents and other caregivers are a part of a system of interacting partners, all of whom affect and are affected by each other. Each of the family members' actions and behaviors are intricately interconnected and the roles and responsibilities that parents and other caregivers assume are interdependent and continually negotiated. Thus, families have unique tempos and thresholds for change and transformation that determine how individuals negotiate and move through the new cultural world. Acculturation introduces families to new sociocultural contexts that can either expand or restrain their behaviors, attitudes, and relationships with each other (Chun, 2006). As Oppedal (2006) stressed, acculturation should be understood as an integral part of, or as embedded within, development as individuals learn to function effectively in one or more cultural contexts.

Focusing on the socialization of ethnic minority children, Harrison, Wilson, Pine, Chan, and Buriel (1990) used an ecological orientation perspective. They conceptualized the socialization process as the interconnectedness among the status of the families, adaptive strategies (e.g., maintaining extended family relations), socialization goals (e.g., inculcate ethnic pride and interdependence in children to promote self-worth and strengthen intergroup solidarity), and child outcomes. Included in their exploration was biculturalism, the simultaneous adoption of two cultural orientations.

Multidimensional Perspectives

In an attempt to recognize and more accurately reflect the complexity of the change inherent in the acculturation process, researchers developed a number of multidimensional models that reflect differential change along different planes or axis (Berry, 2003; Gonzales, Knight, Morgan-Lopez, Saenz, & Sirolli, 2002; Ryder, Alden, & Paulhus, 2000). One such model has been offered by Marin (1992). He proposed that acculturation occurs at various levels. First, changes such as dietary preferences and accepting the foods from the dominant society are those that occur at a superficial level. Whereas changes such as language use, social networks, and media preferences are indicative of changes that occur at an intermediate level. Lastly, changes in beliefs, values, and norms are changes at the significant level. Although, Marin's model provides a stratified view of acculturation, it does not differ markedly from previous unidimensional models.

Another example, and among the most widely used, is Berry's (2003) dual axis acculturation strategies framework. His framework is focused on two acculturation levels: the individual (maintaining one's identity and characteristics) and group (maintaining relationships with the host society). Depending on the responses, individuals may form one of four acculturation attitudes or strategies: assimilation (adopting the culture of the host society and rejecting one's own cultural identity), integration (maintaining their cultural identity and adopting aspects of the host society), separation (maintaining all their own cultural identity and rejecting the culture of the host society), and marginalization (rejecting both their own culture and the host society). These acculturation strategies are to be distinguished from how well immigrants interact and engage in their new surroundings (adaptation). An immigrant's ability to adapt is reflected in his or her ability to successfully navigate the institutions of one's new context such as schools, work, and the broader community (sociocultural adaptation), as well as overall life satisfaction and well-being (psychological adaptation) (Ward, 1996).

It is important to note, however, that successful adaptation is a function of both acculturation strategies and the policies and practices of the receiving culture (Sabatier & Berry, 2008; Suárez-Orozco, Carhill, & Chuang, 2011). For example, Berry and Sabatier (2011) compared acculturation strategies and the adaptation of immigrant youth in the Canadian cities of Toronto and Montreal. Whereas Toronto follows the Multiculturalism Act, Montreal maintains an interculturalism policy that has an "assimilationist flavor" in which the French language and culture have privileged status (Bouchard & Taylor, 2008). Their comparison suggests that a policy on multiculturalism was associated with youth who had adopted integration acculturation strategies, which, in turn, tended to have higher levels of self-esteem as compared to their counterparts (Berry & Sabetier, 2011).

THE CONTEXT OF FAMILIES AND IMMIGRATION

Focusing on the cultural orientation differences (between the native and host countries), researchers have explored how families have adjusted to their receiving countries and the extent to which they retain or lose their native cultural beliefs and customs (see Arends-Tóth & van de Vijver, 2006). During these family changes and transformations, parents not only need to ensure the physical health and survival of their children but also the need to inculcate the values and behaviors that they believe will facilitate their children's adaptation to the new environment (Buriel & Ment, 1997). Especially when immigrants' native cultural orientation is substantially different from the orientation of the host (e.g., the emphasis on interdependence versus independence), the clash of cultures may modify immigrants' perspectives on the importance of family relationships and functioning. Thus, when researchers explore the immigration process in relation to families, two primary processes are investigated: (1) the cultural orientations of native and host countries; and (2) the rates or levels of acculturation processes at the individual levels.

WORLDVIEWS ON CULTURAL ORIENTATION

A major distinction made between cultures is the degree to which they possess a worldview that emphasizes the individual or the collective as core tenets of the culture (Triandis, 1995). Specifically, Triandis (1995) argued that a culture could be broadly classified based on interpersonal and intergroup behaviors. He proposed two general worldview models: individualistic (I) and collectivistic (C) orientations. Individualistic societies emphasize personal uniqueness, individual goals and choice. The focus on family revolves around the immediate family members. Conversely, collectivistic societies promote interdependence, relatedness, group well-being (Hsu, 1983; Kagitcibasi, 1994; Kim, 1994; Markus & Kitayama, 1991; Oyserman, Coon, & Kemmelmeier, 2002; Triandis, 1995). These broad worldviews are reflected in the values and practices of parents as they socialize their children.

Parents in individualistic cultures such as Canada and the US tend to stress and foster the development autonomy and self-actualization in their children, whereas interpersonal relationships and a sense of responsibility to the collective is comparatively downplayed. According to Tamis-LeMonda et al. (2008), parents in individualistic cultures are guided by four central values that foster the broader development goal of autonomy: personal choice; intrinsic forms of motivation and persistence, self-esteem, and self-maximization.

The focus on personal choice affords the opportunity for children to act upon their personal preferences, thereby establishing a unique identity and to some extent taking on responsibility for their decisions ("children need to learn to make good choices") (Iyengar & Lepper, 1999). Closely related to personal choice is parents' focus on the development of intrinsically motivated children. Intrinsic motivation, the internal drive or desire to achieve one's own goal is highly valued (a child who is successful in school because he or she wants to learn) and preferred over extrinsic motivation, the desire to achieve a goal for the sake of a secondary goal (achieving in school for good grades to please one's parents) (Iyengar & Lepper, 1999).

Another primary value among individualistic cultures is that of self-maximization (achieving one's full potential as individuals). Among these cultures, parents, even when interacting with their infants emphasize the importance of self-maximization as compared with their more collectivistic counterparts (Harwood, Miller, & Irizarry, 1995). Finally, parents in individualistic cultures view self-esteem (a positive self-esteem is the belief that one is good and worthy) as central to children's well-being. Parents see themselves as particularly responsible to ensure that their child has good self-esteem (Harwood et al., 1995; Miller, Wang, Sandel, & Cho, 2002). Collectively, these values are manifested in parents' beliefs and childrearing practices, and represent their desire for independent and autonomous individuals.

Collectivistic cultures, on the other hand, differ significantly in their orientation and expectations for their children. Parents in collectivistic cultures are guided by values that encourage interdependence and relatedness in their children. The values are represented in parents' emphasis on the importance of family relationships (immediate as well as extended family members), and the importance and sense of responsibility to the group. The need for respect and obedience to maintain social order and recognize social status is also stressed (Grotevant, 1998; Marin & Marin, 1991; Tamis-LeMonda et al., 2008).

Asian countries have been characterized as collectivistic due to the influence of Confucianism. Briefly, Confucianism is grounded in the basic tenets of the common good and social harmony over individual interests. Social responsibilities are designated by clear lines of authority. Respect for the status of others and the subordination of the self for the good of the collective is deemed necessary if peace and prosperity are to follow. Consequently, the collective group is the ultimate measure for approval or rejection of behavior. The family represents one type of collective group. A cornerstone of Confucianism is filial piety. Filial piety refers to the principle that one behaves in a manner that will bring honor and not disgrace to the family name. Children are to be devoted and obedient to their parents (Chao & Tseng, 2002). Therefore, filial piety justifies adult authority over children and authority for elders over members of younger generations. Thus, filial piety serves as a building principle that governs the general behavioral patterns of socialization. It provides specific rules of intergenerational conduct applicable throughout life (see Chuang, 2009).

Latino families have similar family values, with researchers focusing on three particular values: *familismo, respeto,* and *educación. Familismo* includes a strong sense of loyalty, reciprocity, and solidarity among immediate and extended family members. Family members are viewed as the primary source of support and the needs of the family are prioritized over those of the individual. *Respeto* emphasizes dignity and respect toward others, particularly parents and other authority figures (Grau, Azmitia, & Quattlebaum, 2009; Marin & Marin, 1991; Valdés 1996). *Educación* is a set of beliefs and practices that focus on a moral upbringing and being a good person (Marin & Marin, 1991; Sarkisian, Gerena, & Gerstel, 2006; Valdés 1996).

Although the theoretical distinction between individualism and collectivism may be useful as an initial step towards understanding cultural differences in family processes, it does not fully account for the vast sociocultural variability within and across cultural groups, nor does it capture the fluidity of cultures across time. Such perspectives run the risk of oversimplifying and even stereotyping family processes as either collectivistic or individualistic. As Kagitcibasi (1980) warned, "There is a danger that Individualism/Collectivism is too readily used as an explanation for every behavioral variation between so-called individualistic and collectivistic cultures—an all-purpose contrast. If Individualism/Collectivism is used to explain everything, it may explain nothing" (p. 9).

As families immigrate to a new country, parents' values and practices change and adapt in accordance to their new social surroundings. For example, in a recent comparative study, Chuang and Su (2008) revealed that immigrant Chinese-Canadian fathers generally spent more time with their infants than did Chinese fathers in mainland China. However, both immigrant Chinese-Canadian and mainland Chinese fathers were involved in various aspects of childcare (e.g., changing diapers, playing) and household duties (e.g., cooking, cleaning the house, laundry). Chuang (2006) found that Chinese-Canadian mothers' views on their children's decision-making power on everyday events supported an "individualistic" view, promoting independence, as well as "collectivistic," one that was seen as promoting self-reliance.

The role of acculturation on family outcomes, however, has not been consistent (Chun & Akutsu, 2003). Some researchers reported that when family members adapted more to the dominant culture, there was less family cohesion, less mutual support, and more family conflict (e.g., Brooks, Stuewig, & Lecroy, 1998). Others, however, found that acculturation influenced only some components of family relationships (e.g., perceived emotional support was not linked to acculturation) (Cortes, 1995) and others reported no significant findings (e.g., Fuligni, 1998).

ACCULTURATION PROCESSES AND THE DISCREPANCIES BETWEEN PARENTS AND CHILDREN

Although family members may have a sense of shared experiences, individuals may differ in the nature, degree, and rate of these processes, which in turn, influence the interpersonal relations between and among family members (Parke, 2004; White, Roosa, Weaver, & Nair, 2009). This variation is dependent on a host of factors such as native cultural customs and beliefs, the age of immigration, language abilities, previous experiences (e.g., education, employment history), and the extent to which family members can retain ties and relationships with their native culture (Chun, Organista, & Marin, 2002). As stressed by Elder (1998) and others (Harrison et al., 1990; Tamis-LeMonda, 2004), a family systems model is needed to recognize the interdependence and interconnectedness of each family members' lives, and how their stressors and adjustment experiences will affect others.

For example, Durgel, Leyendecker, Yagmurlu, and Harwood (2009) indicated that there is a significant difference between mothers who possessed an integrated versus separated acculturation strategy. Specifically, immigrant Turkish mothers living in Germany who were more integrated in the German culture were found to value individualistic goals much more than Turkish mothers who were more separated from the German culture. It is important to note, however, the individualistic orientation displayed by integrated immigrant mothers were less than the individualistic orientation displayed by native German mothers (Durgel et al., 2009). Moreover, differences in parenting behaviors can be persistent and continue to exist between second-generation immigrants and native mothers (Moreno, 1997; Yaman, Mesman, van Ijzendoorn, Bakermans-Kranenburg, & Linting, 2010).

One of the frameworks that have been used to explore the intergenerational changes between parents and their children is Portes and Rumbaut's (1996) Generational Consonance versus Dissonance theory. They posited that differences between the levels of the parents' and children's acculturation will result in either consonance or dissonance in the family. Specifically, when parents and children are similar in their acculturation process, there is generational consonance. However, dissimilar levels among family members will result in generational dissonance. Based on this framework, Portes and Rumbaut (1996) developed four types of families on the basis of levels of congruency and acculturation. Three types of generationally consonant families were proposed: consonant resistance to acculturation, consonant acculturation, and selective acculturation. The last type was dissonant acculturation. Briefly, consonant resistance to acculturation families are when children and parents are being resistant to the host culture, such as learning English. This results in families being isolated within their communities. In contrast, consonant acculturation families have members actively learning the host language and its culture, integrating into the new culture. For selective acculturation families, families are learning English and the new culture, as well as maintaining their involvement with their ethnic community in efforts to preserve their ethnic heritage. Dissonant acculturation families are families where members are incongruent in their levels of acculturation/assimilation. For example, children may be more active in learning English as their parents' efforts in learning English remain minimal.

Researchers have explored the rates of acculturation and potential discrepancies between parents and their children as each member is exposed to different levels of their ethnic (native) and host cultures. Taking life stage into consideration and a developmental ecological orientation, parents have matured in their ethnic culture, whereas their children may have limited exposure to their ethnic culture or exclusive experience in the new one. Also, children and youth face different adaptation challenges than their parents (Zhou, 1997). For example, immigrant parents experience their own adaptation challenges as they simultaneously must socialize their children to be successful in the new sociocultural environment (Plalet & Schönpflug, 2001; Szapocznik & Kurtines, 1993). Parents strive to transmit their ethnic culture to their children while children face the task of interpreting and making meaning of their parents' teachings of their ethnic culture in a new culture (Costigan & Dokis, 2006b; Kwak, 2003). Moreover, many parents face challenges in learning the new language and culture, which may result in less willingness to adapt to the new norms and customs (Matsuoka, 1990; Phinney, Ong, & Madden, 2000). Children, in contrast, are more likely to have intensive exposure to the new culture at school and with peers (Okagaki & Bojczyk, 2002). With their psychological needs of social acceptance and inclusion, and to academically excel, children may adapt more quickly to the values and customs of the new culture than their parents (Chuang et al., 2011; Phinney et al., 2000). When there are substantial differences between the two cultures, these discrepancies may heighten the pressures on immigrant families to adopt the customs and values of the new country (Costigan & Dokis, 2006b).

However, there may be greater parent–child discrepancies in some domains of life than others (Costigan & Dokis, 2006b). To address these variations, some researchers have focused on private and public domains of acculturation. The private domain includes the socioemotional and value-related aspects of psychological and interpersonal acculturation such as ethnic identity and parenting practices. The public domain refers to the functional and utilitarian aspects of acculturation, such as schooling and language use (Arends-Tóth & van de Vijver, 2003, 2004). Comparing children's and parents' acculturation levels, Costigan and Dokis (2006b) explored the extent to which immigrant Asian parents' and children's acculturation affected their private and public domains of acculturation. Although past findings revealed that compared to their children, adults were more adaptive of the host's lifestyle, the largest difference between parents and children was found in the public domain. Closer examination revealed that even though parents were more willing to modify their public behaviors compared with their private identity and cultural values, their children had greater modification, resulting in a continued discrepancy between parents and children. Generally, children preferred to speak English and used English language media much more than did their parents. In addition, children endorsed independence values more highly than did their parents. This may be expected as children have significant exposure to the host's culture via school, media, and peers. For the private domain, parents and children were similar in their ethnic identity and values. This may reflect the parents' effectiveness in value transmission, emphasizing the importance of cultural values. The effectiveness of value and ethnic transmission was linked to high levels of parental warmth (Knafo & Schwartz, 2001).

Arends-Tóth and van de Vijver (2004) examined how parents and children differed on the various acculturation issues in Turkish immigrant families in the Netherlands. Particular attention focused on three domains of parent–child acculturation, including: (1) behavioral practices as defined as one's participation in ethnic and host cultures such as language use and media preferences (Tsai, Chentsova-Dutton, & Wong, 2002); (2) ethnic identity; and (3) cultural values. Behavioral practices were viewed as a part of the public domain, whereas the other two domains, ethnic identity and cultural values, were within the private domain. Immigrant adults were more willing to adopt and change their behaviors and activity engagements in the public than private domain. For example, Turkish immigrant adults were more integrated in these public domains (participating in the host cultures' activities while retaining their ethnic practices), but maintained their ethnic values and identity (private domains). These findings were similar among Moroccan and Turkish immigrants in Belgium (Snauwaert, Soenens, Vanbeselaere, & Boen, 2003).

Different rates of acculturation within families may also create discrepancies in cultural values and beliefs between children and their parents that affect family relationships (Berry, Phinney, Sam, & Vedder, 2006). In Szapocznik and Kurtines's (1993) review of clinical work with Puerto Rican families, they found that one of the key effects of acculturation gaps between parents and their children was heightened parent–child conflict due to discrepancies in values, interests, and language competencies. These findings of acculturation gaps leading to family conflict were also found among Indian families (Farver et al., 2002) and Soviet Jewish refugee families (Birman, 2006). Similarly, Martinez (2006) reported that parent–child acculturation gaps were linked to increased levels of family stress and decreased effectiveness in parenting practices. Intergenerational acculturation gaps have also been related to the quality of family relationships (Lau et al., 2005; Sluzki, 1979). For example, Chinese-American immigrant parents who were more oriented to their culture and ways of parenting were less effective with children who were quickly adopting the host culture (Buki, Ma, Strom, & Strom, 2003). As Chun (2004) reported, immigrant Chinese parents stated that, "things move too fast in America" and believed that this accelerated developmental tempo (children becoming more independent at a faster pace than desired by parents) had compromised their parenting. These parents also mentioned that this fast pace of change also impacted their time spent with their children and their children's ties to their cultural heritage.

However, parents were not uniformly more likely to retain their native culture and adolescents to the host culture, especially with respect to the identity dimension of acculturation. Ho's (2009) study on Vietnamese immigrant families found that although Vietnamese parents identified themselves as generally more Vietnamese and less American in three acculturation domains (language competence, identity acculturation, and behavioral acculturation) compared to their adolescents, a substantial number of parents' views on their Vietnamese and American identities were unexpected. Specifically, many parents scored higher on American identity than did their adolescents, whereas adolescents scored higher than did their parents on their Vietnamese identity. Birman (2006) found similar results with immigrant adolescents and parents from the former Soviet Union, in the US. Perhaps these findings reflect adolescents' need to embrace their ethnic identity as they struggle to re-create their new identity. Adolescents may also have desires to preserve their self-identification and pride of being "Vietnamese" as their non-immigrant peers may have socially excluded them based on their "ethnicity." Parents, on the other hand, may view "being American" as a reflection of their decisions to leave Vietnam due to ideological and political reasons. Only the discrepancies between parents and children in the Vietnamese identity acculturation predicted less family cohesion and adolescents being less satisfied with their parents (Ho, 2009). These comparisons between adolescents' and parents' scores on identity, however, need to be viewed cautiously. The meaning of "Vietnamese" and "American" identities may be conceptualized differently by children and parents as each represent a different generation and were of different ages when they immigrated, having different developmental needs and expectations (Birman & Trickett, 2001; Tsai, Ying, & Lee, 2001).

Child–parent conflicts have been associated with adolescent depression, delinquency (Crane, Ngai, Larson, & Hafen, 2005), and low family cohesion, which, in turn, led to poor adolescent adjustment (Crane et al., 2005; Tseng & Fuligni, 2000). As autonomy and independence have been found to be more developmentally relevant for youth, most acculturation studies on parent–child conflicts have focused on this age stage. However, few have attempted to disentangle normative developmental factors from acculturation issues (Chun, 2006).

Researchers have also examined issues of language and communication between immigrant parents and their children and found some level of decline in family functioning and parental coping (e.g., Trickett & Jones, 2007; Martinez, McClure, & Eddy, 2009; Weisskirch, 2005) and deterioration in parent–child relationships (Luo & Wiseman, 2000; Santisteban & Mitrani, 2003). As Hernandez et al. (2008) reported, half of the immigrant parents (mothers and fathers) have limited proficiency in speaking English. However, about 60% of immigrant families have at least one parent in the home who is fluent in English or speaks English exclusively. Moreover, one-quarter of children in newcomer families (child aged 13 or over) do not speak English very well or exclusively, and the same proportion of newcomer families live in linguistically isolated households. As children learn the host language and culture quicker than their parents, parents then rely on them (as well as on other members of their social network) to serve as language and cultural brokers for their parents (Suárez-Orozco & Suárez-Orozco, 2001; Jones & Trickett, 2005; Santisteban, Muir-Malcolm, Mitrani, & Szapocznik, 2002; Tse, 1995a).

Children become intermediaries between their parents and the host society as they assist their parents by translating, interpreting, and navigating often complex situations (Hernandez et al., 2008). Examples include healthcare visits (Cohen, Moran-Ellis, & Smaje, 1999), parent–teacher school conferences (Orellana, Dorner, & Pulido, 2003), and bank transactions (McQuillan & Tse, 1995). Children can also become unintentionally the primary navigators of their family's access to valuable services, information, or material resources (Martinez et al., 2009). Language brokering places children in very influential roles in families, roles that may or may not be developmentally appropriate (Tse, 1995b). Especially with the significant number of parents who may have limited or no language competence of the dominant culture, children as brokers for their parents and the impact on family relationships and functioning have received considerable attention.

To date, the overall findings are inconsistent with respect to the positive or negative outcomes of language brokering. Some researchers have found positive effects of language brokering on children, including the development of strong metalinguistic and interpersonal skills (Malakoff & Hakuta, 1991; Valdés, 2003), increased confidence and maturity (McQuillan & Tse, 1995; Walinchowski, 2001), academic self-efficacy (Buriel, Perez, De Ment, Chavez, & Moran, 1998) and achievement (Orellana, & Li-Grining, 2007; Orellana et al., 2003), and pride at being able to help out their families (DeMent & Buriel, 1999; Tse, 1995a, 1996).

In contrast, other researchers have reported negative consequences of language brokering at the individual level (for children and parents) and family level (family dynamics and relationships). Immigrant parents' reliance on their children may create role reversals that negatively affect the power and control dynamics within the family (Buki et al., 2003; Kibria, 1996; Umaña-Taylor, 2003). Especially when parents rely a great deal on their children, children become increasingly powerful cultural agents, often leading to parents deferring to their children when faced with important family decisions (Martinez, 2006; Santisteban et al., 2002; Tse, 1995b). These situations in which brokering may undermine the traditional parent–child roles and parental authority can lead to parent–child conflicts (Park, 2001, 2002; Portes & Rumbaut, 2001). When parents feel disempowered, especially when children's experiences of language brokering are negative (DeMent & Buriel, 1999; McQuillan & Tse, 1995; Ng, 1998; Valenzuela, 1999; Weisskirch & Alva, 2002), brokering may lead to poorer outcomes for children. Also, it is not only the pragmatics of translating and interpreting the language for their parents, but the interpretation of the subtle cultural norms that are part of the interactions of families with various social systems may be equally as important and stressful (Martinez et al., 2009). Children may not be cognizant of or experienced enough to understand these subtleties, the technical vocabulary, or the vocabulary in the parents' origin-country language (Hernandez et al., 2008).

GENDERED ACCULTURATION AND PARENTING

More recently, researchers have given greater attention to the issue of gender in acculturation processes (see Chuang & Moreno, 2008; Chuang & Tamis-LeMonda, 2009). Gendered acculturation provides greater insight into the complexities of the challenges that families face as it impacts family dynamics and functioning (Dion & Dion, 2001). Due to the challenges of adjustment and settlement, gender roles in families may alter how mothers and fathers interact with and socialize their children. For example, Jain and Belsky (1997) found that highly acculturated South Asian fathers were more likely to teach, discipline, play with, and care for their children than their less acculturated counterparts. Also among South Asian families, Patel, Power, and Bhavnagri (1996) reported that mothers and fathers may alter their parenting practices differently as they acculturate to their new host country. Specifically, mothers were found to be more encouraging of American cultural characteristics for their children, whereas the fathers were emphasizing their Indian values, especially for girls, such as deference to authority, manners, and politeness (Patel et al., 1996). In contrast, Costigan and Dokis (2006a) reported that for Chinese parents, fathers were more oriented to the new culture, whereas the mothers were more oriented to the ethnic culture. Others have also found that it was the mothers who viewed themselves as more responsible for the ethnic cultural maintenance than did their spouses (Davey, Fish, Askew, & Robila, 2003; Phinney, Horenczyk, Leibkind, & Vedder, 2001).

For family dynamics, Qin's (2009) study on immigration processes for Chinese American fathers and mothers showed that as they settled and adapted to their new homeland, this transition often led to growing alienation with their children. Specifically, compared with mothers, fathers were more likely to have their stress and dissatisfaction affect their relationships with their children. Even though children were found to spend less actual time with their fathers after migration, children stated that the loss of time with their mothers was more pronounced, especially because they generally spent more time with them in their home country.

LIMITATIONS OF CURRENT THEORY USAGE AND SUGGESTIONS FOR MOVING FORWARD

As the fields of immigration, culture, and ethnic minority families move forward, researchers have acknowledged the complexities of children and their families (Parke & Chuang, 2011). Attempts to capture change and transformation in immigrant families with a "single" acculturation construct (such as a single index like language) or a proxy measure (e.g., generational level, years of residence in host country) are now being recognized for their limitations. Rather, researchers are more culturally sensitive to the multidimensionality of the immigration process and have attempted to develop more comprehensive measures that reflect the multiple domains of life (e.g., private, public domains). As Arends-Tóth and van de Vijver (2006) stressed, acculturation measures need to assess both mainstream and heritage cultures, with equal emphasis on the maintenance of the heritage culture rather than a focus on how immigrants are adapting to the receiving society. Moreover, the capacity of immigrants to develop bicultural competencies and adaptive skills needs greater attention (Chun & Akutsu, 2003). It is important to note that perhaps various acculturation indexes would be an effective strategy as each index has been found to have different outcome effects. For example, Jain and Belsky (1997) reported that years of residency in the US was not associated with the fathers' levels of involvement in their children's lives but other indexes such as cultural attitudes and feelings were significant predictors.

The assessment of acculturation experiences must also be viewed as dynamic and highly variable for individual members (e.g., young children versus adolescents versus parents) as each face unique challenges based on their developmental stage. Families are also not passive agents that are subject to their environments but rather may also influence their environments. Especially when many families are transnational, moving back and forth between the two countries, and do not forsake or decrease their ties with their heritage country, this bidirectionally of social influence on the host societies needs greater attention (Chun & Akutsu, 2003; Parke & Chuang, 2011). Thus, an ecological perspective needs to take into consideration *both* countries and their social, political, and cultural contexts to better understand the dynamics in families.

Thus, no one single aspect of acculturation is sufficient for understanding the pathways of immigration and how the challenges and barriers that family members face may impact their development and interpersonal relationships. Rather, researchers need to first gain greater insight into the pre-immigration situation such as the motivations for leaving one's country (voluntary or forced, and under what conditions) and the characteristics of the family before migration. For example, their socioeconomic status and economic resources, social skills, human and social capital, knowledge of the receiving country, and language abilities are of a few factors that will have some influence in determining how they will successfully adjust to the host country. Next, researchers would need to better understand the historical and political context of the migration, and the characteristics of the receiving country (e.g., communities of similar ethnic groups, social and class structure, the attitudes of the host in accepting new immigrants), and whether the receiving country has institutional support (e.g., settlement serving agencies in Canada) to assist immigrant families upon arrival (Guarnaccia, 1997; Parke & Chuang, 2011; Suárez-Orozco et al., 2011). This means a reconceptualization of the immigration research, placing some attention to the family dynamics and relationships before immigrating to a new country so that the findings can be used as a baseline to then compare how immigrant families have adjusted in their new homelands. This approach creates a more accurate and appropriate portrait of immigration as a multiphase cross-time process that recognizes pre-immigration, migration transition, and post-immigration phases. Moreover, by viewing immigration as a cross-time and cross boundary issue, it underscores that immigration, like all transitions, is a process and not an event (Parke & Chuang, 2011).

CONCLUSION

Taking a multidisciplinary and multimethodological approach to immigration research has gained recent attention. This is evident in special issues of scholarly journals (Chuang & Gielen, 2009; Chuang & Tamis-LeMonda, 2009) and edited books (Chuang & Moreno, 2008, 2011; also see Bornstein & Cote, 2006). Scholars are slowly recognizing that immigration should be the medium from which to explain family functioning, rather than treating immigration as a peripheral variable or as a "one time event." With the multitude of variations of families' sociocultural, socioeconomic status, and immigrant backgrounds, researchers will need to use and refine theoretical and methodological frameworks that will accurately capture the nuances and complexities of families. However, disentangling these factors is not simple and, thus, no one theory can exclusively address the various complexities and dynamic processes of development, family functioning and relationships, and sociocultural context. As others have stressed, it is important to address the sociocultural processes in all aspects of the research agenda, including the conceptual framework and hypotheses of the study, the ethnic appropriateness of the informants, the use of culturally sensitive and relevant methodological strategies, and interpreting the findings within a cultural context (Quintana et al., 2006). Thus, we need to critically assess our current research tools and to develop more innovative methodologies such as the utilization of both qualitative and quantitative methods and multiple informants to tap into the dynamics and ever-changing social relationships among various family members (Chuang, 2009).

However, we believe current theoretical models (i.e., family systems theory, ecological theories, acculturation typologies) fall short in capturing the significant variability inherent in understanding culture and family processes between groups and across historical time, and inadvertently imply a level of sociocultural stability that is unwarranted. To capture the influence of immigration on families, researchers need to use a more critical ecological approach to family functioning, one that more fully accounts for ongoing transitions in context and meaning among and between groups over time (Chuang, 2009). Such an approach questions the utility of an immigrant experience to one that focuses on a particular profile of immigrant and conditions. Not delving deeper into the dynamics and intricacies of culture, immigration, development of each family member, and how these factors intertwine with parenting and family functioning will inadvertently or implicitly add credence to over-generalizations of and support to stereotypic characterizations of certain immigrant and ethnic groups. Although the various factors to consider are numerous and may be difficult to disentangle (e.g., SES factors, family structure, reasons for immigrating, one's SES in the native country), researchers need to be mindful of the complexities, and attempt to further explore these issues among various cultural and ethnic groups. Better understanding how cultural processes influence family dynamics and relationships will provide greater insight into the boundaries, meanings, and functions of child and family development.

REFERENCES

Arends-Tóth, J., & van de Vijver, F. J. R. (2003). Multiculturalism and acculturation: Views of Dutch and Turkish-Dutch. *European Journal of Social Psychology*, *33*, 259–266.

Arends-Tóth, J., & van de Vijver, F. J. R. (2004). Domains and dimensions in acculturation: Implicit theories of Turkish-Dutch. *International Journal of Intercultural Relations*, *28*, 19–35.

Arends-Tóth, J., & van de Vijver, F. J. R. (2006). Issues in the conceptualization and assessment of acculturation. In M. H. Bornstein & L. R. Cote (Eds.), *Acculturation and parent-child relationships* (pp. 33–62). Mahwah, NJ: Erlbaum.

Bennett, N. (1976). *Teaching styles and pupils progress*. Cambridge, MA: Harvard University Press.

Berry, J. W. (1980). Acculturation as varieties of adaptation. In A. Padilla (Ed.), *Acculturation: Theory, models, and new findings* (pp. 9–25). Bounder, CO: Westview Press.

Berry, J. W. (2003). Conceptual approaches to acculturation. In K. Chun, P. Balls-Organista, & G. Marin (Eds.), *Acculturation: Advances in theory, measurement, and applied research* (pp. 17–37). Washington, DC: APA Press.

Berry, J. W. (2008). Globalisation and acculturation. *International Journal of Intercultural Relations*, *32*, 328–336.

Berry, J. W., Phinney, J. S., Sam, D. L., & Vedder, P. (2006). Immigrant youth: Acculturation, identity, and adaptation. *Applied Psychology: An International Review*, *55*, 303–332.

Berry, J. W., Poortinga, Y. H., Segall, M. H., & Dasen, P. R. (2002). *Cross-cultural psychology: Research and applications* (2nd ed.). New York: Cambridge University Press.

Berry, J. W., & Sabatier, C. (2011). The acculturation and adaptation of second generation immigrant youth in Toronto and Montreal. In S. S. Chuang & R. P. Moreno (Eds.), *Immigrant children: Change, adaptation, and cultural transformation* (pp. 125–148). Lanham, MD: Lexington Books.

Birman, D. (2006). Acculturation gap and family adjustment: Findings with Soviet Jewish refugees in the U.S. and implications for measurement. *Journal of Cross Cultural Psychology*, *37*, 568–589.

Birman, D., & Trickett, E. J. (2001). Cultural transitions in first-generation immigrants: Acculturation of Soviet Jewish refugee adolescents and parents. *Journal of Cross Cultural Psychology*, *32*, 456–477.

Blake, J. (1989). *Family size and achievement*. Berkeley, CA: University of California Press.

Bornstein, M. H., & Cote, L. R. (2004). Mothers' parenting cognitions in cultures of origin, acculturating cultures, and cultures of destination. *Child Development*, *75*, 221–235.

Bornstein, M. H., & Cote, L. R. (Eds.) (2006). *Acculturation and parent-children relationships: Measurement and development*. Mahwah, NJ: Erlbaum.

Bouchard, G., & Taylor, C. (2008). *Fonder l'avenir. Le temps de la conciliation. Rapport de la Commission de consultation sur les pratiques d'accommodement reliées aux différences culturelles* (Building the future: A Time for reconciliation). Montréal, ON: Commission de consultation sur les pratiques d'accommodement reliées aux différences culturelles.

Bourhis, R. Y., Moïse, L. C., Perreault, S., & Senécal, S. (1997). Towards an interactive acculturation model: A social-psychological approach. *International Journal of Psychology*, *32*, 369–386.

Bronfenbrenner, U. (1979). *The ecology of human development: Experiments by nature and design*. Cambridge, MA: Harvard University Press.

Bronfenbrenner, U. (1986). The ecology of the family as a context for human development. *Developmental Psychology*, *22*, 723–742.

Bronfenbrenner, U., & Morris, P. A. (2006). The bioecological model of human development. In W. Damon & R. M. Lerner (Eds.), *Handbook of child psychology, Vol. 1: Theoretical models of human development* (6th ed., pp. 793–828). New York: John Wiley.

Brooks, A. J., Stuewig, J., & Lecroy, C. W. (1998). A family-based model of Hispanic adolescent substance use. *Journal of Drug Education*, *28*, 65–86.

Buki, L. P., Ma, T. C., Strom, R. D., & Strom, S. K. (2003). Chinese immigrant mothers of adolescents: Self-perceptions of acculturation effects on parenting. *Cultural Diversity and Ethnic Minority Psychology*, *9*, 127–140.

Buriel, R., & Ment, T. D. (1997). Immigration and sociocultural change in Mexican, Chinese, and Vietnamese American families. In A. Booth, A. C. Crouter, & N. Landale (Eds.), *Immigration and the family* (pp. 165–200). Mahwah, NJ: Erlbaum.

Buriel, R., Perez, W., De Ment, T. L., Chavez, D. V., & Moran, V. R. (1998). The relationship of language brokering to academic performance, biculturalism, and self-efficacy among Latino adolescents. *Hispanic Journal of Behavioral Sciences*, *20*, 283–297.

Chao, R., & Tseng, V. (2002). Parenting of Asians. In M. H. Bornstein (Ed.), *Handbook of parenting, Vol. 4 Social conditions and applied parenting* (2nd ed., pp. 59–93). Mahwah, NJ: Erlbaum.

Chuang, S. S. (2006). Taiwanese-Canadian mothers' beliefs about personal freedom for their young children. *Social Development*, *15*, 520–536.

Chuang, S. S. (2009). Transformation and change: Parenting in Chinese societies. In J. Mancini & K. A. Roberto (Eds.), *Pathways of development: Explorations of change* (pp. 191–206). Lanham, MA: Lexington Books.

Chuang, S. S., & Gielen, U. (2009). Understanding immigrant families from around the world: Introduction to the special issue. *Journal of Family Psychology*, *23*, 275–278.

Chuang, S. S., & Moreno, R. P. (Eds.) (2008). *On new shores: Understanding immigrant fathers in North America*. Lanham, MD: Lexington Books.

Chuang, S. S., & Moreno, R. P. (Eds.) (2011). *Immigrant children: Change, adaptation, and cultural transformation*. Lanham, MD: Lexington Books.

Chuang, S. S., Rasmi, S. S., & Friesen, C. (2011). Service providers' perspectives on the pathways of adjustment for newcomer children and youth in Canada. In S. S. Chuang & R. P. Moreno (Eds.), *Immigrant children: Change, adaptation, and cultural transformation* (pp. 149–170). Lanham, MA: Lexington Books.

Chuang, S. S., & Su, Y. (2008). Transcending Confucian teachings on fathering: A sign of the times or acculturation? In S. S. Chuang & R. P. Moreno (Eds.), *On new shores: Understanding immigrant fathers in North America* (pp. 129–150). Lanham, MD: Lexington Books.

Chuang, S. S., & Tamis-LeMonda, C. S. (Eds.) (2009). From shore to shore: Understanding fathers, mothers, and children in North America. *Sex Roles*, *60* (7/8).

Chun, G. H. (2004). Shifting ethnic identity and consciousness: U.S.-born Chinese American youth in the 1930s and 1950s. In J. Lee & M. Zhou (Eds.), *Asian American youth: Culture, identity and ethnicity* (pp. 113–141). New York: Routledge.

Chun, K. M. (2006). Conceptual and measurement issues in family acculturation research. In M. H. Bornstein & L. R. Cote (Eds.), *Acculturation and parent-child relationships* (pp. 63–78). Mahwah, NJ: Erlbaum.

Chun, K. M., & Akutsu, P. D. (2003). Acculturation among ethnic minority families. In K. M. Chun, P. B. Organista, & G. Marín (Eds.), *Acculturation: Advances in theory, measurement, and applied research* (pp. 95–119). Washington, DC: American Psychological Association.

Chun, K. M., Organista, P. B., & Marin, G. (Eds.). (2002). *Acculturation: Advances in theory, measurement, and applied research*. Hong Kong: City University of Hong Kong Press.

Citizenship and Immigration Canada. (2007). *Facts and figures*. Retrieved from http://www.cic.gc.ca/english/resources/statistics/menu-fact.asp.

Cohen, S., Moran-Ellis, J., & Smaje, C. (1999). Children as informal interpreters in GP consultations: Pragmatics and ideology. *Sociology of Health and Illness, 21*, 163–186.

Cortes, D. E. (1995). Variations in familism in two generations of Puerto Ricans. *Hispanic Journal of Behavioral Sciences, 17*, 249–255.

Costigan, C. L., & Dokis, D. P. (2006a). Similarities and differences in acculturation among mothers, fathers, and children in immigrant Chinese families. *Journal of Cross-Cultural Psychology, 37*, 723–741.

Costigan, C. L., & Dokis, D. P. (2006b). Relations between parent-child acculturation differences and adjustment within immigrant Chinese families. *Child Development, 77*, 1252–1267.

Crane, D. R., Ngai, S. W., Larson, J. H., & Hafen, M. (2005). The influence of family functioning and parent-adolescent acculturation on North American Chinese adolescent outcomes. *Family Relations, 54*, 400–410.

Davey, M., Fish, L.S., Askew, J., & Robila, M. (2003). Parenting practices and the transmission of ethnic identity. *Journal of Marital and Family Therapy, 29*, 195–208.

DeMent, T., & Buriel, R. (1999, August). Children as cultural brokers: Recollections of college students. Paper presented at the SPSSI Conference on Immigrants and Immigration, Toronto, Canada.

Dion, K. K., & Dion, K. L. (2001). Gender and cultural adaptation in immigrant families. *Journal of Social Issues, 57*, 511–521.

Durgel, E. S., Leyendecker, B., Yagmurlu, B., & Harwood, R. (2009). Sociocultural influences on German and Turkish immigrant mothers' long-term socialization goals. *Journal of Cross-Cultural Psychology, 40*, 834–852.

Elder, G. H. (1998). The life course and human development. In W. Damon (Series Ed.) & N. Eisenberg (Vol. Ed.), *Handbook of child psychology. Vol. 1. Theoretical models of human development* (5th ed., pp. 939–991). New York: Wiley.

Evans, W. G., Saegert, S., & Harris, R. (2001). Residential density and psychological health among children in low-income families. *Environment and Behavior, 33*, 165–180.

Farver, J. M., Narang, S. K., & Bhadha, B. R. (2002). East meets West: Ethnic identity, acculturation, and conflict in Asian Indian families. *Journal of Family Psychology, 16*, 338–350.

Fuligni, A. J. (1998). Authority, autonomy, and parent-adolescent conflict and cohesion: A study of adolescents from Mexican, Chinese, and Filipino, and European backgrounds. *Developmental Psychology, 34*, 782–792.

Gonzales, N. A., Knight, G. P., Morgan-Lopez, A., Saenz, D., & Sirolli, A. (2002). Acculturation and the mental health of Latino youths: An integration and critique of the literature. In J. M. Contreras, K. A. Kerns, & A. M. Neal-Barnett (Eds.), *Latino children and families in the United States* (pp. 45–74). Westport, CT: Greenwood.

Gordon, M. M. (1964). *Assimilation in American life*. New York: Oxford University Press.

Grau, J. M., Azmitia, M., & Quattlebaum, J. (2009). Latino families: Parenting, relational, and development processes. In F. A. Villarruel, G. Carlo, J. M. Grau, M. Azmitia, N. J. Cabrera, & T. J. Chahin (Eds.), *Handbook of U.S. Latino psychology: Developmental and community-based perspectives* (pp. 153–169). Thousand Oaks, CA: Sage.

Green, A. G. (2003). "What is the role of immigration in Canada's future?" In C. M. Beach, A. G. Green, & J. G. Reitz (Eds.), *Canadian Immigration Policy for the 21st Century* (pp. 33–45). Kingston, ON: John Deutsch Institute for the Study of Economic Policy, Queen's University.

Grotevant, H. D. (1998). Adolescent development in family contexts. In W. Damon & N. Eisenberg (Eds.), *Handbook of Child Psychology; Vol. 3: Social, Emotional, and Personality Development* (5th ed., pp. 1097–1149). New York: Wiley.

Guarnaccia, P. J. (1997). Social stress and psychological distress among Latinos in the United States. In I. Al-Issa & M. Tousignant (Eds.), *Ethnicity, immigration, and psychopathology* (pp. 71–94). New York: Plenum Press.

Harrison, A. O., Wilson, M. N., Pine, C. J., Chan, S. Q., & Buriel, R. (1990). Family ecologies of ethnic minority children. *Child Development, 61*, 347–362.

Harwood, R. L., Miller, J. G., & Irizarry, N. L. (1995). *Culture and attachment: Perceptions of the child in context*. New York: Guilford Press.

Hernandez, D. J. (1986). Childhood in sociodemographic perspective. In R. H. Turner & J. H. Short, Jr. (Eds.), *Annual review of Sociology, Volume 12* (pp. 159–180). Palo Alto, CA: Annual Reviews.

Hernandez, D. J. (2004). Children and youth in immigrant families. In J. A. Banks & C. A. McGee Banks (Eds.), *Handbooks of research on multicultural education* (2nd ed., pp. 404–419). San Francisco, CA: Jossey-Bass.

Hernandez, D. J., & Charney, E. (Eds.) (1998). *From generation to generation: The health and well-being of children in immigrant families*. Washington, DC: National Academy Press.

Hernandez, D. J., Denton, N. A., & MacCartney, S. E. (2008). Immigrant fathers: A demographic portrait. In S. S. Chuang & R. P. Moreno (Eds.), *On new shores: Understanding immigrant fathers in North America* (pp. 47–103). Lanham, MD: Lexington Books.

Ho, J. (2009). Acculturation gaps in Vietnamese immigrant families: Impact on family relationships. *International Journal of Intercultural Relations, 34*, 22–33.

Hoffman, L. (1981). *Foundations of family therapy*. New York: Basic Books.

Hsu, F. L. K. (1983). *Rugged individualism reconsidered*. Knoxville, TN: University of Tennessee Press.

Iyengar, S. S., & Lepper, M. R. (1999). Rethinking the value of choice: A cultural perspective on intrinsic motivation. *Journal of Personality and Social Psychology, 76*, 349–366.

Jain, A., & Belsky, J. (1997). Fathering and acculturation: Immigrant Indian families with young children. *Journal of Marriage and the Family, 59*, 873–883.

Jones, C. J., & Trickett, E. J. (2005). Immigrant adolescents behaving as culture brokers: A study of families from the Former Soviet Union. *Journal of Social Psychology, 145*, 405–427.

Kagitçibasi, C. (1980). Individualism and collectivism. In J. W. Berry, M. H. Segall, & C. Kagitçibasi (Eds.), *Handbook of cross-cultural psychology. Vol. 3. Social behavior and applications* (pp. 1–50). Needham Heights, MA: Allyn and Bacon.

Kagitçibasi, C. (1994). A critical appraisal of individualism and collectivism: Toward a new formulation. In U. Kim, H.C. Triandis, C. Kagitçibasi, S.C. Choi, and G. Yoon (Eds.), *Individualism and collectivism: Theory, method, and applications* (pp. 52–65). Thousand Oaks, CA: Sage.

Kao, G. (1999). Psychological well-being and educational achievement among immigrant youth. In D. J. Hernandez (Ed.), *Children of immigrants: Health, adjustment, and public assistance* (pp. 410–477). Washington, DC: National Academy Press.

Kibria, N. (1996). Power, patriarchy, and gender conflict in the Vietnamese immigrant community. In E. N. Chow, D. Y. Wilkinson, & M. Baca Zinn (Eds.), *Race, class, and gender: Common bonds, different voices* (pp. 206–222). Thousand Oaks, CA: Sage.

Kim, U. (1994). Individualism and collectivism: Conceptual clarification and elaboration. In U. Kim, H.C. Triandis, C. Kagitçibasi, S.C. Choi, & G. Yoon (Eds.), *Individualism and collectivism: Theory, method, and application* (pp. 19–40). Thousand Oaks, CA: Sage.

Knafo, A., & Schwartz, S. H. (2001). Value socialization in families of Israeli-born and Soviet-born adolescents in Israel. *Journal of Cross-Cultural Psychology, 32*, 213–228.

Kwak, K. (2003). Adolescents and their parents: A review of intergenerational family relations for immigrant and nonimmigrant families. *Human Development, 46*, 115–136.

Lau, A. S., McCabe, K. M., Yeh, M., Garland, A. F., Wood, P. A., & Hough, R. L. (2005). The acculturation gap-distress hypothesis among high-risk Mexican American families. *Journal of Family Psychology, 19*, 367–375.

Luo, S. H., & Wiseman, R. L. (2000). Ethnic language maintenance among Chinese immigrant children in the United States. *International Journal of Intercultural Relations, 24*, 307–324.

Malakoff, M., & Hakuta, K. (1991). Translation skill and metalinguistic awareness in bilinguals. In E. Bialystok (Ed.), *Language processing in bilingual children* (pp. 141–166). Cambridge, England: Cambridge University Press.

Marin, G. (1992). Issues in the measurement of acculturation among Hispanics. In K. F. Geisinger (Ed.), *Psychological testing of Hispanics* (pp. 235–251). Washington, DC: American Psychological Association.

Marin, G., & Marin, B. (1991). *Research with Hispanic populations*. Newbury Park, CA: Sage.

Markus, H., & Kitayama, S. (1991). Culture and the self: Implications for cognition, emotion, and motivation. *Psychological Review*, *98*, 224–253.

Martin, P., & Midgely, E. (2003). Immigration: Shaping and reshaping America. *Population Bulletin*, *58*, 1–43.

Martinez, C. R. Jr. (2006). Effects of differential family acculturation on Latino adolescent substance use. *Family Relations*, *55*, 306–317.

Martinez, J. R., McClure, H. H., & Eddy, J. (2009). Language brokering contexts and behavioral and emotional adjustment among Latino parents and adolescents. *Journal of Early Adolescence*, *29*, 71–98.

Matsuoka, J. K. (1990). Differential acculturation among Vietnamese refugees. *Social Work*, *35*, 341–345.

McLanahan, S., & Sandefur, G. (1994). *Growing up with a single parent: What hurts, what helps*. Cambridge, MA: Harvard University Press.

McQuillan, J., & Tse, L. (1995). Child language brokering in linguistic minority communities: Effects on cultural interaction, cognition, and literacy. *Language and Education*, *9*, 195–215.

Miller, P. J., Wang, S., Sandel, T., & Cho, G. E. (2002). Self-esteem as folk theory: A comparison of European American and Taiwanese mothers' beliefs. *Parenting: Science and Practice*, *2*, 209–239.

Moreno, R. P. (1997). Everyday instruction: A comparison of Mexican American and Anglo mothers and their preschool children. *Hispanic Journal of Behavioral Sciences*, *19*, 527–539.

Nauck, B. (2001). Intercultural contact and intergenerational transmission in immigrant families. *Journal of Cross-Cultural Psychology*, *32*, 159–173.

Ng, J. (1998). From kitchen to classroom: Reflections of a language broker. *Voices from the Middle*, *6*, 38–40.

Okagaki, L., & Bojczyk, K. E. (2002). Perspectives on Asian American development. In G. C. Nagayama Hall & S. Okazaki (Eds.), *Asian American psychology: The science of lives in context* (pp. 67–104). Washington, DC: American Psychological Association.

Oppedal, B. (2006). Acculturation development. In D. L. Sam & J. W. Berry (Eds.), *Cambridge handbook of acculturation psychology* (pp. 97–112). Cambridge, England: Cambridge University Press.

Orellana, M. F., Dorner, L., & Pulido, L. (2003). Accessing assets: Immigrant youth's work as family translators or "para-phrasers". *Social Problems*, *50*, 505–524.

Orellana, M. F., & Li-Grining, C. P. (2007). "I helped my Mom," and it helped me: Translating the skills of language brokers into improved standardized test scores. *American Journal of Education*, *113*, 451–478.

Oyserman, D., Coon, H. M., & Kemmelmeier, M. (2002). Rethinking individualism and collectivism: Evaluation of theoretical assumptions and meta-analyses. *Psychological Bulletin*, *128*, 3–72.

Palameta, B. (2004). Low income among immigrants and visible minorities. *Perspectives on Labour and Income*, *5*. Retrieved from http://www.statcan.ca/english/freepub/75–ca001-XIE/10404/art-2.htm (accessed July 4, 2011).

Park, L. (2001). Between adulthood and children: The boundary work of immigrant entrepreneurial children. *Berkley Journal of Sociology*, *45*, 114–135.

Park, L. (2002). Asian immigrant entrepreneurial children. In L. T. Lo & R. Bonus (Eds.), *Contemporary Asian American communities* (pp. 161–174). Philadelphia, PA: Temple University Press.

Parke, R. D. (2004). The Society for Research in Child Development at 70: Progress and promise. *Child Development*, *75*, 1–24.

Parke, R. D., & Chuang, S. S. (2011). New arrivals: Past advances and future directions in research and policy. In S. S. Chuang & R. P. Moreno (Eds.), *Immigrant children: Change, adaptation, and cultural transformation* (pp. 271–295). Lanham, MA: Lexington Books.

Patel, N., Power, T., & Bhavnagri, H. (1996). Socialization values and practices of Indian immigration parents: Correlates of modernity and acculturation. *Child Development*, *67*, 302–313.

Phinney, J. S., Horenczyk, G., Liebkind, K., & Vedder, P. (2001). Ethnic identity, immigration, and well-being: An interactional perspective. *Journal of Social Issues*, *57*, 493–510.

Phinney, J. S., Ong, A. D., & Madden, T. (2000). Cultural values and intergenerational value discrepancies. *Child Development*, *71*, 528–539.

Plalet, K., & Schönpflug, U. (2001). Intergenerational transmission of collectivism and achievement values in two acculturation contexts: the case of Turkish families in Germany and Turkish and Moroccan families in the Netherlands. *Journal of Cross-Cultural Psychology*, *32*, 186–201.

Portes, A., & Rumbaut, R. G. (1996). *Immigrant America: A portrait* (2nd ed.). Berkeley, CA: University of California Press.

Portes, A., & Rumbaut, R. G. (2001). *Legacies: The story of the immigrant second generation*. New York: Sage.

Qin, D. (2009). Gendered processes of adaptation: Understanding parent-child relations in Chinese immigrant families. *Sex Roles*, *60*, 467–481.

Quintana, S. M., Aboud, F. E., Chao, R. K., Contreras-Grau, J., Cross, W. E., Hudley, C., ... Vietze, D. L. (2006). Race, ethnicity, and culture in child development: contemporary research and future directions. *Child Development*, *77*, 1129–1141.

Ray, B. (2005). *Canada: policy changes integration challenges in an increasingly diverse society*. Washington, DC: Migration Information Source, Migration Policy Institute. Retrieved from http://www.migrationinformation.org/Profiles/display.cfm?ID=348 (accessed September 18, 2006).

Rumbaut, R. G. (1999). Passages to adulthood: The adaptation of children and youth of immigrants in Southern California. In D. J. Herandez (Ed.), *Children of immigrants: Health, adjustment, and public assistance* (pp. 478–545). Washington, DC: National Academic Press.

Redfield, R., Linton, R., & Herskovits, M. (1936). Memorandum on the study of acculturation. *American Anthropologist*, *38*, 149–152.

Rudmin, F. (2009). Constructs, measurements and models of acculturation and acculturative stress. *International Journal of Intercultural Relations*, *33*, 106–123.

Ruesch, J., Jacobsen, A., & Loeb, M. B. (1948). Acculturation and illness. *Psychological Monographs*, *62*, 1–40.

Ryder, A. G., Alden, L. E., & Paulhus, D. L. (2000). Is acculturation unidimensional or bidimensional? A head- to-head comparison in the prediction of personality, self-identity, and adjustment. *Journal of Personality and Social Psychology*, *79*, 49–65.

Sabatier, C., & Berry, J. W. (2008). The role of family acculturation, parental style and perceived discrimination in the adaptation of second generation immigrant youth in France and Canada. *European Journal of Developmental Psychology*, *5*, 159–185.

Sam, D., & Berry, I. W. (Eds). (2006). *Cambridge handbook of acculturation psychology*. Cambridge, England: Cambridge University Press.

Santisteban, D.A., & Mitrani, V. B. (2003). The influence of acculturation processes on the family. In K. M. Chun, P. B. Organista, & G. Marin (Eds.), *Acculturation: Advances in theory, measurement, and applied research* (pp. 121–135). Washington, DC: American Psychological Association.

Santisteban, D. A., Muir-Malcolm, J. A., Mitrani, V. B., & Szapocznik, J. (2002). Integrating the study of ethnic culture and family psychology intervention science. In H. A. Liddle, D. A. Santisteban, D. A. Levant, & H. J. Bray (Eds.), *Family psychology: Science-based interventions* (pp. 331–351). Washington, DC: American Psychological Association.

Sarkisian, N., Gerena, M., & Gerstel, N. (2006). Extended family ties among Mexican, Puerto Ricans, and Whites: Superintegration or disintegration? *Family Relations*, *55*, 331–344.

Schmidt, R. (2007). Comparing federal government immigrant settlement policies in Canada and the United States. *American Review of Canadian Studies*, *37*, 103–122.

Sewell, W. H., Hauser, R. M., & Wolf, W. C. (1980). Sex, schooling, and occupational status. *American Journal of Sociology*, *83*, 551–583.

Sluzki, C. E. (1979). Migration and family conflict. *Family Process*, *18*, 379–390.

Snauwaert, B., Soenens, B., Vanbeselaere, N., & Boen, F. (2003). When integration does not necessarily imply integration: Different conceptualizations of acculturation orientations lead to different classifications. *Journal of Cross-Cultural Psychology*, *32*, 231–239.

Statistics Canada (2006). *2006 Census: Immigration in Canada: A portrait of the foreign-born population, 2006 Census: Highlights*. Retrieved from http://www.census2006.ca/census-recensement/2006/as-sa/97–ca/census- recensement/200557/p1-eng.cfm (accessed April 8, 2010).

Stonequest, E. (1961). *The marginal man: A study in personality and culture conflict*. New York: Russel and Russel Inc.

Suárez-Orozco, C., Carhill, A., & Chuang, S. S. (2011). Immigrant children: Making a new life. In S. S. Chuang & R. P. Moreno (Eds.), *Immigrant children: Change, adaptation, and cultural transformation* (pp. 7–26). Lanham, MA: Lexington Books.

Suárez-Orozco, C., & Suárez-Orozco, M. M. (2001). *Children of immigration. Cambridge*, MA: Harvard University Press.

Super, S., & Harkness, C. M. (2002). Culture and parenting. In M. H. Bornstein (Ed.), *Handbook of parenting: Vol. 4 Social conditions and applied parenting* (2nd ed., pp. 59–93). Mahwah, NJ: Erlbaum.

Szapocznik, J., & Kurtines, W. M. (1993). Family psychology and cultural diversity: Opportunities for theory, research, and application. *American Psychologist*, *48*, 400–407. DOI: 10.1037/0003–1037/066X.48.4.400.

Tamis-LeMonda, C. S. (2004). Conceptualizing fathers' roles: Playmates and more. *Human Development, 47,* 220–227.

Tamis-LeMonda, C. S., Way, N., Hughes, D., Yoshikawa, H., Kahana-Kalman, R. & Niwa, E. (2008). Parents' goals for children: The dynamic co-existence of collectivism and individualism. *Social Development, 17,* 183–209.

Triandis, H. C. (1995). *Individualism and collectivism.* Boulder, CO: Westview Press.

Trickett, E. J., & Jones, C. J. (2007). Adolescent culture brokering and family functioning: A study of families from Vietnam. *Cultural Diversity and Ethnic Minority Psychology, 13,* 143–150.

Tsai, J. L., Chentsova-Dutton, Y., & Wong, Y. (2002). Why and how researchers should study ethnic identity, acculturation, and cultural orientation. In G. C. N. Hall & M. H. Bond (Eds.), *Asian American psychology: The science of lives in context* (pp. 41–66). Washington, DC: American Psychological Association.

Tsai, J. L., Ying, Y. W., & Lee, P. A. (2001). Cultural predictors of self-esteem: A study of Chinese American female and male young adults. *Cultural Diversity and Ethnic Minority Psychology, 7,* 284–297.

Tse, L. (1995a). Language brokering among Latino adolescents: Prevalence, attitudes, and school performance. *Hispanic Journal of Behavioral Sciences, 17,* 180–193.

Tse, L. (1995b). When students translate for parents: Effects of language brokering. *CABE Newsletter, 17,* 16–17.

Tse, L. (1996). Language brokering in linguistic minority communities: The case of Chinese and Vietnamese-American students. *Bilingual Research Journal, 20,* 485–498.

Tseng, V., & Fuligni, A. (2000). Parent-adolescent language use and relationships among immigrant families with East Asian, Filipino, and Latin American backgrounds. *Journal of Marriage and Family, 62,* 465–476.

Umaña-Taylor, A. (2003). Language brokering as a stressor for immigrant children and their families. In M. Coleman & L. Ganong (Eds.), *Points and counterpoints: Controversial relationship and family issues in the 21st century: An anthology* (pp. 157–159). Los Angeles, CA: Roxbury.

United Nations. (2005). Trends in the total migrant stock. *Department of Economic and Social Affairs: Population Division.* Retrieved from http://www.un.org/esa/population/publications/migration/UN_Migrant_Stock_Documentation_2005.pdf (accessed July 4, 2011).

U.S. Census Bureau. (1992). *General population characteristics: United States (Current Population Reports CP-1–CP-1).* Washington, DC: Department of Commerce.

U.S. Census Bureau. (2006). *Census Bureau data shows key population changes across nation.* Press release on August 15, 2006.

Valdés, G. (1996). *Con respeto: Bridging the distances between culturally diverse families and schools.* New York: Teachers College Press.

Valdés, G. (Ed.). (2003). *Expanding definitions of giftedness: The case of young interpreters from immigrant countries.* Mahwah, NJ: Erlbaum.

Valenzuela, A. (1999). Gender roles and settlement activities among children and their immigrant families. *American Behavioral Scientist, 42,* 720–742.

Van Oudenhoven, J. P. (2006). Immigrants. In D. L. Sam & J. W. Berry (Eds.), *Cambridge handbook of acculturation psychology* (pp.163–180). Cambridge, MA: Cambridge University Press.

Walinchowski, M. (2001). Language brokering: Laying the foundation for success and bilingualism. In R. Lara-Alecio (Chair), *Symposium conducted at the Annual Educational Research Exchange,* College Station, TX.

Ward, C. (1996). Acculturation. In D. Landis & R. Bhagat (Eds.), *Handbook of intercultural training* (2nd ed., pp. 124–147). Newbury Park, CA: Sage.

Weisskirch, R. S. (2005). The relationship of language brokering to ethnic identity for Latino early adolescents. *Hispanic Journal of Behavioral Sciences, 27,* 286–299.

Weisskirch, R. S., & Alva, S. A. (2002). Language brokering and the acculturation of Latino children. *Hispanic Journal of Behavioral Sciences, 24,* 369–378.

White, R. M. B., Roosa, M. W., Weaver, S. R., & Nair, R. L. (2009). Cultural and contextual influences on parenting in Mexican American families. *Journal of Marriage and Family, 71,* 61–79.

Whiting, B. B. (1974). Folk wisdom and child rearing. *Merrill-Palmer Quarterly, 20,* 9–19.

Yaman, A., Mesman, J., van IJzendoorn, M. H., Bakermans-Kranenburg, M. J., & Linting, M. (2010). Parenting in an individualistic culture with a collectivistic background: The case of Turkish immigrant families with toddlers in the Netherlands. *Journal of Child and Family Studies*, *19*, 617–628.

Zhou, M. (1997). Segmented assimilation: Issues, controversies, and recent research on the new second generation. *International Migration Review*, *31*, 975–1008.

19 Economic Distress and Poverty in Families

M. Brent Donnellan, Monica J. Martin,
Katherine J. Conger, and Rand D. Conger

The first decade of the twenty-first century was characterized by relatively high levels of economic distress in the US. For example, the decade saw the highest level of unemployment since the early 1980s (Gomstyn, 2009; Irwin & Shin, 2009); economic growth averaged slightly over 2% per year since 2000, compared with 3% per year during the previous two decades and 4% in the 1960s (U.S. Department of Commerce, 2009); and there were declines in the median family income adjusted for inflation from 2000 to 2009 (U.S. Bureau of the Census, 2010). In fact, according to the National Bureau of Economic Research, two periods of recession occurred in the US during the years between 2001 and 2010: the period from March of 2001 to November of 2001 and again from December of 2007 to June of 2009. This second recession represented the longest period of economic decline in the US since the Second World War, leading many to refer to it as the Great Recession. The Great Recession produced high levels of unemployment (9.6% from January to December of 2010 as opposed to 4.0% in 2000; U.S. Bureau of Labor Statistics, 2011) and high levels of poverty (13.5% of families in 2009 and 42.6 million people; DeNavas-Walt, Proctor, & Smith, 2010; additional economic trends can be found in Edin & Kissane, 2010 and the National Center for Family and Marriage Research, 2011). The unfortunate reality is that the economic conditions of many families deteriorated in the first decade of the new millennium (Conger, Conger, & Martin, 2010).

In light of these trends, the goal of this chapter is to provide an overview of contemporary perspectives linking economic conditions to family processes and child development. We first provide a broad summary of the existing literature evaluating the correlates of low income and low socioeconomic status (SES). We then describe three theoretical models linking economic distress to family processes and developmental outcomes, and summarize research providing support for these models. We conclude by identifying directions for future theoretical development and outlining limitations in the existing literature.

KEY ISSUES OF SOCIOECONOMIC STATUS (SES) AND HUMAN DEVELOPMENT

The literature evaluating the association between socioeconomic status and adult romantic relationships and developmental outcomes supports two broad generalizations: (1) low socioeconomic status is negatively related to adult romantic relationship quality and stability; and (2) low socioeconomic status is negatively related to developmental outcomes in children and adults including achievement, physical health, and mental health. Our review is relatively brief and selective, given space constraints; we provide illustrative findings and reference major review articles.

Throughout the chapter, we use terms such as low income and low SES more or less interchangeably. Strictly speaking, income is only one aspect of SES, which also includes education and occupational prestige (see Conger & Donnellan, 2007; Conger et al., 2010). Duncan and Magnuson (2003) have suggested that researchers disaggregate these components of SES because they may have different trajectories and differentially predict family processes and developmental outcomes. This is an important conceptual point but researchers often struggle to attain this ideal in practice. Fortunately, measures of income, occupational prestige, and education are generally positively correlated. Thus, our review will treat the finer distinctions between SES and income somewhat loosely with the caveat that it might be difficult to precisely judge which aspects of SES are driving the reported effects. We revisit this issue in our discussion of future directions.

Indicators of Low SES are Associated with Relationship Distress and Divorce

Karney, Garvan, and Thomas (2003) conducted a survey of over 6,000 residents of Florida, Texas, California, and New York and found that individuals with lower incomes were less satisfied with their relationships in comparison with individuals from higher income brackets. Similar associations between economic distress and relationship satisfaction have been reported by others (e.g., Fox & Chancey, 1998; Hardie & Lucas, 2010; Rauer, Karney, Garvan, & Hou, 2008).

Past explanations for the connection between income and relationship difficulties have alluded to the idea that values about marriage and committed partnerships may vary by social class or income. However, Karney et al. (2003) found that individuals from all income groups valued marriage in their sample of 4,008 residents of Florida. In particular, 91% of the low income sample agreed or strongly agreed with the question: "A happy, healthy marriage is one of the most important things in life." The percentages were nearly identical to the middle and high incomes groups (92.1 and 93.8%). In addition, never married participants from lower income groups were more likely to want to be married (90%) than unmarried participants with middle and high incomes (76.1 and 63.1%, respectively). Based on these and other similar findings, Karney and Bradbury (2005) concluded that there was little reason to support interventions aimed at strengthening values associated with marriage among lower income populations, because pro-relationship values do not seem to be a viable explanation for the connections between income and relationship difficulties. A more plausible explanation is that couples with fewer resources must simply cope with a greater number of stressful conditions than more affluent couples.

Indeed, a straightforward explanation for the associations between income and relationship difficulties comes from a detailed study of conflict reported by Papp, Cummings, and Goeke-Morey (2009) using a diary study of 100 married couples. Although money was not the most common source of conflict, conflicts that involved money were more intense and difficult to resolve than non-money conflicts. Likewise, Karney et al. (2003) found that a lack of money was a frequent source of disagreements in relationships and that there was a negative association between financial strain and relationship satisfaction. In short, economic distress may generate the kinds of conflicts that are particularly detrimental to relationship quality.

Past research has shown that marital quality or satisfaction is one of the primary predictors of relationship instability (e.g., Karney & Bradbury, 1995); thus, it is not that surprising that there is also evidence linking SES with rates of divorce (Amato, Booth, Johnson, & Rogers, 2007; Karney & Bradbury, 2005; Popenoe, 2007). For example, Bramlett and Mosher (2002) estimated that 44% of low income first marriages dissolve within 10 years, whereas that figure was 23% for high income unions. Consistent with these findings is evidence pointing to increased marital stability for college graduates (Amato, 2010). In short, there appear to be robust connections between economic stress and relationship conflict, dissatisfaction, and instability.

Low SES is Negatively Associated with Developmental Outcomes for both Children and Adults

A succinct generalization of the vast literature evaluating associations between socioeconomic conditions and the developmental outcomes of children (e.g., Bradley & Corwyn, 2002) is provided by Huston and Bentley (2010): "Children growing up in poverty are at a disadvantage in almost every domain of development" (p. 417). Although the effects for income tend to be small (e.g., Votruba-Drzal, 2006), some very large effects for cognitive outcomes have been reported (e.g., Noble, Norman, & Farah, 2005). Previous research has indicated that the deleterious effects of income may be more pronounced at extremely low levels; thus, an important caveat is that aggregated effect sizes may obscure these types of non-linear effects for income (Duncan & Brooks-Gunn, 2000; Huston & Bentley, 2010). It is also possible that overall effect sizes may vary by domain (e.g., cognitive versus emotional outcomes). And even small effect sizes are important, especially given that some outcomes in this literature actually involve matters of life and death. For example, Duncan and Brooks-Gunn (2000) noted that the risk for child mortality is 1.7 times higher for poor as opposed to non-poor children (p. 188). Indeed, SES has been linked to a range of injuries, developmental insults (e.g., levels of lead in the blood), and childhood diseases (see Bradley & Corwyn, 2002).

In addition to health outcomes, SES is negatively associated with indices of childhood cognitive development and achievement like IQ scores, language development, and high school drop-out rates (see Bradley & Corwyn, 2002; Brooks-Gunn & Duncan, 1997). Some evidence suggests that early exposure to poverty is particularly deleterious for achievement outcomes (Huston & Bentley, 2010). For example, Duncan, Yeung, Brooks-Gunn, and Smith (1998) found economic conditions in early childhood had pronounced effects on achievement outcomes like the total years of schooling and high-school completion. One explanation is that low SES has important effects on developing brains such that exposure to disadvantage in the first several years of life may negatively impact brain systems and regions such as those involved in language (e.g., Noble, McCandliss, & Farah, 2007). It is not difficult to imagine how early impairments involving language development have the ability to generate longer-term difficulties in achievement-oriented contexts because of their accumulating effects over the course of development (see also Votruba-Drzal, 2006).

Socioeconomic conditions are also associated with child social and emotional outcomes, although research findings in this area have not been as consistent nor have effects been as strong as those findings linking SES with cognitive ability and health (see Bradley & Corwyn, 2002). Nonetheless, low SES still appears to be an important predictor of higher rates of internalizing and externalizing problems in children. For instance, Kim-Cohen, Moffitt, Caspi, and Taylor (2004) reported that socioeconomic disadvantage was positively correlated with antisocial behavior in children. Likewise, Votruba-Drzal (2006) found that both family income during early childhood and middle-childhood were related to behavior problems in middle childhood. In contrast, middle childhood academic skills were only related to early income. This pattern is consistent with the idea that early socioeconomic deprivation may impair or delay the development of basic cognitive abilities, which sets up a cascade of difficulties (see Masten et al., 2005). On the other hand, the processes linking income and behavior problems might involve the kinds of parenting practices like monitoring and warmth that are more immediately responsive to income changes (Votruba-Drzal, 2006).

Research has also revealed links between SES and adult developmental outcomes. For example, low SES in the family of origin was associated with internalizing and externalizing psychiatric problems in adulthood (Johnson, Cohen, Dohrenwend, Link, & Brook, 1999). Likewise, Miech, Caspi, Moffitt, Wright, and Silva (1999) found that low family of origin SES predicted anxiety problems in young adulthood. Miech and colleagues also reported that low SES in the family of origin predicted antisocial disorders in young adulthood controlling for earlier behavioral problems, while antisocial disorders in adolescence also predicted later educational attainment. This analytic strategy helps address potential selection effects whereby individuals with certain behavioral tendencies are at risk both for attaining low social status and for developing antisocial disorders (see also Dohrenwend et al., 1992). The Miech et al. report increases confidence in possible causal connections between early SES and later development. In addition, there is evidence linking socioeconomic disadvantage with depression (Lorant et al., 2003) and other mental health conditions in adults (Sareen, Afifi, McMillian, & Asmundson, 2011). In particular, Sareen et al. (2011) demonstrated that a longitudinal drop in household income was associated with increased risk of psychiatric disorders in a two-wave national survey that occurred during the recent economic downturn.

SES also appears to have impacts on adult health outcomes. Chapman, Fiscella, Kawachi, and Duberstein (2010) found that SES was associated with all causes of mortality using a cohort study of individuals in midlife. Of note, the impact of low SES was not statistically significant when controlling for personality attributes and risky health behaviors like smoking. This suggests that particular behaviors and personal characteristics may help to explain connections between SES and early mortality (see Mackenbach, 2010).

THEORIES LINKING ECONOMIC CONDITIONS TO FAMILY FUNCTIONING AND CHILD DEVELOPMENT

As reviewed in the last section, there is considerable evidence suggesting that socioeconomic disadvantage is correlated with negative outcomes for adults and children (see also Haas, 2006). This research can be seen as a subset of work on health disparities from social epidemiology indicating that socially and economically disadvantaged adults and children are at increased risk for physical, emotional, and behavioral problems (Berkman & Kawachi, 2000; Bradley & Corwyn, 2002; McLeod & Shanahan, 1996; Oakes & Rossi, 2003). Beyond simply documenting associations between SES and individual well-being, developmental researchers are particularly interested in uncovering the proximal mechanisms that link socioeconomic conditions to human health and behavior. In this section, we focus on family processes as an important conduit for understanding how socioeconomic conditions are translated into differences in physical health and psychological functioning.

We want to be explicit that the three models described in this section are only a part of the complicated web of factors that connect broader socioeconomic conditions with developmental outcomes. There are a number of other plausible mediators beyond the family that are likely to be important including, but certainly not limited to, childcare settings, qualities of the physical environment, schools, neighborhoods, and peers (see Huston & Bentley, 2010). However, the point of a conceptual model is to provide a simplified account of reality that has scientific and practical value. Thus, we begin this section with a brief discussion about theoretical frameworks and assumptions about human development.

A COMMENT ON PERSPECTIVES ON HUMAN BEHAVIOR AND THE UTILITY OF MODELS

Social scientists use theoretical frameworks to generate testable models to better understand and explain human behavior. Theoretical frameworks, and thus models, are rooted in broader principles about the causes of human behavior. The first two models that we describe in this section—the *family stress model* and the *parental investment model*—stem from what can be termed a *social influence* (or *social causation*) perspective (see e.g., Conger & Donnellan, 2007; Dohrenwend et al., 1992; Haas, 2006; Johnson et al., 1999). As the name implies, the assumption is that economic conditions create variations in psychological and physical outcomes.

The opposing *social selection* perspective posits that economic conditions are largely created by personal characteristics through processes of evocation and selection (e.g., Scarr & McCartney, 1983). From this perspective, individual differences in traits such as intelligence and personality facilitate the development of social advantages (e.g., SES) and are also transmitted from parents to children. That is, certain parental characteristics help account for both their economic success and the adjustment of their children. One potential mechanism for such a connection is through the genetic transmission of SES-promoting attributes like cognitive abilities and self-control (see Rowe & Rodgers, 1997). To be sure, there is intriguing evidence that levels of self-control and IQ, two genetically influenced attributes, are prospectively linked with SES (e.g., Moffitt et al., 2011).[1]

---

[1] These issues are further complicated by research indicating that SES moderates the impact of genetic factors on the IQ of children (e.g., Tucker-Drob, Rhemtulla, Harden, Turkheimer, & Fask, 2011; Turkheimer, Haley, Waldron, D'Onofrio, & Gottesman, 2003).

Regardless of the mode of transmission, central to the social selection perspective is the proposition that the observed associations among SES, family processes, and child and adolescent development result from their common dependence on antecedent personal characteristics and dispositions.

Dichotomies rooted in internal versus external causes of human behavior are common in the social sciences and they have a long intellectual history (see Turkheimer, 2004). Debates between social influence and social selection perspectives are similar to debates about nature versus nature (e.g., Rutter, 2002) and the importance of personality factors versus situational factors in explaining behavior (e.g., Donnellan, Lucas, & Fleeson, 2009). Our perspective is that these either/or arguments fail to account for the complexity of the existing research findings. A strict social influence perspective is hard to reconcile with evidence pointing to the life course consequences of individual differences in cognitive ability and personality (see e.g., Roberts, Kuncel, Shiner, Caspi, & Goldberg, 2007), whereas a strict social selection perspective is hard to reconcile with experimental and quasi-experimental research linking income supplementation to improvements in child outcomes (see Huston & Bentley, 2010, for a summary). Likewise, strict social selection arguments are difficult to reconcile with genetically-informed research suggesting that there are shared environmental influences on child and adolescent psychopathology (Burt, 2009).

In light of these considerations, we believe that *both* social influence and social selection likely characterize the processes linking socioeconomic conditions and human development. Such a position is consistent with *transactional models of human development* (e.g., Sameroff, 2010) that offer the insight that, "developmental outcomes are neither a function of the individual alone nor a function of the experiential context alone" (Sameroff & MacKenzie, 2003, p. 614). Accordingly, Conger and his colleagues have proposed an interactionist (Conger et al., 2010; Conger & Donnellan, 2007) or transactional model (Donnellan, Conger, McAdams, & Neppl, 2009) linking personal characteristics and economic distress with child development.[2] This interactionist model is the third model described in this section and is one way to characterize the interplay between social influence and social selection. This model also embodies our expectations for future research connecting economic conditions and human development as researchers move to more formally embrace transactional perspectives.

Nonetheless, it is important to acknowledge that all models are wrong (Box, 1976; Meehl, 1990) because a model simply, "cannot capture the complexities of the real world which they purport to represent" (MacCallum, 2003, p. 114). Models are therefore evaluated in terms of how well they aid in the understanding complex phenomena, their usefulness in accurately predicting outcomes, and in some cases, for how well they provide an empirically supported rationale for designing intervention and prevention programs. This last consideration is a major reason why we highlight social influence models. Social influence models highlight the proximal environmental processes linking economic conditions and psychological outcomes, and thus have seemingly straightforward implications for prevention and intervention efforts (see e.g., Gershoff, Aber, Raver, & Lennon, 2007, p. 92).

THE FAMILY STRESS MODEL (FSM)

The family stress model[3] was initially described and evaluated using data from 451 families with adolescents from rural Iowa in a series of papers published in the early 1990s (Conger et al., 1992, 1993).

---

[2] Conger and Donnellan (2007) and Conger et al. (2010) used the term interactionist to describe this model, whereas Donnellan et al. (2009) used the term transactional. Donnellan et al. suggested that the transactional label avoids any confusion stemming from the fact that interaction has both a conceptual meaning and a stricter statistical meaning in the literature (see also Caspi, 1998). We use the term interactionist here to maintain consistency with the bulk of the previous work on this model.

[3] There is a long tradition of conceptualizing how stress is related to family processes in the social sciences. The most famous of these models include Reuben Hill's (1949) ABC-X model and McCubbin and Patterson's (1983) Double

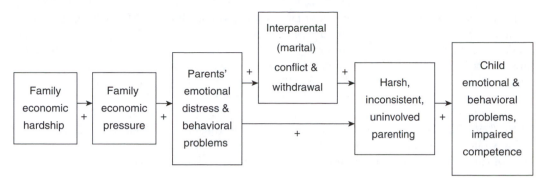

FIGURE 19.1 The family stress model.

A general outline of the FSM is presented in Figure 19.1, beginning with the proposal that economic hardship leads to economic pressure in families. Economic hardships such as income reductions (either through unemployment or underemployment) and financial obligations impose difficulties in daily living that are expected to affect intrapersonal and interpersonal distress, and thus family functioning. Thus, hardship is expected to influence family members primarily through the economic pressures it generates. Put differently, pressures give psychological meaning to the economic hardship experienced by families.

Economic pressure involves the sometimes severe problems created by financial hardships, such as being unable to afford the basic necessities of life or being unable to keep up with monthly bills. The rationale for the claim that economic pressure is linked to distress is based on the idea that economic pressure is a frustrating event and therefore creates a negative affective state (see e.g., Berkowitz, 1989). The FSM proposes that this negative affective state includes parental emotional distress and even behavioral problems, which lead to disruptions in couple functioning because of increased conflicts in the relationship stemming from financial concerns (see Papp et al., 2009). These negative interactions generate global dissatisfaction and even relationship instability. This process then has intergenerational consequences when parental affective states disrupt supportive parent–child relationships and effective parenting practices (see also Gershoff et al., 2007). In other words, disruptions in the marital dyad spillover to the parent–child relationship to exacerbate psychosocial difficulties in children and adolescents according to the FSM. It is also theoretically plausible that conflict and discord in the marital dyad may have relatively direct effects on children and adolescents independent of parenting practices (see e.g., Davies & Woitach, 2008; Grych & Fincham, 1990); however, the canonical FSM emphasizes the spill-over from disrupted marriages to disrupted parent–child relationships.

The promising initial support for the FSM found in the Iowa sample (summarized in Conger & Conger, 2002) has been since replicated in a diverse set of studies. In particular, the basic pattern of predictions specified by the FSM have been supported by results from: (1) a national sample of families with preschool-aged boys and girls (Yeung, Linver, & Brooks-Gunn, 2002); (2) a national sample of young children and their families (Gershoff et al., 2007); (3) an urban sample of primarily low income minority families headed by a single-parent (Mistry, Lowe, Benner, & Chien, 2008);

ABC-X model. In these models, a stressor is any event that demands a behavioral response. We use the term "Family Stress Model" in the current chapter to refer to the specific model linking economic hardship to family process developed by Conger and his colleagues beginning in the early 1990s. It is important to emphasize that the Conger Family Stress Model is broadly compatible with these other models of family stress that describe how factors external to the family unit impinge upon the family system to generate both intrapersonal and interpersonal difficulties.

(4) an ethnically-diverse national sample of families with young children (Mistry, Biesanz, Taylor, Burchinal, & Cox, 2004); (5) two samples of African American families living in urban and rural locations (Conger, Wallace, Sun, Simons, McLoyd, & Brody, 2002; Scaramella, Sohr-Preston, Callahan, & Mirabile, 2008); (6) samples of European American and Mexican American families living in Southern California (Behnke et al., 2008; Parke et al., 2004); and (7) a sample of Chinese American families living in Northern California (Benner & Kim, 2010). Moreover, key predictions from the FSM have been tested and empirically supported in families living outside of the US (Aytaç & Rankin, 2009; Kinnunen & Feldt, 2004; Kwon, Rueter, Lee, Koh, & Ok, 2003; Lorenz, Hraba, Conger, & Pechacova, 1996; Solantaus, Leinonen, & Punamäki, 2004). In short, a wide range of studies have found support for the processes embodied in the FSM.

The Parental Investment Model (PIM)

A second influential model linking economic conditions with child development is the parental investment model (Becker & Tomes, 1986; Bradley & Corwyn, 2002; Corcoran & Adams, 1997; Duncan & Magnuson, 2003; Linver, Brooks-Gunn, & Kohen, 2002). The PIM is based on an economic tradition in developmental science that focuses on how resources are allocated and invested to produce desired outcomes in the face of constraints (see Foster, 2002). The PIM focuses on how resources are generated and distributed within families. Resources in this perspective cover commodities such as parental time and money, and take the specific form of the number of books and other learning-related materials that are provided in the home, the time parents spend assisting children with schoolwork, as well as financial expenditures on tutoring, training, and other cognitively enriching activities (e.g., music lessons). Other investments such as financial expenditures on health through nutrition and medical care, and the choice of neighborhoods where the family resides can be considered under the PIM (see e.g., Gershoff et al., 2007). The starting point of the PIM is the idea that families differ in how they invest their limited resources.

Ultimately, the PIM generates a fairly straightforward prediction that more economically advantaged families have more resources to invest in their children's long-term developmental outcomes (e.g., educational attainment). Families who are faced with a severely constrained financial budget will likely consume much of their resources to survive in the short-term (e.g., by buying food and paying rent), whereas families with greater economic resources are able to make significant long-term investments in the development of their children. Different parents may also make different decisions about resource allocation depending on their expectations for the future. Parents may also differ in terms of the value they place on certain developmental outcomes (e.g., Foster, 2002). Different parents may place more or less importance on certain developmental outcomes. Indeed, there is a long sociological tradition pointing to a connection between occupational status and values related to childrearing (e.g., Kohn, 1959, 1963). These considerations can affect how parents invest their limited resources.

The core propositions of the PIM have empirical support as there is evidence that family income affects the types of investments parents make in their children (Bradley & Corwyn, 2002; Bradley, Corwyn, McAdoo, & García Coll, 2001; Davis-Kean, 2005). Likewise, family income during childhood and adolescence is positively related to academic, financial, and occupational success in adulthood (Bradley & Corwyn, 2002; Corcoran & Adams, 1997; Teachman, Paasch, Day, & Carver 1997; but see Mayer, 1997). Especially important, Linver et al. (2002) found that the connection between income and early cognitive development was largely explained by the parental investments such as providing educational materials and learning opportunities. Similar findings were reported by Yeung, Linver, and Brooks-Gunn (2002). More recently, Gershoff et al. (2007) reported that parental investments were associated with children's cognitive development. In short, there is support for the mediating processes between income and child development proposed by the PIM.

An intriguing possibility emerging from the findings of recent studies (e.g., Gershoff et al., 2007; Yeung et al., 2002) is that PIM processes may explain the connections between family financial resources and children's cognitive development, whereas FSM processes may account for connections between family financial conditions and children's social and emotional functioning (Conger et al., 2010). Limited economic resources may constrain the ability of parents to provide books and other educational materials to their children, limit their efforts to get involved in their children's school, and prevent them from exposing children to intellectually enriching activities like trips to the library or zoo. It may be that these kinds of parental investments and behaviors have more direct links with the development of cognitive skills than with self-regulation and social skills (see Gershoff et al., 2007). Thus, there is the possibility that both PIM and FSM accounts may have merit in terms of explaining the connections between economic conditions and child development, but the two models may be more appropriate for predicting different types of outcomes. The PIM might better account for cognitive outcomes whereas the FSM might better explain socioemotional outcomes. For example, the FSM emphasizes the stress-related emotional and behavioral disruptions in the lives of parents that may affect similar responses by their children. We revisit this possibility in our concluding discussions about future directions.

The Interactionist Model of Socioeconomic Influence (IMSI)

The preceding discussion demonstrates that there is empirical support for the social influence processes specified by both the FSM and PIM. Yet, there is also increasing evidence supporting the alternative social selection perspective—the idea that the characteristics of individuals shape both their socioeconomic attainments and the qualities of their family relationships. For instance, there is growing recognition that relatively enduring personal characteristics are associated with family dynamics such as relationship satisfaction and stability (e.g., Asendorpf, 2002; Dyrenforth, Kashy, Donnellan, & Lucas, 2010; Karney & Bradbury, 1995; Robins, Caspi, & Moffit, 2000) and parenting behaviors (Belsky, 1984; Prinzie, Stams, Deković, Reijntjes, & Belsky, 2009). Likewise, certain early emerging individual differences like self-control appear to promote economic success (e.g., Moffitt et al., 2011) and job performance (Judge, Higgins, Thoresen, & Barrick, 1999). Thus, extant research supports both a social influence and a social selection perspective. For that reason, an inclusive model that incorporates both the processes of social influence and social selection to explain the associations between family dynamics and SES may hold the most theoretical promise.

Indeed, several studies have presented evidence that suggests the utility of such an approach. For example, as previously reviewed, Miech and colleagues (1999) showed that individuals with early proclivities toward antisocial behavior had lower educational attainment, and at the same time low attainment contributed to increased risk for antisocial disorders. Schoon et al. (2002) used data from two birth cohort studies in Britain and found that low SES in the family of origin predicted lower academic achievement and continuing life stress. Moreover, children's lower academic competence and higher life stress were associated with lower SES attainment in adulthood. Similarly, Wickrama, Conger, Lorenz, and Jung (2008) found that low SES in the family of origin increased risk for both mental and physical health problems during the transition to adulthood, which, in turn, predicted economic problems and poorer social circumstances during the early adult years.

These kinds of findings motivated the *Interactionist Model of Socioeconomic Influence* (IMSI) as described in Conger and Donnellan (2007). A version of this model is displayed in Figure 19.2. This model has explicit roles for both social selection mechanisms along with social influence mechanisms. Accordingly, the IMSI represents a transactional perspective on the connections between socioeconomic conditions and life span development. Consistent with the social influence perspective, the model presented in Figure 19.2 proposes that the SES of the first generation parents (G1) will directly impact family processes, which includes family stress processes like economic pressure, marital conflict, and parenting practices as well as specific parental investments as proposed by the PIM. Also consistent with the social influence perspective is the prediction that G1 SES will affect the second generation child's (G2) personal characteristics directly, as well as indirectly through these family processes. The IMSI also specifies continuity in SES and family processes from one generation to the next. The dashed pathways in Figure 19.2 illustrate how the IMSI incorporates social selection mechanisms: G2 personal characteristics predict G2's SES, family processes, and the adjustment of G2's children (G3). However, the IMSI does not propose that these selection mechanisms operate alone: G2 SES and family processes also are hypothesized to directly influence G3 children's development. Most important, the IMSI predicts that these G2 family processes and SES will affect G3 above and beyond the potential influence of G2 personal characteristics.

We should emphasize that aspects of the IMSI are consistent with earlier theoretical models in developmental psychology (e.g., Gottlieb, 1996; Magnusson & Stattin, 1998; Sameroff, 1995), which suggest that individual attributes and socioeconomic conditions will be interrelated across time and generations. For instance, Belsky (1984, p. 84) proposed that parental personality characteristics are associated with marital relationships, parenting, and working conditions in his model of the determinants of parenting, consistent with predictions from the IMSI.

Two recent reports from an intensive three generation study provide preliminary support for the dynamic interplay between social influence and social selection predicted by the IMSI. Schofield et al. (2011) demonstrated that family of origin SES and family processes during adolescence were associated with personality characteristics such as emotional stability and conscientiousness. These personal characteristics, in turn, predicted greater SES attainment in adulthood. Moreover, these attributes predicted less economic pressure, better intrapersonal functioning, and less conflict in relationships. Consistent with the emphasis on family processes in the IMSI, intrapersonal and parenting variables such as distressed marital relationships and warm parenting accounted for most of the observed connections between parent personality and child outcomes.

Martin et al. (2010) used data from the same project but focused on antisocial behavior as a key conduit for the intergenerational processes depicted by the IMSI. Martin and her colleagues showed that SES in the family of origin was negatively related to adolescent antisocial behaviors. These behaviors then predicted diminished SES in adulthood as well as fewer investments in offspring and heightened interpersonal disruptions and conflict. Intrapersonal disruptions such as emotional

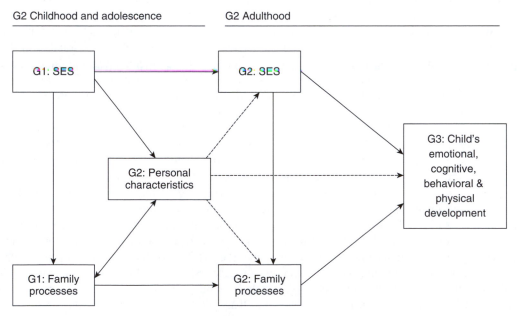

FIGURE 19.2   The Interactionist Model of Socioeconomic Influence (IMSI). Note: Solid arrows represent predictions consistent with the social influence perspective. Dashed arrows represent predictions consistent with the social selection perspective.

distress in parents, interpersonal hostility, and hostile parenting were consistent predictors of childhood expressions of antisocial behavior in the offspring of the focal participants in line with predictions from the IMSI. Other research from this three-generation study continues to produce similar findings (Conger et al., 2012). In short, existing research from a life span developmental perspective underscores our contention that both social influence and social selection processes are responsible for the coupling of SES and individual development. Likewise, these recent studies highlight the importance of family processes.

LIMITATIONS WITH EXISTING THEORY USE AND FUTURE THEORETICAL DIRECTIONS

Although we believe that the FSM, PIM, and IMSI are useful models for understanding how economic conditions are linked with family processes and individual development, we can offer several suggestions for additional theoretical development. As noted in the opening sections, we focused this chapter on family processes because we assume that the family is an important nexus for understanding connections between SES and developmental outcomes. However, contemporary ecological perspectives acknowledge that the family is only one context of human development among several (see Huston & Bentley, 2010). Thus, it will be important to position family processes within the context of neighborhoods, schools, and other microsystems identified by ecological perspectives on the family.

One example of this kind of theoretical extension comes from Gutman, McLoyd, and Tokoyawa (2005), who suggested that economic disadvantage can generate additional stress because of neighborhood conditions. Challenging neighborhood conditions, in turn, generate additional family stress. Thus, low income may contribute to parental distress both by intensifying economic pressure and by contributing to a stressful local ecology. An additional possibility is that low income and neighborhood disadvantage position children in school settings that are not maximally supportive of achievement. Challenges in school settings may act as an additional source of distress for parents and adversely impact the achievement of children. In short, we believe that the processes identified by the three models can be enriched by looking to systems beyond the family to better understand the multiple factors that contribute to broad connections between SES and developmental outcomes.

The possible moderating effects of personal, social, and cultural factors on SES, family stress, and family investment processes are also important arenas for future theoretical development. To be sure, socioeconomic distress does not have the same effects on all individuals and children (e.g., Kim-Cohen et al., 2004). Therefore, an important task is to specify and test those factors that attenuate or exacerbate the pathways highlighted by the models described in this chapter. Although very large sample sizes are often required to detect such statistical interactions reliably (see Donnellan, Conger, McAdams, & Neppl, 2009), there are hints that personality dispositions like mastery may help protect families from the adverse impact of economic pressure on family processes (Conger & Conger, 2002). Researchers have long proposed that some personal characteristics like a general sense of self-efficacy and personal mastery have "stress-suppressing" effects (e.g., Ensel & Lin, 1991; Thoits, 2006), whereas other attributes like neuroticism may exacerbate the distressing consequences of stressful events and interpersonal conflict (e.g., Bolger & Shilling, 1991; Bolger & Zuckerman, 1995). In light of these considerations, there is an increasing appreciation for the role that individual differences and social resources may play in the processes linking economic conditions with family functioning (e.g., Conger & Conger, 2002).

In particular, Conger and Conger (2002) suggested that personal characteristics and social resources can have both main effects on the elements of the FSM as well as moderating effects on the connections between the elements specified in the FSM. For instance, they described evidence that a sense of personal agency and mastery predicted longitudinal declines in economic pressure and helped to buffer the impact of economic pressure on depression. Thus, an internal locus of control and personal sense of effectiveness may help parents cope with economic pressure and may moderate the connections between economic pressure and their psychological distress. Likewise, social resources may also play a moderating role in the family stress process. For example, Conger, Rueter, and Elder (1999) found that high levels of spousal supportiveness could also attenuate the connection between economic pressure and emotional distress. Thus, an important extension of the FSM is to conceptualize and then empirically evaluate those factors that moderate the pathways identified in the model.

We also suspect that cultural factors modify some of the key family processes linking economic hardship with the development of children and adolescents discussed in this chapter. For example, Conger and Donnellan (2007) noted that interparental conflict demonstrated a substantial direct path with child adjustment problems in the Parke et al. (2004) study of Mexican American families, whereas such a direct effect is not consistently found in the Iowa dataset, or in Parke's European American sample.[4] Interparental conflict may be especially counter-normative in Mexican and Mexican American families, and therefore, especially distressing for children in those families. This possibility led Conger and Donnellan to speculate that cultural values that strongly emphasize the importance of the family unit may explain the differences between the results for the Iowa and Parke et al. samples. Additional research and theoretical development is needed to understand how cultural values and norms may attenuate or accentuate pathways linking SES to human development. Likewise, additional research is needed to isolate direct and indirect associations between disrupted marriages and the development of children and adolescents.

A final important moderator of the effects of socioeconomic disadvantage on developmental outcomes is the age of the child. Families can experience economic hardships at different points in the family life cycle (e.g., job losses that accompany recessions can hit when children are infants, toddlers, or older). As we noted, it appears that early exposure to income deprivation is associated with difficulties in achievement-related domains of development, whereas both early exposure and more contemporaneous economic conditions are linked with behavioral and emotional difficulties. Much of the research investigating the PIM has involved younger children, whereas research investigating the FSM has involved older children. Rather than family stress processes being especially sensitive to economic conditions and more strongly associated with social and emotional problems, it may be that the greatest period of risk for such problems occurs in adolescence and, to a lesser extent, middle childhood. Studies that investigate parental investments with adolescent samples, as well as additional studies of family stress processes with young children are needed to definitively address these possibilities.

As suggested in a recent review by Conger et al. (2010), future theoretical developments would also benefit from a more nuanced view of SES. A more comprehensive assessment of SES by studying income, occupational status, and educational attainment from both a dynamic and interactive perspective is needed. All three of these SES-linked variables may change at different rates over time and these components of SES may interact with each other (i.e., combine in non-additive ways) to statistically predict outcomes of interest. For instance, Conger et al. (2010) noted that high educational attainment might be able to buffer or soften the impact of income reduction during periods of economic recession. In light of this possibility, we hope that future theories will strive to incorporate all three aspects of SES comprehensively and intensively.

In addition to future theoretical development, there is a pressing need to use better research designs to test the theoretical propositions embodied by the three models. A stronger empirical test of theoretical models generates increased confidence in those models. For instance, much of the

---

[4] The issue of whether interparental conflict has effects on children and adolescents apart from the proposed connection between marital conflict and disrupted parenting in the FSM is an issue of ongoing debate in the literature. We acknowledge there is research indicating that interparental conflict has a more or less direct impact on offspring apart from disrupted parenting (see e.g., Amato & Booth, 2001). Our point here is not to advocate for the canonical FSM position over other viewpoints; instead, we simply wish to emphasize that this topic represents an important area for future theoretical development and empirical work.

extant literature is based on correlational and observational studies, and many of the studies are cross-sectional. These designs limit theory evaluation because they provide weak grounds for making causal inferences about the processes under investigation. Fortunately, there is also an experimental literature involving intervention programs for low income families. Although the effects are often small and qualified by a number of factors, these kinds of studies provide some evidence for the general proposition that money causally matters for families and children (Gennetian & Miller, 2002; Huston et al., 2005; Leventhal & Brooks-Gunn, 2003; Morris, Duncan, & Clark-Kauffman, 2005; but see Leventhal, Fauth, & Brooks-Gunn, 2005). Taken as a whole, the experimental literature suggests that inferences about social influence processes are, at the very least, plausible. A limitation of experimental studies is that many of them have not directly measured family processes, making it difficult to determine whether the processes outlined by the FSM and PIM are the precise mechanisms responsible for any of the experimental effects.

An important quasi-experimental study, however, provided insights into the sorts of mediating processes that might explain the connections between income and child outcomes (Costello, Compton, Keeler, & Angold, 2003). Costello and her colleagues took advantage of a naturally occurring income supplementation in the form of a casino that opened on an American Indian reservation. Those families that received added income from the casino had children with fewer symptoms of externalizing problems. The primary mediator of these statistical effects involved family processes (especially those related to the FSM), as predicted by the models described in this chapter. To be sure, a precise understanding of intervening processes that connect SES with developmental outcomes is critical for designing effective interventions. This is one reason the FSM is valuable because it specifies family interactional processes as key conduits through which socioeconomic factors are connected with human development. We hope that future experimental and quasi-experimental research incorporates in-depth assessments of parenting practices and family investment processes to test whether these potentially mediating processes (derived from the models described in this chapter) are directly impacted by changes in socioeconomic conditions.

Perhaps the largest unresolved issue complicating the interpretation of the bulk of the existing evidence supporting the importance of family processes for understanding the connections between economic disadvantage and child development involves unmeasured genetic factors shared by parents and offspring (see D'Onofrio & Lahey, 2010). Thus, genetically-informed research will prove to be particularly important in addressing this concern. We should note that preliminary evidence by D'Onofrio and his colleagues (2009) suggests that social influence processes related to low income remain a factor in the association between family income and conduct problems in children even in genetically-informed research. That is, there is evidence that the association between family income and conduct problems is not purely genetic in origin—social environmental factors appear to be a factor in this connection.

More broadly, there is emerging evidence that environmental stress interacts with genetic factors to impact individual development (e.g., Guo, Roettger, & Cai, 2008; Moffitt, Caspi, & Rutter, 2006). Thus, we expect that both social influence and social selection processes will characterize the connections among SES, family processes, and individual lives as played out across generations and over the course of the life span. We do not expect that passive genetic factors are the sole explanation for associations among SES, family processes, and human development. Last, regardless of our intuitions, support for any theoretical model must ultimately be found from repeated testing of its predictions using multiple groups and multiple datasets with different research designs. We expect that such tests will be conducted with more frequency in the coming years.

CONCLUSION

The recent downturn in the global economy has underscored the fact that economic distress is a significant hardship faced by many families in the US and other developed countries. There is considerable evidence connecting low SES with a wide range of interpersonal challenges, physical health problems, and psychological difficulties in children and adults. The models in this chapter provide three different but ultimately complimentary perspectives on the processes connecting SES and developmental outcomes. The first two models reviewed, the FSM and PIM, stem from a social influence perspective, a perspective that has traditionally been assumed to be directly opposed to the social selection perspective. However, new theoretical developments have progressed beyond these assumptions to incorporate the interplay among individual differences, SES, and family relationships such as those proposed by the IMSI. Compared with models that are built exclusively on one tradition or the other, attention to these interactionist models may better account for the complexity of the existing research findings, and may inform the development of additional integrative theoretical frameworks.

To be sure, there are enduring tensions between social influence and social selection perspectives in discussions linking economic conditions with human development. To our minds, theoretical and empirical progress often stalls when proponents of one perspective ignore the potential insights from the other perspective (see also D'Onofrio & Lahey, 2010). There are signs that this kind of counterproductive polarization is waning as transactional perspectives on the connections between SES and human development gain in acceptance (see Huston & Bentley, 2010). Indeed, exposure to high levels of economic stress is an unfortunate reality for many families and we believe that those theoretical models that more closely approximate reality will prove more useful for those researchers, practitioners, and policy-makers who are interested in improving the lives of families and children facing economic distress.

REFERENCES

Amato, P. R. (2010). Research on divorce: Continuing trends and new developments. *Journal of Marriage and Family*, *72*, 650–666.

Amato, P. R., & Booth, A. (2001). The legacy of parents' marital discord: Consequences for children's marital quality. *Journal of Personality and Social Psychology*, *81*, 627–638.

Amato, P. R., Booth, A., Johnson, D. R., & Rogers, S. J. (2007). *Alone together: How marriage in America is changing*. Boston, MA: Harvard University Press.

Asendorpf, J. B. (2002). Personality effects on personal relationships over the life span. In A. L. Vangelisti, H. T. Reis, & M. A. Fitzpatrick (Eds.), *Stability and change in relationships* (pp. 35–56). New York: Cambridge University Press.

Aytaç, I. A., & Rankin, B. H. (2009). Economic crisis and marital problems in Turkey: Testing the family stress model. *Journal of Marriage and Family*, *71*, 756–767.

Becker, G. S., & Tomes, N. (1986). Human capital and the rise and fall of families. *Journal of Labor Economics*, *4*, S1–S139.

Behnke, A. O., MacDermid, S. M., Coltrane, S. L., Parke, R. D., Duffy, S., & Widaman, K. F. (2008). Family cohesion in the lives of Mexican American and European American parents. *Journal of Marriage and Family*, *70*, 1045–1059.

Belsky, J. (1984). The determinants of parenting: A process model. *Child Development*, *55*, 83–96.

Benner, A. D., & Kim, S. Y. (2010). Understanding Chinese American adolescents' developmental outcomes: Insights from the family stress model. *Journal of Research on Adolescence*, *20*, 1–12.

Berkman, L. F., & Kawachi, I. (Eds.). (2000). *Social epidemiology*. New York: Oxford University Press.

Berkowitz, L. (1989). Frustration–aggression hypothesis: Examination and reformulation. *Psychological Bulletin*, *106*, 59–73.

Bolger, N., & Shilling, E. A. (1991). Personality and the problems of everyday life: The role of neuroticism in exposure and reactivity to daily stressors. *Journal of Personality*, *59*, 355–386.

Bolger, N., & Zuckerman, A. (1995). A framework for studying personality in the stress process. *Journal of Personality and Social Psychology*, *69*, 890–902.

Box, G. E. P. (1976). Science and statistics. *Journal of the American Statistical Association*, *71*, 791–799.

Bradley, R. H., & Corwyn, R. F. (2002). Socioeconomic status and child development. *Annual Review of Psychology*, *53*, 371–399.

Bradley, R. H., Corwyn, R. F., McAdoo, H. P., & García Coll, C. (2001). The home environments of children in the United States: Part I. Variations by age, ethnicity, and poverty status. *Child Development*, *72*, 1844–1867.

Bramlett, M. D, & Mosher, W. D. (2002). *Cohabitation, marriage, divorce, and remarriage in the United States*. Vital and Health Statistics, Series 23. Washington, DC: U.S. Government Printing Office.

Brooks-Gunn, J. & Duncan, G. (1997). The effects of poverty on children and youth. *The Future of Children*, *7*, 55–71.

Burt, S. A. (2009). Rethinking environmental contributions to child and adolescent psychopathology: A meta-analysis of shared environmental influences. *Psychological Bulletin*, *135*, 608–637.

Caspi, A. (1998). Personality development across the life course. In W. Damon, & N. Eisenberg, (Eds.), *Handbook of Child Psychology* (Vol. 3, pp. 311–388). New York: Wiley.

Chapman, B. P., Fiscella, K., Kawachi, I., & Duberstein, P. R. (2010). Personality, socioeconomic status, and all-cause mortality in the United States. *American Journal of Epidemiology*, *171*, 83–92.

Conger, K. J., Martin, M., Reeb, B. T., Little, W. M., Craine, J. L., Shebloski, B., & Conger, R. D. (2012). Economic hardship and its consequences across generations. In V. Maholmes & R. B. King (Eds.), *Oxford Handbook of Child Development and Poverty*. Oxford, England: Oxford University Press.

Conger, R. D., & Conger, K. J. (2002). Resilience in Midwestern families: Selected findings from the first decade of a prospective, longitudinal study. *Journal of Marriage and Family*, *64*, 361–373.

Conger, R. D., Conger, K. J., & Martin, M. J. (2010). Socioeconomic status, family processes, and individual development. *Journal of Marriage and Family*, *72*, 685–704.

Conger, R.D., Conger, K.J., Elder, G.H., Lorenz, F.O., Simons, R. L., & Whitbeck, L. B. (1992). A family process model of economic hardship and adjustment of early adolescent boys. *Child Development*, *63*, 526–541.

Conger, R. D., Conger, K. J., Elder, G. H., Jr., Lorenz, F. O., Simons, R. L., & Whitbeck, L. B. (1993). Family economic stress and adjustment of early adolescent girls. *Developmental Psychology*, *29*, 206–219.

Conger, R. D., & Donnellan, M. B. (2007). An interactionist perspective on the socioeconomic context of human development. *Annual Review of Psychology*, *58*, 175–199.

Conger, R. D., Rueter, M. A., & Elder, G. H., Jr. (1999). Couple resilience to economic pressure. *Journal of Personality and Social Psychology*, *76*, 54–71.

Conger, R. D., Wallace, L. E., Sun, Y., Simons, R. L., McLoyd, V. C., & Brody, G. (2002). Economic pressure in African American families: A replication and extension of the family stress model. *Developmental Psychology*, *38*, 179–193.

Corcoran, M., & Adams, T. (1997). Race, sex, and the intergenerational transmission of poverty. In G. J. Duncan & J. Brooks-Gunn (Eds.), *Consequences of growing up poor* (pp. 461–517). New York: Russell Sage Foundation Press.

Costello, E. J., Compton, S. N., Keeler, G., & Angold, A. (2003). Relationships between poverty and psycho-pathology: A natural experiment. *Journal of the American Medical Association*, *290*, 2023–2029.

DeNavas-Walt, C., Proctor, B. D., & Smith, J. C. (2010). *Income, poverty, and health insurance coverage in the United States: 2009*. CPR Report P60–238. Washington, DC: Census Bureau.

Davies, P. T., & Woitach, M. J. (2008). Children's emotional security in the interparental relationship. *Current Directions in Psychological Science*, *17*, 269–274.

Davis-Kean, P.E. (2005). The influence of parent education and family income on child achievement: The indirect role of parent expectations and the home environment. *Journal of Family Psychology*, *19*, 294–304.

Dohrenwend, B. P., Levav, I., Shrout, P. E., Schwartz, S., Naveh, G., Link, B. G., Skodol, A. E., & Stueve, A. (1992). Socioeconomic status and psychiatric disorders: The causation-selection issue. *Science*, *255*, 946–952.

Donnellan, M. B., Conger, K. J., McAdams, K. K., & Neppl, T. K. (2009). Personal characteristics and resilience to economic hardship and its consequences: Conceptual issues and empirical illustrations. *Journal of Personality*, *77*, 1645–1676.

Donnellan, M. B. Lucas, R. E., & Fleeson, W. (2009). Introduction to *Personality and Assessment* at age 40: Reflections on the legacy of the person-situation debate and the future of person-situation integration. *Journal of Research in Personality*, *43*, 117–119.

D'Onofrio, B.M., & Lahey, B. B. (2010). Biosocial influences on the family: A decade review. *Journal of Marriage and Family*, *72*, 762–782.

D'Onofrio, B.M., Goodnight, J.A., Van Hulle, C.A., Rodgers, J.L., Rathouz, P.J., Waldman, I.D., & Lahey, B.B. (2009). A quasi-experimental analysis of the association between family income and offspring conduct problems. *Journal of Abnormal Child Psychology, 37*, 415–429.

Dyrenforth, P. S., Kashy, D. A., Donnellan, M. B., & Lucas, R. E. (2010). Predicting relationship and life satisfaction in nationally representative samples from three countries: The relative importance of actor, partner, and couple similarity effects for personality traits. *Journal of Personality and Social Psychology, 99*, 690–702.

Duncan, G. J., & Brooks-Gunn, J. (2000). Family poverty, welfare reform, and child development. *Child Development, 71*, 188–196.

Duncan, G. J., & Magnuson, K. A. (2003). Off with Hollingshead: Socioeconomic resources, parenting, and child development. In M. H. Bornstein & R. H. Bradley (Eds.), *Socioeconomic status, parenting, and child development* (pp. 83–106). Mahwah, NJ: Erlbaum.

Duncan, G., J. Yeung, W. J., Brooks-Gunn, J., & Smith, J. R. (1998). How much does childhood poverty affect the life chances of children? *American Sociological Review, 63*, 406–423.

Edin, K., & Kissane, R. J. (2010). Poverty and the American family: A decade in review. *Journal of Marriage and Family, 72*, 460–479.

Ensel, W. M., & Lin, N. (1991). The life stress paradigm and psychological distress. *Journal of Health and Social Behavior, 32*, 321–341.

Foster, E. M. (2002). How economists think about family resources and child development. *Child Development, 73*, 1904–1914.

Fox, G. L., & Chancey, D. (1998). Sources of economic distress: Individual and family outcomes. *Journal of Family Issues, 19*, 725–749.

Gennetian, L. A., & Miller, C. (2002). Children and welfare reform: A view from an experimental welfare program in Minnesota. *Child Development, 73*, 601–620.

Gershoff, E. T., Aber, J. L., Raver, C. C., & Lennon, M. C. (2007). Income is not enough: Incorporating material hardship into models of income associations with parenting and child development. *Child Development, 78*, 70–95.

Gomstyn, A. (2009). 663,000 unemployed ask, what recovery? *ABC News*, April 3.

Gottlieb, G. (1996). A systems view of psychobiological development. In D. Magnusson (Ed.), *The lifespan development of individuals: Behavioral, neurobiological, and psychosocial perspectives* (pp. 76–103). Cambridge, UK: University of Cambridge Press.

Grych, J. H., & Fincham, F. D. (1990). Marital conflict and children's adjustment: A cognitive-contextual framework. *Psychological Bulletin, 108*, 267–290.

Guo, G., Roettger, M. E., & Cai, T. (2008). The integration of genetic propensities into social-control models of delinquency and violence among male youths. *American Sociological Review, 73*, 543–568.

Gutman, L. M., McLoyd, V. C., & Tokoyawa, T. (2005). Financial strain, neighborhood stress, parenting behaviors, and adolescent adjustment in urban African American Families. *Journal of Research on Adolescence, 15*, 425–449.

Hardie, J. H., & Lucas, A. (2010). Economic factors and relationship quality among young couples: Comparing cohabitation and marriage. *Journal of Marriage and Family, 72*, 1141–1154.

Haas, S. A. (2006). Health selection and the process of social stratification: The effect of childhood health on socioeconomic attainment. *Journal of Health and Social Behavior, 47*, 339–354.

Hill, R. (1949). *Families under stress*. New York: Harper & Row.

Huston, A. C., & Bentley, A. C. (2010). Human development in societal context. *Annual Review of Psychology, 61*, 411–437.

Huston, A. C., Duncan, G. J., McLoyd, V. C., Crosby, D. A., Ripke, M. N., Weisner, T. S., & Eldred, C. A. (2005). Impacts on children of a policy to promote employment and reduce poverty for low-income parents: New Hope after 5 years. *Developmental Psychology, 41*, 902–918.

Irwin, N., & Shin, A. (2009). Job losses could drown stimulus. *Washington Post*, March 7.

Johnson, J. G., Cohen, P. Dohrenwend, B. P., Link, B. G., & Brook, J. S. (1999). A longitudinal investigation of social causation and social selection processes involved in the association between socioeconomic status and psychiatric disorders. *Journal of Abnormal Psychology, 108*, 490–499.

Judge, T.A., Higgins, C.A., Thoresen, C.J., & Barrick, M.R. (1999). The Big Five personality traits, general mental ability, and career success across the life span. *Personnel Psychology, 52*, 621–652.

Karney, B. R., & Bradbury, T. N. (1995). The longitudinal course of marital quality and stability: A review of theory, method, and research. *Psychological Bulletin, 118*, 3–34.

Karney, B. R., & Bradbury, T. N. (2005). Contextual influences on marriage: Implications for policy and intervention. *Current Directions in Psychological Science*, *14*, 171–174.

Karney, B. R., Garvan, C. W., & Thomas, M. S. (2003). *Family formation in Florida: 2003 baseline survey of attitudes, beliefs and demographics relating marriage and family formation*. Gainesville, FL: University of Florida.

Kim-Cohen, J., Moffitt, T. E., Caspi, A., & Taylor, A. (2004). Genetic and environmental processes in young children's resilience and vulnerability to socioeconomic deprivation. *Child Development*, *75*, 651–668.

Kinnunen, U., & Feldt, T. (2004). Economic stress and marital adjustment among couples: Analyses at the dyadic level. *European Journal of Social Psychology*, *34*, 519–532.

Kohn, M. L. (1959). Social class and parental values. *American Journal of Sociology*, *64*, 337–351.

Kohn, M. L. (1963). Social class and parent-child relationships: An interpretation. *American Journal of Sociology*, *68*, 471–480.

Kwon, H. K., Rueter, M. A., Lee, M. S., Koh, S., & Ok, S. W. (2003). Marital relationships following the Korean economic crisis: Applying the family stress model. *Journal of Marriage and Family*, *65*, 316–325.

Leventhal, T., & Brooks-Gunn, J. (2003). Moving on up: Neighborhood effects on children and families. In M. H. Bornstein & R. H. Bradley (Eds.), *Socioeconomic status, parenting, and child development* (pp. 209–230). Mahwah, NJ: Erlbaum.

Leventhal, T., Fauth, R. C., & Brooks-Gunn, J. (2005). Neighborhood poverty and public policy: A 5-year follow-up of children's educational outcomes in the New York City Moving to Opportunity demonstration. *Developmental Psychology*, *41*, 933–952.

Linver, M. R., Brooks-Gunn, J., & Kohen, D. (2002). Family processes as pathways from income to young children's development. *Developmental Psychology*, *38*, 719–734.

Lorant, V., Deliège, D., Eaton, W. Robert, A., Phillippot, P., & Ansseau, M. (2003). Socioeconomic inequalities in depression: A meta-analysis. *American Journal of Epidemiology*, *157*, 98–112.

Lorenz, F. O., Hraba, J., Conger, R. D., & Pechacova. Z. (1996). Economic change and change in well-being in the Czech Republic, with comparisons to married women in the United States. *Czech Sociological Review*, *4*, 43–62.

MacCallum, R. C. (2003). Working with imperfect models. *Multivariate Behavioral Research*, *38*, 113–139.

Mackenbach, J. P. (2010). New trends in health inequalities research: Now it's personal. *Lancet*, *376*, 854–855.

Magnusson, D., & Stattin, H. (1998). Person-context interaction theories. In W. Damon & R. M. Lerner (Eds.), *Handbook of child psychology: Theoretical models of human development* (5th ed., pp. 685–759). New York: Wiley.

Martin, M. J., Conger, R. D., Schofield, T. J., Dogan, S. J., Widaman, K. F., Donnellan, M. B., & Neppl, T. K. (2010). Evaluation of the interactionist model of socioeconomic status and problem behavior: A developmental cascade across generations. *Development and Psychopathology*, *22*, 695–713.

Masten, A.S., Roisman, G.I., Long, J.D., Burt, K.B., Obradović, J., Riley, J.R., Boelcke-Stennes, K., & Tellegen, A. (2005). Developmental cascades: Linking academic achievement and externalizing and internalizing symptoms over 20 years. *Developmental Psychology*, *41*, 733–746.

Mayer, S. (1997). *What money can't buy: Family income and children's life chances*. Cambridge, MA: Harvard University Press.

McCubbin, H. I., & Patterson, J. M. (1983). The family stress process: The double ABCX model of adjustment and adaptation. *Marriage and Family Review*, *6*, 7–37.

McLeod, J. D., & Shanahan, M. J. (1996). Trajectories of poverty and children's mental health. *Journal of Health and Social Behavior*, *37*, 207–220.

Meehl, P. E. (1990). Appraising and amending theories: The strategy of Lakatosian defense and two principles that warrant it. *Psychological Inquiry*, *1*, 108–141.

Miech, R. A., Caspi, A., Moffitt, T. E., Wright, B. R. E., & Silva, P. A. (1999). Low socioeconomic status and mental disorders: A longitudinal study of selection and causation during young adulthood. *American Journal of Sociology*, *104*, 1096–1131.

Mistry, R. S., Biesanz, J. C., Taylor, L. C., Burchinal, M., & Cox, M. J. (2004). Family income and its relation to preschool children's adjustment for families in the NICHD study of early child care. *Developmental Psychology*, *40*, 727–745.

Mistry, R. S., Lowe, E. D., Benner, A. D., & Chien, N. (2008). Expanding the family economic stress model: Insights from a mixed-methods approach. *Journal of Marriage and Family*, *70*, 196–209.

Moffitt, T. E., Caspi, A., & Rutter, M. (2006). Measured gene-environment interactions in psychopathology. *Perspectives on Psychological Science, 1,* 5–27.

Moffitt, T. E., Arseneault, L., Belsky, D., Dickson, N., Hancox, R., Harrington, H. L., ... Caspi. A. (2011). A gradient of childhood self-control predicts health, wealth, and public safety. *Proceedings of the National Academy of Science, 108,* 2693–2698.

Morris, P., Duncan, G. J., & Clark-Kauffman, E. (2005). Child well-being in an era of welfare reform: The sensitivity of transitions in development to policy change. *Developmental Psychology, 41,* 919–932.

National Center for Family and Marriage Research (2011, March). *Families and households: Economic Well-being.* Family Profiles: FP-11–FP-01. Retrieved from http://ncfmr.bgsu.edu/ pdf/family_profiles/ file94189.pdf.

Noble, K. G., McCandliss, B. D., & Farah, M. J. (2007). Socioeconomic gradients predict individual differences in neurocognitive abilities. *Developmental Science, 10,* 464–480.

Noble, K. G., Norman, M. F., & Farah, M. J. (2005). Neurocognitive correlates of socioeconomic status in kindergarten children. *Developmental Science, 8,* 74–87.

Oakes, J. M., & Rossi, P. H. (2003). The measurement of SES in health research: Current practice and steps toward a new approach. *Social Science and Medicine, 56,* 769–784.

Papp, L. M., Cummings, E. M., & Goeke-Morey, M. C. (2009). For richer, for poorer: Money as a topic of marital conflict in the home. *Family Relations, 58,* 91–103.

Parke, R. D., Coltrane, S., Duffy, S., Buriel, R., Dennis, J., Powers, J., French, S., & Widaman, K. F. (2004). Economic stress, parenting, and child adjustment in Mexican American and European American families. *Child Development, 75,* 1632–1656.

Popenoe, D. (2007). *The state of our unions: The social health of marriage in America.* Piscataway, NJ: The National Marriage Project.

Prinzie, P., Stams, G. J. J. M., Deković, M., Reijntjes, A. H. A., & Belsky, J. (2009). The relations between parents' Big Five personality factors and parenting: A meta-analytic review. *Journal of Personality and Social Psychology, 97,* 351–362.

Rauer, A. J., Karney, B. R., Garvan, C. W., & Hou, W. (2008). Relationship risks in context: A cumulative risk approach to understanding relationship satisfaction. *Journal of Marriage and Family, 70,* 1122–1135.

Roberts, B. W., Kuncel, N. R., Shiner, R., Caspi, A., & Goldberg, L. R. (2007). The power of personality: The comparative validity of personality traits, socioeconomic status, and cognitive ability for predicting important life outcomes. *Perspectives on Psychological Science, 2,* 313–345.

Robins, R. W., Caspi, A., & Moffitt, T. E. (2000). Two personalities, one relationship: Both partners' personality traits shape the quality of their relationship. *Journal of Personality and Social Psychology, 79,* 251–259.

Rowe, D. C., & Rodgers, J. L. (1997). Poverty and behavior: Are environmental measures nature and nurture? *Developmental Review, 17,* 358–375.

Rutter, M. (2002). Nature, nurture, and development: From evangelism through science toward policy and practice. *Child Development, 73,* 1–21.

Sameroff, A. J. (2010). A unified theory of development: A dialectic integration of nature and nurture. *Child Development, 81,* 6–22.

Sameroff, A. J. & MacKenzie, M. J. (2003). Research strategies for capturing transactional models of development: The limits of the possible. *Development and Psychopathology, 15,* 613–640.

Sareen, J., Afifi, T. O., McMillan, K. A., & Asmundson, G. J. G. (2011). Relationship between household income and mental disorders: Findings from a population-based longitudinal study. *Archives of General Psychiatry, 68,* 419–427.

Scaramella, L. V., Sohr-Preston, S. L., Callahan, K. L., & Mirabile, S. P. (2008). A test of the Family Stress Model on toddler-aged children's adjustment among Hurricane Katrina impacted and nonimpacted low-income families. *Journal of Clinical Child and Adolescent Psychology, 37,* 530–541.

Scarr, S., & McCartney, K. (1983). How people make their own environments: A theory of genotype greater than environment effects. *Child Development, 54,* 424–435.

Schofield, T., Martin, M. J., Conger, K. J., Donnellan, M. B., Neppl, T., & Conger, R. D. (2011). Intergenerational transmission of adaptive functioning: A test of the interactionist model of SES and human development. *Child Development, 82,* 33–47.

Schoon, I., Bynner, J., Joshi, H., Parsons, S., Wiggins, R. D., & Sacker, A. (2002). The influence of context, timing, and duration of risk experiences for the passage from childhood to midadulthood. *Child Development*, *73*, 1486–1504.

Solantaus, T., Leinonen, J., & Punamäki, R. L. (2004). Children's mental health in times of economic recession: Replication and extension of the family economic stress model in Finland. *Developmental Psychology*, *40*, 412–429.

Teachman, J. D., Paasch, K. M., Day, R. D., & Carver, K. P. (1997). Poverty during adolescence and subsequent educational attainment. In G. J. Duncan & J. Brooks-Gunn (Eds.), *Consequences of growing up poor* (pp. 382–418). New York: Russell Sage.

Thoits, P. A. (2006). Personal agency in the stress process. *Journal of Health and Social Behavior*, *47*, 309–323.

Tucker-Drob, E. M., Rhemtulla, M., Harden, K. P., Turkheimer, E., & Fask, D. (2011). Emergence of a gene x socioeconomic status interaction on infant mental ability between 10 months and 2 years. *Psychological Science*, *22*, 125–133.

Turkheimer, E. (2004). Spinach and ice cream: Why social science is so difficult. In L. F. DiLalla (Ed.). *Behavior genetics principles: Perspectives in development, personality, and psychopathology* (pp. 161–189). Washington DC: American Psychological Association.

Turkheimer, E., Haley, A., Waldron, M., D'Onofrio, B. & Gottesman, I. I. (2003). Socioeconomic status modifies heritability of IQ in young children. *Psychological Science*, *14*, 623–628.

U.S. Bureau of the Census. (2010). Historical income data: Current Population Survey tables. Retrieved from http://www.census.gov/hhes/www/income/data/historical/families/index.html (accessed January 31, 2011).

U.S. Bureau of Labor Statistics (2011). Labor force statistics from the Current Population Survey. Seasonal Unemployment Rate (2000–2010). Retrieved from http://data.bls.gov/cgi-bin/surveymost (accessed February 21, 2011).

U.S. Department of Commerce, Bureau of Economic Analysis. (August 27, 2009). Table 1.1.1. Percent change from preceding period in real gross domestic product [percent]. Retrieved from http://www.bea.gov/national/nipaweb/ (accessed September 25, 2009).

Votruba-Drzal, E. (2006). Economic disparities in middle childhood development: Does income matter? *Developmental Psychology*, *42*, 1154–1167.

Wickrama, K. A. S., Conger, R. D., Lorenz, F. O., & Jung, T. (2008). Family antecedents and consequences of trajectories of depressive symptoms from adolescence to young adulthood: A life course investigation. *Journal of Health and Social Behavior*, *49*, 468–483.

Yeung, W. J., Linver, M. R., & Brooks-Gunn, J. (2002). How money matters for young children's development: Parental investment and family processes. *Child Development*, *73*, 1861–1879.

20 Theories and their Empirical Support in the Study of Intergenerational Family Relationships in Adulthood

Teresa M. Cooney and Pearl A. Dykstra

The shared lives of parents and offspring are longer today than ever before. It is not until their sixth decade of life that most adults in developed countries will occupy the "orphan" status, having experienced the death of their last remaining parent (Puur, Sakkeus, Põldma, & Herm, 2011; Soldo, 1996; Uhlenberg, 1996). Even after this transition occurs, most late middle-aged persons will still be part of a parent–adult child relationship—in this case as the older generation member (Matthews & Sun, 2006; Soldo, 1996). Given that much of one's life course is spent in at least one adult intergenerational relationship, the significance of these ties for everyday living and personal well-being cannot be over-stated. This chapter reviews conceptualization of and research on the central dimensions of adult child–parent relationships, their manifestation in contemporary family life, and theoretical explanations for the variability that is seen in them.

It is important to note at the outset that scholarship on adult intergenerational relations is often criticized for neglect or narrow application of theory (Marshall, Matthews, & Rosenthal, 1993). This weakness may be largely attributed to the fact that both family studies and gerontology (the fields in which most of this scholarship is produced) are largely problem-driven, applied disciplines. As such, Silverstein (2005) notes that conceptual development and theory building are often secondary to more practical, applied concerns. This reasoning may also explain the specific topics that attract the greatest attention within the literature on aging families. To illustrate, though caregiving for frail and functionally impaired parents occupies a very small portion of adulthood for a select group of individuals (Rosenthal, Matthews, & Marshall, 1989), the topic of family caregiving dominates this research literature (Allen, Blieszner, & Roberto, 2000). We largely omit the caregiving literature from our discussion here, however, because of our decision to address more commonly experienced, long-term aspects of parent–adult child relationships that characterize this family tie for most adults.

We focus primarily on theorizing regarding four domains of intergenerational relations—association, exchange of support, affective or emotional closeness, and conflict. These dimensions are key components of Bengtson's solidarity paradigm, the predominant conceptualization in the adult intergenerational relations literature. Moreover, these domains (with the exception of conflict) have attracted attention from intergenerational relations scholars for the past 50 years, dating back to classic studies by Shanas et al. (1968) and Sussman (Sussman, 1953; Sussman & Burchinal, 1962). Their preoccupation with levels of intergenerational contact and aid was a likely reaction to family theorizing of the time (Burgess, 1960; Parsons & Bales, 1955) that emphasized the centrality of the nuclear family, isolation of older family members (Marshall et al., 1993), and social disengagement by older adults more generally (Cumming & Henry, 1961). Fueled by social and political upheaval, research in the 1960s and 1970s added concern for attitudinal differences between the generations, though this research on the "generation gap" peaked in the early to mid-1970s (Smith, 2000). Therefore, our discussion largely omits this latter domain, referred to as consensual solidarity by Bengtson, and instead addresses issues of intergenerational closeness and conflict more generally and the increasingly popular concept of intergenerational ambivalence.

Greater internationalization has spurred cross-national research initiatives, including multinational data collections and the careful harmonizing of data gathered in different countries by different research teams. Consequently, the last decade has produced more comparative research on intergenerational relations, which examines how relational processes vary across cultural, political, and social contexts (Silverstein & Giarrusso, 2010). In addressing theories used to understand variations in intergenerational processes, we thus attend to individual, micro-level factors as well as cultural and policy explanations at the macro-level. This approach requires that we draw broadly from both the US and European literatures.

Because the *intergenerational solidarity framework* guides our presentation of research findings, it is useful to briefly describe this formulation. Proposed by Vern Bengtson and his colleagues, the solidarity perspective has been expanded and refined over the past four decades. When initially conceived in the 1970s (Bengtson, Olander, & Haddad, 1976), family solidarity was proposed as "a unidimensional metaconstruct subsuming affection, association and consensus"—components that were considered highly interdependent relationship features (Bengtson & Roberts, 1991, p. 859). Empirical testing with a variety of data sources prompted reformulation of the model over time. In 1982, Bengtson and Schrader offered the six dimensions of intergenerational solidarity still acknowledged today: the original three dimensions of association, affection and consensus (labeled associational, affectual and consensual solidarity, respectively), as well as functional solidarity (intergenerational exchanges), normative solidarity (obligation to family members) and structural solidarity (factors shaping opportunity for intergenerational relating, such as proximity and family size).

Bengtson's formulation of intergenerational solidarity builds on ideas central to Durkheim's (1893/1933) theorizing on social organization, and on social psychology theories outlined by Homans (1950) and others. Simply put, the solidarity model asserts that a critical part of what creates and maintains behavioral and emotional bonds between family members (e.g., parents and adult offspring) is shared norms and beliefs, and behavioral interdependence.

The last 25 years have seen a proliferation of research on the various solidarity dimensions, notably the associational, functional and affective forms. Structural and normative solidarity are generally considered as factors influencing these other dimensions. Over time, family scholars have become increasingly aware of the challenges of addressing the complexity of intergenerational relationships. One challenge is how to investigate family conflict as well as positive exchanges and sentiment (Bengtson, Rosenthal, & Burton, 1996), an issue that critics accused Bengtson of ignoring in early formulations of his solidarity model (Connidis & McMullin, 2002; Luescher & Pillemer, 1998). More recent discussions of solidarity have included attention to conflict (Bengtson, Giarrusso, Mabry, & Silverstein, 2002), and research and theorizing about ambivalence are widespread today (Connidis & McMullin, 2002; Luescher & Pillemer, 1998). We address empirical findings pertaining to these relational dimensions and the theorizing used to understand them in this chapter.

KEY FINDINGS

Interaction between Generations: Associational and Structural Solidarity

The level of interaction between generations in the family is captured primarily by the concept of associational solidarity, typically operationalized as frequency of in-person visits or other contact between family members. Though often studied along with functional solidarity, even when examined alone the potential for association to offer more than just companionship—also instrumental and emotional support—is generally noted (Soldo & Hill, 1993). Frequent face-to-face contact facilitates the provision of practical assistance and may alert support providers to the recipient's needs. Furthermore, contact can be viewed as a form of support in itself, given that it meets a social need. It is also an indirect indicator of forms of instrumental support that are too idiosyncratic to measure in large-scale surveys (Kalmijn & Dykstra, 2006).

Associational solidarity is strong between adult offspring and parents despite geographic distance that may separate family members. This is true whether rates of contact are reported by the parent or the adult children. In the US, the majority of adults with living parents have at least weekly contact with their mothers and over half note such frequent contact with their fathers (Lawton, Silverstein, & Bengtson, 1994). Similarly, from the parents' perspective, most have at least weekly contact with one or more children, the exception being recently divorced fathers (Shapiro, 2003). Data for 10 European countries collected in the context of the Survey of Health and Retirement in Europe (SHARE) also reveal that half of the pooled sample of older parents reported more than weekly contact with their "most in-touch" non-resident child. Cross-national variation exists however, as over 60% of older persons from Greece, Spain and Italy note such high contact levels, compared with 40–50% of respondents from Austria, Denmark, France, Germany, the Netherlands, Sweden, and Switzerland (Hank, 2007).

With the spread of such technologies as email and cell phones, levels of contact are likely to increase. Internet users claim that e-mail facilitates communication with family members (Howard, Rainie, & Jones, 2001). Though in-person visits and contact by other means tend to show moderate positive correlations (Cherlin & Furstenberg, 1986), they appear to tap into different dimensions of intergenerational ties. Frequent in-person interactions more strongly predict various forms of instrumental help exchange, whereas other forms of frequent contact are more strongly associated with affection and emotional support (Van Gaalen & Dykstra, 2006).

Levels of functional solidarity are modest in most families. Fingerman and her associates (2011) used a regional US sample of persons ages 40–60 to document exchanges of support with two generations—aging parents and adult offspring. They found that 53% of respondents helped grown offspring more than parents, with frequency of aid to offspring averaging a few times a month to weekly. Support was given at about this same rate in 28% of families where aged parents were the typical recipients. Overall, the frequency of intergenerational support provided by middle-aged respondents averaged a few times a month to monthly; in contrast, they received support from their aged parents and adult offspring monthly to a few times a year.

European studies reveal moderate levels of intergenerational support exchange as well. Using SHARE data, Albertini, Kohli, and Vogel (2007) reported that 21% of older parents noted providing monetary help to an adult child in the last year, with only 3% receiving such help. Regarding instrumental support, 16% of elders were recipients and 9% were contributors of help to offspring. The proportion giving assistance to offspring, however, jumped to 37% when childcare was included in support measures. An important finding in this work is that while fewer than half of European adults engage in regular exchanges of help with offspring, for those who do, the intensity of support exchange is high. Aged parents reporting childcare assistance averaged 902 hours per year—a substantial amount of time. As in US studies, the predominant pattern of parents being the primary giver of support does shift as parents reach advanced ages.

CONDITIONS FOR INTERACTION BETWEEN THE GENERATIONS

Two factors, geographic proximity and normative beliefs, are known to strongly influence intergenerational interaction. Research findings pertaining to each are summarized here.

Geographic Proximity

Physical proximity, a component of structural solidarity, increases opportunities for intergenerational association, companionship and practical help exchange. Proximity, however, may not be exogenous to intergenerational support and contact (Grundy & Shelton, 2001; Tomassini, Wolf, & Rosina, 2003). That is, family members might choose to move closer to one another because support is required and expected by one or both generations. To illustrate, Silverstein and Angelelli (1998) found that older parents who are in poor health and live alone are more likely to voice intentions of moving nearer to adult offspring than are healthier, partnered elders. Using Dutch registry data, Smits, Van Gaalen, and Mulder (2010) revealed that needs determine who moves in with whom. Divorce and a loss of income prompted adult children to move in with their parents, while widowhood and receiving disability benefits led parents to move in with offspring. The person in need was most likely to move. Adult children derive benefits from nearby parents as well. A study in former western Germany found that women were more likely to have a first child if their parents were local than if they lived further away (Hank & Kreyenfeld, 2003). Studies on "boomerang children" also underscore adult children's reliance on their parents when they experience job loss or personal setbacks in their lives (Mitchell, 2005). Proximity allows for intergenerational dependence as well as interdependence.

Norms

Another solidarity dimension proposed as critical in explaining associational and functional solidarity is normative solidarity, which includes views about family obligations or responsibility. Family obligations are beliefs about family members' responsibilities to care for and support one another, which supposedly offer guidelines for family behavior (Finch & Mason, 1990). Scholars typically focus on filial responsibility—adult children's responsibilities towards aged parents (Herlofson, Hagestad, Slagsvold, & Sørensen, 2011). Much less attention addresses feelings of obligation in the opposite direction, that is, parents' responsibility towards adult children. With few exceptions (De Vries, Kalmijn, & Liefbroer, 2009; Finch & Mason, 1993), the term parental responsibility refers to parents' responsibility for young children. Little is known about how people view their responsibilities as parents in middle and late life.

Research linking family obligation to support behavior has produced inconsistent findings, especially in cross-sectional investigations. Several studies report that providers and/or receivers of support score higher on measures of filial responsibility compared with those who are not involved in intergenerational exchanges (Ikkink, Van Tilburg, & Knipscheer, 1999; Stein et al., 1998). Other research finds no association between the endorsement of filial responsibility and actual support (Lee, Netzer, & Coward, 1994; Peek, Coward, Peek, & Lee, 1998). Daatland and Herlofson (2003b) document inconsistencies across countries. Older persons receiving family help more strongly endorsed filial obligations than did those without such support, but only in Spain and Israel and not in Germany, England and Norway. Cooney and Dykstra (2011) considered distinct attitudes regarding obligations to adult offspring and to aged parents in national samples from the US and the Netherlands; they found limited evidence that obligations influenced the provision of functional support once the recipient's needs and the provider's resources were controlled. Only in the case of providing assistance to aged parents in the US sample were normative feelings predictive of functional support. They argue that norms are more powerful determinants of behaviors in countries with limited public support systems. This view is discussed more below.

Longitudinal findings regarding the role of family obligations in support behavior are also mixed. Using data from the first three waves of the Longitudinal Study of Generations (LSG), Silverstein,

Parrott, and Bengtson (1995) showed that sons', but not daughters' endorsement of filial responsibility predicted support to parents measured three years later. Yet, a later study, using more recent waves of LSG data, showed that daughters' rather than sons' espoused filial obligations were predictive of increased support to mothers (but not fathers) in need (Silverstein, Gans, & Yang, 2006). Results from the Norwegian Life-course, Ageing and Generations Panel study (NorLAG) revealed that attitudes towards filial responsibility predicted the provision of support to parents, but more so for sons than for daughters (Herlofson et al., 2011). Analyzing Dutch panel data, Dykstra and Fokkema (2009) also found sons were more responsive than daughters to norms of filial obligation when maternal need increased. Overall, the balance of evidence suggests that filial obligations have a stronger motivational component for sons than daughters. Females appear less sensitive to social prescriptions, perhaps because they take support provision for granted, are more likely to incorporate support tasks into their daily schedules, or are more intrinsically motivated than males. Appeals to social duty and responsibility seem to work better for sons than for daughters.

Failure to demonstrate a strong and consistent role of family obligations in explaining intergenerational support provision also may be understood by considering the resources and needs of each generation—part of what Silverstein and Bengtson (1997) refer to as the "opportunity structure" for exchange behavior. Intergenerational transfers require the resources of time and money, which, if available to the giver, are provided when the recipient has needs. Silverstein et al. (2006) point out that strong family obligations may be a necessary factor in intergenerational support exchange, but not sufficient for explaining support patterns. That is, strong feelings of family responsibility may predispose individuals to be supportive, but whether assistance actually materializes depends on the specific context of need. To illustrate, they found that only under conditions of declining parental health was the strength of filial norms significant in increasing levels of help provided by offspring.

AFFECTIVE DIMENSIONS OF INTERGENERATIONAL RELATIONSHIPS

Affectual Solidarity

The emotional or affective bond between parents and adult offspring is central to both generations as they engage in companionship, advice giving, and sharing of emotional support (Wenger & Jerrome, 1999). For aging parents, emotional ties with offspring may be especially valued given the loss of other significant social relationships (e.g., spouse, siblings) due to death, and the relinquishment of social roles, such as worker (Szinovacz & Davey, 2001). Most aged parents identify one of their offspring as a close confidant (Connidis & Davies, 1992). This is especially the case for women, who are less likely than men to name their spouse as their preferred confidant (Robertson & Mosher-Ashley, 2002). Relationships with parents also tend to be judged favorably from the perspective of adult offspring. The majority of adults report high quality ties with parents, but this finding holds true in relation to mothers more so than fathers (Silverstein & Bengtson, 1997; Silverstein, Gans, Lowenstein, Giarrusso, & Bengtson, 2010; Van Gaalen & Dykstra, 2006). Moreover, compared with their parents' ratings of their relationship, adult children report less closeness and attribute less importance to the parent–child bond (Albrecht, Coward, & Shapiro, 1997; Aquilino, 1999; Fingerman et al., 2011; Giarrusso, Stallings, & Bengtson, 1995; Shapiro, 2004).

Conflict

The affective component of parent–adult child relationships, particularly when viewed from the solidarity perspective, generated substantial debate in the literature in the last 20 years. Strong opposition has been voiced regarding what is perceived as an overly-positive, idealized view of parent–adult child relations (Marshall et al., 1993; Luescher & Pillemer, 1998) and neglect of intergenerational conflict and strain in discussions of the solidarity perspective.

Conflict between adults and their parents has attracted more empirical attention in the last 15 years. Clarke, Preston, Raksin and Bengtson (1999) report that most adults identify some problems with their adult offspring and parents. Often noted are communication and interaction problems and tensions over personal habits and lifestyle choices.

Problems between the generations are often expressed outright, and criticism and yelling are not uncommon (Parrot, Giarrusso, & Bengtson, 1997). The open expression of conflict is not necessarily undesirable. By openly airing their problems, family members can release built-up negative emotion and initiate problem-solving (Parrot & Bengtson, 1999). Unresolved tensions between parents and offspring can detract from affectual solidarity (Birditt, Miller, Fingerman, & Lefkowitz, 2009).

Ambivalence

According to classical sociologists, the coexistence of closeness and tension is inherent to close relationships (Coser, 1956; Simmel, 1904). Nevertheless, until recently, intergenerational solidarity and conflict were generally studied separately. Numerous investigations into the co-occurring positive and negative elements of intergenerational relationships have been conducted since the introduction of the ambivalence perspective in the late 1990s. The psychological view of ambivalence is that family members may simultaneously have both warm and antagonistic feelings toward one another (Luescher & Pillemer, 1998). The sociological view of ambivalence is that institutional forces exert competing and contradictory demands on the resources of family members (Connidis & McMullin, 2002).

Ambivalent feelings have been identified in a variety of family situations, with levels varying with the degree of family relatedness. In their comparison of expressed sentiment in a wide set of social relationships, Fingerman, Hay, and Birditt (2004) found more ambivalence in close family ties (e.g., parents and offspring) than in relations with distant relatives, friends and acquaintances. Comparing adults' reports of relationships with in-laws versus parents of both sexes, however, Willson, Shuey, & Elder (2003) found greater ambivalence in in-law ties.

One set of factors that influence ambivalence fall under what is referred to as structural solidarity—including demographic factors such as geographic proximity, the sex and age of offspring or parents, and parental marital status. For example, adults living in closer proximity to parents report more mixed feelings in their relationships with them (Willson et al., 2003). In a longitudinal study carried out in the Netherlands, moving away by either the adult child or the aging parent resulted in a shift from an ambivalent type of relationship to a more harmonious type (Schenk & Dykstra, 2012). Dutch data also reveal that adult offspring are more likely to be classified as having ambivalent relationships with fathers than mothers, and with parents who are currently unmarried compared with partnered. Increasing age also results in a greater likelihood that daughters compared with sons report ambivalent relationships with parents that involve high levels of assistance but less than ideal affective quality (Van Gaalen, Dykstra, & Komter, 2010).

Empirical results like these suggest that ambivalence possibly results when issues of dependence-independence are challenged in intergenerational relationships (Willson, Shuey, Elder, & Wickrama, 2006). Health factors, which may impact relational dependency and need for assistance, are significant predictors of ambivalence. When parents are in poorer health they report greater intergenerational ambivalence (Pillemer et al., 2007), as do their offspring (Willson et al., 2003, 2006), although Fingerman, Pitzer, Lefkowitz, Birditt, & Mroczek, (2008) only found this to be the case for adult children's reports in relation to mothers', but not fathers' physical health. Similarly, mothers (Pillemer et al., 2007) and fathers (Fingerman et al., 2008) report higher levels of ambivalence when their adult children have health problems, and mothers also express greater ambivalence when offspring have issues with the law or chemical dependency (Pillemer & Suitor, 2002; Pillemer et al., 2007). Not surprisingly, greater relational ambivalence is reported by offspring whose parents require care, (Van Gaalen & Dykstra, 2006; Willson et al., 2003), as well as by mothers whose adult children get more parental assistance (Pillemer & Suitor, 2002; Pillemer et al., 2007). Yet, in the study conducted by Willson et al. (2003), it was only daughters providing care—not sons, who expressed heightened ambivalence in relation to their dependent aging parents.

Though numerous findings indicate connections between intergenerational assistance and ambivalence, or factors that would imply a greater need for familial assistance, the association between giving help and feeling ambivalent is not simply linear and positive. In comparing reports of ambivalence for middle-aged offspring and their young–old mothers, Willson et al. (2006) found that even though mothers provided more assistance to their offspring than vice-versa, greater relational ambivalence was reported by adult children of both sexes than mothers. Which generation is reporting their feelings appears to matter, perhaps because of relational expectations and how they vary for parents and offspring across the life course. This issue is addressed by theories pertaining to intergenerational ambivalence, as discussed below.

THEORY OVERVIEW

THEORIZING ABOUT INTERGENERATIONAL INTERACTION

Social Exchange

The literature presents numerous arguments for why parents and adult children help each other. One perspective starts from a rational choice framework and regards intergenerational support as a form of exchange (Emerson, 1976; Homans, 1961). All social exchange involves costs and rewards: giving support is a cost for the giver, and receiving support is a benefit for the receiver. *Exchange theory* posits that people will incur the costs of giving in anticipation of the rewards of receiving.

Exchange can take different forms (Komter, 2005; Offer, 1997). One is delayed exchange. Parents provide substantial support early on to their young children, in anticipation of future reciprocity from their offspring as the parents' needs grow. And, adult children reciprocate to aging parents for earlier contributions of support received. A second form is a different type of delayed exchange, referred to as prospective exchange. Adult children provide support to their parents to enhance the likelihood of receiving money or property from their parents when they die. A third form is direct exchange: parents and children exchange time and services more or less concurrently. An example is a gift to the parent in exchange for watching the grandchildren.

Antonucci's (1990) concept of a support bank is particularly useful for describing how reciprocity is achieved in the long-term relationships of parents and children. She argues that investments in the form of support to others are made, or "banked," over time in anticipation of drawing on them later when one's own needs arise. Antonucci proposes a lifespan view of the exchange process where reciprocity is not calculated in the present, but is assessed across the entirety of a relationship.

One of the most consistent sets of findings in support of delayed exchange is the body of literature regarding support and contact in the context of parental divorce. Several studies reveal the significant negative impact of parental divorce on contacts with older parents, especially divorced fathers who tend to have a history of less involvement and support than divorced mothers (Aquilino, 1994a,b; Cooney & Uhlenberg, 1990; Shapiro, 2003). Research also shows detrimental effects of divorce for older parents' receipt of instrumental care or coresidential support from adult offspring, even when faced with severe functional limitations (Pezzin, Pollak, & Schone, 2008). Lin (2008) found that care and monetary support were less likely for divorced than widowed fathers, though this difference did not hold for mothers. Data from Europe generally reveal similar patterns of a dampening effect of divorce on intergenerational solidarity (Daatland, 2007; Kalmijn, 2007). Such results are often explained by citing the limited contact and support provided by divorced fathers, which reduces the need for reciprocity from children later in life.

Evidence for prospective exchange comes from research showing that the more wealthy parents are, the more attention and support they receive from their adult offspring (Cox & Rank, 1992).

Bernheim, Shleifer and Summers (1985) found that parent–child contact was greater when the parents had a larger amount of bequeathable wealth, but only in multiple-child families. They suggested that parents use bequests to influence child behavior and that manipulation of children works only when threats to disinherit are credible. McGarry and Schoeni (1997) add more evidence for prospective exchange with their finding that older parents' expectations for future care from specific offspring were associated with the amount of monetary support they had recently provided to the particular child. Thus, aging parents seem to expect their financial investments in their children to be repaid through future care and support as needed.

Direct exchange can be examined by comparing concurrent support up and down generational lines. Suitor, Pillemer, & Sechrist (2006) found that mothers were more likely to report giving emotional and practical support, and sick care in the past year to offspring who had given them support during the same timeframe. This study did not offer evidence, however, regarding reciprocity in levels of exchange.

In general, balanced exchanges turn out to be rare according to most research, with studies consistently indicating that intergenerational support flows primarily downward, from parents to offspring (Albertini et al., 2007; Attias-Donfut, Ogg, & Wolff, 2005; Fingerman et al., 2011; Kohli, 1999). A lack of reciprocal transfers between parents and adult offspring was evident in the empirically-derived typology of late-life families that Dykstra and Fokkema (2011) based on SHARE data. They found no pattern in these data that could be labeled "concurrent reciprocal transfers" between parents and adult children, as depicted by high probabilities of both downward and upward support. Rather, in addition to an autonomous type relationship (characterized by not living nearby, little contact or support exchange, and the refutation of family obligation norms), there were several types of relationships reflecting unbalanced exchange: a supportive at a distance type (not living nearby, frequent contact, refutation of family obligation norms, and primarily financial transfers from parents to adult children); a descending familialism type (living nearby, frequent contact, endorsement of family obligation norms, and primarily help in kind from parents to children); and, an ascending familialism type (living nearby, frequent contact, endorsement of family obligation norms, and primarily help in kind from children to parents). The youngest respondents in this sample were most likely to be classified in the supportive at a distance and the descending familialism types, whereas the oldest respondents were most likely to be in the ascending familialism type. The exchange of support among parents and adult children resembled a pattern of reciprocity in the long run, akin to Antonucci's (1990) support bank.

Equity Theory

A specific form of exchange theory, equity theory emphasizes the pursuit of balanced costs and rewards in social relationships. As a result, reciprocity is central to this theory and giving assistance to a parent or child is thus viewed as part of a fairly balanced pattern of dyadic interactions. Equity theorists (Walster, Walster, & Berscheid, 1978) acknowledge the importance of social norms in individuals' adherence to relational give and take. Given social expectations that relationships be balanced or fair, feelings of guilt may result if one benefits significantly more from a relationship than does the relationship partner, or than is deserved given one's input to the relationship. Further, being the recipient of unbalanced support can contribute unfavorably to feelings of dependency (McCulloch, 1990), a particularly salient issue in parent–child relationships across the lifespan. As noted above, there is a lack of empirical evidence for equitable relationships, at least in the short-term, for parents and adult offspring.

Demonstration Theory

Another unique form of exchange theory that has been applied to intergenerational relations is demonstration theory (Stark, 1999). It seeks to explain the motives behind the upward flow of assistance by introducing a third family generation. According to this view, the principal motive for upward transfers is not repayment, but serving as example for the youngest generation so that in adulthood they will replicate the supportive behavior modeled by their own parents. Evidence of greater assistance to and more frequent contact with aging parents among offspring with children compared with childless adults is consistent with this theory (Cox & Stark, 2005). Nevertheless, as Wolff (2001) shows, alternative interpretations cannot be ruled out, such as the possibility that higher levels of contact by offspring with children may be attributable to childcare being provided by the grandparents. Other tests of demonstration theory have focused on the gender of grandchildren. According to the theory, parents of daughters would invest more in being "proper" role models than parents of sons because females are expected to help their parents more than are males. In support of this hypothesis, Mitrut and Wolff (2009) found that parents of girls visit grandparents more often than do parents of boys.

Altruism

Whereas exchange theory posits that intergenerational behavior is motivated by self-interest, *altruism theory* starts from the perspective that beneficence guides parent–offspring interactions (Wade-Benzoni & Tost, 2009). The basic idea of altruism theory is that because parents and adult children care about each other, they monitor each other's well-being and make transfers as required to enhance or maintain the other's well-being (Becker, 1974). Support is thus contingent on the needs of parents and children, which is consistent with another theoretical explanation referred to as *contingency theory* (Deutsch, 1975). The critical influence in whether support is given (as well as one's response to both giving and receiving support—see Davey & Eggebeen, 1998) is not how the support figures into some grand accounting scheme of exchanges in the relationship, but rather the level of need relational partners are experiencing.

Need is often inferred from the statuses family members hold. Regarding adult offspring, for example, parents provide more help when the adult child has health problems (Suitor et al., 2006), is a student or out-of-work (Attias-Donfut & Wolff, 2000; Fingerman, Miller, Birditt, & Zarit, 2009; Kohli, 1999; Schenk, Dykstra, & Maas, 2010), or is a parent—especially a single parent (Aquilino, 2006; Fingerman et al., 2009; Schenk et al., 2010). For aging parents, statuses that tend to attract greater support based on inferred need are widowhood (Ha, 2008; Dykstra & Fokkema, 2009; Kalmijn, 2007; Silverstein et al., 2006), lone residence (Cooney & Dykstra, 2011), and having functional limitations (Eggebeen & Davey, 1998; Fingerman et al., 2011).

Of interest, however, is that individual statuses such as these, whether pertaining to adult offspring or aged parents, are less influential in determining familial support in countries with more extensive social welfare systems than in those that rely heavily on familial assistance such as the US (Cooney & Dykstra, 2011). This comparative finding is consistent with Kalmijn and Saraceno's work (2008) that revealed that filial responsiveness to parental needs varied widely across European countries, in line with overarching views of state versus family responsibility. In more "familialistic" countries, where residents feel strongly that aging parents should be cared for by their families, the association between the support provided by adult children and parental need is stronger than in more "individualistic" countries, where residents are less likely to feel that eldercare is primarily a family responsibility. Similarly, Viazzo (2010) argues that different explanatory models apply to exchanges in Northern and Southern Europe. In the Northern countries (e.g., Scandinavia, the Netherlands) with more generous welfare systems, transfers flow to the neediest, irrespective of any present or future reciprocating help, consistent with the altruistic model. In the Southern countries (e.g., Italy, Spain) with less generous welfare systems, transfers reflect the payment of services and visits, which are embedded in current and future obligations of reciprocity. Ultimately, transfers in Southern Europe are "driven by more binding moral obligations" (Viazzo, 2010, p. 147).

The complementarity of the exchange and altruism models of support also emerges in the work of Silverstein and colleagues (2002) in which they tested various theories of intergenerational support. First, they posed an "*investment model*", whereby parents can expect to receive support from their offspring proportional to levels of assistance they provided earlier to the younger generation. Next, their "*insurance model*" builds on the investment model by applying a second condition—parental need. This model predicts parental support based on past level of assistance to offspring, plus parents' current need for help. Insurance "kicks in" when it is most needed, with one's benefits level depending on how much support was contributed earlier to the younger generation. In discussing reciprocity, Silverstein emphasizes the social components of this explanation, noting that social norms about the appropriateness of repayment are the force underlying reciprocal acts. He also refers to Homans' (1950) early writings on social groups, theorizing that long-term reciprocal exchanges between individuals promote group bonding and stability. Using 26 years of LSG data to examine instrumental and emotional support to aging parents, Silverstein's group finds merit for both models. Respondents who in their youth reported more activities with a parent reported higher levels of functional solidarity with aging parents over the subsequent two decades, confirming the investment model. Yet, evidence was found for the insurance model too, as parents' early financial investments in offspring (as teens and young adults) did not result in reciprocal support across all subsequent years, but instead predicted accelerated rates of help giving by offspring 25 years later when the parents reached older ages and likely needed more assistance.

Silverstein's team offered altruism as a possible explanation for intergenerational functional solidarity, noting that some studies have lent support for the idea that family members assist others in need, regardless of any past social exchange. Indeed, they found that children's functional and emotional support to parents increased as the older generation moved into advanced ages, "even under what may be considered to be estranged circumstances—when the early parent–child relationship was emotionally distant, had no time commitment, and involved no financial support" (Silverstein et al., 2002, p. S10). Of course, these authors recognize that underlying what they interpret as altruistic behaviors may be strong feelings of obligation (though we noted above the mixed evidence that obligations explain functional support). The findings noted here do suggest, however, that individuals may act in an altruistic manner—reflecting generic goodwill and concern for others in need, without having a particularly strong, positive relationship to the care recipient.

Attachment

Like altruism theory, *attachment theory* views intergenerational support as a means of assisting a parent or child in need. A distinction between the two theories, however, is the nature of the relationship between the provider and recipient of support. General beneficence motivates support to others in need, according to altruism theory. Thus, altruistic acts may be directed toward parents, adult children, or even strangers, who are in need. But, in attachment theory, it is the significant, unique relationship between parent and child, developed over time from early childhood, that is believed to motivate continued intergenerational contact and closeness, and later support in adulthood.

Attachment theory was originally formulated by child development scholars (Bowlby, 1969); Cicirelli (1983; 1993) is best known for extending attachment theory to adult late-life relationships. He contends that actions taken to protect the attachment figure (a parent for a child; an adult child for a parent) are motivated by the strong emotional bonds in the attachment relationship. Supportive helping behaviors are interpreted by attachment theorists as a means of protecting the attachment figure who is in need, or, in attachment language, who is faced with threats to survival (Klaus, 2009). By protecting the attachment figure, the relationship partner is assured the continuance of this unique and valued emotional bond, as well as potential support from the attachment figure in the future (Schwarz & Trommsdorff, 2005). Such theorizing applies to functional solidarity demonstrated by either adult offspring or their parents.

There is evidence that attachment to parents is associated with support provision for them. Sorensen, Webster, & Roggman (2002) found that middle-generation persons reporting a secure attachment to parents reported feeling more prepared to assist them in the future. Cicirelli (1993) found correlations between the amount of time daughters spent providing instrumental support to their mothers and their secure, positive attachment to them. Using a German sample of adult daughter-mother dyads, Schwarz and Trommsdorff (2005) revealed a connection between attachment and provision of instrumental support to mothers.

Repudiation of attachment theory, however, comes from studies that fail to reveal consistent links between the emotional bond of parents and children and support provision. Using an established measure of adult attachment, Carpenter (2001), for example, found no association between attachment (as reported by the child) and the instrumental support provided to mothers by adult daughters. Yet, he did find that emotional support of mothers was linked to daughters' attachment scores. Similarly, Parrot and Bengtson (1999) analyzed two waves of LSG data and found that adult children's reports of felt affection toward each parent (closeness, understanding, and communication used as indicators of attachment) were predictive of the levels of emotional support offered to each parent, but not the extent of instrumental support given, nor the amount of total support (financial, expressive, and instrumental) provided by the grown child to each parent three years later.

Application of attachment theory to intergenerational relationships in mid to later life has been limited (see Merz, 2010). Though often referred to in the background sections of empirical studies, direct tests of the theory are rare. Moreover, studies applying attachment theory to adult intergenerational relations mostly consider it as an explanation for adults' support of aging parents. Less common is its use in explaining aging parents' continued support to children.

Furthermore, researchers often use reports of affection as a measure of attachment, even though the two concepts are distinct. Cicirelli (1993) employs a global index of attachment that assesses feelings adults experience regarding love for the parent, as well as feelings of security and comfort derived from the parent, and emotions that result from being apart and being reunited with the parent. Other scholars conceptualize adult attachment as reflecting qualitatively different types or styles of relating to the caregiver (Carpenter, 2001). Other debates pose challenges for the use of attachment theory as well, such as whether attachment style reflects an individual trait or whether it is an aspect of a particular social relationship (e.g., a specific parent–child dyad) (Bartholomew & Shaver, 1998). These debates are not widely discussed by intergenerational scholars who use attachment explanations in their research on parents and adult children, and thus the theory has not advanced far in this literature.

EXPLAINING GENERATIONAL DIFFERENCES IN SOLIDARITY RATINGS

In reporting on adult intergenerational relations, the older generation fairly consistently offers a more favorable view than the younger generation. Bengtson and Kuypers (1971) formulated the notion of the developmental stake to explain their finding that young adults reported less closeness and discussion, and more disagreement in interactions with their parents than did the older generation. They attributed generational differences in perceptions of the relationship to the distinct developmental status and challenges of each generation. Drawing on Erikson's theory of psychosocial development, Bengtson and Kuypers posited that each generation's evaluation of the relationship promotes their own current developmental needs. Thus, middle-aged parents, who are dealing with generativity issues, benefit from evaluating their relationships with offspring in a positive way that reflects their influence on and importance to the next generation. Conversely, the struggle to develop an individual identity and achieve intimacy compels young adults to minimize closeness and consensus with parents, thereby promoting a view of themselves as unique, independent adults.

Subsequent work by Thompson, Clark, and Gunn (1985) provided additional evidence of these generational differences, in this case regarding attitudes on a variety of social and lifestyle issues. They went one step further however, to directly test whether psychosocial development accounted for these generational differences and found no support for the reasoning underlying the development stake. Moreover, the original reasoning offered by Bengtson and Kuypers in the formulation of the developmental stake fails to adequately explain why even very old parents report more favorable relationships than do their middle-aged offspring (Fingerman, 2001; Giarrusso, Stallings, & Bengtson, 1995; Thompson & Walker, 1984).

The revised formulation of the idea—now referred to as the "intergenerational stake," (Giarrusso et al., 1995) focuses on exchange between the generations and their differential level of resources, rather than on distinct developmental goals. It is argued that parents' generational position, and their resource advantage for most of adulthood, promotes their greater material and instrumental investment in their offspring than vice versa. This exchange pattern, discussed earlier, is thought to contribute to parents' perception of greater closeness in their relationship with offspring, compared with the view of the younger generation. The intergenerational stake notion is also supported by evidence of a similar generational discrepancy in relationship ratings by grandparents and adult grandchildren (Bengtson, Giarrusso, Silverstein & Wang, 2000).

Finally, comparisons of parent–child reports of forms of solidarity other than affective closeness have not revealed these consistent generational differences. Shapiro's (2004) dyadic analysis found that although parents rated relational quality (affectual solidarity) higher than did their adult children, the younger generation reported greater intergenerational contact and support than parents. Perhaps parents downplay their assessment of giving to promote the view of having independent, successful children; they also may report conservative estimates of received support so as to maintain their sense of competence and independence. Indeed, Shapiro found that adult children's over-reporting was correlated with increasing parental age. Yet, in another study, Mandemakers and Dykstra (2008) found that both generations over-reported giving and underreported receiving of support when compared with the other's reports. These authors offer a self-enhancement explanation for their findings.

EXPLAINING CONFLICT AND AMBIVALENCE

Conflict between adult offspring and parents, as noted, typically centers on communication differences, lifestyle choices, and different expectations and desire for interaction. Fingerman (2001) attributes much of the tension between aging mothers and adult daughters in her research to their mutual struggle for independence and the older generation's desire and demand for more contact and involvement than the younger one. She coins the term *developmental schisms* to refer to the fact that the two generations have different, competing developmental needs at their respective points in the lifespan. While adult children need space and time to deal with their multiple roles (e.g., spouse, parent, worker), aging parents often desire more closeness and attention due to retirement, loss of partner, and friends. As a result, relational tensions may mount. Findings from Fingerman's work, that of Clarke et al. (1999) and Schenk and Dykstra (2012) also align with social conflict theories that explain conflict as resulting from differing attitudes, values and behavioral choices of family members or competition for scarce and valued resources (Farrington & Chertok, 1993).

With regard to relational ambivalence, Van Gaalen, Dykstra and Komter (2010) hypothesize that ambivalence is most prevalent when structural conditions offer few "escape options" for the relationship. This explanation applies well to situations where there are limited options to defer responsibilities to other family members, such as when an adult child lives close to parents (Willson et al., 2003), or has a widowed parent (Van Gaalen et al., 2010). Few escape options also exist in situations strongly governed by social norms, as in the case of daughters providing care to aged parents, given gendered expectations about caregiving (Connidis & McMullin, 2002; Willson et al., 2003). Dependence limits escape options as well, such as when offspring depend on parental assistance in young adulthood (Pillemer et al., 2007) or parents require filial care in late life (Van Gaalen & Dykstra, 2006). Similarly, the finding reported by Fingerman et al. (2004), that the closest family ties exhibit the greatest ambivalence, is consistent with the escape options argument, because close relationships are typically viewed as less volitional than ties to distant relatives and non-family members. Also proposed by Fingerman et al. (2004), however, is the argument that because individuals hold stronger expectations for closer relationships to be supportive and positive, when such expectations are violated ambivalence is likely to arise.

Another explanation offered for the existence of intergenerational ambivalence focuses on the competing social expectations that exist for intergenerational relationships—specifically those of parents and of offspring. According to Pillemer and Suitor's research group (2007), central to the ambivalence in parent–adult child relationships are the competing social pressures to maintain solidarity in this relationship while at the same time managing independent, adult lives. This argument is substantiated by their findings that when adult children are less independent (e.g., unmarried or have serious health or other problems), mothers report greater ambivalence (Pillemer et al., 2007). It also gains support from several studies linking poor health (and possibly care demands) to ambivalent parent–adult child relationships (Fingerman et al., 2008; Pillemer et al., 2007; Willson et al., 2003). Although receiving support from parents or adult offspring may reaffirm feelings of care and concern, it can also threaten feelings of independence for the recipient, and put heightened demands on the support provider.

Finally, it is argued that ambivalence results in relationships when normative expectations are violated, because norms set standards by which to evaluate situations and relationships, and they determine what we anticipate in relationships at different points in the lifespan. This theory is posed by Pillemer and Suitor (2002) and supported by their findings that mothers report greater ambivalence in relation to their children whose life progress violates normative pathways than with those who are moving along as expected.

MACRO-LEVEL THEORIZING ON INTERGENERATIONAL RELATIONSHIPS

In all advanced societies, responsibility for the old and the young is shared in some manner between the family and the state. Interdependencies between generations (and between men and women) in families are built and reinforced by the legal and policy arrangements in a particular country. Laws define the relationships of dependence and interdependence between generations (and genders), whereas policies reward or discourage particular family patterns and practices. A consideration of legal norms and public policies draws attention to cultural specificity. Countries differ in their understanding of "proper" intergenerational family relations (Reher, 1998; Therborn, 2004; Viazzo, 2010). For that reason, when explaining cross-national differences in patterns of intergenerational exchange in families it is difficult to disentangle culturalist explanations, which focus on differences in norms and values, and structuralist explanations, which address differences in welfare state arrangements and economic wealth.

Intergenerational Regimes

To understand the family/state division of responsibility for the old and the young, three patterns in legal and policy frameworks have been distinguished (Saraceno, 2010; Saraceno & Keck, 2010), building on the writings of Esping-Andersen (1999), Korpi (2000) and Leitner (2003). These patterns differentiate between the degree to which country-specific institutional frameworks support the desire to be responsible towards one's children and frail aged parents and/or support individual autonomy, thereby partially lightening intergenerational dependencies and the gendered division of family labor. The first pattern is familialism by default, and pertains to countries where there are few or no publicly provided alternatives to family care and financial support. The second is supported familialism, where there are policies, usually in the form of financial transfers, which support families in keeping up their financial and caring responsibilities. The third is defamilializa- tion, where needs are partly addressed through public provision (services, basic income). An analy- sis of policies in all 27 countries of the European Union showed that the same pattern did not always emerge regarding responsibilities for the young and those for the old (Saraceno & Keck, 2010). Furthermore, contrary to widespread opinion, supported familialism and defamilialization are not always contrasting policy approaches. In some countries, they actually represent part of an inte- grated approach to public support of intergenerational responsibilities.

This categorization goes beyond the dichotomy of public/private responsibilities, showing that public support may both motivate and lighten private, family responsibilities. It emphasizes that country-specific institutional frameworks can impose dependencies that limit the autonomy of individuals, but they can also support individuals' choices to assume intergenerational obligations.

According to Saraceno's *intergenerational regime framework*, public family provisions (or the lack thereof) can create differential opportunities for individual autonomy for young and old, men and women. For example, generous parental leave policies support parental care for children, and, in the case of fathers' quotas specifically, support the caring role of fathers, thus de-gendering family care while supporting the "familialization" of fathers (Brandth & Kvande, 2009). Childcare services instead lighten—without fully substituting for—parental care and education responsibilities. At-home care, adult day programs or institutional services for the frail elderly partly substitute for family care. The same occurs when payments for care can only be used to hire someone in a formal way. Non-earmarked payments for care maintain informal family care but also encourage recourse to the often irregular market of domestic helpers, as is happening in some Southern European countries, where migrant workers are hired to provide childcare and eldercare at home (Ayalon, 2009).

Saraceno (2010) argues that intergenerational care regimes have different implications for social class inequalities and gender inequalities. One of the issues is whether policies involve payments for care, (paid) leaves, or the provision of care services. For example, when public support is offered in money rather than in kind, trade-offs between using it to buy services or to keep it for the family budget while providing care directly, are different for families in different socioeconomic circumstances. The strategy of staying at home to provide care is more likely to be adopted by members of the working-class (in practice: women), reducing their ability to remain in the labor market and hence contributing to the likelihood of old-age poverty for themselves.

Crowding in and Crowding Out

Another perspective on the balance of responsibility between the family and the state is that of "moral hazard" (Wolfe, 1989), the notion that people are less inclined to care for family members if public provisions are available. Empirical studies have repeatedly failed to find that provisions of the welfare state "crowd out" family care. Research consistently shows that generous welfare state services actually complement rather than substitute for family care (Chappell & Blandford, 1991; Daatland & Lowenstein, 2005; Künemund & Rein, 1999; Litwin & Attias-Donfut, 2009; Motel-Klingebiel, Tesch-Römer, & Von Kondratowitz, 2005). Moreover, it appears that welfare state support may actually "crowd in" family involvement because it allows for specialization to emerge; that is, when professional care providers take over the medically demanding, strenuous and regular physical care, family members willingly offer less demanding, spontaneous help (Bonsang, 2009; Brandt, Haberkern, & Szydlik, 2009) because they are less overwhelmed by other roles. With regard to downward family support, monetary welfare provisions enable family members to respond to those with the greatest financial needs (Deindl & Brandt, 2011; Kohli, 1999; Schenk et al., 2010).

THEORY LIMITATIONS

The study of adult intergenerational family bonds is a popular and relevant area of inquiry today given population aging. Yet this field, at least that part focused on the manifest forms of family bonds—intergenerational contact and support (Silverstein & Bengtson, 1997), is characterized by more significant recent advancements in data gathering and analysis than by theoretical contributions.

Versions of exchange theory are among the most widely used explanations for making sense of variations in intergenerational relating. As reviewed though, evidence for their utility is mixed. Inconsistent support for exchange theories may be partly due to the complexity and problems involved in operationalizing exchange principles for family ties that span decades and that have distinct features in comparison to other relationship types (Dykstra, 2009). Forged by blood, marriage, co-residence, or caring responsibilities, family bonds are virtually inalienable. Hence, it may be nonsensical to think that exchange theories, which are founded on assumptions of rational human behavior and that emphasize selfish concern, can provide strong explanations for intimate family relationships involving intense intrapersonal affective components (Rossi, 1995). The normative dimension of parent–child ties is another distinguishing characteristic. There is an "ought" to these relationships, which arguably has weakened over recent decades and differs widely across societies, but is nevertheless unmistakable (Daatland & Herlofson, 2003a). As a result, the possibility of relationship dissolution and voluntary involvement is relatively limited for parents and offspring (Van Gaalen et al., 2010), calling into question the value of exchange principles. Theory focused instead on altruistic concerns and moral obligations, including the ways in which they are negotiated in families, may provide a more true-to-life representation of the bonds between children and parents in middle and late life.

Calls to move away from theories based on rational choice have also advocated for greater consideration of intrapersonal characteristics, such as personality factors, and their role in family relationships (Rossi & Rossi, 1990). Yet, few studies in the past two decades have explored such factors (aside from attachment style—see below) and researchers have been slow to include them in their theoretical formulations. Sechrist, Suitor, Vargas and Pillemer (2011) provide one example of this approach in work revealing a significant association between shared religious values and parent–adult child relationship quality. Citing Merton and other theorists, they speculate that attitudinal similarity facilitates the establishment and maintenance of relational bonds. Studies like this one, however, require greater attention to the processes linking values and relational quality. For example, an alternative to theorizing that intrapersonal characteristics, like values, develop and then influence relationship quality is the possibility that relationship processes influence values and other intrapersonal characteristics. Glass, Bengtson, & Dunham (1986) found that intergenerational similarity in values regarding religion, politics and gender roles was as likely to result from parental influences on adult children's values as the reverse. The fact that parents' reported values were influenced as much by those of their grown children as vice-versa suggests that perhaps open, on-going association and communication between the generations over time—an aspect of relational solidarity—shapes intergenerational similarity in values. Theorizing of this sort requires researchers to be sensitive to the developmental nature of both intrapersonal factors, including personality, and relationship quality over time.

Attachment theory is the one theoretical approach based on intrapersonal psychological features that has been more extensively used to explain intergenerational relationship processes. Greater attention is needed, however, concerning conceptualization and measurement issues in applying this theory. Though two measurement approaches dominate the study of attachment in adulthood—one using a clinically scored Adult Attachment Interview and the other depending on a self-report of attachment styles in relationships (Bartholomew & Shaver, 1998), only the latter is used in the study of later life parent–offspring relationships. A problem with this measurement approach is that it assumes that adults are fully aware of the attachment dynamics in their relationships and can clearly summarize them in response to structured questions (Bartholomew & Shaver, 1998). This assumption is questionable given attachment theorists' claim that individuals develop cognitive/affective representations of themselves as relational partners based on early childhood experience, and the extent to which individuals are consciously aware of these mental schemas is not evident. Researchers who apply attachment theory and concepts to their empirical work should explicitly address such theoretical issues as they make measurement and analytic choices.

Additionally, researchers must recognize that the adult attachment system is theorized to kick in under conditions that pose a high level of threat to self or one's relational partner (Kobak & Duemmler, 1994). Consequently, strong tests of attachment theory may require examination of situations that involve relatively high intensity care demands for an aging parent or adult child, rather than the day-to-day exchanges that are the focus of most studies reported herein.

Finally, attachment theorists argue that attachment styles/patterns are reflected not only by behaviors exhibited in a given relationship, but also in terms of one's sensitivity to the needs of the relational partner and one's emotional reaction to providing care or support (Mikulincer & Shaver, 2007). Thus, to more adequately assess the role of attachment style in adult intergenerational relationships, researchers should look beyond whether support or companionship is offered to an aging parent or adult child, to how appropriate the behavior is given the needs of the relational partner (similar to contingency theory), as well as the subjective experience (e.g., discomfort, burden) of the person offering the helping behavior.

Even for scholars using theories other than attachment theory, more attention should be directed to understanding the subjective experience of intergenerational interactions, such as what motivates specific behaviors and what their outcomes are in terms of emotional well-being and perceived closeness. Help provided out of affection is likely to be less costly to the provider and more rewarding for the recipient than help given in return for earlier favors or because it is the normatively "correct" path to follow (Komter, 2005). Unraveling, both theoretically and empirically, the subjective experiences leading to, underlying, and ensuing from intergenerational exchanges, will help capture the complexities of adult childparent relationships (Silverstein & Giarrusso, 2010).

Despite calls for increased attention to intrapersonal factors and individual's subjective experience of family relationships, there remains concern that too much attention has been directed at the individuals in intergenerational relationships, thereby neglecting important higher-order relational properties and processes. According to Marshall et al. (1993), intergenerational scholars need "to entertain the idea that characteristics of the families of individual respondents may be important explanations of their behavior," (p. 62). This approach, however, raises conceptual issues in defining "family," along with challenges of adequately operationalizing and analyzing abstract "family" phenomenon and characteristics (Copeland & White, 1991). Recent work using typologies could advance this effort at both theoretical and methodological levels, though presently even typologies tend to be applied only to parent–child dyads in families (e.g. Silverstein et al., 2010; Van Gaalen & Dykstra, 2006). Qualitative approaches used in combination with quantitative data are a possible alternative for capturing these higher-order family features.

Beyond the family level, greater attention needs to be devoted to building social structural factors, such as ethnicity, race, and social class into our theories. Such factors may not only produce contextual variation in empirical findings, but also call into question the applicability and adequacy of commonly used theories. Do the key theories apply better to some family types than others? Giarrusso and colleagues (1995) question, for example, whether the intergenerational stake is as evident in ethnic groups where family members possess a stronger collective identity and downplay individualism. We also need to expand on the limited attention (Sechrist et al., 2011; Suitor, Sechrist, & Pillemer, 2007; Wong, Kitayama, & Soldo, 1999) that has been given to diversity issues. A stronger focus on the influence of unique features of various ethnic and racial groups, including their cultural history and current status in society, may aid development of theories that facilitate understanding not only of variation in the behavioral aspects of parent–adult child relations, but also in the meaning and subjective experience of these relationships, between and within various racial and ethnic groups (Becker, Beyene, Newsom, & Mayen, 2003). As Bengtson et al. (1996) argued, failure to recognize and understand the variability that exists within specific minority groups can have serious policy implications.

Finally, the explosion of cross-national work in the past decade opens the door to enhanced theorizing about macro-structural forces and their interplay with micro-level interpersonal processes. Much can be gained from a consideration of the social-structural forces that shape intergenerational dependencies: economic circumstances, legal arrangements, and public care services. A challenge is to clearly theorize about the linkages that connect these structural features with aspects of family life. It would also be of value to directly test the utility of particular theories in different sociopolitical contexts. For example, the persistent contrasts in family patterns between Anglo-Saxon, Scandinavian, Continental European, Mediterranean, and former Communist countries (Kertzer, 1991; Therborn, 2004; Viazzo, 2010), which have been traced to differences in inheritance laws, religious traditions, and means of economic production, underscore the need to analyze the applicability of altruism and reciprocity in motivating assistance between relatives. Given our increasing awareness of the complexity of intergenerational family relationships and the influences on them, it is likely that a variety of "conceptual and theoretical lenses" are required to view them clearly (Katz, Lowenstein, Phillips, & Daatland, 2005) across contexts.

CONCLUSION

Clearly, parent–adult child relationships constitute a critical domain in family studies, and one that will likely remain so in years to come. Reductions in mortality translate into more years together for adults and their parents. Thus, understanding what produces variability in parent–adult child bonds, and why, will continue to be important questions. Furthermore, growing diversity in couple and family forms will likely impact adult child–parent bonds, raising new research questions and theoretical explanations. Finally, current economic pressures around the globe will surely affect family relationships, especially those involving adults and increasingly dependent aging parents. Because times of economic austerity usually lead to retrenchment of government support and programs (Starke, 2006), family members are likely to face heightened demands for support from one another. Understanding macro-level situations of this type and how they impact intergenerational bonds across countries will become increasingly important in the future.

REFERENCES

Albertini, M., Kohli, M., & Vogel, C. (2007). Intergenerational transfers of time and money in European families: Common patterns – different regimes? *Journal of European Social Policy, 17*, 319–334.

Albrecht, S. L., Coward, R. T., & Shapiro, A. (1997). Effects of potential changes in coresidence on matched older parent-adult child dyads. *Journal of Aging Studies, 1*, 81–96.

Allen, K. R., Blieszner, R., & Roberto, K. (2000). Families in the middle and later years: A review and critique of research in the 1990s. *Journal of Marriage and the Family, 62*, 911–926.

Antonucci, T. C. (1990). Social supports and social relationships. In R. Binstock, & L. K. George (Eds.), *Handbook of aging and the social sciences* (3rd ed., pp. 205–226). New York: Academic Press.

Aquilino, W. (1994a). Impact of childhood family structure on young adults' relationships with parents. *Journal of Marriage and the Family, 56*, 295–313.

Aquilino, W. (1994b). Later-life parental divorce and widowhood: Impact on young adults' assessment of parent–child relations. *Journal of Marriage and the Family, 56*, 908–922.

Aquilino, W. (1999). Two views of one relationship: Comparing parents and young adult children's reports of the quality of intergenerational relations. *Journal of Marriage and the Family, 61*, 858–870.

Aquilino, W. (2006). Family relationships and support systems in emerging adulthood. In J. J. Arnett & J. L. Tanner (Eds.), *Emerging adults in America: Coming of age in the 21st Century* (pp. 193–217). Washington, DC: American Psychological Association.

Attias-Donfut, D., Ogg, J., & Wolff, F. (2005). European patterns of intergenerational financial and time transfers. *European Journal of Ageing, 2*, 161–173.

Ayalon, L. (2009). Family and family-like interactions in households with round-the-clock paid foreign carers in Israel. *Ageing & Society, 29*, 671–686.

Bartholomew, K., & Shaver, P. R. (1998). Methods of assessing adult attachment: Do they converge? In J. A. Simpson & W. S. Rholes (Eds.), *Attachment theory and close relationships* (pp. 25–45). New York: Guilford Press.

Becker, G., Beyene, Y., Newsom, E., & Mayen, N. (2003). Creating continuity through mutual assistance: Intergenerational reciprocity in four ethnic groups. *Journal of Gerontology: Social Sciences, 58B*, S151–S159.

Becker, G. S. (1974). A theory of social interactions. *Journal of Political Economy, 82*, 1063–1093.

Bengtson, V. L, Giarrusso, R., Mabry, J. B., & Silverstein, M. (2002). Solidarity, conflict, and ambivalence: Complementary or competing perspectives on intergenerational relationships? *Journal of Marriage and the Family, 64*, 568–576.

Bengtson, V. L, Giarrusso, R., Silverstein, M., & Wang, Q. (2000). Families and intergenerational relationships in aging societies. *Hallym International Journal of Aging, 2*, 3–10.

Bengtson, V. L., & Kuypers, J. A. (1971). Generational differences and the "developmental stake." *Aging and Human Development, 2*, 249–260.

Bengtson, V. L., Olander, E. B., & Haddad, A. A. (1976). The "generation gap" and aging family members: Toward a conceptual model. In J. F. Gubrium (Ed.). *Time, roles and self in old age* (pp. 237–263.) New York: Human Sciences Press.

Bengtson, V. L., & Roberts, R. E. L. (1991). Intergenerational solidarity in aging families: An example of formal theory construction. *Journal of Marriage and the Family*, *53*, 856–870.

Bengtson, V. L., Rosenthal, C., & Burton, L. (1996). Paradoxes of families and aging. In R. H. Binstock & L. K. George (Eds.), *Handbook of aging and the social sciences* (4th ed., pp. 253–282). New York: Academic Press.

Bengtson, V. L., & Schrader, S. S. (1982). Parent–child relations. In D. Mangen & W. Peterson (Eds.), *Handbook of research instruments in social gerontology* (Vol. 2, pp. 115–185). Minneapolis, MN: University of Minnesota Press.

Bernheim, B. D., Shleifer, A., & Summers, L. H. (1985). The strategic bequest motive. *Journal of Political Economy*, *93*, 1045–1076.

Birditt, K. S., Miller, L. M., Fingerman, K. L., & Lefkowitz, E. S. (2009). Tensions in the parent and adult child relationship: Links to solidarity and ambivalence. *Psychology and Aging*, *24*, 287–295.

Bonsang, E. (2009). Does informal care from children to their elderly parents substitute for formal care in Europe? *Journal of Health Economics*, *28*, 143–154.

Bowlby, J. (1969), *Attachment and loss, Vol. 1: Attachment*. New York: Basic Books.

Brandt, M., Haberkern, K., Szydlik, M. (2009). Intergenerational help and care in Europe. *European Sociological Review*, *25*, 585–601.

Brandth, B., & Kvande, E. (2009). Gendered or gender-neutral care politics for fathers? *The ANNALS of the American Academy of Political and Social Science*, *624*, 177–189.

Burgess, E. W. (1960). Aging in western culture. In E. W. Burgess (Ed.), *Aging in Western societies* (pp. 3–28). Chicago: University of Chicago Press.

Carpenter, B. (2001). Attachment bonds between adult daughters and their older mothers: Associations with contemporary caregiving. *Journal of Gerontology: Psychological Sciences*, *56B*, P257–P266.

Chappell, N., & Blandford, A. (1991). Informal and formal care: Exploring the complementarity. *Ageing & Society*, *11*, 299–317.

Cherlin, A. J., & Furstenberg, F. F. Jr. (1986). *The new American grandparent: A place in the family, a life apart*. New York: Basic Books.

Cicirelli, V. G. (1983). Adult children's attachment and helping behavior to elderly parents: A path model. *Journal of Marriage and the Family*, *45*, 815–826.

Cicirelli, V. G. (1993). Attachment and obligation as daughters' motives for caregiving: Behavior and subsequent effect on subjective burden. *Psychology and Aging*, *8*, 144–155.

Clarke, E., Preston, M., Raksin, J., & Bengtson, V. L. (1999). Types of conflict and tensions between older parents and adult children. *The Gerontologist*, *39*, 261–270.

Connidis, I. A., & Davies. L. (1992). Confidants and companions: Choices in later life. *Journal of Gerontology*, *47*, S115–S122.

Connidis, I. A., & McMullin, J. A. (2002). Sociological ambivalence and family ties: A critical perspective. *Journal of Marriage and Family*, *64*, 558–567.

Cooney, T. M., & Dykstra, P. (2011). Family obligations and support behaviour: A United States – Netherlands comparison. *Ageing & Society*, *31*, 1026–1050.

Cooney, T. M., & Uhlenberg, P. (1990). The role of divorce in men's relations with their adult children after mid-life. *Journal of Marriage and the Family*, *52*, 677–688.

Copeland, A. P., & White, K. M. (1991). *Studying families*. Newbury Park: Sage.

Coser, L. A. (1956). *The functions of social conflict*. London: Routledge & Kegan Paul.

Cox, D., & Rank, M. R. (1992). Inter-vivos transfers and intergenerational exchange. *Review of Economics and Statistics*, *74*, 305–314.

Cox, D., & Stark, O. (2005). On the demand for grandchildren: Tied transfers and the demonstration effect. *Journal of Public Economics*, *89*, 665–1697.

Cumming, E., & Henry, W. (1961). *Growing old: The process of disengagement*. New York: Basic Books.

Daatland, S. O. (2007). Marital history and intergenerational solidarity: The impact of divorce and unmarried cohabitation. *Journal of Social Issues*, *63*, 809–825.

Daatland, S. O., & Herlofson, K. (2003a). 'Lost solidarity' or 'changed solidarity': A comparative European view of normative solidarity, *Ageing & Society*, *23*, 537–560.

Daatland, S. O., & Herlofson, K. (2003b). Norms and ideals about elder care. In A. Lowenstein & J. Ogg, (Eds.), *OASIS. Old age and autonomy: The role of service systems and intergenerational family solidarity*. Final report (pp. 125–163). Haifa: University of Haifa.

Daatland, S. O., & Lowenstein, A. (2005). Intergenerational solidarity and the family-welfare state balance. *European Journal of Ageing*, *2*, 174–182.

Davey, A., & Eggebeen, D. (1998). Patterns of intergenerational exchange and mental health. *Journals of Gerontology: Psychological Sciences*, *53B*, P86–P95.

De Vries, J., Kalmijn, M., & Liefbroer, A. C. (2009). Intergenerational transmission of kinship norms? Evidence from siblings in a multi-actor survey. *Social Science Research*, *38*, 188–200.

Deindl, C., & Brandt, M. (2011). Financial support and practical help between older parents and their middle-aged children in Europe. *Ageing & Society*, *31*, 645–662.

Durkheim, E. (1933). *The division of labor in a society* (G. Simpson, trans.). New York: The Free Press (original work published in 1893).

Deutsch, M. (1975). Equity, equality, and need: What determines which value will be used as the basis of distributive justice. *Journal of Social Issues*, *31*, 137–149.

Dykstra, P. A. (2009). Kin relationships. In H. T. Reis & S. Sprecher (Eds.), *Encyclopedia of human relationships* (pp. 951–954). Thousand Oaks, CA: Sage.

Dykstra, P. A., & Fokkema, T. (2009, July). Normative beliefs and responsiveness to increasing parental needs. Paper prepared for the Symposium "Changing families/emerging issues and needs," at the meetings of the International Association of Gerontology and Geriatrics, Paris.

Dykstra, P. A., & Fokkema, T. (2011). Relationships between parents and their adult children: A West European typology of late-life families. *Ageing & Society*, *31*, 545–569.

Eggebeen, D. J., & Davey, A. (1998). Do safety nets work? The role of anticipated help in times of need. *Journal of Marriage and Family*, *60*, 939–950.

Emerson, R. (1976). Social exchange theory. *Annual Review of Sociology*, *2*, 335–362.

Esping-Andersen, G. (1999). *Social foundations of postindustrial economies*. Oxford, England: Oxford University Press.

Farrington, K., & Chertok, E. (1993). Social conflict theories of the family. In P. G. Boss, W. J. Doherty, R. LaRossa, W. R. Schumm, & S. K. Steinmetz (Eds.), *Sourcebook of family theories and methods: A contextual approach* (pp. 357–381). New York: Plenum Press.

Finch, J., & Mason, J. (1990.) Filial obligations and kin support for elderly people. *Ageing & Society*, *10*, 151–175.

Finch, J., & Mason, J. (1993). *Negotiating family responsibilities*. London: Tavistock/Routledge.

Fingerman, K. L. (2001). *Mothers and their adult daughters: Mixed emotions, enduring bonds*. New York: Springer.

Fingerman, K. L., Miller, L., Birditt, K., & Zarit, S. (2009). Giving to the good and the needy: Parental support of grown children. *Journal of Marriage and Family*, *71*, 1220–1233.

Fingerman, K. L., Hay, E. L., & Birditt, K. S. (2004). The best of ties, the worst of ties: Close, problematic, and ambivalent social relationships. *Journal of Marriage and Family*, *66*, 792–808.

Fingerman, K. L., Miller, L., Birditt, K. & Zarit, S. (2009). Giving to the good and the needy: parental support of grown children. *Journal of Marriage and Family*, *71*, 1220–1233.

Fingerman, K. L., Pitzer, L. M., Chan, W., Birditt, K., Franks, M. M., & Zarit, S. (2011). Who gets what and why? Help middle-aged adults provide to parents and grown children. *Journal of Gerontology: Social Sciences*, *66B* (1), 87–98.

Fingerman, K. L., Pitzer, L. M., Lefkowitz, E. S., Birditt, K., & Mroczek, D. (2008). Ambivalent relationship qualities between adults and their parents: Implications for the well-being of both parties. *Journal of Gerontology: Psychological Sciences*, *63B*, P362–P371.

Giarrusso, R., Stallings, M., & Bengtson, V. L. (1995). The "intergenerational stake" hypothesis revisited: Parent-adult child differences in perceptions of relationships 20 years later. In V. L. Bengtson, K. W. Schaie, & L. M. Burton (Eds.), *Adult intergenerational relations: Effects of social change* (pp. 227–263). New York: Springer.

Glass, J., Bengtson, V. L., & Dunham, C. C. (1986). Attitude similarity in three-generation families: Socialization, status inheritance, or reciprocal influence? *American Sociological Review*, *51*, 685–698.

Grundy, E., & Shelton, N. (2001). Contact between adult children and their parents in Great Britain 1986–1999. *Environment and Planning A*, *33*, 685–697.

Ha, J. (2008). Changes in support from confidants, children, and friends following widowhood. *Journal of Marriage and Family*, *70*, 306–318.

Hank, K. (2007). Proximity and contacts between older parents and their children: A European comparison. *Journal of Marriage and Family*, *69*, 157–173.

Hank, K., & Kreyenfeld, M. (2003). A multilevel analysis of child care and women's fertility decisions in Western Germany. *Journal of Marriage and Family*, *65*, 584–596.

Herlofson, K., Hagestad, G., Slagsvold, B., & Sørensen, A.-M. (2011). *Intergenerational family responsibility and solidarity in Europe*. Deliverable 4.3 for the European Commission Seventh Framework funded project MULTILINKS (#217523). Retrieved from http://www.multilinks-project.eu/uploads/papers/0000/0038/herlofson_deliverable.pdf.

Homans, G. C. (1950). *The human group*. New York: Harcourt, Brace and World.

Homans, G. C. (1961). *Social behavior: Its elementary forms*. New York: Harcourt.

Howard, P. E. N., Rainie, L., & Jones, S. (2001). Days and night on the Internet: The impact of diffusing technology. *American Behavioral Scientist*, *45*, 383–404.

Ikkink, K. K., Van Tilburg, T., & Knipscheer, K. C. P. M. (1999). Perceived instrumental support exchanges in relationships between elderly parents and their adult children: Normative and structural explanations. *Journal of Marriage and the Family*, *61*, 831–833.

Katz, R., Lowenstein, A., Phillips, J., & Daatland, S. O. (2005). Theorizing intergenerational family relations: Solidarity, conflict, and ambivalence in cross-national contexts. In V. L. Bengtson, A. C. Acock, K. R. Allen, P. Dilworth-Anderson, & D. Klein (Eds.), *Sourcebook of family theory and research* (pp. 393–407). Thousand Oaks, CA: Sage.

Kalmijn, M. (2007). Gender differences in the effects of divorce, widowhood and remarriage on intergenerational support: Does marriage protect fathers? *Social Forces*, *85*, 1079–1104.

Kalmijn, M., & Dykstra, P. A. (2006). Differentials in face-to-face contact between parents and their grown-up children. In P. A. Dykstra, M. Kalmijn, T. C.M. Knijn, A. E. Komter, A. C. Liefbroer, & C. H. Mulder (Eds.), *Family solidarity in the Netherlands* (pp. 63–87). Amsterdam: Dutch University Press.

Kalmijn, M., & Saraceno, C. (2008). A comparative perspective on intergenerational support: Responsiveness to parental needs in individualistic and familistic countries. *European Societies*, *10*, 479–508.

Kertzer, D. I. (1991). Household history and sociological theory. *Annual Review of Sociology*, *17*, 155–179.

Klaus, D. (2009). Why do adult children support their parents? *Journal of Comparative Family Studies*, *40* (2), 227–241.

Kobak, R. R., & Duemmler, S. (1994). Attachment and conversation: Toward a discourse analysis of adolescent and adult security. In K. Bartholomew & D. Perlman (Eds.), *Attachment processes in adulthood* (pp. 121–149). London, England: Jessica Kingsley.

Kohli, M. (1999). Private and public transfers between generations: Linking the family and the state. *European Societies*, *1*, 81–104.

Komter, A. E. (2005). *Social solidarity and the gift*. Cambridge, England: Cambridge University Press.

Korpi, W. (2000). Faces of inequality: Gender, class and patterns of inequality in different of welfare states. *Social Politics*, *7*, 127–191.

Künemund, H., & Rein, M. (1999). There is more to receiving than needing: Theoretical arguments and empirical explorations of crowding in and crowding out. *Ageing & Society*, *19*, 93–121.

Lawton, L., Silverstein, M., & Bengtson, V. (1994). Affection, social contact, and geographic distance between adult children and their parents. *Journal of Marriage and the Family*, *56*, 57–68.

Lee, G. R., Netzer, J. K., & Coward, R. T. (1994). Filial responsibility expectations and patterns of intergenerational assistance. *Journal of Marriage and the Family*, *56*, 559–565.

Leitner, S. (2003). Varieties of familialism. The caring function of the family in comparative perspective. *European Societies*, *5*, 353–375.

Lin, I. (2008). Consequences of parental divorce for adult children's support to their frail parents. *Journal of Marriage and Family*, *70*, 113–128.

Luescher, K., & Pillemer, K. (1998). Intergenerational ambivalence: A new approach to the study of parent–child relations in later life. *Journal of Marriage and the Family*, *60*, 413–425.

Mandemakers, J. J., & Dykstra, P. A. (2008). Discrepancies in parent's and adult child's reports of support and contact. *Journal of Marriage and Family*, *70*, 495–506.

Marshall, V. W., Matthews, S. H., & Rosenthal, C. J. (1993). Elusiveness of family life: A challenge for the sociology of aging. *Annual Review of Geriatrics*, *13*, 39–72.

Matthews, S., & Sun, R. (2006). Incidence of four-generation family lineages: Is timing of fertility or mortality a better explanation? *Journal of Gerontology: Social Sciences*, *61B*, S99–S106.

McCulloch, B. J. (1990). The relationship of intergenerational reciprocity of aid to the morale of older parents: Equity and exchange theory comparisons. *Journals of Gerontology: Social Sciences, 45*, S150–S155.

McGarry, K., & Schoeni, R. F. (1997). Transfer behavior within the family: Results from the Asset and Health Dynamics study. *Journals of Gerontology: Social Sciences, 52B*, S8292.

Merz, E.-M. (2010). *Caring for your loved ones? An attachment perspective on solidarity between generations*. Saarbrücken, Germany: Lambert Academic.

Mikulincer, M., & Shaver, P. R. (2007). Relations between the attachment and caregiving systems. In Mikulincer, M., & Shaver, P. R. (Eds), *Attachment in adulthood: Structure, dynamics, and change* (pp. 324–345). New York: Guilford Press.

Mitchell, B. A. (2005). *The boomerang age: Transitions to adulthood in families*. New Brunswick, NJ: Transaction Publishers.

Mitrut, A., & Wolff, F.-C. (2009). A causal test of the demonstration effect theory. *Economics Letters, 103*, 52–54.

Motel-Klingebiel, A., Tesch-Römer, C., & Von Kondratowitz, H.-J. (2005). Welfare states do not crowd out the family: Evidence for mixed responsibility from comparative analyses, *Ageing & Society, 25*, 863–882.

Offer, A. (1997). Between the gift and the market: The economy of regard. *The Economic History Review, 50*, 450–476.

Parrot, T. M., & Bengtson, V. L. (1999). The effects of earlier intergenerational affection, normative expectations, and family conflict on contemporary exchanges of help and support. *Research on Aging, 21* (1), 73–105.

Parrot, T., Giarrusso, R., & Bengtson, V. L. (1997). Conflict in adult child-older parent relationships: The paradoxical influence of intergenerational solidarity. Unpublished manuscript.

Parsons, T., & Bales, R. (1955). *Family socialization and interaction process*. New York: The Free Press.

Peek, M. K., Coward, R. T., Peek, C. W., & Lee, G. R. (1998). Are expectations for care related to the receipt of care? An analysis of parent care among disabled elders. *Journal of Gerontology: Social Sciences, 53B*, S127–S136.

Pezzin, L. E., Pollak, R. A., & Schone, B. S. (2008). Parental marital disruption, family type, and transfers to disabled elderly parents. *Journal of Gerontology: Social Sciences, 63B*, S349–S358.

Pillemer, K., & Suitor, J. J. (2002). Explaining mothers' ambivalence toward their adult children. *Journal of Marriage & the Family, 64*, 602–613.

Pillemer, K., Suitor, J. J., Mock, S. E., Sabir, M., Pardo, T. B., & Sechrist, J. (2007). Capturing the complexity of intergenerational relations: Exploring ambivalence within later-life families. *Journal of Social Issues, 63*, 775–791.

Puur, A., Sakkeus, L., Põldma, A., & Herm, A. (2011). Intergenerational family constellations in contemporary Europe: Evidence from the Generations and Gender Survey. *Demographic Research, 25*, 135–172.

Reher, D. S. (1998). Family ties in Western Europe: Persistent contrasts. *Population and Development Review, 24*, 203–234.

Robertson, S., & Mosher-Ashley, P. (2002). Patterns of confiding and factors influencing mental health service use in older adults. *Clinical Gerontology: Journal of Aging and Mental Health, 26*, 101–116.

Rosenthal, D. J., Matthews, S. H., & Marshall, V. W. (1989). Is parent care normative? The experience of a sample of middle-aged women. *Research on Aging, 11*, 244–260.

Rossi, A. S. (1995). Commentary: Wanted: Alternative theories and analysis modes. In V. L. Bengtson, K. W. Schaie, & L. M. Burton (Eds.), *Adult intergenerational relations: Effects of societal change* (pp. 264–276). New York: Springer.

Rossi, A. S., & Rossi, P. H. (1990). *Of human bonding: Parent–child relations across the life course*. New York: Aldine de Gruyter.

Saraceno, C. (2010). Social inequalities in facing old-age dependency: A bi-generational perspective. *Journal of European Social Policy, 20*, 32–44.

Saraceno, C., & Keck, W. (2010). Can we identify intergenerational policy regimes in Europe? *European Societies, 12*, 675–696.

Schenk, N., & Dykstra, P. A. (2012). Continuity and change in intergenerational family relationships: An examination of shifts in relationship type over a three-year period. *Advances in Life Course Research*. Retrieved from http://dx.doi.org/10.1016/j.alcr.2012.01.004 (accessed 30 January 2012).

Schenk, N., Dykstra, P.A., & Maas, I. (2010). The role of European welfare states in intergenerational monetary transfers: A micro-level perspective. *Ageing & Society, 30*, 1315–1342.

Schwarz, B., & Trommsdorff, G. (2005). The relation between attachment and intergenerational support. *European Journal on Ageing*, 2, 192–199.

Sechrist, J., Suitor, J. J., Varga, N., & Pillemer, K. (2011). The role of perceived religious similarity in the quality of mother-child relations in later life: Differences within families and between races. *Research on Aging*, *33*(1), 3–27.

Shanas, E., Townsend, P., Wedderburn, D., Friis, H., Milhoj, P., & Stehouwer, J. (1968). *Old people in three industrial societies*. New York: Atherton Press.

Shapiro, A. (2003). Later-life divorce and parent/adult-child contact and proximity: A longitudinal analysis. *Journal of Family Issues*, *24*, 264–285.

Shapiro, A. (2004). Revisiting the generational gap: Exploring the relationships of parent/adult-child dyads. *International Journal of Aging and Human Development*, *58*, 127–146.

Silverstein, M. (2005). Testing theories about intergenerational exchanges. In V. L. Bengtson, A. C. Acock, K. R. Allen, P. Dilworth-Anderson, & D. Klein (Eds.), *Sourcebook of family theory and research* (pp. 407–410). London, England: Sage.

Silverstein, M., & Angelelli, J. J. (1998). Older parents' expectations of moving closer to their children. *Journals of Gerontology: Social Sciences*, *53B* (3), S153–S163.

Silverstein, M., & Bengtson, V. L. (1997). Intergenerational solidarity and the structure of adult child-parent relationships in American families. *American Journal of Sociology*, *103* (2), 429–460.

Silverstein, M., Conroy, S., Wang, H., Giarrusso, R., & Bengtson, V. (2002). Reciprocity in parent-child relations over the adult life course. *Journals of Gerontology: Social Sciences*, *57B*, S3–S13.

Silverstein, M., Gans, D., Lowenstein, A., Giarrusso, R., & Bengtson, V. L. (2010). Older parent-child relationships in six developed nations: Comparisons at the intersection of affection and conflict. *Journal of Marriage and Family*, *72*, 1006–1021.

Silverstein, M., Gans, D., & Yang, F. M. (2006). Intergenerational support to aging parents: The role of norms and needs. *Journal of Family Issues, 27*, 1068–1084.

Silverstein, M., & Giarrusso, R. (2010). Aging and family life: A decade review. *Journal of Marriage and Family*, *72*, 1039–1058.

Silverstein, M., Parrott, T. M., & Bengtson, V. L. (1995). Factors that predispose middle-aged sons and daughters to provide social support to older parents. *Journal of Marriage and the Family*, *57*, 465–475.

Simmel, G. (1904). The sociology of conflict I. *American Journal of Sociology*, *9*, 490–525.

Smith, T. W. (2000). *Changes in the generation gap, 1972–1998*. Retrieved from http://cloud9.norc.uchicago.edu/dlib/sc-43.htm (accessed January 18, 2011).

Smits, A., Van Gaalen, R. I., & Mulder, C. H. (2010). Parent–child coresidence: Who moves in with whom and for whose needs? *Journal of Marriage and Family*, *72*, 1022–1033.

Soldo, B. J. (1996). Cross pressures on middle-aged adults: A broader view. *Journals of Gerontology: Social Sciences*, *57B*, 271–273.

Soldo, B. J., & Hill, M. S. (1993). Intergenerational transfers: Economic, demographic, and social perspectives. In G. L Maddox & M. P. Lawton, (Eds.), *Annual review of gerontology and geriatrics* (Vol. 13): *Focus on kinship, aging, and social change* (pp. 187–216). New York: Springer.

Sorensen, S., Webster, J. D., & Roggman, L. A. (2002). Adult attachment and preparing to provide care for older relatives. *Attachment and Human Development*, *4* (1), 84–106.

Stark, O. (1999). *Altruism and beyond: An economic analysis of transfers and exchanges within families and groups*. Cambridge, England: Cambridge University Press.

Starke, P. (2006). The politics of welfare state retrenchment: A literature review. *Social Policy & Administration*, *40*, 104–120.

Stein, C. H., Wemmerus, V. A., Ward, M., Gaines, M. E., Freeberg, A. L., & Jewell, T. C. (1998). "Because they're my parents": An intergenerational study of felt obligations and parental caregiving. *Journal of Marriage and the Family*, *60*, 611–622.

Suitor, J. J., Pillemer, K., & Sechrist, J. (2006). Within-family differences in mothers' support to adult children. *Journal of Gerontology: Social Sciences*, *61B (1)*, S10–S17.

Suitor, J. J., Sechrist, J., & Pillemer, K. (2007). Within-family differences in mothers' support to adult children in Black and White families. *Research on Aging*, *29*, 410–435.

Sussman, M. B. (1953). The help pattern in the middle class family. *American Sociological Review*, *18*, 22–28.

Sussman, M. B., & Burchinal, L. (1962). Kin family networks: Unheralded structures in current conceptualizations of family functioning. *Marriage and Family Living*, *24*, 231–240.

Szinovacz, M. E., & Davey, A. (2001). Retirement effects on parent-adult child contacts. *The Gerontologist*, *41*, 191–200.

Therborn, G. (2004). *Between sex and power: Family in the world, 1900–2000*. London, England: Routledge.

Thompson, L., Clark, K., & Gunn, W., Jr. (1985). Developmental stage and perceptions of intergenerational continuity. *Journal of Marriage and the Family*, *47*, 913–920.

Thompson, L., & Walker, A. (1984). Mothers and daughters: Aid patterns and attachment. *Journal of Marriage and the Family*, *56*, 313–322.

Tomassini, C., Wolf, D. A., & Rosina, A. (2003). Parental housing assistance and parent–child proximity in Italy. *Journal of Marriage and Family*, *65*, 700–715.

Uhlenberg, P. (1996). Mortality decline in the Twentieth Century and supply of kin over the life course. *The Gerontologist*, *36*, 681–685.

Van Gaalen, R. I., & Dykstra, P. A. (2006). Solidarity and conflict between adult children and parents: A latent class analysis. *Journal of Marriage and Family*, *68*, 947–960.

Van Gaalen, R. I., Dykstra, P. A. & Komter, A. E. (2010). Where is the exit? Intergenerational ambivalence and relationship quality in high contact ties. *Journal of Aging Studies*, *24*, 105–114.

Viazzo, P. P. (2010). Family, kinship and welfare provision in Europe, past and present: Commonalities and divergences. *Continuity and Change*, *25*, 137–159.

Wade-Benzoni, K., & Tost, L. P. (2009). The egoism and altruism of intergenerational behavior. *Personality and Social Psychology Review*, *13*, 165–193.

Walster, E. G., Walster, W., & Berscheid, E. (1978). *Equity: Theory and research*. Boston, MA: Allyn & Bacon.

Wenger, G. C., & Jerrome, D. (1999). Change and stability in confidant relationships: Findings from the Bangor Longitudinal Study of Ageing. *Journal of Aging Studies*, *13*, 269–294.

Willson, A. E., Shuey, K. M., & Elder, G. H., Jr. (2003). Ambivalence in the relationship of adult children to aging parents and in-laws. *Journal of Marriage and Family*, *65*, 1055–1072.

Willson, A. E., Shuey, K. M., Elder, G. H., Jr., & Wickrama, K. A. S. (2006). Ambivalence in mother-adult child relations: A dyadic analysis. *Social Psychology Quarterly*, *69*, 235–252.

Wolfe, A. (1989). *Whose keeper? Social science and moral obligations*. Berkeley, CA: University of California Press.

Wolff, F.-C. (2001). Private intergenerational contact in France and the demonstration effect. *Applied Economics*, *33*, 143–153.

Wong, R., Kitayama, K. E., & Soldo, B. J. (1999). Ethnic differences in time transfers from adult children to elderly parents: Unobserved heterogeneity across families? *Research on Aging*, *21*, 144–175.

Section VI

Families and Extrafamilial Institutions

21 The State of Theory in Work and Family Research at the Turn of the Twenty-First Century

Maureen Perry-Jenkins and Shelley M. MacDermid

Over 30 years ago, Kanter (1977) proposed a fundamental shift in our understanding of the work–family interface with the simple, yet profound, idea—work and family, far from being separate spheres, are contexts that intersect and interact with each other in a myriad of ways. Since that time, research on work and family has flourished across multiple disciplines, including: psychology, sociology, family studies, economics, communication, organizational behavior, law, political science, social work, and public policy. One consequence of its interdisciplinary roots is that the work–family literature covers topics ranging from the effects of daily work stressors on later family behavior to macro-level studies that examine the ways in which different social norms across countries shape workers commitment to family and employment. Although an exciting and vibrant field of study, work and family scholars face the challenge of integrating research across disciplines, each with its own diverse approaches to studying work–family phenomena, in a way that captures the complexity of the topic while also framing issues in a clear and concise manner. Research in this field has much to offer to the policy arena because it addresses many societal problems such as unemployment, underemployment, recruitment and retention, work–life stress, and productivity, as well as related topics such as healthcare and childcare. Thus, it is important that we identify the most useful theories that not only assist us in organizing the plethora of work and family research that has arisen across disciplines but also moves the field forward in a grounded and coherent way.

Theory is alive and well in the study of work and family, where numerous theories have been used to conceptualize the nature of the interrelationships between the two spheres. Few attempts have been made, however, to consider which theories are most prominent in the field, which theories have provided key insights into understanding work–family processes, and which theories hold the most promise for furthering our field. Kurt Lewin noted long ago that, "There is nothing so practical as a good theory" (Lewin, 1952, p. 169); unfortunately, we have found that there is nothing so overwhelming as too many "good theories" to choose from. Our goal in this chapter is to highlight those theories that have been the most "practical" in furthering our understanding of work–family issues with a critical eye towards not only how these theories have enhanced our knowledge, thus far, but perhaps, at times, have limited our approach to new knowledge.

KEY ISSUES IN WORK AND FAMILY RESEARCH

An analysis of three-decade reviews that have been written about the field of work and family, published in one of the premier outlets for work–family research, the *Journal of Marriage and Family*, highlights a number of key topics in the field that have remained consistent over the years.

Specifically, the topics include: (a) gender, time, and division of labor in the home, and the related topic of the gender gap in wages; (b) paid work (too much or too little); (c) parental (primarily maternal) employment and child outcomes; (d) work–family inter-role conflict; (d) work, family, stress, and health; and (e) work–family policies, both public and private (Bianchi & Milkie, 2010; Menaghan & Parcel, 1990; Perry-Jenkins, Repetti, & Crouter, 2000).

Turning to the first topic, focused on gender, time, and the distribution of paid and unpaid labor in families, research in this vein continues to receive great attention in the field. Although Bianchi and Milkie (2010) document the narrowing gender gap between men's and women's time in paid and unpaid labor, research has consistently shown that even with the movement to greater equality in the division of labor, women continue to spend more time caring for children and more time multitasking (Craig, 2006). Numerous studies have attempted to uncover possible causal explanations for gender inequity in paid work and unpaid work; however, no one theory has proven successful in providing an answer. Theoretical perspectives that have been used to explain the division of labor in families include: (a) relative resources, (b) time availability, (c) gender ideology, and (d) doing gender (Bianchi & Milkie, 2010).

Another theme in the work–family literature focuses on how much and when people work. Jacobs and Gerson (2004) point to the problems of overwork and workplace inflexibility for middle-income and professional workers, while research by Lambert (2009) highlights the challenges of underemployment (e.g., too few hours), the uncertainty of job schedules, and at times "too much flexibility" in low-wage jobs.

A work–family topic that has received less attention over the past decade is parental work conditions, usually mothers' work, as they affect children's development. Interestingly, the field of work and family gained public notice in the 1970s because of societal concerns that the increase in maternal employment rates would have negative implications for child development. When research consistently showed few effects of maternal work hours on child outcomes, studies began to examine how conditions of work (i.e., autonomy, control, support) affected the worker and, in turn, children's outcomes. Parcel and Menaghan (1994), using a work socialization perspective, highlighted the ways in which workplace autonomy and problem solving skills as well as positive workplace relationships enhanced children's developmental outcomes. More recently, using data from the NICHD Study of Early Childcare, Brooks-Gunn, Han, and Waldfogel (2010) examined the effects of maternal employment on children's cognitive and emotional development. In the most comprehensive analysis ever completed with a large, representative sample, the findings document the effects of early maternal work (i.e., work in the first year of life) on children's development across the first 7 years of life. Although pointing to no overall negative or positive effects of maternal employment on child development, the more nuanced analyses point to unique effects of maternal employment at different times during children's development. For example, in families where mothers worked full-time by 3 months, teachers and caregivers were more likely to report externalizing problems at 4.5 years and in first grade. In addition, the findings point to advantages for children whose mothers work part-time rather than full-time. As we will discuss in this chapter, key moderating (e.g., race, ethnicity, social class) and mediating factors (e.g., parental well-being) as well as childcare quality are all critical variables to address in framing these results.

Perhaps the area of greatest research activity over the years has focused on work–family conflict. This topic has been approached from multiple theoretical perspectives including *role theory* and related theories such as *demand–resource theory*, *border and boundary theories*, and *stress theories*. The work–family conflict approach posits that work and family roles are in constant conflict due to incompatibility in role demands from each domain. In contrast, a number of scholars argue for *role expansionist/facilitation theory* (Barnett & Hyde, 2001; Frone, Russell & Cooper, 1992; Grzywacz & Butler, 2005; Marks, 1977), an approach that holds that engagement in multiple roles can be an opportunity to enhance one's energy, which, in turn, can lead to better mental and physical health.

The question of how work stressors can affect the health and well-being of workers and their families has been a frequent topic of study for work–family researchers. Work hours, *per se*, are not strongly linked to mental and physical health, but the time of day that one works does matter. Specifically, non-day shifts for working parents take a toll on both mental health and marital relations (Barnett, Gareis, & Brennan, 2008; Perry-Jenkins, Goldberg, Pierce & Sayer, 2007). In addition to work hours, other critical work stressors include time urgency on the job, lack of autonomy and control, low supervisor support, poor co-worker relations and long and/or alternating work shifts. There are two ways that stress can affect individual and family outcomes. The first is through short-term stress processes whereby daily stressful work conditions lead workers to withdraw from interactions at home and/or engage in more negative interactions (Repetti, 2005). The second way that stress operates is through the long term effects of chronic job stress on physical and emotional well-being.

Finally, work–family research has direct implications for public policy and over the past decade research in this area has increased dramatically. Kossek and Distelberg (2009) argue, however, that most of the research in this area has focused on the availability of policies as opposed to their effectiveness. As Bianchi and Milkie (2010) point out, the effectiveness of any given policy depends on the desired outcomes. At a very global level, theoretical perspectives that have been used to understand both the availability and effectiveness of policy are explained by Folbre (1994) through the societal values of collectivism versus individualism. Are we, as a society, responsible for children and others who may not be able to care for themselves and should our policies reflect that collectivist responsibility or, from an individualistic perspective, is the pervasive view that we are responsible only for ourselves and what is ours? Folbre posits that a deep and abiding social value of individualism, which pervades US ideology, explains the lack of supportive work–family policies in this country. Compared with other industrialized nations, the US has meager public policies and programs for working families. Research that examines the effects of work place policies on family life suggests that the use of work–family supports predicts lower wages for mothers (Glass, 2004), but also predicts higher rates of breastfeeding, better maternal health, and greater job stability, all factors related to better cognitive and emotional outcomes for children (Kelly, 2006).

It is clear from this brief overview that the research on work and family covers numerous topics from multiple perspectives and, consequently, this research has also been approached from a wide range of theoretical perspectives. The goal of this chapter is to provide an overview of those theories that have been influential in the field while presenting a critical analysis of the role of theory in the work–family literature. In addition, a second aim is to offer some recommendations for theory and theory development as we move our field forward.

At the outset, it is fair to say that we were overwhelmed with the enormity of the task we had agreed to complete. Given the vast array of disciplines that address work and family issues and given the sheer number of articles that exist on this topic, we were initially stymied with how to proceed. For example, a search for the phrase "work and family" in PsychINFO yields almost 50,000 references; a similar search in Sociological Abstracts yields over 24,000 results. Clearly an exhaustive review of the literature would be a formidable, if not impossible, undertaking. Given that our aim was to understand how theory has guided the work–family literature, we decided that the best approach would be to examine which theories arose as most prominent over the past decade and we decided to do this by reviewing the top 20 articles chosen each year, over the past 10 years, for the Kanter Award for Excellence in Work–Family Research. Under the leadership of Professor Shelley MacDermid Wadsworth, every year since 1999, a large panel of work–family scholars has been charged with sifting through between 2,000 and 3,000 articles to find the "best of the best" in terms of work and family research. The review committee includes scholars from around the world who review research in over 74 journals across a wide range of disciplines. This data base provides a rich resource of what leading scholars in our field see as the best research in the field on work and family issues. We proceeded to review the top 20 articles nominated from 1999 to 2009 and assessed which theory or theories guided each article, the samples used, and the major themes addressed. In the following section, we identify and briefly describe the theories that have informed the field.

THEORIES THAT HAVE INFLUENCED WORK AND FAMILY RESEARCH

ROLE THEORY AND WORK–FAMILY CONFLICT AND FACILITATION

One of the most influential theories in the field of work and family is *role theory*. A key premise of role theory is that individuals generally occupy multiple roles defined by socially prescribed rules and norms for behavior. Roles, while guiding the behavior of individuals, can be understood from two different vantage points: the structural–functionalist perspective and the interactionist perspective. From a structural–functionalist perspective, roles are conceived of as a set of expectations for individuals constructed and enforced by society. Thus, as a society, we have agreed upon norms and behavioral expectations for roles such as "mother" and "father" or "teacher" and "student." In contrast, from an interactionist perspective, roles are continually being constructed and reconstructed within different social contexts. In one setting, an individual may take on the role of "leader," while in another he or she might be "follower." Thus, the question of whether roles are fixed and static versus fluid and dynamic has been a topic of great theoretical debate. In our review of the Kanter papers over the past 10 years, approximately 22% of the articles used the basic tenets of role theory in conceptualizing their research, and another 25% built on role theory in conceptualizing work–family conflict and facilitation theories.

For example, Dierdoff and Ellington (2008) suggest that work–family conflict emerges from the competing pressures individuals face managing multiple roles across settings. They argue that distinct norms and requirements attached to work and family roles create strain and, "to reduce stress individuals are often forced to make concessions in performing one role over another. In the context of the work and family role interface, such interference can cause inter-role conflict" (p. 884). In their study of 2,765 workers in 126 different occupations, Dierdoff and Ellington found that specific occupational role demands and obligations predicted greater work–family conflict.

As highlighted above, theoretical constructs stemming from role theory play key roles in the work–family literature. Specifically, concepts such as role conflict, role strain, and role boundaries abound in the literature. As early as 1960, Goode presented a theory of *role strain* that described the difficulty of fulfilling multiple role demands. Goode's early theorizing was vital to the work and family field in that he articulated how the concept of role strain captured workers' inability, at times, to handle their work and family obligations and predicted negative psychological outcomes. Given the dramatic shifts that were about to occur in the 1960s and 1970s, regarding the institutions of work and family, Goode's work provided a strong theoretical framework to begin examining the interrelationship of work and family.

Two decades later, Greenhaus and Beutell's (1985) theorizing on inter-role conflict spearheaded the work–family conflict literature. In the 1990s, Frone and colleagues (Frone, Russell, & Cooper, 1992; Frone, Yardley, & Markel, 1997) introduced the concepts of work-family conflict (WFC) and family–work conflict (FWC) that have been used extensively across multiple disciplines. Work–family conflict occurs when a person's participation in his or her work role interferes with family roles and family–work conflict addresses the ways in which family roles and responsibilities impinge upon the work role. In a meta-analysis conducted by Ford, Heinen, and Langkamer (2007) that examined the bidirectional effects of work on family and family on work, it was found that stressors and supports in each domain were related to satisfaction outside of that domain. In short, family conflict negatively affects work satisfaction just as work conflict negatively affects family satisfaction. They also emphasized the important conclusion that objective role demands, such as work hours or time spent in childcare, are perceived and responded to differently by employees. Thus, role researchers must be careful in considering how the meanings attached to certain roles influence how an employee responds to the demands of that role.

In still another application, Westman, Hamilton, Vinokur, and Roziner (2004) studied the crossover of negative concerns about work from one spouse to the other in a sample of Russian Army officers during a period of military downsizing. Results showed that wives were more susceptible to crossover effects than husbands, supporting Pleck's (1977) notion of 'asymmetrical permeability,' which suggests that work and family effects tend to flow more strongly in one direction than the other for husbands and wives. Specifically, Westman et al. found that wives reported negative fallout from their husbands' negative work experiences, but there was little evidence of husbands being negatively influenced by their wives' work experiences.

Although work–family conflict, as a theoretical construct, is by far the most common term used in the work–family literature, there have been many calls from scholars in the field to expand the work–family paradigm to include a positive perspective incorporating what has been coined, "work–family facilitation." Work–family facilitation refers to, "the extent to which individuals' participation in one life domain (e.g., work) is made easier by the skills and experiences, and opportunities gained by their participating in another domain" (Grzywacz & Butler, 2005, p. 97). Barnett (1998) proposed that a holistic conceptualization of work–family fit required attention to both work–family conflict and facilitation. Marks (1977) referred to this process as the role expansion/enhancement theory and proposed that occupying multiple roles provides individuals with greater opportunities and resources.

Voydanoff (2004) provides an empirical example of exploring both work–family conflict and facilitation simultaneously using the National Survey of Midlife Development to study these processes in 2,507 employees ranging in age from 25 to 74 years. Results indicated that work demands were relatively more important than resources in relation to work–family conflict and work resources were more important in relation to work–family facilitation, emphasizing the importance of examining both types of effects in assessing the full valence of work–family effects.

Despite the strong theoretical underpinnings of role theory in much of the work–family literature, a number of critiques of this perspective have been proposed, most notably from feminist theorists. The term "sex role," used to identify distinct roles of women and men, has been rejected by feminist scholars who argue that the concept of a sex role reifies the roles played by women and men and obscures the power inequities inherent in gender. Moreover, early theorizing about gender socialization during early childhood has been called into question. Notions that gender identity and related "normative" behaviors are established early in development and, as such, are fairly immutable (Cahill, 1983) fails to explain how gender-related change in adulthood occurs, and virtually ignores the larger macro-sociopolitical context within which "doing gender" occurs. Thus, a key challenge posed by feminist scholars is to consider how the social construction of work and family roles serves to maintain the status quo and gender inequality.

THEORETICAL PERSPECTIVES ON WORK AND STRESS

Concepts of stress and strain are central to the theoretical underpinnings of the work and family field and reflect the second most common theme in the work and family literature over the past decade. They are discussed in close to one quarter of the Kanter papers (24.8%). Conger and Elder (1994) have demonstrated direct connections between family economic stress and marital distress, negative parent–child relations, and diminished child well-being.

Karasek's (1979) job demand–control model, originally proposed in the mid-1970s, posited that workers will experience the most distress under conditions of high job demands and low control. This model, often referred to as the *job strain model*, has received considerable attention in the field. In a modification of the original model, the *job demand–control–support model* (JDCS) was introduced, which includes the addition of social support as a buffer of demands (Karasek, Triantis, & Chaudhry, 1982; Searle, Bright, & Bochner, 2001). In this theoretical context, social support refers to the interpersonal resources that individuals draw upon to help them cope with stressful situations.

In a qualitative study of executive-level female managers, Ezzedeen and Ritchey (2008) built on the JDCS model and described the critical role of spousal support, especially emotional and esteem support, as a buffer to the demands of CEO positions. In a quantitative test of the JDCS model, Hammer, Saksvik, Nytro, Torvatn, and Bayazit (2004) demonstrated that job demands and stressors were related to work–family conflict in a sample of 1,346 employees in the food and beverage industry, but broad level work performance norms (i.e., indicators of supportive or non-supportive work settings) moderated this relationship. Specifically, organizational norms that encouraged respectful and supportive social relations at work diminished the relationship between job demands and job stress.

SOCIAL EXCHANGE THEORY

About 7% of the Kanter articles over the past decade rested on the basic tenets of exchange theory to explain work and family phenomena. *Social exchange theory*, as originally proposed by Homan (1958), is based upon what Carrol, Knapp, and Holman (2005) refer to as methodological individualism, meaning that all social entities, such as families and work, can be understood at the level of the individual. More specifically, the needs, wants, and desires of an individual account for his or her actions, and individuals are inherently self-interested. According to Thibaut and Kelley (1959), "every individual voluntarily enters and stays in any relationship only as long as it is adequately satisfactory in terms of costs and rewards" (p. 37). This theory does little to address how individual actors come to hold certain values and preferences, but rather examines how these values and preferences shape costs and rewards in everyday life.

From a work and family perspective, this theoretical approach has been used to consider the costs and rewards of work and family life for individual actors, as well as couples, as they make decisions about where to work, how much to work, whether and when to marry, when to have children, and even when to divorce. According to Breen and Cooke (2005), for example, women's employment generally increases their ability to invoke a credible *threat* of divorce if a more favorable division of domestic labor cannot be negotiated. In addition, it follows from an exchange perspective that husbands' greater domestic participation should *decrease* the risk of divorce.

Bittman, England, Sayer, Folbre, and Matheson (2003) used exchange theory to explore bargaining and time in housework using data from Australia and the US. They argued that power flows through resources that are brought to a relationship and that a spouse can use economically based bargaining power to get the other partner to do housework. The authors were especially interested in clarifying the ways in which "money talks" in determining the division of labor and the ways in which gender shapes the process. Results indicated "substantial evidence consistent with exchange-bargaining theories in both societies. At least within the range where women's earnings don't exceed men's, women decrease their housework when they increase their earnings" (p. 209). For men, however, relative levels of income between spouses were unrelated to the division of labor; thus, for men, gender trumps money. While women use relative income to reduce their own housework, it is not used in efforts to increase husbands' housework; rather women replace their time with purchased services or some housework goes undone. This article provides a clear test of exchange theory while also employing both a gender and ecological perspective to consider how the hypothesized processes may differ for women and men across national contexts.

Critics of an exchange theory perspective argue that the general theme of greater resources garnering greater power between individuals fails to address the broader, sociopolitical systems that inequitably distribute resources as a function of race, gender and ethnicity. Risman (1987), proposing a microstructural approach to understanding gender inequality, argued that micro-structural differences between men and women are due to differential experiences, opportunities, and access to social networks, as opposed to biological conditions or early socialization. Moreover, feminist scholars argue that the microstructural processes occur within a macro legal, political, and social environment that differentially shapes access to resources. The failure of social exchange theory to address this social reality raises the risk of interpreting all behavior as a function of individual likes, preferences, and resources with little acknowledgment of the effects of broader social norms and differential access to resources.

ECONOMIC THEORY: MICRO- AND MACRO-PERSPECTIVES

The theoretical links between economic principles and family life were first drawn by Becker (1965) in his *theory of the allocation of time* in which families were considered units of production (Carlin, 1999). In his book, *A Treatise on the Family*, Becker (1981) outlined some key hypotheses linking family income and resources to family behavior. The economic perspective assumes that, "individuals maximize their utility from basic preferences that do not change rapidly over time and that the behavior of different individuals is coordinated by explicit and implicit markets" (1981, p. ix). A key idea is that individuals rationally pursue their self interest except in cases of altruistic behavior, which most often occur around family care giving. In addition, Becker proposed that a specialized division of labor, with women taking on household work and men involved in the labor market, maximizes family production. Although controversial, Becker's theoretical model has stimulated considerable empirical work in areas such as gendered divisions of paid and unpaid work within families, wage inequality between men and women, poverty, welfare reform, income maintenance, dependence, and family stability.

Brennan, Barnett, and Gareis (2001) studied families in which the wife earned more than the husband, in order to examine the consequences of violating typical patterns of gender specialization, hypothesizing that husbands' and wives' satisfaction with their marriage might be compromised. Husbands' evaluations of marriage were less favorable when they earned less than their wives and more favorable when they earned more, consistent with Becker's theory, but wives' assessments of marriage were not sensitive to salary gaps. For both husbands and wives, marital satisfaction was greater when they perceived more subjective rewards associated with salary. Violating the researchers' predictions, gender role attitudes did not appear to play a role in spouses' reactions to salary patterns.

Bargaining theory, built on similar principles to those proposed by Becker, holds that men and women bargain over the allocation of time and goods in the household. Bargain theorists are interested in how resources, such as earned income, affect the type of bargains struck between spouses. For example, Lundberg and Pollak (1993) described "threat points" in relationships such that a "divorce threat point" emphasizes the bargaining that occurs between spouses over power and resources (e.g., financial, time, affection) with the possibility of divorce increasing if a good deal is not agreed upon by both partners. Feminist economists have countered Becker's theory, in particular, and capitalism more generally, as maintaining an ideology of male supremacy and female oppression. A core argument is that no or low wages for women reify a system of oppression in which women are dependent upon men for economic resources and, thus, in the subordinate position take on more of the domestic labor, in turn suppressing options in the paid labor force. Cooke (2006) argues that "The desirability of the gendered division of labor—when husbands specialize in economic production while wives specialize in domestic (re)production—is judged differently depending upon whether one is theorizing about household versus individual outcomes" (p. 444). For example, at the household level, *gender specialization theory* (Becker 1981) predicts that marital stability will be greater when partners specialize in home work (women) and market work (men) and thus family solidarity will be insured; in contrast, from a bargaining or exchange perspective, when women are employed, the division of home labor will be critical to their marital satisfaction. Under this dynamic, husbands' greater domestic participation should *decrease* the risk of divorce (Breen & Cooke, 2005). In contrast to the gender specialization approach to paid and unpaid work, this approach holds that if the division of labor is not equitable, then marriage will be viewed as less advantageous and divorce rates are predicted to rise. Cooke (2006) compared these two theoretical approaches in a study examining the impact of the household division of labor on marital stability.

Results revealed support for both theories depending on the national context. In West Germany, a country with more traditional notions of gender roles and where dual-earner lifestyles are not the norm, employed wives perform more household tasks to compensate for their more non-traditional economic role. In contrast, in the US, employed women perform fewer household tasks. In Germany, moves away from specialized gendered spheres increased the risk of divorce while in the US, gender equity decreased the risk of divorce. As Cooke concludes, "these findings highlight that it is not sufficient to look at individual resources in making predictions regarding the household division of labor; we must situate effects within the institutional setting" (p. 465).

Understanding the Work–Family Interface through a Time Availability Perspective

A central challenge for all families is allocating time for work, family, leisure, and personal needs and researchers have focused great attention on the predictors of time allocation in families and the outcomes of these arrangements. The dramatic increase in women's market work has served to diminish gender specialization in family work, but gender specialization has not disappeared. The main premise of the *time availability perspective* is that husbands and wives divide household tasks based on a rational calculation of time availability. From this perspective, the differential in husbands' and wives' work hours accounts for the gender gap in the division of household labor. Time use studies indicate that the gender gap in unpaid work, such as cooking and cleaning, has diminished in part due to an increase in men's time in these activities, but also a large decline in women's time in these chores (Bianchi, Robinson, & Milkie, 2006). In contrast, in terms of child-care the gap has narrowed primarily due to men's increased involvement with their children (Bianchi & Milkie, 2010). Scholars agree, however, that a time availability perspective explains some, but not all, of the inequity in family labor between women and men.

Institutional Theory

Although interference between work and family is ultimately experienced by individuals, *institutional perspectives* remind us that organizations and institutions play important roles in the work–family interface. At work, individuals are members of organizations that set performance goals, regulate access to resources (i.e., compensation, benefits, and career mobility), and determine the supportiveness of work atmospheres, all of which may affect workers' experience of interference (Blair-Loy & Wharton, 2002). In turn, the resources offered by organizations may depend upon the customs or standards within their industry and laws and regulations in the larger society (e.g., Dimaggio & Powell, 1983; Meyer & Rowan, 1977). Among the Kanter-nominated articles, 11% were guided by institutional perspectives and examined several types of questions.

One set of questions focused on how government policies and regulations in the US and abroad affect organizations and the individuals within them when it comes to family-supportive policies and behavior. Kelly (2003), for example, applied Institutional theory on law and organizations to the problem of why federal incentives in the US failed to expand employer-sponsored child-care, finding that organizations in industries that relied on professionals, managers, or technical workers were more likely to provide childcare, while organization in tight labor markets, or with more workers who were parents or union members were more likely to provide dependent care expense accounts.

A second set of questions focused on how external environments respond to organizations' actions regarding family support. Arthur (2003) used institutional theory to show that certain industries would be especially likely to experience increases in their share prices as a result of media announcements of new work–life initiatives. Findings indicated that the positive return from work–life initiatives exceeded the magnitude of negative returns from layoff announcements.

Finally, studies based on institutional theory focus on how dynamics within organizations shape the opportunities and constraints workers experience regarding work and family. Blair-Loy and

Wharton (2002) aimed to extend institutional theory by examining the connection between organizational factors and individual employees' use of family-friendly benefits, finding that family need had little to do with use of flexibility policies, but was very important for the use of family care policies. Work-group characteristics were strongly related to the use of flexibility but only minimally related to use of family care policies, possibly because the norms regarding use of flexibility are more ambiguous.

Structural Theory

About 12% of the articles we reviewed drew from *structural or social stratification theories* to explain work and family phenomena. According to Chafetz (1997), macrostructural theories fall into two main categories: (1) those that emphasize the primacy of culture and ideology and (2) those that emphasize socioeconomic factors. At their core, macro-structural theories aim to account for variations in social stratification across groups or over time (Chafetz, 1997). From a sociological perspective, Gerstel and Sarkisian (2006) explain that a structural approach posits that if one accounts for structural differences in individuals' lives, differences that emerge from variation in social class, race, ethnicity, and gender, then differences in unpaid work will disappear. In their Kanter Award winning article of 2005, Sarkisian and Gerstel (2004) used a structural analysis to understand the effects of work conditions on men's and women's care giving. They found that, "all things being equal, employed women and employed men give equal amounts of help to parents and parents-in-law. We emphasize, however, that all things are not equal: On average, employed women and men differ in their employment characteristics, and hence, we argue, they differ in the amount of help they give to parents" (p. 444). In short, women in less lucrative jobs and lower status jobs do more caregiving, and we know in the majority of dual-earner families women are more often the ones in the lower status jobs.

Williamson and McNamara (2003) studied the implications of race, class, and gender, for the consequences of unplanned changes in disability or marital status. During the 6 years of their study, almost one-third of the workers in the sample experienced unexpected changes in status such as widowhood, divorce, or injuries that affected their ability to work. They found that race, class, and gender were associated with "patterned vulnerability," such that workers with fewer resources experienced especially negative consequences.

A key theme in the research emerging from a structural perspective is attention to how wider societal, national, international, and historical conditions shape the everyday interactions of family life. In particular, the ways in which these broader conditions value or devalue racial, gender, or class equality, in turn, transform the very nature and meaning of all human interactions (Coontz, 2005; Ferree, 2010).

Theories of Work Socialization

We were surprised that over the past decade only about 5% of the top articles in the field focused on work as a socializer of beliefs and values that affect worker well-being and, in turn, the development of children. The *work socialization perspective* focuses on how occupational conditions, such as self-direction, job complexity, and supervisor support socializes the worker in ways that affect life off of the job. In the 1990s, a number of studies examined how work conditions affected the worker, parenting, and ultimately child development (Cooksey, Menaghan & Jekielek, 1997; Parcel & Menaghan, 1994; Whitbeck, et al., 1997). In short, findings suggested that greater occupational complexity, more autonomy, and more workplace supports have positive effects on family environments and children's social and cognitive development.

In a recent SRCD Monograph, entitled "*First-year Maternal Employment and Child Development in the First 7 years*", Brooks-Gunn and colleagues (2010) presented an analysis of the NICHD Study of Early Childcare data. We recommend that anyone interested in the topic of maternal employment, primarily hours and occupational status, as they affect child development read this monograph. From a work socialization perspective, however, the study did not address how actual conditions of employment influence child development. As the authors note in their conclusion, "We explored some differences between those in professional and nonprofessional occupations, but there is much more to be done to analyze whether and how the effects of parental work might vary depending on the nature, type, and quality of the job. In particular, characteristics such as flexibility, job satisfaction, working hours, and work schedules are likely to be especially consequential" (p. 108).

ECOLOGICAL, LIFE COURSE, AND GENDER PERSPECTIVES ON WORK AND FAMILY RESEARCH

We separated out the "ecological, life course, and gender" perspectives from the theories previously reviewed because we consider these broad perspectives as possible lens through which researchers can consider hypotheses generated from theory. Approximately 20% of the articles reviewed ascribe to the main tenets of the *ecological perspective*, either by using key concepts from Bronfenbrenner's model or identifying the perspective itself. An ecological perspective holds that human development is shaped by a multilevel complex of family, social, and historical contexts in our environments (Bronfenbrenner 1979; Bronfenbrenner & Morris, 2006). In the early 1980s, Bronfenbrenner and Crouter (1982) used an ecological perspective to evaluate the work and family literature, and more recently Perry-Jenkins and MacDermid (2012) extended this early work by examining the work–family literature through an ecological lens from the 1980s until 2010. When we consider the changing racial and ethnic profile of the USA in tandem with the long running income inequality that persists (Weinberg, 1996; U.S. Census Bureau, 2008), it is clear that the social and ecological niches that define the work and family lives of employees and their families are quite unique and variable. It is these unique sociocultural contexts that are likely to promote distinct types of work–family processes and relationships.

Looking within unique social contexts, Newman and Chin (2003) gathered ethnographic data from poor, racial, and ethnic minority families living in New York City in order to understand the impact of welfare reform on working parents living in poverty. The researchers were interested in parents' strategies for dealing with the tension between the need to pursue steady employment and the need to support their children's education, which in combination presented a very taxing load of responsibilities. Although some families were able to develop creative strategies for attending to both priorities, other families felt forced to choose, or if unable to do so experienced a chaotic 'drowning' situation.

A gender perspective was used in almost 40% of the articles we reviewed. A gender perspective goes beyond simply analyzing gender differences and looks at the impact of gender on people's opportunities, social roles, and interactions. As Ferree (2010) highlights, a critical contribution of gender research over the past decade has been the focus on intersectionality. Specifically, intersectional analyses theorize that, "social structures, political discourses, interpersonal practices, and individual experiences of inequality are shaped not by gender alone but in interaction with race, class, age, sexuality, disability, and other relations of inequality" (Ferree, 2010, p. 427). Intersectional research focuses less on differences across social groups and more on inequality, less on "what is" and more on "what is possible" (Allen, 2001). Thus, a gender perspective is not inherent in research that examines differences in the amount of housework or childcare conducted by men and women in families; rather a gender analyst considers the multiple contexts (e.g., work, family, schools, policies, laws) that perpetuate inequalities at all levels of our social world to influence family interaction.

Doucet (2000) combined gender and ecological perspectives to understand the experiences of couples trying to achieve gender symmetry in their daily lives. In-depth interviews revealed that couples struggled to sustain their commitment when dealing with others in the public sphere, and members of the larger community. Specifically, neighbors, other parents, friends, and family and kin, contributed to this tension by conveying expectations for traditional gender specialization. As a result, both men and women felt guilty and particularly vulnerable to the judgments of their gender peers. It seemed very difficult for couples to extend their gender symmetry at home to gender symmetry in the larger community.

Finally, a *life course perspective* was raised in only 10% of the Kanter articles, a surprisingly low percentage given the importance of considering how life course stages are likely to give unique meaning to the challenges and rewards of constructing work and family lives that "fit" (Moen, Kelly, & Huang, 2008). A life course perspective highlights the importance of family, social, and historical time as they influence the ways in which work and family lives play out over time. The critical concept of linked lives also points to the importance of considering how the life courses of spouses, parents, children, and siblings intersect and co-occur and, thus, necessarily affect the strategies and coping mechanisms that individuals used in managing work and family responsibilities. Moen, Kelly, and Huang (2008) argue that the notion of life course fit, as applied to work and family research, shifts our focus from a more traditional conceptualization of the work–family interface to consider how the person–environment fit at both work and home shifts over time as changing resources and needs affect individuals' feelings of vulnerability and control. Surely the challenges of managing two jobs, a marriage, and two young children conjure up very different images of the work–family interface than the benefits that may accrue from the intersection of two vibrant careers for an empty nest couple.

Willson (2003) studied the experiences of financial insecurity among elderly White and African American women as a function of their own and their husbands' employment experiences, exemplifying the principle of 'linked lives' in the life course perspective? Their findings showed that African Americans were doubly disadvantaged—because of their own limited incomes and also because of their husbands' limited incomes relative to their White counterparts. Patterns of income insecurity over the life course are thus very much related to race.

LIMITATIONS IN THE USE OF THEORY IN THE WORK–FAMILY LITERATURE

In tracking the work and family literature for the past 10 years, we have been excited by the vast array of theoretical approaches to the topic and the shifts in level of analysis from micro-processes linking work stress to family interactions to the most macro-analyses comparing work–family values across nations. Nevertheless, what we see as the greatest shortcoming to the use of theory in the work–family literature, and we want to be clear that this is a critique that we level at ourselves as well as the field at large, is a lack of creativity and consistency when it comes to building theory. In our review of the Kanter articles, we found that theory was often used in developing the study rationale, but rarely did researchers spend time at the end of the article discussing how their results supported theory.

Important questions were left unanswered. If hypotheses were not supported, what possible theoretical explanations could the authors offer? Where did the study fall short and in what new ways might we think about these issues? Thus, even when there is empirical consensus about a particular phenomenon in work–family research (e.g., that women do more household tasks than men), it is less clear what theoretical concepts best explain this finding (Bianchi & Milkie, 2010). Commuri (2005) argues that, "a theory builder must first learn to take a current theory apart, turn it upside down, use it out of context, confront it, and contrast it against other theories" (p. 501). Moreover, Commuri goes on to suggest that we must pay attention to the "told and the untold" in work and family phenomenon. What are our blind spots? For example, for years, work–family researchers focused on conflict, stress, inequity, and overload with a blind eye towards how the work–family interface also includes facilitation, growth, and empowerment. This insight, in retrospect, seems so obvious and, yet, for decades it was virtually ignored. It makes us wonder what other blind spots might be limiting our ability to understand the entirety of work–family dynamics. As we examined the research for this review a few of those blind spots became clear. For example, over the past decade, we have been relatively blind to the effects of social class on work–family linkages.

We know little about the differential effects of work conditions, such as pay, hours, shift work, autonomy, and time urgency, on low-income, middle-class, and professional workers. In addition, although many studies have documented the negative effects of work stress and overload on workers' physical and mental health outcomes, far less attention has been paid to the potentially positive effects of supervisor support, collegial co-worker relations and job autonomy on worker well-being. Given our aging population, more attention must also be paid to the role of employment in the lives of older workers, and perhaps as importantly, understanding the effects of the transition out of the workforce on employees' well-being. Finally, the field is just beginning to reap the benefits of randomized, controlled intervention studies (Bailyn, Bookman, Harrington, & Kochan, 2006), in which researchers are testing the effects of workplace interventions on worker well-being; however, we must be cognizant of the "dual agenda" in these experiments that must balance a focus on work performance and profit margins with equal attention to the well-being of workers, their families, and the community.

An especially important tool to building better theory includes testing competing theoretical models in the same study. For example, Lee and Ono (2008) tested an *economic specialization model* against a *bargaining hypothesis* to understand how paid and unpaid work predicted marital happiness. Results indicated support for differing theoretical hypotheses as a function of both gender and country. Specifically, a bargaining perspective explained women's happiness in the US, whereby the more money women earned the greater their marital happiness. In contrast, the economic specialization model explained women's findings in Japan, whereby women specializing in home work and men in market work reported greater marital happiness. Men in both the US and Japan reported the most marital happiness when women specialized in home work and men in market work. Thus, Lee and Ono's (2008) research highlights the importance of using multiple theories to understand work–family processes as well as examining how factors such as culture and gender can moderate the links between work and family.

As we compare theoretical explanations, we begin to decipher which concepts and processes are the most practical in explaining a phenomenon. Theories are not prophetic, static, or written in stone. At their very best, theories clarify, illuminate, and move the field forward. If theory only reifies what is and fails to challenge us to consider what could be, or what is unjust about "what is," then we remain stuck in our own positivistic thinking. As we advance the field, we must attend to how change and innovation may be experienced by some as enhancing life and others as detrimental to the quality of life. As Ferree states, "not every change is progress and nearly all changes have differential effects on those who are more or less powerful and privileged. This is why studying struggles and their outcomes is so important and yet so difficult" (Ferree, 2010, p. 433).

We think a perfect example of studying struggle focuses on the current lack of family friendly policies in the US. Researchers have begun to focus much needed attention on which workplace policies might best support working families struggling with a lack of time and resources. A policy initiative entitled Workplace Flexibility 2010, spearheaded by scholars at Georgetown Law School and the Sloan foundation in 2000, pulled together researchers, policy-makers, and legislators to consider innovative flexibility policies that would enable workers to better manage work and family challenges. Over the course of developing a flexibility proposal, it became clear that the needs of salary and higher-wage workers were different than low-wage workers. Consequently, it was shown that the potential benefits of offering greater workplace flexibility supports, while potentially enhancing work–family facilitation for salary and professional workers, had the potential to actually reduce work hours and stability for low-wage workers (Lambert, 2009). Thus, as Ferree suggests, in monitoring change and "progress" in our field, it is important that we consider how our practices and procedures are set in particular political and economic contexts that differentially affect those with more power from those with less power.

In the spirit of attending to the untold stories, we must go further in contextualizing our understanding of work–family interrelationships. Gender and ecological perspectives have pushed researchers to consider how sociocultural contexts, such as culture, race, ethnicity, and social class, differentially affect the work–family interface. With that said, the majority of studies fail to look within racial and ethnic groups to understand the unique effects of culture on work–family processes. More often, a *social address approach* is taken in which certain groups (i.e., White vs Black; low SES vs high SES; males vs females) are compared on outcomes. We encourage scholars to spend more time looking *within* groups to identify the key variables, above and beyond social addresses, that explain their findings.

SUGGESTIONS FOR THE USE OF THEORY IN THE WORK AND FAMILY LITERATURE

As we move forward, we challenge work–family researchers to answer some important questions related to theory, specifically: (1) Was an explicit theoretical perspective used in the study?; (2) Did the theoretical concepts turn out to be useful?; (3) How should the theory be altered as a result?; and (4) What aspects of the theory should be tested next? As we reviewed the work–family literature, we struggled, at times, to determine what theoretical frameworks were implicit in studies. By addressing these fairly basic questions, we not only take the guess work out of attempts to codify our research, but we may also enhance the precision of our research.

In almost every review of theory in the family and work literature, there is a call for greater clarity and consensus regarding language and terminology, and we echo that sentiment. For example, we found ourselves continually struggling with terms like "structural theory", "institutional theory", and "resource theory" that are used across disciplines and often refer to quite different things. In the sociological literature, the terms structural theory and institutional theory seem to be used interchangeably to address the ways in which structural inequality, like occupational segregation for example, shapes inequity in family life. In contrast, in the business and occupational psychology literature institutional frameworks include a focus on workplace benefits and resources, policies, and workplace conditions. We recommend that researchers use greater precision in explicating the origins of the theories and concepts they use in their empirical work.

In a related vein, defining the terms "work" and "family" is an exercise that never gets old. In that these terms are socially constructed notions, their meaning and function changes across contexts and over time. In contrast to our call above to more explicitly define theoretical terms and concepts in our empirical work, we think about the concepts of work and family in a slightly different way. Although we encourage researchers to explicitly define the concepts of work and family in their own work, we hesitate to recommend that scholars spend time trying to come to consensus on any one definition or conceptualization of these terms; rather, we encourage continual exploration as "work" and "family" take on new and different meanings across countries, geographical areas, and across all types of social groups defined by race, ethnicity, social class, religion, and gender. In addition, families are complicated networks of kin, extended kin, step parents, grandparents and the like, and our methods must do a better job of capturing that complexity, especially since kin networks often provide some of the most critical support to families juggling the demands of work and family. One only needs to look at the family literature in the mid-1900s and in the first decade of the twenty-first century to see how the structure of families and their functions have shifted over time. In our minds, this points to perhaps some "real" changes in families, but we hope and suspect that it also highlights the ability of work and family scholars to widen the lens used to study work–family phenomena and to look a little more carefully for our "blind spots," such as how we define "family."

FUTURE THEORETICAL DEVELOPMENT IN THE WORK AND FAMILY FIELD

Decades of research on work and family have documented the complex and multiple factors that influence the ways in which these two spheres intersect. Given that 2,000–3,000 articles are being published every year on the topic of work and family, we have our work cut out for us as theorists to consolidate and organize our empirical findings in a logical and useful theoretical frame.

Within disciplines, we recommend that researchers: (1) specify the theories that guide research; (2) define terms and concepts; (3) return to theory in the conclusion and critically evaluate its utility; (4) "tinker" with the theory, make suggestions, and/or pose new hypotheses.

Across disciplines, we challenge researchers to look beyond their usual frame of reference to see what can be learned as we move our unit of analysis from the individual, to the family, the workplace, the community and the country. One way to stay informed is to review the Kanter award winners every year, as they reflect some of the best research in the field and represent multiple perspectives and frameworks. In addition, the inaugural conference of the Work and Family Researchers Network was held in the Spring of 2012 with a goal to, "advance, promote and disseminate interdisciplinary research on work and family." This was the first ever international conference on work–family research and our hope is that it will foster stronger collaborations across disciplines and lead to a more coherent and theoretically rich approach to the field.

We have mentioned a number of times here that "who" we study is as important as "what" we study. As of 2008, 66% of the US population was non-Hispanic White; 15% Hispanic; 14% African American; and 5% Asian American. By 2050, the U.S. Census Bureau projects the population will be 46% non-Hispanic whites; 30% Hispanic; 15% African American; and 9% Asian (U.S. Census Bureau, 2008). Suarez-Orozco and Suarez-Orozco (2001) highlight the fact that the US is in the midst of the largest wave of immigration in our nation's history. Thus, the cultural context of work and family life will be changing over the next half century and important questions as to how sociocultural contexts shape the nature of work–family relations will need to be addressed.

CONCLUSION

Many of the theories we have reviewed in this chapter have withstood the test of time. It is likely that the broader structural and contextual theories and perspectives that we reviewed (e.g., structural theory, gender theory, ecological perspective) work best when integrated with more micro-level theories, such as work–family spillover or role theory. This review gives us a starting point from which to develop more integrated models to understand work–family dynamics and we encourage researchers in the field to consider, if they have not already, what theories or competing theories best explain the phenomena they study, test their hypotheses, share the results and suggests revisions or challenges to current theory.

REFERENCES

Allen, K. R. (2001). Feminist visions for transforming families: Desire and equality, then and now. *Journal of Family Issues, 22*, 791–809.

Arthur, M. M. (2003). Share price reactions to work–family initiatives: an institutional perspective. *Academy of Management Journal, 46*(4), 497–505.

Bailyn, L, Bookman, A., Harrington, M. & Kochan, T. A. (2006). Work–family interventions and experiments: Workplaces, communities, and society. In M. Pitt-Catsouphes, E. Kossek, S. Sweet, M. Pitt-Catsouphes, E. Kossek, & S. Sweet (Eds.), *The work and family handbook: Multi-disciplinary perspectives, methods, and approaches* (pp. 237–265). Mahwah, NJ: Erlbaum.

Barnett, R. C. (1998). Toward a review and reconceptualization of the work/family literature. *Genetic, Social, and General Psychology Monographs, 124*(2), 125–182.

Barnett, R. C., Gareis, K. C., & Brennan, R. T. (2008). Wives' shift work schedules and husbands 'and wives' well-being in dual-earner couples with children: A within couple analysis. *Journal of Family Issues, 29*, 396–422.

Barnett, R. C., & Hyde, J. S. (2001). Women, men, work and family: An expansionist theory. *American Psychologist, 56*, 781–796.

Becker, G. S. (1965). A theory of time allocation. *Economic Journal, 75*(299), 493–517.

Becker, G. S. (1981). *A treatise on the family*. Cambridge, MA: Harvard University Press.

Bianchi, S., & Milkie, M. A. (2010). Work and family research in the first decade of the 21st Century. *Journal of Marriage and Family*, *72*, 705–725.

Bianchi, S., Robinson, J. P., & Milkie, M. A. (2006). *Changing rhythms of American family life*. New York: Russell Sage Foundation.

Bittman, M., England, P., Sayer, L., Folbre, N., & Matheson, G. (2003). When does gender trump money? Bargaining and time in household work. *American Journal of Sociology*, *109*, *186–214*.

Blair-Loy, M., & Wharton, A. S. (2002). Employees' use of work–family policies and the workplace social context. *Social Forces*, *80*, 813–845.

Breen, R., & Cooke, L. P. (2005). The persistence of the gendered division of domestic labour. *European Sociological Review*, *21*, 43–57.

Brennan, R. T, Barnett, R. C., & Gareis, K. C. (2001). When she earns more than he does: A longitudinal study of dual-earner couples. *Journal of Marriage and Family*, *63*, 168–182.

Brooks-Gunn, J., Han, W., & Waldfogel, J. (2010). First-year maternal employment and child development in the first 7 years. *Monographs of the Society for Research in Child Development*, *75*(2), 1–113.

Bronfenbrenner, U. (1979). *The ecology of human development*. Cambridge, MA: Harvard University Press.

Bronfenbrenner, U. & Crouter, A. C. (1982). Work and family through time and space. In S. B. Kamerman & C. D. Hayes (Eds.), *Families that work: Children in a changing world* (pp. 39–83). Washington, DC: National Academy Press.

Bronfenbrenner, U. & Morris, P. A. (2006). The bioecological model of human development. In R. M. Lerner & W. Damon (Eds.), *Theoretical models of human development*, Vol. 1 (pp. 793–828). Hoboken, NJ: Wiley.

Cahill, S. (1983). Reexamining the acquisition of sex roles: a symbolic interactionist approach. *Sex Roles*, *9*, 1–15.

Carlin, P. S. (1999). Economics and the family. In M. B. Sussman, S. K. Steinmetz, C. W. Peterson (Eds.), *Handbook of Marriage and the Family* (pp. 525–551). New York: Plenum Press.

Carrol, J. S., Knapp, S. J., & Holman, T. B. (2005) Theorizing about marriage. In V. L. Bengston, A. C. Acock, K. R. Allen, P. Dilworth-Anderson, & D. Klein (Eds.), *Sourcebook of family theory and research* (pp. 263–278). Thousand Oaks, CA: Sage.

Chafetz, J. S. (1997). Feminist theory and sociology: Underutilized contributions for mainstream theory. *Annual Review of Sociology*, *23*, 97–120.

Commuri, S. (2005) Methodological challenges in theorizing work–family conflict. In V. L. Bengston, A. C. Acock, K. R. Allen, P. Dilworth-Anderson, & D. Klein (Eds.), *Sourcebook of family theory and research* (pp. 501–506). Thousand Oaks, CA: Sage.

Conger, R. D., & Elder, G. H. Jr. (1994). *Families in troubled times*. New York: DeGruyter.

Cooke, L. P. (2006). "Doing" gender in context: Household bargaining and risk of divorce in Germany and the United States. *American Journal of Sociology*, *112*, 442–472.

Cooksey, E. C., Menaghan, E. G., & Jekielek, S. M. (1997). Life course effects of work and family circumstances on children. *Social Forces*, *76*, 637–667.

Coontz, S. (2005). *Marriage, a history: From obedience to intimacy or how love conquered marriage*. New York: Viking.

Craig, L. (2006). Does father care mean fathers share? A comparison of how mothers and fathers in intact families spend time with children. *Gender and Society*, *20*, 259–281.

Dierdoff, E. C., & Ellington, J. K. (2008). It's the nature of the work: Examining behavior-based sources of work–family conflict across occupations. *Journal of Applied Psychology*, *93*, 883–892.

Dimaggio, P. J. & Powell, W. W. (1983). The iron cage revisited: Institutional isomorphism and collective rationality in organizational fields. *American Sociological Review*, *48*, 147–160.

Doucet, A. (2000). 'There's a huge difference between me as a male career and women': Gender, domestic responsibility, and the community as an institutional arena. *Community, Work and Family*, *3*(2), 163–184.

Ezzedeen, S. R., & Ritchey, K. G. (2008). The man behind the woman: A qualitative study of the spousal support received and valued by executive women. *Journal of Family Issues*, *29*, 1107–1135.

Ferree, M. M. (2010). Filling the glass: Gender perspectives on families. *Journal of Marriage and Family*, *72*, 420–439.

Folbre, N. (1994). *Who pays for the kids?: Gender and the structures of constraint*. New York: Routledge.

Ford, M. T., Heinan, B. A., & Langkamer, K. L. (2007). Work and family satisfaction and conflict: A meta-analysis of cross-domain relations. *Journal of Applied Psychology*, *92*, 57–80.

Frone, M. R., Yardley, J. K., & Markel, K. S. (1997). Developing and testing an integrative model of the work–family interface. *Journal of Vocational Behavior*, *50*(2), 145–167.

Frone, M. R., Russell, M., & Cooper, M. L. (1992). Antecedents and outcomes of work–family conflict: Testing a model of the work–family interface. *Journal of Applied Psychology*, *77*, 65–78.

Gerstel, N., & Sarkisian, N. (2006). Sociological perspectives on families and work: the import of gender, class, and race. In M. Pitt-Catsouphes, E. Kossek, & S. Sweet (Eds.), *The work and family handbook: Multi-disciplinary perspectives, methods, and approaches* (pp. 237–265). Mahwah, NJ: Erlbaum.

Glass, J. (2004). Blessing or curse? Work–family policies and mother's wage growth. *Work and Occupations*, *31*(3), 367–394.

Goode, W. J. (1960). A theory of role strain. *American Sociological Review*, *25*, 483–496.

Greenhaus, J. H., & Beutell, N. J. (1985). Sources of conflict between work and family roles. *Academy of Management Review*, *10*, 76–88.

Grzywacz, J. G., & Butler, A. B. (2005). The impact of job characteristics on work-to-family facilitation: testing a theory and distinguishing a construct. *Journal of Occupational Health Psychology*, *10*, 97–109.

Hammer, T. H., Saksvik, P. O., Nytro, K., Torvatn, H., & Bayazit, M. (2004). Expanding the psychosocial work environment: Workplace norms and work–family conflict as correlates of stress and health. *Journal of Occupational Health Psychology*, *9*, 83–97.

Homan, G. C. (1958). Social behavior as exchange. *American Journal of Sociology*, *63*(6), 597–606.

Jacobs, J. A., & Gerson, K. (2004). *The time divide: Work, family and gender inequality*. Cambridge, MA: Harvard University Press.

Kanter, R. M. (1977). *Work and family in the United States: A critical review and agenda for research and policy*. New York: Russell Sage Foundation.

Karasek, R. A. (1979). Job demands, job decision latitude, and mental strain: Implications for job redesign. *Administrative Science Quarterly*, *24*, 285–308.

Karasek, R. A., Triantis, K. P., & Chaudhry, S. S. ((1982). Coworker and supervisor support as moderators of the association between task characteristics and mental strain. *Journal of Occupational Behaviour*, *3*, 181–200.

Kelly, E. L. (2006). Work–family policies: The United States in international perspective. In M. Pitt-Catsouphes, E. Kossek, S. Sweet (Eds.), *The work and family handbook: Multi-disciplinary perspectives, methods, and approaches* (pp. 99–124). Mahwah, NJ: Erlbaum.

Kelly, E. L. (2003). The strange history of employer-sponsored childcare: Interested actors, uncertainty, and the transformation of law in organizational fields. *American Journal of Sociology*, *109*(3), 606–649.

Kossek, E. E., & Distelberg, B. (2009). Workplace policies: Opportunities to improve health and well-being. In A. C. Crouter & A Booth (Eds.) *Work–life policies* (pp. 3–50). Washington, DC: Urban Institute Press.

Lambert, S. J. (2009). Lessons from the policy world: How the economy, work supports, and education matter for low-income workers. *Work and Occupations, 36*, 56–65.

Lee, K. S., & Ono, H. (2008). Specialization and happiness in marriage: A U.S.-Japan comparison. *Social Science Research*, *37*, 1216–1234.

Lewin, K. (1952) *Field theory in social science; Selected theoretical papers by Kurt Lewin*. London, England: Tavistock.

Lundberg, S. & Pollak, R. A. (1993). Separate spheres bargaining and the marriage market. *Journal of Political Economy*, *101*, 988–1010.

Marks, S. R. (1977). Multiple roles and role strain: Some notes on human energy, time and commitment. *American Sociological Review*, *42*, 921–936.

Menaghan, E. G., & Parcel, T. L. (1990). Parental employment and family life: Research in the 1980s. *Journal of Marriage and the Family*, *52*, 1079–1098.

Meyer, J. W. & Rowan, B. (1977). Institutionalized organizations: Formal structure as myth and ceremony. *American Journal of Sociology*, *83*, 340–363.

Moen, P., Kelly, E., & Huang, Q. (2008). Work, family, and life-course fit: Does control over work time matter? *Journal of Vocational Behavior*, *73*, 414–425.

Newman, K. S., & Chin, M. M. (2003). High stakes: time poverty, testing, and the children of the working poor. *Qualitative Sociology*, *26*, 3–34.

Parcel, T. L., & Menaghan, E. G. (1994). *Parents' jobs and children's lives*. New York: Aldine de Gruyter.

Perry-Jenkins, M., Goldberg, A., Pierce, C. & Sayer, A. (2007) Shift work, role overload, and the transition to parenthood. *Journal of Marriage and Family*, *69*, 123–138.

Perry-Jenkins, M. & MacDermid, S. (2012) Work and family through time and space: Revisiting old themes and charting new directions. In G. W. Peterson & K. R. Bush (Eds.). *The handbook of marriage and the family*. New York: Springer.

Perry-Jenkins, M. Repetti, R. L., & Crouter, A. C. (2000). Work and family in the 1990s. *Journal of Marriage and the Family*, *62*, 981–998.

Pleck, J. H. (1977). The work–family role system. *Social Problems*, *24*, 417–427.

Repetti, R. (2005). A Psychological Perspective on the Health and Well-Being Consequences of Parental Employment. In S. M. Bianchi, L. M. Casper, B. King, S. M. Bianchi, L. M. Casper, B. King (Eds.), *Work, family, health, and well-being* (pp. 245–258). Mahwah, NJ: Erlbaum.

Risman, B. J., (1987). Intimate relationships from a microstructural perspective: Men who Mother. *Gender and Society*, *1*(1), 6–32.

Sarkisian, N., & Gerstel, N. (2004). Explaining the gender gap in help to parents: The importance of employment. *Journal of Marriage and Family*, *66*, 431–451.

Searle, B., Bright, J. E. H., & Bochner, S. (2001). Helping people sort it out: The role of social support in the job strain model. *Work and Stress*, *15*, 328–346.

Suarez-Orozco, C., & Suarez-Orozco, M. M. (2001). *Children of immigration*. Cambridge, MA: Harvard University Press.

Thibaut, J. W., & Kelley, H. H. (1959). *The social psychology of groups*. Oxford, England: John Wiley.

U.S. Bureau of the Census. (2008). *Household income rises, poverty rate unchanged, number of uninsured down*. Washington, DC: Government Printing Office.

Voydanoff, P. (2004). Implications of work and community demands and resources for work-to- family conflict and facilitation. *Journal of Occupational Health Psychology*, *9*, 275–285.

Weinberg, D. H. (1996). *A brief look at postwar U.S. income inequality*. Retrieved from www.census.gov (accessed September 21, 2009).

Westman, M., Hamilton, V. L., Vinokur, A. D., & Roziner, I. (2004). Crossover of marital dissatisfaction during military downsizing among Russian army officers and their spouses. *Journal of Applied Psychology*, *89*, 769–779.

Whitbeck, L. B., Simons, R. L., Conger, R. D., Wickrama, K. A. S., Ackley, K. A., & Elder, G. H., Jr. (1997). The effects of parents' working conditions and family economic hardship on parenting behaviors and children's self efficacy. *Social Psychology Quarterly*, *60*, 291–303.

Williamson, J. B. & McNamara, T. K. (2003). Interrupted trajectories and labor force participation. *Research on Aging*, *25*, 87–121.

Willson, A. E. (2003). Race and women's income trajectories: Employment, marriage, and income security over the life course. *Social Problems*, *50*, 87–110.

22 Theories of Family Health
An Integrative Perspective and Look Towards the Future

Barbara H. Fiese and Amber Hammons[1]

All families face daily challenges in managing the health of their members. These challenges may range from maintaining a healthy lifestyle (e.g., promoting good eating habits and regular physical activity) to complex medical regimens associated with chronic health conditions. Family health encompasses the activities and beliefs that guide behavior, as individuals face transitions, experience chronic health conditions, adhere to medical regimens, deliberately attempt to prevent disease or complications arising from disease states, and interact with the healthcare community. Family health is not just the absence of disease or symptoms. Rather it is a dynamic process reflecting how the group, as a whole, goes about developing strategies and ideas about what constitutes healthy living and how the group responds to stressful situations brought upon by afflictions as well as normative transitions. Thus, family health is a complex part of life in need of theories that are on the one hand comprehensive enough to account for a variety of circumstances but on the other hand specific enough to make precise predictions about how the family will behave.

Contemporary family theory is often organized around the symbolic interaction, life course development, social exchange, family systems, ecological, and feminist perspectives (Dilworth-Anderson, Burton, & Klein, 2005). Family health theories incorporate aspects of these higher order theories, often with an eye towards intervention and prevention. For example, many of the approaches we discuss consider how family social interaction patterns may affect individual health outcomes. Thus, our attention is directed towards mid-level theories in which predictions are made about the likelihood that families will engage in particular behaviors in response to health challenges. We review *family stress theory, the biopsychosocial model, family resilience and routines*, and *the integrative model of medical traumatic stress*. We conclude with a discussion of new directions including biological approaches and the effects of shifting demographics on health.

KEY ISSUES IN THE STUDY OF FAMILY HEALTH

Theorizing about family health is a complicated affair because health is not merely the absence of disease, but is also a state of physical, mental, and social well-being (World Health Organization, 1946). Theories on family health must account for how individual states of wellbeing are reached within the context of the family environment. Theories are also evaluated according to unit of analysis, description versus explanation, and proposed mechanisms of change (Crosbie-Burnett & Klein, 2009).

[1] Preparation of this manuscript was supported in part by grants from the National Institute of Child Health and Human Development (HD057447), and the United States Department of Agriculture (Hatch 793–328), and The Christopher Family Foundation Food and Family Program.

TABLE 22.1
Summary of Four Family Health Theories

Theory	Unit of analysis	Description	Mechanism of change	Mediators/ moderators
Family stress and coping	Individual family members, marital system, relational subsystems, community	Pile-up of stressors creates strain. Resources and capabilities are challenged which in turn compromise health	Improve decision-making skills through coping strategies to acquire resistance to strain	Severity of illness. Number of stressors
Integrative medical traumatic stress	Subjective experience of family members	Post-traumatic symptoms develop in multiple family members in response to life-threatening illness	Whole family treatment using cognitive–behavioral approaches to recognize normative reactions	Stage of cognitive development. Time since diagnosis. Pre-existing conditions (psychopathologies)
Biopsychosocial	Biological disease state of individual, psychological functioning of individual, social interaction and relationship quality with family	Bidirectional influence of family relationships and social interaction on individual health	Change in quality of family relationships and social interaction should improve health outcomes	Disease severity. Individual psychological functioning. Socioeconomic resources
Family resilience	Whole family within sociocultural context. Attention to beliefs, communication patterns, routines, and rituals	Family practices and meaning-making processes include being able to normalizeand contextualize adversity	Create a sense of coherence in response to challenging events. Establish regular routines and meaningful rituals in context of health challenges	Life course of illness. Medical regimen demands. Socioeconomic context

Central to our concern is the degree to which the theory proposes that family processes directly cause health outcomes, mediate the relation between individual characteristics and health outcomes, or act as moderators under specified risk conditions. Thus, we provide a brief overview of the unit of analysis, description of primary tenet(s), proposed mechanism(s) of change, and potential mediators/moderators of each theory (see Table 22.1 for a Summary).

Contemporary theories of family health are often embedded in a *socioecological framework* (Bronfenbrenner, 1979) recognizing the complex interplay among individual functioning, family processes, and sociocultural context. The theories we review vary in terms of how explicit the socioecological framework is recognized. However, it does provide a unifying paradigm to evaluate the comprehensiveness of the different theories. We consider five aspects of the socioecological framework applicable to theories of family health: (1) developmental context; (2) environmental stress, including family level stressors; (3) maintenance and prevention with particular attention to adherence to medical regimens and promotion of healthy lifestyles; (4) the intersection of the family with healthcare institutions and communication with healthcare providers; and (5) the broader socioeconomic context of health (Figure 22.1). This multi-layered approach provides guidance regarding

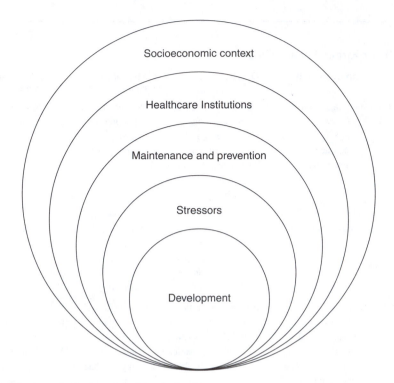

FIGURE 22.1 Socioecological model of family health.

how well the theory attends to the normative challenges presented by development, how the intersection of environmental stress sometimes outside the family's control may affect health outcomes, how engaged the family is in promoting health, and how the theory takes into account broader system influences such as the healthcare system and socioeconomic context.

Although there are specific treatments to address health conditions that include multiple family members such as the *behavioral family systems approach* (Wysocki et al., 2006), we opted not to focus on therapy models *per se* but rather focus on theories that attempt to describe the relation between family functioning and health outcomes. We appreciate the role that different therapy models may play in elucidating health processes, but reviewing these was beyond the scope of this chapter.

OVERVIEW OF THEORIES OF FAMILY HEALTH

FAMILY STRESS AND COPING THEORIES

Family stress and coping theories take, as a starting point, that all families face daily challenges and develop coping mechanisms to face these challenges (Hill, 1958; McCubbin & Patterson, 1983). A variant of the stress and coping theories is the *family adjustment and adaption (FAAR) model* (Patterson, 1988). The model proposes that families actively engage in processes to balance demands with capabilities and that these interact with family meanings to arrive at a level of adjustment. When there is an imbalance between demands and capabilities, a crisis results and health is compromised.

The stress and coping model as developed by Patterson and colleagues has emphasized the universal experience that many families go through as they manage chronic health conditions. Rather than focus on a particular disease state and predict pathways of influence, this theory emphasizes the amount of stress in the environment and its impact on functioning. For example, parents of children with chronic health conditions are more likely to experience compromises in family functioning when their child's condition is more severe and requires more time and management on the part of the family (Rodriques & Patterson, 2007).

Growth and development is considered a normative demand (Patterson, 1988). How well the family system copes with developmental challenges such as the birth of a child with a chronic health condition will depend on its capabilities and number of stressors and strains. In this regard, parents of young infants who are ill-prepared to receive the news that their child has a life-long condition that requires additional resources may experience added strains that compromise their marital relationship, which, in turn, reduce capabilities to care for their child and affects the child's health (Rodriques & Patterson, 2007). If the family is able to resolve the crises, it is possible to readjust and create a healthier child raising environment.

The pile-up of stressors over time can tax the family's resources and capabilities and has been found to be negatively associated with health outcomes within families (McCubbin & Patterson, 1983). This pile-up threatens the family's ability to maintain good health behaviors and has been found to be associated with poorer adherence to prescribed medical protocols for children with chronic health conditions (Patterson, Wall, Berge, & Milla, 2007, 2009). Thus, health maintenance is threatened when there is a pile-up of stressors and the family environment is characterized by strain and tension.

According to the theory, a prime opportunity to resolve a crisis around disease management would be improved decision-making skills through partnership with healthcare providers. Healthcare providers can deliver educational information to the family about effective coping strategies, minimize counterproductive strategies, prevent unnecessary demands, anticipate strains, and teach the family how to acquire resistance capabilities (Patterson, 1988). An expanded version of the model places importance on how the family creates meaning and an identity around illness-related tasks (Patterson & Garwick, 1994). Theory-driven recommendations for working with healthcare providers are consistent with the family resilience theories discussed later, including focusing on beliefs and structuring routines and rituals.

A central aspect of the family stress model is the relative balance between resources and capabilities. Lack of economic resources can tax the family system and place added strain on caregivers. However, the effect may be indirect through access to care and health literacy. For example, children with special healthcare needs are more likely to be raised in low income households with low levels of parental education. Children with special healthcare needs, in general, have less access to health services, which in turn is accentuated when parents do not recognize the need for assistance (Porterfield & McBride, 2007). According to the family stress model, the effects of poverty will present added strain and pile-up of stress by blocking access to adequate care and gaining knowledge to improve capabilities.

The family stress theory focuses primarily on the process of explaining family functioning and adaptation in response to the stress of chronic health conditions. With the exception of attention to disease management and medical adherence, it does not directly address pathways of disease or health processes of the individual. In this regard, family stress and coping models contribute primarily to our understanding of how the system as a whole functions in response to disease states of the individual rather than predict individual variability in health status. Although the developmental context is recognized as a source of demand on the system, it is seen as a broad and general context rather than from a life course perspective. Further, the socioeconomic context is considered as a source of strain for the system rather than a modifier of health outcomes. It is important, to note however, that the family stress model played a seminal role in laying the groundwork for recognizing the important role of beliefs in maintaining health outcomes.

BIOPSYCHOSOCIAL SYSTEMS APPROACH

The *biospychosocial theory* evolved from the work of Engel (1977), who recognized that the physical and psychological could not be separated when considering disease states. Biopsychosocial theories propose that health is the result of a complex interplay between biological factors and the social context. Biopsychosocial theories have been expanded to include principles of general systems theory, including hierarchical organization, boundaries, feedback loops of communication, and notions of equilibrium and disequilibrium (Wynne, 2003).

The relationships among the psychological, biological, and social contexts are reciprocal rather than linear and constitute a system of health. This system is divided into three levels: biological (disease processes), psychological (psychological and emotional functioning), and social (family and social functioning (e.g., school, work, friends) (Wood, 1993). Health is achieved when there is a balance among the three aspects of the system and threatened when there is disequilibrium within the system. For example, the family may engage in attentive disease management strategies to monitor blood glucose levels in an adolescent with diabetes. This in turn may compromise striving for independence, which may impair development within the peer group. From the family functioning perspective, time consuming attention to disease management activities may threaten the marital relationship or attention to siblings without the disease. Thus, family health in this theory is defined by the dynamic balance between individual (both biological and psychological) and family level functioning (Wood, 1995).

Wood has proposed an integration of developmental and biopsychosocial theories with the incorporation of principles of *attachment theory* (Wood, 1993; Wood, Klebba, & Miller, 2000). In this theory, patterns of family interaction (e.g., proximity, hierarchy, triangulation) intersect with characteristics of the individual to either buffer or exacerbate biological processes related to disease activity. The integration of attachment theory to the biopsychosocial theory provides a link between the child's attachment history and relationship formation in the broader family system. Further, the potential for attachment relationships to act as a buffer between biological reactivity and family level processes is proposed. Consequently, the developmental features of this theory include establishing a secure base with reliable family members such that exploration can be supported. Wood has proposed that family proximity seeking includes the use of personal space, sharing of private information, emotion regulation, and decision-making (Wood, 1995). Added to proximity seeking is the importance of hierarchy in the family, in which parents are in charge of their children by setting limits in a nurturing environment. For the entire family, responsivity to emotions and personal needs is essential to maintaining health and well-being. Thus, patterns of social interaction are an important feature of this theory.

During developmental transitions (e.g., entry to school, adolescence), intrafamilial boundaries may be challenged and affect disease processes. For example, during adolescence the need for autonomy may increase the need for greater personal space of the adolescent, less sharing of private information, and more individual decision-making. This shift has the potential to threaten individual health, however, if the disease management skills of the adolescent are not mature enough to handle a complex medical regimen such as diabetes or cystic fibrosis.

Validation of the biopsychosocial theory has occurred in studies on chronic illnesses such as asthma, cardiac disease, irritable bowel disease, and pediatric depression (Wood et al., 2006). Specific patterns of family interaction have been identified in children and adolescents that predict disease severity and symptoms. For example, negative family emotional climate has been found to predict child depression (even after controlling for adherence to treatment for depression), which was in turn related to asthma severity (Wood et al., 2006, 2008). The work by Wood and colleagues has elegantly demonstrated pathways of influence on disease states that include relationship quality of the parents, felt security between the child and parent, and affect regulation and reactivity of the child (Wood et al., 2006). The theory is relatively specific in predicting direct pathways from family climate to disease severity mediated by the psychological functioning of the individual (Lim, Wood, Miller, & Simmens, 2011; Wood et al., 2007; Wood, Miller, Jungha et al., 2006). The significance of this theory for family health is the central role that family functioning and process plays in the balance between individual psychological functioning and disease states. Further, the testing of specific pathways of effect has significantly advanced both theory and application in the field of family health.

Biopsychosocial theories are deeply embedded in models of family oriented primary care (McDaniel, Campbell, Hepworth, & Lorenz, 2005). Primary care family psychology grew out of an integration of the biopsychosocial approach and *family systems theories* at the University of Rochester Department of Family Medicine (McDaniel & LeRoux, 2007). At the root of family oriented primary care is an emphasis on educating physicians to understand illness and symptoms from the perspective of the family, improve physician–family communication patterns, and respect how the social context may influence the family's ability to manage complex medical regimens. This theory-driven approach expands treatment of disease processes to not only provide psychoeducation to patients, families, and primary care providers from a biopsychosocial perspective but also consider characteristics of the broader healthcare system and how it may influence health outcomes of the individual and ability of the family to effectively respond and manage resources. For example, collaboration with primary healthcare providers also involves learning to interact under time constraints, educating medical personnel about the connections between psychological and biological processes, and the role that personal disclosure of the provider may play in managing sharing distressing news with family members (McDaniel et al., 2007).

An important contribution of biospsychosocial theories is the equal weight given to individual psychological functioning, family processes, and the social context in predicting health outcomes. Biopsychosocial theories are frequently used as frameworks to explain health disparities, or the increased risk for low income and ethnic minorities to experience health problems (Adler & Rehkopf, 2008; Chen, Matthews, & Boyce, 2002; Myers, 2009). However, family processes are considered but one of many risk factors for poor health outcomes rather than as a potential resource to reduce disparities. Consistent with biopsychosocial theories is a resiliency framework whereby individuals and families develop reserve capacities to function well even in the face of adversity (Gallo, de los Monteros, & Shivpuri, 2009). We now address the family resilience framework with a focus on the development of health promoting routines.

FAMILY RESILIENCE AND HEALTH PROMOTING ROUTINES

Resilience can be defined as doing well in the face of adversity. In the context of family health, the adversity may be facing the challenge of a chronic health condition, seeking healthcare with limited economic resources, or accessing healthy food in low income neighborhoods. We focus our attention on the processes by which families become resilient in the face of adversity and how these processes can promote health.

The vast majority of family resilience theories incorporate two aspects of family functioning as influential on health: family practices that organize daily life through routines and family beliefs that guide behavior and interpretation of experiences (Fiese & Spagnola, 2007). Patterson proposes that family meaning-making or the family's creation of a world view can influence how it manages daily demands and respond to the pile-up of stressors (Patterson, 2002). The appraisal or meaning of an event can promote healthy adaptation to stressful conditions. Walsh proposes that the meaning-making process associated with resiliency includes being able to normalize and contextualize adversity as well as create a sense of coherence out of challenging events (Walsh, 2003). Rolland and Walsh (2006) go on to emphasize that families can be assisted in creating positive meanings about health and wellbeing in the face of adversity by building a sense of competence and mastery.

A resiliency approach is consistent with biopsychosocial theories in that it theorizes that health is the result of multiple influences including risk in the environment and protective processes available to the family. Further, a resiliency approach is consistent with a developmental framework in that normative and non-normative transitions are seen as both potential resources as well as challenges to the family system. For example, the normative event of sending a child to school may call upon the organizational resources of the family to alter schedules, coordinate communication with school personnel, and arrange transportation. For a family with a child with a chronic health condition, this normative transition may be complicated when there is also the need to arrange for medical supervision while at school.

Rolland (1987) has identified the life course of illness and health from a resilience framework. He argues that it is not only important to consider the developmental period of the family but also the phase of a particular condition. Rolland identifies the crisis phase, which typically occurs soon after a diagnosis; the chronic phase, which may last throughout much of an individual's life; and the terminal phase. From a resilience framework, the phase of the illness is important because different resources may be available at different points of the illness. During the crisis phase, it is important to engage the meaning-making capacity of the family to redefine new roles and create a positive story of the illness or condition for the family. During the chronic phase. it is important to maintain normative routines and open lines of communication. During the terminal phase, it is important to be able to openly express grief and solicit support from family members.

The family resilience approach identifies two features of family life that may serve as protective factors under challenging conditions: (1) the meaning-making process and (2) family routines and rituals. We briefly provide evidence of how these aspects of family life may promote healthy outcomes under varying conditions of risk.

Families vary considerably in how they interpret health conditions and develop strategies based on their beliefs. Parents of children with persistent asthma were interviewed about the time their child was diagnosed with the disease, how they typically manage the disease, and what was the worse experience they had in managing their child's disease (Fiese & Wamboldt, 2003b). Parents differed in the types of beliefs they held in terms of how well they could control the condition and the strategies they developed in response to severe symptoms. Parents who expressed that they had little control over their child's symptoms and waited until the symptoms were quite severe to seek care had the highest rates of emergency care one year following the interview and their children experienced the lowest quality of life. The relative coherence of tales told about chronic illnesses has also been found to be related to family functioning (Fiese & Wamboldt, 2003a). From a theory building perspective, how the family makes sense of disease states and its belief system about the likelihood the family will be effective in controlling the disease may affect family level behaviors, such as cooperative disease prevention strategies that in turn affect symptom severity.

Family resilience is also evident in the promotion of regular and meaningful family routines and rituals (Fiese, 2006; Patterson, 2002; Walsh, 2003). Family routines have health promoting features in that they provide an organizational structure and predictability to daily life, include an element of planning ahead, promote the assignment of roles, and over time can provide meaning and reduce strain in stressful environments. The regularity of family routines has been found to be associated with adherence to medical regimens (Fiese, Wamboldt, & Anbar, 2005). Interestingly, if carrying out medication routines were considered a burden, then quality of life was compromised for both the parent and child. Thus, the meaning behind routines is integrally tied to both health outcomes as well as the mechanics of disease management.

A daily routine that has the potential for promoting healthy outcomes under a variety of circumstances is the practice of regular and meaningful mealtimes. In a meta-analytic review of family mealtimes, it was found that families who regularly ate together three or more times a week reduced their child's odds for obesity by 12%, disordered eating by 35%, eating unhealthy foods by 20% and increased their odds for eating healthy foods by 24% (Hammons & Fiese, 2011). Family process variables observed during family mealtimes such as positive communication have also been related to positive health outcomes including better lung functioning, better quality of life, and reduced risk for severe asthma symptoms (Fiese, Winter, & Botti, 2011; Fiese, Winter, Wamboldt, Wamboldt, & Anbar, 2010).

Pertinent to our discussion is the important role that socioeconomic and ethnic context plays in the practice of family routines. There is some evidence to suggest that low income single parents practice fewer and less regular routines than middle income dual household parents (Bradley, Corwyn, Burchinal, McAdoo, & Coll, 2001; Fiese et al., 2011). However, it has also been demonstrated that regular family routines can serve as a protective factor for low income high risk families (Brody, Flor, & Gibson, 1999). From a theoretical perspective, it is important to consider under which conditions it is easier to develop routines and which barriers may exist to sustain routines under challenging conditions. For low income ethnic minority families, lack of time due to long work hours, accommodating public transportation schedules, juggling multiple childcare arrangements, and lack of access to adequate healthcare have been identified as barriers to sustaining health promoting and regular family routines (Roy, Tubbs, & Burton, 2004; Tubbs, Roy, & Burton, 2005).

Creating health promoting routines can be used as part of educational strategies in healthcare settings and tailored to fit individual family needs (Fiese, 2006, 2007; Fiese & Wamboldt, 2001). The central elements to routine interventions are being able to identify the family's past experience and success in creating routines, supporting self-efficacy in sustaining routines, and tailoring the routine to fit in to the family's unique circumstances. The multi-generational history of routines and rituals and cultural context can be sources of strength and capacity building for vulnerable families (McAdoo, 1993; Rolland & Walsh, 2006).

Family resilience theories add to the understanding of family health by attention to the role that environmental risk may play in exacerbating an existing health condition. The practice of regular and meaningful routines may be one pathway by which risk is buffered to promote better health outcomes. The beliefs family members create about health experiences appear to be crucial mediators of behaviors that may be moderated by the life-course of a particular condition.

Summary

We have reviewed some of the major contemporary theories of family health. While not exhaustive, this brief overview highlights some of the contributions that systems approaches have made to understanding the health and well-being of individuals. The majority of these theories assume that the disease state of an individual will be stressful for families and requires coping mechanisms. The success of these coping mechanisms will depend, in part, on the resources available to the family, the psychological functioning of individuals, and patterns of social interaction that include open lines of communication and responsiveness to emotional needs. In this regard, theories of family health build upon general systems theory with an emphasis on health and disease as both a context and outcome.

A consistent thread throughout these theories is the pivotal role of beliefs about disease and experiences surrounding healthcare (both personal and institutional). It is important to distinguish the role that beliefs play in many of the family health theories from general health belief models. Very simply put, contemporary health belief theories such as the health belief model (Janz & Becker, 1984) propose that individuals are motivated to preserve their health based on their belief that likelihood that their actions will have an effect and their perception about the severity of the condition (Weinstein, 1993). In contrast, family health theories tend to emphasize general beliefs about disease that are deeply rooted in generational experiences (Rolland, 1994) and may or may not be directly accessible through self-report but are accessed through narratives and stories told about illness (Brody, 1987). In this regard, the severity of the illness (or perceived susceptibility to disease severity) is not as crucial as the ability to create a coherent narrative about the family's experience with challenging conditions and identify possible coping strategies (Fiese & Wamboldt, 2003a; Walsh, 2003).

Generally speaking, the family health theories developed thus far are primarily descriptive with less emphasis on evaluating the direct links between disease processes and family functioning. The biopsychosocial theories come closest to identifying pathways of influence taking into account the role that individual psychological functioning may play in mediating the effects of family functioning on disease severity. Further, the role that socioeconomic and cultural contexts may play has been greatly under-specified in the theories to date. New directions in family health theorizing and research may provide guidance in addressing these gaps. One such approach is the integrative theory of medical traumatic stress.

An Integrative Theory of Medical Traumatic Stress

In contrast to the stress and coping theory that considers family adaptation across disease states, the *integrative theory of medical traumatic stress* was designed to facilitate the understanding of short- and long-term psychological consequences of responses to pain, injury, and serious illness such as cancer (Kazak et al., 2006). This theory focuses on the development of post-traumatic stress symptoms and from the outset considered the important role that the family played in supporting healthy outcomes (Kazak, Rourke, & Crump, 2003). The development of symptoms is divided into three phases corresponding to an illness phase. The first phase is "peritrauma" and concerns the period during and immediately following the potentially traumatic medical event. The theory emphasizes the importance of taking the 'subjective' nature of the trauma into account by looking at the family's beliefs and overall perception of the trauma. Trauma itself is considered subjective because what is determined to be traumatic for one family may not be traumatic to another family. Thus, this subjective appraisal is coined "potentially traumatic events" (PTE). Responses in this phase may be influenced by pre-existing conditions such as anxiety disorders (Kazak et al., 1998), suggesting that overall family functioning may be either a resource or obstacle to healthy outcomes during this phase.

In Phase II, early, ongoing, and evolving responses are examined. Once the acute phase of the trauma is over, there is concern that post-traumatic stress symptoms (PTSS) may occur. The presence of PTSS influences not only the child's functioning but can impair the parent's ability to adequately care for the child, which in turn affects adherence to medical regimens. In the third phase, longer-term pediatric medical traumatic stress (PMTS) may be present. Long-term PTSS and/or post-traumatic stress disorder (PTSD) in family members of childhood cancer survivors is not uncommon. In a study of 150 families of adolescent survivors of cancer, nearly all families had at least one parent who had symptoms of re-experiencing the trauma and 20% of the families had a parent with current (PTSD) (Kazak et al., 2004). The long-lasting effects of trauma are important because the family, as a system, may be less capable to care for the ill member due to avoidance reactions that prevent good health maintenance behaviors.

The developmental context is an essential part of this theory. In order to understand how individuals process traumatic events, it is essential to consider their level of cognitive development and at what point in development they experienced the event. For example, adolescence is considered a particularly vulnerable period as cognitive maturation, need for autonomy, and the central role of interpersonal relationships can collide with intensive medical treatments that include missed school days, time away from peers, and changes in physical appearance. Indeed, recent research has indicated that individuals diagnosed with cancer as adolescents were more likely to experience PTSS than those who were diagnosed when they were of elementary school age (Kazak et al., 2010).

PTSS extends beyond the patient to include parents (Kazak, Boeving, Alderfer, Hwang, & Reilly, 2005) and to a lesser extent siblings (Alderfer, Labay, & Kazak, 2003). From a life-course perspective, parents of very young children may be particularly vulnerable to PTSS when their child faces an injury or life-threatening condition. In this regard, the trauma experienced by the entire family becomes a target for intervention and prevention. The Surviving Cancer Competently Intervention Program (SCCIP) was designed for parents of children who survived cancer. The approach integrates cognitive behavior with family therapy approaches and has proven to reduce the frequency of PTSS (Kazak et al., 2004). Reasoning that post-traumatic stress symptoms could be prevented if family members were approached soon after the diagnosis of their child's condition, a newly diagnosed version of SCCIP was developed (Stehl et al., 2009). This approach was less feasible in recruiting families to participate. Thus, the treatment of traumatic symptoms may be more efficacious after family members have had an opportunity to process their experience during Phase II, and less accepting of intervention during Phase I when the trauma is new and other aspects of health care are a priority.

The *integrative theory of medical traumatic stress* has been integrated with the *pediatric psychosocial preventative health model* (PPPHM) to provide a comprehensive "blueprint" for evidence-based healthcare delivery (Kazak et al., 2007). This empirically derived theory posits that most families with a child with a serious health condition are competent and are able to adjust well over time despite an initial period and/or recurring periods of distress. However, targeted interventions are delivered to families that experience several risk factors and persistent or escalating distress. The SCCIP program is an example of a preventative intervention aimed at reducing post-traumatic symptoms before they develop into a disorder. Consultation with the family in healthcare settings may be necessary to assure that the family as a system is functioning competently to receive care (Kazak, Simms, & Rourke, 2002). In some cases, pre-existing family problems may present obstacles to the healthcare team in delivering adequate care. In these circumstances, consultation is offered to promote family competency, set realistic goals, and reduce acute distress without an attempt to change longstanding family dynamics. Finally, survivors of life-threatening conditions such as pediatric cancer may re-experience traumatic symptoms during important life transitions. Family members may not always connect the re-emergence of symptoms with such transitions as marriage, new jobs, and school graduations. Healthcare providers are in a unique position to provide anticipatory guidance and serve as a resource during these vulnerable periods (Kazak et al., 2007).

The *integrative medical traumatic stress theory* expands upon the stress and coping theory through its specification of the role that trauma may play in response to life-threatening health conditions. Cognitions and beliefs about the health condition are central to this theory. Further, theory-driven treatment models have been developed including the SSCIP, family systems oriented consultation, and *PPPHM*. It is not surprising that this theory is patient-oriented as it grew out of clinical practice based in hospital settings (Kazak et al., 2007). In this regard, it reflects theory development based on family experiences within a healthcare setting emphasizing the role that healthcare providers can play in supporting families to manage acute and chronic health conditions. This theory is also developmentally specific with its attention to the role that cognitive development may play in the expression of symptoms and the role that life transitions may play in triggering the re-experience of trauma. In this regard, the individual is first and foremost a developing organism that influences how health conditions will be experienced. The family serves as a source of support through its presumed competence to deal with challenges over the long haul. However, the family is considered a whole system such that the experience and condition of the individual patient can influence the health of other members including parents and siblings. Less attention is paid to the socioeconomic context and the role that depletion or reduction of economic resources may play in increasing risk for symptoms.

LIMITATIONS OF EXISTING FAMILY HEALTH THEORIES AND SUGGESTIONS FOR NEW THEORETICAL DEVELOPMENTS

Recent advances in biobehavioral research methods, the expanding literature on the cumulative effects of early adverse life events on health, and the changing demographic and cultural mix of families point to new directions for family health theories. To date, much of the work of family health theorists has been driven by the intersection of family therapy models, developmental theories, and to some extent healthcare system practices. The emergent fields in health, in general, require a transdisciplinary approach, whereby new theories are developed that transcend a single discipline (Nash, 2008; Rosenfield, 1992). In the case of family health, the relevant disciplines may include biology, psychophysiology, nutrition sciences, developmental sciences, neuroscience, pediatrics, family medicine, gerontology, health economics, and public health to name a few. The theories that evolve draw from the methods and principles of each discipline but the resulting knowledge cannot be predicted from the postulates of any single discipline. We provide an overview of new developments in health and biobehavioral reactivity, the impact of early adverse life events on adult health, and socioeconomic and cultural context. We conclude with recommendations for a transdisciplinary integration of these approaches for emerging theories in family health.

BIOBEHAVIORAL APPROACHES

An emerging and important direction in understanding health is the role that genetics and biologic processes play in regulating health and gene environment interactions (Reiss, 2010). It is beyond the scope of this section to provide a comprehensive review of all the advances that have been made in linking biological variations with family process (for an excellent review, see D'Onofrio & Lahey, 2010). Rather, we aim to highlight some key findings that illustrate how individual biological characteristics interact with the family context to lead to significant variations in health outcomes.

Context specific factors that have been shown to affect children's psychobiological responses include early mother–child attachment disruptions, early contact with stressors, abuse related PTSD, impoverishment and low SES (Boyce & Ellis, 2005). Boyce and colleagues challenge traditional research that postulates stress reactions to be unidirectional and cite evidence in support of a bivalent (or two possible pathways) stress response. They propose an *evolutionary–developmental theory* of biological sensitivity to context. Their theory posits that, highly reactive individuals do poorly in high stress environments but do well in low stress environments, typically revealing lower than normal stress responses. For example, highly reactive children in high stress families had higher rates of respiratory illness than their low reactive peers, but children in low stress environments who were highly reactive were the healthiest of all the children. Because response to stress has been an implicit core construct of contemporary theories of family health, future approaches need to consider the complex interplay between individual biological reactivity that can be moderated by levels of stress in the family environment. To date, family health theories have focused primarily on the pile-up of stressors and/or perceived strain as critical to predicting health outcomes or severity of disease. Recent evidence suggests that particular forms of early adverse life events may be particularly toxic for later health conditions.

CUMULATIVE EFFECTS OF EARLY ADVERSE LIFE EVENTS

It is well established that individuals who are less well educated, have low status jobs, and earn little to no income experience poorer health than their counterparts at higher socioeconomic levels (Adler et al., 1994). There is a monotonic function between increasing levels of disadvantage and risk for poor health outcomes including risk for injury, cancer, chronic health conditions such as diabetes, and premature death. Although the link between low socioeconomic status (SES) and poor health has been recognized for some time, recent research has pointed to the importance of early adverse life events in low income neighborhoods and potential impact on biological functioning.

Two lines of research illustrate how adverse life events may contribute to poor health outcomes and have the potential to inform family health theories. First, Evans and colleagues have elegantly demonstrated the cumulative effects of poverty on child and adolescent health (Evans & Kim, 2007; Evans, Kim, Ting, Tesher, & Shannis, 2007). Rather than focusing on a particular disease outcome, Evans and colleagues identify health processes such as allostatic load, which reflect the overall wear and tear on the body caused by the mobilization of different biological systems in response to environmental stressors (Evans, 2003). For example, allostatic load can be measured through summing physiological indicators of overnight cortisol, epinephrine and norepinephrine, resting diastolic and systolic blood pressure, and body mass index. Taken together, these measurements provide an overall index of health and risk for morbidity (McEwen, 1998). In a sample of over 200 young adolescents, Evans and colleagues report that children exposed to more environmental risk (e.g., family chaos, poverty, crowding) experienced more allostatic load. However, the effect was only significant for those youth raised in households where there were low levels of maternal responsiveness.

In a longitudinal analysis of the cumulative effects of poverty on stress regulation, Evans also reports that children who experience poverty for longer periods of time are at increased risk for stress reactivity (Evans & Kim, 2007). These findings underscore the importance of carefully examining the role of poverty in the family not just as a source of economic resources but also in terms of the types of stressors that may be present. In addition, there is also evidence that family processes may be protective in these high risk environments (Repetti, Taylor, & Seeman, 2002).

A second line of research that points to the importance of early adverse life events and health is the evidence linking childhood SES and adult health. Cohen and colleagues have provided a conceptual model linking the physical and psychosocial environments that associate early SES with adult health (Cohen, Jankicki-Deverts, Chen, & Matthews, 2010). While it is beyond the scope of this chapter to thoroughly discuss all the points of the proposed model, there are two key points that can contribute to theories of family health. First, characteristics of the physical and psychosocial home environments in childhood have been found to be associated with poor adult health. Homes that are characterized by substandard quality, crowding, and toxic exposures (i.e., lead, tobacco smoke) have been found to be associated with increased risk for infections and cancer. Psychosocial risks include "risky families" (Repetti, et al., 2002) characterized by high levels of conflict, inconsistent parenting practices, and low levels of warmth and attentive relationships. Environmental chaos identified as the lack of routines in childhood is also identified as having an impact on adult health. Risks in the psychosocial environment have been associated with more severe symptoms of chronic diseases such as asthma, accelerated puberty, and addictions. The physical and psychosocial environments set the stage for biological outcomes potentially through the regulation of health behaviors. Thus, it is important to consider not only the family environment in terms of psychosocial processes but also physical characteristics of the households that may constrain social interactions.

The cumulative effects of adverse early life events on health, point to the importance of including an analysis of the early social environment in theories of family health. Although family theorists have long recognized the importance of family history and early experiences in predicting current patterns of interaction and health symptoms, current models of health emphasize the important role of the physical as well as the psychosocial environment. Features such as overcrowding and high levels of ambient noise may be associated with chaos in the environment which in turn may affect proximal processes such as social interaction and the practice of regular routines (Evans, Gonnella, Marcynyszyn, Gentile, & Salpekar, 2005). Because physical and psychosocial environmental risk factors are over-represented in low income neighborhoods and low income individuals are at increased risk for poor health outcomes, new directions in family health theories must take into account the role that poverty plays in predicting health outcomes. Another area of increasing importance is the role that shifting demographics and cultural context plays in health.

Family Demographics

There have been two dramatic demographic changes in the past decade that have consequences for family health. First, family living arrangements have become increasingly complex and varied in the US. Second, there has been a rapid increase in immigration in the past ten years. These two demographic shifts have consequences for family health as family structure (and instability) and immigration patterns have been found to be related to health outcomes in significant ways. Although it is beyond the scope of this chapter to review to all the available literature in this domain, we highlight some key findings that can inform theory development.

Cohabitation is now the typical first union for couples in the US (Brown, 2010). Although the link between marriage, *per se*, and child well-being has given rise to research and policy controversies over the past decade, the relevant issue for family health theories is the relative stability of relationships within the household and availability of resources. Family stability refers to whether children grow up with the same parent(s) that were present at their birth. Stability is further assessed by the number of relationship transitions the child experiences in their life. These transitions may, or may not, be associated with marriage in that there may be multiple intimate relationships formed that include an adult moving in or out of the household. In general, children's health has been reported to fare better when raised in two-parent than single-parent households (Wen, 2008). What is less clear, however, is the role that relationship stability plays in fostering health outcomes. Using the Fragile Families dataset, Schmeer (2011) reports that parent report of child general health at 5 years of age was best predicted by marital status at the time of the child's birth. Children born to cohabiting parents were less likely to be in excellent health than children born to married parents 5 years later, controlling for maternal health and household economic factors. Findings associated with relationship instability were somewhat mixed as there was a slight increase in health status for those children whose cohabiting parents married sometime in the 5-year time period but this was a small advantage. Using the same dataset and controlling for possible mediating effects of family structure (i.e., maternal depression, parenting quality, income level) Waldfogel and colleagues found that relationship instability rather than marital status was the strongest predictor of child health status that included obesity and asthma (Waldfogel, Craigie, & Brooks-Gunn, 2010).

Whereas the direct link between family structure and health outcomes is inconclusive, it is important to consider how relationship instability and availability of resources brought to bear by added income and social support may influence health. In a recent Institute of Medicine Workshop Report, the topics of cohabitation, fluidity in family relationships, and the complexity of living arrangements were raised as core measurement issues to advance the science of family research (Institute of Medicine, 2011). For theory development, it will be important to consider how commitment and stability in relationships may be either a risk or protective factor for long-term health.

A second demographic shift to consider is the role that immigration may play in health. Over the past decade, there has been a tremendous growth in immigration with the largest increase seen in the Hispanic population (Martin & Midgley, 2006). There is frequently a health advantage to immigration as foreign-born immigrant children often experience better health than their US-born peers. This is likely due to a variety of factors including the fact that recent immigrant children tend to live in two parent households, eat less snack foods, and smoke and drink less alcoholic beverages (Perreira & Ornelas, 2011). Family level factors can also act as a protective factor against the stress of immigration. For example, familism or the presence of strong family ties may reduce burden and provide additional means of social support to promote resiliency under the stresses of immigration and living in low income circumstances (Gallo, Penedo, de los Monteros, & Arguelles, 2009).

The apparent paradox of experiencing good health following immigration may be short-lived, however. For the vast majority of health outcomes, the benefits of immigration are soon lost by the second generation and sometimes by adolescence if immigration occurs when children are very young (Perreira & Ornelas, 2011). One explanatory mechanism linking poor health and immigration is the role of perceived discrimination. Perceived discrimination has been linked to a variety of poor health outcomes including compromised mental and physical health in adults (Paradies, 2006). Recent evidence suggests that for first and second generation Latin American youth, perceived discrimination is associated with somatic complaints and depressive symptoms (Huynh & Fuligni, 2010). Yet to be determined is whether family level factors may act as a protective factor under conditions of perceived discrimination.

An Integrative Approach

Recent research highlighting the complex interplay between biological reactivity and the social environment and the important role that demographic factors may play in health calls for an expansion of family theories. From the outset it is important to consider the role that individual variations in biological reactivity and genetic risk may play in the expression and risk for disease. Each individual brings to the social environment a propensity to react to stress in particular ways. Current knowledge indicates biological reactivity extends beyond personality characteristics or temperament. Rather, it is a physiological substrate that intersects with the social environment in predictable

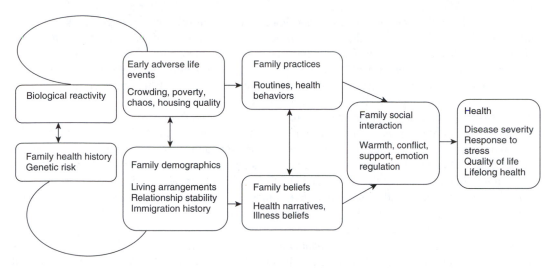

FIGURE 22.2 New directions for the integrative model of family health.

ways to regulate important behaviors such as eating, sleeping, and activity levels. Important features of the social environment include early adverse life events, and family and neighborhood demographics. These aspects of the social environment can moderate aspects of individual biology in the prediction of health outcomes.

The family is a very important part of the social environment and operates on both a macro- and micro-level in influencing health. The macro-level influences tend to be extended over long periods of time through family practices and beliefs. These include family routines that promote health and narratives created about health and illness. Most proximal to daily experiences is the micro-family environment that occurs on a momentary basis. The family micro-environment includes social interaction patterns supportive of positive health outcomes such as warmth, responsiveness to emotions, and social support. An expanded view of family health includes not only disease outcomes but also quality of life and lifelong health. We present this model in Figure 22.2.

The model includes biological contributions to health, including individual variability in reactivity and family health history. The connections to the social environment are not clearly identified as yet, but may influence the degree to which early adverse life events and family demographics such as instability may have as negative consequences on health. The social environment, early adverse life events and family demographics, serve as moderators on important health outcomes and act synergistically between each other. The family environment includes both the macro-environment (practices and beliefs) and the micro-environment (social interaction). The family environment serves to mediate the effects of biological vulnerabilities on health outcomes. We recognize that this model may be overly complex. On the other hand, it may also be simplistic given the multi-determined nature of health.

CONCLUSION

We began this chapter by noting that family health is a complicated construct. We conclude with a brief summary highlighting the overlap across the different theoretical approaches to reveal the core aspects of health that can be addressed from a family perspective.

An overarching theme provided by the theories we reviewed is the role of interpreting events and then taking action within the confines of the psychological and socioeconomic context of the family. Health, or symptoms of a disease, is not something that happens as the result of a prescribed order given by a professional but rather is a dynamic quality experienced by the individual, supported or derailed by the family, and lived in a neighborhood or community. When a diagnosis is given the interpretive process begins immediately. This process is framed by the developmental status of the individual, the life course of the family, and previous experiences with illness and health of the family members. To maintain health, the family must rally economic and collective resources. If these resources are drained either through economic or psychological burden, then the health of individuals is compromised. In the case of chronic health conditions, family disease management strategies such as medical adherence become disorganized and ineffective such that the individual's symptoms become more severe. In the case of diseases that are the result of environmental conditions such as poverty, crowding, or lack of access to care, the family may withdraw from supportive interactions and become less attentive to daily routines that have the potential to promote health and well-being. Although yet to be clearly established on the family level, reactivity to stress will vary from individual to individual. The family environment may be a prime resource to protect highly reactive individuals most susceptible to poor health outcomes.

The theories that have been developed thus far still rely heavily on stress and coping models rather than health promotion. On the one hand, this is perfectly understandable. Many of the theories have grown from the desire to address the family's need to cope with a chronic health condition and thus the first point of theorizing is how the family reacts or copes under pressure. In this regard, theories that include allocation of resources and interpretation of traumatic events provide a window into how family members rally together in the face of unanticipated stressful events. The stress and coping models, however, offer little direction as to important mediating and moderating variables.

The biopsychosocial theory, on the other hand, more clearly elucidates pathways of effect and takes into account the reciprocal nature of disease symptoms, individual psychological functioning, and family processes. Although there is recognition that the social context is an important moderator of health outcomes from a biopsychosocial perspective, less systematic attention has been paid to the cumulative effects of social disadvantage on health outcomes from a family systems perspective. (For exceptions, see Chen et al., 2002; Evans & Kim, 2007; Everhart, Fiese, & Smyth, 2008). The family resilience perspective begins to offer a more comprehensive view of the social ecologies of health with a focus on health promotion. However, it, too, has its limitations. To date, the resilience model is still a descriptive model with little attention to mechanisms of effect. Future theoretical work is warranted to more clearly specify how the creation of meaning-making representations and family practices centered in routines may be the active ingredients in family resilience (Fiese & Spagnola, 2007).

Considerable advances in biobehavioral technologies have revealed the complex intersection between health and environmental context. Further, the ever-changing nature of what constitutes a family calls into question how researchers will define family influences on health. To address the grand health challenges that face the world (e.g., obesity prevention, cardiovascular health, and hunger), family theorists have the opportunity to integrate principles of general systems, biopsychosocial, and resilience theories to create a new paradigm for health. The next generation of family health theories will advance our knowledge of how beliefs and practices at the family level influence biology and the course of disease over time. There is a cautionary note, however. Biological pathways will never "explain" how family processes influence health. As George Engel stated over 30 years ago, "The boundaries between health and disease, between well and sick, are far from clear and never will be clear, for they are diffused by cultural, social and psychological considerations." (Engel, 1977, p. 196). The challenge for the future is to create theory-driven research agendas that account for the bidirectional influence of family processes and biological processes within complex environments.

REFERENCES

Adler, N. E., Boyce, T., Chesney, M. A., Cohen, S., Folkman, S., Kahn, R. L., & Syme, S. L. (1994). Socioeconomic status and health: The challenge of the gradient. *American Psychologist, 49*, 15–24.

Adler, N. E., & Rehkopf, D. H. (2008). US disparities in health: Descriptions, causes and mechanisms. *Annual Review of Public Health, 29*, 235–252.

Alderfer, M. A., Labay, L., & Kazak, A. E. (2003). Brief report: Does posttraumatic stress apply to siblings of childhood cancer survivors? *Journal of Pediatric Psychology, 28*, 281–286.

Boyce W.T., & Ellis, B.J. (2005). Biological sensitivity to context: I. An evolutionary-developmental theory of the origins and functions of stress reactivity. *Development and Psychopathology, 17*, 271–301.

Bradley, R. H., Corwyn, R. F., Burchinal, M., McAdoo, H. P., & Coll, C. G. (2001). The home environments of children in the United States Part II: Relations with behavioral development through age thirteen. *Child Development, 72*, 1868–1886.

Brody, G. H., Flor, D. L., & Gibson, N. M. (1999). Linking maternal efficacy beliefs, developmental goals, parenting practices, and child competence in rural single-parent African American families. *Child Development, 70*, 1197–1208.

Brody, H. (1987). *Stories of sickness*. New Haven, CT: Yale University Press.

Bronfenbrenner, U. (1979). *The ecology of human development*. Cambridge, MA: Harvard University Press.

Brown, S. L. (2010). Marriage and child well-being: Research and policy perspectives. *Journal of Marriage and Family, 72*, 1059–1077.

Chen, E., Matthews, K. A., & Boyce, W. T. (2002). Socioeconomic differences in children's health: How and why do these relationships change with age? *Psychological Bulletin, 128*, 295–329.

Cohen, S., Jankicki-Deverts, D., Chen, E., & Matthews, K. A. (2010). Childhood socioeconomic status and adult health. *Annals of the New York Academy of Sciences, 1186*, 37–55.

Crosbie-Burnett, M., & Klein, D. M. (2009). The fascinating story of family theories. In J. H. Bray & M. Stanton (Eds.), *The Wiley-Blackwell handbook of family psychology* (pp. 37–52). Malden, MA: Wiley-Blackwell.

D'Onofrio, B. M., & Lahey, B. (2010). Biosocial influences on the family: A decade review. *Journal of Marriage and Family, 72*, 762–782.

Dilworth-Anderson, P., Burton, L. M., & Klein, D. F. (2005). Contemporary and emerging theories in studying families. In V. L. Bengston, A. C. Acock, K. R. Allen, P. Dilworth-Anderseon & D. F. Klein (Eds.), *Sourcebook of family theory & research* (pp. 35–50). Thousand Oaks, CA: Sage.

Engel, G. L. (1977). The need of a new medical model: A challenge for biomedicine. *Science, 196*, 129–136.

Evans, G. W. (2003). A multimethodological analysis of cumulative risk and allostatic load among rural children. *Developmental Psychology, 39*, 924–933.

Evans, G. W., Gonnella, C., Marcynyszyn, L. A., Gentile, L., & Salpekar, N. (2005). The role of chaos and poverty and children's socioemotional adjustment. *Psychological Science, 16*, 560–565.

Evans, G. W., & Kim, P. (2007). Childhood poverty and health: cumulative risk exposure and stress dysregulation. *Psychological Science, 18*, 953–957.

Evans, G. W., Kim, P., Ting, A. H., Tesher, H. B., & Shannis, D. (2007). Cumulative risk, maternal responsiveness, and allostatic load among young adolescents. *Developmental Psychology, 43*, 341–351.

Everhart, R. S., Fiese, B. H., & Smyth, J. M. (2008). A cumulative risk model predicting caregiver quality of life in pediatric asthma. *Journal of Pediatric Psychology, 33*, 809–818.

Fiese, B. H. (2006). *Family routines and rituals*. New Haven, CT: Yale University Press.

Fiese, B. H. (2007). Routines and rituals: Opportunities for participation in family health. *OTJR-Occupation, Participation, and Health, 27*, S41–S49.

Fiese, B. H., & Spagnola, M. (2007). The interior life of the family: Looking from the inside out and outside in. In A. S. Masten (Ed.), *Multilevel dynamics in developmental psychopathology: pathways to the future*. (pp. 119–150). Mahwah, New Jersey: Lawrence Erlbaum.

Fiese, B. H., & Wamboldt, F. S. (2001). Family routines, rituals, and asthma management: A proposal for family based strategies to increase treatment adherence. *Families, Systems, and Health, 18*, 405–418.

Fiese, B. H., & Wamboldt, F. S. (2003a). Coherent accounts of coping with a chronic illness: Convergences and divergences in family measurement using a narrative analysis. *Family Process, 42*, 439–451.

Fiese, B. H., & Wamboldt, F. S. (2003b). Tales of pediatric asthma management: Family based strategies related to medical adherence and healthcare utilization. *Journal of Pediatrics, 143*, 457–462.

Fiese, B. H., Wamboldt, F. S., & Anbar, R. D. (2005). Family asthma management routines: Connections to medical adherence and quality of life. *Journal of Pediatrics, 146*, 171–176.

Fiese, B. H., Winter, M. A., & Botti, J. C. (2011). The ABC's of family mealtimes: Observational lessons for promoting healthy outcomes for children with persistent asthma. *Child Development, 82*, 133–145.

Fiese, B. H., Winter, M. A., Wamboldt, F. S., Wamboldt, M. Z., & Anbar, R. D. (2010). Do family mealtime behaviors predict separation anxiety symptoms in children with persistent asthma? *Journal of Child Psychology and Psychiatry*, *51*, 144–151.

Gallo, L. C., de los Monteros, K. E., & Shivpuri, S. (2009). Socioeconomic status and health: What is the role of reserve capacity? *Current Directions in Psychological Science*, *18*, 269–274.

Gallo, L. C., Penedo, F. J., de los Monteros, K. E., & Arguelles, W. (2009). Resiliency in the face of disadvantage: Do Hispanic cultural characteristics protect health outcomes? *Journal of Personality 77*, 1707–1746.

Hammons, A., & Fiese, B. H. (2011). Is frequency of shared family meals related to the nutritional health of children and adolescents? A meta-analysis. *Pediatrics*, *127*(6), e1565–e1574.

Hill, R. (1958). Generic features of families under stress. *Social Casework*, *49*, 139–150.

Huynh, V. W., & Fuligni, A. J. (2010). Discrimination hurts: The academic, psychological and physical well-being of adolescents. *Journal of Research on Adolescence*, *20*, 916–941.

Institute of Medicine and National Resource Council (2011). *Toward an Integrated Science of Research on Families: Workshop Report.*

Janz, N. K., & Becker, M. H. (1984). The Health Belief Model: A decade later. *Health Education Quarterly*, *11*, 1–47.

Kazak, A. E., Alderfer, M. A., Rourke, M. T., Simms, S., Streisand, R., & Grossman, J. R. (2004). Posttraumatic Stress Disorder (PTSD) and Posttraumatic Stress Symptoms (PTSS) in families of adolescents childhood cancer survivors. *Journal of Pediatric Psychology*, *29*, 211–219.

Kazak, A. E., Boeving, A., Alderfer, M. A., Hwang, W. T., & Reilly, A. (2005). Posttraumatic stress symptoms during treatment in parents of children with cancer. *Journal of Clinical Oncology*, *23*, 7405–7410.

Kazak, A. E., DeRosa, B. W., Schwartz, L. A., Hobbie, W., Carlson, C., Ittenbach, R. F., …, Ginsberg, J. P. (2010). Psychological outcomes and health beliefs in adolescent and young adult survivors of childhood cancer and controls. *Journal of Clinical Oncology*, *28*, 2002–2007.

Kazak, A. E., Kassam-Adams, N., Schneider, S., Zelikovsky, N., Alderfer, M. A., & Rourke, M. (2006). An integrative model of pediatric medical traumatic stress. *Journal of Pediatric Psychology*, *31*, 343–355.

Kazak, A. E., Rourke, M. T., Alderfer, M. A., Pai, A., Reilly, A. F., & Meadows, A. T. (2007). Evidence-based assessment, intervention, and psychosocial care in pediatric oncology: A blueprint for comprehensive services across treatment. *Journal of Pediatric Psychology*, *32*, 1099–1110.

Kazak, A. E., Rourke, M. T., & Crump, T. A. (2003). Families and other systems in pediatric psychology. In M. C. Roberts (Ed.), *Handbook of Pediatric Psychology* (pp. 159–175). New York: Guilford Press.

Kazak, A. E., Simms, S., & Rourke, M. T. (2002). Family systems practice in pediatric psychology. *Journal of Pediatric Psychology*, *27*, 133–144.

Kazak, A. E., Stuber, M., Barakat, L. P., Meesek, K., Guthrie, D., & Meadows, A. (1998). Predicting posttraumatic stress symptoms in mothers and fathers of survivors of childhood cancer. *Journal of the American Academy of Child and Adolescent Psychiatry*, *37*, 823–831.

Lim, J., Wood, B. L., Miller, B. D., & Simmens, S. J. (2011). Effects on paternal and maternal depressive symptoms on internalizing symptoms and asthma disease activity: Mediation by interparental negativity and parenting. *Journal of Family Psychology*, *25*, 137–146.

Martin, P., & Midgley, E. (2006). Immigration: Shaping and reshaping America. *Population Bulletin 61* (4).

McAdoo, H. P. (1993). *Ethnic families: Strength in diversity*. Newbury Park, CA: Sage.

Mccubbin, H. I., & Patterson, J. M. (1983). The family stress process: The double ABCX model of family adjustment and adaptation. *Marriage and Family Review*, *6*, 7–37.

McDaniel, S. H., Beckman, H. B., Morse, D. S., Silberman, J., Seaburn, D. B., & Epstein, R. M. (2007). Physician self-disclosure in primary care visits. Enough about you, what about me? *Archives of Internal Medicine*, *167*, 1321–1326.

McDaniel, S. H., Campbell, T. L., Hepworth, J., & Lorenz, A. (Eds.). (2005). *Family-oriented primary care* (2nd ed.). New York: Springer.

McDaniel, S. H., & LeRoux, P. (2007). An overview of primary care family psychology. *Journal Clinical Psychology Medical Settings*, *14*, 23–32.

McEwen, B. S. (1998). Protective and damaging effects of stress mediators. *New England Journal of Medicine*, *338*, 171–179.

Myers, H. F. (2009). Ethnicity- and socioeconomic status-related stresses in context: An integrative review and conceptual model. *Journal of Behavioral Medicine*, *32*, 9–19.

Nash, J. M. (2008). Transdisciplinary training: Key components and prerequisites for success. *American Journal of Preventive Medicine, 35*, S133–S140.

Paradies, Y. (2006). A systematic review of empirical research on self-reported racism and health. *International Journal of Epidemiology, 35*, 888–901.

Patterson, J. M. (1988). Families experiencing stress: The family adjustment and adaptation response model. *Family Systems Medicine, 5*, 202–237.

Patterson, J. M. (2002). Understanding family resilience. *Journal of Clinical Psychology, 2002*, 233–246.

Patterson, J. M., & Garwick, A. W. (1994). Levels of meaning in family stress theory. *Family Process, 33*, 287–304.

Patterson, J. M., Wall, M., Berge, J., & Milla, C. (2007). Gender differences in treatment adherence among youth with cystic fibrosis: Development of a new questionnaire. *Journal of Cystic Fibrosis, 7*, 154–164.

Patterson, J. M., Wall, M., Berge, J., & Milla, C. (2009). Associations of psychological factors with health outcomes among youth with cystic fibrosis. *Pediatric Pulmonology, 44*, 46–53.

Perreira, K. M., & Ornelas, I. J. (2011). The physical and psychological well-being of immigrant children. *The Future of Children, 21*, 195–218.

Porterfield, S. L., & McBride, T. D. (2007). Perceived need and access to health services among children with special healthcare needs. *American Journal of Public Health, 97*, 323–329.

Reiss, D. (2010). Genetic thinking in the study of social relationships: Five points of entry. *Perspectives on Psychological Science, 5*, 502–515.

Repetti, R. L., Taylor, S. E., & Seeman, T. E. (2002). Risky families: Family social environments and the mental and physical health of offspring. *Psychological Bulletin, 128*, 330–366.

Rodriques, N., & Patterson, J. M. (2007). Impact of severity of a child's chronic health condition on the functioning of two-parent families. *Journal of Pediatric Psychology, 32*, 417–426.

Rolland, J. S. (1987). Chronic illness and the life cycle: A conceptual framework. *Family Process, 26*, 203–221.

Rolland, J. S. (1994). *Families, illness, and disability*. New York: Basic Books.

Rolland, J. S., & Walsh, F. (2006). Facilitating family resilience with childhood illness and disability. *Current Opinion in Pediatrics, 18*, 527–538.

Rosenfield, P. L. (1992). The potential of transdisciplinary research for sustaining and extending linkages between health and social sciences. *Social Science and Medicine*, 1343–1357.

Roy, K. M., Tubbs, C. Y., & Burton, L. M. (2004). Don't have no time: Daily rhythms and the organization of time for low-income families. *Family Relations, 53*, 168–178.

Schmeer, K. K. (2011). The child health disadvantage of parental cohabitation. *Journal of Marriage and Family, 73*, 181–193.

Stehl, M. L., Kazak, A. E., Alderfer, M. A., Rodriguez, A., Hwang, W. T., Pai, A. L., …, Reilly, A. (2009). Conducting a randomized clinical trial of an psychological intervention for parents/caregivers of children with cancer shortly after diagnosis. *Journal of Pediatric Psychology, 34*, 803–816.

Tubbs, C. Y., Roy, K. M., & Burton, L. M. (2005). Family ties: Constructing family time in low-income families. *Family Process, 44*, 77–91.

Waldfogel, J., Craigie, T., & Brooks-Gunn, J. (2010). Fragile families and child wellbeing. *The Future of Children, 20*, 87–112.

Walsh, F. (2003). Family resilience: A framework for clinical practice. *Family Process, 42*, 1–18.

Weinstein, N. D. (1993). Testing four competing theories of health-protective behavior. *Health Psychology, 12*, 324–333.

Wen, M. (2008). Family structure and children's health and behavior data from 1999 National Survey of America's Families. *Journal of Family Issues, 29*, 1492–1519.

Wood, B. L. (1993). Beyond the "psychosomatic family": A biobehavioral model of pediatric illness. *Family Process, 32*, 261–278.

Wood, B. L. (1995). A developmental biopsychosocial approach to the treatment of chronic illness in children and adolescence. In R. H. Mikesell, D. D. Lusterman & S. H. McDaniel (Eds.), *Integrating family therapy: handbook of family psychology and family systems* (pp. 437–455). Washington, DC: American Psychological Association.

Wood, B. L., Klebba, K. B., & Miller, B. D. (2000). Evolving the Biobehavioral Family Model: The fit of attachment. *Family Process, 39*, 319–344.

Wood, B. L., Lim, J., Miller, B. D., Cheah, P., Zwetsch, T., Ramesh, S., & Simmens, S. (2008). Testing the biobehavioral family model in pediatric asthma: Pathways of effect. *Family Process, 47*, 21–40.

Wood, B. L., Miller, B. D., Lim, J., Lillis, K., Ballow, M., & Stern, T., (2006). Family relational factors in pediatric depression and asthma: Pathways of effect. *Journal American Academy Child and Adolescent Psychiatry*, *45*, 1494–1502.

World Health Organization (1946). *Preamble to the Constitution of the World Health Organization as adopted by the International Health Conference*. Retrieved from http://www.who.int/about/definition/en/print.html.

Wynne, L. C. (2003). Systems theory and the biopsychosocial model. In R. Frankel, T. Quill & S. H. McDaniel (Eds.), *The biopsychosocial approach: Past, present, and future*. (pp. 219–230). Rochester, NY: University of Rochester Press.

Wysocki, T., Harris, M. A., Buckloh, L. M., Mertlich, D., Lochrie, A. S., Taylor, A., … White, N. H. (2006). Effects of behavioral family systems therapy for diabetes on adolescents' family relationships, treatment adherence, and metabolic control. *Journal of Pediatric Psychology*, *31*, 928–938.

23 The Resilience of Military Families
Theoretical Perspectives

Gary L. Bowen, James A. Martin, and Jay A. Mancini

Since 2001, more than 2 million service men and women have been deployed to Afghanistan and Iraq and by the end of 2010, combat deployments had resulted in some 5,500 service member deaths and more than 37,000 serious injuries. Paralleling these operational causalities, our military forces have also experienced a large number of stress-related causalities, including service members demonstrating post-traumatic stress symptoms, as well as evidence of depression, anxiety disorders, substance abuse, and suicidal behaviors. For some service members, these symptoms actually emerge after their return home from the war zone and/or after their return to civilian life (AFHSC, 2010; Institute of Medicine, 2010).

Service members do not face problems alone—the majority are married, others are involved in serious romantic relationships, approximately two in five have children in the household, and almost all are part of an extended family (ICF International, 2010). In effect, families also "serve and sacrifice" because all family members are profoundly affected by military service and military family life, especially wartime separations and the physical, emotional, and social sequelae of war that often persists well beyond the service member's homecoming (Institute of Medicine, 2010).

Behavioral and social scientists have made significant efforts to understand variations in the responses of military families to the many challenges posed by military service, including the adversities associated with wartime service (MacDermid Wadsworth, 2010). The concept of resilience is often used to describe those families that successfully adapt over time in the face of significant adversities and continue to get the day-to-day tasks of life done (e.g., bills paid, children to school, dog fed, and so forth; Bowen & Martin, 2011).

This chapter addresses military family resilience in today's Active and Reserve Components—the US Armed Forces that emerged from the 1990s and a period of profound and stressful downsizing (in the overall number of military bases, units, and people) and were thrown into an unexpected decade of war. Our focus is on married service members with and without dependent children in the home as well as single service members with dependent children in the home. In addition, we focus on the resilience of the family as a group. In agreement with Patterson (2002), this requires a shift in the unit of analysis from the individual to a system level that involves two or more family members.

We review three theories that provide perspectives on the capacity of military families (defined here as Afghanistan and Iraq War era military families) to demonstrate resilience. The first two theories are larger conceptual frameworks in the field of family studies: *life course theory* (sometimes referred to as life course perspective) and *symbolic interactionism*. The third, *family stress theory*, emerged directly from the study of military families in crisis (e.g., Hill, 1949). We examine how each theory addresses one or more of the four dimensions that Hawley and DeHaan (1996) associate with variation in the capacity of families to demonstrate resilience: "context, developmental level, the interactive combination of risk and protective factors, and the family's shared outlook" (p. 293). Limitations in the application of these perspectives are discussed, in particular, the lack of attention to the broader community context. We then offer a theory of community action and change, which effectively examines military family resilience in the context of the formal and informal community networks in which military families are embedded. This community perspective shifts the focus to include larger contextual effects that frame and inform military family resilience.

KEY ISSUES IN THE STUDY OF MILITARY FAMILY RESILIENCE

We begin by discussing both military demands and stressors and marital and family outcomes. This is followed by a discussion of the concept of resilience—a brief history of the concept and its current use in the family studies literature.

MILITARY DEMANDS AND STRESSORS

America's military is an all-volunteer force (AVF)—well-educated, well-trained, well-equipped, well-led, and proud of its professional warrior identity and service to the nation. Our Armed Forces are built around a small Active Component force and a readily available National Guard and other Reserve Components, designed and intended to perform global military missions across a spectrum from warfighting to humanitarian operations.

Because of its small size and the challenges of simultaneously conducting two prolonged, major combat operations during the first decade of the twenty-first century, America's Armed Forces have been severely stressed—including an unprecedented mobilization of the National Guard and other Reserve Components (Hoge, et al., 2004). Meeting the combat and other operational challenges in Afghanistan and Iraq, while maintaining an array of ongoing, worldwide military missions, have required many Active and Reserve Component military members (especially Soldiers and Marines) to serve multiple combat deployments with limited recovery time at home between these deployments. To a lesser extent, Active and Reserve Air Force and Navy personnel have also been deployed to Afghanistan and Iraq often as "filler" personnel (medical, logistical, communications, transportation, civil affairs, and other military specialties) to support the Army and Marine Corps. At the same time, Air Force and Navy units have experienced an increase in operational tempo associated with sustaining America's global military presence. Examples of these missions include the co-occurring air and sea-based combat and humanitarian engagements in Libya and the massive humanitarian aid provided in response to the earthquake in Haiti and the multiple disasters in Japan.

Like other segments of society, the Armed Forces contain a diverse array of family types whose membership and structure often place added stress on family life (Department of Defense, 2009). These family types include single parent families, dual military career couples, as well as a significant number of military families where there is a child or adult in the family with a special need. Many military spouses are also in the civilian workforce, often because of economic necessity.

As Segal (1989) first described them, the family and the military are both "greedy institutions" demanding much of their members. From the perspective of today's military family, especially non-traditional families, the challenges of military life are increasingly complex and the duty demands of current military service cause many of these families to feel overwhelmed. Although military duties and service life have always been stressful, the pace, intensity, and dangers associated with today's operational requirements, place a particularly heavy load on military families (Chandra, Burns, Tanielian, & Jaycox, 2011). As noted more than 20 years ago by Bowen and Orthner (1989), military families are a type of "organization family"—families where the needs of the employing organization usually take priority over the needs of the family.

MARITAL AND FAMILY OUTCOMES

Despite the challenges of a demanding military lifestyle, most military families do well and many military families thrive, often benefiting from positive life experiences like those associated with living and traveling overseas (Martin & Sherman, 2009). Most military families also experience a personal satisfaction and feel a sense of pride that typically comes with awareness that the service and sacrifice associated with being a military family are important and valued.

For some military members and their families, however, the service member is not able to successfully complete his or her military service obligation or the spouse may not be willing to continue in the marriage and remain in military life (Martin & Sherman, 2012). Although the military divorce rate has been relatively steady even in this current wartime period, about 3% per year, there is obvious stress on military marriages associated with this challenging lifestyle, especially for those families in both the Active and Reserve Components who have experienced the frequent, often lengthy, and always dangerous combat deployments to Afghanistan and Iraq (Karney & Crown, 2007).

The adversities and challenges faced by families during wartime may also have negative repercussions on the nature of the parent–child relationship, as well as child and adolescent adjustment. For example, each stage of deployment may present challenges for military children and adolescents, as evidenced in their lower academic performance and elevated risk for mental health problems (Chandra, et al., 2011; Huebner, Mancini, Wilcox, Grass, & Grass, 2007). The impacts of military service may also influence the child or adolescent directly or indirectly through increasing problems in the marital relationship (Dekel & Monson, 2010; Sheppard, Malatras, & Israel, 2010).

In recognition of these many wartime challenges, DOD and the military services have made considerable efforts to provide couples and families with primary, secondary, and tertiary support to enrich, sustain, and support marriages and family life (Institute of Medicine, 2010). While many of the stressors associated with military duties and military life are not new, the challenges of today's wartime military service, including lengthy, repeated combat deployments and the associated family separations, represent unprecedented threats to the integrity and well-being of service members and their families. Stress is cumulative, and the demands currently being made on our all-volunteer military and their family members are not likely to substantially lessen in the foreseeable future.

THE CONCEPT OF RESILIENCE

Many men and women in the Armed Forces overcome war-related trauma and disabling physical and psychological wounds and return to productive roles in both the military and the larger society. In other words, they demonstrate resilience.

The concept of resilience first appeared in the developmental psychopathology literature in the 1980s and was used to describe children and adolescents who evidenced normal developmental trajectories despite facing significant individual and/or environmental adversities. The work of Norman Garmezy, Suniya Luthar, Ann Masten, Sir Michael Rutter, and Emmy Werner is representative of this literature. In part, the concept of resilience arose to replace the misleading idea in the literature that some children were "invulnerable" to the consequences of adversities in their lives (*cf.* Earvolino-Ramirez, 2007).

The concept of resilience can be applied to individuals, dyads, families, groups, communities, and even larger units of analysis (Bowen & Martin, 2011). In each case, the central question remains the same: What distinguishes those who are able to avoid or overcome the potential negative effects of adversity over time (successful adaptation) from those who are not? Addressing this question involves unpacking the concept of resilience in the context of current literature, as well as introducing several additional concepts to this discussion (Fergus & Zimmerman, 2005; Luthar, Cicchetti, & Becker, 2000; MacDermid Wadsworth, 2010).

First, resilience is evaluated in the context of adversity that is associated with an increased probability of negative outcomes. Second, the determination of resilience requires a longitudinal perspective with at least three time periods: (1) a baseline period before the adversity appears; (2) the time period during and immediately following the adversity; and (3) the longer-term time period for monitoring the response trajectory, which can range from days to decades (*cf.* Werner & Smith, 1992). Thus, resilience refers to a "dynamic process" rather than a trait, state, or a particular outcome (Luthar, et al., 2000, p. 543). Third, the overcoming of adversity requires some evaluative or normative point of comparison (Bowen & Martin, 2011). For example, what is positive adjustment or competence and how does the floor of adjustment or competence vary for individuals and groups across time and situations? Reiss and Oliveri (1991) describe how the larger social community shapes an understanding of both the seriousness of a stressor event and the expected competence when confronted with the stressor event.

In addition to the concepts of adversity, time, and a normative point of comparison, assets play a critical role in models of risk and resilience. Assets are internal strengths and resources that reside within the individual or group and the nature of opportunities and supports within the environment (Bowen & Martin, 2011). Building on the work of L'Abate (1990), who defines "personal and interpersonal competence" by what a person "is, does, and has" (p. 258), we have defined three sets of assets: (a) *Being*, (b) *Having*, and (c) *Doing* (Bowen & Martin, 2011). *Being* assets involve innate individual attributes anchored in genetics, such as intelligence, personality, and physical abilities, which are enhanced by life experiences. *Having* assets involve the possession of financial capital, the availability of opportunities, and the presence of social connections, including both formal and informal support systems. *Doing* assets involve behavioral competencies that reflect specific knowledge, training, and skills at both the individual and the group level.

Whatever the type, assets function in at least one of three ways in the relationship between adversity (risk) and outcomes. Assets may decrease the occurrence or the intensity of adversity (prevent), increase the probability of positive outcomes (promote), or buffer the negative influence of adversity on outcomes (protect). Bowen (1998), in examining the relationship between work spillover and family adaptation in the US Army, demonstrated that the asset of unit leadership support functioned in all three ways. It is also important to note that we do not assume a one-to-one correspondence between assets and resiliency outcomes, either directly or indirectly. Upper and lower threshold points may be present where the relationship between particular assets and specified outcome shifts more dramatically (Crane, 1991).

McCubbin and McCubbin and their colleagues, as part of the Family Stress, Coping and Health Project at the University of Wisconsin, played an instrumental role in introducing the idea of resilient families into the discipline of family studies (McCubbin & McCubbin, 1988). They equated the study of resilient families to "the search for characteristics, dimensions, and properties of families which help families to be resistant to disruption in the face of change and adaptive in the face of crisis situations" (1988, p. 247). McCubbin and McCubbin's definition of family resilience raised an important question in the literature about whether family resilience referred to the capacity of the family, as inferred from their definition, or to a process of adjustment and adaptation (*cf.* Patterson, 2002).

An important contribution in the study of family resilience from our perspective appeared in an article published by Hawley and DeHaan (1996). In addition to providing an excellent historical review of the concept of family resilience, as well as discussing its conceptual mooring in the study of individual resilience, the authors posed an important conceptual question: "Is resilience mutually constructed and shared by the family as a whole, or is it a collective of individual resiliencies exhibited by family members?" (p. 290). In other words, as the authors posed, "is there a basis for believing that families as units can exhibit resiliency?" (p. 5). The authors concluded that resilience as a family-level construct had theoretical promise, although they noted the challenges in measuring and assessing this construct.

Drawing upon both the individual and family resilience literatures, Hawley and DeHaan offered the following definition:

> Family resilience describes the path a family follows as it adapts and prospers in the face of stress, both in the present and over time. Resilient families respond positively to these conditions in unique ways, depending on the context, developmental level, the interactive combination of risk and protective factors, and the family's shared outlook. (p. 293)

This definition of family resilience generally aligns with other definitions in the literature (Boss, 2002; Conger & Conger, 2002; Patterson, 2002; Walsh, 1996), Consequently, we use Hawley and DeHaan's definition to anchor our review, although we acknowledge that definitional ambiguity and confusion remain in the literature with family resilience also defined as a characteristic, capacity, and as an outcome (*cf.* Ganong & Coleman, 2002).

In the next section, we consider family theories that address one or more dimensions that Hawley and DeHaan associate with variation in the ability of families to demonstrate resilience: "context, developmental level, the interactive combination of risk and protective factors, and the family's shared outlook" (p. 293). This approach is consistent with what Walsh (1996) describes as the focus on family resilience: "to identify and foster key processes that enable families to cope more effectively and emerge hardier from crises or persistent stresses, whether from within or from outside the family" (p. 263).

THEORIES OF RESILIENCE IN MILITARY FAMILIES

We focus on three theories that contribute to our understanding of military family resilience: life course theory, symbolic interactionism, and family stress theory. Several additional theories have implications for the study of military family resilience, such as systems theory, bioecological theory, and family development theory, that are often discussed in the context of these three theories (*cf.* Walsh, 1996). However, aspects of these theories that address process, context, and development are included in our discussions. Although we do not discuss theories addressing particular genetic or hereditary influences, such as the stress-diathesis model, we acknowledge that these theories offer future promise to the study of military family resilience (Bowen & Martin, 2011).

LIFE COURSE THEORY

Interest in the life course as a theoretical approach for understanding both micro- and macro-aspects of human development across time emerged in the latter decades of the twentieth century particularly in sociology and psychology (Bengtson & Allen, 1993; Elder & Shanahan, 2006; George, 2003). Early interest focused primarily on what has been described as culturally and normatively constructed life stages and age roles, biographical meanings, the aging processes, outcomes of institutional regulations and policies, and demographic accounts of individual and collective lives (Mayer, 2009). Today, life course theory (LCT) continues to evolve within and across the social sciences and reflects emerging efforts to integrate the physical, psychological, and social mechanisms that underlie human development with the individual, meso-, and macro-level contexts that frame human development (Mayer).

LCT is particularly pertinent to two of the four dimensions that Hawley and DeHaan associate with family resilience: context and developmental level. The dimension of risk (e.g., life events) and protective factors (e.g., social supports), is also effectively captured by LCT, as described below. The theory is perhaps least applicable to the dimension of the family's shared outlook, although the family was the focus of analysis in early life course studies during the period of the Great Depression (e.g., Angell, 1936; Cavan & Ranck, 1938).

The life course paradigm (represented here in the context of military service and principally by the writings of Glen Elder) is grounded in the assumption that earlier and ongoing life experiences help to shape both our life journey and the life outcomes we experience at any point in time. Important concepts anchoring this paradigm are life trajectories (the major life paths that comprise our life experience) and life transitions (important life events that in some way alter our life path) that are embedded in these trajectories. For example a military member's service experience would be identified as a career trajectory and a promotion in rank as a transition. The timing and sequencing associated with any transition is also considered important in understanding the effects of the transition across the life course, including consideration of any single transition in the context of other trajectories and transitions. For example, the same period in a military career when one may be moving into a higher leadership position (promotion in rank) may be occurring at a time when one is also taking on important family obligations like the birth of a child. If a single recruit becomes pregnant during basic training, the family life trajectory is thrown out of sync with the military life trajectory—the timing and sequencing of transitions on each life trajectory (family life, education, and career) have implications for the others; each is informed by normative considerations that provide guidelines and standards for social comparison. The timing and sequencing of these various life transitions are important in understanding their impact on subsequent life course outcomes.

According to Gade (1991), it is necessary to locate an individual in three related time dimensions: historical time (what is occurring in the macro-environment), family time (important family developmental stages and events), and individual time (a biopsychosocial dimension). For today's military family, this means understanding what it means to be in an all-volunteer military and serving during a period of prolonged war with multiple deployments and possible combat exposures. It means understanding how these conditions influence and interact with personal, marital, and family relationships and other normative life events, as well as having an appreciation for the personal and family biopsychosocial factors that are the fabric for this paradigm and serve as the catalyst for associated life course outcomes. Elder (1990) observed that "the study of human lives in a changing society must relate the micro experience of lives and the macro level of institutions and structures" (p. 240).

Related life course concepts that have been applied to the topic of military family resilience include: "(a) human agency, (b) location in time and place, (c) timing, (d) linked lives, and (e) life-long development" (MacLean & Elder, 2007, p. 177). These concepts, and the application of LCT, provide a unique perspective for understanding the military family and nature of military service in larger sociohistorical context. For example, the response by citizens and the media to the veterans of the wars in Afghanistan and Iraq is quite different from the response received by an earlier generation of Vietnam War veterans. Clearly, the nature of this sociohistorical context plays an important role in the ability of military families to demonstrate resilience and to sustain resilience across time and life experiences.

LCT has been used to explain some of the long-term effects of military service (MacLean & Elder, 2007). Another broad area of military interest for life course research has been the long-term effects of specific events and experiences, in particular combat exposure and its immediate and long-term physical and behavioral health implications, as well as other life adjustment implications across various life stages (Elder, 1987; Elder & Clipp, 1989; Elder, Gimbel, & Ivie, 1991; Gimbel & Booth, 1994; Little & Friedlander, 1979; Pavalko & Elder, 1990).

A core concept incorporated here flows from the earlier mentioned life course description of "linked lives" and is represented in the related concept of "social convoys" across the life course (Kahn & Antonucci 1980). Kahn and Antonucci developed the *convoy model* to provide a developmental and life-span perspective on what was at the time a new concept of interpersonal relationships. The term convoy was originally used by Kahn and Antonucci to incorporate the perspectives of attachment, social roles, and social support within a lifespan perspective and to describe a hierarchy of relationships within personal networks, based on emotional closeness in the relationship. The concept of a convoy is used here to highlight the dynamic aspects of our relationships, taking account of qualitative changes at the level of the individual, the couple, or family, as well as our larger network of family, friends, colleagues, and acquaintances.

In the present context, the concept of a convoy of social relationships is a powerful metaphor— for both the military member and for the military family. It is a metaphor that has application within a LCT framework applied to military members in which unit-based, "buddy" relationships established and defined by shared combat experiences typically become life-long relationships that have a meaning like no other. While less recognized, spouse and family relationships forged in the shared experiences and stress of military life frequently become life-long connections as well, connections that are maintained even as individual and family life trajectories evolve as families transition from military to civilian life.

SYMBOLIC INTERACTIONISM

Symbolic interaction (SI) explores how individuals and families construct their worlds and determine what their experiences mean, accounts for how families adjust and adapt, and the processes and mechanisms they employ in doing so. Consequently, SI is highly applicable to addressing the "family's shared outlook" dimension identified by Hawley and DeHaan (1996). SI also speaks to the importance of "context" in Hawley and DeHaan's discussion of resilience, as social norms, reference groups, and ongoing intra- and extra-familial patterns of interaction influence how family members and families define presenting situations.

SI theory has a long history of use in family science (see Burr, Leigh, Day, & Constantine, 1979; LaRossa & Rietzes, 1993). In this approach interpretation intervenes between what might be considered an objective event and the experienced event. Thus, from an SI perspective, humans are assumed to be actors in their physical and social worlds, and not solely reactors.

Meaning is a central concept in SI theory, because it is the significance or importance that individuals and families attach to their experience that form the basis of actions they take (Blumer, 1969; Manis & Meltzer, 1972). Hawley and DeHaan (1996) note the critical role that meaning plays in understanding resilience through the concept of family ethos: "a shared set of values and attitudes held by a family unit that serves as the linchpin of its resilience" (p. 290).

Social relationships provide an important context for how individuals and families define and respond to presenting situations and circumstances. Whether it is the formation of opinions, deciding a course of action, or determining that a circumstance or experience is normal and tolerable, stressful and manageable, or significant and leading to crisis, social interaction has an important place. People in our lives have been referred to as "orientational others" by Kuhn (1972), and reference group is another term often used to describe collections of people who have some say in the sense we make of our lives; a reference group may be friends, family members, work associates, or a community (Shibutani, 1986).

A significant term that comes into play when describing SI is the *definition of the situation* (Thomas & Znaniecki, 1918). According to these early symbolic interactionists, if a situation is defined as real by a family then it is real in its consequences, that is, what a family does next. Intertwined with the establishment of meaning is this process of weighing, examining, and evaluating what is occurring and its significance. In the mix of this defining process is the social environment, that is, people (family, friends, neighbors, co-workers, officials, supervisors, leaders, and so on) with whom individuals and families interact. Defining situations involves learning how to navigate the social and cultural world early in life, as well as learning to deal with specific situations (for example, whether an event is considered a change that a person must cope with, or a crisis that has far-reaching and life-changing implications). Patterson (2002) discusses family definitions of situations with regard to family meanings, stating there are three levels of those meanings: "(a) families' definitions of their demands (primary appraisal) and capabilities (secondary appraisal); (b) their identity as a family (how they see themselves internally as a unit); and (c) their world view (how they see their family in relationship to systems outside of their family)" (p. 351).

SI theory elevates *the self* in explaining what motivates people to act. According to Mead (1934), one's self is ever-changing and malleable and results from the ongoing interaction a person has with others. Social interactions are powerful agents in shaping views of self, including self-views that are related to resilience, that is, feeling competent to deal with uncertainty or adversity. From a collective point of view, the concept of self shaped by social interaction can be applied to the family level as well, which is broadly reflected in the work of Reiss (1981) on family paradigms.

Boss's (2002, 2006) theorizing and research on military personnel and families has provided a core and significant SI understanding of what families' experience. In the early 1970s, Boss studied the families of American soldiers missing in action in Vietnam and Laos. Subsequently, Boss (2002) studied numerous other family situations where separation and loss were present. Two interrelated concepts emerged from her work that have been highly heuristic in studies of military family resilience: (a) ambiguous stressor events, including ambiguous loss, and (b) boundary ambiguity. The first concept, ambiguous stressor events, focused on the "A" or the "event or situation" (stressor variable) in the ABCX Model. In some cases, it is difficult to obtain the facts necessary to understand the stressor event itself, which results in an ambiguous or uncertain situation. For example, will the combat injury result in a long-term disability or not? The family's coping process is hampered when members have difficulty understanding exactly what they are dealing with.

The concept of boundary ambiguity focused directly on the "C" or "meaning component" in the ABCX model, which Boss (2002) defined as the "perceptual outcome" of ambiguous loss (p. 30). It contains two elements or situations, one being where a family member is physically missing (not present) but psychologically present, perhaps because her/his status of being alive is not known (an example is a soldier missing in action). A second type of boundary ambiguity occurs when a family member is physically present but psychologically absent, as in the situation when a service member has suffered profound brain damage with associated memory loss as a result of a blast injury (TBI). In both instances, families are unsure, disorganized, and in a sense "frozen" (Boss, 2006, pp. 7–8). In Boss's theory, boundary ambiguity occurs when it is unclear who is in and who is out of the family, who is a real and functioning family member, and who can be counted on and who cannot (Boss, 2006, p. 12). Boundary ambiguity is a risk factor for families. When circumstances such as family separation occur (deployment as one example), families draw on their inner strengths, as well as their social connections, to maintain balance, certainty, and predictability.

Recently, Huebner, et al. (2007) accessed Boss's theorizing to examine adjustment among youth in military families when a parent is deployed. This study examined four categories of data including overall perceptions of loss, boundary ambiguity, changes in mental health, and relationship conflict. Findings revealed broad-based concern over the deployed parents' welfare, and their own welfare as the deployment progressed. Adolescents acted out toward others and had a greater tendency for emotional outbursts. Their depression and anxiety were related to persistent uncertainty about the well-being of the deployed parent. Boundary ambiguity was evident because of the deployed parent's status of being present psychologically, but not present physically, during the deployment; and being present physically but sometimes not psychologically present during the subsequent reintegration period that follows deployment.

A final example is Huebner's (2009) discussion of meaning and attachment related internal working models as applied to military deployment and families, which is rooted in SI. In discussing contrasting reactions to separation due to deployment ("This deployment separation is scary and I can't cope" versus "This deployment separation is a challenge to be dealt with"), Huebner suggests an amplified way of looking at the relationships between the resources that families have that can support them during stressful times ("B" factors in the ABC-X framework), and how families perceive and define their circumstances ("C" factor in the model). Her goal was to explain how military families can best access resources available to them, and she suggests that an important primary resource is *attachment security* (the bond a person has with important others; this is akin to social attachment). Also discussed are *internal working models*, essentially views of self and of others that often form through early experiences in relationships.

In sum, SI theory is well-aligned with accounting for variation in family resilience. As a theory, SI opens up the "black box" of "family shared outlook," and captures the construction of meaning in "context." As seen in the work of Boss above, SI is a theoretical cornerstone in family stress theory, which is discussed next.

FAMILY STRESS THEORY

Family stress theory is the most explicit of the theories reviewed in its application to military family resilience during a time of war (MacDermid Wadsworth, 2010). Family stress theory in its different variations draws upon both LCT and SI theory, as well as other conceptual frameworks, including systems theory, ecological theory, and family developmental theory (Bowen, Richman, & Bowen, 2000; Everson & Camp, 2011; Walsh, 1996).

Family stress theory has its origin in Hill's (1949) seminal study, *Families under stress: Adjustment to the crisis of war separation and reunion*, which he later described as the ABCX model (Hill, 1958). In Chapter 2 of his book, which addressed the sociology of family crisis and family adjustment, Hill described this model:

> At least three variables are at work to determine whether a given event becomes a crisis [the X factor] for any given family: (1) the hardships of the situation or event itself [the A factor], (2) the resources of the family, its role structure, flexibility, and previous history with crisis [the B factor), and (3) the definition the family makes of the event [the C factor]; that is, whether family members treat the event as if it were or as if it were not a threat to their status, their goals, and objectives. (p. 9)

Although the outcomes in Hill's model were family adjustment and family crisis rather than family resilience, they are relevant in that his focus was on a family versus an individual outcome. Hill recognized that he was pushing into uncharted territory in his focus on the family system. In his discussion of crisis and adjustment, he noted that "Thinking at the family level is third dimensional in a sense, and we have only recently attempted it" (p. 11).

Hill focused on the process of family adjustment in response to the family confronting a crisis situation (e.g., "angle of recovery" and "level of reorganization"), which is consistent with our conceptualization of family resilience as the process rather than the outcome. His "truncated roller-coaster pattern of adjustment to crisis" is foundational to his family stress theory, which involves going from crisis to disorganization to recovery to reorganization (p. 14). The "angle of recovery" for the family system was dependent on its crisis-meeting resources and the meaning that the family system gave to its situation. Hill identified a number of family-level resources that he predicted were potentially predictive of positive adjustment to the crisis associated with war separation and reunion, including the level of family integration and family adaptability.

In the context of the four dimensions that Hawley and DeHaan (1996) associate with the ability of families to demonstrate resilience, Hill's work was particularly instructive to the interaction of risk and protective factors and to the family's shared outlook. Both dimensions were instrumental in his ABCX model. For example, Hill (1949) offered what he termed a "classification of family breakdowns, which sorted stressors or risk factors into groups depending on their source (extra-family versus intra-family) and nature (dismemberment only, accession only, demoralization only, and demoralization plus dismemberment or accession) (pp. 9–10). In Hill's model, war separation and reunion were viewed as stressor events that had the potential of producing stress and crisis depending on the resources available to the family and its appraisal or definition of its presenting situation.

Hill proposed a number of resources (protective factors or assets) that he hypothesized were potentially predictive of adjustment to war separation and reunion. In some cases, he softened his predictions from hypotheses to "hunches" (p. 18). Although his subsequent work focused on the role of family development (e.g., Mederer & Hill, 1983), this was not addressed in the 1949 work.

Neither did he address the role of context. In fact, the first chapter of the book is titled, "The Family as a Closed System" (p. 3). Although Hill discussed the challenges of the researcher entering the privacy of the home in this chapter, he also noted the "internal" nature of his study. As he stated, "Residual categories that receive scant attention are extra-family influences, such as, interfamily operations, social forces of urbanization, secularization, and war itself" (p. 7). However, the extensions of his work in the literature have addressed each of the four dimensions, including family development and context, although not necessarily in a resilience framework.

Hill's early work built the cornerstones for the work of many others. H. McCubbin and his colleagues were instrumental in extending Hill's work. McCubbin and Patterson (1983) extended the original ABC-X model to include post-crisis variables and the build-up of stressors from previous crises (the Double ABC-X model and the Family Adjustment and Adaptation Response model), and McCubbin and McCubbin (1988) further extended this work by adding family types (T-Double ABCX model) and a focus on family resiliency (Resiliency Model of Family Adjustment and Adaptation). McCubbin's collaboration with Olson (Olson, McCubbin, & Associates, 1983) combined a focus on family stress and change with the Circumplex Model of Families (a three-dimensional model including a focus on family cohesion, adaptability, and communication) within a developmental family life cycle perspective. In 1983, McCubbin, Patterson, and Lavee used the Double ABC-X model and the FAAR model to frame a study of 1,000 Army families who had faced relocation to West Germany. A series of resulting empirical articles (e.g., Bowen, 1989; Lavee, McCubbin, & Patterson, 1985; McCubbin & Lavee, 1986), included attention to family diversity in the military in the form of social class and ethnicity (McCubbin & McCubbin, 1988).

In 2002, Patterson published an article in which she attempted to integrate family resilience and family stress theory. The Family Adjustment and Adaptation Response (FAAR) model was used as the family stress model. Patterson, a former student and colleague of McCubbin, specified four central constructs in the FAAR model, which she italicized in describing the focus of the model: "families engage in active processes to balance *family demands* with *family capabilities* as these interact with *family meanings* to arrive at a level of *family adjustment and adaptation*" (p. 350).

Patterson (2002) offered two important conceptual clarifications. First, she distinguished family resilience from individual resilience: "To be considered family resilience (in contrast to individual resilience), the outcome of interest should be at the family system level, where a minimum of two family members are involved; that is, it should represent the product of family relationship(s)" (p. 352). In addition, she distinguished family resilience as a process from family resiliency, which reflects the family's capacity to handle its presenting circumstances: "*family resiliency* could be used to describe the capacity of a family system to successfully manage their life circumstances and *family resilience* could be used to describe the processes by which families are able to adapt and function competently following exposure to significant adversity or crises" (p. 352). Although social scientists seem to agree that family resilience refers to a process, the concept of family resiliency lacks consistent definition in the literature (cf., Bowen & Martin, 2011).

In making these distinctions, Patterson (2002) focused the study of family resilience on what Hawley and DeHaan (1996) described as "the interactive combination of risk and protective factors" (p. 7). As factors and processes that moderate the relationship between adversity and family-level outcomes, risk and protective factors can be across units of analysis: individual, family, and community (cf. Patterson, p. 356). In support of Angell's (1936) study of depression era families and the work of Olson, et al. (1983), Patterson notes the importance of family cohesiveness and family flexibility as protective factors in the ability of families to adjust and adapt in the context of adversity.

Boss's contextual model of family stress builds directly on Hill's ABCX model (Boss, 2002). Unlike McCubbin, whose theoretical attention has focused more on the post-crisis adaptation of families, Boss's work has focused more on what keeps families from experiencing crisis. In addition, although great care needs to be taken in overgeneralizing, McCubbin's work, like Hill's, has focused relatively more on the internal workings of families rather than the larger context in which families are embedded. Boss, on the other hand, gives considerable attention both to the family's internal and external contexts.

In her contextual model of family stress management, Boss (2002) discusses five components of the family's external context: heredity, development, economy, history, and culture. Unlike the internal context of the family (structural, psychological, and philosophical), the external context is outside of the control of the family. Boss, who describes her model as grounded in symbolic inter-actionism within a larger postmodern perspective of social constructionism, clearly addresses Hawley and DeHaan's dimension of context, which includes concepts addressing the developmental level of the family and its sociohistorical and cultural context. Yet, as mentioned above in our application of symbolic interactionism, we believe that Boss's greatest contribution to the study of family resilience is her focus in her model on the construction of meaning (the family's construction of shared meaning). Boss defines a family perception as "the group's unified view of a particular stressor event or situation" (p. 23). In describing her work with distressed families, Boss describes her efforts in helping each family and individual family members give new meaning to their presenting situation in a way that promotes their management of stress and their adaptation as a family unit: "How are you going to make this a story you can live with as a family and as individuals?" (p. 13).

An excellent example of Boss's model applied to military family resilience is her recent co-authored chapter (Wiens & Boss, 2006). In the chapter, Wiens and Boss identify both protective factors, including attention to community supports, and risk factors associated with military family separation. They also present Boss's conceptual family stress model. Particularly helpful in understanding military family resilience is their discussion of the cultural context of life in the military that places normative constraints on families and their coping patterns, such as the potential stigma of having and reporting problems in a "warrior-oriented" organization that extols physical and mental hardiness for both service members and their families.

A number of studies with military samples have been framed and informed by family stress theory (e.g., Bowen, Orthner, & Zimmerman, 1993), although relatively few have focused on the family system as the unit of analysis (e.g., McCubbin & Lavee, 1986). Following Hill's focus on war separation and reunion, the issue of deployment continues to receive a significant level of attention as a family stressor event, especially deployments during a time of war (Mmari, Roche, Sudhinaraset, & Blum, 2009; Pincus, House, Christensen, & Adler, 2001; Sheppard, et al., 2010). Unique stressors have been associated with each phase of the combat deployment experience: before deployment, during deployment, and after deployment (*cf.*, MacDermid Wadsworth, 2010). Other military-related and family-related stressors may compound the influence of wartime deployment on the family. For example, MacDermid Wadsworth (2010) discussed the notion of "trauma transmission" (p. 539) among family members from the combat experiences of the service member, including physical and psychological injuries that result from war. Importantly, life in the military is inherently stressful for families even in peacetime, including deployment and training related family separations, relocations, and remote assignments, and dangerous jobs and challenging duty assignments for the service member are customary and usual in the military.

Before closing this discussion of family stress theory, it is important to identify a modified version of Hill's traditional ABCX model of family stress that explicitly addresses the context of racism in American society: The *Mundane Extreme Environmental Stress (MEES) model* by Peters and Massey (1983). The MEES model has implications for the study of military family resilience, although we were unable to identify literature that had applied this model to military families. Framed from the perspective of Black American families, three additional terms are added into the model. An additional A factor reflects specific acts of racial discrimination; a D factor represents ongoing and pervasive (mundane) racism in society; and a Y factor describes the reactions of

Black families to the A and D factors (Murry, 2000). The MEES model provides an opportunity to examine the additional burden on families in the military fueled by oppression and discrimination. In the context of increasing racial and ethnic diversity in the military services, the MEES model has rich potential to examine a critical aspect of context in the lives of many military families, as well as to examine other types and forms of oppression and discrimination (e.g., gender, social class, family background, religion, and sexual orientation or at the intersection of these statuses). This includes attention to the relatively small proportion and the disadvantaged nature of the US population that volunteer for military service (Elder, Wang, Spence, Adkins, & Brown, 2010).

LIMITATIONS OF THEORY USAGE IN UNDERSTANDING MILITARY FAMILIES

We contend that most studies of military family resilience have given insufficient attention to the community context in which families are embedded, and moreover have typically assessed community context from the perspective of the individual. In this micro-level approach, the grouping or clustering of individuals is ignored, as is families do not interface with other families (Mancini, Bowen, & Martin, 2005a). In other cases, proxy variables are used to reflect community context, such as its physical and demographic infrastructure. From our perspective, a full appreciation of military family resilience requires attention to the larger community context in which families work and live.

We recently proposed a social organizational approach to capture community-level processes that may influence family outcomes (cf. Mancini & Bowen, 2013). Such contextual effects theories attempt to account for variations in individual outcomes by calling attention to variables at the individual level and to larger group-level processes, including those at the collective family and community levels (Jacard & Jacoby, 2010; White & Teachman, 2005). In the next section, we present our attempt to understand families in their larger community context. This analysis involves more explicit attention to the role of context as a dimension in understanding variations in military family resilience.

FUTURE THEORETICAL DIRECTIONS: THEORY OF COMMUNITY ACTION AND CHANGE

In 1985, Walker, in a critique of Hill's (1949) model, called for a "contextual study of families under stress" (p. 834). From our perspective, although the original ABCX model has been conceptually embellished by the work of McCubbin, Boss, and others (Burr, Klein, & Associates, 1994) to embrace contextual influences, the role of communities as social organizational settings in which families experience and cope with stressor events has not received sufficient attention. In particular, community has been evaluated from the perceptions of family members as a mechanism of social support (a micro perspective) (e.g., Lavee, McCubbin, & Patterson, 1985) rather than a larger context in which family life in a community is enacted (a macro-perspective). From the perspective of Boss's Contextual Model of Family Stress, we describe a third band of influence on family stress management: community context. This band of influence lies between the external context ("heredity, development, economy, history, culture"), which Boss considers to be outside of the family's control, and the internal context ("structural, psychological, philosophical") of the family in Boss's (2002) model. Like the internal context from Boss's perspective, the family does have influence on this community context.

We turn to review our work on community context factors, which we consider to be significant elements for understanding military family resilience. In support of an ecological perspective to the study of military family resilience, families are considered to be nested in larger community networks that shape, inform, and constrain patterns of interaction (Bowen & Martin, 2011; Bowen, Martin, Mancini, & Nelson, 2000). In turn, families have a reciprocal impact on these larger community network forces. Families act upon their environments, and they are not simply passive units entirely receptive to environmental actions. We take the position that families are largely embedded in the layers and levels of social life, rather than largely insulated from social life. We also contend the aggregation of families, through the networks they form become primary enactors of change in community contexts which in turns influences family situations and experiences.

The *theory of community action and change* was developed as a framework for informing assessment efforts, and the associated prevention and intervention programming used by the US military to promote military family and community resilience (Mancini & Bowen, 2013). Mancini and Bowen recently provided a detailed review of the history and development of the theory, and the basic tenets of the theory have been published elsewhere as well (Bowen, et al., 2000; Mancini & Bowen, 2009; Mancini, Bowen, & Martin, 2005a,b; Mancini, Martin, & Bowen, 2003). Consequently, we focus our attention on key assumptions and concepts from the theory for understanding variations in military family resilience.

First, families are assumed to be open systems that are situated in dynamic interaction with the environment in which they are embedded. This environment has many different features that frame and inform family functioning and interaction, and family members are not necessarily aware of how this environment shapes and constrains them or how they necessarily influence the environment. As noted above, Boss (2002) has identified some important aspects of this broader environment in her discussion of the external context. However, we focus on an aspect of the environment that is more immediate and proximal in the lives of families: the social organizational processes in the local community in which families live (e.g., urban neighborhoods, suburban subdivisions, military bases, or communities in rural areas).

Social organization is used as an umbrella term to describe ''the collection of values, norms, processes, and behavior patterns within a community that organize, facilitate, and constrain the interactions among community members'' (Mancini et al., 2003, p. 319). From an action theory perspective, the operation of formal (e.g., military and civilian community agencies, the unit chain of command) and informal networks (e.g., extended family, friends, work associates, neighbors) is the major focus of interaction and prevention efforts to influence military family resilience (Bowen, et al., 2000). Formal and informal networks operate within a larger physical (i.e., built community) and social (i.e., demographic composition) infrastructure that frame and inform their operation (Mancini & Bowen, 2013). Adopting a contextual effects perspective (Bowen & Pittman, 1995), the operation of these networks is assumed to be more or less exogenous to any one family. Thus, the unit of analysis is extended from the individual family (a micro-level orientation) to also consider families in their community context (a macro-level orientation).

Community capacity is an emergent outcome in communities that results from the social capital found in the particular configuration and operation of formal and informal networks. Community capacity has two components: "the extent to which community members (a) demonstrate a sense of shared responsibilities for the general welfare of the community and its members and (b) demonstrate collective competence in taking advantage of opportunities for addressing community needs and confronting situations that threaten the safety and well-being of community members" (Bowen, et al., 2000, p. 7). From the perspective of the theory, the nature, level, and pattern of shared responsibility and collective competence in a community influences the results that families are able to achieve over time. From a military family resilience perspective, this would include the trajectories of individual families in achieving family-level results in the context of adversity.

Importantly, families may not be aware of the influence of the larger community on their processes and outcomes. However, in our most recent work (Mancini & Bowen, 2013), we propose that a sense of community is a potential social psychological mediator between social organizational processes and family results at the micro-level, such as military family resilience. We defined sense of community as "the extent to which individuals and families feel a sense of identification, esprit de corps, and attachment with their community." We assume that families are more likely to achieve favorable results in the context of a high sense of community. This aspect of the theory requires further elaboration and testing, although our earlier research demonstrated a positive link between the perceived sense of community and the self-reported family adaptation of married Air Force members (Bowen, Mancini, Martin, Ware, & Nelson, 2003). The challenge as discussed by Zelditch (1991) is to begin to specify the social psychological links between structure and action.

The theory of community action and change has many nuances and caveats that were not discussed in the context of this short overview, such as the fact that communities, like individuals and families, have developmental pathways and rhythms—their own life course (The Harwood Group, 1999). For example, communities that surround military installations often change significantly during times of large-scale deployments, which have effects on the local economy, the larger opportunity structure, and the demographic composition of the community (e.g., increase in number of temporary single adult households). In addition, families may need communities to operate differently in support of resilient outcomes at different stages in the family life cycle and in the context of different types of adversities (Bowen, Richman, & Bowen, 2000). For example, a high casualty rate in a particular military unit may have devastating effects on the community in which the unit is embedded.

CONCLUSION

We have discussed three theoretical frameworks from family science that have applicability to understanding military family resilience—life course theory, symbolic interactionism, and family stress theory. Each has merit in understanding the nuances of family life through the lens of context and developmental level (life course), the family's shared outlook (symbolic interaction), and the combination of risk and protective factors (stress theory). We have added a theory of community action and change to the mix that draws attention to local geographic networks that frame and inform family functioning and interaction and from which families may derive resources and support. This community approach elevates the significance of networks of families for affecting the quality of family life. At the least, a more intentional approach to research on military families using any one of these lens represents an advance, because it will lend to a more coherent body of knowledge, one that provides clearer guidance on improving the theorizing and also improving the research. Of greater potential significance is examining military family resilience through the intersection of these theories.

The understanding of military family resilience will benefit from greater intentionality about marking where these theories intersect and overlap. As one example, life course theory is a broad lens that captures the dynamic nature of families in historical, family, and individual time. It also enlightens us about contexts in which military families live; individuals in military families are part of a much larger cohort that has an influence on their lives. Consequently, families where one spouse or adult partner is a military member may be mainly interacting with civilian families (particularly the case with Guard and Reserve families). Their reference group (cohort) is likely to have remote experience with separation, transition, and change, compared with military families. Therefore the understanding they have of deployment experiences is very limited, and military families may not feel their situation is well understood. They may even question their own motives for continuing a military lifestyle.

Using this same example, symbolic interaction contributes a lens that elevates what happens within a family that is connected with these contexts, for instance, Blumer's (1969) suggestion that meanings originate through social interactions. In addition, "orientational others" (Kuhn, 1972) may be mainly other military families (more likely with the Active force, and especially those who live on or near the base or installation), or mainly non-military. The impacts of these orientational others on the military family's shared outlook will vary dramatically.

In many respects, family stress theory is the most encompassing of the three theories; it contains elements of contexts (e.g., the external context in Boss's model, which includes attention to time and history), attention to both risk and protective factors (the "A" and "B" components), and elements of attaching meaning (the "C" component). In addition, the family stress approach incorporates vividly possible outcomes, such as military family resilience. As discussed earlier, the concepts of stressor events, especially ambiguous loss, and the family's perception of who is in and out of the family (boundary ambiguity) that may result from ambiguous loss provide a rich set of conceptual lenses to understand military family resilience. Yet, family stress theory does not give sufficient attention to the community context in which families are embedded—the primary community structures (formal and informal networks) in which family life is enacted. The theory of community action and change offers "grist for the mill" in future applications of family stress theory to understanding military family resilience—a band of influence on the family system that lies between the internal and the external context in Boss's (2002) model.

An important challenge for future theoretical development is to ensure a greater correspondence between the concept of military family resilience and its measurement. The empirical testing of theory requires such alignment. Drawing upon the definition of family resilience from Hawley and DeHaan (1996) and the integrative review by Patterson (2002) of family resilience and family stress theory, we concluded that the study of military family resilience was distinguished from the study of individual resilience by its focus on the family unit as the outcome of interest (e.g., couples, parent–child dyads, siblings, or the family itself). As mentioned earlier, the resilience of the family is determined by a focus on at least one system-level outcome from two or more family members over time in the context of adversity.

In the time since Hawley and DeHaan (1996) published their article, statistical developments have provided a means to better capture these system-level outcomes, even when the data are collected at the individual level. For example, Sayer and Klute (2005) present the use of multilevel models to study dyads, such as husbands and wives or parents and children, in which both members of the dyad are nested in a relationship and provide the same information (i.e., relational data about themselves or about their relationship). The authors also discuss extensions of the model to handle data from more than two group members and longitudinal data that capture group members at more than one time point, which are essential in the study of military family resilience (cf. DeHaan, Hawley, & Deal, 2002). Importantly, in the context of our theory of community action and change, the multilevel approach can capture the nesting of the dyads and families in larger systems, such as the neighborhood or community. Unfortunately, we are not aware of military datasets that include multiple members from the same family, that examine military families over time, and that capture the functioning of families within higher levels of aggregation, such as neighborhoods, military bases, or local communities.

In addition to quantitative approaches, such as the use of multilevel models, qualitative approaches have rich potential for understanding military family resilience, especially examining families as a unit over time in the context of adversity. A primary merit of qualitative analyses lies in elaborating meaning and explanation. These qualitative methods are ideally suited for examining the family qua unit rather than as a single individual (e.g., spouse, child) or group of individuals over time, and they provide an opportunity to illuminate the nuances in the different paths that families may follow in response to adversity. These methods provide a means to capture what we described earlier as "noise amplification" in the study of military family resilience.

Several recent studies have applied qualitative approaches to the study of military family resilience (e.g., Faber, Willerton, Clymer, MacDermid, & Weiss, 2008; Huebner, et al., 2007; Mmari, et al., 2009; Wiens & Boss, 2006). Yet, none of these studies meet the three main requirements for the examination of military family resilience: the presence of adversity; longitudinal data involving at least three time points, including at least one observation prior to the adversity; and family-level data.

In conclusion, theory, research design, measurement, and analysis need to work in concert in future studies of military family resilience. Clearly, in the case of military family resilience, research methods and the application of these methods lag behind the theoretical richness and anchoring of the concept. Yet, on a positive note, LCT, SI theory, and family stress theory provide three corner-stones from which to build conceptual models of military family resilience for empirical testing. The incorporation of the theory of community action and change will bring greater attention to the community context in which military families are embedded. The incorporation of theories that fall within the critical/emancipatory paradigm (*cf.* Burr, 1995), such as feminist family theories and critical race theory, will direct more attention to issues of power, status and differential access to resources in the study of military family resilience, including attention to the demography of those who serve and those who go to war. To end on a positive note, we see the study of military family resilience to have a rich theoretical history and foundation from which to build.

REFERENCES

Angell, R. C. (1936). *The family encounters the depression*. New York: Charles Scribner.

Armed Forces Health Surveillance Center (AFHSC) (2010, November). Selected mental health disorders among active component members, U.S. Armed Forces, 2007–2010. *Medical Surveillance Monthly Report (MSMR), 17(11)*.

Bengtson, V. L. & Allen, K. R. (1993). The life course perspective applied to families over time. In P. G. Boss, W. J. Doherty, R. LaRossa, W. R. Schumm, & S. K. Steinmetz (Eds.), *Sourcebook of Family Theories and Methods* (pp. 469–504). New York: Plenum.

Blumer, H. (1969). *Symbolic interactionism: Perspective and method*. Englewood Cliffs, NJ: Prentice-Hall.

Boss, P. (2002). *Family stress management: A contextual approach* (2nd ed.). Thousand Oaks, CA: Sage.

Boss, P. (2006). *Loss, trauma, and resilience: Therapeutic work with ambiguous loss*. New York: W. W. Norton.

Bowen, G. L. (1998). Effects of leader support in the work unit on the relationship between work spillover and family adaptation. *Journal of Family and Economic Issues, 19*, 25–52.

Bowen, G. L. (1989). *Family adaptation to relocation: An empirical analysis of family stressors, family resources, and sense of coherence*. (Technical Report, ARI TR 856). Washington, DC: U.S. Army Research Institute for the Behavioral and Social Sciences.

Bowen, G. L., Mancini, J. A., Martin, J. A., Ware, W. B., & Nelson, J. P. (2003). Promoting the adaptation of military families: An empirical test of a community practice model. *Family Relations, 52*, 33–44.

Bowen, G. L., & Martin, J. A. (2011). The resiliency model of role performance for service members, veterans, and their families: A focus on social connections and individual assets. *Journal of Human Behavior in the Social Environment, 21*, 162–178.

Bowen, G. L., Martin, J. A., Mancini, J. A., & Nelson, J. P. (2000). Community capacity: Antecedents and consequences. *Journal of Community Practice, 8*, 1–21.

Bowen, G. L., & Orthner, D. K. (Eds.) (1989). *The organization family: Work and family linkages in the U.S. Military*. New York: Praeger.

Bowen, G. L., Orthner, D. K., & Zimmerman, L. I. (1993). Family adaptation of single parents in the United States Army: An empirical analysis of work stressors and adaptive resources. *Family Relations, 42*, 293–304.

Bowen, G. L., & Pittman, J. F. (1995). Introduction. In G. L. Bowen & J. F. Pittman (Eds.), *The work and family interface: Toward a contextual effects perspective* (pp. 1–13). Minneapolis, MN: The National Council on Family Relations.

Bowen, G. L., Richman, J. M., & Bowen, N. K. (2000). Families in the context of communities across time. In S. J. Price, P. C. McKenry, & M. J. Murphy (Eds.), *Families across time: A life course perspective* (pp. 117–128). Los Angeles: Roxbury.

Burr, W. R. (1995). Using theories in family science. In R. D. Day, K. R. Gilbert, B. H. Settles, & W. R. Burr (Eds.), *Research and theory in family science* (pp. 73–90). New York: Free Press.

Burr, W. R., Klein, S. R., & Associates (1994). *Reexamining family stress: New theory and research*. Thousand Oaks, CA: Sage.

Burr, W. R., Leigh, G. K., Day, R. D., & Constantine, J. (1979). Symbolic interaction and the family. In W. R. Burr, R. Hill, F. I. Nye, & I. L. Reiss (Eds.), *Contemporary theories about the family, Volume II.* (pp. 42–111). New York: The Free Press.

Cavan, R., & Ranck, K. (1938). *The family and the depression.* Chicago: University of Chicago Press.

Chandra, A., Burns, R. M., Tanielian, T., & Jaycox, L. H. (2011). Understanding the deployment experience for children and youth from military families. In S. MacDermid Wadsworth & D. Riggs (Eds.), *Risk and resilience in U.S. military families* (pp. 175–192). New York: Springer.

Conger, R. D., & Conger, K. J. (2002). Resilience in Midwestern families: Selected findings from the first decade of a prospective, longitudinal study. *Journal of Marriage and Family, 64,* 361–373.

Crane, J. (1991). The epidemic theory of ghettos and neighborhood effects on dropping out and teenage childbearing. *American Journal of Sociology, 96,* 1226–1259.

Department of Defense (DOD) (2009). Office of the Under Secretary of Defense, Personnel and Readiness. *Population Representation in the Military Services: Fiscal Year 2009* Report. Retrieved from http:// prhome.defense.gov/MPP/ACCESSION%20POLICY/PopRep2009/index.html. (accessed March 29, 2011).

DeHaan, L., Hawley, D. R., & Deal, J. E. (2002). Operationalizing family resilience: A methodological strategy. *American Journal of Family Therapy, 30,* 275–291.

Dekel, R., & Monson, C. M. (2010). Military-related post-traumatic stress disorder and family relations: Current knowledge and future directions. *Aggression and Violent Behavior, 15,* 303–309.

Earvolino-Ramirez, M. (2007). Resilience: A concept analysis. *Nursing Forum, 42(2),* 73–82.

Elder, G. H., Jr. (1987). War mobilization and the life course: A cohort of World War II veterans. *Sociological Forum, 2,* 449–472.

Elder, G. H., Jr. (1990). Foreword. In A. Kerckhoff (Ed.), Getting started: the transition to adulthood in Great Britain. Boulder, CO: Westview Press.

Elder, G. H., Jr. & Clipp, E. C. (1989). Combat experience and emotional health: Impairment and resilience in later life. *Journal of Personality, 57,* 311–341.

Elder, G. H., Jr., Gimbel, C., & Ivie, R. (1991). Turning points in life: The case of military service and war. *Military Psychology, 3,* 215–231.

Elder, G. H. Jr., & Shanahan, M. J. (2006). The life course and human development. In W. Damon & R. M. Lerner (Eds.), *Handbook of child psychology: Theoretical models of human development* (pp. 665–715). New York: Wiley and Stone.

Elder, G. H., Jr., Wang, L., Spence, N. J., Adkins, D. E., & Brown, T. H. (2010). Pathways to the All-Voluntary Military. *Social Science Quarterly, 91,* 455–475.

Everson, R. B., & Camp, T. G. (2011). Seeing systems: An introduction to systemic approaches with military families. In R. B. Everson & C. R. Figley (Eds.), *Families under fire: Systematic therapy with military families* (pp. 3–29). New York: Routledge.

Faber, A. J., Willerton, E., Clymer, S. R., MacDermid, S. M., & Weiss, H. M. (2008). Ambiguous absence, ambiguous presence: A qualitative study of military Reserve families in wartime. *Journal of Family Psychology, 22,* 222–230.

Fergus, S., & Zimmerman, M. A. (2005). Adolescent resilience: A framework for understanding healthy development in the face of risk. *Annual Review of Public Health, 26,* 399–419.

Gade, P. A. (1991). Military service and the life-course perspective: A turning point for military personnel research. *Military Psychology, 3(4),* 187–199.

Ganong, L. H., & Coleman, M. (2002). Family resilience in multiple contexts. *Journal of Marriage and Family, 64,* 346–348.

George, L. K. (2003). Life course research: Achievements and potential. In J. T. Mortimer & M. J. Shanaha (Eds.), *Handbook of the life course* (pp. 671–680). New York: Kluwer Academic Publishers.

Gimbel, C. & Booth, A. (1994). Why does military combat experience adversely affect marital relations? *Journal of Marriage and the Family, 56,* 691–703.

Hawley, D. R., & DeHaan, L. (1996). Toward a definition of family resilience: Integrating life-span and family perspectives. *Family Process, 35,* 283–298.

Hill, R. (1949). *Families under stress: Adjustment to the crisis of war separation and reunion.* New York: Harper and Brothers.

Hill, R. (1958). Generic features of families under stress. *Social Casework, 49,* 139–150.

Hoge, C. W., Castro, C. A., Messer, S. C., McGurk, D., Cotting, D. & Koffman, R. I. (2004). Combat duty in Iraq and Afghanistan, mental health problems, and barriers to care. *New England Journal of Medicine*, *351*, 13–22.

Huebner, A. J. (2009). Exploring processes of family stress and adaptation: An expanded model. In J. A. Mancini, & K. A Roberto (Eds.), *Pathways of human development: Explorations of change*. (pp. 227–242). Lanham, MD: Lexington.

Huebner, A. J., Mancini, J. A., Wilcox, R. M., Grass, S. R., & Grass, G. A. (2007). Parental deployment and youth in military families: Exploring uncertainty and ambiguous loss. *Family Relations*, *56*, 112–122.

ICF International (2010). *Demographics 2008: Profile of the military community*. Washington, DC: Office of the Deputy Under Secretary of Defense (Military Community and Family Policy).

Institute of Medicine. (2010). *Returning home from Iraq and Afghanistan: Preliminary assessment of readjustment needs of veterans, service members, and their families*. Washington, DC: The National Academies Press.

Jacard, J. & Jacoby, J. (2010). *Theory construction and model-building skills: A practical guide for social scientists*. New York: Guilford Press.

Kahn, R. L., & Antonucci, T. C. (1980). Convoys over the life course: Attachment, roles, and social support. In P. B. Baltes & O. Brim (Eds.), *Life-span development and behavior* (Vol. 3, pp. 253–268), New York: Academic Press.

Karney, B. R., & Crown, J. S. (2007). *Families under stress: An assessment of data, theory, and research on marriage and divorce in the military*. Santa Monica, CA: RAND Corporation.

Kuhn, M. H. (1972). The reference group reconsidered. In J. G. Manis & B. N. Meltzer (Eds.), *Symbolic interaction: A reader in social psychology* (pp. 171–184). Boston: Allyn & Bacon.

L'Abate, L. (1990). A theory of competencies x settings interactions. *Marriage and Family Review*, *15*, 253–269.

LaRossa, R., and Rietzes, D. C. (1993). Symbolic interactionism and family studies. In Boss, P. G., Doherty, W. J., LaRossa, R., Schumm, W. R., & Steinmetz, S. K. (Eds), *Sourcebook of family theories and methods: A contextual approach*. (pp. 135–162). New York: Plenum.

Lavee, Y., McCubbin, H. I., & Patterson, J. M. (1985). The Double ABCX Model of Family Stress and Adaptation: An empirical test by analysis of structural equations with latent variables. *Journal of Marriage and the Family*, *47*, 811–825.

Little, R. D., & Friedlander, J. E. (1979). Veterans' status, earnings, and race: Some long term results. *Armed Forces and Society*, *13*, 244–260.

Luthar, S. S., Cicchetti, D., & Becker, B. (2000). The construct of resilience: A critical evaluation and guidelines for future work. *Child Development*, *71*, 543–562.

Mancini, J. A., & Bowen, G. L. (2009). Community resilience: A social organization theory of action and change. In J. A. Mancini & K. A. Roberto (Eds.). *Pathways of human development: Explorations of change* (pp. 245–265). Lanham, MD: Lexington Books.

Mancini, J. A., & Bowen, G. L. (2013). Families and communities: A social organization theory of action and change. In Peterson, G. W., & Bush, K. R. (Eds), *Handbook of marriage and the family* (3rd ed. pp. 781–813). New York: Springer.

Mancini, J. A., Bowen, G. L., & Martin, J. A. (2005a). Community social organization: A conceptual linchpin in examining families in the context of communities. *Family Relations: Interdisciplinary Journal of Applied Family Studies*, *54*, 570–582.

Mancini, J. A., Bowen, G. L., & Martin, J. A. (2005b). Spotlight on theory: Families in community contexts. In V. L. Bengtson, A. C. Acock, K. R. Allen, P. Dilworth-Anderson, & D. M. Klein (Eds.), *Sourcebook of family theory and research* (pp. 293–306). Thousand Oaks, CA: Sage.

Mancini, J. A., Martin, J. A., & Bowen, G. L. (2003). Community capacity. In Gullotta, T. P., & Bloom, M. (Eds.), *Encyclopedia of primary prevention and health promotion* (pp. 319–330). New York: Kluwer Academic/Plenum.

Manis, J. G., & Meltzer, B. N. (1972). *Symbolic interaction: A reader in social psychology, (2nd ed.)*. Boston, MA: Allyn & Bacon.

Martin, J. A., & Sherman, M. D. (2009). The impact of military life on individuals and families: Resources and intervention. In S. Price & C. Price (Eds.), *Families and change: Coping with stressful events and transitions* (4th ed., pp. 381–397). Thousand Oaks, CA: Sage.

Martin, J. A., & Sherman, M. D. (2012). *Understanding the effects of military life and deployment on couples and families*. In D. K. Snyder and C. M. Monson (Eds.), *Couple-based interventions for military and Veteran families: Promoting individual and relationship well-being*. New York: Guilford Press.

Mayer, K. U. (2009). New directions in life course research. *Annual Review of Sociology*, *35*, 413–433.

MacDermid Wadsworth, S. M. (2010). Family risk and resilience in the context of war and terrorism. *Journal of Marriage and Family*, *72*, 537–556.

MacLean, A., & Elder, G. H. (2007). Military service in the life course. *Annual Review of Sociology*, *33*, 175–196.

McCubbin, H. I., & Lavee, Y. (1986). Strengthening Army families: A family life cycle stage perspective. *Evaluation and Program Planning*, *9*, 221–231.

McCubbin, H. I., & McCubbin, M. A. (1988). Typologies of resilient families: Emerging roles of social class and ethnicity. *Family Relations*, *37*, 247–254.

McCubbin, H. I., & Patterson, J. M. (1983). The family process: The Double ABCX Model of Adjustment and Adaptation. In H. I. McCubbin, M. B. Sussman, & J. M. Patterson (Eds.), *Social stress and the family: Advances and developments in family stress theory and research* (pp. 7–37). New York: Haworth Press.

McCubbin, H. I., Patterson, J. M., & Lavee, Y. (1983). *One thousand army families: Strengths, coping and supports*. St Paul, MN: University of Minnesota, Family Social Science.

Mead, G. H. (1934). *Mind, self and society*. Chicago: University of Chicago Press.

Mederer, H., & Hill, R. (1983). Critical transitions over the family life span: Theory and research. In H. I. McCubbin, M. B. Sussman, & J. M. Patterson (Eds.), *Social stress and the family: Advances and developments in family stress theory and research* (pp. 39–60). New York: Haworth Press.

Mmari, K., Roche, K. M., Sudhinaraset, M. & Blum, R. (2009). When a parent goes off to war: Exploring the issues faced by adolescents and their families. *Youth & Society*, *40*, 455–475.

Murry, V. M. (2000). Challenges and life experiences of Black American families. In P. C. McKenry & S. J. Price (Eds.), *Families & change* (2nd ed., pp. 333–358). Thousand Oaks, CA: Sage.

Olson, D. H., McCubbin, H. I., & Associates (1983). *Families: What makes them work*. Beverly Hills, CA: Sage.

Pavalko, E. K., Elder, G. H. Jr. (1990). World War II and divorce: A life-course perspective. *American Journal of Sociology*, *95*, 1213–1234.

Patterson, J. M. (2002). Integrating family resilience and family stress theory. *Journal of Marriage and Family*, *64*, 349–360.

Peters, M. F., & Massey, G. (1983). Chronic vs. mundane stress in family stress theories: The case of black families in white America. *Marriage and Family Review*, *6*, 193–218.

Pincus, S. H., House, R., Christensen, J., & Adler, L. E. (2001). The emotional cycle of deployment: A military family perspective. *Journal of the Army Medical Department*, *2*, 15–23.

Reiss, D. (1981). *The family's construction of reality*. Cambridge, MA: Harvard University Press.

Reiss, D., & Oliveri, M. E. (1991). The family's conception of accountability and competence: A new approach to the conceptualization and assessment of family stress. *Family Process*, *30*, 193–214.

Sayer, A. G., & Klute, M. M. (2005). Analyzing couples and families: Multilevel methods. In V. L. Bengtson, A. C. Acock, K. R. Allen, P. Dilworth-Anderson, & D. M. Klein (Eds.), *Sourcebook of family theory & research* (pp. 289–313). Thousand Oaks, CA: Sage.

Segal, M. W. (1989). The nature of work and family linkages: A theoretical perspective. In G. L. Bowen & D. K. Orthner (Eds.), *The organization family: Work and family linkages in the U.S. Military* (pp. 3–36). New York: Praeger.

Sheppard, S. C., Malatras, J. W., & Israel, A. C. (2010). The impact of deployment on U.S. *military families*. *American Psychologist*, *65*, 599–609.

Shibutani, T. (1986). *Social processes*. Berkeley, CA: University of California Press.

The Harwood Group (1999). *Community rhythms: Five stages of community life*. Bethesda, MD: The Harwood Group and the Charles Stewart Mott Foundation.

Thomas, W. I. & Znaniecki, F. (1918). *The Polish peasant in Europe and America*. Boston, MA: Badger.

Walsh, F. (1996). The concept of family resilience: Crisis and challenge. *Family Process*, *35*, 261–281.

White, J. M., & Teachman, J. D. (2005). Discussion and extension: A comment on the use of multilevel methods in family research. In V. L. Bengtson, A. C. Acock, K. R. Allen, P. Dilworth-Anderson, & D. M. Klein (Eds.), *Sourcebook of family theory and research* (pp. 307–314). Thousand Oaks, CA: Sage.

Wiens, T. W., & Boss, P. (2006). Maintaining family resiliency before, during, and after military separation. In C. A. Castro, A. B. Adler and T. W. Britt (Eds.), *Military life: The psychology of serving in peace and combat* (Vol. 3). *The military family* (pp. 13–38). Westport, CT: Praeger Security International.

Walker, A. J. (1985). Reconceptualizing family stress. *Journal of Marriage and the Family, 47,* 827–837.

Werner, E. E., & Smith, R. S. (1992). *Overcoming the odds: High risk children from birth to adulthood.* Ithaca, NY: Cornell University Press.

Zelditch, M. Jr. (1991). Levels in the logic of macro-historical explanation. In J. Huber (Ed.), *Macro-micro linkages in sociology* (pp. 101–106). Newbury Park, CA: Sage.

24 Individuation and Differentiation in Families Across Cultures

Camillo Regalia, Claudia Manzi, and Eugenia Scabini

Know thyself. These two words of the Oracle at Delphi summarize the main task of identity development. Scholars interested in identity development have focused on the intrapsychic process, whereby young people begin to explore (or discover) who they might become. Through this individuation process, which begins in infancy and culminates in adulthood, an individual develops a unique and autonomous self-concept distinct from others. However, the individuation process does not take place in a social vacuum; family context has a great influence on, and is very much involved in, the process of defining one's identity. Accordingly, family scholars have focused attention on the differentiation process, a family process that regulates distance between family members and affects the development of individual identity (Sabatelli & Mazor, 1985).

Contemporary research in this field has examined the universal validity of individuation and differentiation processes. However, contrasting results from studies using different cultural groups make the theoretical interpretation of these processes challenging. Accordingly, we analyze individuation and differentiation processes in the family, focusing on the usefulness of these processes for understanding human development in different cultural contexts. First, we define the processes and present key theories that address them. Second, we show how the assumption of a more culturally oriented perspective gives new insight into individuation/differentiation processes in families. Finally, we discuss the implications of a more inclusive understanding of family dynamics within a cultural perspective for theory development.

KEY ISSUES IN INDIVIDUATION AND DIFFERENTIATION

Individuation and differentiation can be seen as two sides of the same coin underlying identity formation: the individual perspective, which mainly focuses on the process through which an individual develops his/her identity (i.e., the individuation process), and the family perspective, which examines the parents' and the family's attempt to support or hinder the individual process (i.e., the differentiation process). Most theories on this subject tend to focus on one of the two perspectives. For this reason, we begin by reviewing the main individuation theories as well as the main differentiation theories. We then address theories that integrate both of these two processes.

THEORIES OF INDIVIDUATION AND DIFFERENTIATION

THEORIES OF INDIVIDUATION

Individuation as Separation

There are two different definitions of the term *individuation*. The first is psychoanalytic and is principally defined in terms of *separation*. Margaret Mahler (1963) argued that the psychological birth
of the human infant occurs when the child attains an initial concept of him- or herself as a separate
individual following a period of psychological oneness or symbiosis with the mother. Individuation
occurs after a long developmental process between mother and child; this process normally ends
towards the end of the child's third year of life, with the attainment of object constancy and a stable
sense of self. According to Mahler, the individuation process is strictly tied to the complementary
separation process, which allows for the self to be disentangled from the other, while individuation
describes who and what the separate self is.

Peter Blos (1967) has extended the concept of individuation to adolescence, defining this period
as the second individuation process. Blos emphasized that adolescents have the developmental task
of separating themselves from the internalized figures of the parents in order to become a member
of the adult world. These ongoing changes assist adolescents in becoming more responsible for
themselves and to separate, both physically and psychologically, from their parents.

Interestingly, according to the original psychoanalytic perspective, the second individuation process refers to an adolescent's intrapsychic or internal distancing from the infantile object representations of parents. In other words, separation is an emotional process that refers to the de-idealization
of parents in favor of a more realistic appraisal of their identity. This process does not necessary
imply an effective movement away from interpersonal relations with parents. The controversial
term "emotional autonomy" was coined by Steinberg and Silverberg (1986) to reinforce the idea
that an affective disengagement of adolescents from their parents is a necessary step for individuation and healthy development. However, the idea that an adolescent needs to become emotionally
distant from parents was later equated with the more radical assumption that detachment from
parents is needed for identity development in adolescence.

Related Individuation

Concepts of emotional separation and detachment have been mixed together for a long time, and
their significance for the development of the adolescent are difficult to understand. Recent studies
have shown how these constructs, despite their association, are distinct dimensions of parent–children relationships (see Beyers, Goosens, Vansant, & Moors, 2003; Beyers Goossens, Van Calster,
& Duriez, 2005; Ingoglia, Lo Coco, Liga, & Lo Cricchio, 2011). An alternative conception of individuation starts from the awareness that "individuation is not something that happens *from* parents,
but rather *with* them" (Ryan & Lynch, 1989, p. 341). That is, individuation is a process through
which the individual builds a sense of self in relation to others. This can be defined, according to
Stierlin (1974), as *related individuation*, an ongoing process in which a higher level of individuation
both demands and makes possible a corresponding higher level of relatedness. The press toward
individuation requires adolescents to develop more realistic and de-idealized perceptions of their
parents, to reduce parental emotional dependency and assume primary responsibilities without
impairing close family ties. The goal of individuation, however, is the attainment of relational
autonomy, whereby autonomy and self-governance are affirmed within the context of continuous,
mutually validating relationships (Josselson, 1988).

Several different theoretical perspectives, such as *attachment theory* and *self-determination
theory* (SDT), have endorsed this view of related individuation. According to Bowlby's theoretical
framework, attachment consists of a system of intertwined parent–child behaviors whose functions
are two-fold: to maximize and assure the physical safety of the child and to enable the child to
explore the environment (Bowlby, 1969). Since its early formulation, attachment theory has strictly

linked the attachment system to autonomy. Successful attachment experiences lead to firmer individuation and positive feelings with regards to autonomy. Securely attached adolescents and their parents are more able to negotiate the balance between maintaining relatedness and supporting autonomy development. The more an adolescent is securely attached to his or her parents, the more likely he or she will feel free to enter into new social relationships, generally enhancing the individuation process (for a review, see McElhaney, Allen, Stephenson, & Hare, 2009). Accordingly, the view of the adolescence as a necessary period of emotional and relational upset due to the need to separate from parents is no longer regarded as normative, but a function of insecure attachment (Ainsworth, Blehar, Waters, & Wall, 1978).

Self-determination theory also challenges the assumption that separation from parents is necessary for individuation. SDT is a motivational theory in which individuals must satisfy three basic needs—the need for competence, autonomy, and relatedness—in order to attain optimal development and psychological health (Deci & Vansteenkiste, 2004).

According to SDT, the experience of autonomy does not stand in opposition to relatedness and does not imply detachment from the influences of the social context (Ryan & Lynch, 1989). Ryan (1993) asserts that the relationship between autonomy and relatedness is nevertheless complex because the intrinsic needs for autonomy and relatedness often oppose one another. One can relinquish autonomy in order to secure the esteem or approval of an attachment figure just as one can relinquish relatedness in order to preserve autonomy (i.e., teenagers who detach themselves from overly controlling parents). Nevertheless, theoretically both autonomy and relatedness are required for optimal individual development. Typically, SDT predicts and empirically confirms that families that are responsive to and supportive of the autonomy of adolescents promote the development of volitional or self-governing functioning (Soenens, Berzonsky, Vansteenkiste, Beyers, & Goossens, 2005), which, in turn, leads to better adjustment and higher levels of psychosocial functioning (Deci & Ryan, 2000). Similarly, family and developmental scholars consistently find that relatedness with parents leads to increased individuality (Buhl, 2008a; Grotevant & Cooper, 1986; Kruse & Walper, 2008; McClanahan & Holmbeck, 1992).

In summary, individuation mainly concerns the developmental task of building a personal identity. The different perspectives presented in this chapter come together in the identification of the two polarities involved in the individuation process: autonomy and relatedness. Many scholars have viewed these two polarities as basic human needs (Baumeister & Leary, 1995; Brewer, 1991; Snyder & Fromkin, 1980). Although early theorists considered autonomy and relatedness as opposite dimensions, newer theories view autonomy and relatedness as complementary; increased relatedness enhances a person's ability to be more autonomous. As will be seen in the next section, cross-cultural research on the individuation process has put into debate both the universal presence of the autonomy and relatedness human dimensions, and the nature of their relationship. As a consequence, the individuation process itself has been questioned, at least in some of the cross-cultural perspectives.

THEORIES OF DIFFERENTIATION

Different theoretical perspectives have focused on the concept of individuation, whereas differentiation stems mainly from *family systems theory* (Bowen, 1978), and primarily concerns the aspects of family functioning that may influence or thwart the individuation process and threaten the needs for relatedness and autonomy. Family systems theory provides a framework for defining and understanding relationships between family members as well as the boundaries that characterize these relationships. Three principles of family systems theory are particularly relevant: the family as a whole is the unit of analysis; the family is composed of subsystems (e.g., individual, sibling, parent–child) defined by internal boundaries, and these subsystems are organized hierarchically; the family has external boundaries that differentiate it from the social world. The concept of boundary and, in particular, the focus on boundary definition or boundary dissolution within the family is one core aspect of the family systems theory. The concept of differentiation stems from the process of regulation of the boundaries sustained by the family during the lifespan.

According to prevailing models of family functioning, *family cohesion* (also described as tolerance for intimacy, closeness–caregiving, involvement, and connectedness or communion) and *enmeshment* (also described as lack of tolerance for individuality, lack of separateness, intrusiveness, and psychological control or dependency) are important aspects of family differentiation (e.g., Anderson & Sabatelli, 1992; Bowen, 1978; Olson, 1982). There is considerable disagreement, however, about the relationship between these two properties (Green & Werner, 1996). Manzi, Vignoles, Regalia, and Scabini (2006) have identified two different perspectives on this issue—the *one-dimensional model of family differentiation*, in which family cohesion and enmeshment are considered the two opposite ends of one continuum, and the *two-dimensional model*, in which cohesion and enmeshment are considered to be separate dimensions and the optimal situation is a combination of both high levels of cohesion and low levels of enmeshment achieved within the family. We briefly describe these two perspectives with reference to the work of Salvator Minuchin and Murray Bowen, whose theories gave rise to these concepts.

The One-Dimensional Model

Minuchin argued that families vary in their degree of emotional and physical proximity or distance (Minuchin, 1974; Minuchin & Fishman, 1981). He described family functioning through the concept of boundary regulation and, in particular, proposed that the regulation of family boundaries may be represented by a continuum with two extremes. At one end, there are families with rigid boundaries in which relationships are characterized by distance or separation (disengagement). The other end shows families with fused boundaries, in which members demonstrate emotional and physical proximity that is too close (enmeshment). Minuchin's continuum portrays the need for balance in family relationships, between disengagement and enmeshment closeness. Typically, too rigid boundaries within the family cause members to become disengaged, or to lack feelings of intimacy and connectedness. At the other end of the continuum, however, boundaries that are too loose cause members to lack a sense of autonomy and become enmeshed with other members of their system. In the latter case, boundaries are diffuse and even small amounts of stress can immediately affect other members. Minuchin was the first to combine enmeshment and disengagement into a single continuum of "boundary clarity", but other scholars have also embraced this perspective, such as Skinner, Steinhauer, and Santa-Barbara (1983), Epstein, Bishop, and Baldwin (1982), and Olson (1982).

The Two-Dimensional Model

Bowen (1976, 1978) viewed differentiation as the primary indicator of an individual's emotional health. At an interpersonal level, differentiation is defined as the family's ability to separate the emotional and intellectual spheres of its members. Its antithesis is what Bowen called the undifferentiated family ego mass, a situation of emotional fusion in a family in which all members are similar in emotional expression and assume to know each others' thoughts, feelings, and fantasies. In times of relative calm, undifferentiated families may appear to function normally, but stress causes them to break down.

According to Bowen, the level of differentiation of a person is determined by the level of differentiation from one's parents, by the type of relationship the child has with the parents, and the way one's unresolved emotional attachment to his/her parents is handled in young adulthood. In contrast to Minuchin, Bowen's asserts that a well-differentiated family has the ability to both experience intimacy with others and preserve autonomy; "the more differentiated a self, the more a person can be an individual, while in emotional contact with the group" (Kerr & Bowen, 1988, p. 94). This means that disengagement and enmeshment in the family context are not seen as opposite ends of the same continuum, but as different dimensions. Typically, the dimension of closeness–disengagement and the dimension of differentiation–enmeshment reciprocally reinforce each other, even though this idea was not specifically expressed in Bowen's writings.

Many authors have distinguished between the dimensions of closeness and differentiation. Anderson and Sabatelli (1990), for instance, conceptualize differentiation as a bidimensional construct that encompasses both degree of individuality and the degree of intimacy. Gavazzi and colleagues (Gavazzi, 1993; Cohen, Vasey, & Gavazzi, 2003) stress that well-differentiated families are characterized by high tolerance for both individuality and intimacy, and members have feelings of closeness and belonging while maintaining their individuality and agency.

In summary, the dichotomy between closeness and differentiation seems just as controversial in the literature on family differentiation as it does in the literature on the individuation process. According to the one-dimensional model, family patterns that promote autonomy are in contrast with processes linked to relatedness. A family must find the right balance between closeness and autonomy; thus, optimal family functioning is found at intermediate levels of cohesion, or, in statistical terms, cohesion is supposed to have a curvilinear effect on individual adjustment. According to the bidimensional model, autonomy and relatedness dimensions are different and optimal family functioning derives from the highest level of closeness and differentiation. Thus, these dimensions are supposed to be statistically distinguishable and to each have a linear effect on well-being. Empirical evidence has mainly supported the bidimensional model with most studies indicating that the dimensions of cohesion and enmeshment are statistically distinguishable and that these two dimensions have a linear rather than a curvilinear effect on well-being (Anderson, 1986; Cluff, Hicks, & Madsen, 1994; Farrell & Barnes, 1993). In any case, as we will see in the next section, the cross-cultural findings have questioned the differentiation process as the individuation process. In particular, a more culturally sensitive view of the family system states that we should not define an optimal family function and ignore the cultural context in which the family lives. Most of the family patterns in fact assume a particular and specific meaning according to the culture in which the family lives.

The Mutual Differentiation Process

Many scholars agree that understanding identity development in families requires joint consideration of individuation and differentiation processes as a systemic co-construction process (e.g., Buhl, 2008b). To understand how individual family members understand life and define their identity within the family context, we consider the interdependence that characterizes the family. The whole family system is involved in the process of defining identity subsystems, not only the identities of individuals.

Anderson and Sabatelli (1990) and Bell and Bell (2009) argue that positive individuation is the outcome of the family's ability to promote positive differentiation, escaping the traps of fusion and disengagement. Parenting style plays a key role in the process of identity construction for an adolescent. The more parents' caregiving efforts are directed toward promoting a family system with clear interpersonal boundaries, in which members are encouraged to think for themselves, speak for themselves, and accept others' differences, the more children develop a differentiated self and a capacity for autonomous action, learning how to direct their efforts effectively toward mastering the environment and supporting their sense of psychological well-being (Bell & Bell, 2009).

In the *symbolic–relational perspective*, Scabini and Manzi (2011) have recently proposed an integrative model that combines individuation and differentiation into a single process called *mutual differentiation*. Mutual differentiation is the dialectic process of individuals and families freeing themselves from each other, while at the same time remaining emotionally related. It is a relational process that deals with the ethical (justice–loyalty) and affective (trust–hope) symbolic aspects of the family system (see Cigoli & Scabini, 2006). The term *mutual* is used because the identity development of a family subsystem involves other family subsystems, the overall family system, and the relations between the two as they grow together. Thus, not only do individuals and family dyads have to individuate from the family, but the family itself must also permit and encourage this process.

The term *differentiation* is used because the basic human needs of relatedness and autonomy must be satisfied for the family and its subsystems to function adequately. According to this perspective, there are two dimensions of the family system that can satisfy or threaten both the basic human needs of relatedness and autonomy: *family cohesion* and *family respect of boundaries*.

Family cohesion is defined as the *strength* of the family bond, which includes feelings and behaviors such as emotional closeness, social support, and so on. Conversely, *family respect of boundaries* is defined as a particular *characteristic* of the family bond, which reflects how family members deal with psychological boundaries.[1] Scabini (1995) has emphasized the importance of considering two kinds of boundaries: interpersonal boundaries within the family, and boundaries between the family and the community or social environment. The first boundary reflects the amount of concern for the psychological difference of each individual family member: when an individual's boundaries are not respected, his or her ability to feel, perceive, and develop individual opinions within the family is weakened. The second boundary refers to the relationship between the family and its social context: when a family builds rigid boundaries with the outside world, individual members are forced to sustain their needs and find gratification only within the family.

In sum, optimal family functioning consists of family respect for boundaries (both in terms of well-defined interpersonal boundaries and a permeable boundary between the family and the outside world) together with the family promotion of close and tight bonds. The combination of family cohesion and family respect of boundaries is likely to lead to the promotion of well-differentiated family relationships, an appropriate relational context for the individual to satisfy the personal needs of autonomy and relatedness. Note that the symbolic–relational paradigm stresses the idea that the successful outcome of the mutual differentiation process is not only a well-differentiated self, but also a well-differentiated family bond. In this perspective, family bonds mutually linking family members are the central focus of analysis.

Figure 24.1 synthesizes the symbolic–relational perspective on the mutual differentiation process.

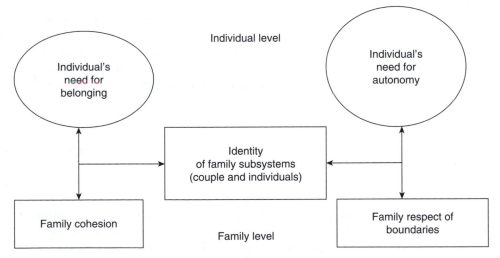

FIGURE 24.1 Mutual differentiation process. Identity is the outcome of the relationships between individual and family systems with regard to the dimensions of belonging and autonomy.

---

1 With reference to this dimension, Kerig (2005) has outlined several constructs that may have a negative effect on family boundaries: intrusiveness (i.e., controlling and coercive parenting), parentification (i.e., the dynamic in which the parent turns to the child for nurturance and assistance), spousification (i.e., the parent turns to the child to meet his/her need for intimacy and affection that is not fulfilled within the marriage relationship), and triangulation (i.e., the child becomes entangled in conflictual family interactions and is caught in the middle).

THE ROLE OF CULTURE IN THE PROCESS OF INDIVIDUATION AND DIFFERENTIATION

In the last few decades, there has been a dramatic increase in the number of studies acknowledging cultural variations in family functioning across the world. Findings from research in cross-cultural psychology and studies on the family relationships of immigrants belonging to different cultural groups have challenged assumptions and beliefs about what constitutes the nature and optimal functioning of family relationships (Santisteban, Muir-Malcolm, Mitrani, & Szapocznik, 2002).

In the first section of this chapter, individuation and differentiation were presented as two sides of the same process that involves the task of identity formation and the fundamental human needs of autonomy and relatedness. Identity formation and the needs of autonomy and relatedness have been the center of debate within the cultural perspective. The concept of self is one of the issues most questioned from this point of view: Does culture affect the meaning and function of the self in different contexts? Also, the universality of the needs of autonomy and relatedness and, consequently, the universality of the individuation/differentiation process, has been questioned: Are these needs culture specific or are they universal? Is the individuation/differentiation process a product of the Western concept of self?

In the following section, we present the cultural debate on identity. We then highlight the debate on autonomy and relatedness across cultures, providing an outline of three different theories found in the literature. Finally, we present our own perspective on how culture influences these processes and draw some conclusions.

THE CULTURAL SHAPE OF THE SELF

Research in the last three decades has emphasized the cultural variation in the way people construe the concept of self. According to Kirmayer (2007), much psychological theory has been supported by implicit notions of the person in US society. The North American concept of the self centers on individualism: to be a person means to be an independent individual, a self-made man or woman. People are valued for how richly developed and articulated their inner sense of self is and for how strong and coherent their self-direction is. In his influential work on emerging adulthood, Arnett (2004) showed that for the majority of young people in North American society, most shared criteria of adulthood—accepting responsibility for one's own actions, making independent decisions, and being financially independent—all refer to a dimension of independence. Consequently, Arnett holds that adult status in Western societies means achieving independence from others and learning how to become self-sufficient.

This concept of the person has been culturally questioned, and in particular the idea that the Western conceptualization of the self can be meaningfully applied to non-Western cultural contexts. In fact, many scholars agree that the structure of the self is not identical in every culture. The normal or psychologically "healthy" structure of the self may be markedly different across cultures. For instance, Roland (1987), after spending a period of time in India, concluded that the structure of the "self" among Indian people was deeply rooted in the bonds linking the individual to the extended family and community. After identifying the individual with the family and *jati* (community), the author coined the expression "familial self" to describe how the self was rooted in the subtle emotional hierarchical relationships of the family and group, as opposed to the "individualized self."

Similar observations can be made for other cultures and societies. Chinese Confucian culture (along with Japanese, Korean, and many Southeast Asian cultures) is essentially sociocentric and includes relationships with others in the definition of the self (Tu Wei-Ming, 1985). This idea is captured in the Chinese word for character or personality, *ren*. A person with *ren* is fundamentally a social being—he or she expresses unique qualities through a mature commitment to family or some larger social group. Another example can be found in Japanese culture. The term *Jibun* means self, but originally meant "one's share" of something beyond oneself. According to Hamaguchi (1985), the self is a fluid essence that changes according to interpersonal relationships.

In sum, it seems that in individualistic societies a person perceives the self as independent from others, self-expressive, and self-centered. A sharp line between the self and the other may be found. In collectivistic societies, a person sees the self as interdependent, highly connected, egalitarian, and following group interests (Markus & Kitayama, 1991; Triandis, 1995).

This conclusion has challenged the common view in personality and social psychology that people strive to distinguish themselves from others, that they have a basic motive to achieve distinctiveness (Brewer, 1991; Snyder & Fromkin, 1980). Thus, in some cultures, it is claimed, people want to be distinguished as individuals, whereas, in others, people want to be part of larger entities and may even seek to avoid distinctiveness from other members of those entities (Triandis, 1995; see also Kim & Markus, 1999; Markus & Kitayama, 1991). However, in a recent study, Becker et al. (2012) found that culture moderated the ways in which feelings of distinctiveness were constructed but not the strength of the distinctiveness need itself. In particular, distinctiveness was associated more closely with difference and separateness in more individualistic cultures, and more closely with social position in more collectivistic cultures (see also Vignoles, Chryssochoou, & Breakwell, 2000).

Cultural Views of Autonomy and Relatedness in the Family Context

Drawing from their awareness of different cultural forms of self and identity, family scholars have focused attention on how these forms result in different family patterns. In particular, families in Western societies are more inclined to promote autonomy among their members, especially children, emphasizing and supporting the values of personal choice, intrinsic motivation, self-esteem, and self-maximization. Parents alternate between closeness and distance with children and direct their attention outward in order to enhance the individuation process. In contrast, a strong sense of relatedness in non-Western families promotes family connectedness, positive group orientation, and upholds the qualities of respect and obedience in order to enhance relationships and interdependence (Grotevant, 1998; Harwood, Schoelmerich, Schulze, & Gonzalez, 1999; Rothbaum & Trommsdorff, 2007; Tamis-LeMonda et al., 2008).

Individualistic societies put more emphasis on autonomy within the family, whereas collectivistic societies emphasize family relatedness, and recognition of this difference has led scholars to develop three different theories or models.

The Oppositional Model

This perspective reconfirms the idea that autonomy and relatedness are opposite ends of the same continuum. Promoting relatedness in the family context brings about the suppression of autonomy. Cultures that promote relatedness in the family context consequently suppress both autonomy and the individuation/differentiation process.

Evidence for this relativistic view of the individuation/differentiation process is found in many studies. Roland's (1987) observations on the styles of childrearing in Indian families showed that parenting style was partially at odds with the Western emphasis on individuation and separation. Strikingly, Roland remarked that the types of parent–child relationships that would be considered problematic according to Western psychology were not only valued in India, but considered a source of well-being: "one can view the more symbiotic mothering and modes of relationships, with a relative inhibition of separation and autonomy, as being highly adaptive" (Roland, 1987, p. 242). Similarly, parenting styles aimed at controlling and limiting the autonomy of children have no negative influence on children's psychological adjustment in interdependent cultures, as can be seen among the Chinese (Chao 2001; Leung, Lau, & Lam, 1998), African Americans (McWayne, Owsianik, Green, & Fantuzzo, 2008; Randolph 1995), Korean (Rohner & Pettengill 1985) Turkish

(Kagitçibasi, 2005), Hongkongese and Pakistani (Stewart, Bond, Kennard, Ho, & Zaman, 2002), Algerians, and Saudi Arabians (Dwairi & Achoui, 2010).

In conclusion, scholars affirm that the high value attributed to interdependence in collectivistic cultures has important consequences for the way family patterns generally labeled in Western culture as inadequate or maladaptive are interpreted. In other words, living in an undifferentiated family with loose, overlapping boundaries and a high amount of control may not be problematic in a non-Western cultural context.

The Additive Model

An alternative perspective emphasizes the additive relations between the values of autonomy and relatedness (Tamis-LeMonda et al., 2008) and, to some extent, runs parallel to the concept of related individuation and the bi-dimensional model of differentiation outlined earlier. The model assumes that families in most cultures and societies still appreciate and support the efforts of family members to become autonomous and maintain strong relationships and ties (Bush, 2000; Helwig, 2006), though they may prioritize them differently (Yeh, Liu, Huang, & Yang, 2007).

This view is consistent with the idea that in all cultures individuals have to both assimilate to and distinguish themselves from the families and communities of which they are members. Thus, this perspective affirms the universality of the individuation/ differentiation process. Rogoff (2003), for instance, shows that in several interdependent cultures parental childrearing practices support autonomous children's decisions and behaviors. Interestingly, the goal of autonomy was consistent with the cultural framework of these groups: autonomy was not conceived in order to promote independence or psychological separation, but was designed to nurture empathy, the valuing of harmony, and other characteristics of cooperative societies.

Helwig's (2006) re-examination of the literature on autonomy shows how the developmental pathway toward autonomy presents many similarities across diverse cultures. Throughout childhood and into adolescence, children struggle to expand their personal sphere of decision-making by regulating concrete activities (e.g., recreational choices) and claiming more personal rights (e.g., privacy or freedom of expression). Common negative outcomes associated with the over-restriction of personal autonomy can be seen in both individualistic and collectivistic cultures. Contrary to the assumption that children obey the rules established by their parents and do not question parental authority in interdependent cultures, the development of personal autonomy is likely to require a common process of negotiation, and conflicts between children and adults are not infrequent, as children tend to push the boundaries, overcoming parental reluctance or even displaying explicit opposition.

The Contextual Model

A third perspective proposes that the values of autonomy and relatedness can be associated in different ways according to the context in which the family lives. From a culture-informed perspective, Kagitçibasi states that the development of a specific type of self is linked to the interplay of cultural, socioeconomic, and family variables that the author describes in her model of family change. According to Kagitçibasi (1996; 2005; 2007), autonomy and relatedness are two different dimensions that are related in different ways according to the sociocultural context. She claims that relatedness deals with interpersonal distance, or rather, the degree of connection with others, and ranges from separateness to connectedness. Separate selves are distanced from others with well-defined self-boundaries, whereas the boundaries of connected selves may be fused with others. Autonomy relates to volitional agency, a concept borrowed from self determination theory: "it is to be an agent and at the same point to act willingly, without a sense of coercion" (Kagitçibasi, 2007, p. 164). The opposite of autonomy is not dependence (i.e., reliance on parental or societal regulations), but heteronomy (i.e., the experience of pressure and coercion).

The basic tenet of the contextual model is recognition of the primacy of the context in which the family is situated, as it affects the interplay of autonomy and relatedness in family relationship patterns.

According to Kagitçibasi, this context includes both the cultural environment (i.e., individualistic or collectivistic orientations) and living conditions (e.g., urban–rural residence; socioeconomic development status, level of affluence). This context is likely to affect family functioning in terms of family values and, consequently, family interaction and socialization patterns.

This cultural, socioeconomic system gives rise to three prototypical family models, each characterized by specific interpersonal and intergenerational relationships that, in turn, are specifically linked to the development of the self. The *family model of total interdependence* is considered prototypical of the traditional, collectivistic rural agrarian family, even if it is also prevalent in urban low-income groups with limited resources. This model entails functionally extended family structures and affirms a child's economic and utilitarian value that provides a source of security for their parents in old age, ensuring family survival. In this model, family material and emotional interdependence are highly valued: individuation and, thus, the autonomy of the child is undesirable as it may be detrimental to family integrity and survival. Consequently, obedience-oriented childrearing and authoritarian parenting are common and socialization processes are aimed at enhancing strong, lasting, binding family relations. Thus, autonomy and relatedness are seen as opposites in these kinds of families.

A contrasting family model is that of the *family model of independence*, which is prototypical of the more individualistic Western, industrial, affluent, middle-class, and urban society. It essentially entails the nuclear family structure. Children are no longer regarded as having economic value, but an emotional and psychological value for the parents. This family model entails a self-reliance orientation in childrearing and relatively permissive parenting. Individual autonomy is adaptive and desirable in such a sociocultural context and separation of adult offspring is not considered a threat to the family.

The third model is particularly noteworthy and is what Kagitçibasi defines as the *family model of psychological/emotional interdependence*. This model appears in collectivistic countries when material interdependencies in the family decrease with urban lifestyles, but psychological interdependence continues to be valued, given the continuing "culture of relatedness." Autonomy in these contexts is allowed for two main reasons: it is no longer a threat to family livelihood and is highly adaptive in urbanized lifestyles. However, strong family ties and parental control are maintained because socialization values continue to emphasize family loyalties. The relation of autonomy and relatedness, of individual and family loyalties, leads to the emergence of the "autonomous-related self." As Gupta and Panda (2003) underlined with reference to Indian families, this self can also be defined as an "individualized familial self." Empirical evidence for this model is particularly consistent across several countries (for more extensive empirical research, see Kagitçibasi, 2005, 2007) and can be observed in several countries across the world where deep cultural changes occur as a result of increasing urbanization, affluence, and globalization.

China is an excellent example, as it has been widely recognized as a collectivistic culture (Triandis, 1995) that abides by the basic tenets of Confucianism, which emphasize greater importance of the common good and social harmony over individual interests. Chuang and Moreno (2008), however, affirm that China has undergone significant social and economic changes that have altered China's cultural context and, consequently, have also altered parenting beliefs and values. The one-child policy and economic reform may have created a more child-centered, Westernized parenting approach, especially among the urban and well-educated population (Chang, Schwartz, Dodge, & McBride-Chang, 2003). As Chen, Bian, Xin, Wang, and Silbereisen (2010) emphasize, parents "seem to realize that it is important for their children to learn independent and initiative-taking skills in order to explore the environment and that controlling and restrictive parenting styles may not be conducive to the development of these skills" (p. 267). This new parental trend does not necessarily go against the traditional value of relatedness. In fact, there are studies showing that the young still seem to internalize values regarding filial piety and, in particular, are socialized to demonstrate respect toward parents in public and reverence of family values and traditions (Leung, Wang, Wang & McBride-Chang, 2010; Wong, Leung & McBride-Chang, 2010).

Similar trends can be observed in other countries traditionally labeled as collectivistic, like India (Sharma, 2003). Increasing urbanization and rapid changes in life styles under the influence of an ongoing process of modernization are altering the structures of Indian families, which are now increasingly nuclear and small. In fact, more autonomous-oriented parenting practices are becoming common. Mothers in modern cities, for instance, encourage their children to be self-reliant, an attitude that is needed to live in an increasingly competitive society (Seymour, 1999). At the same time, studies have reported the sustaining influence of familial interchanges and traditional relationships (Sharma, 2003).

Critique

We presented different perspectives that explained how cultural context might affect the dimensions of autonomy and relatedness and the individuation/differentiation process. The oppositional model argues that there is no need for autonomy in a cultural context that values relatedness. Consequently, individuation/differentiation is seen as a product of Western industrialized countries. However, the view that individualistic societies promote autonomy and collectivistic societies are only concerned with relatedness is, at least, limited. In fact, scholars from the additive model have demonstrated that the need for autonomy is universal and, thus, individuation/differentiation can be regarded as a common process worldwide. We agree that autonomy and relatedness are not only distinct and universal dimensions, but are also part of the cultural context. Kagitçibasi's contextual model provides a useful framework for understanding how family values and, in particular, family promotion of relatedness and autonomy are a function of the changes in socioeconomic conditions. Nevertheless, the rationale of the model seems to reinforce the idea that both individuation and family differentiation are more likely to occur only in some cultural contexts. There is no room for autonomy in the traditional family model of total interdependence, and the value of individualism emphasizes separation between and among family members in the modern family model of independence.

We do not believe that the three models fully explain individuation/differentiation across cultures. An account is needed that is universal, but also context-sensitive and culture-inclusive (Valsiner, 2009). The experience of autonomy is influenced by the cultural process of meaning-making. Meaning is formulated within a context in which culture plays an important role; culture influences how an individual interprets a specific set of behaviors as controlling or autonomy supporting. This idea has been supported by recent frameworks that provide more culturally oriented definitions of autonomy.

One example is the *dual model of autonomy* (Yeh & Yang, 2006), which posits the coexistence at the individual level of two forms of autonomy: individuating autonomy and relating autonomy. Both forms encompass a definition of autonomy in terms of volitional agency. Individuating autonomy represents a volitional capacity to define specific goals, develop strategies to promote identity, and uniquely express the self in relation with others. Relating autonomy represents a volitional capacity to act in a way that takes into account the harmony of self in relation to others, the quality of interpersonal relationships, and self-transcendence. Individuals can alternate between both forms of autonomy depending on the context, and each form of autonomy has a dominant, but not necessarily exclusive, domain of functioning (Yeh, Bedford, & Yang, 2009). Similarly, Rudy, Sheldon, Awong, and Tan (2007) distinguish between *individual relative autonomy* and *inclusive relative autonomy*, in which the motivation for action is the determining factor. Individual autonomy entails an action performed by an individual who perceives himself/herself as independent (e.g., "I work hard because I think it's important to achieve a good position"). Inclusive autonomy entails an action performed by an individual who perceives himself/herself as interdependent, with boundaries that overlap with others (e.g., "I work hard because, in my family, we think it's important to achieve a good position"). In both cases, autonomy is an expression of personal motivation, but the source of motivation is culturally defined in accordance with the importance attributed to others in self definition. In other words, it is plausible that in specific cultures individuals feels autonomous when behaving in accordance with a choice made by someone they trust (e.g., their mother) because that person has been greatly included within their sense of self.

An explanation of how culture influences the needs of autonomy and relatedness as a consequence of the individuation/differentiation process, in line with Luciano (2010), is what we call the domain-specific approach (Manzi, Regalia, Pelucchi, & Fincham, 2012). The main question this perspective examines is not *if* autonomy and relatedness can coexist in different cultural contexts, but *how* they coexist. The answer to this question pertains to the meaning-making process and, in particular, to the meaning that autonomy may assume in different cultural contexts.

THE DOMAIN-SPECIFIC APPROACH

The domain-specific approach emphasizes that the cultural context does not affect the meaning an individual attributes to the need for autonomy, but the specific domain in which the individual expects to act in an autonomous way. In this regard, Luciano (2010) gives us an insightful definition of autonomy. The need for autonomy describes the extent to which one functions with autonomous volitional choice, but the notion of choice is an ambiguous concept that makes it difficult to clearly define autonomy. "Choice can be viewed as the process of choosing—but choosing what?" (Luciano, 2010, p. 499). The influence culture has on autonomy within the family context plays on this last question. Without considering the role of pervasiveness in the need for autonomy, culture influences the domain in which an individual is allowed and expects to choose autonomously.

A child's experience of autonomy is thus influenced by the cultural context of the domain the autonomous choice is allowed in. For example, in one cultural context, a child's autonomous decision-making is supported by the parent in the domain of choosing what to wear, but not in choosing which clothes to purchase (Tuli & Chaudhari, 2010). Another example of a domain in which the expectations of autonomy vary to a large extent across cultures concerns marriage. In Western societies, marriage is seen as a matter of individual choice, and any type of familial interference is seen as maladaptive and detrimental. In several North-African and Eastern societies, marriage is still essentially a family issue. Even if, under the force of modernization, there is a gradual decline of arranged marriages, the level of interference and control by parents and relatives is high and culturally expected as normative (Breger & Hill, 1998; Buunk, Parker, & Duncan, 2010).

If culture deeply influences the domain in which autonomy can be expressed, then it should be stressed that parenting is the first, and probably the most important, means through which the cultural meaning of autonomy is reproduced. Identical parenting strategies can, thus, have different meanings or may be based on different parenting goals (Mason et al., 2004).

As seen in the first section of this chapter, the individuation/differentiation process has been elaborated through two Western theoretical perspectives—psychoanalytic theory and family systems theory. Both theories uphold autonomy as a developmental ideal (Sampson, 1988). We have also seen that other cultures, however, view relatedness as the ultimate goal for individual development. This does not mean, however, that an individual's need to develop his or her own individuality is not present in such cultures. According to the domain-specific approach, we can argue that autonomy and individuality are always valued, but the domain in which an individual expects to act autonomously is likely to vary according to the context. Thus, a parenting style that controls a child's particular domain of choice may lead one young person to feel controlled or manipulated in one cultural context, but may be associated with feelings of love and concern in a different culture (Mason et al., 2004).

A clear example can be found in Manzi et al.'s (2006) study that showed that young Italian adults do not consider family control over the organization of their leisure time and personal space as a violation of autonomy, but as a manifestation of closeness within the family. However, young British adults viewed these same controlling behaviors as negative family patterns that threatened their sense of self. According to the domain specific perspective, it should not to be concluded that young Italian adults have no need for autonomy, but that they express autonomy in different domains.

This issue has been further investigated by Manzi et al. (2012), in a cross-cultural study aimed at comparing child perceptions of intrusive parenting over three different domains: promotion of autonomous thought, promotion of autonomous decision-making, and promotion of physical separation. It was found that control over physical separation was considered an indicator of positive family functioning for Italians, while participants living in the US, Belgium, and China viewed this behavior as negative and controlling. US children differed significantly from the other three groups when evaluating the effects of parental control. Only North American children perceived the control of parents in this domain as harmful, while other participants, especially children in China, did not percieve this kind of parental control as detrimental.

In sum, the domain-specific approach seems to address the different and apparently contrasting results the individuation/differentiation process has across cultures. On one hand, it supposes that the need for autonomy is universal and, consequently, the process of individuation/differentiation is pervasive across cultures. On the other hand, it takes into consideration the cultural variability of this process, affirming that culture delineates the possible meanings of autonomy and, in particular, the specific domains in which an individual expects to act autonomously.

LIMITATIONS OF THE EXISTING USE OF THEORY AND SUGGESTIONS FOR FUTURE THEORETICAL DEVELOPMENT

Three issues need to be taken into account so that future theory and research can be more culturally informed. The first concerns the *level of analysis of the individuation process*. As we have seen, family systems theory as well as the symbolic–relational paradigm have underscored that the individuation/differentiation process involves the entire family system and not only the parent–child dyad. Nevertheless, the majority of empirical studies have used the single individual in the parent–child relationship as the unit of analysis. Analyzing this process from a more comprehensive view of the family system could be particularly useful for a better understanding of the individuation/differentiation process across cultures. Evidence gained from clinicians who work with an approach aimed to understand the ethnic and cultural dimensions of mental illnesses or relational sufferings would be very useful.

For example Moro, Neuman, and Real (2008) report that in several countries of sub-Saharan Africa, the parents' main concern when a child is born is to name him/her adequately, in order to separate the child from the family ancestors who live in a supernatural world where the child is believed to come from. In these cultures, the first separation enabling the individuation of the child as a person with his/her own identity is therefore not from the mother, but from the ancestors. It seems then that the individuation process lies here not in the parent–child relationship, but in the wider relationships linking the child, the parents, and their ancestors from previous family generations. In Western industrialized cultures, even Bowen (1978) emphasized that the extent to which individuation in a family is achieved is likely to be determined by the degree of differentiation of marital couples in relation with previous generations. Thus, what is needed is an increase in multigenerational family studies, namely theory and research that analyzes the patterns of functioning of families as a whole with a specific focus on the relationships between different family subsystems across cultures. This aspect can be particularly relevant for families in interdependent cultures, in which there are strong bonds among generations and older generations are likely to have a great influence on the family patterns of new generations.

A second point of discussion focusses on the *outcomes of this process*. Most of the theories on individuation, and in particular the self-determination theory, seem to consider the achievement of autonomy as the final milestone of the individuation process, like an intrinsic value. One can speculate whether the development of an autonomous identity can be regarded as a developmental step toward a more mature state of personal identity, whose main features are intimacy and "generativity" (Erikson, 1982; McAdams & de St. Aubin, 1998). In other terms, resolving the issue of relationships to parents enhances a sense of personal authority and distinctive identity, but it also raises questions concerning the goal of autonomy. Cultural variations seem particularly relevant at this level and have to be investigated.

Western societies seem to consider these goals within a perspective that stresses the importance of free choice. To become an adult seems to be more a matter of self-sufficiency and is relatively independent of the traditional role transitions an individual goes through, like marriage and becoming a parent (Arnett, 2004). In several non-Western cultures, reaching autonomy primarily entitles the individual to take family and social responsibilities in a direction of a generative stance. One is expected to differentiate from one's own family of origin in order to generate one's own family. Empirical evidence shows that the absence of family generativity can be stigmatized by family members as a personal failure (Moro, Neuman, & Real, 2008).

It must be emphasized that in several Western developmental and personality theories the idea that the achievement of an autonomous identity itself represents the endpoint of adult development is not present at all. Starting from Erikson's psychosocial developmental theory (Erikson, 1982) through McAdam's generativity model (McAdams & de St. Aubin, 1992), the optimal outcome for individual development is reached when the individual devotes considerable effort toward the well-being of future generations. The generativity experience presents itself as a recursive interplay between autonomy and relatedness. According to McAdams and de St. Aubin, (1992) the truly generative parent "works hard and long to promote the development of his child and to nurture all that is good and desirable in the child. But he must eventually grant the child his or her own autonomy, letting go when the time is right, letting the child develop his or her own identity, make his or her own decisions and commitments, and ultimately create those offerings of generativity that will distinguish that child as someone who was 'given birth to' in order to 'give birth to.'" (p. 1006). The symbolic–relational paradigm also regards generativity not as the outcome of an individual personality process, but as the result of the couple and intergenerational bond's optimal functioning (Cigoli & Scabini, 2006).

A third issue to address concerns *variability within cultures*. As we have seen, the oppositional model, the additive model, and the contextual model all use the dichotomy between individualism and collectivism to explain the cultural impact on the individuation/differentiation process. Although the distinction between individualistic and collective cultures provides a useful theoretical orientation to cultural differences, finer distinctions are required to avoid excessive simplification. In their meta-analytic review of the literature on country differences and the individualism-collectivism dichotomy, Oyserman, Coon, and Kemmelmeier (2002, p. 3) found that contrary to expectations, "European Americans were not more individualistic than African Americans, or Latinos, and not less collectivistic than Japanese or Koreans".

The mainstream conceptions of culture reflect an essentialist and classificatory approach to culture and the self that risks confusion. As Hermans and Kempen (1998) emphasized several years ago, the real world is difficult to understand based on broad dichotomies. The process of globalization and the increasing interconnections among people around the world result in the emergence of cultural mixtures or hybridization. Consequently, the question of boundary regulation and differentiation does not only concern individuals and families, but also cultural systems. The need to integrate cultural systems into our theories is apparent.

CONCLUSION

In this chapter, we have shown how the related processes of individuation and differentiation are at the core of identity formation. In order to build a personal identity, an individual must negotiate the tension between the two basic and apparently contrasting dimensions of autonomy and relatedness. This developmental task requires the ability to maintain connections and regulate closeness with family members, especially parents. This process is enhanced by the extent to which the family system can ensure respect for interpersonal boundaries. Two major theoretical perspectives have been developed, both at the individual and family levels, to explain the relationships between relatedness and autonomy, which are at the core of individuation and differentiation. One perspective, comprising the Mahlerian psychoanalytic point of view and Minuchin's Family System theory, claims that these two dimensions act in opposition and that one is fulfilled at the expense of the other. A second perspective claims that these aspects do not represent two extremes of the same dimension, but are expressions of different dimensions. In this case, adequate personal and family functioning requires both to be met (see self-determination theory, attachment theory, and Bowen's family system theory).

The universality of the individuation/differentiation process has been addressed by models that have described different relationships between the dimensions of autonomy and relatedness across cultures. In cross-cultural psychology, the prevailing model for a long time has been the oppositional model, which posits an inverse relation between autonomy and relatedness. Other models have shown a possible positive correlation between them and have emphasized the need to consider economic and social variables within different individualistic or collectivistic orientations.

Finally, the domain-specific approach claims that culture moderates the way both autonomy and relatedness are satisfied: both needs can be considered cultural and flexible universals guiding the process of individuation. This means that individuals and families can be guided by a common set of underlying individual needs, but that each cultural group develops different, culturally specific, ways of satisfying such needs depending on the specific domains taken into account.

In conclusion, cultures are changing systems characterized by a high level of variability and we need to capture this in our theories. One must not overgeneralize when trying to understand a culture, but assume an "emic" perspective. It is only possible to understand the full meaning of individuation and differentiation processes by looking inside a cultural system, and by considering the variation of these meanings in light of social change and through the same economic and cultural areas of reference. Building such perspectives into our theories will inevitably provide a more complete understanding of the processes we seek to understand.

REFERENCES

Ainsworth, M. D. S., Blehar, M. C., Waters, E., & Wall, S. (1978). *Patterns of attachment: A psychological study of the strange situation*. Hillsdale, NJ: Erlbaum.

Anderson, S. A. (1986). Cohesion, adaptability, and communication: A test of an Olson Circumplex Model hypothesis. *Family Relations: Interdisciplinary Journal of Applied Family Studies, 35*, 289–293.

Anderson, S. A., & Sabatelli, R. M., (1990). Differentiating differentiation and individuation: Conceptual and operational challenges. *American Journal of Family Therapy, 18*, 32–50.

Anderson, S. A., & Sabatelli, R. M. (1992). The differentiation in the family system scale (DIFS). *American Journal of Family Therapy, 20*, 77–89.

Arnett, J. J. (2004). Emerging adulthood: The winding road from the late teens through the twenties. New York: Oxford University Press.

Baumeister, R. F., & Leary, M. R. (1995) The need to belong: Desire for interpersonal attachments as a fundamental human motivation. *Psychological Bulletin, 117*, 497–529.

Becker, M., Vignoles, V. L., Owe, E., Brown, R., Smith, P. B., Easterbrook, M., … Yamako lu, N. (2012). Culture and the distinctiveness motive: constructing identity in individualistic and collectivistic contexts. *Journal of Personality and Social Psychology, 102*, 833–855.

Bell, L. G. & Bell, D. C. (2009) Effects of family connection and family individuation. *Attachment and Human Development, 11*, 471–490.

Beyers, W., Goossens, L., Van Calster, B., & Duriez, B. (2005). An alternative substantive factor structure of the emotional autonomy scale. *European Journal of Psychological Assessment, 21*, 147–155.

Beyers, W., Goossens, L., Vansant, I., & Moors, E. (2003). Structural model of autonomy in middle and late adolescence: connectedness, separation, detachment, and agency. *Journal of Youth and Adolescence, 32*, 351–365.

Blos, P. (1967). The second individuation process of adolescence. *The Psychoanalytic Study of the Child, 22*, 162–186.

Bowen, M. (1976). Theory in the practice of psychotherapy. In P. J. Guerin Jr. (Ed.), *Family therapy* (pp. 42–90). New York: Gardner.

Bowen, M. (1978) *Family therapy in clinical practice*. New York: Aronson.

Bowlby, J. (1969). *Attachment and loss:* Vol. 1. *Attachment*. New York: Basic Books.

Breger, R., & Hill, R. (1998). Cross-cultural marriage. Oxford, England: Berg.

Brewer, M. B., (1991). The social self: On being the same and different at the same time. *Personality and Social Psychology Bulletin, 17*, 475–482.

Buhl, H. M. (2008a). Development of a model describing individuated adult child-parent relationships. *International Journal of Behavioral Development, 32*, 381–389.

Buhl, H. M. (2008b). Significance of individuation in adult child–parent relationships. *Journal of Family Issues, 29*, 262–281.

Buunk, A., Parker, J., Duncan, L. (2010). Cultural variation in parental influence on mate choice, *Cross-Cultural Research: Journal of Comparative Social Science, 44*, 23–40.

Bush, K. (2000). Separateness and connectedness in the parent adolescent relationship as predictors of adolescent self-esteem in US and Chinese samples. *Marriage and Family Review, 30*, 153–178.

Chang, L., Schwartz, D., Dodge, K., McBride-Chang, C. (2003). Harsh parenting in relation to child emotion regulation and aggression. *Journal of Family Psychology, 17*, 598–606.

Chao, R. K. (2001). Extending research on the consequences of parenting style for Chinese Americans and European Americans. *Child Development, 72*, 1832–1843.

Chen, X., Bian, Y., Xin, T., Wang, L., & Silbereisen, R. K. (2010). Perceived social change and childrearing attitudes in China. *European Psychologist, 15*, 260–270.

Chuang, S. S., & Moreno, R. P. (Eds.) (2008). *On new shores: Understanding immigrant fathers in North America*. Lanham, MD: Lexington Books.

Cigoli, V., & Scabini, E. (2006). *Family identity. Ties, symbols, and transitions*. Mahwah, NJ: Lawrence Erlbaum.

Cluff, R. B., Hicks, M., & Madsen, C. H., Jr. (1994). Beyond the circumplex model: A moratorium on curvilinearity. *Family Process, 33*, 74–79.

Cohen, E. A., Vasey, M. W., & Gavazzi, S. M. (2003). Family differentiation as individuality and intimacy tolerance: Multiple family perspectives and the dimensionality of family distance regulation. *Journal of Family Issues, 24*, 99–123.

Deci, E. L. & Vansteenkiste, M. (2004). Self-determination theory and basic need satisfaction: Understanding human development in positive psychology. *Ricerche di Psicologia*. Special Issue: *Positive Psychology, 27*, 23–40.

Deci, E. L., & Ryan, R. M. (2000). The "what" and "why" of goal pursuits: Human needs and the self-determination of behavior. *Psychological Inquiry, 11*, 227–268.

Dwairi, M. & Achoui, M. (2010), Parental control: a second cross-cultural research on parenting and psychological adjustment of children *Journal of Child and Family Studies, 19*, 16–22.

Epstein, N. B., Bishop, D. S., & Baldwin, L. M. (1982). McMaster model of family functioning: A view of the normal family. In F. Walsh (Ed.), *Normal family processes* (pp. 115–141). New York: Guilford Press.

Erikson, E. H. (1982). *The life cycle completed*. New York: Norton.

Farrell, M. P. & Barnes, G. M. (1993). Family systems and social support: A test of the effects of cohesion and adaptability on the functioning of parents and adolescents. *Journal of Marriage and the Family, 55*, 119–132.

Gavazzi, S. M. (1993). The relation between family differentiation levels in families with adolescents and the severity of presenting problems. *Family Relations, 42*, 463–468.

Green, R. J., & Werner, P. D. (1996). Intrusiveness and closeness-caregiving: Rethinking the concept of family "enmeshment". *Family Process, 35*, 115–136.

Grotevant, H. D. (1998). Adolescent development in family contexts. In Damon, W., & Eisenberg, N. (Eds) *Handbook of child psychology* (Vol. 3). Social, emotional, and personality development (5th ed., pp. 1097–1149). Hoboken, NJ: Wiley.

Grotevant, H. D., & Cooper, C. R. (1986) Individuation in family relationships: A perspective on individual differences in the development of identity and role-taking skill in adolescence. *Human Development, 29*, 82–100.

Gupta, R. K., & Panda, A. (2003). Individualised familial self: The evolving self of qualified technocrats in India. *Psychology and Developing Societies, 15*, 1–29.

Hamaguchi, E. (1985). A contextual model of the Japanese: Toward a methodological innovation in Japan studies. *Journal of Japanese Studies*, *11*, 289–321.

Harwood, R. L., Schoelmerich, A., Schulze, P. A., & Gonzalez, Z. (1999). Cultural differences in maternal beliefs and behaviors: A study of middle-class Anglo and Puerto Rican mother–infant pairs in four everyday situations. *Child Development*, *70*, 1005–1016.

Helwig, C. C. (2006). The development of personal autonomy throughout cultures. *Cognitive Development*, *21*, 458–473.

Hermans, H. J. M., & Kempen, H. J. G. (1998). Moving cultures: the perilous problems of cultural dichotomies in a globalizing society. *American Psychologist*, 53, 1111–1120.

Ingoglia, S., Lo Coco, A., Liga, F., & Lo Cricchio, M. G. (2011). Emotional separation and detachment as two distinct dimensions of parent-adolescent relationships. *International Journal of Behavioral Development*, *10*, 123–139.

Josselson, R. (1988). The embedded self: I and thou revisited. In D. K. Lapsley & F. C. Power (Eds.), *Self, ego, and identity: Integrative approaches* (pp. 91–106). New York: Springer-Verlag.

Kagitçibasi, C. (1996). The autonomous-relational self: A new synthesis. *European Psychologist*, *1*, 180–186.

Kagitçibasi, C. (2005). Autonomy and relatedness in cultural context: implications for self and family. *Journal of Cross-Cultural Psychology*, *36*, 403–422.

Kagitçibasi, C. (2007) *Family, self, and human development across cultures* (2nd ed.) Mahwah, NJ: Lawrence Erlbaum.

Kerig, P. K. (2005). Revisiting the construct of boundary dissolution: A multidimensional perspective. In P. K. Kerig (Ed.), *Implications of parent-child boundary dissolution for developmental psychopathology* (pp. 5–42). New York: The Haworth Press.

Kerr, M. E., & Bowen, M. (1988). *Family evaluation: An approach based on Bowen theory*. New York: Norton.

Kim, H., & Markus, H. R. (1999), "Deviance or uniqueness, harmony or conformity? A cultural analysis". *Journal of Personality and Social Psychology*, *77*, 785–800.

Kirmayer, L. J. (2007). Refugees and forced migration: hardening of the arteries in the global reign of insecurity. *Transcultural Psychiatry*, *44*, 307–310.

Kruse, J. & Walper, S. (2008). Types of individuation in relation to parents: Predictors and outcomes. *International Journal of Behavioral Development*, *32*, 390–400.

Leung, K., Lau, S., & Lam, W. (1998). Parenting styles and academic achievement: A cross-cultural study. *Merrill-Palmer Quarterly: Journal of Developmental Psychology*, *44*, 157–172.

Leung, A., Wang, S., Wang, I. & McBride-Chang, C. (2010). Filial piety and psychosocial adjustment in Hong Kong Chinese early adolescents. *Journal of Early Adolescence*, *30*, 651–667.

Luciano, M. M. (2010). Commentary: Autonomy and relatedness reconsidered: Learning from Indian families. *Culture Psychology*, *16*, 497–505.

Mahler, M. S. (1963). Thoughts about development and individuation. *The Psychoanalytic Study of the Child*, *18*, 307–324.

Manzi, C., Vignoles, V. L., Regalia, C., & Scabini, E. (2006). Cohesion and enmeshment revisited: Differentiation, identity, and well-being in two European cultures. *Journal of Marriage and Family*, *68*, 673–689.

Manzi, C., Regalia, C., Pelucchi, S., Fincham, F. D. (2012). *Documenting different domains of promotion of autonomy in families, Journal of Adolescence*, *10*, 289–298.

Markus, H., & Kitayama, S. (1991). Culture and the self: Implications for cognition, emotion, and motivation. *Psychological Review, 98*, 224–253.

Mason, C. A., Walker-Barnes, C. J., Tu, S., Simons, J., & Martinez-Arrue, R. (2004). Ethnic differences in the affective meaning of parental control behaviors. *Journal of Primary Prevention*, *25*, 59–79.

McAdams, D. P., de St. Aubin, E. (1992). A theory of generativity and its assessment through self-report, behavioral acts, and narrative themes in autobiography. *Journal of Personality and Social Psychology*, *62*, 1003–1015.

McAdams, D. P., & de St. Aubin, E. (Eds.) (1998). *Generativity and adult development: How and why we care for the next generation*. Washington, DC: American Psychological Association Press.

McClanahan, G., & Holmbeck, G. N. (1992). Separation-individuation, family functioning, and psychological adjustment in college students: A construct validity study of the Separation-Individuation Test of Adolescence. *Journal of Personality Assessment*, *59*, 468–485.

McElhaney, K. B., Allen, J. P., Stephenson, J. C., & Hare, A. L. (2009). Attachment and autonomy during adolescence. In R. Lerner, & L. Steinberg, L. (Eds.) *Handbook of adolescent psychology* (3rd ed., Vol. 1, pp. 358–403). Hoboken, NJ: Wiley.

McWayne, C. M., Owsianik, M., Green, L. E., & Fantuzzo, J. W. (2008). Parenting behaviors and preschool children's social and emotional skills: A question of the consequential validity of traditional parenting constructs for low-income African Americans. *Early Childhood Research Quarterly, 23,* 173–192.

Minuchin, S. (1974). *Families and family therapy.* Cambridge, MA: Harvard University Press.

Minuchin, S., & Fishman, H. C. (1981). *Family therapy techniques.* Cambridge, MA: Harvard University Press.

Moro, M., Neuman, D., Real, I. (2008). *Maternités en exil.* Paris: La Pensée Sauvage.

Olson, D. H. (1982). Circumplex model of marital and family system. In F. Walsh (Ed.), *Normal family processes* (pp. 115–132). New York: Guilford Press.

Oyserman, D., Coon, H., & Kemmelmeier, M. (2002). Rethinking individualism and collectivism: Evaluation of theoretical assumptions and meta-analyses. *Psychological Bulletin, 128,* 3–73.

Randolph, S. M. (1995). African American children in single-mother families. In Dickerson, B. J. (Eds) *African American single mothers: Understanding their lives and families.* (pp. 117–145). Thousand Oaks, CA: Sage.

Rogoff, B. (2003). *The cultural nature of human development.* New York: Oxford University Press.

Rohner, R. P., & Pettengill, S. M. (1985). Perceived parental acceptance-rejection and parental control among Korean adolescents. *Child Development. Special Issue: Family Development, 56,* 524–528.

Roland, A. (1987). The familial self, the individualized self and the transcendent self. *Psychoanalytic Review, 74,* 237–250.

Rothbaum, F., & Trommsdorff, G. (2007). *Do roots and wings complement or oppose one another? The socialization of relatedness and autonomy in cultural context.* In J. E. Grusec & P. Hastings (Eds.), The handbook of socialization (pp. 461–489). New York: Guilford Press.

Rudy, D., Sheldon, K. M., Awong, T., & Tan, H. H, (2007). Autonomy, culture, and well-being: The benefits of inclusive autonomy. *Journal of Research in Personality, 41,* 983–1007.

Ryan, R. M., & Lynch, J. H. (1989). Emotional autonomy versus detachment: Revisiting the vicissitudes of adolescence and young adulthood. *Child Development, 60,* 340–356.

Ryan, R. M. (1993). Agency and organization: Intrinsic motivation, autonomy, and the self in psychological development. In J. E. Jacobs (Ed.), *Nebraska Symposium on Motivation: Developmental perspectives on motivation* (Vol. 40, pp. 1–56). Lincoln: University of Nebraska Press.

Sabatelli, R. M., & Mazor, A. (1985). Differentiation, individuation, and identity formation: The integration of family system and individual developmental perspectives. *Adolescence, 20,* 619–633.

Sampson, E. E. (1988). The debate on individualism: Indigenous psychologies of the individual and their role in personal and societal functioning. *American Psychologist, 43,* 15–22.

Santisteban, D. A., Muir-Malcolm, J. A., Mitrani, V. B., & Szapocznik, J. (2002*). Integrating the study of ethnic culture and family psychology intervention science.* In H. Liddle, R. Levant, D. A. Santiste-ban, & J. Bray (Eds.), *Family psychology: Science-based interventions* (pp. 331–352) Washington, DC: American Psychological Association.

Scabini, E. (1995). *Psicologia sociale della famiglia [Family social psychology].* Turin: Bollati Boringhieri.

Scabini, E., Manzi, C. (2011). Identity in family processes. In S. J. Schwartz, K. Luyckx, & V. L. Vignoles (Eds), *Handbook of identity theory and research* (pp. 569–588). New York: Springer.

Seymour, S. C. (1999). *Women, family, and child care in India: a world in transition.* Cambridge, MA: Cambridge University Press.

Sharma, N. (2003). *Understanding adolescence.* Delhi: National Book Trust.

Skinner, H. A., Steinhauer, P. D., & Santa-Barbara, J. (1983). Family assessment measure. *Canadian Journal of Mental Health, 2,* 91–105.

Snyder, C. R., & Fromkin, H. L. (1980). *Uniqueness: The human pursuit of difference.* New York: Plenum.

Soenens, B., Berzonsky, M. D., Vansteenkiste, M., Beyers, W., & Goossens, L. (2005). Identity styles and causality orientations: In search of the motivational underpinnings of the identity exploration process. *European Journal of Personality, 19,* 427–442.

Steinberg, L., & Silverberg, S. B. (1986). The vicissitudes of autonomy in early adolescence. *Child Development, 57,* 841–851.

Stewart, S. M. Bond, M. H., Kennard, B. D., Ho, L. M., & Zaman, R. M. (2002). Does the Chinese construct of guan export to the West? *International Journal of Psychology, 37*, 74–82.

Stierlin, H. (1974). Separating parents and adolescents. New York: Quadrangle.

Tamis-LeMonda, C. S., Way, N., Hughes, D., Yoshikawa, H., Kahana-Kalman, R. & Niwa, E. (2008). Parents' goals for children: the dynamic co-existence of collectivism and individualism. *Social Development, 17*, 183–209.

Triandis, H. C. (1995) The self and social behavior in differing cultural contexts. In N. R. Goldberger, & J. B. Veroff. *The culture and psychology reader* (pp. 326–365). New York: New York University Press.

Tu Wei-Ming, (1985). Selfhood and otherness in Confucian thought. In A. Marsella, G. DeVos & F. Hsu (Eds.), *Culture and self* (pp. 231–251). New York: Tavistock/Wiley.

Tuli, M., & Chaudhari, N. (2010) Elective interdependence: Understanding individual agency and interpersonal relationships in Indian families. *Culture & Psychology, 16*, 477–496.

Valsiner, J. (2009). Integrating psychology within the globalizing world. *Integrative Psychological & Behavioral Science, 43*, 1–16.

Vignoles, V. L., Chryssochoou, X. & Breakwell, G. M. (2000). The distinctiveness principle Identity, meaning and the bounds of cultural relativity. *Personality and Social Psychology Review, 4*, 337–354.

Wong, S. M., Leung, A. N.-M., & McBride-Chang, C. (2010). Adolescent filial piety as a moderator between perceived maternal control and mother-adolescent relationship quality in Hong Kong. *Social Development, 19*, 187–201.

Yeh, K., & Yang, Y. (2006). Construct validation of individuating and relating autonomy orientations in culturally Chinese adolescents. *Asian Journal of Social Psychology, 9*, 79–106.

Yeh, K., Liu, Y., Huang, H., & Yang, Y. (2007). Individuating and relating autonomy. In J. Liu, C. Ward, A. Bernardo, M. Karasawa, & R. Fischer (Eds.), *Casting the individual in societal and cultural contexts* (2nd ed., pp. 123–146). Korea: Kyoyook- Kwahak-Sa Publishing.

Yeh, K-H., Bedford, O., & Yang, Y-J. (2009). A cross cultural comparison of the coexistence and domain superiority of individuating and relating autonomy. *International Journal of Psychology, 44*, 213–221.

Author Index

Subject Index